Film Propaganda in Britain and Nazi Germany

Film Propaganda in Britain and Nazi Germany

World War II Cinema

Jo Fox

Oxford • New York

English edition
First published in 2007 by
Berg
Editorial offices:
First Floor, Angel Court, 81 St Clements Street, Oxford OX4 1AW, UK
175 Fifth Avenue, New York, NY 10010, USA

Berg is the imprint of Oxford International Publishers Ltd.

Library of Congress Cataloging-in-Publication Data

Fox, Jo.
　　Film propaganda in Britain and Nazi Germany : World War II cinema /
Jo Fox.—English ed.
　　　p. cm.
　　Includes bibliographical references and index.
　　ISBN-13: 978-1-85973-891-7 (cloth)
　　ISBN-10: 1-85973-891-5 (cloth)
　　ISBN-13: 978-1-85973-896-2 (pbk.)
　　ISBN-10: 1-85973-896-6 (pbk.)
　　1. Motion pictures in propaganda—Great Britain—History. 2. Motion pictures in
propaganda—Germany—History. 3. World War, 1939–1945—Motion pictures and the
war. I. Title.

　　PN1993.5.G7F68 2007
　　791.43'658—dc22

2006031633

British Library Cataloguing-in-Publication Data

A catalogue record for this book is available from the British Library.

ISBN-13　978 1 85973 891 7 (Cloth)
　　　　　978 1 85973 896 2 (Paper)

ISBN-10　1 85973 891 5 (Cloth)
　　　　　1 85973 896 6 (Paper)

Typeset by JS Typesetting Ltd, Porthcawl, Mid Glamorgan
Printed in the United Kingdom by Biddles Ltd, King's Lynn

www.bergpublishers.com

CONTENTS

LIST OF FILM STILLS

For Jonathan

ACKNOWLEDGEMENTS

Naturally, as with any publication, there are so many people to whom I am indebted. Firstly, I would like to thank Collingwood College, the University of Durham, the Department of History at the University of Durham, but, in particular, the British Academy for providing the funds for my research programme at the numerous archives I visited in both Germany and Britain.

The archivists I met in the course of my research have been unfailingly helpful. In particular, for their assistance and their permission to publish materials from their collections, I would like to offer my thanks to the following: the archivists of the special collections at the University of Stirling; the trustees and staff of the Mass-Observation Archive at the University of Sussex; the trustees and staff of the Churchill Archives Centre, Churchill College, Cambridge; the staff at the British Film Institute Library, Stills Collection and the National Film Archive; the trustees and archivists of the Walter Monckton Papers at Balliol College and the Department of Special Collections and Western Manuscripts at the Bodleian Library, University of Oxford; the trustees and archivists of the Laurence Olivier Papers at the British Library, London; the trustees and archivists of the Kenneth Clark Papers at the Tate Gallery, London, the archivists at the Bundesarchiv and the Stiftung Deutsche Kinematek, Berlin. I would like to thank Canal+ for their permission to reproduce a still from *Went the Day Well?* and Granada International Media for their permission to reproduce stills from several of their films. Every effort has been made to contact the copyright holders for permission to cite from materials. I extend my apologies for any omissions. I would like to say a special thank you to Janet Moat, archivist of the Special Collections at the British Film Institute, for answering endless questions and locating relevant materials from the papers of Anthony Asquith, Michael Balcon, Thorold Dickinson and Humphrey Jennings. I would like to extend my thanks to the trustees of these collections for their kind permission to publish excerpts from various sources. I am particularly grateful to Jonathan Balcon for his permission to cite from the Balcon Collection and to Laurence Harbottle for permission to cite from the Olivier Archives. The archivists at the Imperial War Museum in London and Duxford have also been consistently helpful, offering both their time and considerable expertise. I would like to thank, in particular, Matt Lee, who always has the answers to my questions and whose own interest in Polish film-makers in Britain pushed my research in new directions.

I was also fortune enough to make contact with a number of actors of the period, and would like to thank Sir John Mills, Phyllis Calvert and George Cole for agreeing to answer some questions. Phyllis Calvert, in particular, who invited me to her home for tea and scones, revealed much about film-making during World War II. She was so kind and generous with her time and remained exceptionally beautiful and graceful. I was much saddened to hear of her death in 2002.

Over the past few years, I have taught a special subject on British and German propaganda during World War II and have been blessed with very gifted students, whose own enthusiasm for the subject has been a constant source of inspiration. Each group brought fresh ideas and perspectives to the topic, prompting me to revisit and develop my ideas further. I would also like to thank my students for their patience whilst I finished this book. Their encouragement has kept me going!

I would like to express my gratitude to the translators I have worked with on this project, Simone Meakin, Christine Bohlander and, in particular, Steffi Boothroyd, who worked exceptionally hard to reproduce the particular style of Nazi rhetoric which dominates many of the sources.

I have also received a great deal of help from colleagues who were kind enough to cast their expert eye over draft chapters of this book. In particular, I would like to thank Lawrence Black, Sarah Davies, Mark Connelly, Susan Tegel and Oliver Zimmer for their advice. David Welch, who kindly offered his time to look over some of my work, has been a constant source of inspiration to me, his own pioneering research in the field of propaganda and his encouragement over the years motivating my desire to push the boundaries of my subject further. I would like to reserve a special mention for my best friend, Ulf Schmidt. It seems a lifetime ago that we met at the Bundesarchiv in Koblenz. But since that day, he has offered me constant support and companionship. His comments on this work were, as always, perceptive and helped me to realize the real significance of its central arguments.

I would like to thank my family, my grandparents, Richard and Sarah Shrimpton, and my parents, Maureen and Brian Fox, for their unending support and encouragement. Above all, I would like to thank my husband, Jonathan Pearson, to whom this book is dedicated, for without him, it would never have seen the light of day. He has been there to read draft after draft, ask question after question. His patience has been unlimited and for this, and for his love and support, I will be eternally grateful.

1 FILM PROPAGANDA AND WORLD WAR II
DEBATES AND CONTEXTS

> The film appeals to all classes and speaks in a universal language. It is brief, vivid and simple in getting across its message... As a means of disseminating public information and propaganda it is often more striking and thus more effective than the written or spoken word... Under present circumstances no considered public service of information can disregard the tremendous value of films.[1]

On 15 September 1939, writing from his hotel in Hollywood, John Grierson, the legendary realist film-maker, was constructing his plan for the use of film propaganda in Canada. In addition to being a pioneer of the documentary movement, Grierson was a scholar of the medium of film, deeply understanding and appreciating its power and ability to influence both the individual and the mass. That Grierson chose to re-emphasize this just twelve days after the outbreak of war in Europe is of particular significance. For Grierson, film was the primary medium for communicating with the public, for disseminating information and for circulating government propaganda during World War II. For others, it was the primary source of entertainment. It offered a distraction from the realities of everyday lives, an escape from the death and destruction which was all around. It was a means of persuading and communicating but it was also a spectacle.

This dualistic function of film was clearly recognized both before and during World War II. However, the debate over the efficacy of the entertainment and propagandistic functions of cinema is not confined to contemporary scrutiny. Such debates exist within today's historiography of both Britain and Germany in this period. This is not surprising since many of the key questions relating to the use of film as either a medium of propaganda or entertainment or both naturally require the attention of the film scholar. In order to contextualize the central contentions of this book, an analytical and historiographical framework needs to be established to raise issues germane to the study of film in both Britain and Germany, but which also recognizes some specific differences which must necessarily inform this comparison.

In recent years, historiographical debates surrounding films produced under the Third Reich centred on the distinction between what could be termed *Tendenzfilme* (films 'exhibiting strong National Socialist tendencies'[2]) and *Unterhaltungsfilme* (entertainment films). For Siegfried Kracauer, 'all Nazi films were more or less propaganda films – even the mere entertainment pictures which seem to be remote from politics'.[3] Within Kracauer's analysis, *Unterhaltungsfilme* had been falsely merged with the *Tendenzfilme*, creating, as Sabine Hake has noted, an 'undistinguished formless mass'.[4] This initial observation raises some problematic issues. Hake argued that such sweeping assumptions about the totalitarian control of the *Reichsministerium für Volksaufklärung und Propaganda* (Reich Ministry for Popular Enlightenment and Propaganda, RMVP) over the industry served to 'protect against uncomfortable questions about the continuities of popular cinema and the social practices, attitudes and mentalities that sustain it and, in turn, are sustained by it'.[5] Ultimately, there was an initial willingness to characterize Nazi cinema as 'the Other'. However, as the research of Karsten Witte and others has demonstrated, 'German cinema of the Third Reich had little to call its own. It was a borrower'. If that was indeed the case, the historian must be clear as to what she or he perceives to be a 'Nazi film'. As Witte noted, 'there were fascist films. And there were films made under fascist regimes',[6] highlighting a particular dilemma facing the scholar of film of the National Socialist period.

Discourses of politics and entertainment naturally enter into this debate. They lie at the heart of any analysis of the function of film within a conflict scenario. Within the existing historiography, these discourses have essentially produced dichotomous methodologies and foci for historians of 'totalitarian' cinema. In the early 1980s, the field of study emanated from a core of distinguished scholars of propaganda theory and practice, such as David Welch, Richard Taylor, and Erwin Leiser, to name but a few. Their approach to the subject was quite clear: 'to examine Nazi film propaganda as a reflection of National Socialist ideology'.[7] The intention behind the work of Welch, for example, was to 'trace various components of the ideology which recur in the cinema of the Third Reich, in order to discover what this reveals about the nature of propaganda in general and the ideology of National Socialism in particular'. In other words, it was a case study, in which film was a microscope through which to observe the nature and processes of propaganda. *Propaganda and the German Cinema, 1933–1945* was intended to promote the empirical use of film in the field of history, to 'broaden the scope of [historians'] professional dialogue', pioneering the discovery of new 'ways of dealing with the problem of film as evidence'[8] and indeed the past. This contribution to the wider discourse did not intend to engage with films of an 'escapist' nature. The author made this clear at the outset.[9] Emphasis was placed firmly on the propagandistic nature of politically motivated films. In reconstructing the film, historians seek to establish intent, analyse content, locate the film in its historical context, and, where possible, attempt to discern and interpret 'public reaction'. The selection of films for this purpose is located within strictly defined parameters. As Richard Taylor noted, if 'the conscious purpose is to lull the audience in order to manipulate its opinions for political ends, then we are concerned with film propaganda: if not, then we are concerned with entertainment pure and simple'.[10] Furthermore, according to scholars of propaganda and persuasion techniques, even films which fall into the latter category can have a political role, particularly within a society at war. 'Pure' entertainment films were a diversion, aiming to sustain morale and provide opportunities for the population to escape their trials and tribulations through a diet of romantic comedies, musicals and drama. This was not without political significance in the Third Reich. As Welch argued, 'in a highly politicized society, even the apolitical becomes significant, in that so-called entertainment films tend to promote the official "world view" of things and reinforce the existing economic and social order',[11] further blurring the distinction between the escapist and the political.

This method of reconstructing the filmic past has been scrutinized in recent years. A new generation of film scholars has begun to search for an alternative methodology, attempting to redefine the parameters of research into the cinematic culture of the Third Reich. The emerging theories sought to move away from 'propaganda studies' and what Linda Schulte-Sasse described as their 'blissful orderliness and simplicity'. Rather, she argued, 'Nazi films, regardless of genre, need to be studied in themselves *and* anchored in the context of their culture's moral and aesthetic values'.[12] Schulte-Sasse contended that scholars needed to address film's 'internal contradictions as well as its continuities'. To this end, she challenged the concept of the 'coherent and predictable ideological edifice we call "Nazi ideology"'. She used ideological critique as a starting point for the study of films produced in the Third Reich, 'sorting out configurations, establishing unities among film texts as well as references between texts and various subtexts'.[13] This intriguing research methodology produced some fascinating analytical visions of Nazi cinema, cutting deep into the heart of National Socialist culture and its use of the image, and the debate over the entertainment function of films, whilst also fitting with recent historiographical developments in the field tracing patterns of consensus, collaboration and resistance.[14]

Nevertheless, Julian Petley observed that Schulte-Sasse's approach failed to resolve the difficulties of analysing the escapist and the political within cinema, noting that her 'reliance on textual analysis in places leads to an unnecessary and unproductive muddle over the hoary question of the difference between, on the one hand, the "political" and "propaganda" and on the other "entertainment"'.[15] Petley advanced the view that the films were a product of their social and political *milieu*, and as a result, those 'which had non-propagandist, "classical" textual properties nonetheless [could function] as propaganda within the particular social conjuncture of the Third Reich because of the way in which they [might be] placed within the apparatuses involved in their consumption'.[16] In addition, Petley posed a fundamental question. In probing Schulte-Sasse's assertion that the eponymous protagonist of Veit Harlan's notorious 1940 anti-Semitic film, *Jud Süß*, could be 'read' as both hero and anti-hero, he demanded: '[read] by whom? By a reader in the Third Reich? By a film theorist in 1997? Or by critics such as [David Stewart] Hull or Rudolf Oertel, whose complete ignorance of National Socialist ideology, and especially of its crucial "radical" aspect, leads them into ludicrous misreadings of a quite unsustainable kind?'[17] For Petley, the real value of studying the cinema of the Third Reich can be found in an accurate contextualization of film and its meaning, stressing that:

> In a society in which highly mystified representations of the Third Reich abound, be
> they popular fictions set in a largely mythological Nazi Germany, or revisionist accounts

of the Third Reich cinema itself, we need to understand the Third Reich through its own movies, and vice versa. This way we get to know the Third Reich from within, as it were, and to access its own self-image.[18]

In understanding the inherent tensions within films, even the tensions perhaps between ideological and propagandistic intent and contradictory and sometimes incoherent meanings and messages, combined with an appreciation of the cultural, social, economic and political space in which these films were conceived, produced, filmed, edited, and received, the film historian comes not only closer to understanding the films themselves, but their role within society.

Such debates are not confined to historians of totalitarian film, however. The reconciliation of entertainment and propaganda for historians of British cinema has followed a similar pattern. As James Chapman has identified,[19] the development of British cinematic analysis has evolved along three distinct methodological lines: the 'old film historians' who often had direct involvement in film and propaganda work during World War II;[20] the 'empiricist school', a group of academic historians with a focus on and interest in film;[21] and the film theorists, who framed their analysis in semiotic terms.[22] As with research into German film in the period from 1939 to 1945, debates focus on the seemingly dichotomous approaches presented by historical and theoretical analysis. For the historian, film acts as a significant primary source, as a source for the analysis of propaganda, as historical evidence in its own right, and as a means of observing and understanding processes and mentalities associated with the 'immediate past'.[23]

However, the study of propaganda raises some significant questions on a theoretical level, notably, as Steve Neale identified, 'the conceptualisation of and differentiation between modes of address, not only at the level of the text, but also at the level of the institution which produces the text and in which it is embedded; the specification of the relationship between artistic practices and ideological and political apparatuses and institutions; and the relationship of both to the conjuncture'.[24] Fundamentally, Neale sought to 're-cast a set of basic terms, to re-cast the problematic in which propaganda has predominantly been thought', arguing that 'what has to be identified is the use to which a particular text is put, to its function within a particular situation, to its place within cinema conceived as a *social practice*'.[25] By analysing the form of address, text and context, Neale sought to place specific works, touching on the 'poles' of entertainment and propaganda. He recognized that 'books or articles on Nazi propaganda ... constantly hover between conceiving entertainment films as non-ideological and escapist and therefore performing an ideological function in not confronting "reality", or else as embodying Nazi ideology in a "hidden" way through particular modes of characterisation or the portrayal of validated narrative actions'. Critiquing established methodologies of assessing the 'effects of entertainment film on the political level within specific conjunctures', Neale drew on Leif Furhammar and Folke Isaksson's 1968 work, *Politics and Film*, stating that, using this method, such effects 'can only be empirically noted: there is no conceptual apparatus – no theory – with which to handle them. Within a problematic of intentionality and manipulation, the concepts needed are necessarily absent, not least because they would entail entirely different concepts of subjectivity, ideology and politics'.[26] For Neale, this is what semiology and ideological critique could add to the existing field of research.

Such criticisms of empirically executed film research are also articulated within more recent works. In *Waving the Flag: Constructing a National Cinema in Britain*, Andrew Higson challenged the established work of Jeffrey Richards, Anthony Aldgate and Charles Barr among others. 'At best', stated Higson, '[such work] sets out to delineate the pleasures offered and the ideological work performed by such cinema for its audiences, and to situate film texts in their broader institutional contexts…, [allowing historians to make] new connections and links'. Questioning the methodological approaches of the 'social historians of the cinema', Higson claimed that 'much of this work nevertheless remains bound to problematic explanatory frameworks which fail to break with the concerns of earlier discourses, particularly with regard to the relationship posited between films and society, and with the assumptions made about how films produce meanings and pleasures'.[27] In an earlier article, he observed that such approaches limited the theoretical background to film analyses, with films becoming mere 'products, which, … reflect or reproduce the "dominant ideology"'.[28] Moreover, he argued, traditional histories tended to take a linear approach, failing, as a result, to 'deal with the question of the relation between the productivity of the text and the metapsychology of the spectator, and the way in which the spectator is positioned in enunciative address of the text, and the critical discourses which circumscribe the meaning of the text'. Historical approaches, focusing on 'structural and economic determinants', place an emphasis, he furthered, on 'representation … rather than point of view; on narrative closure rather than on permanent struggle between the voyeuristic pull of the narrative and the fetishistic production of visual pleasure; on ideological reproduction rather than tension and excess within the film system'.[29]

For Higson, this methodological approach, with films becoming 'products reflecting pre-determined ideological position', 'lifts the burden' from the shoulders of the film historian, who, avoiding a detailed analysis of the film, 'resorts to journalistic gloss, or the avowed *intentions* of film-makers'.[30] He added that historical accounts of film need to be 'reconceptualised',[31] avoiding the 'sociological desire for neatness and continuity, a desire for a text to be *either* "progressive" *or* "reactionary", and a refusal to pay attention to the permanent and productive tensions, the play of containment and excess, in the film system'.[32] However, through a theorized reconstruction of this process, as John Hill observes, Higson's approach 'tends to depend upon a method of analysis which identifies their significance in terms of internal textual operations'.[33]

It is in the identification of internal and external processes that the tensions between the two sub-disciplines of film are exposed. For the film historian, a focus on representation and its relationship to the specific *milieu* provides, as Petley identified, an opportunity to understand societies through their self-image, in essence to understand them from within.

Empiricists naturally shy away from analysis of the 'metapsychology' of the audience, as the results can be subjective and imprecise. What historians are primarily interested in are the *perceptions* of that 'meta-psychology', and the contemporary interpretations of it. Equally, it is impossible to remove the necessity for analyses of *intent* from any detailed study of a film or cinema, for this elucidates its *purpose*, its *raison d'être*. For the film theorist, emphasis is placed upon the meaning of the film itself; without an understanding of how to 'read' a film, how meaning, and indeed ideology and propaganda, are conveyed, it is difficult to understand the conscious and subconscious processes affecting the spectator. More specifically, such analyses can be fruitful, particularly when exposing contradictions and tensions within the filmic discourse and the social environment in which the film is screened.

It is against this historiographical backdrop that this work is set. Whilst this book recognizes the value of these two streams of highly significant research activity in terms of analysing entertainment and propaganda within the cinema, it does not claim to be able to fuse historical and semiotic approaches to the study of film. This, I believe, is a task for future inter-disciplinary collaborative work, which should be undertaken in order to draw upon the important research findings derived from both methodologies. This work is purely historical and empirical in approach, but will attempt to draw on the work of film theorists where appropriate. The key functions of this work are to analyse historically the relationship between British and German cinema of World War II and compare and contrast their propaganda methods in the tradition of attempting to locate film within its political and historical *milieu*.

The book is a comparative analysis of two national cinemas. Such an approach has been expertly executed for Nazi Germany and the Soviet Union by Richard Taylor in his ground-breaking 1979 book, *Film Propaganda: Soviet Russia and Nazi Germany*.[34] However, in this work I hope to contribute to current debates by moving towards a comparison of the function and nature of film propaganda under democracy and dictatorship. As Chapman has noted, up until the late 1970s and early 1980s, most research relating to the function of film within wartime propaganda campaigns focused on the 'totalitarian states'. For the European dictatorships, propaganda was integrated into the functions of government. Naturally, historians of propaganda gravitated to this well-spring in order to analyse the form, nature and effect of propagandistic activity during the war. With the empirical research of Nicholas Pronay, Philip Taylor, Jeffrey Richards and Anthony Aldgate, amongst others, new pathways began to be forged into the function and nature of film propaganda under democracy. This, in turn, has opened up new opportunities to analyse both democratic and authoritarian film propaganda within a comparative context, and extend conclusions drawn from filmic analysis to a more general historical discussion of the nature of propaganda.

But what is the value of such a comparison? Ian Kershaw has argued that a comparison between British and German propaganda of World War II, as a means of judging the efficacy of propagandistic activities, is 'of limited value because of the radically different aims and ambitions of the two systems'.[35] For Kershaw, the differences between the two systems and the nature of their wartime military experiences preclude any meaningful comparison of effectiveness:

> the task of the British propaganda apparatus was markedly simpler. Building upon the general acceptance of a just and necessary war in defence of existing values and one which, with all its setbacks, could be viewed with increasing optimism, the job of British propaganda in maintaining both civilian and military morale was a relatively easy and straightforward one. German propaganda, on the other hand, was far more ambitious. From the very beginning of the Third Reich it had set itself the task of educating the German people for a new society based upon a drastically restructured value system. The 'revolutionary' task of German propaganda contrasts starkly with the 'conservative' basis of British propaganda aims. Furthermore, German propaganda was faced with a military situation worsening gradually from late 1941 onwards to a point of despair for Germany. Its task in upholding morale in these circumstances was incomparably greater than that of British propaganda.[36]

Naturally the way in which propaganda was used by Britain and Germany during World War II was different in some respects. As Chapman has noted with reference to film propaganda, 'even though democratic governments could increase their powers drastically during wartime, they did not have (or were reluctant to use) the same powers of coercion exercised by the dictatorships'.[37] But, for the historian of film propaganda, these differences are potentially significant. A comparative perspective on propaganda activity under two very different systems poses some intriguing questions, and allows for an understanding of the broader processes, functions, execution and themes of propaganda during World War II.

It also serves to underline the debate over the nature of propaganda in democracies and dictatorships. Propaganda, by which I mean 'the deliberate attempt to influence the opinions of an audience through the transmission of ideas and values for a specific persuasive purpose, consciously designed to serve the interest of the propagandist and their political masters, either directly or indirectly',[38] operates on many levels and in different contexts. But are there specific characteristics associated with the operation and execution of propaganda in democratic and authoritarian states? Jacques Ellul, in attempting to clarify the specific characteristics of democratic propaganda, concluded that, if democratic propaganda is executed according to its ascribed characteristics, it is doomed to failure. For Ellul, 'some of democracy's fundamental aspects paralyse the conduct of propaganda. There is, therefore, no "democratic" propaganda. Propaganda made by the democracies is ineffective, paralysed, mediocre'.[39] In attempting to reconcile the functions of propaganda and the nature of democracy, Ellul observed that

> Precisely to the extent that the propagandist retains his respect for the individual, he denies himself the very penetration that is the ultimate aim of all propaganda: that of provoking action without prior thought. By respecting nuances, he neglects the major law of propaganda: every assertion must be trenchant and total. To the extent that he

remains partial, he fails to use mystique. But that mystique is indispensable for well-made propaganda. To the extent that a democratic propagandist has a bad conscience, he cannot do good work; nor can he when he believes in his own propaganda.[40]

Ellul's analysis raises some problematic issues, not least in his conception of the 'total society' which has been challenged by both distant and recent scholarship into the functioning of the 'totalitarian' state.[41] This aside, the scholar must question whether Ellul intends to suggest that when democracies use effective propaganda the nature of the state fundamentally changes or, alternatively, that propaganda is essentially an activity pursued solely by dictatorships. The first is a troubling assertion which implies that such actions 'no longer have a special democratic character'; the second is unrealistic, because it fails to take into account any specialized definition of propaganda. In addition, such stark juxtapositions are often unhelpful in attempting to analyse such a multi-functional and complex phenomenon. This study will work within these parameters in a comparative context, attempting to shed some new light on these debates by focusing on a defined medium: film. Moreover, it aims to analyse the propagandistic function of the cinema within the context of 'total war'. Whereas Ellul's theories on democratic and authoritarian propaganda operate within a generalized context, this study will seek to examine whether such distinctions become blurred within a conflict situation: in other words, does war affect the way in which democratic and authoritarian propaganda is planned, executed and received? Finally, the book will question in what ways this distinction can be upheld altogether, pointing to definable elements which are similar if not the same, as well as to the essential differences between propaganda in the two states.

In order to grapple with these issues, one must be clear as to the basis on which the comparison will be made. Here the difficulty rests with a comparative evaluation of effectiveness, as Kershaw identified. I share his view that 'assessments of the effectiveness of propaganda cannot be carried out either on the basis of a notional absolute scale of what is "effective" or on a comparative basis with dissimilar systems'.[42] However, a comparative assessment of propaganda activity can reveal the ways in which the state propagandists, operating from within different political systems, dealt with psychological wartime trends in the wider populations, without assessing the impact of these activities comparatively. This study will analyse the impact of film propaganda within its national contexts and against the propagandists' own objectives, rather than attempt to compare the efficacy of the British and German propaganda campaigns during World War II generically. As Kershaw has noted, the contexts within which propaganda was disseminated and consequently received were different. However, at various and sometimes simultaneous times during the conflict, propagandists in both Britain and Germany were focusing on similar themes, albeit from within different state structures, and this is worth closer inspection in order to draw out the specific nature of democratic and authoritarian propaganda. Both British and German propagandists sought to persuade their respective peoples of a 'just war', and attempted to allay fears relating to aerial bombardment, invasion and the possibility of defeat; both had to manage the expectations of a public who experienced the euphoria of victory and the despair associated with loss. The rhetoric of 'total war' in essence was similar in both countries, as David Culbert has observed.[43] It does not always follow that, because of the different characters of the two state systems, propagandist endeavours will merely result in a stark contrast.

A comparative study can also raise some important questions relating to the way in which British and German film propagandists responded to one another's work. Film propaganda did not solely operate in a national context. If the military war was global, so too was the battle for hearts and minds. We need to analyse how British film propaganda reacted to or drew upon German film propaganda and vice versa, and demonstrate the propagandistic interconnectivity of the two nations. Throughout this study, I will draw on examples of such interaction, where possible, in order to emphasize that whilst home propaganda operated within a specific internal context, it was also observed and noted by enemy and ally alike. Throughout the conflict, sources reveal a continuous comparative discourse relating to propaganda outputs, which was only natural for a phenomenon which has a tendency to be reactive as well as proactive. This aspect of propaganda is perhaps best articulated within a comparative study, single nation studies often overlooking this significant aspect of persuasion in World War II. Within a comparative framework, the scholar is drawn to the multiple contexts in which propaganda operated in this period, highlighting the interrelation of filmic productions and thus adding a further dimension to existing studies.

Further, any study of propaganda must consider reception. There is naturally a question-mark over the reliability of sources of popular opinion emanating from within the Third Reich, such as the *Sicherheitsdienst* (SD) reports, which cover the wartime period, and equally over retrospective personal recollections of the impact of a particular film or event. As Marcia Klotz recognized:

> Contemporaneous film reviews or Gau reports on audience responses shed little light on how the films were received on an ideological level. Likewise, there is no way of asking people after the fact whether they 'heard a message' in those grey areas, whether they did in fact 'know' what films allowed them 'not to know'. Any examination of these questions must necessarily remain speculative, for these messages were never intended to be articulated consciously.[44]

Probing further the analyses of Klotz in this respect, the question of popular reactions to cinema in the Third Reich has more recently been re-examined by Hake in her study of popular cinema of the Third Reich. In a superb analysis of the tensions between political and popular discourses in relation to the formation of attitudes and opinions on film in Nazi Germany, Hake has pointed to the need to reintegrate the spectator into filmic analysis. She contends that the 'filmic effect' is not merely produced by film-makers but also by 'spectators, whose imagination gave meaning to the cinema's pleasures beyond the special confines of the auditorium'.[45] Within the historiography, audiences in the Third Reich, she argued, 'continue to be treated as a predictable and therefore negligible group', 'usually vilified as passive and uncritical recipients of film propaganda or, less frequently, vindicated in their individual efforts to escape from the official culture of mass spectacles and collective rituals'.[46] As Hake convincingly demonstrates, the patterns of popular engagement with the cinema are invariably more complex.

Naturally, within the intricate process of reconstructing public responses to film, whether in Britain or in Germany, one needs to be wary of how representative and reliable the data are. British public opinion sources, such as the reports and materials produced by Mass-Observation, the weekly Ministry of Information [MoI] Home Intelligence Reports, produced between September 1940 until the autumn of 1944, and the Wartime Social Survey, are riddled with contradiction and tension.[47] Equally, Michael Balfour, in discussing the historical use of the SD reports in Nazi Germany, commented that they were 'no doubt biased and fallible', but nonetheless 'are the best evidence we are ever likely to have'.[48] Other scholars agree. Hake contends that although 'the positive reception of a propaganda film may have been staged by party members or fabricated by SD agents', this 'does not invalidate the relevance of the agents' observations as constructions of publicly expressed enjoyment and dislike'.[49] It becomes increasingly clear from modern studies of film propaganda that the analysis of reception forms an essential part of the film and propaganda scholars' work.[50]

Much analysis has focused here upon reading popular opinions within a totalitarian system, but we must question how far this was an issue faced by democratic regimes and how far they lend themselves to comparison. Marlis G. Steinert's work on popular opinion in Germany during World War II asserts that 'every state leadership, be it democratic, authoritarian or totalitarian, requires a certain degree of acclamation to exercise power in the long run. Without the consensus, whether forced or passive, of a broad social stratum, no government can long survive in the age of the masses'.[51] Although opinion is sought via different methods, through public opinion surveys, parliamentary elections or other indicators in a democratic state and via surveillance networks within a totalitarian state, no government can afford to ignore the popular voice. Challenging the accepted notion that within totalitarian states 'there is no noteworthy, or only weakly defined, public opinion … and that consequently the fascist states also had "only a very weak and ineffective instrument for public opinion research at their disposal"',[52] Steinert details the specific structures within the Third Reich devoted to collecting and analysing public opinion, noting that 'hardly a National Socialist organisation existed that did not, at least occasionally or in specific areas, deliver public opinion reports'.[53] More significantly in terms of this study, Steinert observed that 'the … propaganda policy of the Third Reich, which was to mould and direct the opinion of the *Volk*, was not only a reaction to public opinion but was also frequently inspired by it, as well as often decisively forming the public mind. It can thus be confirmed … that "public opinion and propaganda mutually limit and influence each other".'[54] Essentially, then, according to Steinert, in both democracies and totalitarian states 'there are … broad opinion trends, typical and representative opinions, and a widespread common mood'[55] which influenced each government during wartime when constructing wartime propaganda policy. As Steinert has effectively demonstrated, it is no longer possible for the historian to speak of an 'unresponsive' totalitarian state completely divorced from its public, thus further facilitating a comparison with the democracies.

Although, at best, as Steinert notes, all such sources can do is help to outline wider trends in popular opinion and perhaps even the meta-psychology to which Higson refers, there is some benefit in exploring phases in opinion within a comparative and perhaps dissimilar context, using the cinema as a prism through which to examine 'public mood'. By raising questions relating to the public desire for particular genres of film at particular times, we can begin to explore the impact of conflict on mood in a more general sense. By comparing public reactions to film genres and to specific films in Britain and Germany, with their very different patterns of wartime experience and fluctuating military successes and failures, we can observe whether these circumstances impacted upon film choice and whether film production responded to these needs and desires, whilst at the same time recognizing the constraints of source materials and the specific nature of the states in question.

In addition, it is important not to forget that cinema, as well as being a tool of the state and vehicle of popular fantasy, is also an industry. As such, film producers were motivated as much by monetary profits as by the desire or requirement to serve the state, particularly in times of crisis. Logically, then, films needed to correspond to public desires both psychologically and in order to maximize profits for the producing studios, helping to resurrect their fortunes after periods of sustained industrial crisis. This was true of both democratic and totalitarian powers and points to the more fragmentary and complex nature of even the most structured of societies, in which no one factor, whether it be ideological, social, economic or political, dominates but rather a multitude of forces pushing the state in various directions. This process naturally raises some problematic questions: Were there tensions between the industry and the official propagandists? Did the official propagandists understand and support the public desire for escapist vehicles, and the industry's need to produce them in order to sustain filmic activity? To what extent did war impact upon resources? This becomes important when one considers that in both Britain and Germany, public interest in fantasy and escapist drama peaked as raw materials for costumes, sets and even raw film stock became increasingly scarce. How did the industry, and the official propagandists, circumnavigate practical concerns, whilst negotiating potentially conflicting interests? Naturally, this leads us back to the intersection between propaganda and entertainment, highlighted in the discussion of historiographical debates above.

Film provides the historian with a prism through which to view the complex relationships between the industry, the government and their peoples, to understand the interplay between propaganda and entertainment and to probe the interaction between conflict, propaganda and morale. This book seeks to analyse some of the key issues highlighted above, concentrating on specific and detailed analyses of the context of and representation within individual films indicative of wider cinematic issues and trends in Britain and Germany from 1939 to 1945. The overall thesis concentrates on conceptions of propaganda. Therefore, films have been selected which specifically met that need. Although I will attempt to highlight areas where propaganda and entertainment intersected and point to tensions within the propagandistic discourse, this work is specific to the propagandistic genre. In short, the book provides snapshots set within a wider analytical framework, focusing on the key themes of justifying war, the impact of aerial bombardment and the glorification of the pilot in popular discourses, the image of the enemy, the manipulation of the past for propagandistic purposes and finally responses to victory and defeat, within the feature and short length film, in order to articulate *propagandistic intent and reception*. At its core, the book seeks to re-examine conceptions of democratic and authoritarian propagandists at war, questioning stark juxtapositions and pointing to the complexities relating to the use of persuasive techniques in both state systems. It argues that each state possessed an intricate and complex relationship with its respective peoples and suggests that at times the propaganda outputs conformed far less to the official rhetoric emanating from the RMVP and the MoI regarding their 'information policies' than might be expected, thus blurring the distinction between democratic and authoritarian propaganda whilst at the same time not forgetting that the state mechanisms were not the same or largely similar. For a comparative study can also give clarity to essential differences, as well as pointing to similarities and unresolved tensions between the proclaimed nature of the state and the reality.

Douglas Fairbanks Jr, in an address to the convention of the National Education Association in the United States on 3 July 1939, asserted that

> the motion picture theatre in those [dictator] nations is almost entirely devoted, under government supervision to telling the audience that it is quite the happiest audience on the face of the earth. In democratic nations on the other hand, the audience itself is the controlling influence. If the audience wants the social order examined, the films will examine; if the audience seeks criticism, the films will criticise; if the audience wants fairy stories – well we have 'Snow White'.[56]

This book questions whether Britain and Germany corresponded to these stereotypes, contending that authoritarian and democratic industries were both sensitive to audience demands and fluctuated between actively creating 'the happiest audience on earth' and allowing forays into the world of the 'fairy tale' as circumstances dictated.

NOTES

1. Grierson Papers, Special Collections, University of Stirling, Scotland (hereafter, GP). John Grierson G3:6:2 'A Plan for a Wartime National Film Propaganda Service in Canada', Lido Hotel Hollywood, 15 September 1939.
2. D. Welch, *Propaganda and the German Cinema, 1933–1945* (I. B. Tauris, London/New York, 2nd edn, 2001), p. 2.
3. S. Kracauer, in S. Hake, *Popular Cinema of the Third Reich* (University of Texas Press, Austin, 2001), p. 3.
4. Ibid.
5. Ibid.

6. K. Witte, 'The Indivisible Legacy of Nazi Cinema', *New German Critique*, vol. 74 (Spring–Summer 1998), pp. 23–31. Here, p. 29.

7. D. Welch, *Propaganda and the German Cinema*, p. 1.

8. Ibid., p. 3.

9. Ibid., p. 2.

10. R. Taylor, *Film Propaganda: Soviet Russia and Nazi Germany*, 2nd edn (I. B. Tauris, London/New York, 1998), p. 210.

11. D. Welch, *Propaganda and the German Cinema*, p. 37.

12. L. Schulte-Sasse, *Entertaining the Third Reich: Illusions of Wholeness in Nazi Cinema* (Duke University Press, Durham, NC and London, 1996), p. 3. Italics in original.

13. Ibid.

14. For a further discussion of these issues, see J. Fox, '"Heavy Hands and Light Touches": Approaches to the Study of Cinematic Culture in the Third Reich', *History Compass* (2003). Excerpts included here are reproduced with the kind permission of Blackwell's publishers. See also excellent articles by E. Carter, 'The New Third Reich Film History', *German History*, vol. 17, no. 4 (April 1999), pp. 565–83, and S. Spector, 'Was the Third Reich Movie-Made? Interdisciplinarity and the Reframing of "Ideology"', *American Historical Review* vol. 106, no. 2, (April 2001), pp. 460–84.

15. J. Petley, 'Review', *Screen*, vol. 38, no. 3 (Autumn 1997), pp. 287–95, pp. 291–2.

16. Ibid., p. 292.

17. Ibid., p. 293.

18. Ibid.

19. J. Chapman, *The British at War. Cinema, State and Propaganda, 1939-1945* (I. B. Tauris, London/New York, 2000), pp. 5–8.

20. For examples of this strand of analysis see B. Wright, *The Use of the Film* (Bodley Head, London, 1948); P. Rotha, *The Film till Now: A Survey of World Cinema* (Vision, London, 1949/1963); *Rotha on the Film: a Selection of Writings about the Cinema* (Faber and Faber, London, 1968); *Documentary Diary: An Informal History of the British Documentary Film 1928–1939* (Secker and Warburg, London, 1973); *Documentary Film: The Use of the Film Medium to Interpret Creatively and in Social Terms the Life of the People as it Exists in Reality* (with Sinclair Road and Richard Griffiths, Faber and Faber, London, 1952); R. Manvell, *The Film and the Public* (Penguin, Harmondsworth, 1955); *What is a Film?* (Macdonald, London, 1965); *Films and the Second World War* (Dent, London, 1952).

21. In particular see N. Pronay and F. Thorpe, *British Official Films in the Second World War: A Descriptive Catalogue* (Clio, Oxford, *c.*1980); N. Pronay and D. W. Spring (eds), *Propaganda, politics, and film, 1918–45* (Macmillan, London, 1982); J. Richards, *The Age of the Dream Palace: Cinema and Society In Britain, 1930–1939* (Routledge & Kegan Paul, London, 1984); *Films and British National Identity: From Dickens to Dad's Army* (Manchester University Press, Manchester, 1997); *Visions of Yesterday* (Routledge & Kegan Paul, London, 1973); J. Richards (ed.), *The Unknown 1930s: An Alternative History of the British Cinema, 1929–39* (I. B. Tauris, London, 1998); J. Richards and A. Aldgate, *Best of British: Cinema and Society, 1930–1970* (Blackwell, London, 1983); *Britain Can Take It: The British Cinema in the Second World War* (Edinburgh University Press, Edinburgh, 1986/1994); P. M. Taylor, *British Propaganda in the Twentieth Century: Selling Democracy* (Edinburgh University Press, Edinburgh, 1999); P. M. Taylor (ed.), *Britain and the Cinema in the Second World War* (St. Martin's Press, New York, 1988); S. Harper, *Picturing the Past: Rise and Fall of the British Costume Film* (Bfi Publishing, London, 1994); *Women in British Cinema: Mad, Bad and Dangerous to Know* (Continuum, London, 2000).

22. In particular see, A. Higson, *Waving the Flag: Constructing a National Cinema in Britain* (Clarendon Press, Oxford, 1995); A. Higson (ed.), *Young and Innocent?: The Cinema in Britain, 1896–1930* (University of

Exeter Press, Exeter, 2002); *Dissolving Views: Key Writings on British Cinema* (Cassell, London, 1996); J. Ashby and A. Higson (eds), *British Cinema, Past and Present* (Routledge, London/New York, 2000); S. Neale, 'Propaganda', *Screen*, vol. 18, no. 3 (1977), pp. 9–40: A. Kuhn, '"Desert Victory" and the People's War', *Screen*, vol. 22, no. 2 (1981), pp. 45–68; 'The Camera I: Observations on Documentary', in *Screen*, vol. 19, no. 2 (1978) pp. 71–83; *An Everyday Magic: Cinema and Cultural Memory* (I. B. Tauris, London, 2002); *Women's Pictures: Feminism and Cinema* (Verso, London, 1994); G. Hurd (ed.), *National Fictions: World War II in British Films and Television* (BFI Publishing, London, 1984). It should be noted that these authors also engage in historical contextualisation, even though their primary methodology is based on an analysis of narrative and textual processes.

23. P. M. Taylor, 'Introduction: Film, the Historian and the Second World War', in P. M. Taylor (ed.), *Britain and the Cinema in World War II*, pp. 1–15, p. 3.

24. S. Neale, 'Propaganda', p. 9.

25. Ibid., p. 39.

26. Ibid., p. 14.

27. A. Higson, *Waving the Flag*, p. 18.

28. A. Higson, 'Critical Theory and "British Cinema"', *Screen*, vol. 24, nos. 4–5 (1983), pp. 80–95, p. 84.

29. Ibid., p. 85.

30. Ibid., p. 86.

31. Ibid., p. 93.

32. Ibid., p. 87.

33. J. Hill, 'Review', *Screen*, vol. 37, no. 1 (Spring 1996), pp. 106–10, p. 107.

34. This work has recently been republished in a second edition in the 'KINO: The Russian Cinema' series.

35. I. Kershaw, 'How Effective was Nazi Propaganda?', in D. Welch (ed.), *Nazi Propaganda. The Power and the Limitations* (Croom Helm, London and Canberra, 1983), pp. 180–206, p. 181.

36. Ibid., pp. 181–2.

37. J. Chapman, *The British at War*, p. 4.

38. D. Welch, 'Propaganda', in N. Cull, D. Culbert and D. Welch (eds), *Propaganda and Mass Persuasion: A Historical Encyclopaedia, 1500 to the Present* (ABC-CLIO, Santa Barbara, 2003), p. 322.

39. J. Ellul, *Propaganda: The Formation of Men's Attitudes* (Vintage, New York, 1973). First published by Alfred A. Knopf, New York, 1965, p. 241.

40. Ibid., pp. 240–1.

41. Notably, the scholarly debates of the 1960s pioneered by, amongst others H. Arendt, specifically, *The Origins of Totalitarianism* (G. Allen & Unwin, London, 1958); R. Dahrendorf, and C. J. Friedrich and Z. K. Brzezinski, *Totalitarian Dictatorship and Autocracy* (Harvard University Press, Cambridge, MA, 1965); as well as by E. Nolte, *Der europäische Bürgerkrieg 1917–1945. Nationalsozialismus und Bolschewismus* (Propyläen, Berlin, 1987); and, more recently, J. Linz, *Totalitarian and Authoritarian Regimes* (Lynne Rienner, Boulder, CO, 2000); but also in the field of modern European history. For an overview of debates specific to the Third Reich, see I. Kershaw, *The Nazi Dictatorship* (Arnold, London, 2000).

42. I. Kershaw, 'How Effective was Nazi Propaganda?', p. 182.

43. D. Culbert, '*Kolberg* (Germany, 1945); The Goebbels Diaries and Poland's Kołobrzeg Today', in J. Whiteclay Chambers II and D. Culbert (eds), *World War II: Film and History* (Oxford University Press, 1996), p. 73.

44. M. Klotz, 'Epistemological Ambiguity and the Fascist Text: *Jew Süss, Carl Peters* and *Ohm Krüger*', *New German Critique*, 74 (Spring–Summer 1998), pp. 91–125. Here, p. 124.

45. S. Hake, *Popular Cinema of the Third Reich*, p. 69.

46. Ibid.

47. Balfour noted that care must be exercised here, especially in the case of Mass-Observation [M-O] as they were 'apt to generalise from inadequate data'. M. Balfour, *Propaganda in War, 1939–1945: Organisations, Policies and Publics in Britain and Germany* (Routledge & Kegan Paul, London/Boston, 1979), p. 447.

48. Ibid., p. 450.

49. S. Hake, *Popular Cinema of the Third Reich*, p. 75.

50. Perhaps the best discussion of SD reports and public opinion sources within the Third Reich can be found in M. G. Steinert, *Hitler's War and the Germans: Public Mood and Attitude during the Second World War* (Ohio University Press, Athens, Ohio, 1977). Edited and translated by T. E. J. De Witt. This work was originally published under the title *Hitler's Krieg und die Deutschen: Stimmung und Haltung der deutschen Bevölkerung im Zweiten Weltkrieg* (Econ Verlagsgruppe, Düsseldorf/Vienna, 1970). See in particular pp. 1–24 for a discussion of the sources and methodological issues.

51. M. G. Steinert, *Hitler's War and the Germans*, p. 1.

52. Ibid., p. 2. Here Steinert is quoting P. R. Höfstätter, *Psychologie der Öffentlichen Meinung* (Vienna, 1949), p. 18.

53. Ibid.

54. Ibid., p. 3. Here Steinert is quoting P. R. Höfstatter, *Psychologie*, p. 148.

55. Ibid., p. 4.

56. Douglas Fairbanks Jr, Address to the Convention of National Educational Association, 3 July 1939. In GP G3:8:2. Papers of John Grierson , 'Some reference notes – In connection with comment by Donald Gledhill, participant in Symposium, July 14 1939 on "Channels of Communication", at a session of the "Institute on Public Opinion and Propaganda, University of California, Los Angeles', p. 1.

> Oh mister, it scared my wits out, thinking of the last war. They said it was going to be
> this week, and I heard my milkman say this morning that the worst has passed now …
> he says Mr. Chamberlain's done it by going in an aeroplane to Hitler.[1]

This opinion, expressed by a woman of 55 from a working-class district of 'Metrop'[2] in September 1938, conveys a little of the sense of relief felt by many after the Munich conference in that same year. The memory of the Great War must have played heavy on the minds of the general population in both Britain and Germany. Almost every household lost a loved one. In addition, both governments stressed that this war, this total war, would be more devastating than the last with the advent of the bomber, its power attested to in the newsreels of the bombing of Guernica in 1937. As one Pathé newsreel pointed out to the British public, the Spanish houses lying in ruins are 'homes just like yours'.[3] Just one year later, Britain and Germany were at war and their governments were faced with justifying to a bewildered public why twenty short years after the 'war to end all wars' the two nations were once again engaged in armed conflict. This chapter intends to explore the ways in which Britain and Germany sought to justify war to their overwhelmingly sceptical populations through film, and to compare and contrast their differing visions of propaganda in the early stages of the conflict from the late pre-war era to the fall of Neville Chamberlain in May 1940. Having established the context in which propaganda was created and received in this period, the chapter will then consider the key themes relating to the justification of war as conveyed in two of the main feature films used for this persuasive purpose: *Feuertaufe* (Baptism of Fire, Hans Bertram, 1940) and *The Lion Has Wings* (Michael Powell, Brian Desmond Hurst, Adrian Brunel, 1939). These two films were regarded by their respective governments as a crucial piece of propaganda in their initial campaigns. The chapter will reconstruct both national responses to each piece but also the international reception of the films, specifically analysing German and British responses to the film propaganda of the enemy, demonstrating the interconnectivity of these filmic outputs and highlighting the fact that propaganda did not solely operate in national contexts but was used as a weapon in the worldwide struggle for hearts and minds.

In Britain and Germany, propagandists faced a complex and difficult task if they were to achieve their aim of persuading their publics that the war was both necessary and winnable. These two aims were at the centre of initial propagandistic activities from August 1939 until mid-1940. Propagandists were also operating within a specific framework, within which their publics demonstrated a mosaic of opinions and were exhibiting a complex series of behaviours which propaganda needed to engage with and in some cases suppress. Fear of the unknown and the threat of mass conflict, including the possibility of aerial bombardment and gas attack, preoccupied the populations, as did the question of the imminence of the first strike.[4] In Britain, a detailed study emanating from Mass-Observation gives some indication of the public sentiments and behaviours with which the government had to contend in the initial crisis of 1938-9. Mass-Observation reported in September 1938 that, on the eve of possible conflict, with Chamberlain travelling to Germany for emergency talks with Hitler, over half of those questioned believed that war would break out in that month. By 27 September, many areas had run out of the smaller sizes of gas masks within 36 hours, 'cellophane sold out in London; it had been recommended for stopping glass splinters in explosions. Hammersmith Borough alone took on 2,000 unemployed to dig trenches, ... suggested by wags as memorials to Chamberlain's Peace with Honour'.[5] Such actions precipitated wider anxiety. Mass-Observation noted the impact on the elderly and women in particular, which resulted in physical symptoms of fear: 'diarrhoea and nervous indigestion'; 'stomach trouble owing to the anxiety of listening to or reading reports of the crisis'; one lady apparently experienced a heart attack whilst having her gas mask fitted.[6]

Given such a widespread sense of dread and foreboding coupled with a lack of effective information management by the Government,[7] it is unsurprising to find examples of more extreme behaviours in the notes of the Mass-Observers who remarked that some individuals were displaying signs of the 'last stage in the collapse of belief in the future': 'suicide talk'. One wife and mother of 42 confessed that she had been 'collecting poisons for some time with guile and cunning', amassing sufficient stocks to administer a lethal dose to her family. She did not 'want to live through another [war], or the children either. I shan't tell them, I shall just do it', she grimly predicted.[8] Overall, Mass-Observation noticed a number of trends in public opinion regarding the imminence of war in 1938–9: 'resistance to the idea that war is coming'; anxiety; 'bewilderment' at 'official secrecy and newspaper contradictions'; and finally a 'sense of helplessness'.[9] Such were the problems with which British propaganda had to contend.

Significantly, similar concerns were expressed in the Third Reich in the lead-up to war. An SD report from Leipzig dated 10 August 1939 noted that the population had begun to recognize that the war was about to commence. Rumour as to the eventual date of the attack on Poland was rife.[10] Amidst the heightened tension, facilitated by the accompanying press hysteria,[11] the people of Leipzig commented that 'the Poles were getting more impudent by the day',[12] a view confirmed by the American journalist William Shirer in conversations in the same month.[13] The idea that the western powers had been pushing for war for some time and that Poland was the true aggressor was promulgated by the press and other media. As Shirer noted, 'Whereas all the rest of the world considers that the peace is about to be broken by Germany, that it is Germany that is threatening to attack Poland over Danzig, here in Germany, in the world the local newspapers create, the very opposite is being maintained'.

Moreover, he commented upon the isolation of the German people in terms of information, and remarked, 'You ask: but the German people can't possibly believe these lies? Then you talk to them. So many do.'[14] Shirer's remarks are confirmed by reports for the German Social Democratic Party (Sopade) in Danzig. Sopade operatives commented in October 1939 that: 'With the outbreak of war, anti-Polish sentiment in Danzig has increased. Our explanation for this is that they [the Germans] did not want war and blamed the Poles for its outbreak'. This was coupled with an increase in 'anti-Polish comments'.[15] Pre-war propaganda against the Poles was intense and was obtaining some success among the population. The Sopade reports from Upper Silesia commented in July–August 1939, in a disheartened tone, that: 'Unfortunately it has to be noted today that anti-Polish propaganda has started to have an effect after all, so much so that even amongst the working people there is now a feeling that if Hitler attacks Poland he will have the majority of people behind him'.[16] They noted pessimistically that the war against Poland was 'absolutely popular amongst the German people'.[17]

Although the German people may have reluctantly, or even in some quarters enthusiastically, supported a quick 'lightning war' with Poland, they were less certain about a major European or even global conflict. Popular opinion was rather less clear-cut when it became obvious from the various reports that Germany was likely to enter a major conflict within the month, even though some continued to believe that it would be averted at the last minute.[18] Sopade reports from August 1939 confirmed that 'a substantial proportion of the population is still hoping that the French will not participate and that therefore the whole thing will come to an end soon'.[19] How broad military action would be, the resultant effects on the home front and how long it would last were primary concerns.[20] Reports from the SD in Leipzig detailed a population who felt unprepared for the coming conflict and concerned about the lack of order and conformity in the city's preparations for aerial attack.[21] In a similar vein to the remarks made by Mass-Observation in Britain, Shirer commented of the state of mind of the German people on the eve of war: 'Everybody is against the war. People talking openly. How can a country go into a major war with a population so dead against it? People also kicking about being kept in the dark. A German said to me last night: "We know nothing. Why don't they tell us what's up?"'[22] As in Britain, tension, nerves and a depressive mood dominated the population. Victor Klemperer, writing from Dresden in August 1939, noted in his diary that the events of that month 'pull too much at my nerves' and that by 3 September, the 'torture of one's nerves [was] ever more unbearable'.[23] Klemperer even suggested that the best thing for him and his wife on the outbreak of war would be 'a morphine injection or something similar'.[24] He added that 'memories of the last war [are] coming to the surface: the ration card. The way it fell upon the people on Sunday afternoon, it must have had a terrible effect on their mood'.[25] For many Germans, the introduction of the ration card signified the inevitability of war. As Shirer confirmed, writing on the same day, 'the average German to-day looks dejected. He can't get over the blow of the ration cards, which to him spells war'.[26]

At the outbreak of war in 1939, both countries can be said to have largely accepted conflict, a feeling accompanied by a sense of helplessness in the face of political decisions, demonstrating what can be best described as 'reluctant loyalty'.[27] Significantly, there 'was no [widespread] evidence of war fever – [but no] … opposition either'.[28] Writing from Berlin on 3 September, Shirer observed there was 'no excitement, no hurrahs, no cheering, no throwing of flowers, no war fever, no war hysteria. There is not even any hate for the French and the British'.[29] Indeed, 'apathy seemed … to be the most prominent characteristic among the Germans on September 1st'.[30] Although Berlin experienced blackouts and air-raid alarms and the population was clearly nervous, life continued as normal with the cafés, restaurants and beer halls packed out on the first night of war.[31] No doubt Berliners hoped that the war would be short and limited. Significantly, as early as October 1939, Sopade were reporting that there was 'no enthusiasm for war', commenting that 'our reports, including recent ones, have shown time and again that the overwhelming majority of the German people did not want war'.[32] Workers, who had been under the stresses and strains of an industrial sector gearing up for a significant conflict, were among the most vocal in expressing their discontent regarding the general European situation. As historian Stephen Salter noted, they 'seem to have experienced disorientation on the outbreak of war – the memories of the slaughter of the First World War concentrating their attention on hopes that they would not be conscripted'. Further, 'the entry of Britain and France into the war was greeted with dismay'.[33] Salter's assertion is confirmed by the Sopade reports of this period detailing workers' reactions to the events of September 1939. One worker stated: 'I hate the war, but it had to happen because the Nazis had no other option. Hitler will lose this war and the Nazis will be brought down. It's just a shame that, once again, it will be the worker who will have to make the most sacrifices'.[34] Despite extensive efforts to justify the conflict, German propagandists were faced, at best, with 'war-weariness' even at this early stage in the war.[35]

Nevertheless, as historian Wolfgang Benz has noted, the German public displayed a mosaic of opinions relating to the outbreak of war lasting from August 1939 to the beginning of the invasion of the Soviet Union in 1941. In addition to the 'apprehension and fear' described by Shirer, Klemperer and others,[36] Benz has added to the portrait of popular opinion constructed by an analysis of more public sources by stressing the importance of private sources such as 'notes, letters, diaries and recollections' which reveal another side to German attitudes at the outbreak of war.[37] Interpretations of popular opinion, argued Benz, had to stress existing alternative views, such as the importance of patriotic duty, which fuelled support for the war but had little to do with support for National Socialist ideology. For Benz, the case of Max Rehm illustrated 'all [the] motivations and explanations of a generation': the Rehm family were 'no model National Socialist family. Rather, they were patriots, with the father and both sons gladly prepared to fulfill what they regarded as their natural duty. However, for the father at least, the uniform of a *Wehrmacht* officer also represented freedom and salvation from the demands and doubts of everyday life'.[38] These views did not find their origins in Nazi militaristic proclamations. Rather they were 'the fruit of older traditions'.[39] In addition, drawing on past sentiments associated with the redemptive qualities of battle, Benz contended that there was an enduring 'fascination with warfare', which manifested itself in the writings of young participants in the conflict, enraptured by 'the grey sheets of dust on all the streets, the noise of engines, the burning and destroyed villages in their apocalyptic grandeur'.[40]

Although presenting the alternative 'voice' of German popular opinion, Benz did not attempt to claim the same levels of jubilation recorded for the outbreak of war in August 1914: 'Experts agree that the August of 1914 and the September of 1939 have little in common'.[41] Similarly, Angus Calder contrasted 'the hysteria of August 1914 and the absence of high spirits' in 1939 in Britain.[42] A sense of 'reluctant loyalty' also pervaded British public opinion. In August 1938, Mass-Observation concluded that the British public were resolved to co-operate with the authorities regardless of their desire to avoid conflict.[43] Despite hopes for a peaceful solution to the European crises between 1936 and 1939, general populations felt powerless to halt the descent into war in August 1939. When their fears were confirmed in the early days of September of that year, people had little choice but to cooperate. But, the decision to go to war, as Tom Harrisson observed, had little to do with the people: it was up to 'Them'.[44] The public did not have to express approval or engage in patriotic celebrations. In order to calm nerves and steel the nation, the government of each country had to persuade its people that their worries were unfounded, that their sacrifices would be needed and that victory was assured. British and German propagandists had to convince the population that war was necessary and justified if they wanted to guarantee full cooperation and high morale.

It was in this climate that both Britain and Germany had come, if by differing degrees, to recognize the importance of justifying war to their populations by September 1939. It had become clear, particularly in the aftermath of World War I, that propaganda was an essential weapon of war, which had the ability, at the very least, to play handmaiden to wider military campaigns. However, the two nations approached the question of propaganda from two very different perspectives, emanating from their respective experiences of public opinion, persuasion and conflict in World War I. Philip Taylor and Michael Sanders argue that the 1914–18 conflict saw belligerents, and in particular the British Government, opening 'a Pandoran Box which unleashed the weapon of propaganda upon the modern world'.[45] War coverage determined that public opinion was to be a key factor in post-war politics. Politicians could not ignore popular opinion, and in turn, the mass publicity surrounding national and international developments meant that the wider population became increasingly politicized. Equally, war was no longer the sole preserve of the soldier. The conflict introduced the concept of 'Total War': an all-embracing effort requiring the contribution of the ordinary man, conscripted to serve on the front lines, the professional soldier and the home populations alike. It was a conflict which affected the everyday lives of citizens. This required total mobilization: not just in military, economic and political terms, but, for the first time in the major sense, in psychological terms as well. If such an effort was required on numerous levels, governments needed to convince their troops and their home populations of the need to enlist, the necessity of the fight and the endurance required to win it. The breakneck speed of modernizing developments, such as the merging of the home and front lines, the employment of women as manual labour in factories and the mass slaughter on the battlefield, required a lubricant – this was to be the fundamental role of state-run propaganda.

Reactions to the propaganda campaigns of the Great War in Britain and Germany partly determined the differing visions of propaganda at the beginning of World War II. In Germany, Nationalist contemporaries claimed that the defeat of 1918 had been brought about by the success of British propaganda in causing German morale to collapse. General Ludendorff famously proclaimed that 'we were hypnotized by the enemy propaganda as a rabbit is by a snake'. In the immediate post-war period, the *Dolchstoßlegende*, the myth of the stab in the back, became a dominant theme of far-right rhetoric, which contended that the defeat was the product of failed German and successful British propaganda.[46] This had a profound impact on the political thinking of Adolf Hitler, who, whilst imprisoned at Landsberg am Lech after the Munich Putsch of 1923, devoted some of his political tract *Mein Kampf* to the theme of propaganda. He stated that British propaganda was regarded as 'a weapon of the first order, while in our country it was the last resort of unemployed politicians and a haven for slackers'.[47] More widely, the legacy of propaganda in World War I was the widespread recognition by government, military and civilian, that it was becoming an intrinsic element of warfare. Methods of persuasion needed to be refined and developed by the state in years to come. For Britain, it also raised certain ethical issues. Britain's success, on the one hand, created a template for future propaganda operations, but it also created numerous problems cutting right to the heart of the very principles that they had claimed to be fighting for: freedom and the rights of the individual. For Britain, the only major result of success was a series of dilemmas – dilemmas which to the contemporary mind were so problematic that successive governments resolved virtually to abandon any involvement in propaganda at state level, partly due to the exposure of the false nature of some of the propaganda employed during the conflict, such as that detailed in Arthur Ponsonby's *Falsehood in Wartime*, published in 1928.[48] There was also a general desire to rid the nation of all weapons of total warfare, including those associated with psychological warfare. Questions pertaining to the accountability of the state also left a rather bitter aftertaste. Issues of class, religion and morality impacted upon government reluctance to use propaganda, and the public became far more sceptical about government information. As Robert Graves observed in his 1929 publication, *Goodbye to all That*, 'It never occurred to me that newspapers and statesmen could lie. I forgot my pacifism – I was ready to believe the worst of the Germans ... I discounted perhaps 20% of the atrocity details as wartime exaggeration. That was not, of course, enough'.[49] Therefore, having forged the way for the use of psychological warfare, persuasion of neutrals, home morale, censorship and espionage, and in order to regain popular trust in politics, the expertise was shelved, only to be reluctantly brought out again in 1935. In the lead-up to World War II, then, as Taylor and Badsey have observed, the British Ministry of Information 'was to a large extent still fighting the last war'.[50]

This was one of the reasons why the Ministry of Information in the first months of World War II was perceived to be so ineffective. Although historians have both confirmed and challenged this perception,[51] the Ministry appeared to struggle to gain public support and trust, and to define its identity and mission. It entered the war 'inarticulate' if not as 'speechless' as it had been in August 1914. Despite the fact that the Ministry had been planned for five years prior to the outbreak of war, 'before Hitler's seizure of Prague in March 1939 few people in British governmental circles were prepared to accept the idea that a Ministry of Information would be necessary. [It did], after all, mean war'.[52] In the early stages of the conflict, the Ministry suffered through its attempts to resolve the dilemma as to whether its primary function would be to 'inform' the public or to use propaganda as an aggressive weapon of war, initially viewing these tasks as being mutually exclusive. In October 1939, *The Times* reported a debate in the House of Lords, in which Lord Macmillan, the then Minister of Information, intimated that there existed 'a false notion that victory required the services of a miscellaneous legion of "specialists", churning out "propaganda"... A Ministry of Information,' he asserted, 'rightly discharging its titular functions, will provide its own answer to the critics'.[53] And the critics were numerous indeed. Nicknamed the 'Ministry of Dis-information' and 'the Ministry of Muddle', the MoI was subject to many satirical critiques, delivered by, amongst others, Evelyn Waugh in his novel *Put Out More Flags* (1942) and the journalist Norman Riley in *999 and All That* (1940), the title ridiculing the announcement that the MoI had employed 999 staff.[54] Perhaps more worrying for the Ministry was the fact that the public perception of the MoI was one of inefficiency, bungling and poor management, and was convinced that it was not up to the task of defeating the juggernaut that was the Nazi propaganda machine. A letter to *The Times* on 30 September 1939 reflected public dissatisfaction with the operation of the Ministry, its author commenting that '[g]enuine sympathy is felt for Lord Macmillan; he is faced with an impossible task as a first-class jockey who had been put up on a carthorse to win the Derby. It is no use the owner (*i.e.* the Government) docking its tail or fitting racing plates in place of iron shoes; it cannot win because its origin, its shape and its action unfit it for the work required of it'.[55] Such feelings were also confirmed by Mass-Observation, who reported in April 1940 that 'the MoI is almost universally discredited in the eyes of the masses'. Propaganda output, they noted, was consistently 'slowed up, muddled or mishandled ever since the war began'. Contrary to Lord Macmillan's claims of the Ministry fulfilling the role indicated by its title, the MoI was perceived as taking up 'a position of under-information'. This had worrying implications:

> It is powerfully affecting voluntary effort, and nothing is answered by a superficial unity
> of compulsion – particularly as propaganda has tried to inform the masses that this

is a war for freedom. The present position of devalued or relatively idle channels of publicity automatically leads to waves of rumour, bewilderment, increasing criticism of the status quo; talk and personal opinion develop as an opposition to inadequate information and instructions not publicized in popular form. The results are deplorable for civilian morale ... public bewilderment is already piling up; the Premier's refusal to clarify war aims has accentuated it. Bewilderment breeds disgust, and suspicion. Disgust and suspicion breeds disunity, defeat.[56]

Unfortunately, the Ministry had not lived up to H. V. Rhodes's advice in November 1938 that it 'should ... start in a Rolls-Royce way and not in a Ford way'.[57]

With such an unpopular Ministry, it is not surprising to find that few were happy with the prospect of becoming Minister of Information. Each incumbent found the post to be tiresome and difficult to manage. After leaving the office in January 1940, Lord Macmillan commented that he watched 'with Lucretian philosophy the vicissitudes of the Ministry which I once adorned and I must confess I cannot regret my emancipation'.[58] His successor Lord John Reith, the former director-general of the BBC, held similar views,[59] as did Duff Cooper, who succeeded Reith as Minister of Information on 12 May 1940 for a short period. Cooper recalled that one of the chief difficulties of his task was coping with the levels of public criticism received by the Ministry. He noted that 'the presence of so many able, undisciplined men in one ministry was bound to lead to a great deal of internal friction, and we were at the same time subjected to a continual bombardment of criticism from without'.[60] This sense of working for an ineffective Ministry, with little public or political respect permeated the structures of the MoI. Indeed, Duff Cooper's despondency at the constant level of press and popular criticism[61] led him to periods of inactivity and indecision at crucial points in the early stages of the war. Walter Monckton, Director of the Press and Censorship Bureau, commented that 'I get so horribly depressed from time to time with the burden of the Ministry. There is so much to do, and with all his great and good qualities my master is very hard to get to the point of drastic action or to take interest in a concrete form'.[62]

Monckton must have been all too aware of the problems outlined in a letter to him from A. P. Ryan, adviser to the BBC on home affairs, in June 1941, in which Ryan noted that, 'the history of animal management contains no more dismal record of failure. No dog has been stopped from barking by the MoI. The public are skeptical and unimpressed ... Ample lip service is paid to the importance of propaganda in wartime, but behind the scenes ... the spirit of skepticism is vocal'.[63] Duff Cooper's rather undistinguished time as Minister caused some fundamental questions to be raised over the nature of British propaganda and its organization. In May 1941, Brendan Bracken, former journalist and Conservative Member of Parliament, in a letter to Monckton, warned:

> I think a storm is brewing over the devoted head of your Minister who is, as you know, the whipping boy of the Government. Your Minister is pushed by a strange pack of

critics. Some say you are doing too much and wasting public money. Others abuse Duff for not trying to turn himself into a little Goebbels. I am afraid that Duff cannot Nazify himself. He is not a congenital liar. He has no concentration camps in which to put editors. And he is even refused facilities for beating journalists... Finally the Service Departments are tighter than oysters... And they have the happiness of knowing that their unreasonable and irritating attitude to the press will not get them into trouble. The MoI exists to bear their burdens.[64]

Just two months after writing this letter, Bracken himself became Minister of Information, succeeding Duff Cooper. He remained in the post until the end of the war. Benefiting from his journalistic background and his close relationship with Winston Churchill, he afforded the Ministry some stability and guaranteed a direct link to the Prime Minister. Nevertheless, the most turbulent time for Britain during the war was also the most insecure for the MoI, leading government officers to chant 'Hush, hush chuckle who dares, Another new Minister's fallen downstairs'.[65]

It was in this atmosphere of concern over the psychological mission of the Ministry and its ability to fulfil it that the MoI had to realize its primary function: that of combating declining morale and enemy propaganda. In this latter task at least, it had a formidable opponent. The two structures and missions of the Ministry and the *Reichsministerium für Volksaufklärung und Propaganda*, at this early stage in the war, could not have been more different. For the British Ministry of Information, the most important tasks were to 'secure and disseminate news ... of the activities of the Government as widely and freely as possible', 'to present the British and Allied case as widely and fully as possible to the world in all its aspects' and 'to watch and check enemy news and propaganda in all countries and to undertake counter-propaganda and [a] counter news service to ensure that the British position ... [is] fully understood'. More importantly, the Ministry set itself the task of watching and recording 'habit and opinion at home with a view to maintaining the integrity and spirit of the people; to guide habit and opinion in directions favourable to the policy and aims of the Government by [the] issue of information, instruction and advice both direct and indirect'.[66] The early years of the MoI's propaganda campaign were characterized by a gentle and 'open' approach to persuasion. On the eve of war, the Home Publicity Sub-Committee determined that, in order to counter the widespread panic and terror that they presumed would ensue with aerial bombardment, an ample supply of tea should be on hand: 'the most comforting thing ... was to have a cup of tea and get together to talk things over', commented Lady Grigg. Professor Hilton added that the Committee needed to consider 'the value of sugar for steadying the nerves'.[67] This approach, as McLaine has pointed out, 'fell rather short of what might have been expected a day or two before the *Luftwaffe* was supposed to launch a heavy attack against the country'.[68] Naturally, such attitudes led to the denunciation of the early propaganda methods of the MoI as 'effeminate and mild-mannered'.[69]

In that meeting, the Home Publicity Division also added that all publicity should avoid sensationalism, 'as was done in the last war'.[70] Fear of the return to World War I propaganda tactics, discredited in the post-war period, determined the course of British propaganda activities in the early years of the conflict.[71] Although officers of the Ministry recognized that 'influencing opinion is just as good a way of helping to win a war as the use of aeroplanes and tanks' and that 'the object of war [propaganda] is to persuade people to do things'[72] their approach to psychological warfare, in the broadest sense of the term, was cautious, and partly a product of the legacy of the Great War. Propaganda was still regarded by the Government as 'an exotic', belonging 'to the dictator regimes'. As Lord Reith observed, 'special care therefore had to be used if it was to be grafted onto the democratic machinery'.[73] Working with a population already suspicious of propaganda required considerable skill if the Ministry was to succeed in guiding the habit and opinion of the British public at war. Accordingly, the MoI projected itself as an 'information'-providing body, and went to considerable lengths to contrast its own activities with those of the RMVP. Broadcasting to the nation in April 1941, Walter Monckton observed that:

> [T]he big difference between our Ministry of Information and the Propaganda Ministry of Dr. Goebbels [is that] ... from the moment our Ministry came into existence it has been subjected to constant criticism... But neither I nor my fellow workers mind this criticism because we realise that it is an essential part of that freedom for which we are fighting this war... Freedom to think, to speak, to worship as we like... [W]e have a hard and fast rule: always to tell the truth. I know our method must seem dull compared to this ... completely unreliable Nazi method. We shall not preserve this freedom by complacency or lying: 'No early hopes or lies shall guide us to the goal; But iron sacrifice of body, will and soul'.[74]

The Ministry was fully conscious that 'propaganda is primarily an offensive act',[75] and that this act had to be perceived to be conducted within limits that were acceptable to a democratic nation. At times, the press supported the mission of the MoI in this respect, seeking to convince the public of the primarily informative nature of the Ministry's work and its potential benefits. As *The Yorkshire Post* commented in February 1940, 'We shall not link our propaganda with such desperate expedients as Goebbels does, however grievous the burdens and exasperations of war become... Our propaganda should be the champion of our deeds'.[76]

The German response to the outbreak of World War II was also partly conditioned by the memory of the propaganda activities during the 1914–18 conflict. Perceiving German propaganda and psychological warfare of the Great War to be weak and a key factor in Germany's defeat, culminating in the *Dolchstoßlegende*, the Nazis took an aggressive and overt approach to propaganda. Unlike in Britain, it was considered to be a positive and essential force in governing the nation, and the Nazis, rather than disguising the state's use of persuasion, promoted it. In September 1934, Goebbels described modern political propaganda as a 'creative art'. For Goebbels, persuasion was just as important as military prowess and might in recasting the German nation, noting that 'it may be a good thing to possess power that rests on arms. But it is better and more lasting to win the heart of a people and to keep it'.[77] Given this constant aim of the Party and, later, of the regime, it is not surprising that one of the first acts of the new administration was to establish the RMVP by Presidential decree on 12 March 1933, one and a half months after the Nazis came to power. Joseph Goebbels was appointed head of the new Ministry, following a successful period organizing the propaganda campaign for the 1930 and 1932 Reichstag elections. It was staffed by 350 civil servants and other employees. Although the Ministry grew throughout the 1930s, by 1 April 1939, it had not surpassed Goebbels' limit of 1,000 due to financial constraints, making it in essence no larger than the MoI's 999.[78] Its task, clarified by Hitler in June 1933, was to assume responsibility for 'all tasks of spiritual direction of the nation',[79] giving the Ministry some flexibility in the interpretation of its role. Just as the title of the Ministry of Information said much about the British approach to propaganda in the aftermath of World War I, so too did the title of its German counterpart. For Goebbels, both propaganda and popular enlightenment had distinct functions to play in the Nazi state.[80] 'Popular enlightenment', he stated, 'is essentially something passive. Propaganda, on the other hand, is something active… It is not enough to reconcile people to our regime, to move them toward a position of neutrality toward us; we would rather work on a people until they are addicted to us'.[81] For the Nazis, propaganda was a 'revolutionary act'.[82]

The organization of the RMVP was seemingly clear cut and delineated, although research suggests that many areas of National Socialist communications were subject to the same overlapping responsibilities and power struggles as other aspects of the regime.[83] Goebbels united the three offices of the Ministry, the *Reichskulturkammer* (Reich Culture Chamber), established on 22 September 1933 to oversee the seven *Kammern* (Chambers) for the individual means of communication and to control personnel in the arts, and the Central Propaganda Office of the Party. These institutions covered all areas of propaganda in the Reich, from film, radio, the press, literature, music, theatre and art to the synchronization of activities on a local and national level.[84] This adhered to the Nazi policy of *Gleichschaltung* – the coordination of state structures and national community under Nazi leadership.

Despite this unification of the media, however, Hitler and his newly appointed minister did not consistently share each other's views on the direction of propaganda policy in the Third Reich. On some issues, they remained in agreement. Both Hitler and Goebbels viewed the masses with equal contempt. In *Mein Kampf*, Hitler maintained that the masses' understanding was, 'feeble'. Goebbels concurred, observing that, 'the rank and file are usually much more primitive than we imagine'. Propaganda, therefore, had to be confined to 'simple and repetitive' terms. Both Hitler and Goebbels concluded that ideas were to be 'reduced to the simplest level', and repeated over and over again, 'until the very last individual has come to grasp the idea that has been put forward'. On the method for the transferral of these ideas, Hitler and Goebbels disagreed. Hitler's vision of the propaganda state, as outlined in *Mein Kampf*, ended upon the acquisition and consolidation of power.[85] Goebbels, however, believed that, once in power, propaganda had to be intensified in order to strengthen the National Socialist position and, more importantly, to change the national consciousness: – to win over the masses – to re-educate them. As he stated in April 1933, 'We are not satisfied with having 52% of the nation and terrorizing the other 48%. We want the people as the people, not only passively but actively'.[86]

By 1939, Nazi propaganda had been institutionalized for six years, and although there remains some debate as to how prepared the RMVP was for the events of 1939,[87] the outbreak of hostilities had been 'preceded by peacetime propaganda, which was seen as an essential part of the prelude to war'.[88] Given the different approaches of Britain and Germany and their respective attitudes towards propaganda in the aftermath of World War I, it is not surprising to find that the rhetoric which marked the first years of the war differed considerably. Whereas Britain pursued a more understated approach, National Socialist propaganda sought to activate the population psychologically. This led Goebbels to proclaim that the British were 'poor psychologists'.[89] Attempting to dispel the myth of 1914-18 psychological warfare, he announced that 'the English have never been good psychologists', rather that the German propagandists failed to appreciate the importance of the battle for hearts and minds. Within this environment, proclaimed Goebbels, it was clear that 'in the kingdom of the blind, the one-eyed man is king'. British dominance in the field of psychological warfare during World War I was deemed by Goebbels to be an 'easy victory'. Times had changed, he announced, and commented that:

> These days, both the German working man and the German intellectual know more about the English character, English politics and the English ways than the 'Gentlemen' in London would think. We have become political psychologists, whereas Churchill and Chamberlain are still employing methods from 25 years ago and think they are still dealing with the Germans of 1918.[90]

There was some truth in this. As Philip Taylor has demonstrated, 'although the means of disseminating propaganda [in Britain] had altered radically through the advance of communications technology..., the methods adopted towards propaganda in the next war were to be essentially those employed in the last'.[91]

The concept that the British propagandists were trapped in the past was a theme often repeated by Goebbels. For the Reich Minister, his opponents were merely 'figures of fun'.[92] He remained confident throughout the initial period of the war, believing that the British had missed significant opportunities to capitalize on key events.[93] German propagandists went to considerable lengths to draw upon the perceived legacy of the British psychological campaigns of the Great War, frequently reminding the public of the atrocity stories published by British newspapers and circulated worldwide.[94] Goebbels capitalized on the belief that British propaganda was renowned for perpetrating falsehoods, proclaiming that Nazi propaganda during the war had 'no need to respond to lies with lies', and that it would confront the 'slander campaign of their enemy with the whole truth'.[95] Claiming that 'truth is our weapon', Nazi propaganda insisted that they did 'not need lies' nor did they 'want them'. English and French propagandists, they asserted, 'lie and will lie further' but 'the truth will always win'.[96] Although outwardly Goebbels did not fear British propaganda in the early years of the conflict, believing it to be impotent in the face of the work conducted by the RMVP, he still took certain measures to discredit the message of the Reich's primary enemy, leading the British in turn to comment: 'In the present struggle, the Germans, despite their huge preponderance in men and materials, have never relaxed their attention to propaganda'.[97] If not in terms of style and content, this, at least, was something the British were keen to emulate.

At the outbreak of war, both Britain and Germany recognized the importance of film as a method of justifying war. Technological advances and the popularization of cinema as a means of information and distraction meant that by 1939 film was regarded as a primary medium of mass communication and, in addition, a weapon in the arsenal for the battle for hearts and minds. By the summer of 1940, both Britain and Germany spoke of film in military terms, with *Filmwelt* proclaiming it to be the ultimate 'weapon of truth'[98] and *The Cinema*, a British trade newspaper, heralding the 'charge of the cinema brigade'.[99] Given their more active attitude to the use of propaganda, it is not surprising that the National Socialists rushed to embrace the most modern of media. By the outbreak of war, the Nazis had already amassed considerable experience in dealing with film, from early attempts during the late 1920s and early 1930s,[100] to constructing and executing film production whilst in power from 1933. By 1939, the RMVP and its subsidiary, the *Reichsfilmkammer* (Reich Film Chamber, RFK), had already devised and managed a well-oiled system in relation to the supervision of the major studios, film financing, industry personnel registration and control, pre- and post-production censorship, and exhibition and distribution.[101] The gradual process of acquiring the various film companies operating within the Reich and its territories, notably Ufa Filmkunst, Terra Filmkunst, Tobis Filmkunst, Bavaria Filmkunst, Prag Film AG and Wien-Film, ended on 10 January 1942 with the creation of Ufa-Film GmbH (Ufi), which became classified as *staatseigen* (state-owned) rather *staatsmittelbar* (indirectly state-controlled).[102] This was supplemented just over one month later, on 29 February 1942, with the introduction of the *Reichsfilmintendanz* to 'concentrate on matters of film "art"', allowing the RMVP to dictate the political affairs of the industry'.[103] In all, war provided the impetus and the opportunity for the full incorporation of the film industry into the National Socialist fold.

As the moves to 'nationalize' the film industry from 1937 to 1942 suggested, film was perceived to be an important method of communication in wartime. War meant specific tasks for film in Nazi Germany. It acted as 'one of the most important means of leading the people', with newsreels presenting a 'real, unvarnished picture of military action [conducted] by German soldiers on all fronts'. Feature films were to be much more than 'sheer entertainment'; they had an 'educational function', with 'high artistic value' and '*weltanschaulich* meaning'.[104] For Goebbels, film in war was 'the most important means of propaganda', its task being 'to strengthen the fighting spirit of every single citizen, so that our warfare will lead to complete success'.[105]

It was essential then, given that film was to play a considerable role in wartime propaganda campaigns, that production and box-office receipts should remain high. In the early years of the war, the RMVP went to considerable lengths to stress the success of the film industry. The press emphasized the impact of the territorial gains made by the Reich on the film industry and the opportunities for exporting German films abroad,[106] as well as maintaining that there had been a substantial increase in attendance in the *Altreich* 'year on year'.[107] Despite the manifold problems which confronted the film industry with the outbreak of war, notably the acquisition of film theatres and audiences with disparate film cultures across Europe,[108] the Nazi propaganda machine continued to present its difficulties as opportunities for the development of the German cinema, reassuring audiences that their enjoyment of German film should not be disrupted. As the *Frankfurter Zeitung* asserted in May 1940, the blackout had not hindered cinema attendance. Indeed, the cinema became a draught-proof, heated place to spend a couple of hours. Even rationing and consumer restrictions became a boon for the film industry, assuming that people's spending power had been freed up to allow for increased expenditure on leisure activities and entertainment.[109] When aerial bombardment commenced, Nazi newspapers were keen to emphasize that not even the bomber could drive the German people from the theatre or cinema, claiming that shows and films were playing to 'packed houses in all Gaus', 'even those where the English love to terrorize the civilian population'.[110] Perhaps as testament to the Nazis' achievement in persuading the population to visit the cinema more regularly, attendance continued to increase throughout the war, only dropping slightly in 1944.[111]

Nevertheless, despite Nazi claims that the German film industry had never been healthier, the number of films exhibited in total and the number of German films produced during the Third Reich, as detailed by the numbers of films passing through the *Filmprüfstelle*, steadily declined (apart from a small rise in 1943), falling from 172 in total in 1937 to just 77 by 1944.[112] Falling production has to be set against increased attendance. The programme often did not fully satisfy the needs of an increased cinema audience, a factor which was not helped by the RFK's decree of 11 November 1939 which detailed that 'no German film should run for less than a week in a German cinema'.[113] With fewer films to screen, cinema owners opted for longer runs of films, leading to a decline in audience interest and satisfaction with the film programme. An SD report of 26 August 1941 from the Leipzig region commented that a number of films were 'running for far too long', complaining that in local cinemas the Arthur Maria Rabenalt film *Reitet für Deutschland* (Riding for Germany) was only replaced by another film after four months and that the run of Günther Rittau's war film *U-Boote westwärts* (U-Boats Westwards) had already reached two months. Significantly, they added that one film, *Frau Luna* (Theo Lingen, 1941), had been well received, commenting that 'Working-class audiences, in particular, were delighted to see a funny and light movie for once. They were glad to be able to have a laugh for a change and rated the film as good'.[114] As war progressed, the problem of re-runs and long runs increased, as evidenced by the programme of 'National Films' to be screened in 1944.[115] Overall, the German film industry was not as successful as the publicity surrounding it had claimed. Despite increased attendance, a by-product of war in many ways, it offered its patrons less; it was not necessarily providing audiences with a varied programme, one which responded to public needs, particularly the need for light entertainment before 1942; it was not producing as much as promised and consequently it did not live up to its claim that Germany was the 'second largest film-producing country in the world'.[116]

With the onset of war, the industry was also faced with further challenges. The cost of producing films, already a difficulty in the pre-war years, once again came to the fore, a problem which was dramatically increased with the interference of the censor, who frequently halted or requested amendments to projects already in the latter stages of production.[117] This problem was exacerbated by increasingly strict controls on film materials in wartime, which limited the amount of negative stock available to film-makers, and the shortage of film workers who were increasingly required to join the armed forces or work in armaments production. Such production difficulties were no doubt aggravated by the studios' increasingly ambitious film projects of the war years.[118]

Foreign policy activities, whilst increasing the potential audience for German films, on the one hand, also reduced the overall global capacity of film importing and exporting, on the other hand. Film-producers, the RFK and the RMVP recognized the importance of global film markets to the German film industry. Nevertheless, exports crashed to a mere 7 per cent of the industry's income for 1939, partly due to the fact that 'many foreign Jewish distributors simply refused to accept German films'[119] and that German restrictions on imports prevented a full exploitation of global markets, due to foreign quota systems.[120] Despite National Socialist attempts to restrict or even ban imported films, films of foreign origin continued to be shown in Germany. The most prolific exporter of films, the United States of America, continued to exhibit films in the Third Reich until February 1941, despite repeated attempts to enact a total ban.[121] Significantly, the decisions, that to avoid banning US films and the ban itself, appear to have been based upon financial reasoning relating to importing, exporting, and the negotiation of favourable contracts. Notably absent from these discussions was mention of ideological factors, demonstrating that the RMVP did not merely regard film as a vehicle for the transmission of propaganda. It was also a business, at times a lucrative one. However, comments relating to the quality and propagandistic value of American features filtered through to the Nazi leadership from below. The SD reports for the Leipzig region relating to the 1940 film *South Sea Nights* (*Südseenächte*) noted that the film was 'heavily criticized'. The report suggested that the RMVP were more concerned with honouring existing contracts with the United States than the spiritual direction of the nation and that 'the showing of such a film, solely in order to make money, is not in keeping with National Socialism'.[122] Moreover, audiences recognized the tension between the war effort and the import of American films. An SD report from May 1940 noted that:

> The main issue is why these films should still be shown now, in times of war, when the American position of neutrality is by no means pro-German. A German war newsreel and then an American feature film to follow would be very much at odds with one another and present the German viewer with contradictions which would be hard to bear.[123]

Thus, war brought significant challenges for the Nazi-controlled film industry in maintaining and strengthening its financial position, ensuring that box-office receipts continued to rise and managing the opportunities presented by the annexation of new territories from 1938, whilst at the same time coping with wartime shortages, increasingly ambitious film projects, and managing a variety of popular needs and desires as expressed by cinema-goers. Although by 1942 the film industry had become *staatseigen*, the RMVP faced considerable difficulties in managing and balancing productions, ideology and popular opinion.

The British, for their part, were well aware of the perceived power of the German film industry and its propaganda outputs. Duff Cooper, Minister of Information in 1940, noted that 'the most prominent minister in Germany today is the Minister of Propaganda, and it is estimated by those who have studied the question very carefully that the German government are spending upon propaganda something in the neighbourhood of £20,000,000 a year. Great are the powers of propaganda'.[124] The comparison with his own situation in the British war cabinet must have been apparent to Cooper and, although the trade newspaper, *Today's Cinema*, urged him that Britain was 'in a position to beat Germany via films',[125] the MoI were not convinced. British propagandists were slow to recognize the immense potential of film, and in particular, the feature film as a means of persuasion, delaying the formulation of a policy regarding suitable approaches to the use of film in the propaganda arsenal. The history of British film during World War II was inextricably tied to the Ministry and its subsidiary, the Films Division.[126] Like the Ministry itself, the Films Division got off to a rather inauspicious and turbulent start. The early years of the conflict were marked by a lack of cooperation between the MoI and the film industry and a lack of effective and trusted leadership. The Films Division experienced three different directors from 1939 to 1945: Sir Joseph Ball (until late 1939), Sir Kenneth Clark (until April 1940), and finally Jack Beddington, who at least possessed some experience of the film industry, albeit in the field of advertising as director of publicity at Shell Mex and BP Ltd in the 1930s. He was not considered to be 'a brash amateur', unlike his predecessor.[127] Although the MoI had officially sponsored around 1,400 short films by 1945, it did not possess the capability of producing its own films until the GPO Film Unit was resurrected in April 1940 under the name 'Crown Film Unit'. Even with its own production apparatus, the Films Division was beset by administrative problems as well as disputes about its role in film production at war, causing a deep rift between John Grierson's 'Documentary Boys' such as Arthur Elton, Basil

Wright, John Taylor and Paul Rotha, and Ministry officials.[128] The public, the film industry and the government regarded the Films Division with a high degree of scepticism.[129] The Select Committee on National Expenditure of August 1940 damningly concluded that 'the work of the Films Division in the home field has been largely ineffective through the lack of clearly defined objectives on the part of the Ministry… This Division had not been presented with a clear conception of the message or messages which were to be conveyed to the public by means of films'.[130]

The Select Committee had, in fact, cut right to the heart of the problem: that, in the early stages of the war, British propagandists and film-makers were themselves divided as to the most effective form of film propaganda. Although Lord Macmillan proclaimed in October 1939 that the Ministry 'recognises how important in the modern arsenal of weapons of the mind the cinema with its vivid appeal to the eye is' and that they were 'most anxious to increase its efficacy',[131] they did not have a set policy for film propaganda until 1940, under the guidance of Kenneth Clark, who circulated a document intended to guide the Films Division as to general principles and suitable themes. It was at this stage that the Co-ordinating Committee recommended the use of a variety of forms of film to convey the message to the public ranging from the documentary, to the feature film, to the informational short, newsreels and even cartoons, which they considered to be 'a very flexible medium of propaganda and [which has] the advantage that ideas can be inserted under cover of absurdity. They can present (as in Mickey Mouse) a system of ethics in which independence and individuality are always successful, bullies are made fools of, the weak can cheek the strong with impunity'.[132] Each form of film propaganda had a specific role to fulfil within the British programme. Short films were viewed as 'an immediate means of communication with the people', whereas documentaries were instructed to focus on the 'fighting [and] subsidiary services'. The MoI encouraged the production of feature films which emphasized 'British life and character … British ideas and institutions … [and] German ideals and institutions in recent history' by way of contrast.[133] Nevertheless, it was still felt that the propaganda plan was too nebulous and indistinct. As the Select Committee commented in the same year:

> British morale stands in so little need of artificial support. This consideration should have led to the conclusion that material for films was not to be found in the interpretation of vague themes of reassurance but in messages to the people precisely related to particular needs. The aim should be not merely the enhancement of patriotic spirit but its direction into channels of activity. What is needed [is] to break down the psychological barriers to the fulfilment of particular national requirements.[134]

This sentiment was echoed by some in the industry, such as the *Documentary News Letter*, who believed that 'you cannot raise morale unless you give the public information and explanation; and our great failing … lies in the fact that most of the information given to the public has no forward looking quality'.[135]

In attempting to combine the informative and escapist function of film, the MoI declared that propaganda films need not be dull. Indeed, they contended that 'film propaganda will be most effective when it is least recognisable as such'. The perfect 'cover', therefore, for government-sponsored propaganda activities was the entertainment feature. The MoI suggested that:

> The film being a popular medium must be good entertainment if it is to be good propaganda. A film which induces boredom antagonises the audience to the cause which it advocates. For this reason, an amusing American film with a few hits at the Nazi regime is probably better propaganda than any number of documentaries showing the making of bullets, etc.[136]

Whilst the sentiment of this statement holds true, it demonstrates that, in the early years of the war, the MoI expressed little confidence in the British film industry's ability to produce entertainment features with propaganda value. Here, escapist entertainment was to be left to the Hollywood dream factory. This, in part, also reflected the government's concerns over investing in such an unpredictable medium as the entertainment feature film for propagandistic purposes. The Select Committee on National Expenditure of August 1940 provides a clear example of the scepticism with which the filmic activities of the MoI and film propaganda more generally were viewed in official circles:

> Of the three main kinds of film, the feature film, the entertainment film which takes the chief place in the ordinary cinema programme, is the most difficult to employ as an instrument of propaganda. That it has a place in any long term policy cannot be doubted. That it has a place in a programme of wartime propaganda is open to question. There are two principal difficulties. One is the great length of time necessary required for the production of a full length feature film. The other and more serious objection is the highly speculative character of feature film production. Effort and experience, art and imagination, genius itself, none nor all of these have the power to command infallible success. One thing only is certain in feature film production – the uncertainty of success.[137]

During the early stages of the conflict, and in particular after the experience of the first major feature film production of the war years made with the support of the MoI, *The Lion Has Wings*, the Ministry was rather cautious about the use of feature length films for official propaganda purposes, despite encouragement from the industry. Although, as Chapman suggests, 'from about 1942–3, it is possible to identify a broad consensus between the MoI and the commercial film-makers over the nature of film propaganda'[138] facilitated by the Ideas Committee which brought together key individuals from the industry and the propagandists of the MoI, the early years were beset with difficulties in establishing a firm basis for cooperation and interference from bodies such as the Select Committee on National Expenditure. With the appointment of Beddington, who devised 'the means whereby Select Committee and Treasury strictures could either be neatly circumvented or fruitfully confronted by documentarists and feature film producers alike',[139] and the increasing cooperation between the MoI and the studios, film was established as a key means of communicating the British wartime message in both an escapist and an informative manner.

The initial reluctance to engage with film as a principal method of propaganda led to despair and frustration within the film industry. Indeed, *Today's Cinema* gloomily proclaimed in November 1940 that 'when the history comes to be told of the terrible messing about that has gone on with the film trade, it will form [some of] the blackest pages in the war organisation'.[140] Castigating the civil servants for their 'smugness' and refusal to 'adjust themselves to the rapid tempo and the iconoclastic urgencies of total war', film-makers feared that cinematic production would be hampered by a 'barricade of precedent, procedure and prejudice' and stalled by 'red-tape and ... official hierarchies'. At the height of the dispute between film-makers and the MoI, *Documentary News Letter* resorted to the words of J. B. Priestley to accuse the Ministry of displaying the characteristics of 'a man who hates democracy, reasonable argument, give and take, tolerance, patience and a humorous equality ... who loves bluster and swagger ... plotting in back-rooms, shouting and bullying'.[141]

The industry's fears were also shared by the public, who informed Mass-Observation in April 1940 that film had been 'neglected' and that 'the Government's only propagandist film so far has been treated as a joke, although it was supposed to instruct people about ARP. Its audience response, in terms of laughter, nearly equals an indifferent Disney'.[142] In the early months of the war, then, the Ministry was undecided about its film propaganda programme, and its activities were hampered by the limited visions of the Treasury and Parliamentary Select Committees. Despite pleas from both the industry and the public, the MoI failed to act quickly to invest in film, adding to its image as an ineffective and impotent body. It was in this environment that the perception that the Nazis were winning the battle of hearts and minds dominated popular and official discourses. Film-makers, such as Michael Balcon, were forced to 'plead' for British Production,[143] whilst Robert Cromie, writing for *Today's Cinema*, encouraged the MoI to 'use the cinema as an asset to the nation!' He warned 'that the Germans have created a form of propaganda founded upon conscientious lying and have developed this with cunning until it assumes the rank and importance of a state service demands a suitable antidote'.[144] *Today's Cinema* even went as far as to claim that 'propaganda films will save lives', arguing that propaganda 'is a weapon we must use to the full and that the Government must be prepared to put to its greatest use – *via the screen*'.[145] The film trade were keen to point out that the cinema also had a specific role to play in the lead-up to the war and in the early days of the 'phoney war'. As Richard Ford of the Odeon Education Department commented, 'even in the crisis of September 1938, the value of the cinemas was clearly evident, not only for disseminating information but in providing an antidote for worry and nervous strain. Indeed the psychological value of the cinema in combating "jitters" may well be its strongest claim to be regarded as a public servant'.[146] Mass-Observation was disappointed to find that 'unfortunately for the cinema, elderly people took charge of the war. Many in our Cabinet are far from cinema fans', concluding that 'the achievements of the film section … are staggeringly little'.[147] It was clear that, as Mass-Observation, the industry and the public had noted, the Ministry remained relatively impervious to the benefits of film propaganda in the initial months of the conflict.

Not only did the British film industry have to contend with internal division and dispute, but it was faced with problems created by the war itself, including the initial decision to close cinemas for the first two weeks of the conflict. A letter from a Mass-Observer to their primary film reporter, Len England, demonstrates that the decision to close the cinemas was an unpopular one. Judging by the levels of public annoyance, he stated, 'you would have imagined that they depended utterly on the films for their entertainment and relaxation, instead of being, with most of them, a matter of an occasional visit'.[148] Fearing that the *Luftwaffe* would target places of mass entertainment, cinemas only began to reopen outside major conurbations on 11 September, with urban areas following shortly after on the 15th, although some cinemas reopened somewhat earlier on 7 September, such as those in Aberystwyth. Early re-openings were on the condition that 'an operator be detailed to listen in for air raid warnings during the whole period of the entertainment, that all exits are properly cleared [and] that a sufficient staff is available to prevent panic in the case of an air raid warning'. Cinema owners were urged to assist the authorities 'not only in carrying out the legal aspect of these regulations, but also their spirit'.[149] By 4 November, permission had been granted for cinemas to remain open until 11 p.m. nationwide[150], and when the doors opened once again, as one contemporary observer noted, 'they were packed from floor to ceiling'.[151]

The government also failed to give wholehearted support to the industry, resisting initial appeals to waive entertainment tax in wartime.[152] The tax was increased three times during the war years and 'by 1945 amounted to 36% of gross receipts'.[153] Naturally, this resulted in increased ticket prices for patrons.[154] Nor did the Government declare film-workers to be engaged in reserved occupations, although some were, notably camera operators, processors and plate, film and paper producers.[155] This made the 'call-up' a very real threat to the British film industry in the early years of the war. The industry called for the 'postponement of the military service of the film-making personnel essential to the fulfilment of important MoI needs'.[156] Michael Balcon begged the Government to recognize the importance of investing in films for both propaganda and mass entertainment, promising full cooperation with MoI objectives and warning them that 'a live industry can make such gestures; a dead one cannot'.[157] Such was the crisis facing them that on 7 September 1939, the C.E.A. urged 'the employment of women projectionists – *for service during [the] war period only*'.[158] Despite the protests of the industry, the threat of enlistment continued throughout the war, with the increasing need to release staff for essential war work and military service. The industry faced losing up to 70 per cent of its key personnel when, in April 1941, the Ministry of Labour and the National Service extended the call-up of film staff, ensuring that 'no employee of the British Film Industry ... under the age of 35' was eligible for the reserve list. The move was nicknamed the 'Massacre on All Fool's Day' by the *Documentary News Letter*.[159] In all, over two-thirds of British film technicians were called up.[160] Not only were human resources scarce, but so were materials essential to film production, including studio space, which 'diminished from 22 (using 65 sound stages) to 9 (with 30 sound stages)'.[161] Although the German film industry faced its own challenges as a result of the outbreak of war, Nazi propagandists were keen to capitalize on the so-called failure of the British film industry to mobilize. In May 1940, the *Frankfurter Zeitung* reported that British 'film production has faltered, with numerous technical staff and even well known actors being out of work. Consequently, the drive in Britain, in particular, to increase the proportion of home-produced films being shown has suffered a setback.[162] The *Hamburger Fremdenblatt* added on 16 February 1941 that, 'in contrast to English film production, which had capitulated rather than face the challenges of war, the German film industry was intensely at work contributing to the war effort'.[163] Not only, then, had the British film industry got off to a rather inauspicious start, it was now the subject of enemy propaganda.

Confronted with the prospect of a curtailment of the film industry and associated enterprises due to the war, the trade newspapers launched themselves into giving advice to cinema-owners which would enable them to keep their premises open and maintain a steady stream of cinema-goers. Naturally, the blackout caused a number of problems for cinema-owners, accounting for a reduction of 27 per cent in male patrons and of 17 per cent in female patrons.[164] As one Mass-Observer commented, the blackout 'kept the more timid sort in their homes'. For others, the blackout drove people into the cinemas, especially as there was nothing to do outside.[165] The blackout threatened to place restrictions on cinema signage, although by 7 December 1939, Scotland Yard had approved a 'new lighting plan' allowing for some advertising, and leading to *Kinematograph Weekly*'s proclamation that 'kinemas will brighten the blackout'.[166] In order to help cinema owners circumnavigate the challenges the dark presented to them, the newspaper resurrected its column 'Showmanship in wartime' to demonstrate that 'British exhibitors are ingenious enough to discover outlets for their capacity for showmanship which meet the needs of the moment'. The column collected numerous ideas for attracting patrons to the cinema without the use of bright lighting and within ARP restrictions, such as the use of fluorescent paints, light traps and ultra-violet lighting, as well as building film advertisements into the torches of the usherettes. 'Street stunts' were also particularly popular. At the Odeon in Balham Hill, the exhibitor adapted 'the Siegfried line, which took the form of a rope stretched across the vestibule, upon which were various articles of "washing", each with the name of a film painted upon it. A prominently placed notice told patrons: "This is not the Siegfried Line, but an Odeon line-up of good things to come"'.[167]

Once patrons had made the decision to go to the cinema, they could be comforted by the knowledge that new regulations were introduced to protect them. Preparations for cinema safety in the event of war had been underway since 1937.[168] *Kinematograph Weekly* informed its readers that, by November 1939, cinemas were required to fit non-splintering sky and lantern lights, that all windows to foyers, street and vestibules should be protected, all refrigeration plants, other than those used for ice-cream, using toxic or flammable refrigerant should be disposed of and that the formerly grand adornments such as chandeliers had to be removed. There were also new rules for employees, who were provided with a shelter in the event of an air-raid. They were to be trained in evacuation, first-aid and anti-gas precautions, and were charged with ensuring that all exits and gangways remained clear, as well as listening for air-raid sirens throughout the performance. Should a siren sound, exhibitors would display a slide 'instructing the audience as to their best course' in consultation with the local ARP, inviting them to go home or move to communal shelters,[169] although many preferred to stay in the cinema.[170] Exhibitors were advised that, in the event of a possible air-raid, 'there is always a danger that a woman may become hysterical and set off others. Women attendants should have specific instructions to remove any such person immediately, and take her to the cloakroom, where smelling salts should be available'.[171] Cinema-owners were encouraged to support government measures, by, for example, refusing to hold special children's matinees in evacuated areas.[172] In some cases, cinemas were to be used as communal air-raid shelters,[173] and some used the fact that they had air-raid shelters as a positive advertisement, such as the Gaiety in Southampton which boasted of its 'century old cellars'.[174]

When eventually cinemas did come under fire from mid-1940, the Blitz seemed to have relatively little effect on film attendance. Mass-Observation reported that 'people have little fear of being caught in the cinema in an air-raid, provided that there's a reasonable chance that the all-clear will sound before they leave'; however, patrons tended to opt for matinees as opposed to evening programmes.[175] It was frequently reported that few left the cinema when advised of a raid in progress or of a warning: 'the majority [saw] the show through', waiting for the all-clear from the comfort of their seats. When sirens sounded in the middle of a performance, 'very few people [were] seriously perturbed'.[176] *Kinematograph Weekly* commented that 'in some cases, [the theatre] management have endeavoured to profit by an untoward incident'. When a shell entered a theatre in the North-East, patrons were invited to inspect the damage for a small contribution to the theatre's 'cigarette fund'.[177] Despite enduring heavy losses at times, cinema-owners were determined to continue to show their pictures.

War presented new challenges and indeed opportunities to the film industries of both Britain and Germany. In some ways, they faced similar problems. Both had to deal with the emerging tension between increased demand and public expectations, as shaped by the war, and diminishing resources in terms of both materials and personnel. This was to become a particular problem for both Britain and Germany from 1942 when the gulf between public desires for the escapist film and resources for production became increasingly wide. However, at this early stage in the war, film in Britain and Germany was also subject to problems specific to national circumstances. Germany had to cope with the difficulties associated with an expanded market and diverse audience preferences, whilst the British were still debating the appropriate use of film as a form of propaganda. The British Ministry of Information was also facing a barrage of press, industry and public criticism, detrimental to the morale of the fledgling Ministry. In Germany, where debates were limited by censorship, the press was used to stress the progress made by the film industry under National Socialism, and where the British press, and indeed the Government, saw obstacles, the German press saw 'opportunities'. It should be no surprise to note the hesitancy of the British Government to invest in such an 'unreliable' means of propaganda as film. The Treasury Select Committee was, after all, responsible to the British taxpayer and owed it to them to allocate their funds judiciously, especially in wartime. In Germany, the RMVP embraced film and the modern media. They had been using it as a tool for propagandistic activities even before the *Machtergreifung*. Perhaps most importantly, the two countries were conducting their early wartime propagandistic activities based on two very different experiences and understandings of propaganda during World War I, and this conditioned both their responses and public perceptions of their work. It was from these two very different social, political and cultural climates that the first major contributions to feature-length film propaganda emerged: *Feuertaufe* and *The Lion Has Wings*.

Still 1   *Feuertaufe*. Illustrierter Film-Kurier, private collection.

Feuertaufe, commissioned by the German Air Ministry in September 1939, was one of the best examples of film propaganda as a weapon of war. Its power, forcefulness and depiction of overwhelming might were used by the Nazi leadership to convey the means and potential for ultimate victory to the home populations and to intimidate foreign powers. Scripted by director Hans Bertram and Wilhelm Stöppler and narrated by actor Herbert Gernot and radio announcer Dr Geschke, the film earned the *Prädikat* of *Staatspolitisch und künstlerisch wertvoll* for its representation of the 'eighteen-day war' against Poland.[178] The film was said by Bertram to have fulfilled a 'higher task', and he prided himself on the acknowledgements he received as a result of his work from the Führer and *Generalfeldmarschall* Hermann Göring,[179] although Goebbels claimed in his diary that Hitler had personally decided, upon his recommendation, that the film should receive the 'second' rather than the 'first' level of *Prädikat* that the RMVP could bestow.[180]

Although little evidence of the process of filming survives,[181] it is possible to reconstruct some of the conditions Bertram's crew of twenty-seven camera and sound men were operating under. As Bertram recalled:

> At the outbreak of war, I was given the task and the authority to create a film about our *Luftwaffe* operations. I only had to report to the OKW (*Wehrmacht*'s Supreme Command), and my staff and I had complete freedom. The only problem was that time was short: the eighteen-day lightning war demanded that we worked at lightning speed.[182]

Such momentum in the field meant that Bertram's crew always had to be in the right place at the right time to capture the shot. The crew, as Bertram suggested, were afforded much cooperation from the air force, including the use of three aeroplanes, a He 111 for filming the battle, a Ju 52 for transport and general use, and a slow-flying 'Stork' for the aerial shots including surveying the scenes over Warsaw after its destruction.[183] They also received eight motor vehicles for transporting men and materials.[184] The provision of equipment for filming during an active campaign is suggestive of the importance propagandists placed upon cinema as a means of both conveying and conducting warfare. Military cooperation was not restricted to the 'documentary' form, as Bertram himself was to discover during the production of his feature film based on a similar theme to *Feuertaufe*, *Kampfgeschwader Lützow* (Fighter Squadron Lützow, 1941).[185] Although Bertram received much technical and material cooperation from the *Luftwaffe*, he was no novice in the field of aviation, having piloted many flights around the world, particularly in Asia and the Far East, and as the co-creator of the earlier air force film *D III 88* (Herbert Maisch, 1939).[186]

The filming of *Feuertaufe* created numerous difficulties, even for such experienced aviation film-makers as Bertram and his *Sondertruppe*. Aiming to create a 'total experience' of war for the film audience, they found themselves located within a combat zone with wide-ranging battle fronts, specifically the Corridor, the Vistula and Warsaw, which roughly equated to 'film-sets' for Bertram's crew.[187] Resources were spread thinly, and this problem was exacerbated by the speed of the conflict itself. The success of advancing German troops, the nature of *Blitzkrieg* and the short duration of the campaign meant that the cameramen had to react quickly and make lightning decisions as to what was valuable to shoot and which setting would be the most effective in achieving the overall aims of the film.[188] Within this environment, Bertram was forced to squeeze the entire filming for a feature-length production into a few days, leaving little room for error or sub-standard shots. In order to minimize the amount of poor-quality footage, Bertram devised installations for his cameras which would prevent the inevitable shake on screen produced by the engines of the aircraft and used cameras with greater focal length to capture key shots from greater distances.[189] Filming conflict in such a short period of time and with the volatile nature of the battle, no preparatory script was available to Bertram's crew, nor could they predict where the action would take place from one day to the next. Plans had to be flexible, according to Bertram, so that they could capture the best shots.[190] Little on-the-spot editing was possible and, in total, the film's editor, Karl Otto Bartning, had to reduce 17,000 metres of film shot in the field to just 2,465.[191]

For a film-crew operating primarily from within a combat zone, the dangers were all too real. Seven of Bertram's original crew lost their lives whilst making *Feuertaufe*. However, this provided the film's producers, Tobis, with an unexpected opportunity to stress the reality of the war-experience as depicted in the film and to promote the ultimate message of many war films of the Third Reich: sacrifice and heroic death. The seven men were accorded a soldier's death, a 'heroic death for Führer and Fatherland',[192] paying the 'highest price, their lives, for this [filmic] work', although the press was quick to remind the audiences that 'Our fate is not death, but fighting, and that means living!'[193] It was within this rhetoric that film-makers became an integral part of the military machine and were afforded heroic status akin to that of soldiers. Kurt Hubert, export director for Tobis, announced that the army cameramen were 'regular soldiers, doing a soldier's full duty, always in the first lines … [and] this explains the realistic pictures we show'.[194] This dimension of wartime film production becomes apparent from the promotional materials for *Feuertaufe*. A 10-pfennig book produced to accompany the release of the film described the cameramen of the *Propagandakompanien* as 'soldiers, like gunners, artillerymen, airmen, sailors. They join in the attack, they shoot and they fight side by side with the fighting units'.[195] The public were reminded that the PK-men were also 'the *Führer's soldiers*'.[196] Through *Feuertaufe*, as cinema-owners were informed by Tobis, 'films, too, are part of German warfare',[197] and its cameramen became front-line fighters.

Bertram's cameramen were not only an important part of the fighting forces of the nation, they also presented themselves as 'observers of history' in keeping with the classification of *Feuertaufe* as a 'documentary'. The film was promoted as a true reflection of war, with Bertram's *Sondertruppe* as witnesses to momentous events in history, as mere recorders of the national struggle against the western powers and their allies. Hubert claimed that the feature-length documentaries produced at the beginning of the war were 'perfect document[s] of historical truth and nothing but the truth, therefore answering the demand for a good substantial report in every way'.[198] As Bertram recalled, 'Right at the beginning, when we went to war, we realized the significance of this film: that it would need to show the decisive battle and that it would be a milestone in our people's ... revolution'.[199] Much publicity was given to the status of the film crew, stressing their links to the *Wochenschauen* and official film units such as the *Kriegsberichterkompanien* and the film-men of the *Reichs-luftfahrtsministeriums*. Bertram claimed that the film had employed the most talented documentary cameramen available to the Reich.[200] That his crew were tied to film units previously associated with reportage gave *Feuertaufe* an air of authenticity and presumed objectivity. Publicists could also capitalize on the perceived popularity of the *Wochenschauen* and exploit the popular desire to be transported to the frontlines, integrated into the action and to receive news of German troop successes. The press book for the film reminded cinema-owners 'how audience numbers everywhere rose to extraordinary figures when the newsreels showed reports of the battles in Poland'.[201] Now the public could be sated with a feature-length production drawing on prior events with which they would have had some familiarity and which elicited a favourable reaction. Presenting the people once again with the conflict in Poland, both film-makers and propagandists could profit from the audiences' previous engagement with the subject matter. To this end, the film was advertised as a purely historical document with little added meaning or interpretation.[202] As recorders of history, the film-makers could attest to *Feuertaufe*'s documentary legitimacy and claim that the film was a 'living document' of the German *Luftwaffe* in action. Bertram focused on the enormity of the task in hand, stressing that 'the wealth of experiences was such that is almost impossible to relate individual episodes'.[203] In espousing a grand narrative of the conflict, emphasis was placed upon German superiority and dominance. In this way, the film was intended as a 'lasting document' attesting to the strength, courage and the professionalism of the *Luftwaffe*,[204] one devoid of personalized and individualized meanings, representing the eternal unity of the German fighting peoples and the righteousness of their cause.

The emphasis placed upon 'realism' within *Feuertaufe* also fulfilled another propagandistic function for the RMVP: it served as a counterpoint to the presentation of British propaganda seeking to justify war, targeting in particular the first feature-length production of the war years, *The Lion Has Wings*. Publicity for Bertram's film drew upon the fictionalized aspects of the British film to highlight the German approach to war propaganda: '*Truth is our weapon*'.[205] *Filmwelt* proclaimed that

> They have lied, the news agencies and 'information offices' in England and France, the gentlemen at Reuters and Havas – they have lied, they are lying now and they will continue to lie. With both words and images. But they have not realized that lies are amongst the poorest and least effective weapons one could think of in political and military operations. The truth is always victorious. It will be victorious in this war too – as sweeping as the German *Wehrmacht*.[206]

Feuertaufe acted as the prime example by which to contrast the so-called truthful approach of the German film propagandists with the 'trick-photographers' of British cinema. Bertram's film had

> no scenes set up in the manner of the pitiful English 'film reportages chronicling success' about a supposed attack on Wilhelmshaven, which was actually created in the special effects studio of an English company. Hence, the film *Feuertaufe* represents the victory of truth of the Germany documentary film over the English lies and hypocrisies in their mendacious and malicious films.[207]

This comparative approach underlined the outward commitment of both the film and the propagandists to 'inform' their public of events in the war and to warn the German people against British 'agitation'.

Although German propagandists were careful to stress the factual element within *Feuertaufe* and the spirit of the collective might of the armed forces, they were also conscious of the impact of entertainment on morale and of the total propaganda environment. *Feuertaufe* was frequently linked to fictionalized productions depicting the same events of September 1939, the most obvious example being Bertram's 1941 film *Kampfgeschwader Lützow*. Explicit references were drawn between the two films in the promotional literature, and the same music and newsreel footage was used in the fictional piece to sharpen the relationship between the two films in the minds of the audience.[208] The press book recognized the different functions of the documentary and fictional feature films, but in essence advocated that audiences might read them together:

> we may indeed describe the aviation film *Kampfgeschwader Lützow* as simply unique in form and design. The documentaries were factual reports of historic significance. They brought the battle of our *Wehrmacht* closer to millions of strongly sympathetic Germans. Through bold editing, artful fading, the magnificent wealth of the material and through the burning proximity of the battle itself, documentaries managed to achieve similarly outstanding results as the war newsreels. A feature film is governed by different laws: it requires a dramatic storyline, internal dynamics and demands a convincing dramatic structure… It has to possess the same mobilizing genuineness as the best documentary.[209]

In some senses then, feature and documentary films were united in their aims, although governed by different rules. It was through this integrated approach to film propaganda that Bertram was able to produce two complementary films; whereas he was viewing the events of September 1939 as presented in *Feuertaufe* in terms of realistic, historical images of the frontlines akin to the reportage of the *Wochenschauen* with its focus on the bigger picture, his feature film was able to intensify the emotional experience of the cinema audience with its concentration on individualized and specific stories set within a dramatic and potentially entertaining *milieu*. This served to merge fiction and fact: Bertram was blurring the boundaries between the real and the imagined, audiences being encouraged to conceive of the two aspects of propaganda as one entity. The effect was to reinforce mutually the messages presented and to work within the total media environment of the Third Reich.

The main aims of Bertram's 1940 production centred on the justification of Germany's decision to go to war, placing the blame squarely upon the shoulders of the western plutocratic powers and the aggression of Germany's Polish neighbour whilst convincing the public at home and, to a lesser extent abroad, of the overwhelming strength of the German armed forces and, in particular, the *Luftwaffe*. Reflecting the conditions of its production, *Feuertaufe*'s opening credits emphasize the 'authenticity' and the historicity of the film: '*These pictures are genuine and simple, hard and relentless like war itself*'. In order to underscore the reality of both the conflict and the film, the names of the fallen cameramen are presented to the audience, a sequence broken by the bugle call announcing the commencement of the narrative, which focuses upon the 'historical' antecedents of the war with Poland. The realization that the German public were reluctant to embrace the wider European conflict in the early months of the war brought an increasing need to justify hostilities. The film attempted to persuade its audience that conflict was an unavoidable situation, blaming Polish belligerence in the first instance, underpinned by British warmongering. War is presented as having been forced upon an overwhelmingly peaceful Führer, who when provoked is compelled to respond with the might of the German armed forces to defend the common interest. The threat to Reich borders, implicit in the narrator's commentary on escalating Polish militarism, is visualized in the subsequent sequence depicting potential enemy troop movements over the Reich border. The narrator predicts that '*it would suit these gentlemen just fine if Polish tanks pushed the Reich frontier back to the Elbe, back to Bremen, Hanover or Kassel – the next town is Nuremberg*'. The black, menacing mass pours over a map of white German territory, emphasizing the Reich's status as 'an entirely innocent, harmless creature … in symbolic contrast to the black of Poland, England and France'. The starkness of the imagery in which 'this world of light is opposed by one of darkness with no softening shades' supplements the master narrative of the film:[210] that the onset of the war can be seen and justified in similarly simplistic terms.

Focus shifts away from predictive narration to the 'historical facts' of August 1939. In a scene designed to affirm German cultural, political and ethnic rights over the free port of Danzig, once again, Bertram merges symbol and realism, combining this visual with newsreel footage of *Gauleiter* Albert Forster's rousing speech encouraging the people of Danzig to resist fear of invasion: '*However they provoke us, we must in no way react*', a statement which served to complement the earlier scenes of Polish aggression and German passivity. In this sequence, German militarism is defensive but decisive. The narrator reassures the audience that '*Danzig may be calm. Adolf Hitler's armed forces are ready to fight in Greater Germany's struggle for freedom. The German forces are armed!*' And here they are represented in their entirety: from the *Heimwehr*, to the army and the navy. Special mention is reserved the *Luftwaffe*, who '*like a sword in the sky, … is ready for action, to strike anyone who tries to break the peace of Europe*'.

By way of contrast to the heroic deeds of the German forces, the film proceeds to address the intentions of the enemies of the Reich: Poland, France and England. The film contends that this triumvirate is responsible for escalating tensions in Europe. Particular attention is given to the role of Britain. Depicted as plutocratic warmongers deeply engrossed in their political machinations and power games, the British leaders are held accountable for the outbreak of the war:

> London is the centre of the warmongers. The British plutocrats have their puppets dancing back and forth between Downing Street and the Houses of Parliament. It is a fateful hour, now that England has issued Poland with a carte blanche. The diplomats play their cards. Poland will be let loose, and Germany will strike back. Then you'll have your war, Herr Chamberlain!

The focus upon leadership, explicit within the commentary of *Feuertaufe*, reflected the wider propagandistic aims of the RMVP. Nazi propaganda increasingly identified Neville Chamberlain as the key instigator of World War II, his image evolving as the conflict intensified. Whilst on 18 November 1939 the ministerial conference minute reported that 'the press is to publish a cartoon of Chamberlain in slippers', by December Goebbels had requested that he 'must no longer be portrayed ... as an incompetent, helpless figure with an umbrella, but as a vicious old man',[211] a directive adhered to by Bertram's depiction of the British prime minister as a vindictive warmonger controlled by the forces behind western plutocracy, Judaism and Freemasonry.[212] Such representations of the British leadership seemed to be relatively popular, an SD report from the Leipzig region noting that 'they, who have unleashed the war must relentlessly be shown to the German people as they really are', such propaganda being received with enthusiasm.[213] In this and other respects, *Feuertaufe* responded to popular and governmental demands to shift the burden of guilt onto the western plutocratic powers. As the ministerial conference of 28 June 1940 revealed, '[our propaganda] must emphasize that Britain wants this war and that she shall have it now, and it must further emphasize that Britain is governed by war criminals and that she cannot expect anything but war from us until she comes to her senses',[214] a message which was reinforced across the different media of the Reich. In particular, Fritz Hippler's 1939 production, *Feldzug in Polen* (Campaign in Poland), served to underline the central political contentions of *Feuertaufe*, emphasizing Britain's status as a '*capitalist exploiter of the peoples of the world*' and the hypocrisy of its leaders in portraying themselves as the guardians of '*freedom, justice, truth and morality*'. In *Feldzug in Polen*, as in *Feuertaufe*, 'London is the hub of warmongers'. Justification of war based around these themes was not limited to the documentary form, however. Bertram's feature-length production, *Kampfgeschwader Lützow*, viewed as the fictional representation of *Feuertaufe*, contended that the war had been provoked by the 'eternal war-mongering in the West...', the megalomaniacal Poles in the East' and Britain, 'the arch-enemy of a Germany striving for progress'.[215]

Particular emphasis was to be placed by Nazi propagandists upon the plutocratic nature of democracies, thus standing in stark contrast to the 'modern and progressive dictatorship' of the Third Reich. The RMVP stressed that plutocracy was to be the keystone of 'the ideological struggle', and prided itself, in December 1939, that 'the propaganda against plutocracy in Britain is attracting notice and beginning to be effective'.[216] This assault was to have two primary targets: for the German public, 'it must be explained ... that the plutocratic caste can be knocked out of its stupid and impertinent sense of superiority only by blows from our weapons', whereas propaganda to the British home audience was aimed at driving a wedge between government and people, stressing that 'the plutocratic clique ruling them has nothing in common with them nor does it feel any ties to them'.[217] To this end, Goebbels claimed in February 1940 that 'there is but one war aim: victory over western plutocracy'.[218] Nazi propaganda emphasized that Britain and Germany were natural adversaries, the publicity for *Feuertaufe* stressing that 'Great Britain does not want a Greater Germany at her side'.[219] The RMVP ministerial minutes instructed the media to develop the idea that 'Britain ... is waging this war to get rid of a troublesome German competitor – not in order to present a shining example of her love of freedom'.[220] This was to be presented as a decisive conflict between the forces of retrogression and progression in Europe, the victor assuming the mantle for the cultural, political and social direction of the continent. Nazi propaganda characterized the war as the culmination of a historical process, a struggle between modernity and tradition. For Nazi Germany, it was a revolutionary battle to defend the nation, to avenge the Peace Treaties of 1919 and to fulfil a historic mission. Propaganda consistently claimed that the western plutocracies, threatened by the 'new, modern, socialist Germany', would not be satisfied until the German nation was completely 'annihilated'. It fell, therefore, to the people to subvert the 'destructive will' of their opponent and protect the 'national way of life' reflected in the National Socialist movement. After all, it was the party who had facilitated the *Volk*'s awakening from the 'political narcosis' of the past, and now the nation they had created was to be called upon to defend their new status as a 'political people' against the subversive intentions of the plutocrats.[221] This propagandistic theme, as Steinert has asserted, had some success in the initial years of the war, predominantly in the aftermath of the Poland campaign, the SD reporting in November 1939 that 'the *Volk* realized that England only wants Germany's annihilation; thus trusting completely in the Führer, the *Volk* has resolved more than ever to see this imposed war through to the victorious end'.[222] Nazi film reflected these propagandistic trends, suggesting 'a war of life against death, of future against past', supplemented by 'politico-historical records' and set against a 'panorama of ... manipulated topical events', contextualized within the justification of war.[223]

To heighten sentiments directed against the enemy, the RMVP infused their propaganda with injustice and atrocity, focusing on the plight of ethnic Germans under Polish control. The narrative of *Feuertaufe* moves seamlessly between the images of English warmongering and agitation to the visual representation of Polish atrocity against the *Volksdeutsche*: 'the *helpless are murdered in a cowardly and treacherous manner. Thousands flee to the Reich. The elderly, women and children are forced to hide in the forests and then slip over the border through the back door. Why do these people have to suffer? Just because they are German*. The SD reported that atrocity propaganda of this nature, acting as a smoke-screen to the German offensive action on 1 September and subsequent violence against Polish nationals, was having some impact upon the German public, noting in October 1939 that reports of 'the bestial Polish atrocities against ethnic Germans' was producing 'a profound and vehement indignation by the German *Volk*'.[224] There were, however, some reservations. Rumours circulating at the time of the Poland campaign suggested that the public had already begun to '[doubt] German news, especially reports about cruelties against Germans by Poland and other enemy powers'.[225] In addition, there was 'general recognition of the fact that a civilized nation cannot retaliate measure for measure'.[226] Clearly, newsreel and documentary was only of limited value to the propagandist.

It was within this environment that 'realistic' images which served to generate a sense of the wider justification for war were to be supplemented by highly individualized and emotional representations within the feature film, with the experience of ethnic Germans in Poland treated by prominent productions of the early war years such as *Kampfgeschwader Lützow*, *Feinde* (Enemies, Viktor Tournjansky, 1940) and *Heimkehr* (Homecoming, Gustav Ucicky, 1941). Capitalizing on reports that the German people were responding relatively well to films depicting the 'struggle for freedom by oppressed peoples',[227] fictionalized representations of Polish aggression towards ethnic Germans were fairly prolific in the initial years of World War II. These films sought to give powerful visual expression to the reports of atrocity contained within the newsreels and documentaries, perhaps the most potent sequence being the murder of an innocent ethnic German woman in Gustav Ucicky's 1941 production, *Heimkehr*, stoned to death by a murderous horde, her necklace bearing the swastika ripped from her neck as she lay slain on the floor. Such images brought wider discourses on the causes of the war down to an individual, and therefore more identifiable, level, and supplemented the newsreel footage with dramatic reconstructions of atrocity stories which added emphasis to the claims made by earlier documentary productions. The publicity material for Bertram's *Kampfgeschwader Lützow* reflected the passionate language of the fictional representations of the trauma of the ethnic Germans in the Polish Corridor: '[The Poles] wanted to annihilate all Germanness in the East. Relentlessly, Polish soldiers and police whip and push the expellees. They don't care if those damned Germans suffer hunger and thirst, illness and fatigue. Whoever can't go on, will stay behind with a mercy bullet'.[228] As opposed to documentary reportage, audiences were offered the opportunity to 'experience the terrible fate of the ethnic Germans, terrorized by the brutal Polish murderers, and their liberation by German troops'.[229] Through fictional feature films, such as *Kampfgeschwader Lützow*, the propagandist was able to create emotionally charged environments on the screen, whilst exploiting audiences' previous filmic encounters with the subject matter. Here, feature film worked in unison with the documentary to create personal and expressive accounts. These accounts were underpinned by 'objective' reports and served to heighten the senses in relation to and forge identification with the 'realism' propaganda they had already viewed through the newsreel and films such as *Feuertaufe* and *Feldzug in Polen*.

Like Bertram, Viktor Tourjansky, in his 1940 film, *Feinde*, used the image of the ethnic Germans to intensify the identification of the audience with their own national identity, further personalizing the propaganda message. In *Feinde*, described as the filmic representation of 'a chapter in our generation's German history', it is the refugees' 'deep love of their homeland' that enabled them to endure 'being expelled from their houses and homesteads, even being sent to their deaths in cold blood by bestial and agitated soldiers of a foreign country'.[230] The film's publicity explicitly encouraged cinema-goers to reflect upon the sacrifice of the ethnic Germans trapped in Poland and to internalize the meaning of the film, stressing that 'This is a film that every German will understand and sympathize with. It has a lot to give to its audience and will strengthen their belief and love of their fatherland'.[231] Once again, *Feinde* was intended to be seen alongside the newsreel footage, providing mutual reinforcement of principal propagandistic ideas and creating a sense of unity with fellow ethnic Germans, in doing so further buttressing Nazi justifications for entry into the war. Such images were intended as 'a kind of reminder and as pieces of historical evidence from the documents of indelible blood-guilt, those *Wochenschauen*, which are beyond all imagination. For they are anchored in our hearts as a memorial to the unforgettable heroism of our German brothers and sisters'.[232] By using a variety of different film formats to reinforce the same message, the RMVP sought to saturate the public space with a single conception of the origins of World War II: that the western plutocratic nations, motivated by an insatiable power-lust and maniacal jealousy of modern Germany, had manipulated Poland into conflict with the Reich, thus setting the stage for the final reckoning with an age-old system, embodied in Britain and her empire. Added to this was the highly charged agitational propaganda describing atrocities against ethnic Germans in the Polish zone, which was explicitly designed to heighten German anger and indignation at the actions of her eastern neighbour. It was in the face of such pronounced provocation that Germany was forced into armed conflict to defend her honour, to avenge the past and to protect her compatriots.

In contrast to the portrayal of an enemy clamouring for war, *Feuertaufe* depicted the German forces and, in particular, their Führer as inherently peaceful. Emphasis was placed upon the possibility of a surprise attack and on the justification for extensive rearmament: '*Whoever wants peace must be armed for war*'. The narrator explains that, despite endless provocations, '*the Führer still attempts to salvage the peace, even at the eleventh hour. The world holds its breath*'. The Führer-image in the film is pacifistic and yet resolute, *Filmwelt* affirming that 'The Führer is saying "As far as this but no further!"'[233] He is endowed with the benevolence and might of a monarch. *Nationalsozialistische Landpost* claimed that Hitler's decision-making as presented in *Feuertaufe* enabled the public to understand what was meant by the term '*ultima ratio regis*' to previous generations,[234] a vision reinforced in a subsequent scene in which Hitler surveys his victorious troops. He commands the sequence. It was an image matched in both newsreels and other documentary productions of the period. The combined effect of these portrayals was to underpin the Führer-myth and uphold the justification for war.

Once the Führer-decision has been made, the film gathers speed in its depiction of the military might of the German forces and in particular, its 'brand spanking new' weapon, the *Luftwaffe*.[235] With the 'Polish attack' on Beuthen on 1 September 1939, the wrath of the *Luftwaffe* is visited upon Germany's eastern neighbour, the narrator opining that '*The almighty strength of the German air force has unleashed a mighty torrent of steel ... the Poles are firing in the flight path! We'll answer them with bombs!*' The film is at pains to stress that the target is purely strategic and that the *Luftwaffe* is not vengeful, heading home immediately after the military objective has been achieved. The impact of the first bombing raid is displayed for the audience: '*Railway tracks are ripped up. Stations lie in rubble and ashes. Kilometer-long trains have been abandoned. An indescribable chaos*'. This sequence of destruction and devastation is rapidly followed with yet another description of a successful bombing raid. Once again, the camera surveys the damage: bombed-out trains, railway lines shattered, a mass of twisted steel and rubble littered with the debris of train wreckage. Here the viewer can make out the shadow of the cameraman, reinforcing the reality of the images being portrayed and yet, in a later sequence, war is treated as a game, the description of a raid on Polish rail infrastructure referring to the *Luftwaffe*'s potential to throw an armoured train from the tracks '*like a toy*'.

The action shifts to show the demolition of the Polish air force. A hanger and the aero-planes lie in ruins. The score swings from the menacing soundtrack of destruction to the upbeat tempo of occupation and reconstruction. The Germans, having conquered the airfield, set about rebuilding it. Bertram positively contrasts the constructive activities of the occupying force with the destructive tendencies of the Polish army, who are shown to blow up their own property to thwart the German advance, a futile activity as '*the Germans march ever onwards*', unrestricted and unhindered. Within this sequence, the peace-loving and creative soldiers are seen at leisure, shaving and cooking, such images normalizing warfare. Here, the troops exhibit a private existence and are thrown violently and suddenly into the public sphere. Again, Bertram's film responded to the need to make the filmic experience both individualized, in the identification of the character of each soldier, and collective. The fusion of the public and the private, of the collective and the individual, in the midst of the wider context of war fulfilled a similar function to the blurring of fact and fiction within the feature and documentary films of the Third Reich.

Set against the 'normal' within *Feuertaufe* is the extraordinary. The technical skill and lightning speed of the *Luftwaffe* occupies a central position within Bertram's narrative. Planes dominate enemy skies, '*as quick as the wind, [buzzing] around the conquered airspace*', such comments intended to deepen the sense of control and dominance over the battlefield.

Propagandists were keen to promote the idea that '1940 is not 1914'.[236] The lightning strikes of the initial years of the war stood in stark contrast to the Great War, a war of attrition with troops and machinery mired in the trenches of northern Europe. Here was a different kind of conflict: technical superiority was heralded as the means to pursue a less discriminate war, one in which the bomber and his target were at a distance, a point frequently reinforced in Bertram's film by aerial shots of the battlefield. The film stressed advanced technologies, resonating with the general propaganda contrasting the modernity of the Reich with the sterility and tradition of the western plutocrats. The collective and unified air and ground forces are supported by a team of logistical experts equipped with surveillance apparatus, including an on-the-ground film processing laboratory to develop reconnaissance pictures. *Feuertaufe* presents a well-oiled machine, with the ability to wreak destruction and devastation, a vision bolstered by the quick turn-around of aircraft for sorties into enemy territory: the narrator informs the audience that '*Back at base, our Stukas are some hundred kilos lighter. But the lost weight will soon be replaced*', as the ground crew are seen to reload the undercarriages of the bombers with its '*dangerous cargo that will break any resistance*'. The sequences of the battle of Warsaw, in which the '*land is set ablaze*', confirm that '*resistance will be ruthlessly crushed*'.

With each act of Polish defiance, the rage of the *Luftwaffe* is unleashed. In a series of apocalyptic images, Bertram brings his film to a terrifying crescendo. Viewing the scenes of annihilation from on high, the audience sees the city reduced to rubble and in flames. Smoke plumes rise up into the skies, and a cloud covers Warsaw. The panoramic shots taken from the slow-flying Stork reveal the devastation caused by the bombing raids. The spectator, accompanying the air crews, is struck by the serenity of the sequences from the sky, but as the narrator reminds the audience, the *Blitzkrieg* has been relentless and '*below is hell*': '*Only the chimneys are left standing – like tombstones in a graveyard*'. Within 36 hours of continual bombardment, the city capitulates. Yet, the bombers are not accountable for the obliteration of the streets and buildings: this was the '*criminal responsibility*' of those who instructed the populace to turn Warsaw into a fortress and demanded that they participate in '*senseless resistance*'. Above all, it is the western plutocrats who have to answer for their crimes:

> As the negotiations progress, we fly once again over the city. And Herr Chamberlain should accompany us. What have you got to say now, Herr Chamberlain? You can see the catastrophe into which you plunged the Polish capital for yourself. Can you feel the curse of a people betrayed? Here you can see the results of your pointless war policies. This is all your work! One day you will have to answer for it before the world. And take heed: this is what happens when the Luftwaffe strikes. It knows how to seek out the guiltiest of the guilty.

The shot continues to survey the destruction of the city, preparing the viewer for the surrender of Poland and the triumphant march of the German troops into the city.

As the film draws to its conclusion with the cessation of active hostilities in the east and the occupation of Poland, the audience is reminded that as one chapter in the grand narrative of World War II closes, another one begins. In the closing scenes of the film, Göring addresses the audience directly, informing them that:

> At Versailles, when the air force was taken from the German people, no one thought that our Führer, Adolf Hitler, would restore this weapon, now stronger and more powerful than ever before. Now, we are at the end of the first phase of our wider struggle. And what the *Luftwaffe* promised in Poland will, through [them], be fulfilled in England and France: that means, every enemy will be struck, beaten and annihilated.

Thus the wider conflict is once again justified in terms of the fulfilment of historical destiny, through Göring's reference to the injustices of the Peace Treaties of 1919. This was a line consistently peddled by the RMVP, the ministerial conference minutes of 12 December 1940 emphasizing that 'Europe was atomized at Versailles according to the laws of political reason. Britain has been a poor guardian of a great European cause. She has made a whole continent unhappy. Indeed that was what led to the war'.[237] Throughout *Feuertaufe*, and again in its filmic conclusion, Bertram crafts the image of a defensive and long-awaited war. It is within this context that the final sequence delivers an explicit and direct threat to the western enemy nations: that there 'are no longer any islands',[238] and that the *Luftwaffe* is poised to destroy them. The magnificence of the *Luftwaffe* and their future plans are brought to the fore in the march played at the end of the film, *Bombs on England*, its music composed by Norbert Schultze and words by the film's scriptwriter, Wilhelm Stöppler. Likening the air force to an eagle, soaring from its eyrie up to gates of the sun, the song, *Bombs on England*, reflects the central theme of the film:

> We flew to the Vistula and the Warthe / We flew into Polish territory / We struck the enemy army hard with lightning strikes, bombs and fire.
> So the youngest of all weapons was baptized and consecrated by fire / From the Rhine to the sea, the air force is ready for action.
> We're preparing the final, decisive blow to the British lion / We're sitting in judgement, smashing a world power to pieces; and this will be our proudest day.

To accompany the march, the camera switches its focus to a map of England, the audience viewing it through the nose of a Stuka dive-bomber. With a screech of the engines, the Stuka plummets to the earth and England explodes in a mass of fire and smoke. As the closing shots of the film suggest, the film was clearly designed to have a significant impact upon the hearts and minds of home audiences, in justifying German entry into the war, and on foreign audiences, acting as a direct threat to them and warning against resistance.

Feuertaufe was premiered at the Ufa-Palast am Zoo in Berlin on 5 April 1940, having been passed by the censor two days before. As an indication of the significance of the film to the propaganda campaigns of the Third Reich, it was attended by leading personalities; the commanding officers of the *Luftwaffe*, Field Marshal Hermann Göring, Field Marshal

Walther von Brauchitsch, Reichsminister Dr Goebbels, Wilhelm Frick, Hans Lammers, and other dignitaries from the German army and navy, the Government, the Party and the diplomatic corps. Music was provided by the *Musikkorps* of the Hermann Göring regiment.[239] This was to be followed by screenings across Germany, showing at 170 cinemas in the first instance. Unsurprisingly, *Feuertaufe* met with the characteristically favourable press response induced by Goebbels' restriction of arts criticism to nothing more than description and exultation. Press reaction was designed to condition the responses of the public, ultimately the key concern for the RMVP, and, in the wider distribution of the film, the studio went to some lengths to control audience reaction, particularly in the publicity produced for cinema-owners. The RMVP were conscious of how the general cinema-going experience could impact upon the popularity of film, campaigning in February 1940 for 'a better relationship between sales staff and their customers',[240] and were concerned with creating the right conditions in which to showcase their filmic propaganda. The publicity materials for Bertram's 1940 production give some indication of the levels of planning for the launch of the film as well as the atmosphere in cinemas across the Reich. It is clear from the SD report of 14 May 1940 that Tobis invested much time, money and effort in publicizing the film's release, which created a sense of anticipation prior to local premieres. They reported that: 'the particularly heavy advertising for the film *Feuertaufe*, in the press, on posters and elsewhere, ensured that in the whole of the Reich, in both cities and the countryside, its cinema release was anticipated with the utmost excitement'.[241] The key operatives in these publicity initiatives were to be the cinema-owners, who were expected to play a significant role in advertising the film and attracting a large audience. As with the shooting of the film itself, the promotion of *Feuertaufe* at a local level was militarized and politicized, serving to create a sense of collective responsibility in achieving state objectives. It was to be emphasized that it was the 'national duty' of the individual both to screen and to see this film. Accordingly, cinema-owners were told that they were the RMVP's 'most important aides in looking after this politically significant film, which needs to be brought to the whole of the German people',[242] and, to this end, they were encouraged to produce detailed publicity plans and to promote the film enthusiastically through a variety of channels.

Their task was difficult. Cinema-owners were faced with selling a feature length documentary to a public who preferred entertainment films and an evening of escapist drama. Promotional materials for the film drew upon the public's desire for fantasy and excitement by endorsing *Feuertaufe* in similar ways, Tobis advising cinema-owners to inform their audiences that the film was just as 'gripping and dramatic as even the greatest works of fiction'. Proprietors were instructed to trade on the name of Bertram in the first instance and to draw on his 'star-power', connecting *Feuertaufe* with other popular films, such as *D III 88*. Posters and leaflets were to convince the patron that *Feuertaufe* was even more true to life than Maisch's 1939 production, for which Bertram wrote the script, capitalizing on the fact that this film had been particularly popular at the box-office.[243] Audiences were also to be enticed by the prospect of seeing new footage that had not been screened in either the *Wochenschauen* or the first Poland campaign film. This was to be something different, which reflected the public's desire to be both informed and entertained.

The SD report of 14 May 1940 detailed that the publicity campaign for Bertram's film was extraordinarily wide-ranging, from national publicity to individual initiatives on a local level. Posters, leaflets and more traditional advertisements were to be supplemented by promotional spectaculars. The SD commented that 'in many towns, the film's first showing was organized as a special celebratory event, with decorations put up in the rooms and representatives of the *Wehrmacht*, the party and the authorities present'.[244] Cinema-owners were advised to stage musical extravaganzas, asking the local *Luftwaffe* or anti-aircraft division's orchestra to perform the signature tune of the film, *Bombs on England*, on the cinema stage prior to the first screening of the film, preferably accompanied by a soldier's choir. More specific audiences were also to be targeted: Tobis encouraged special screenings for schools, organizations, party members or the armed forces, publicized by small posters in educational establishments, offices and barracks. In addition to fulfilling their 'national duty' in promoting the film, cinemas could benefit financially from their activities, with the studios offering incentives to successful advertisers. A series of four postcards with stills from the film were available for purchase at 5½ Pf. apiece which could then be sold on at 10 Pf. Alternatively, they could be distributed free of charge at the box-office. A further enticement to visit their local cinema was printed on the back: 'I've seen … the Tobis film of the deployment of the German *Luftwaffe* in Poland, and would like to recommend strongly that you go and see this gripping [piece of] photo-reportage too. The film *Feuertaufe* is showing from the [insert date] in the [insert name] cinema [insert address] daily at 4:00, 6:00 [and] 8:30'.[245] This brief analysis of the promotional activities surrounding *Feuertaufe* points to the nexus of commercialism and propaganda in the cinema of the Third Reich. Even the most propagandistic of films produced under National Socialism, such as Bertram's 1940 epic, were underpinned by a sense of escapism and had their own commercial identity. This dimension of the industry proved that commercialism and propaganda could be mutually beneficial and reinforcing. With such a strong sense of collective responsibility informing the publicity materials and the promotional activities generating widespread excitement and interest in the film, it is unsurprising to find that *Feuertaufe* was relatively successful at the box-office, with 'some showings … sold out days in advance'.[246]

Despite the fact that the distributors invested a great deal of time in attempting to mould popular reactions to *Feuertaufe*, contemporary reception tended to be affected by more widespread trends in opinion. Both the SD and Sopade reports demonstrate an observable correlation between audience responses to the film and wider beliefs about the film's central themes. Naturally, the delay between the events of September 1939 and the release of the film in April 1940 meant that propagandists could not capitalize upon the initial and immediate public euphoria specific to the war in Poland.[247] Rather, they could bask in the glory of the victories of the early months of 1940, resulting in the fall of France in June, and create a nostalgia for the first major skirmish of World War II, allowing the audience to reflect upon the speed and power of the German armed forces during the 'eighteen-day war', subsequently confirmed by military events in the west.

It is clear from numerous reports emanating from within the Reich that the film's central aim, justifying war and absolving Germany from any responsibility for the outbreak of hostilities, was relatively successful in the period from September 1939 to the film's release in April 1940 and beyond, particularly in its assignation of blame to the western plutocratic powers. The SD reported that the opening sequences depicting English and Polish war aims had 'proved to be extraordinarily effective'.[248] In addition, a variety of contemporary sources confirm that the general mood reflected the views presented in Bertram's film. A Sopade report from Berlin in December 1939 noted that opinion tended to agree that 'the English have started the war, the English are continuing the war, the English have no reason to wage war'.[249] A similar report from the Rhineland emphasized that:

> We have got a culprit! This culprit is England and, in particular, her propaganda minister Churchill. Many would still like to believe that England has no right to meddle in eastern European affairs... Poland was none of England's business... Danzig and the corridor were issues for Germany alone to deal with... The English had no right to interfere. [250]

The British MoI recognized too that the RMVP had some success in promoting this aspect of the conflict, a Ministry memorandum noting that the Germans had been particularly careful to 'maintain that the Polish German dispute was strictly an internal affair to be dealt with between the two countries and that it is no business of any other country to meddle with Germany's domestic affairs'.[251] But the feeling had gone beyond mere annoyance in relation to foreign intervention in 'domestic' matters, the SD in Leipzig stating that, at times, this feeling of indignation had developed into outright hatred,[252] which in turn resulted in calls for the 'immediate destruction of the British Empire'. The SD noted that the public felt that any acceptance of peace terms was 'wholly undesirable' and that 'the Führer can face the world without criticism and there will be no reproach for this war which makes no sense for England'. This led the SD to conclude that 'the propaganda effort which has been directed against England since September 1939 has meant that people are dying to annihilate the arch-enemy. The fact that this is going to happen now or soon is being fanatically welcomed here'.[253] Complementing the findings of local SD operatives, a national SD report of October 1939 noted that such propaganda had prompted widespread reactions in various sections of society, commenting that 'people are aware that England is Germany's main enemy and the *general mood* is so solidly *against England* that even children in the streets are singing satirical songs about Chamberlain'.[254] Naturally, it was within this climate of popular opinion, that some of the key aspects of Bertram's film, such as the closing sequence involving the 'trick photography' of the Stuka bomber nose diving and annihilating the British Isles and the accompanying song, *Bombs on England*, found significant success.[255] This success was more closely tied to prevailing contemporary views which were reinforced by Bertram's film rather than generated by it, pointing to multiple determinants in the formation of popular opinion and the impact of various manifestations of propagandistic intent.

The 'trick-sequence', although recognized as such by audiences, did little to undermine the sense of authenticity generated by the film and its publicity. Cinema-goers responded well to and were 'deeply impressed' by the opening credits in which the fallen cameramen were mentioned,[256] a scene deliberately designed to generate an impression of reality and sacrifice. Many were excited by the prospect of being able to see new footage, particularly shots which had not yet been included in the *Wochenschauen*.[257] However, although the novelty of the film created considerable interest in its initial release period, it often took some time for particular productions to reach the suburban or rural districts. Whilst national SD reports commented upon the positive responses to fresh reportage in Bertram's film, a regional report from Oschatz noted that *Feuertaufe* had first been screened locally on 5–7 July 1940, exactly three months after the Berlin premiere. Here, cinema-goers were leaving the film theatre remarking, 'we've seen all this before in the *Wochenschau*',[258] demonstrating that Reich audiences were not necessarily undergoing the same cinematic experiences and that this potentially negated the propagandistic impact of a film in certain regions. For these audiences, the Tobis publicity claiming that *Feuertaufe* gave the individual the opportunity to see new perspectives on the Poland campaign did not correspond to their own experience of the film. Even where the propagandistic timing was accurate, success could not be guaranteed. National SD reports stressed that some cinema-goers were unaccustomed to the 'realistic' aerial shots and found them 'tiring'.[259] A similar reaction was felt by Reich Minister Goebbels, who, having attended the premiere in Berlin, noted in his diary that the 'excessive realism' in the film was somewhat 'trying'.[260] Nevertheless, he admitted that he 'was glad to see German soldiers again', adding that 'the war is cruel, but a law of nature and necessary'.[261] German audiences shared his relief at the shots of the armed forces, and scenes glorifying the *Luftwaffe* were also reported to have been well-received. After initial screenings, the SD observed that the public commented upon their 'pride' in the *Luftwaffe* and 'satisfaction that Germany was now in possession of such [a force], which had, in Poland, spectacularly endured its first great trial'.[262] Again, such views were mirrored more widely. The SD in Leipzig reported widespread admiration for pilots, a sentiment reflected in the relative popularity of the early aviation films of the Third Reich, and that there was 'immense [public] confidence' in the *Luftwaffe*.[263] Sopade confirmed in December 1939 that 'in general, there is a lot of pride in the German weapons, particularly the German artillery and the *Luftwaffe*'.[264] Given the final sequences of *Feuertaufe* and the continued fascination with the air force, it is unsurprising that audiences reported that they felt increasingly 'secure in the face of military threats from the western powers' after having seen the film.[265] The most striking and memorable scenes were reported to have been those involving aerial shots of the remnants of Warsaw and the closing words of Hermann Göring.

The immense destructive power of the *Luftwaffe*, however, was not greeted with universal admiration. Although some viewers would have preferred more battle sequences, a number of women commented that the aerial shots of the city in ruins generated compassion for the Poles, not the 'heroic pride' other cinema-goers had experienced. Rather, these scenes led some to reflect upon the 'horror of war'.[266] Echoing the more reserved sentiments of some Germans who felt that war always resulted in the suffering and hunger of the innocent,[267] it became increasingly apparent that Bertram's film had terrified and appalled some viewers, a factor used to great effect in the export of the film to neutral and targeted foreign nations.

Although it has been argued that *Feuertaufe* was primarily intended for German home audiences, the film had a considerable impact abroad. In April 1940, the press reported that 'special screenings' had been arranged for Rome, Copenhagen, Oslo, Brussels and The Hague.[268] Organized by the *Wehrmacht* and the Foreign Office, such 'screenings' echoed Tobis' desire to promote the film as '*a serious warning to our enemies*'. They emphasized that 'film, too, is a means of German warfare',[269] and it was in this spirit that Bertram's film was exported. As Thomas Sakmyster has shown, 'considerable effort and financial support' was ploughed into the distribution of the early war documentaries, with key productions 'subtitled or dubbed into many languages, including English, Portuguese and Spanish' and some reworked to fulfil better the propagandistic objectives of the regime as the war took shape.[270] By June 1940, distribution had been extended beyond Europe to the Soviet Union, the United States and South America. Although some neutral countries, such as the United States, recognized that screenings of *Feuertaufe* to military attachés could only be read as psychological intimidation, others, notably Hungary and Finland, used the images of the awesome power of the *Luftwaffe* to bolster support for military and political intervention alongside the Axis Powers. Of particular significance were the 'special screenings' to potential targets of Nazi aggression or nations 'under strong diplomatic pressure to cooperate with the Third Reich', such as Denmark and Norway, where the film was shown shortly before the German offensive of April 1940.[271] Contemporary reports suggested that, whilst foreign audiences did not necessarily sympathize with German justifications for war, the images of Warsaw lying in ruins after an aerial and ground assault by German forces left an indelible print on the minds of viewers.[272] It was through fear of creating public panic and a disastrous fall in morale, and prompted by reports submitted to the Foreign Office through its network of diplomats, that the British Government decided that *Feuertaufe* was not to be shown in the United Kingdom. Moreover, they held it up to be the epitome of aggressive Nazi propaganda, an example of the kind of psychological intimidation that democratic nations would not engage in at any price.

Initial British reactions to Bertram's film appeared just days after the Berlin premiere, with *The Times* reporting on 8 April 1940 that *Feuertaufe* was 'an unparalleled pictorial record of the horror and beastliness of war' in which 'the spectator is treated to an hour and a half of ruthless destruction'. Attempting to rebut the central claims made by the opening sequences of the film, *The Times* pointed to the inaccuracies in Bertram's account of the initial attack on Poland and noted that the resultant product was 'one long record of massacre and destruction'. Of particular note to British audiences, the newspaper informed its readers, was the 'new Nazi "hymn of hate"', *Bombs over England*, a song complete with 'a realistic swish and bang on the drum'. If the film was insufficient to create dread and fear in any foreign audiences, *The Times* reported that Bertram had the audacity to broadcast the song 'sung by "the choir of an artillery patrol"' and introduced by the director himself 'who asked foreign listeners to take particular note of it'.[273]

The film, however, seems to have had a prolonged impact upon the British propagandists who viewed it; for in 1942–3 *Feuertaufe* became the focus for renewed criticism of German war aims and methods. The campaign against the film in this period, and the concepts associated with it, began with a broadcast by the popular radio presenter J. B. Priestley on 7 May 1942. Taking the opportunity to attack Goebbels, 'a detestable fellow … possessed of a devilish cunning', and his propaganda machine, Priestley focused on Bertram's film as the embodiment of totalitarian psychological intimidation, a film which 'tells the world that any country which has the temerity to defy Hitler will be mercilessly bombed'. 'The film', he commented, 'has a kind of sinister refrain – *bomben, bomben, bomben*'. Contrasting Goebbels' 'sadistic delight [that] cities were being wrecked and thousands of British men, women and children were being blown to bits, buried or burnt alive' with the British decision to 'set their jaws and [mutter] that they could take it', Priestley suggested a 'repayment' to their 'clucking and crowing': 'they screamed with joy about their *bomben, bomben, bomben*. Now they could have some and see how they liked it'. He concluded that 'it's high time the average German is shown that war doesn't mean merely motion pictures for other people's capital cities, toppling and blazing, but also means fire and slaughter on your own doorstep, that other people can play at this terrible game of *bomben, bomben, bomben*'.[274] For Priestley, *Feuertaufe* 'revealed the habits of mind of the people who made it', showing that the Nazis 'only thought in terms of Force and Fear'. Having viewed the film in June 1940, he believed that it 'was a characteristic product – in spite of considerable technical merits – of half-crazy, haunted, fearful minds' and, above all, it was a product 'of a people who, for some reason best known to themselves, are ready to sacrifice liberty, scholarship, art, philosophy, and all the humanities, in order to turn themselves into a kind of overgrown species of warrior-ant'.[275] It was in this spirit that the Prime Minister, Winston Churchill, decided to commission a film to reflect the sentiments of Priestley's broadcast and to challenge the filmic 'blood-and-thunder' of the Third Reich.[276]

In 1943, Churchill wrote that 'Our enemies have consumed celluloid in large quantities not only to drug their own people, but to intimidate and bewitch their unwary neighbours. In doing so, they have recorded not only their pattern of aggression and destruction, but their own basic and barbaric cynicism'.[277] With this in mind, Churchill commissioned a filmic response to Bertram's 1940 production. Writing to Brendan Bracken, then Minister of Information, on 16 April 1943, the Prime Minister requested that *Feuertaufe* be 'considerably shortened' and screened 'with an English commentary'. He believed that it would make for 'very good propaganda', showing 'how ruthless the Germans were, and how they were prepared to use the weapon of the air to subjugate all other countries'. He even suggested the title: *The Biter Bit*.[278] Bracken concurred, suggesting that 'we ought . . . to have some good shots of heavy bombers and the dusting they are giving to Germany', a statement resonating with Priestley's earlier broadcast. However, there were some practical obstacles to the production of *The Biter Bit*. Bracken informed the Prime Minister that:

> Alas, it may take much time to produce this picture. Our small film division, which has done priceless propaganda work, is being broken up in order that the Army may have more raw warriors. In no far distant time, the Ministry may have to abandon film production. The army and the Ministry of Labour apparently look upon it as work of no importance.[279]

Bracken's predecessors lacked the political clout that personal relations with the Prime Minister could bring. This memorandum is testament to how far the Ministry and its incumbent chief officer had come since the early days of World War II. Although the seeds of discontent over the use of film as a weapon of war were still apparent in Bracken's blatant defence of the film work of the MoI, the Minister had learnt how to manoeuvre propaganda to the forefront of the political and military agenda. His minute was intended to touch a nerve by raising the question of human resources in connection with the Prime Minister's personal project, and in this aim, it was successful. Churchill wrote in the margin 'tell me what elements have been taken'.[280] By 5 July, the MoI reported that *The Biter Bit* would be ready by 26 July, under the direction of Alexander Korda.[281]

The film, intended to show 'how the Germans in the early days of the war vaunted the power of their air force' and to compare 'this with the blows they are receiving now', was released in September 1943.[282] It was a response to *Feuertaufe*, as is demonstrated in its opening sequence, the narrator, Ralph Richardson, commenting, '*We all like the cinema. It was invented for your amusement, to make your lives happier. It was left to the Germans to debase films, to use them as a weapon of blackmail and terror*'. The film reconstructed the 'special screening' of *Feuertaufe* to diplomats and other dignitaries in Oslo, where '*even a social event had been turned into an instrument of total war*'. *The Biter Bit* was unequivocal in its condemnation of National Socialist film propaganda, and using original footage from the 1940 production in line with Churchill's request, it drew attention to the specifics of Bertram's film to illuminate the barbarity of the Nazi war machine and the insidiousness of their propaganda: '*The film's object was to terrify the neutral countries and blackmail them into submission . . . The film even had a theme song: the song of the German airmen – WE BLITZ AND BOMB AND BURN. This is the voice of the happy German warrior*'. Richardson stressed that '*copies of "Baptism of Fire" were shown in . . . neutral countries to warn them of their doom. And where the film failed to blackmail them into submission, doomed they were. . . The Germans prided themselves on the use of the Luftwaffe against the defenceless population*'.

The wrath of the *Luftwaffe* was soon turned upon England. Korda's film sought to weave the dramatic story of the Battle of Britain and British resilience with the failure of the German air force to penetrate the British Isles and to achieve its war objectives. The narrative of the film maintains its connection with *Feuertaufe*, this time demonstrating the emptiness of Nazi propaganda claims: '[*Göring*] *thought it was safe to begin the destruction of Britain. He sent out his cameramen to record a new "Baptism of Fire": the annihilation of our island from the air*'. Korda contrasted the impersonal film propaganda of the Third Reich with the individualized documentaries reflecting the people's experience of the first days, Richardson informing the audience: '*we too made films of those historic days. Do you remember "Front Line" in August 1940?*' (Dover Frontline, Harry Watt, 1940). *The Biter Bit* seeks to provide a further distinction between British and German propaganda in the analysis of German reactions to the bombardment of British cities. Once again underlining the German desire to capture the brutalities of war on film, Korda informs the audience that the German response to the Blitz on London was to send in '*an observer in one of their aircraft to give a running commentary on the raid as if it were a football match*'. In a heavy German accent, the narrator mimics the remarks of the commentator as well as the wider themes of Nazi propaganda, as expressed in *Feuertaufe*: '*We see the red blazing metropolis of England, the culture of plutocrats and slave-holders, the capital of world-enemy number one*'.

In keeping with the original desires of both Churchill and his Minister of Information, the early images of Nazi *blitzkriege* were to be set against the retaliatory measures of Britain and her Allies, with British and Commonwealth bombers being instructed to '*Go out into the night and give him a real good medicine*' by their commanders. Now, proclaims the film, reflecting the words of the Prime Minister, '*the biter is bit*'. Although the film was intended to stand in contrast to Bertram's production, it attempts to match the destructive power of the *Luftwaffe* with that of the allied air forces, expressing this through similar vocabulary to earlier National Socialist propaganda, the narrator stating that a '*ring of aluminium and steel, of fire and explosives*' is closing in on the Reich. It is, '*for the Germans…, a ring of doom*'. The film depicts wave after wave of raids upon German territory, predominantly in Cologne and Hamburg. However, Korda is at pains to stress that, unlike the *Luftwaffe*, the Allies' '*targets are not defenceless Warsaws, Rotterdams or Belgrades*' but military and industrial targets, hit with '*mathematical*' precision. In the sequences of devastation within the borders of the Reich, war and retaliation were justified as a response to the Blitz and terror wreaked upon a defenceless Europe, a terror reflected in the horrifying aerial shots in *Feuertaufe*. Naturally, within this justification, the Allied forces are presented as above reproach, merely delivering decisive blows to targets of military significance. No mention is made of civilian casualties.

Although some critics were less than complimentary about the finished product, calling it 'dogmatic and optimistic in its assertions' and likening it to 'a pendant to the Disney-Seversky film *Victory through Air Power*,'[283] Churchill was pleased with *The Biter Bit*. In the introduction to the film, he wrote, '*when [the Germans] sent their Luftwaffe over Warsaw and Rotterdam and London, their cameras were as pitiless as their bombers, and the record of violence was presented with gloating and glee. We have returned their bombs. We now return their film*.[284] Despite Bracken's concern that Britain was still not taking film propaganda seriously, it appears that Churchill, for one, had begun to conceive of the cinema as a valuable weapon of war, to be used alongside conventional combat methods, a sentiment reflected in his commission of and introduction to *The Biter Bit*. This film, however, was not the only British film to be made as a reaction to *Feuertaufe*. Roy Boulting recalled viewing both Bertram's film and *Sieg im Westen* (Victory in the West, Svend Noldan, 1941), commenting that they 'thoroughly intimidated all those who saw them'. He was resolved to 'do something that was the equivalent': his 1943 film *Desert Victory* was the product.[285] This response also gives some indication of the impact of Bertram's 1940 production. That the British were still considering a rebuttal of *Feuertaufe* three years after its initial release speaks to the significant affect it had upon British propagandists and their leaders and points to the international context of film propaganda during World War II. International responses to cinematic propaganda could, as in the case of *The Biter Bit*, be protracted over a period of months and years, but they could also be immediate, as with Korda's other significant film taking air power as its central theme, *The Lion Has Wings*, Britain's feature-length equivalent to *Feuertaufe*, and its main film setting out its justification for war.

THE LION HAS WINGS

It did not go unnoticed that, in the early years of World War II, 'whereas German propaganda … is developed to a fine art, British propaganda … is unfortunately conspicuous by its shortcomings'.[286] Even by the admission of one of the directors of *The Lion Has Wings*, Michael Powell, whilst 'the drums of Hitler were beating louder and louder' and 'Mussolini yapped away in his corner of Europe', 'we at Denham were making fairy-tales'.[287] Goebbels was to claim that Powell's 1939 film was indeed a great work of fiction and set it against the 'realism' of German wartime cinema.[288] The 'brief' of *The Lion Has Wings* was 'to build the main case against Hitler as a war-monger and butcher of his fellow men, to show Britain's potential for men and munitions in the coming struggle and, above all, to star the Royal Air Force'.[289] In this sense, it provides a contrast to Bertram's *Feuertaufe* and allows for a comparative analysis, the two films having similar aims in terms of justifying conflict and showcasing the new aerial weaponry of modern warfare. Nonetheless, for all the similarities in intent, the outcomes of each film were arguably quite different and reflected the status of each power in the war and the nature of their propagandistic output.

The Lion Has Wings was conceived and produced by Alexander Korda. From the earliest indications that war might erupt in 1939, Korda resolved to contribute to the war effort in cinematic terms and, in early September, called a meeting of his 'principal contract people – people he could depend upon and who depended upon him', among them his wife, Merle Oberon, Ralph Richardson, Brian Desmond Hurst and Michael Powell. He informed his colleagues that his studio, Denham, 'was already a classified area' and that 'the next day, everybody ... would start working on a feature propaganda film which [Korda] had promised Churchill would be ready in one month',[290] temporarily abandoning the production of *The Thief of Baghdad* (1940). Korda expected that his 'mixed bag of directors',[291] Brian Desmond Hurst, Michael Powell and Adrian Brunel, should 'go with heart, mind and soul into making this picture, and work with whomever [they] were assigned to'.[292] It was no surprise that Korda expected such devotion from his crew and cast, given his own escape from authoritarianism under Admiral Horthy in Hungary. It came to his attention, probably from his acquaintance Ernst Udet, premier flying ace of the Third Reich, that he had been placed on the Gestapo list for suppressing resistance in the event of invasion of Britain, and Korda was not prepared to undergo further persecution and torture at the hands of the invaders. He did not possess 'romantic fantasies of heroism', commenting that occupation would be 'dull, nasty and very German'.[293] It was with this in mind that he was said to have 'cashed in his life insurance policies to finance [*The Lion Has Wings*], and completed it ... without any assistance from the government',[294] personally guaranteeing 'the salaries of all his contract people'.[295] In keeping with the low budget of the film, the final production costs were reported to be £30,000. The salaries were not befitting of the talent Korda had assembled: the directors received a flat fee of £50 each, along with prominent members of the cast, who also received a share of the profits, whilst minor cast members earned £5 per day of filming. Oberon and Richardson did not, however, accept a salary, choosing to donate their services to the war effort.[296] Oberon reflected that this was indicative of 'everyone ... doing their bit'. Going a step further, she told *The New York Times* that she often lay awake at night thinking 'of the many things I would do to Hitler if I could just get my hands on him'.[297] However, as K. R. M. Short has demonstrated, reports of the financing of the film have been somewhat lost in the rhetoric of the 'People's War' and patriotic duty. The Films Division of the MoI under the director of Sir Joseph Ball and his deputy, G. E. Forbes, had successfully bargained for '50% of Korda's worldwide profits in the event of the film's commercial distribution and [added] a contractual clause which entitled the government to take over production "at any stage at cost, plus ten per cent"'.[298] Needless to say, 'the British government made no financial investment of its own', causing indignation amongst Korda's production team, in particular Dalrymple who contended that if the MoI were to benefit from the profits of the film, they should also contribute to the costs, which they duly did, on 23 November 1939. The princely sum of £3,000 was forwarded to Korda 'to secure distribution of dubbed or subtitled copies of the film for distribution in Portugal, Spain, Italy and France', the same target regions for the export of *Feuertaufe* in 1940: naturally, the Ministry's investment was 'to be deducted from the profits accruing' to them.[299] Short reported that, by 1944, both the MoI and the production company, Korda's *London Film Productions*, had each earned £25,140 in box-office receipts.[300]

As the urgency of Korda's initial meeting with his cast and crew suggests, time was of the essence, and *The Lion Has Wings* was 'shop-made, edited and directed in less than a month'. Powell reported that 'the labs worked day and night, and the film was playing in about sixty countries all over the world a week or ten days later',[301] placed on general release from 3 November, just two months after the outbreak of war.[302] This, in itself, was an extraordinary feat, given the mobilization of film-workers to munitions production, the armed forces or the ranks of the documentarists, and the conversion of studios into factories.[303] Mass-Observation speculated that 'the haste [of production] is understandable, for obviously the sooner such a film could be released the greater would be its topical value'. In the rush to produce the film, they noted, 'Korda must have been much helped by the existence of previous pictures of which large portions would be of value'.[304] Although contemporary footage may have added a sense of realism to the film, it compounded the fact that it was rather disjointed and hastily composed. With three different directors each responsible for a section of the finished piece (Powell for operations, Hurst for the dramatic scenes and Brunel for the opening sequence[305]), *The Lion Has Wings* emerged as a 'hodgepodge',[306] the MoI commenting that it 'may be reckoned as three documentaries strung together to attain a feature length'. 'This', they claimed, 'was its principal defect'.[307] Moreover, that the MoI asserted that Korda's film was a 'documentary' was much in contention by the father of the documentary movement, John Grierson, who, in his constant attempts to lobby the MoI to employ documentarists more frequently in government propaganda, commented that it was telling that 'when [they] wanted to project a positive and constructive democratic England', the directors of the 1939 production, 'had to go to the documentaries for [their] key images'.[308] In this sense, the film fell short of both the expectations of feature and documentary film producers. Scenes in the film had either been reconstructed, such as the sequence of the Kiel raid, or had been drawn from other films, notably, *The Conquest of the Air*, *Fire Over England*, *The Gap*, and various newsreels. The former led to accusations of an intent to deceive, the film being described by Powell as 'an outrageous piece of propaganda, full of half-truths and half-lies, with some stagy episodes which were embarrassing and with actual facts which were highly distorted';[309] the latter caused the audience to become bored and leave the film theatre deeply unimpressed. Significantly, Mass-Observation commented that several cinema-goers noticed the duplication of footage.[310]

The use of newsreel footage in *The Lion Has Wings* created additional practical problems for Korda, who had negotiated its purchase 'well below the usual price'. As Short noted, the relationship between London Film Productions and the newsreel companies collapsed when the latter argued that 'their significant contribution went unacknowledged in the film and, even worse, that they would not share in its potential profits', a claim unsubstantiated considering its opening credits. But these allegations had significant impacts upon British film production during World War II. Short observed that 'the result of this controversy led [the Newsreel Association] to ban future provision of material for feature film production, unless the studio was an associate of the newsreel company'[311] on 30 October 1939, a ban which had immediate impacts: Associated Talking Pictures had already begun production on the new George Formby feature-length film, *Let George Do It*, which included a sequence using newsreel footage of a Nazi rally.[312]

However, for all the criticisms made of this aspect of Korda's 1939 film, the production team were left with very little choice. In fact, they were keen to inject some realism and include original shots in *The Lion Has Wings*. Powell recalled that, despite his lack of aviation experience, a contrast to Hans Bertram in this respect, he was eager to fly with the RAF for their raid on Kiel, asking his acquaintance Air Vice-Marshal Sholto Douglas whether he could arrange it. Sholto's response was to inform Squadron Leader Wright, the liaison officer for the film, to 'take Micky Powell back to Denham and drop him there without a parachute'.[313] Frustrated, Powell vowed to reconstruct the Kiel raid using trick photography, montage and scripted sequences. Even here, he attempted to give the sequence a sense of realism, but this too was denied. As *The Lion Has Wings: The Epic of the Famous Korda Film*, a book intended to promote the film, claimed:

> As soon as the producers knew the full story of the raid, and prepared to reconstruct it from the first instruction from the Chief of Air Staff to the actual return, they suggested that the names and some of the personal history of the men on screen should be included on the screen. This was refused, on the grounds which Sir Kingsley Wood has stated in other circumstances, that individuals do not carry out these daring adventures, but that it is the work of the Royal Air Force; the team spirit.[314]

The failure to give full support to the production team in this respect of the MoI and other governmental agencies meant that Goebbels and the RMVP were able to exploit the fact that large sections of the British film were either reconstructed or fictional dramatizations, fuelling their claims to have presented the 'truth' though reportage without needing to fabricate materials and conquests.

It was for this reason, amongst others, that the film was accused of being overtly propagandistic, which, given the genesis of the MoI and its campaigns, was problematic. Many film-goers claimed that it 'was propaganda pure and simple'. Drawing on memories of the inter-war period and the disastrous effect of the revelations of 'falsehoods' during World War I, audiences (not surprisingly) commented that they thought it was 'un-British to shove propaganda down your throat like that. They should regard us as more intelligent than that'.[315] In the publicity for Korda's film, the producers contended that the press had generated the idea that the film was primarily intended for a persuasive purpose. Forwarding their own definition of 'propaganda', they argued that:

> A propaganda film, like any other vehicle of propaganda, is made specifically by or at the instruction of an authority responsible for the object to be publicised or propagated. But *The Lion Has Wings* ... was neither originated by the Air Ministry nor the Ministry of Information; nor was it sponsored by them in any other way than by placing at the disposal of the producers the facilities of the Royal Air Force, in the same way as other fighting services and government institutions have collaborated with film producers in the past. As the result seems to have achieved a first class propaganda picture which is also first class entertainment, it may be said that it does not matter how the film came to be made.[316]

However, contrary to the producers' expectations, *The Lion Has Wings* did not strike a happy balance between propaganda and entertainment, although this was the original intention in casting Oberon and Richardson to give the film some 'star power', fusing the personal stories with the documentary footage.[317] The 'human interest stories' were supposed to 'link each separate incident [in the film] and make it a combined whole', hoping to 'add vitality to what otherwise might have been a colourless account'.[318] However, many film-goers, particularly from the 'lower classes', complained that they were 'disappointed because Merle Oberon and Ralph Richardson are billed yet given little to do'.[319] Indeed, Oberon's scenes lasted little more than three minutes in total. Len England, chief film reporter for Mass-Observation, commented that, in this instance, 'famous actors only confuse matters if they are dragged into the picture only because of the box-office value of their names'.[320] Therefore, although the inclusion of film stars may have increased initial profits, it did little to aid the propaganda message of the film.

The overtly propagandistic tenor of the film is apparent from the opening sequences. Korda commissioned the voice of E. V. H. Emmett, the Gaumont British newsreel commentator, for the narration, providing a link to footage that audiences had seen before and giving the early scenes a 'newsreel' feel. The purpose of the introduction was to frame the later activities of the RAF and raids on German territory. Like the German commentator of *Feuertaufe*, Emmett was to explain that World War II had been forced upon a peace-loving people by a barbaric aggressor nation and that the only course of action to protect freedom was to retaliate, preserving Britain's heritage and identity. This purpose was forwarded in the opening lines, Emmett announcing that:

> *This is Britain, where we believe in freedom. For over eight hundred years, we have kept our shores safe from invaders, and for eight hundred years, we have opposed every dictator who arose and tried to enslave Europe. For this is Britain, where we believe in freedom. We also believe in peace, peace to develop our inheritance… We have no use for war.*

The commentary was supplemented with images of rural and industrial England, from the chocolate-box cottages to clean and functional conurbations. Emphasis was placed on improved social conditions, and the film drew attention to schools, producing '*good citizens of the world*', working mothers, happy children playing contentedly, the benefits of paid holidays and plentiful leisure time. *The Lion Has Wings*, as Short has noted, depicted 'an emerging British nation worth fighting for', expressed through Dalrymple's distinctively 'optimistic [and] non-partisan ideology'. He explicitly chose to omit footage of 'dole queues, … shuttered cotton mills, … silent Durham and South Wales pits, … deserted ship yards on the Clyde and Tyne, … and Jarrow marchers', for 'movie audiences did not need to be reminded … of those tragic facts'.[321] Nor did he depict a divided nation, separated by class or status. Rather he chose to create a rural and urban idyll, where all are supported and cared for by a nation determined to defeat the dual spectres of Fascism and Nazism which cast their shadow over Europe. Nowhere is this aim more apparent than in the sequence of the King, Queen and young princesses joining the 'ordinary' people in a popular song. Here was an egalitarian Britain, which, whilst 'broadly committed to safeguarding its time-tested traditions, particularly the Royal Family', was also 'a socially responsible industrial democracy in transition'.[322] At the heart of this image was the presentation of improved facilities, health care, education and sports. This was in direct response to Nazi propaganda, which consistently pointed to social deprivation in Britain, specifically the themes of 'health insurance in England' and 'unemployment benefit' as well as class distinction and inequality, purportedly evidence of the failure of democratic systems of government to provide for the masses.[323] The thrust of this argument was not lost on British contemporary observers who recognized that the claims made by Korda's film were at odds with the experience of the 'common-man'. Even the ordinary cinema-goer noticed that romantic images of the nation's social life left British propagandists hostage to the claims of the RMVP. As one man commented to Mass-Observation in 1940, the film's opening sequence lost 'a good deal of support of those who unfortunately know that life in Britain today (while much better than in Nazi Germany) is nothing like what it might be... [T]his sort of stuff provides ample excuse for Dr. Goebbels and co. to attack Britain for trying to deceive the people of Britain and of neutral countries',[324] a comment reflected in *Documentary Newsletter* in March 1940. In an attempt to persuade film-makers to take a more realistic tone in their propaganda work, one more in line with the experiences of 'everyman', they reminded them that Goebbels was 'unlikely to be kept in ignorance of any British social problem by its absence from the screen. He is in fact more likely to make capital of suppression than of frank admission'. They questioned whether 'British morale [would] be weakened' by 'films fairly representing the critical domestic issues of the day' or 'which articulated the inevitable dislocations of war', arguing that 'the man-in-the-street must believe it is his war or lose it; and he cannot fight blindfold.[325] By choosing to idealize everyday life in Britain, Dalrymple created a tension between the film and the audience's prior and contemporary experiences, which in turn led cinema-goers to question the veracity of the film's message, potentially undermining its propagandistic impact from the outset.

Supplementing the narrative of peace and social development, the film moves on to consider the differences between the German and British people. Korda chose to highlight these divisions through images of leisure and sport. As *Kinematograph Weekly* observed, 'a contrast of ideals marks the opening – Britain is shown in the pre-war days equipping herself mentally and physically for industry, peace and play, while Germany is depicted [as having] only one thought and aim – power and aggression'.[326] Questioning enemy propaganda which claimed that the British were '*effete and decadent*', '*a characteristically unfortunate lie – as they would find to their cost*', the commentary focuses upon each nation's interpretation of competitiveness. The narrator notes that '*we [the British] have long made up our minds that we should use our bodies for games and sport and not for building up vast armies with which to terrorize and ultimately subdue our weaker neighbours*'. Above images of the 'gentlemanly' sport of football, Emmett announces '*We like to win matches not wars*', reassuring the audience: '*although if we must have wars we can win those too*'. Set against the good-natured, sportsmanlike and fun-loving scenes of Britons at play, at fairgrounds, rowing on the river and at the races, Korda switches his focus to Nazi Germany, contrasting the lively and unpredictable activities in the previous frames with the regimented and militarized lives of the Germans. The scene cuts back and forth from '*friendly battles*' to the vast columns of storm-troopers; from the joyous and playful rendition of 'hands-knees and bumpsy-daisy' to the mechanized and controlled ranks of the Nazi Party members. This approach met with some success with certain film-goers, one man commenting to Mass-Observation that these scenes 'appealed in just the right proportion to the English self-righteousness, supercilious good-humoured tolerance … their fighting instincts were awoken, fully clothed by the traditional fair-play of the race'.[327] However, if the audience had not yet grasped the central theme of the sequence, the director cuts to images of the Nazi rallies synchronized with the sound of sheep baaing, the commentator asking '*Are these men or [is it] dipping day on the sheep farm?*' Within this sequence, as *Kinematograph Weekly* noted, 'the British and German mentalities are stripped and it is easy to see which is on the side of peace and which on war',[328] a sentiment picked up by contemporary audiences: Mass-Observation recorded that film-goers stated that 'the contrast between the peaceful England and the military Germany was most vivid', one woman reporting that she 'did enjoy hissing Hitler',[329] although this may have been due to the overall cinema experience, peer pressure and patriotic fervour that marked a number of screenings of *The Lion Has Wings* as reported by Mass-Observers in their studies of reactions in Streatham, Leicester Square, Tottenham Court Road, Cricklewood and Bolton.[330]

This contrast was the springboard from which Korda's production lays blame for the conflict. The 'guilty men' are the Nazi leaders, in keeping with the British hope that the German people, subjugated under a ruler in need of armed protection as the film emphasizes, will rise up and overthrow the regime, a theme reflected in numerous contemporary films such as Anthony Asquith's *Freedom Radio* (1940). Here Korda represented 'Hitler's parade of broken promises' alongside Chamberlain's declaration of war, which 'is delivered in a tender domestic scene'.[331] Playing upon Hitler's assertion that he had 'no territorial demands in Europe', the narrator tracks the pervasive occupation of eastern Europe by the National Socialists, the black mass of the Nazi empire pouring over the map of the continent in a scene remarkably reminiscent of the depiction of the proclaimed Polish intent to invade the Reich in *Feuertaufe*. The sequence is set against a distorted score of the *Horst Wessel Lied* and *Deutschland über Alles*, further reinforcing the connection to the Party. As if to emphasize that war had been planned from the outset, Korda cuts to excerpts from *Mein Kampf*, stressing that it was clear that '*Hitler's ambition lay naked in the cold light of truth*'. As *Kinematograph Weekly* stressed, 'the righteousness of Britain's cause is plainly stated'.[332]

Korda is also careful to draw a link between Germany of the past and present, Emmett noting that '*history repeats itself – as in 1914 the world has no choice*'. The history of the German past is presented as one of belligerence, the present conflict merely a continuum with aggression portrayed as a national characteristic. Britain's past, by contrast, is presented as illustrious, Korda demonstrating that contemporary experience is underpinned by the glories of the past. In World War II, the pilots of the RAF, the focus of the film, were standing upon the shoulders of giants. To heighten the emotions, Emmett reminds them that '*Britain founded her greatness on the sea, but the spirit of those great names of old lives once more in those who dare the uncharted heights of heaven: Nelson, Drake, Frobisher, Raleigh. The dauntless courage that made them famous is born anew in these young captains of the clouds*'. Just as their forefathers had learnt to craft their weapons, he continued, so too would the armourers of 1939 rise to the task: '*We learned early in our history to study our weapons as well as our men. Cressy and Agincourt were won partly because the English archers were the best in the world, but partly also because they carried the best bows*'. Now '*the strength of the nation*' is found in '*bullets, guns, shells; bullets, guns, shells*'. This is not the only scene in *The Lion Has Wings* which draws parallels with the distant past. In a later sequence demonstrating the ability of the British to repel invaders, Emmett compares the defence of the island in 1940 to events '*three and a half centuries ago when the proud Armada sailed up the English channel*'. This analogy is reinforced by the inclusion of a sequence from *Fire over England* (William K. Howard, 1937) with Flora Robson as Elizabeth I who tells her people: '*Not Spain nor any prince of Europe shall dare to invade the borders of my realm*'. Although historical comparison could have been drawn with Napoleonic France, 'lest French audiences be scandalised', Dalrymple chose to focus on the Elizabethan period, partly because 'it was the only footage available … to prove the point' and partly because 'there was no necessity to court favour with Spain's fascist dictator, General Franco'.[333] However obvious the propagandistic message of the film, though, Mass-Observation reported that the historical analogy was far from successful, leaving audiences '[bewildered] at the sudden change of setting'.[334]

Like its German counterpart, *The Lion Has Wings*' central aim was to justify entry into World War II by using the motif of peaceful resilience in the face of unacceptable aggression, followed by a determination to eradicate tyranny to preserve justice and freedom. In both films, the propagandists base their claims around reports of atrocity. Using a similar technique as Bertram in *Feuertaufe*, a series of headlines appear on the screen as a means of justifying British entry into the conflict: '*Polish Peasants Machine-Gunned*'; '*311 Americans in Torpedoed British Liner*'; '*Athenia: American Horror*'; '*Refugee Train Bombed*'; '*Red Cross Train Bombed*'; '*Frightfulness in Occupied Poland*'. In each case, the British rush to defend other nations from Nazi belligerence: Poland and, significantly, the neutral United States of America. It is the attack on the *Athenia*, suggests Emmett, that prompts '*the battleships of the skies*' to mobilize: '*while pilots passed the time waiting for orders to avenge the outrage of the* Athenia*, orders were on the way*'. Within the film, the focus is firmly placed on the RAF, and their '*sky battleships, armed and equipped with all that military science and technical skills could devise*'. Korda sought to fuse romantic and industrial images, reflecting his perception of the nature of Britain at war. A premium is placed upon the technical wizardry of the RAF and their crews and the power of their machines. The narrator informs the audience of the speed, might and prowess of the soldiers of the skies, their machine guns that '*spit out a stream of bullets swifter than thought itself*'. Fuelled by petrol, described by Emmett as '*the life-blood of modern war*', the planes are '*loaded with their cargo of destruction*' for their raid which is '*exact and mathematical*'. At the same time, Korda injects romantic images of their mission into the mechanical science of warfare. Fighters are described as '*messengers of heaven*', a comment reflected in the publicity materials for the film. In a promotional book to accompany Korda's production, Lloyd George avows that the crews' 'daily and nightly struggles are like the Miltonic conflict between the winged hosts of light and darkness. They fight the foe up high and they fight him low down… Every fight is a romance; every record is an epic'. Opining that 'the heavens are their battlefield', he continued, 'they are the knighthood of this war, without fear and without reproach. They recall the old legends of chivalry, not merely by daring individuality, but by the nobility of their spirit, and among the multitudes of heroes let us think of the chivalry of the air'.[335] Yet the 'ordinary' is not lost in these idealistic visions. As the narrator states, '*But even on a job that carries a 50-50 chance of death, these wonderful boys start out with a light heart and a joke*'. The shot focuses on a bomb being loaded onto an aircraft, upon which is chalked the message '*One for Adolf*'. For Priestley, it was this aspect of Korda's production that set it apart from its German counterpart. He commented in June 1940 that *Feuertaufe*

> [is] the opposite of *The Lion Has Wings* – and I mean by that, that it presents all the contrary qualities. Our film didn't take itself too solemnly; it showed our airmen as likeable human beings, cracking jokes with their wives and sweethearts. But this Nazi picture is all 'drums and trombones' – gloom and threats. A loud German voice bullies you through it all. There's a lot about destruction and death and not a glimmer of humour, or fun, or ordinary relationships.[336]

Finally, '*the engines throb and leap to life*'. The RAF are '*heading East on a great adventure*', a raid on the Kiel Canal. Although the focus is upon the air force, Korda is careful to show the camaraderie of the armed forces and 'how Britain's might is assembled'. Here, argued *Kinematograph Weekly*, 'the picture really comes into its own. The Navy on the high seas, the soldier on the barracks square, tanks on manoeuvres, aeroplanes being manufactured and civilian services being organised, all take authentic place in the ruthless war scheme'.[337] Powell emphasized that their assignment is an honourable one: the marks are purely military, with the crew destroying a German navy vessel and '*a heavily protected naval base – a legitimate target of modern warfare*'. Unlike their German counterparts, the RAF does not, Emmett asserts, '[drop] *their bombs … on unfortified towns*', arriving in daylight and not under the cover of night, like the cowardly *Luftwaffe*. Although he was not able to film the actual Kiel raid, Powell attempted to infuse his re-enactment with the reality of the operation, the narrative informing the audience that '*although you have been watching a reconstruction of that raid upon the Kiel Canal, the men you now see stepping out of these bombers are the officers and men of the RAF who carried our that heroic raid. These are the men that flew the planes and dropped the bombs on Hitler's battleships*'. This sequence, this '*epic of the skies, carried* out with brilliant dash and matchless courage', provided, according to *Kinematograph Weekly*, 'inspiration and comfort'[338] to those on the home front and the front lines.

Powell wanted not only to call attention to Britain's ability to attack but also her capacity for defence. The narrator points out *'how we can protect our own country from undesirable visitors. What is the organization that exists to counter and eventually to conquer German bombing attacks? Vast machines, fighters, interceptors, pursuit planes and personnel ... a train of blimps that trail invisible steel wires'* spell *'death to the invader!'* This sequence was designed to demonstrate the multi-layered defence system of the United Kingdom, conceived to repel any Nazi invasion or bombing raid. The film focused its attention upon the anti-aircraft gunners on the ground, the network of blimps lacing the skies and the airborne defence of the fighter pilots. Again, Powell devised a scenario in which each of the methods of defending the island are employed to the full and are each seen to be successful. For this sequence, Squadron Leader Wright provided Denham with 'the fuselage of a crashed spitfire, plus two odd wings from some other station', which were 'set ... up on one of the big stages with lots of room around it'. Powell added 'wind machines and sound machines' and mounted the construction upon 'a platform that could be tipped and turned and made to do all sorts of things, including dips and swings against a night background'.[339] He was also able to simulate the action of battle 'with lighting effects, sound effects, playbacks, back projection, recordings of shells exploding and machine gun fire, prop men throwing firecrackers – the works in fact- [I] really had a high old time', he commented. Powell also needed to reconstruct some enemy aircraft, taking a little less care as 'anything would do for them, they were going to be sitting ducks for the RAF anyway', manning them with 'three dastardly *Luftwaffe* pilots'.[340] Within Powell's sequence, the Nazi bombers are met with a *'hail of metal that changes the sky into an inferno'*, the A.A.'s *'searchlights [stabbing] the blackness with a silver sword'*, whilst Fighter Command protects the nation *'day and night'*. The *'raiders'*, cowardly at heart, do not risk low-level bombing amongst the complex of blimps over the cities and industrial centres. To ensure that the *'bandits'* are driven back, Fighter Command instructs their units to pursue the *Luftwaffe*, to bring them down and to escort them from the British Isles. Eventually, *'they turn and make for home ... yes they're on the run'*.

These scenes met with a mixed reaction. *Kinematograph Weekly* commented that this sequence was 'a sight for sore eyes' and that audiences should feel reassured that '"Jerry" has a poor chance of bombing London'.[341] This was a sentiment reflected in some comments reported by Mass-Observation, with some exiting the cinema feeling an increased sense of 'safety' and overwhelmingly reassurance.[342] One viewer remarked that *The Lion Has Wings* 'blew away the cobwebs of fear spun by the Nazi spider-propaganda. I thought the Germans were almighty when war was declared, and it's films like that one about the RAF which make me feel secure'.[343] However, some film-goers did not agree. They commented that they noticed 'the absolute immunity of the British fighter and the extraordinarily easy manner in which the German fighter was blasted out of the sky',[344] which underestimated

Still 2 *The Lion Has Wings*: Oberon and Richardson take a stroll
by the river. Still from Bfi Stills, Posters and Designs Archive.
Reproduced with the permission of Granada International Media.

the nature of the struggle ahead and the reality of the threat from the *Luftwaffe*. Some
complained of the 'portrayal of the Germans as swarthy villains', claiming that it gave 'a
false impression of the weakness of the German air-force'.[345] This reaction was enhanced by
the depiction of the British 'being shown as handsome young men who were doing their bit
and playing the white-man on the Kipling and Rupert Brooke model, whilst the Germans
were shown as saturnine and rather cowardly men who turned tail at the slightest hint of
resistance and could not fight at all'.[346] Popular comments were matched by criticism from
the documentarists, their publication, *Documentary News Letter*, proclaiming in January
1940 that 'puerile it is that all the successes should be on our side, that the Nazi pilots are
cowardly morons'.[347] When the raiders did come in 1940, these comments proved to be
sadly accurate. Although *The Lion Has Wings* temporarily allayed the all-pervasive fear of
the bomber displayed by the public and reported by Mass-Observation in 1938–9, it had
encouraged the view that Britain would be able to repel its 'undesirable visitors', and when
its major cities felt the full force of the *Luftwaffe*, they realized that they were not facing
'swarthy' cowards who fled at the sight of barrage balloons, but a powerful destructive
machine with the ability to reduce their targets to rubble.

The film's final sequence ensured that 'the woman's angle', 'principally illustrated by
the agony of waiting', was covered.[348] After a strenuous night repelling the Nazi invader,

Richardson drifts into slumber under the shade of a tree, whilst Oberon appeals to the nation. Women should again be ready to give 'their lovers, husbands, sons ... to the earth to defend their land ... to the sea and now ... to the air', such sacrifices necessary to 'keep our land... We must keep our freedom. We must fight for what we believe in: truth and beauty and fair play and kindness, so that even if we don't live to enjoy life founded in the good things, at least our children may'. This too came in for strong criticism from Documentary News Letter. Reviewing the scene, the journal ranted:

> Merle Oberon sums up for the women of England. She starts talking to Ralph Richardson beneath a Denham tree. The camera moves up until, as she gulps 'and – kindliness', she is in full close-up. Sadly, she turns from the audience to Richardson – her audience. He is asleep, a smile of forbearance lingering on his face. This may be 'realism' but it is poor understanding of the psychology of film propaganda.[349]

As if this were not enough for Documentary News Letter, Oberon casts her eyes to the sky to watch the RAF fly past in formation. Emmett closes the film by informing the audience that 'no longer do we fight wars for jealousy or greed. Nor do we fight in anger'. Reinforcing Oberon's speech, he continues: 'we fight because we must for just those things that we hold so dear'. The audience are instructed to learn from the RAF squadrons by internalizing their motto: 'per ardua ad astra – through ordeal to the stars, through endeavour to triumph, through trial to victory'. The film ends with the RAF insignia blazoned across the skies.

The film opened on 3 November 1939 amid much pomp and circumstance. The distributor, United Artists, ensured that it was widely screened, enticing cinema-owners to take The Lion Has Wings by reducing the normal rate 'on condition that the exhibitors, on their side, waive their usual barring clauses'.[350] This meant that Korda's film could run in a particular region in a number of cinemas simultaneously, in keeping with the MoI's request that 'the film be shown in as many kinemas [sic] as early as possible'.[351] The film was screened by all the major outlets, Gaumont, Odeon, Granada and County, with the exception of ABC.[352] The Times reported on 24 November that 200 copies of the film were to be shown in north London alone. 'No other film', they commented, 'however successful, has been distributed on this scale'.[353] Mass-Observation noted that 'the film was widely seen; in at least two cinemas it broke all existing records despite concurrent showings'.[354] The extent of the distribution was matched by the publicity. Tom Harrisson, co-founder of Mass-Observation, reported that local premieres were transformed into social celebrations, often including 'civic receptions or formal parades of soldiers or air-force men'[355] or involving the decoration of cinema foyers.[356] Some cinema-owners undertook more adventurous promotional activities. W. J. Rawkins, the proprietor of the Savoy in Burnt Oak, staged an elaborate display in his foyer consisting of:

> A realistic balloon barrage [above which] was suspended model airplanes in formation flight. On one side of the floor, amidst model shrubs and trees was a miniature anti-aircraft battery and every type of Army transport lorry. On the opposite side, partially hidden by foliage, lay field ambulances and a fire-fighting unit, each complete in detail.

The whole scheme was shrouded in fine white silk net which gave a truly cloudy effect and was surmounted by a Royal Air Force pilot's wings 20 feet in length.[357]

Other cinema managers created similar public spectacles. Two proprietors in Norwich mounted 'a large lion's head with wings attached … on three-ply and pushed it through all the main streets of the city with a special 12-sheet poster carrying the title of the film with time of screenings' at their respective cinemas. Unsurprisingly, this display 'drew considerable attention'.[358] In the most bizarre advertisement, the Odeon, Edgware Road, hired 'a scale model of a Hampden twin-engine bomber' and placed it alongside a 'stuffed lion loaned by a Piccadilly taxidermist' in the foyer.[359]

Publicists also drew upon patronage offered by leading political or royal figures to promote the film. Whilst *The Times* reported that Sir Kingsley Wood, Secretary of State for Air, and officials of the MoI attended a screening in the West-End,[360] much public attention focused on the fact that *The Lion Has Wings* was 'the first film seen by King George VI and Queen Elizabeth after the outbreak of war'.[361] Local proprietors capitalized on the publicity surrounding 'celebrity' screenings to encourage a growth in box-office receipts, the Majestic, High Wycombe '[loaning] a special illuminated display cabinet which carried a moving band on which was written: "The King and Queen paid their first visit to the Cinema since the war commenced to see *The Lion Has Wings*. See it yourself at the Majestic"'.[362] All of this film advertising, from 'air-displays, civic receptions [and] formal parades' to the attendance of local and national dignitaries from mayors to the King, created 'a sense of duty' to see the film, equating individual viewings to the patriotic message promoted in the film.[363] The excessive promotional activities surrounding the release of Korda's film were also translated into profits, underlining 'the correlation between a high level of publicity and success at the box-office'.[364]

However, as historian Julian Poole has observed, 'weekly returns only tell us about attendance figures, they do not tell us about personal reactions. They do not tell us why people went to see a particular film or whether they enjoyed it'.[365] For this, historians have to probe problematic sources. It is difficult to gauge the extent to which audiences believed, internalized and acted upon the film's message or, in other words, to ascertain how successful it was as propaganda, a difficulty highlighted by Harrisson in 1940. In analysing the findings of Mass-Observation, he concluded that '71% of those who had seen the film *said* they had liked it, 38% of them liking it very much, these being mainly women and, to a lesser extent, older men'. Nevertheless, Harrisson questioned the reasons behind reports of this favourable reaction, forwarding the theory that 'many of those who said they liked the film apparently only did so because they thought it the right thing to say'.[366] This revealed a distinct division between public, private and published reactions to Korda's production. As Harrisson noted, press reviews of the film had been almost entirely positive, with the exception of Graham Greene who had criticized the over-use of old footage and the depiction of German airmen as 'an evil-looking lot'. A number of reviewers had praised the film as a 'wonderful pictorial tribute to the RAF', giving the audience 'courage and confidence on the darkest days' with its 'stirring and good-humoured' tenor,[367] claiming that it was a 'mighty piece of propaganda'.[368] To some extent, these comments reflected popular opinions of the film, Harrisson potentially exaggerating his qualitative data to underline the disparity between press and public opinion, a central political aim of Mass-Observation.[369] Sequences in the film seem to have generated genuine excitement in the audience, particularly amongst younger viewers.[370] The overall message of the film elicited a feeling of security in individual film-goers, challenging previous fears that 'the bomber will always get through', and generated some resentment towards Hitler for plunging Europe into yet another conflict, one Mass-Observer overhearing jokes about 'giving Adolf a kick in the pants' and concluding that the film was 'well-received'.[371] Such reactions have prompted some historians to argue that, contrary to Harrisson's views, 'Korda's team ... had succeeded in their effort to take their message to the British nation'. Supported by superb box-office receipts, a measure of success by the studio and distributors, Short contended that 'the film succeeded in drawing an approval rating from 61.8% men and 83.6% of women' questioned by Harrisson's own organization.[372]

Nonetheless, Harrisson continued to contend that *The Lion Has Wings* 'misfired rather badly', asserting in 1973 that it remained 'a very good case of hamming, underestimating the intelligence of your audience'.[373] Indeed, if the historian looks to the qualitative as opposed to the quantitative data unearthed by Mass-Observation from October 1939 to March 1940, there are numerous individual comments to support Harrisson's thesis. Audience disapproval centred on three key criticisms of the film: poor entertainment and storyline, realism and propaganda. Film-goers frequently commented upon the propagandistic content of Korda's film in a negative manner, feeling deceived and suspicious. One comment from a twenty-year-old male illustrates this view perfectly:

> God knows we have plenty of propaganda ammunition without descending to the use of lies and half-truths. For instance, trying to make out that all Britain's battles in the past have been for the sake of humanity (tell that to the Indians)... Such things will deceive some people in England into an unnatural belief that Britain is 100% right – always.[374]

Audiences did not respond well to the 'usual tripe' and 'flag-wagging'.[375] Complaining that the film was too full of propaganda,[376] film-goers resented the political content of films, arguing that 'you want something to cheer you up'.[377] One woman lamented that the film was 'all propaganda. Nobody wants to see that sort of thing. It's not entertainment. [We] get enough of that in the news'.[378] These comments were indicative of a wider trend observable in the British cinema-going public. Although his study of the Majestic at Macclesfield suggested that *The Lion Has Wings* 'did reasonable business', Poole has noted that Ealing's George Formby comedies found significant audiences, as did American escapist films.[379] *Kinematograph Weekly* recognized that, as early as October 1939, the public were imploring 'no war pictures, please!' and were in desperate need of 'something that will offer as good a relief as possible from the anxiety which is never far below the surface of the British citizen these days'. The public were 'in a mood that demands vigorous, lively entertainment, with no harping upon a string that must in the nature of things be discordant'.[380] Yet, despite Korda's attempt to fuse propaganda and entertainment in *The Lion Has Wings*, the public recognized that the film possessed a weak story line and was loaded with 'Kordage and Merlery'.[381] The film, therefore, did not seem to enjoy the magic ingredient for cinematic propagandistic success: 'the film being a popular medium must be good entertainment if it is to be good propaganda'.[382] Although an analysis of the quantitative data suggests that *The Lion Has Wings* was enjoyed by most cinema-goers, there is a tension with the qualitative evidence provided by Mass-Observation. It is entirely possible that, as Harrisson suggested, the public flocked to their local cinemas prompted by widespread publicity and patriotic fervour and either felt compelled or wanted to offer positive comments to observers, whilst at the same time criticizing certain aspects of the film such as propagandistic content, storyline and the absence of realism. This mixed, and potentially simultaneous, reaction within the cinema-going public and the individual patron is likely to have prompted Harrisson to comment that 'the film may not have had such an encouraging effect as was hoped'.[383]

If the film caused such mixed reactions at home, it caused even more consternation abroad, its export raising uncomfortable questions about the nature of British propaganda. On 24 November 1939, *The Times* reported that copies of the film were being prepared for dispatch to France, Belgium, Switzerland, Portugal, Spain, Scandinavia, Canada, Australia, New Zealand, South Africa, Singapore, India and Egypt. The most important delivery was made by Alexander Korda himself, travelling on a transatlantic clipper to New York and 'personally supervising [the film's] release in America'.[384] However, Korda found himself in an extremely sensitive diplomatic environment. The Foreign Office was fearful that Korda could be perceived to be 'plugging the place full of British propaganda'. They lamented, 'if this news gets round in America nothing will more successfully kill the film, ruin Korda's reputation and generally defeat every purpose which the film may have been designed to promote'.[385] The Foreign Office and the MoI held that propaganda to the United States should not be traced back to the British Government, fearful that memories of the Bryce Report (1915) and the Zimmermann Telegram (1917) and their propagandistic exploitation by British agents in the United States might hold significant implications for the promotion of Britain's cause in 1939–40.[386] The Foreign Office deliberately distanced itself from the Korda production and its promotion in North America, noting on 17 November 1939 that 'the very unfortunate publicity given to this film in relation to the United States of America has ... excited the gravest misgivings here and it is absolutely essential that there should be no suspicion of government support behind any efforts to secure its distribution here'.[387] Moreover, the Foreign Office and the Ministry recognized that this kind of activity breached the undertaking of the House of Commons that Britain would not actively seek to conduct propaganda operations in the US.[388]

Evidence from Grierson, now working at the National Film Board of Canada, suggested that British fears were justified. Although he reported that *The Lion Has Wings* was 'the most useful job sent over', he added that the Canadians had felt the film to be 'too obvious propaganda', pointing to the same criticisms as British audiences. The Canadians noticed too that 'only Germans were killed and were made gratuitously – and against all good sense – to look very much wickeder young men than their British counterparts'. In a scathing appraisal of Oberon's concluding speech, Grierson reported that the scene 'tended to sicken people on recollection'. More seriously and underlining Foreign Office fears, Grierson lamented that 'the criticism [in the United States] was much more pronounced and sufficient to make the film an indifferent commercial proposition. In this case, according to general comment, the propaganda was thought too raw'.[389] *The Lion Has Wings* was not an extraordinary success abroad, perhaps due to the fact that it was primarily designed to appeal to the British sense of humour and the home audience's understanding of their own nation and heritage. In the export of the film, at least, Korda's film was no match for the awesome terror tactics employed by Bertram, the *Wehrmacht* and the German Foreign Office in their aggressive distribution of *Feuertaufe* across Europe and the world.

It was clear, therefore, that by early 1940, British propaganda was not living up to expectations. Even if the historian or the contemporary observer looks favourably upon popular reactions to *The Lion Has Wings*, as *Today's Cinema's* 'onlooker' commented in November 1939, 'one propaganda picture, however marvelous, doesn't make a publicity campaign'.[390] Questions were being asked of the film policy of the MoI. *Today's Cinema* commented two weeks earlier that 'from all accounts, [Korda's film is] calculated to make every man and woman in this county proud of being English-born. But that's only one film. Where is the big campaign for film propaganda that we had every reason to believe would be forthcoming from the Ministry?'[391] This was a view championed by many, including the Film Centre's publication, *Documentary News Letter*, who complained that although 'the value of this weapon [film] has been ... denied by no-one..., its use ... after four months of war ... appears to be in danger of neglect'.[392] Not only was the MoI in danger of allowing the RMVP to forge ahead in its cinematic propaganda, the Ministry's failure to foster and support British film production for the war effort in the early years of the conflict left producers wide open to scathing criticism from their enemy. Of all the films produced by the British in World War II, none was to receive more criticism from Goebbels than *The Lion Has Wings*.

For Goebbels and the RMVP, Korda's film offered them the opportunity to juxtapose British and German propaganda methods. The two films were consistently and repetitively contrasted in Nazi literature and by officials of the RMVP, such comparisons supposedly demonstrative of the British intent to deceive. In the publicity for Bertram's *Feuertaufe*, *The Lion Has Wings* played a significant role in underlining Tobis' assertion that their film was pure reportage, a realistic reflection of the battle for Poland. According to *Filmwelt*, in April 1940, the month of *Feuertaufe's* release, Bertram had no need for trick photography, montage sequences and other cinematic deception techniques. The National Socialist press contended that, in direct contrast to the 'pretend aerial attack by the English on Wilhelmshaven', 'the shots in … *Feuertaufe* speak the language of facts'.[393] Nazi propaganda stressed that its campaigns were generated out of the desire to inform the public, rather than to lull them into a false sense of security or to mislead them in any way. Depicting film in the Third Reich as a living 'document' of contemporary history, *Filmwelt* stated that:

> Lying is hardest to do in films. That is why the gentlemen from the Thames or the Seine are found out so quickly. For example, in a plot featuring an air attack, it makes a huge difference whether German *Stukas* are shown attacking Warsaw, as in the film *Feuertaufe*, or model airplanes built in an English special effects studio attack an artificially created Wilhelmshaven in order to show a heroic deed by the 'winged lion'. The film itself proves that, rather than a flying king of the animal world, what we are dealing with is at best a rat cowardly hiding in its hole.[394]

The German press even suggested that the title be changed to *Puss in Boots* to reflect the nature of Korda's film, the *Berliner Börsen-Zeitung* apparently commenting that 'this animal out of the fairy-story clearly has a better idea how to deceive successfully than the senile British Lion'.[395] Such was the propagandistic value of the British film for the Nazis that, in May 1940, Goebbels resolved to arrange a special screening of the Korda production in Berlin, predicting that it would 'get a first-class burial in a storm of hilarity'.[396]

It was in relation to the RMVP's intention to show *The Lion Has Wings* that *Filmwelt* reviewed the film in June 1940. Asking his readers whether 'the lion really has wings', Günther Sawatzki delivered a scathing response to the claims made by Korda and his production team. Commenting on the opening sequences of 'a series of atmospheric landscape shots with grazing flocks of sheep, children playing and people dancing happily', Sawatzki demanded why Korda had excluded

> the infamous slums of London's East End, where dozens of sick, malnourished and depraved people are crouching on a few square metres between rotten walls. Instead, the eye is presented with the pleasant sight of fancy and comfortable housing estates such as they are available to any English worker who earns around 1000 Marks a month.[397]

The reviewer not only suggested that Korda's production was perpetrating a monumental deception in its depiction of British social conditions, but that the film erroneously placed blame upon 'these wicked Germans with their war re-armament' for interrupting her 'struggle against social misery' by causing the outbreak of war. 'Of course', claimed Sawatzki, 'for all English misfortunes the Führer is responsible'. Challenging the film's interpretation of life in the Third Reich with its 'disciplined columns … instead of football matches', he pointed to the ridiculous portrait of leadership through the royal family, with its depiction of the 'royal couple in one of those funny sketches where, surrounded by well-behaved members of the plutocracy, they beat time with their hands, first on the knee, then the head, then wiggle their ears and stamp their feet whilst looking majestic and dignified as well as jovially displaying the common touch'. Naturally, the point of this sequence was to demonstrate the personal leadership of George VI and his connection to his people, able to walk amongst them without having to be protected by a phalanx such was his popularity. However, Sawatzki argued that 'when immediately afterwards the Führer appears and, in front of the marching columns of the National Socialist Germany, speaks of the people in need and of the fight for freedom, which has been forced upon us by the rich, then this contrast speaks very honourably in our favour'.[398]

Sawatzki then turns his attention to the outbreak of war and the principal characters, Wing Commander Richardson and his wife. Apart from the criticism offered in other publications of the period on the fictionalized representations of conflict and battle, he pointed to the fact that Richardson was cowardly by hiding away 'for the entire night ... in a bomb-proof command bunker' whilst his men were facing the onslaught of the *Luftwaffe*. *Filmwelt* also drew attention to apparent mistakes in the reconstruction of the Kiel raid, alluding to the possibility that the ship under attack by the RAF was actually bearing a German flag of the Great War, calling into question the veracity of the footage presented. Singled out for special comment was Oberon's final speech, for which Sawatzki reserved his most searing commentary:

> At the end of this strange film, one of the girls, having spent all night on Red Cross duty, lies down in the garden with the victorious air force commander who has emerged from a secure bomb shelter. She gives him a tearful speech about the British philosophy of life whose necessary conclusion is unfortunately that the evil Germans must be eradicated...
> The German audience bursts into one last roar of laughter, as the hero of the air and the shelter has by now fallen asleep. This is how peaceful his hard-boiled heart is. The film of the winged lion thus ends in the same ridiculous fashion as it started.[399]

He concluded that 'the film Jew Korda', in the employ of the 'Jewish war-mongers', had deceived the public into conceiving of the war in an idealized manner: 'the war looks bloody different', Sawatzki reminded him.[400] He encouraged the RMVP to proceed with its plan of distributing *The Lion Has Wings*, commenting that 'this British film deserves our *Prädikat "staatspolitisch wertvoll"* – that's how good its propaganda is. But in our favour!'[401] However, as Willi Boelcke noted, 'before a suitable German version of the film could be completed, the RAF's bombing raids proved that the British lion did indeed have wings and that there were no longer any grounds for hilarity'.[402] In Germany, like Britain, the war had entered a new phase, its propaganda adapting to meet the new challenges the conflict presented.

CONCLUSIONS

> In a war to the death like this one, endurance means everything; morale means every-thing... This war will not be won on the military front, but on the psychological front. It will be won because one group of people have the heart and the will to stay the course: it will be lost because one group of people have failed to find the unity that comes with a clear and inspiring purpose.[403]

Thus film-maker John Grierson described the situation in which propagandists and their film-makers found themselves in 1940. Grierson found that British film-makers were not up to this task in the early years of the war. In contrast to the 'blood-and-thunder' propaganda emanating from the RMVP and in particular the 'documentaries of intimidation', British film elicited at best mixed reactions from home audiences, at worst ridicule from the enemy. He informed his acolytes back home that 'England should thank heaven for the BBC',[404] as the film-makers were not contributing significant works to the propaganda arsenal. As Grierson and the film industry recognized, the MoI was not paying sufficient attention to film as a weapon of war, all the more disturbing as they were faced with a formidable opponent, an enemy who could produce such psychologically powerful films as *Feuertaufe*.

But the two propagandas were, and in many senses had to be, very different, their propagandists working within dissimilar military circumstances and with very different mechanisms for controlling popular opinion. It was in this environment that contrary conceptions of propaganda began to emerge. As film-maker Basil Wright wrote in *The Spectator* in October 1939, 'It is not our part to attempt, as do the Nazis, to persuade others by means of intellectual bludgeoning, perverted half-truths and screams of hate. We need to present the world with a series of truthful pictures of the manner in which we of Great Britain live'.[405] Despite German claims to the contrary, British propagandists continued to assert that their propaganda was grounded in truth, while their adversary's campaigns were marked with 'the abuse, sarcasm, lies and rhetoric with which [they] shouted their way to power'.[406] Although *The Lion Has Wings* did not reflect this sentiment in itself, with its staged reconstructions, 'half-truths and half-lies', it taught the MoI and film-makers a valuable lesson about war propaganda. They not only faced criticism at home but provided the grist for Goebbels' propagandistic mill. It spoke to the inexperience of the British in the propaganda of the modern age, their lack of preparedness in September 1939 and their naivety in facing the Nazi propaganda machine. Meanwhile, Bertram's film attested to the eighteen-month preparation period of the RMVP for the conflict and its six years of experience in the persuasive arts. Both *The Lion Has Wings* and *Feuertaufe*, however, were products of their time. Neither was relevant for more than one year after their release and suggests the short life of propaganda feature films. The message of Korda's film, that Britain could easily repel the *Luftwaffe*, was clearly called into question with the extensive aerial bombardment beginning in 1940. Ultimately, Bertram's film fared no better. Although in the short term the ideal of a blitzkrieg was demonstrated by the western conquests, when Hitler invaded the Soviet Union in June 1941, the German population recognized that there were to be no more 'eighteen-day campaigns'. A study of the history of the two films also reveals that cinematic propaganda operated and was received in a global context, by targeted nations, by neutrals and, significantly, by enemy nations. Both Britain and Germany responded to each other's filmic justifications for war, offering a rare insight into the reception of film propaganda by the enemy and demonstrating that such responses were needed to counter enemy claims.

By May 1940, the war had progressed. Justifying war was no longer the main concern. The 'Sitzkrieg' and the 'Bore War' was over. The propaganda campaigns of the early years focusing on the assignation of blame dissolved into a fight to sustain morale. Mass bombardment replaced the endless waiting for the war to start in earnest, and bombers darkened the skies of both Britain and Germany. Ultimately, Göring's threats delivered in the concluding sequences of *Feuertaufe* were realized in Britain and the idyllic repulsion of the *Luftwaffe* and romantic notions of defence portrayed in *The Lion Has Wings* were to be no more than 'fairytales' concocted by the 'wizard of Denham'. Now the war was in full swing, and film propaganda changed to reflect the shifting nature of warfare. Now film was 'not a mirror but a hammer'. As Grierson told his compatriots, 'it is a weapon in our hands to see and to say what is right and good and beautiful and hammer it out as the mould and pattern of men's action'.[407] And in their depiction of the Blitz that is exactly what the propagandists of Britain and Germany set out to do.

NOTES

1. Survey conducted in September 1938, quoted in C. Madge and T. Harrisson, *Britain by Mass-Observation* (Penguin, Harmondsworth, 1939), p. 66.
2. 'Metrop' was a pseudonym used by Mass-Observation to describe a district of South-West London.
3. P. M. Taylor, *British Propaganda in the Twentieth Century*, p. 104.
4. See for example, T. Harrisson, *Living through the Blitz* (Collins, London, 1976), pp. 19–30.
5. C. Madge and T. Harrisson, *Britain*, p. 88.
6. A selection of responses gathered by Mass-Observation as reported in C. Madge and T. Harrisson, *Britain*, pp. 88–9.
7. Ibid., pp. 40–2. Mass-Observation points in particular to the 1930s being an 'era in which Those Who Know won't tell, and the newspapers tell whatever suits their book'. (p. 41).
8. Ibid., p. 49. This was not an isolated comment. A number of other respondents answered in a similar fashion. See pp. 49–50.
9. Ibid., p. 50.
10. Imperial War Museum, Duxford. Foreign Documents Collection. (Hereafter IWM FDC) Unidentified and uncatalogued box of materials. SD report of the *Unterabschnitt-Leipzig*, II 225 B. – Nr. 1495/39. Ho. 10 August 1939. 'Stimmung in der Bevölkerung', p. 1.
11. Reported in W. Shirer, *Berlin Diary. The Journal of a Foreign Correspondent, 1934–1941* (Hamish Hamilton, London, 1941), despite Goebbels' desire to maintain 'moderation' and 'self-control' in media outputs. See, R. G. Reuth, *Goebbels*, trans. K. Winston (Constable, London, 1993), pp. 247–55. Naturally, the press played a significant role in shaping popular opinion in this period. For a further discussion, see O. J. Hale, *The Captive Press in the Third Reich* (Princeton University Press, Princeton NJ, 1973) and N. Frei and J. Schmitz, *Journalismus im Dritten Reich* (C. H. Beck, Munich, 1989).
12. IWM FDC Unidentified and uncatalogued box of materials. SD report of the *Unterabschnitt-Leipzig*, II 225 B. – Nr. 1495/39. Ho. 10 August 1939. 'Stimmung in der Bevölkerung', p. 1.
13. W. Shirer, *Berlin Diary*, p. 139. Entry for 9 August 1939.
14. Ibid. Diary entry for 10 August 1939.
15. *Deutschland –Berichte der Sozialdemokratischen Partei Deutschlands (Sopade)*. (Verlag Petra Nettelbeck, Zweitausendeins, Frankfurt am Main, 1980). 6. Jahrgang 1939. Nr. 8. A 4, p. 965.
16. Ibid., 6 Jahrgang 1939. Nr. 7. A 8, p. 818. Report from Upper Silesia.
17. Ibid., 6 Jahrgang 1939. Nr. 8. A 6, p. 967. Report from South West Germany.

18. W. Shirer, *Berlin Diary*, p. 141. Shirer commented on 11 August that his observations in Danzig confirmed that there was still a belief that 'Hitler … will effect their return from the Reich without war'. This is in contrast to the views expressed in Leipzig. IWM FDC Unidentified and uncatalogued box of materials. SD report of the *Unterabschnitt-Leipzig*, II 225 B. – Nr. 1495/39. Ho. 10 August 1939. 'Stimmung in der Bevölkerung'. For the view that war was imminent and could not be avoided, see *Deutschland-Berichte der Sopade*, 6 Jahrgang 1939, Nr 8. A 32–3, p. 990.

19. *Deutschland-Berichte der Sopade*, 6 Jahrgang 1939, Nr. 8, A21, 980. Report from Bavaria.

20. IWM FDC Unidentified and uncatalogued box of materials. SD report of the *Unterabschnitt-Leipzig*, II 225 B. – Nr. 1495/39. Ho. 10 August 1939. 'Stimmung in der Bevölkerung', p. 1. The population of Leipzig were particularly concerned about the role of the Soviet Union in the potential conflict.

21. Ibid., pp. 3–4.

22. W. Shirer, *Berlin Diary*, p. 154. Entry for 31 August 1939.

23. M. Chalmers (ed.), *The Diaries of Victor Klemperer 1933–1945: I Shall Bear Witness – To the Bitter End* (Phoenix Press, London, 1998; 2nd edn, 2000), pp. 292–3. Diary entries for 29 August and 3 September 1939.

24. Ibid., p. 294. Diary entry for 3 September 1939.

25. Ibid., p. 293. Diary entry for 29 August 1939.

26. W. Shirer, *Berlin Diary*, p. 152. Diary entry for 29 August 1939.

27. M. Steinert, *Hitler's War and the Germans*, p. 50.

28. Ibid.

29. W. Shirer, *Berlin Diary*, p. 162. Diary entry for 3 September 1939.

30. M. Steinert, *Hitler's War and the Germans*, p. 50.

31. W. Shirer, *Berlin Diary*, p. 160. Diary entry for 1 September 1939.

32. *Deutschland-Berichte der Sopade*, 6 Jahrgang 1939, Nr 8. A21, p. 980.

33. S. Salter, 'Structures of Consensus and Coercion: Workers' Morale and the Maintenance of Work Discipline', in D. Welch (ed.), *Nazi Propaganda*, pp. 88–116. Here, p. 90.

34. *Deutschland-Berichte der Sopade*, 6 Jahrgang 1939, Nr 8. A33, p. 991.

35. Ibid. , Nr 8. A21, p. 980.

36. W. Benz, *Herrschaft und Gesellschaft im nationalsozialistischen Staat* (Fischer, Frankfurt am Main, 1990), p. 63.

37. Ibid., p. 66.

38. Ibid., p. 68.

39. Ibid., p. 67.

40. Ibid., p. 69.

41. Ibid., p. 63.

42. A. Calder, *The People's War. Britain 1939–45* (The Literary Guild, London, 1969), p. 34.

43. C. Madge and T. Harrisson, *Britain*, p. 49.

44. T. Harrisson, *Living through the Blitz*, p. 30.

45. M. L. Sanders and P. Taylor, *British Propaganda during the First World War, 1914–18* (Macmillan, London, 1982), p. 1.

46. Although a popular perception amongst certain sections of the far right in Germany in the post-war era, this has largely been contested by existing historical works. See in particular D. Welch, *Germany, Propaganda and Total War, 1914–1918: The Sins of Omission* (Rutgers University Press, New Brunswick, NJ, 2000).

47. A. Hitler, *Mein Kampf*, trans. R. Manheim (London, Pimlico, 1992), p. 169.

48. A. Ponsonby, *Falsehood in War-Time: Containing an Assortment of Lies Circulated throughout the Nations during the Great War* (G. Allen & Unwin Ltd., London, 1936; first published, 1928).

49. R. Graves, *Goodbye to All That*, 4th edn (Book Club Associates, London, 1966; first published 1929).

50. S. Badsey and P. M. Taylor, 'The Experience of Manipulation: Propaganda in Press and Radio', in J. Bourne, P. Liddle, and I. Whitehead, *The Great World War 1914–45. Vol. 2 The People's Experience* (HarperCollins, London, 2001), pp. 41–57, p. 43.

51. The first major book detailing the work of the MoI was Ian McLaine's *Ministry of Morale. Home Front Morale and the Ministry of Information in World War II* (George Allen & Unwin, London, 1979). In this work, McLaine asserted that 'for nearly two years the measures taken by the propagandists were unnecessary and inept, based as they were on misunderstanding and distrust of the British public which, in turn, were products of the class and background of the propagandists themselves' (p. 10–11). McLaine concedes certain achievements, such as the eventual realization of the importance of civilian morale in determining propaganda policy, the increasing strength of the MoI in the face of conflict with the services, other ministries and the Prime Minister and their insistence that British propaganda should be markedly different from that of the enemy' (p. 11). More recently, James Chapman, in his superb study of British cinema during World War II, *The British at War: Cinema, State and Propaganda, 1939–1945*, has challenged McLaine's views of the MoI, Chapman has argued that the Ministry suffered from the appalling publicity it received in the early years of the war, despite having some significant successes later. He noted: 'Although the MoI was to function quite efficiently later in the war, ... it never completely shook off the negative impression that it had made at the beginning and was stuck thereafter with a reputation for blundering and incompetence' (p. 14). Chapman has also challenged McLaine's lack of analysis of films (p. 5) and his assessment of the Crown Film Unit (p. 137). For more on the MoI, see also M. Balfour, *Propaganda in War, 1939–1945*, esp. pp. 53–88.

52. P. M. Taylor, '"If War Should Come": Preparing the Fifth Arm for Total War 1935–1939', *Journal of Contemporary History*, vol. 16, no. 1, The Second World War: Part 1 (January, 1981), pp. 27–51, p. 48.

53. *The Times*, 26 October 1939.

54. J. Chapman, *The British at War*, pp. 13–14.

55. *The Times*, 30 September 1939. 'Letters to the Editor'.

56. Mass-Observation (hereafter M-O A) File Report (hereafter FR) 90, 'Morale: Channels of publicity: press, radio, pamphlets and leaflets, posters and films', 14 April 1940.

57. H. V. Rhodes, Memorandum, 16 November 1938, in the National Archives (hereafter TNA), Public Record Office (PRO) INF 1/727, as quoted in I. McLaine, *Ministry of Morale*, p. 21.

58. Monckton Papers, Department of Special Collections and Western Manuscripts, New Bodleian Library, University of Oxford (hereafter Monckton papers). MSS DEP Monckton Trustees Papers (Balliol). Box 4. Lord Macmillan to Walter Monckton, from Killin, Perthshire, 25 January 1941.

59. Lord Reith, *The Reith Diaries* (London, Collins, 1975), 27 March 1940, p. 244.

60. Duff Cooper, *Old Men Forget* (Hart-Davis, London, 1953), pp. 276–7. For reactions to Duff Cooper's despondency see, I. McLaine, *The Ministry of Morale*, p. 233.

61. For the extent to which the press was responsible for the criticism relating to the MoI (and how it occasionally contrasted to public views), see the 'Cooper's Snoopers' incident. M-O A: FR 325 '"Cooper's Snoopers": Press Campaign against the Ministry of Information and Duff Cooper', 5 August 1940.

62. Monckton papers. MSS DEP Monckton Trustees Papers (Balliol). Box 4, f. 147. Monckton to Leonora Corbett, 27 March 1941.

63. Monckton papers. MSS DEP Monckton Trustees Papers (Balliol). Box 5. A. P. Ryan to Walter Monckton, 4 June 1941.

64. Monckton papers. MSS DEP Monckton Trustees Papers (Balliol). Box 5. Brendan Bracken to Monckton, 2 May 1941.

65. F. Williams, *Press, Parliament and People* (Heinemann, London, 1946), p. 10. Quoted in I. McLaine, *Ministry of Morale*, p. 6.

66. Monckton papers. MSS DEP Monckton Trustees Papers (Balliol). Box 4. Comments on the purpose of the Ministry of Information and its organization, 23 January 1941.

67. TNA PRO INF 1/316, Home Publicity Division minutes, 1 September 1939, as quoted in I. McLaine, *Ministry of Morale*, p. 27.

68. I. McLaine, *Ministry of Morale*, p. 27.

69. John Marchbank, the Secretary of the Northern Union of Railway Workers, writing in *The Manchester Guardian*, 24 February 1941. Wiener Library cuttings collection, PC5/209B, reel 140.

70. TNA PRO INF 1/316, Home Publicity Division minutes, 1 September 1939, as quoted in I. McLaine, *Ministry of Morale*, p. 27.

71. See P. M. Taylor, 'Techniques of Persuasion: Basic Ground Rules of British Propaganda during the Second World War', *Historical Journal of Film, Radio and Television*, vol. 1, no. 1 (1981), pp. 57–65.

72. Monckton papers. MSS DEP Monckton Trustees Papers (Balliol). Box 5. f. 93. Unattributed document, n/d.

73. Lord Reith, *The Reith Diaries*, 27 March 1940, p. 244.

74. Monckton papers. MSS DEP Monckton Trustees Papers (Balliol). Box 4. f. 152. 'Matters of Moment', Walter Monckton, 31 March 1941. 1st draft.

75. Monckton papers. MSS DEP Monckton Trustees Papers (Balliol). Box 6. f. 61. On Political Warfare, 12 September 1941.

76. *The Yorkshire Post*, 26 February 1940. Wiener Library cuttings collection. PC5/ 101c. Reel 98.

77. See R. Taylor, *Film Propaganda*, p. 142; D. Welch, *Propaganda and the German Cinema*, p. 35.

78. M. Balfour, *Propaganda in War*, p. 15.

79. Reproduced in D. Welch, *Propaganda and the German Cinema*, p. 9.

80. The *New York Times* challenged the distinction between 'popular enlightenment' and 'propaganda', commenting that 'both terms . . . may be considered synonymous, for both have the same didactic, crusading connotation'. *New York Times*, 19 November 1939, p. E5.

81. D. Welch, 'Nazi Film Policy: Control, Ideology, and Propaganda', in G. R. Cuomo (ed.), *National Socialist Cultural Policy* (St. Martin's Press, New York, 1995), pp. 95–121, 96. Balfour notes that Goebbels did not wish to use the word 'propaganda' in the title of the new Ministry 'on the ground that it would be counter-productive', but was said to have been overridden by Hitler. However, he provides little substantive evidence for this assertion. See M. Balfour, *Propaganda in War*, p. 13.

82. M. Balfour, *Propaganda in War*, p. 13.

83. D. Welch, 'Nazi Film Policy', pp. 96–7.

84. Information here from D. Welch, *Propaganda and the German Cinema*, p. 9. See also Z. A. B. Zeman, *Nazi Propaganda* (Oxford University Press, Oxford, 1964), esp. pp. 39–42. See also D. Welch, 'Nazi Film Policy', pp. 96–9.

85. R. Taylor, 'Goebbels and the Function of Propaganda', in D. Welch (ed.), *Nazi Propaganda*, pp. 29–44. Here, pp. 31–2.

86. R. Taylor, *Film Propaganda*, p. 143. A similar speech is reported in M. Balfour, *Propaganda in War*, p. 12, although he gives the date as 16 March 1933.

87. P. Taylor, '"If War Should Come"', p. 48.

88. S. Badsey and P. M. Taylor, 'The Experience of Manipulation', p. 50. See also D. Welch, *The Third Reich: Politics and Propaganda* (Routledge, London, 1993), p. 92.

89. '"Engländer – schlechte Psychologen". Unterredung mit Dr. Goebbels über die Kapitalfehler der Plutokraten', in *Der Angriff*, 24 March 1940. Wiener Library cuttings collection PC 5/101c.

90. Ibid.

91. P. M. Taylor, 'Techniques of Persuasion', p. 57.

92. 'Erlebnisvolle Filmfeierstunde der Hitlerjugend', *Völkischer Beobachter*, 6 November 1939. Wiener Library cuttings collection, PC5/101c. Reel 98.

93. I. Fetscher, *Joseph Goebbels im Berliner Sportpalast 1943. 'Wollt ihr den totalen Krieg?'* (Europäische Verlagsanstalt, Hamburg, 1998), p. 15.

94. For example, see F. A. Koeniger, 'Britische Propaganda', *Der Angriff*, 21 November 1939. Wiener Library cuttings collection PC 5/119D.

95. 'Erlebnisvolle Filmfeierstunde der Hitlerjugend', *Völkischer Beobachter*, 6 November 1939. Wiener Library cuttings collection, PC5/101c. Reel 98.

96. 'Die Wahrheit als Waffe', *Filmwelt*, no. 26, 28 June 1940, pp. 4–5.

97. Monckton papers. MSS DEP Monckton Trustees Papers (Balliol). Box 6. f. 61. On Political Warfare, 12 September 1941.

98. 'Die Kamera – Waffe der Wahrheit', *Filmwelt*, 23 August 1940, p. 4.

99. *The Cinema*, 26 June 1940, p. 5.

100. For more on these activities see in particular, T. Hanna-Daoud, *Die NSDAP und der Film bis zur Machtergreifung* (Böhlau, Cologne, 1996). For details of censorship and its role in promoting right-wing groupings, see D. Welch, 'The Proletarian Cinema and the Weimar Republic', in *Historical Journal of Film, Radio and Television*, vol. 1, no. 1 (1981), pp. 3–18.

101. For details see in particular: W. Becker, *Film und Herrschaft. Organisationsprinzipien und Organisationsstrukturen der nationalsozialistischen Filmpropaganda* (Volker Spiess, Berlin, 1973); J. Petley, *Capital and Culture. German Cinema 1933 -1945* (Bfi publishing, London, 1979); J. Petley, 'Film Policy in the Third Reich' in T. Bergfelder, E. Carter and D. Göktürk (eds), *The German Cinema Book* (Bfi publishing, London, 2002); J. Spiker, *Film und Kapital. Der Weg der deutschen Filmwirtschaft zum nationalsozialistischen Einheitskonzern* (Volker Spiess, Berlin, 1975); D. Welch, 'Nazi Film Policy'; D. Welch, *Propaganda and the German Cinema*, pp. 5–32.

102. D. Welch, *Propaganda and the German Cinema*, pp. 25–9.

103. Ibid., pp. 28–9.

104. 'Die Leistung des deutschen Films im kriege', *Hamburger Fremdenblatt*, 16 February 1941.Wiener Library cuttings collection, PC5/101c. Educational function also stressed in 'Erlebnisvolle Filmfeierstunde der Hitlerjugend', *Völkischer Beobachter*, 6 November 1939. Wiener Library cuttings collection, PC5/101c. Reel 98.

105. 'Dr Goebbels: "Der Film ist das wichtigste Propagandamittel"', *Das 12 Uhr Blatt*, no. 30, 3 February 1940. Wiener Library cuttings collection, PC5/101c. Reel 98.

106. For more on Nazi film export and NS 'cultural imperialism' with reference to the cinema, see R. Van der Winkel and D. Welch (eds), *Cinema and the Swastika: The International Expansion of the Third Reich Cinema* (Palgrave, Basingstoke, 2007).

107. 'Volle Filmtheater, beschäftigte Ateliers', *Frankfurter Zeitung*, no. 250, 19 May 1940. Wiener Library cuttings collection, PC5/106E. Petley has questioned the attendance figures produced for the period. For further details, see J. Petley, *Capital and Culture*, p. 60.

108. Ibid.

109. 'Volle Filmtheater, beschäftigte Ateliers', *Frankfurter Zeitung*, no. 250, 19 May 1940. Wiener Library cuttings collection, PC5/106E.

110. 'Europäischer Film', *Hamburger Fremdenblatt*, Nr. 266, 25 September 1941. Wiener Library cuttings collection, PC5/106E.

111. For details on attendance, see J. Spiker, *Film und Kapital*, pp. 197–8 and J. Petley, *Capital and Culture*, pp. 75–6.

112. J. Spiker, *Film und Kapital*, p. 198.

113. J. Petley, *Capital and Culture*, p. 76.
114. IWM FDC Unidentified and uncatalogued box of materials. SD report of the *Unterabschnitt-Leipzig, Lu/Oe III c 3 (neu)*, 26 August 1941.
115. *Bundesarchiv* (hereafter, BArch), R 55/663, *Reichsfilmintendant* to Goebbels, 15 November 1944.
116. 'Deutschland das Zweitgrößte Filmland der Welt', *Hamburger Tageblatt*, no. 53, 23 February 1940. Weiner Library cuttings collection, PC5/106E.
117. J. Petley, *Capital and Culture*, p. 80.
118. See for example, BArch R55/656, Hinkel Minutes of meeting with Goebbels, 29 July 1944; BArch R56I/110. Memorandum from Hinkel, 21 July 1944.
119. D. Welch, *Propaganda and the German Cinema*, p. 24.
120. Ibid.
121. W. Boelcke, *The Secret Conferences of Dr. Goebbels. October 1939–March 1943*, trans. E. Osers (Weidenfeld and Nicolson, London, 1966 and 1967), p. 3. Minute for 6 November 1939. Requests were made on 12 January and again on 14 February 1940 (reported in the minutes under 16 February 1940, see p. 21). A further and final request is recorded on 28 February 1941, p. 123; Minute for 16 February 1940, p. 21; Minute for 28 February 1941, pp. 123–4.
122. IWM FDC Unidentified and uncatalogued box of materials. SD report of the *Unterabschnitt-Leipzig*, II 225 Tgb. Nr. 3/40 Wa. 1 August 1940. II 214.
123. SD report, 90, 23 May 1940, in H. Boberach (ed.), Meldungen aus dem Reich Die geheimen Lageberichte des Sicherheitsdieastes der SS, 1938–1945 (Pawlak Verlag, Herrsching, 1984), vol. 4, p. 1168.
124. *Today's Cinema*, 15 May 1940, p. 3.
125. Ibid.
126. For a superb account of the history of the Films Division and the MoI's approach to film, see J. Chapman, *The British at War*, pp. 13–138.
127. *Daily Mirror*, 16 April 1940. Quoted in J. Chapman, *The British at War*, p. 29.
128. For more details of this and the relationship between John Grierson and the MoI during the war years, see J. Fox, 'John Grierson, his "Documentary Boys" and the British Ministry of Information, 1939–1942', *Historical Journal of Film, Radio and Television*, vol. 25, no. 3 (August 2005), pp. 345–69.
129. See J. Chapman, *The British at War*, pp. 13–41.
130. TNA PRO INF 1/59, Report of the Select Committee on National Expenditure, August 1940.
131. Lord Macmillan quoted in *Today's Cinema*, 27 October 1939, pp. 1–2.
132. TNA PRO INF 1/867, 'Programme for Film Propaganda', revised copy. Co-ordinating Committee Paper 1. This document was circulated under the instructions of Kenneth Clark. For more details see A. Aldgate and J. Richards, *Britain Can Take It*, p. 6.
133. TNA PRO INF 1/867, 'Programme for Film Propaganda', revised copy. Co-ordinating Committee Paper 1.
134. TNA PRO INF 1/59, Report of the Select Committee on National Expenditure, August 1940.
135. *Documentary Newsletter*, vol. 3, no. 2, February 1942, p. 17.
136. TNA PRO INF 1/867, 'Programme for Film Propaganda', revised copy. Co-ordinating Committee Paper 1
137. TNA PRO INF 1/59, Report of the Select Committee on National Expenditure, August 1940.
138. J. Chapman, *The British at War*, p. 81.
139. A. Aldgate and J. Richards, *Britain Can Take It*, p. 7.
140. *Today's Cinema*, 6 November 1940, p. 7.
141. *Documentary News Letter*, July 1940.
142. M-O A: FR 90, Morale: Channels of publicity: press, radio, pamphlets and leaflets, posters and films, 14 April 1940.

143. *Today's Cinema*, 26 September 1939.

144. *Today's Cinema*, 3 January 1940, p. 162.

145. *Today's Cinema*, 27 September 1939.

146. M-O A: FR 24, 'The Cinema in the First Three Months of War', January 1940. Also in D. Sheridan and J. Richards (eds), *Mass-Observation at the Movies* (Routledge & Kegan Paul, London/New York, 1987), p. 140.

147. Ibid., p. 141.

148. M-O A: Topic Collection (hereafter TC), 17/1/C, R.C. to Len England, 25 January 1940.

149. *Kinematograph Weekly*, 7 September 1939.

150. A. Aldgate and J. Richards, *Britain Can Take It*, p. 1.

151. M-O A: TC 17/1/C, R.C. to Len England, 25 January 1940.

152. *Today's Cinema*, 24 April 1940, p. 3.

153. A. Aldgate and J. Richards, *Britain Can Take It*, p. 2.

154. 43% of cinema-goers in Britain in 1939 paid 'no more than 7d', another 37% 'no more than 1/-.' TNA PRO INF1/ 724, Memorandum by the International Broadcasting and Propaganda Enquiry, 21 June 1939. Reproduced in P. M. Taylor, 'Techniques of Persuasion, p. 60.

155. *Today' Cinema*, 9 September 1939, p. 5.

156. *Documentary News Letter*, June 1941, p. 101.

157. *Today's Cinema*, 26 September 1939.

158. *Kinematograph Weekly*, 7 September 1939. My italics.

159. *Documentary News Letter*, April 1941, p. 63.

160. A. Aldgate and J. Richards, *Britain Can Take It*, p. 2.

161. Ibid.

162. 'Volle Filmtheater, beschäftigte Ateliers', *Frankfurter Zeitung*, no. 250, 19 May 1940. Wiener Library cuttings collection, PC5/106E.

163. 'Die Leistung des deutschen Films im Kriege', *Hamburger Fremdenblatt*, 16 February 1941.Wiener Library cuttings collection, PC5/101c.

164. M-O A: FR 24, 'The Cinema in the First Three Months of War', January 1940. Also in D. Sheridan and J. Richards (eds), *Mass-Observation at the Movies*, p. 139.

165. M-O A: TC 17/1/C, R.C. to Len England, 25 January 1940.

166. *Kinematograph Weekly*, 7 December 1939.

167. *Kinematograph Weekly*, 16 November 1939.

168. *Today's Cinema*, 22 April 1937.

169. *Kinematograph Weekly*, 2 November 1939.

170. M-O A: TC 17/1/C, R.C. to Len England, 25 January 1940.

171. *Kinematograph Weekly*, 2 November 1939.

172. All information here from *Today's Cinema*, 1 December 1939.

173. *Today's Cinema*, 1 November 1939.

174. *Kinematograph Weekly*, 21 September 1939.

175. M-O A: FR 394, 'Mass-Observation Film Work', 10 September 1940.

176. *Kinematograph Weekly*, 22 August 1940, p. 22.

177. Ibid.

178. Credits information from 'So entstand der Film *Feuertaufe*', *Filmwelt*, 19 April 1940. Prädikat information from *Der Angriff* (Berlin), 7 April 1940, p. 3. Wiener Library cuttings collection, 106E. *Filmwelt* also claims that the film was awarded the following *Prädikate: jugendwert, volksbildend, Lehrfilm* and that the film was *jugend – und feiertagsfrei* (15).

179. 'So entstand der Film *Feuertaufe*', *Filmwelt*, 19 April 1940.

180. E. Fröhlich (ed.), *Die Tagebücher von Joseph Goebbels. Sämtliche Fragmente. Teil I: Aufzeichnungen 1924–1941*, vol. 4 (K. G. Saur, Munich/New York/London/Paris, 1987), diary entry for 7 April 1940, p. 100.

181. T. Sakmyster, 'Nazi Documentaries of Intimidation: "Feldzug in Polen" (1940), "Feuertaufe" (1940) and "Sieg im Westen"', *Historical Journal of Film, Radio and Television*, vol. 16, no. 4 (1996), pp. 485–514, pp. 489–90.

182. *Der Angriff* (Berlin), 7 April 1940, p. 3. Wiener Library cuttings collection, 106E.

183. Ibid.

184. *Neues Wiener Tagblatt*, 16 April 1940. Wiener Library cuttings collection, 106E.

185. Stiftung Deutsche Kinemathek, Schriftgutarchiv, Berlin (hereafter SDK Berlin), file 3709 *Kampfgeschwader Lützow*. Press book.

186. On Bertram's aviation experience in preparation for *Feuertaufe*, see *Der Angriff* (Berlin), 7 April 1940, p. 3. Wiener Library cuttings collection, 106E and 'So entstand der Film *Feuertaufe*', *Filmwelt*, 19 April 1940.

187. *Neues Wiener Tagblatt*, 16 April 1940. Wiener Library cuttings collection, 106E.

188. 'So entstand der Film *Feuertaufe*', *Filmwelt*, 19 April 1940.

189. *Der Angriff* (Berlin), 7 April 1940, p. 3. Wiener Library cuttings collection, 106E.

190. *Neues Wiener Tagblatt*, 16 April 1940. Wiener Library cuttings collection, 106E.

191. *Filmwelt*, 19 April 1940, p. 15. This is the official figure given in contemporary publications.

192. 'So entstand der Film *Feuertaufe*', *Filmwelt*, 19 April 1940. I have amended the names to correspond with those presented in the opening credits of the film. The cameramen were Erich Uffel, Arthur Pieper, Erich Weström, Paul Thiel, Werner Bold, Willy Gerlach and Heinz Freyer.

193. *Neues Wiener Tagblatt*, 16 April 1940. Wiener Library cuttings collection, 106E.

194. Kurt Hubert quoted in S. Kracauer, *From Caligari to Hitler. A Psychological History of German Film* (Princeton University Press, Princeton, NJ, 1947), p. 276.

195. SDK Berlin, 12193 *Feuertaufe*. K. F. Frentzel, *Feuertaufe. Der Film vom Einsatz der deutschen Luftwaffe in Polen* (Karl Curtis, Berlin, 1940).

196. E. Schröder, 'Soldaten der PK', *NSZ-Rheinfront*, 4 March 1940. Wiener Library cuttings collection.

197. SDK Berlin, 12193 *Feuertaufe*. Tobis press book.

198. Kurt Hubert quoted in S. Kracauer, *From Caligari to Hitler*, p. 276.

199. *Neues Wiener Tagblatt*, 16 April 1940. Wiener Library cuttings collection, 106E.

200. Ibid.

201. SDK Berlin, 12193, *Feuertaufe*. Tobis press book.

202. SDK Berlin, 12193 *Feuertaufe*. K. F. Frentzel, *Feuertaufe. Der Film vom Einsatz der deutschen Luftwaffe in Polen*. This point was also stressed in 'So entstand der Film *Feuertaufe*', *Filmwelt*, 19 April 1940.

203. *Neues Wiener Tagblatt*, 16 April 1940. Wiener Library cuttings collection, 106E.

204. SDK Berlin, 12193 *Feuertaufe*. Tobis press book.

205. 'Die Wahrheit als Waffe', *Filmwelt*, 28 June 1940.

206. Ibid.

207. *Filmwelt*, 19 April 1940, p. 15.

208. D. Welch, *Propaganda and the German Cinema*, p. 180.

209. SDK Berlin, 3709 *Kampfgeschwader Lützow*. Press book.

210. S. Kracauer, *From Caligari to Hitler*, p. 291.

211. RMVP Ministerial Conference minutes, 18 November and 16 December 1939 in W. Boelcke (ed.), *The Secret Conferences of Dr. Goebbels*, p. 6. An example of the depiction of Chamberlain, which uses much of the symbolism associated with many descriptions of the British prime minister in NS propaganda, can be found in IWM FDC Unidentified and uncatalogued box of materials. Attached to the back of SD report of the *Abschnitt-Leipzig*, II 225 Tgb. Nr 461/39. Wa. 13 December 1939.

212. *Illustrierter Film-Kurier*, 3097, *Feuertaufe* (1940).

213. See, for example, IWM FDC Unidentified and uncatalogued box of materials. SD *Abschnitt-Leipzig*, II 225 Tgb. Nr. 3.40. Wa. 12 April 1940.

214. RMVP Ministerial Conference minutes, 28 June 1940 in W. Boelcke (ed.), *The Secret Conferences of Dr. Goebbels*, p. 62.

215. SDK Berlin, 3709 *Kampfgeschwader Lützow*. Press book.

216. RMVP Ministerial Conference minutes, 23 December 1939 in W. Boelcke (ed.), *The Secret Conferences of Dr. Goebbels*, pp. 10–11.

217. Ibid., 24 July 1940, p. 70.

218. Goebbels in *Frankfurter Zeitung*, 14 February 1940. Wiener Library cuttings collection, 101c.

219. SDK Berlin, 12193 *Feuertaufe*, press book.

220. RMVP Ministerial Conference minutes, 3 September 1940 in W. Boelcke (ed.), *The Secret Conferences of Dr. Goebbels*, p. 84.

221. *Völkischer Beobachter*, 21 January 1940. Wiener Library cuttings collection, 101c.

222. Monthly report of the *Regierungspräsident* for Upper and Middle Franconia, 7 November 1939 quoted in M. Steinert, *Hitler's War and the Germans*, p. 59.

223. S. Kracauer, *From Caligari to Hitler*, p. 287.

224. SD Section Leipzig, report of 12 October 1939, IWM FD 332/46, quoted in M. Steinert, *Hitler's War and the Germans*, p. 56.

225. Correspondence of Commander of Corps area XIII, quoted in M. Steinert, *Hitler's War and the Germans*, p. 54.

226. SD Section Leipzig, report of 12 October 1939, IWM FD 332/46, quoted in M. Steinert, *Hitler's War and the Germans*, p. 56.

227. SD report, no. 89, 20 May 1940, in H. Boberach (ed.), *Meldungen*, vol. 4, p. 1155.

228. SDK Berlin, 3709 *Kampfgeschwader Lützow*. Press book.

229. SDK Berlin, 3709 *Kampfgeschwader Lützow*. Press cuttings. 'Start des *Kampfgeschwader Lützow*. Uraufführung in München und Berlin', 28 February 1941.

230. SDK Berlin 6115 *Feinde*. Publicity phrases from the press book.

231. Ibid., press book.

232. Ibid., press cutting, n.d.

233. *Filmwelt*, 19 April 1940, p. 15.

234. *Nationalsozialistische Landpost*, 12 April 1940. Wiener Library cuttings collection, 106E.

235. Ibid.

236. *Völkischer Beobachter*, 21 January 1940. Wiener Library cuttings collection, 101c.

237. RMVP Ministerial Conference minutes, 12 December 1940 in W. Boelcke (ed.), *The Secret Conferences of Dr. Goebbels*, p. 113.

238. *Illustrierter Film-Kurier*, 3097, *Feuertaufe*.

239. See *Der Angriff* (Berlin), 7 April 1940, 3. Wiener Library cuttings collection, 106E and *Filmwelt*, 19 April 1940, p. 15.

240. RMVP Ministerial Conference minutes, 1 February 1940 in W. Boelcke (ed.), *The Secret Conferences of Dr. Goebbels*, p. 18.

241. BArch R58/184, SD report 87, 14 May 1940, also in H. Boberach (ed.), *Meldungen*, vol. 4, p. 1131.

242. SDK Berlin, 12193 *Feuertaufe*, 'Advice to Cinema-Owners', p. 3.

243. SD report 24, 4 December 1939, in H. Boberach (ed.), *Meldungen*, vol. 3, p. 527.

244. BArch R58/184, SD report 87, 14 May 1940, also in H. Boberach (ed.), *Meldungen*, vol. 4, p. 1131.

245. SDK Berlin, 12193 *Feuertaufe*, 'Advice to Cinema-Owners', p. 13.

246. BArch R58/184, SD report 87, 14 May 1940, also in H. Boberach (ed.), *Meldungen*, vol. 4, p. 1131.

247. See for example IWM FDC Unidentified and uncatalogued box of materials. SD *Abschnitt-Leipzig*, 'Inlandslagebericht', 7 and 21 September 1939.

248. BArch R58/184, SD report 87, 14 May 1940, also in H. Boberach (ed.), *Meldungen*, vol. 4, p. 1131.

249. *Deutschland-Berichte der Sopade*, 6 Jahrgang 1939, Nr 9, 2 December 1939, p. 1028.

250. Ibid., p. 1029.

251. TNA PRO INF 1/ 867, 'German versus British Propaganda', n.d. c. late 1939, p. 2.

252. See for example IWM FDC Unidentified and uncatalogued box of materials. SD *Abschnitt-Leipzig*, 'Inlandslagebericht', 3 October 1939.

253. IWM FDC Unidentified and uncatalogued box of materials. SD *Abschnitt-Leipzig- Außenstelle Oschatz*, 'Stimmung in der Bevölkerung', II 225 Tgb. Nr.3/40. Wa., 25 July 1940.

254. SD report, 16 October 1939, quoted in M. Steinert, *Hitler's War*, p. 59.

255. BArch R58/184, SD report 87, 14 May 1940, also in H. Boberach (ed.), *Meldungen*, vol. 4, pp. 1131–2.

256. Ibid., p. 1131.

257. Ibid.

258. IWM FDC Unidentified and uncatalogued box of materials. SD *Abschnitt-Leipzig- Außenstelle Oschatz*, 'Stimmung in der Bevölkerung', II 225 Tgb. Nr.3/40. Wa., 10 July 1940.

259. BArch R58/184, SD report 87, 14 May 1940, also in H. Boberach (ed.), *Meldungen*, vol. 4, p. 1132.

260. E. Fröhlich (ed.), *Die Tagebücher von Joseph Goebbels. Sämtliche Fragmente*, Vol. 4, diary entry for 6 April 1940, p. 99.

261. Ibid.

262. BArch R58/184, SD report 87, 14 May 1940, also in H. Boberach (ed.), *Meldungen*, vol. 4, p. 1131.

263. BArch NS29/ 775, SD *Abschnitt-Leipzig*, 15 May 1940. These documents can also be found in IWM FDC, SD *Abschnitt-Leipzig*.

264. *Deutschland-Berichte der Sopade*, 6 Jahrgang 1939, Nr. 9, 2 December 1939, p. 1029.

265. BArch R58/184, SD report 87, 14 May 1940, also in H. Boberach (ed.), *Meldungen*, vol. 4, p. 1131.

266. Ibid.

267. *Deutschland-Berichte der Sopade*, 6 Jahrgang 1939, Nr. 9, 2 December 1939, p. 1029.

268. *Neues Wiener Tagblatt*, 16 April 1940. Wiener Library cuttings collection, 106E.

269. SDK Berlin, 12193 *Feuertaufe*, 'Advice to Cinema-Owners', p. 3.

270. T. Sakmyster, 'Nazi Documentaries of Intimidation', p. 498.

271. Ibid., p. 499.

272. Ibid.

273. *The Times,* 8 April 1940, p. 7.

274. Imperial War Museum Sound Archive (Hereafter, IWMS), J. B. Priestley, 7012/B/B. Cat B. BBC broadcast, 7–8 May 1942, 'Britain Speaks', 12 minutes, 7 seconds.

275. J. B. Priestley, *All England Listened. The Wartime Broadcasts of J. B. Priestley* (Chilmark Press, New York, 1967), pp. 12–13.

276. *The Times*, 19 June 1941, p. 6.

277. TNA PRO PREM 4/99/5, Churchill's introduction to *The Biter Bit*, 1943.

278. TNA PRO PREM 4/99/5, Prime Minister's personal minute. M. 273/3 Churchill to the MoI, 16 April 1943.

279. TNA PRO PREM 4/99/5, Bracken to Churchill, m. 273/3, 23 April 1943.

280. TNA PRO PREM 4/99/5, Churchill's annotation to Bracken's minute to Churchill, 273/3 (23 April 1943), 24 April 1943.

281. TNA PRO PREM 4/99/5, F.D. Brown (Downing Street staff) to A. S. Hodge (MoI), 13 July 1943.

282. *The Times*, 22 September 1943, p. 7. In addition, the film was released in the United States. See *The New York Times*, 22. October 1943, p. 21.
283. Ibid.
284. TNA PRO PREM 4/99/5, Churchill's introduction to *The Biter Bit*, 1943.
285. IWMS Roy Boulting, 4627/6, Interview, March 1980. Reel 2.
286. TNA PRO INF 1/867, 'German versus British Propaganda', n.d. c. late 1939.
287. M. Powell, *A Life in Movies. An Autobiography* (Methuen, London, 1987), p. 328.
288. See, for example, 'Der Film als Dokument' *Filmwelt*, 10 May 1940, p. 5.
289. M. Powell, *A Life in Movies*, p. 330.
290. Ibid., p. 329.
291. Ibid., p. 331.
292. Ibid., p. 329.
293. M. Korda, *Charmed Lives. A Family Romance* (Allen Lane, London, 1979), p. 136.
294. Ibid., p. 137. This was a claim also repeated by the film's associate producer, Ian Dalrymple. See K. R. M. Short, *Screening the Propaganda of British Air Power. From RAF (1935) to The Lion Has Wings* (Flicks, Trowbridge, 1997), p. 86.
295. M. Powell, *A Life in Movies*, p. 329.
296. K. R. M. Short, *Screening the Propaganda of British Air Power*, p. 86.
297. *The New York Times*, 8 October 1939, p. 139.
298. K. R. M. Short, *Screening the Propaganda of British Air Power*, p. 87.
299. Ibid.
300. Ibid., p. 88.
301. M. Powell, *A Life in Movies*, p. 335.
302. A. Aldgate and J. Richards, *Britain Can Take It*, p. 23.
303. M. Korda, *Charmed Lives*, p. 136.
304. M-O A: FR 24, 'Cinema in the First Three Months of War', January 1940. Also in D. Sheridan and J. Richards (eds), *Mass-Observation at the Movies*, p. 153.
305. A. Aldgate and J. Richards, *Britain Can Take It*, pp. 21–2.
306. M. Powell, *A Life in Movies,* p. 330.
307. TNA PRO INF 1/867, 'Programme for Film Propaganda', revised copy. Co-ordinating Committee Paper 1, n.d.
308. GP 4:20:3, comments by John Grierson on early British war film production, 10 August 1940.
309. M. Powell, *A Life in Movies*, p. 335.
310. M-O A: FR 15, 'The Lion Has Wings', December 1939. Details of this report can also be found in K. R. M. Short, *Screening the Propaganda of British Air Power* and D. Sheridan and J. Richards (eds), *Mass-Observation at the Movies*.
311. K. R. M. Short, *Screening the Propaganda of British Air Power*, pp. 21–2.
312. A. Aldgate and J. Richards, *Britain Can Take It*, p. 25.
313. M. Powell, *A Life in Movies*, p. 334.
314. J. Ware, *The Lion Has Wings: The Epic of the Famous Korda Film*, (Collins, London, January 1940), p. 172.
315. M-O A: FR 15, 'The Lion Has Wings', December 1939.
316. J. Ware, *The Lion Has Wings*, pp. 166–7.
317. M-O A: FR 15, 'The Lion Has Wings', December 1939.
318. M-O A: FR 24, 'Cinema in the first three months of war', January 1940.
319. M-O A: TC 17/3/ B, Len England, report on *The Lion Has Wings*, 18–24 December 1939, 10 January 1940.

320. M-O A: TC 17/3/ B, Len England, report on *The Lion Has Wings*, 15 January 1940.

321. K. R. M. Short, *Screening the Propaganda of British Air Power*, p. 104.

322. Ibid.

323. See for example, SD report 46, 29 January 1940, in H. Boberach (ed.), *Meldungen*, vol. 3, p. 700.

324. M-O A: TC 17/1/C, Box 3, Len England, 'Film Report', 17 March 1940.

325. 'National Publicity', *Documentary News Letter*, March 1940, p. 3.

326. *Kinematograph Weekly*, 2 November 1939, p. 10.

327. M-O A: TC 17/1/C, Box 3, Len England, 'Film Report', M, 20, A, 17 March 1940.

328. *Kinematograph Weekly*, 2 November 1939, p. 10.

329. M-O A: TC 17/1/C, Box 3, Len England, 'Film Report', F, 40, B, 17 March 1940.

330. M-O A: FR 15, 'The Lion Has Wings', December 1939.

331. *Kinematograph Weekly*, 2 November 1939, p. 10.

332. Ibid.

333. K. R. M. Short, *Screening the Propaganda of British Air Power*, p. 25.

334. M-O A: TC 17/3/ B, Len England, report on *The Lion Has Wings*, 15 January 1940.

335. Lloyd George in the foreword to J. Ware, *The Lion Has Wings*.

336. J. B. Priestley, *All England Listened*, p. 12.

337. *Kinematograph Weekly*, 2 November 1939, p. 10.

338. Ibid.

339. M. Powell, *A Life in Movies*, p. 335.

340. Ibid.

341. *Kinematograph Weekly*, 2 November 1939, p. 10.

342. M-O A: FR 15, 'The Lion Has Wings', December 1939.

343. M-O A: TC 17/1/C, film report from a volunteer, J.T., 28, Preston.

344. M-O A: FR 15, 'The Lion Has Wings', December 1939.

345. M-O A: TC 17/1/C, Box 3, Len England, 'Film Report', M, 50, B, 17 March 1940.

346. Ibid., M, 20 C.

347. *Documentary News Letter*, January 1940, p. 8.

348. *Kinematograph Weekly*, 2 November 1939, p. 10.

349. *Documentary News Letter*, January 1940, p. 8.

350. *Kinematograph Weekly*, 2 November 1939, p. 4. Quoted in J. Chapman, *The British at War*, p. 62.

351. *Daily Film Renter*, 29 November 1939, p. 2. Quoted in J. Chapman, *The British at War*, p. 63.

352. J. Chapman, *The British at War*, p. 63.

353. *The Times*, 24 November 1939, p. 6.

354. T. Harrisson, 'Public Reaction: *The Lion Has Wings*', *Documentary News Letter*, February 1940, p. 5.

355. Ibid.

356. *Kinematograph Weekly*, 4 January 1940. Quoted in K. R. M. Short, *Screening the Propaganda of British Air Power*, p. 161.

357. *Kinematograph Weekly*, 7 December 1939. Quoted in K. R. M. Short, *Screening the Propaganda of British Air Power*, p. 159.

358. *Kinematograph Weekly*, 28 December 1939. Quoted in K. R. M. Short, *Screening the Propaganda of British Air Power*, p. 160.

359. *Kinematograph Weekly*, 7 December 1939. Quoted in K. R. M. Short, *Screening the Propaganda of British Air Power*, p. 159.

360. *The Times*, 21 October 1939.

361. J. Chapman, *The British at War*, p. 63.

362. *Kinematograph Weekly*, 4 January 1940. Quoted in K. R. M. Short, *Screening the Propaganda of British Air Power*, p. 161.

363. M-O A: TC 17/3/ B, Len England, report on *The Lion Has Wings*, 15 January 1940.

364. J. Poole, 'British Cinema Attendance in Wartime: Audience Preference at the Majestic, Macclesfield, 1939–1946', *Historical Journal of Film, Radio and Television*, vol. 7, no. 1 (1987), pp. 15- 34. Here, p. 29.

365. Ibid.

366. T. Harrisson, 'Public Reaction: *The Lion Has Wings*', *Documentary News Letter*, February 1940, p. 5.

367. Press reactions included in M-O A: FR 15, 'The Lion Has Wings', December 1939. See also, K. R. M. Short, *Screening the Propaganda of British Air Power*, pp. 158–9.

368. *Kinematograph Weekly*, 2 November 1939, p. 10. For more specific discussion of press reactions and Dalrymple's response to criticism, see K. R. M. Short, *Screening the Propaganda of British Air Power*, pp. 88–93.

369. See P. Summerfield , 'Mass-Observation: Social Research or Social Movement?', *Journal of Contemporary History*, vol. 20, no. 3 (1985), pp. 439–53. Here, p. 440.

370. M-O A: FR 15, 'The Lion Has Wings', December 1939.

371. M-O A: TC 17/3/ B, 'Report of Film by an Observer', Len England, 30 October 1939.

372. K. R. M. Short, *Screening the Propaganda of British Air Power*, p. 137.

373. T. Harrisson, 'Films and the Home Front – the Evaluation of their Effectiveness by Mass-Observation', 1973. Quoted in K. R. M. Short, *Screening the Propaganda of British Air Power*, p. 137.

374. M-O A: TC 17/1/C, Box 3, Len England, 'Film Report', M, 20, A, 17 March 1940.

375. M-O A: TC 17/3/ B, Len England, report on *The Lion Has Wings*, M, 50, B, 15 January 1940.

376. M-O A: FR 15, 'The Lion Has Wings', December 1939.

377. M-O A: TC 17/3/ B, Len England, report on *The Lion Has Wings*, M, 40, B, 15 January 1940.

378. M-O A: TC 17/1/C, Box 3, Len England, 'Film Report', F, 30, D, 17 March 1940

379. J. Poole, 'British Cinema Attendance in Wartime', pp. 19–20. In particular, *First Love* (Henry Koster, 1939), *It's a Date* (William A. Seiter, 1940), *Susannah of the Mounties* (William A. Seiter, 1939) and Disney's *Pinocchio* (Hamilton Luske/Ben Sharpsteen, 1940) were popular amongst British audiences in the same period.

380. *Kinematograph Weekly*, 19 October 1939, p. 4.

381. M-O A: TC 17/3/ B, Len England, report on *The Lion Has Wings*, M, 50, B, 15 January 1940. For comments on the storyline, see M-O A FR 15, 'The Lion Has Wings', December 1939.

382. TNA PRO INF 1/867, 'Programme for Film Propaganda', revised copy. Co-ordinating Committee Paper 1.

383. T. Harrisson, 'Public Reaction: *The Lion Has Wings*', *Documentary News Letter*, February 1940, p. 5.

384. *The Times,* 24 November 1939, p. 6. The film received some pre-release promotion in the United States. See, *The New York Times*, 9 September 1939, p. 8, primarily centred on Merle Oberon. *The Lion Has Wings* was also reviewed in the press after initial release and re-runs. For example, see *The New York Times*, 22 January 1940, p. 17 and *The Los Angeles Times*, 31 July 1942.

385. TNA PRO FO 371/22840, FO Memorandum. Hughes Roberts (Government Cinematic Advisor), 3 November 1939.

386. For details of the resistance to British propaganda distribution, see S. A. Brewer, *To Win the Peace. British Propaganda in the United States During World War II* (Cornell University Press, Ithaca and London, 1997) and N. J. Cull, *Selling War: The British Propaganda Campaign against American 'Neutrality' in World War II* (Oxford University Press, New York, 1995).

387. TNA PRO FO 371/22840, Memorandum. Cowell to Hughes Roberts, 17 November 1939.

388. TNA PRO FO 371/22840, Cowell to Forbes, 19 November 1939. Information here reproduced by kind permission of Carfax publishing and the editorial team of the *Historical Journal of Film, Radio and Television*. For the full article, see J. Fox, 'John Grierson, his "Documentary Boys"'.

389. GP 4:20:3, comments by John Grierson on early British war film production, 10 August 1940.

390. *Today's Cinema*, 15 November 1939, p. 5.

391. *Today's Cinema*, 25 October 1939, p. 5.

392. *Documentary News Letter*, January 1940, p. 2.

393. 'So entstand der Film "Feuertaufe"', *Filmwelt*, 19 April 1940.

394. 'Der Film als Dokument' *Filmwelt*, 10 May 1940, p. 5.

395. Reported in *The Times*, 6 November 1939, p. 5. I am grateful to Frances Gunnell for drawing my attention to this reference.

396. W. Boelcke (ed.), *The Secret Conferences of Dr. Goebbels*, p. 28.

397. 'Hat der Löwe wirklich Flügel?', Günther Sawatzki, *Filmwelt*, 14 June 1940, p. 14.

398. Ibid.

399. Ibid.

400. Ibid.

401. Ibid.

402. W. Boelcke (ed.), *The Secret Conferences of Dr. Goebbels*, p. 28.

403. GP G4: 21: 3, miscellaneous writings on propaganda n.d. (c. 1940–1).

404. GP 4:20: 3, comments by John Grierson on early British war film production, 1 August 1940.

405. Basil Wright, 'Films and the War', *The Spectator*, 1 October 1939, Grierson Papers, 3:17:5.

406. *The Times,* December 1939.

407. GP G4: 21: 3, miscellaneous writings on propaganda n.d (c. 1940–1).

> The world often watched patiently the lightning flash of the conquerors sword
>
> August von Platen[1]

It was clear from the bombing of Guernica in 1937 by the Condor Legion in the Spanish Civil War that air power would be at the forefront of any modern conflict. It was the weapon which many thought would prevent wars of attrition. The concept of the 'lightning war' was not new.[2] However, the means of its prosecution and its impact were. Public perceptions of future war centred upon the concept of the bomber and Stanley Baldwin's oft-cited view that it 'will always get through'. The mass-bombardment of towns and cities was expected should a major conflict once again darken the continent. It was predicted that war would be delivered from the skies, levelling homes and factories and annihilating the population. This was both a political and cultural prediction and was a subject which excited film-makers. Alexander Korda's controversial 1936 film, *Things to Come*, was said to have had an extraordinary impact upon the psyche, Leslie Halliwell's recollection that 'from the opening titles we were awed, gripped and frightened'[3] tying in with popular concerns about future military engagement and new forms of 'total war'. Although, as Michael Paris points out, the events predicted in Korda's adaptation of the prophecies of H. G. Wells were initially dismissed as 'childish, uncontrolled fantasy', the newsreel footage from Guernica made these images seem horribly real.[4] In Britain, people 'regarded the raids as inevitable and expected them to be heavy, even awful'.[5] There was also the realization that the home front would be the new front line: civilians would now be just as legitimate a target as soldiers. This essentially blurred the distinction between the home front and the front lines for the first time in a real sense and meant that the two arenas of war would have to forge an indestructible bond, the Third Reich proclaiming that 'the front line and the homeland are one, both coexisting in unbreakable solidarity'.[6] It was in this atmosphere of unified struggle with each member of society fulfilling a specific function in the war effort that propagandists recognized that public morale would play a role in victory as never before.

Yet, despite the fear of aerial bombardment, both the British and German people seemed to be endlessly fascinated with flight, an obsession which increased as the apparatus of the air war came to dominate the everyday lives of individuals. In a world in which the skyline was laced with blimps and daily routine disrupted by the constant shrieks of the 'Moaning Minnies' or the 'Howling Horaces',[7] the public found that air power was an omnipresent force in World War II. The soundtrack to life in wartime had become the echo of the most modern form of warfare, from the groan of the bombers to the screech of the fighter's engines to the ack-ack of the anti-aircraft guns. The public was absorbed in the romance of the skies, its glamour, eloquence, grace and power. As John Grierson noted in 1943, 'we bring the airplane into our imagination'. Air power 'beat out a rhythm for our time: a hard, tough and exacting rhythm which takes the head higher and the shoulders back a little further'. It was in the glorification of air power that the propagandist sought to 'sustain this rhythm, to crystallise these images' to become a 'positive and necessary force, providing the patterns of thought and feeling which [made] for an active and imaginative citizenship in the particular circumstances [of its] time'.[8]

Not only did air power pervade the everyday space but it also came increasingly to dominate the cinematic space. The conquest of the air and the cinema complemented each other, both products of the modern age, both occupying a central place in the public imagination. In this respect, the delivery mechanism was as significant as the theme. Images of the air war formed a nexus of escapism and realism so essential to the success of wartime propaganda, especially after 1942 when war-weariness began to take its toll and audiences increasingly demanded that cinema draw them out of their everyday existence in favour of a fantasy world of glamour and adventure. The theme of air power straddled the two genres, providing an insight into the thrilling world of the pilot whilst maintaining a focus on the contemporary and the topical. It also offered a key point of identification for audiences, familiar with the sights and sounds of the air force, and yet embodied something mystical and enchanting in its world above the clouds in pursuit of victory, a world many would not experience at first-hand. In this sense, it was the perfect vehicle for propaganda. This chapter will explore some of the images of aerial warfare in the early years of World War II. Naturally, the experience of bombardment is dualistic and it is with this in mind that it is imperative to explore the two sides of the air war: that of the bomber and that of the bombed. An analysis of the period produces some significant, if unsurprising, contrasts between British and German propaganda. With Germany in the ascendancy militarily by 1940, German propaganda centred on the *Luftwaffe* and sought to glorify the world of the pilot and his crew whilst at the same time providing a point of identification with the audience through individual characters. The *Luftwaffe*, holding much of the public's attention and at the forefront of the conflict in the popular imagination, became a symbol of the Third Reich's success in the field. However, with the losses of the Battle of Britain and the onset of conflict in the east, film-makers turned emphatically towards the subject of death and survival, an issue which occupied British film-producerss from 1940 as the Blitz rained down on the towns and cities of the United Kingdom. It was predictable that the British propagandists chose to focus on the impact of bombardment in the early years of war, as it was the most obvious reflection of the contemporary wartime experience. It was in this context that the Crown Film Unit portrayed the British character in a series of short films produced from 1940 to 1941. Feature film depictions of the Blitz experience served to lighten the public mood or to memorialize the sacrifice of the dark days of 1940, a signal that the 'myth of the Blitz' began at a relatively early stage. Although British film-makers subsequently produced some of the most significant feature films about air power such as *One of Our Aircraft is Missing* (Michael Powell and Emeric Pressburger, 1942), *The First of the Few* (Leslie Howard, 1942), *The Way to the Stars* (Anthony Asquith, 1945), a film so emotionally powerful to airmen that the RAF unit that helped director Anthony Asquith make it left tributes at his graveside many years later,[9] and the lesser known *Journey Together* (John Boulting, 1945–6), the initial years of the war were characterized by films attempting to make sense of or commemorate the Blitz, providing a contrast to the German films of aerial superiority, at least until the decision by British propagandists to begin exploiting raids over Germany in 1941, commensurate with the changing fortunes of war. It is this filmic contrast between 'blitzer' and 'blitzed' which embodies the German and British wartime experience of the early years of the war and allows the film historian to probe both sides of the propaganda relating to aerial conflict, both offensive and defensive. A comparison of British and German approaches to the air war also raises some significant questions about the intrinsic values and style of democratic and authoritarian propaganda, and suggests where, at times, they are forced to merge.

FLIEGER SIND SIEGER: IMAGES OF THE PILOT IN FEATURE FILMS OF THE THIRD REICH

'*Flieger sind Sieger*' (*Pilots are Victors*) was a fitting theme tune for Herbert Maisch's 1939 film *D III 88* and an indication of the importance of air power in the propagandistic discourse of the Third Reich. It reflected the fact that the *Luftwaffe* was accorded special status during the conflict, Hitler proclaiming that it was 'the most effective strategic weapon' and informing the other services that Germany 'should never have been able to hold [its] own in this war if we had not had an undivided *Luftwaffe*'.[10] Given that air power was generally seen to be the driving force behind Nazi successes in the field, particularly from the onset of the war and throughout 1940, it is unsurprising to find that it also occupied a dominant position in the filmic representation of World War II in the same period and beyond. The skill of Nazi propaganda lay in its ability to align its central messages with the broader trends in public opinion. The interest in films centring on the *Luftwaffe* was partly conditioned by the popular fascination with air power, films such as *D III 88*, *Kampfgeschwader Lützow* and *Stukas* (Karl Ritter, 1941) capitalizing upon pre-existing values and beliefs surrounding the air force. From the outset, the *Luftwaffe* occupied a prominent space in the public imagination. At both regional and national level, the SD reported that the public were particularly proud of its pilots.[11] The Security Service in Leipzig testified that 'the German pilots are regarded with utmost admiration, and an enormous amount of trust has been placed in them',[12] whilst a national report of May 1940 confirmed that 'there is particular pride in the German *Luftwaffe*, which has fulfilled all expectations'.[13] Fascination with the aerial forces reached a peak in the early days of the attack on England. As the SD reported in September 1940, 'it is clear from conversations amongst our citizens that there has been great interest in the ongoing reports on the German *Luftwaffe*'s successes against England'.[14]

It is not surprising, therefore, that the German population were attracted to cinematic productions which focused upon air power, their interest in filmic representations of the *Luftwaffe* undoubtedly intensified by the 'realistic' footage sent to the screens by the PK-men in the newsreels in the early stages of the war.[15] The desire to 'experience' the front, and in particular the life of the *Frontflieger*, led to the production of films specifically designed to promote the *Luftwaffe* and its attributes (comradeship, sacrifice, bravery, technological skill and power) and create a sense of individual identification with the pilots and their crew on the part of the audience.[16] This was in many ways best achieved through the fictional feature film, and it was, according to Tobis, 'no coincidence that all the film-makers have long been toying with the idea of a film about the *Luftwaffe*'. After all, 'could there possibly be a subject which is cinematographically more interesting or better suited than the young German *Luftwaffe*?' No other subject, the studio argued, tapped into the public imagination in the same way, defining the individual's role within the mass, whilst at the same time offering the film-maker opportunities for stunning cinematography. They proselytized:

> There is nothing visually stronger than these fast, streamlined giant birds, which race through the air and whose thundering engines proclaim to the world their makers' power. Nothing prompts more admiration than these technological wonders, with which we have turned into reality mankind's centuries-old dream of flying. And above all, the community of our pilots and their crews has become so popular with the people that barely any other community of men comes close.[17]

In short, the air film offered Nazi propagandists the opportunity to promote military superiority alongside the ideal of *Kameradschaft*, whilst demonstrating their mastery of modernity and technology, the Reich superior to its competitors in all aspects of man's greatest desire for millennia: flight.

The focus on the fictional feature to promote these values was used in conjunction with specialized, 'documentary' productions such as Bertram's feature-length *Feuertaufe* and the weekly newsreels. Whilst the documentarists were charged with showing the wider perspective on the air war, fictional film directors created highly personalized identities for their protagonists, their aim being to intensify the sense of identification on the part of the audience and to merge entertainment with politics. Hake has acknowledged that film popularity was highly dependent on 'the attainment of a perfect fit between films and audiences'.[18] As the SD noted, 'ideal conditions ... existed whenever "the film fully satisfied the desire [of the masses] for diversity and topicality"'.[19] It was with this fusion between the topical and the 'escapist' that the *Fliegerfilme* capitalized on scenarios involving human interest set within a contemporary and often political theme.

Moreover, the idealized image of the pilot in fictional feature films in the Third Reich was consistently reinforced across the medium in numerous productions. It is noticeable that the pilot formed the backbone of many an audience fantasy as well as being a reflection of contemporary events. Pilots were not only the masculine fighting force of the air with their bravery, courage and comradeship appealing to male cinema-goers and the troops, but also the heroes of romantic dramas with a specific focus on the needs of the female audience: in two of the most popular films of the war years, *Wunschkonzert* (*Request Concert*, Eduard Von Borsody, 1940) and *Die große Liebe* (*The Great Love*, Rolf Hansen, 1942), the male lead and love-interest of the female protagonist was an airman. The image, therefore, of the pilot in the films of the Third Reich was multi-faceted, performing simultaneous propaganda functions, and stood at the heart of the attempt to merge entertainment, escapism and fantasy with modern political and contemporary propaganda, at the same time working in conjunction with and alongside 'realist' footage provided by the PK units and distributed in the newsreels and feature-length documentaries. Thus, Nazi propagandists were able to create holistic viewing environments by connecting genres via thematic focus. As Julian Petley has convincingly argued, although documentary, political feature films and 'escapist' fiction all possess different modes of address and structure, the collective propagandist function centred upon 'the *way* in which they were placed within the apparatuses involved in their consumption, and this is turn relates both to the organisation of the ideological apparatuses within the Third Reich and to the conjuncture'. The wider context of the production and release of a film dictates 'how films *function* ideologically at any given historical moment',[20] and it was the saturation of the public sphere with a specific and focused set of images relating to air power which simultaneously tapped into topicality and interest which generated such fascination with these films. Moreover, in order to give voice to this, the studio publicity explicitly drew connections between genres and films, encouraging audiences to view the films collectively. This was not only a means of increasing box-office receipts, but, as Petley argues, a means by which 'the RKK and the RMVP were able to initiate publicity material that would help to structure the "preferred reading" of individual films'.[21] This technique was used extensively in the campaigns relating to the *Luftwaffe* films.

Given the future direction of the National Socialist war film, it is ironic that the outbreak of war in 1939 and diplomatic events surrounding it should have interrupted one of the first Ufa productions to focus on air power. Karl Ritter, a director with a specific interest in 'educat[ing] for war', was filming *Legion Condor* set in the Spanish Civil War, *Luftwaffe* General Wilberg acting as a consultant with Paul Hartmann in the leading role.[22] In August, Ritter had been informed by the studio that production was to be halted due to the Nazi–Soviet Pact and the desire to calm relations with Germany's new ally. Ritter's other film, a documentary entitled *Im Kampf gegen den Weltfeind: Deutsche Freiwillige in Spanien* (In Battle with the Enemy of the World: German Volunteers in Spain), was also unsurprisingly withdrawn from circulation.[23] Although this was a blow for Ritter, he would later return to the theme of the *Luftwaffe* for his 1941 production *Stukas*. Instead, the first major production centring on the role of the air force was to be Herbert Maisch's *D III 88*, a film sponsored by Göring 'much to the annoyance of Goebbels who disliked interference of any kind'.[24] Indeed, the *Reichsmarshall* sent the Head of the Press Department of the *Luftfahrtministeriums*, Heinz Orlovius, to aid Maisch in the production of the film.[25] Maisch and the film's co-author, Hans Bertram, however, were already sufficiently experienced in warfare and aviation, the former having served and been wounded at the front in the Great War, the latter a well-known pilot.[26] Tobis went to considerable lengths to assert the director's credentials, informing the press that Maisch had been wounded on three occasions in World War I, after each injury returning to the front lines. Such awareness, argued the studio, ensured that he was able to convey the 'obedience and duty, steady willingness and comradely loyalty' that he himself experienced. Here, in combining the man with the artist, Maisch could merge reality with emotion so that 'the gap between two generations was not so much bridged but rather filled with the spirit of a masculinity that has to prove itself afresh now that Germany is at war again'.[27]

The aim of the film was to represent the 'spirit' of the pilot, to recreate his 'everyday' experience[28] and to mobilize the German population behind the war effort.[29] In particular, the film was to focus on the *Luftwaffe* and the military attributes Maisch wished to portray: comradeship, unquestioning loyalty, discipline and bravery. The film spotlights the friendship of two pilots, Fritz Paulsen (Heinz Welzel) and Robert Eckhardt (Hermann Braun), who flagrantly disregard comradely behaviour and find themselves forced to make an emergency landing during operations as a result. The young pilots are given a second chance, thanks to the encouragement of a veteran fighter pilot of the Great War, who persuades their commander that they should be entrusted with an important mission.

Still 3   *D III 88. Illustrierter Film-Kurier, D III 88,*
private collection.

When this is successfully completed, both Eckhardt and Paulsen rejoin their division, having learned that duty, discipline and comradeship are values which should never be abandoned or subordinated.

Primarily, the film was intended to showcase the new *Luftwaffe*, reinstated by Hitler despite the Treaty of Versailles forbidding Germany to construct and train an air force, as demonstrated by the range of machinery in the film, from the older Fokker Dr. 1 to the He. 60 and 46 through to the Junkers. In this sense, it is the aeroplane which takes the 'starring role' in the production.[30] The aircraft are infused with life and are 'not inanimate objects, not lifeless things made of steel and struts, but giant, dangerous birds, with no enemy or opponent left to fear'.[31] Here, air power is simultaneously modern and technological, mystical and extraordinary, a sentiment typified in another piece in the film's soundtrack, *Wir jagen durch die Lüfte wie Wotans wildes Heer* ('We're racing through the air like Wotan's wild army').

Moreover, in highlighting the influence of the first fighter pilots of 1914–18 on the modern generation of aviators, Maisch built a direct link between past and present, embodied in the film's title, underlining the importance of Germany's aeronautical heritage, denied by the Peace Treaty of 1919 but restored by the Führer. Reviewers stressed that there was

> an obvious link between the German pilots of the Great War and those of today. It is this connection that gives this film the utmost … significance. The pilots of the Great War who stormed the sky and conquered the enemy wherever confronted, those men whose names have lived on in the hearts and minds of the German people, set the great soldierly example that has been a holy legacy for our soldiers.[32]

In constructing this bridge between the past and present alongside tradition and modernity, *D III 88* asserted the Reich's right to possess the means to prosecute air war. The film added to the propagandistic campaign by reinstating the air force psychologically as well as physically through political means. Within this context, the film sought to re-establish continuity in German military history and reinterpret the period of treaty fulfilment. This not only embodied the popular fascination with aviation but also emphasized Hitler's victory over the 'November criminals', a process which refashioned the defeat of 1918 into a source of pride and future strength. After all, *D III 88* promoted an understanding of what the men of the Great War were fighting and dying for: 'a strong and free, proud and successful Germany'.[33]

The central message of *D III 88* is the connection between the individual and the mass and between comrades. The private disagreements between Paulsen and Eckhardt were intended to demonstrate that only unity will achieve ultimate victory. In war, there is no room for private conflict, just as there is little room for individual identity outside the mass.[34] Their commanding officer reminds them that '*there will always be personal differences, but on duty the whole person is required. As is smooth cooperation and unquestioning loyalty. That is the only way for our force to become an instrument upon which Hitler, in case of an emergency, can totally rely*.[35] It is significant that Maisch not only attempted to create a visual bond between contemporaries, in which the youth 'stand shoulder to shoulder', but that an impenetrable union was forged between the officers and their men, an 'indissoluble comradeship' that no situation or conflict could dissolve.[36] Once again, the film highlighted the need to bridge the generations, the elders respected and cast as educators. Tobis emphasized that, 'comradeship is paramount, and one of the most moving scenes in the film is when we … witness the old man giving his life joyfully in order to set an example for the young of soldierly comradeship stronger than both life and death'.[37] Within the theme of comradeship, there is a natural tension within Maisch's production, particularly visible within the context of the Third Reich. For whilst the film functions by creating audience interest in the personalized and individualized identities and stories of the two protagonists, ultimately their distinctiveness is submerged within the master narrative of *Gemeinnutz vor Eigennutz*. Both Paulsen and Eckhardt submit their individual personas to the military discipline of their unit, conforming to be accepted. They come to learn and accept that the individual is no longer of significance, rather that the bonds of comradeship are defined by their selflessness.

It was this aspect of *D III 88* that created public interest, the film being singled out for particular mention by the SD in December 1939.[38] The popularity of Maisch's production prompted a sequel, released in February 1941, directed by Hans Bertram and starring many of the original cast. *Kampfgeschwader Lützow* capitalized on the popularity of Paulsen and Eckhardt, following their stories into the Polish campaign and operations against the British Isles. This generated engagement with contemporary events by exploiting the cinema-goers' desire to track the protagonists through the next chapters of their lives and attesting to the popularity of the human interest angle within military films. Bertram's film offered audiences the opportunity to discover the destiny of the two young pilots in their own age, to share in their fortunes and disappointments. Now, Paulsen and Eckhardt, like the audience themselves, have been plunged into World War II, joining a bomber squadron and awaiting orders. Their competition is reignited by their shared love-interest, Grethe Kubath (Marietheres Angerpointner), a *Volksdeutsche* liberated from Poland. Nevertheless, comradeship prevails, as in *D III 88*. Paulsen and Eckhardt are finally parted when Paulsen, having saved his comrades in an heroic action, dies. Drawing on *D III 88*'s success in 'strengthening the feeling of heartfelt affection for the men of the German *Luftwaffe*', *Kampfgeschwader Lützow*, like its predecessor, claimed to be a tribute from the 'entire German *Volk* to its *Luftwaffe*, to its creator, *Reichsmarshall* Hermann Göring, but also to each individual unknown pilot'.[39] Above all, the film stressed the higher values of the forces, 'comradeship, the fighting spirit and a sense of duty', but at the same time humanized the characters by showing their personal lives, represented by the love story embedded within the film.[40]

In order to heighten the propagandistic impact and to intensify the audiences' belief in the fictional aspect of the scenario, Bertram chose to fuse the imaginary with the real, interspersing acted scenes with documentary footage. In both the location of appropriate copy and the production of the film, he was assisted by the *Luftwaffe*, the Army, the *Waffen-SS* and the Navy, as the opening credits suggest, attesting to the importance that propaganda as a weapon of war assumed under the Nazis. Although Bertram retained a sense of the mystical in his depiction of the *Luftwaffe*, much like the surreal aerial shots in *Feuertaufe* commented upon by audiences in 1940, it was the emphasis upon the authenticity of the imagery which was the dominant factor in *Kampfgeschwader Lützow*. Tobis was proud to announce that the film contained 'genuine and real images of battle. These tanks, fighter planes and batteries are no background scenery!' Audiences were witnessing the 'iron sound of real war'.[41] In addition, Bertram was able to utilize his earlier production, *Feuertaufe*, for a similar purpose, some of the newsreel images and music being incorporated into the later fictionalized representation of the events of 1939–40. This use of documentary footage lodged within the main fictional narrative was intended to blur the distinction between the real and the illusory within *Kampfgeschwader Lützow*, and was a familiar technique used elsewhere (Von Borsody's *Wunschkonzert*, for example) for the same propagandistic purpose: to ensure that the film's message was delivered in a context in which the audience could easily mistake fictional for actual events, creating a psychological impact only intensified by the emotional bond cinema-goers forged with the individual characters of the film. That the publicity for the film promoted *Luftwaffe* involvement in its production only served to heighten the perception of its authenticity.

Once again, the *Luftwaffe* became the star of the film. As with his previous 'documentary' production, Bertram sought to shape the public's perception of air power by asserting that German aircraft were technically superior, 'the German wonder of our age'.[42] That air power was a specifically German phenomenon was a theme emphasized elsewhere, in particular in Gerhard Lamprecht's 1942 biopic *Diesel* starring Willy Birgel as the inventor of the diesel engine. The original synopsis of the film stressed that the engine, a German invention, lay at the heart of military might, the physical power behind aeroplanes, tanks and U-boats.[43] Despite retrogressive propaganda which highlighted the past and heritage, persuasive discourse in National Socialist films also pointed to the fact that Germany was a modern nation, which embraced technological advancement, indeed pioneered it. This marriage between machine and man was not only played out in stories of innovation, but in the natural connection between youth and the future. War, and in particular air power, offered the RMVP the perfect opportunity to propagate this idea. After all, amid the 'eternal thunder of the engines', a perfect harmony between 'man, machine and weapon' could be found. Air power, the youngest of the arms of warfare, was the modern expression of the 'young, faithful and courageous soldierly unit and followers, inspired and led by the Führer and the first soldier of the Nation'.[44] Bertram visualized this power and devotion in his battle sequences, designed to demonstrate the awesome destructive force of the *Luftwaffe*. *Kampfgeschwader Lützow* was yet another example of the supremacy of the German air force, its images of devastation in Poland a testament to military success. Echoing the narrative of *Feuertaufe*, the promotional materials for the film stressed that the audience would 'experience the devastating effects of arms, see the Polish airfields, stations, tracks and bridges under fire from our bombs and machine guns and surrounded by rubble and smoke, and witness the paralysing fear of the Polish regiments, motorized, on foot and on horses, under attack by the Germany's *Luftwaffe* and its tanks'.[45] Audiences were invited into the heart of the action, to relive the 'wonder of the eighteen-day battle' all over again, through the 'grey bird' of the 'Kampfgeschwaders Lützow' in the east.[46] The film was intended to pull the cinema-goer into the experience of 'total war', its modernity, its weaponry and its spirit. Reviewers suggested after its premiere in February 1941 that:

> The force of contemporary global developments has brought about a natural and solid bond of our people with the most visible new weapons and their carriers in this utterly new and revolutionary kind of warfare… The film *Kampfgeschwader Lützow* takes us right into the world of this bond where our new, sharp weapons have liberated us from the squalor of the Polish hell.[47]

Bertram provoked his audience to position themselves within 'the world of the pilots of 1939, 1940, 1941', absorbing them simultaneously not only in the lives of the characters but also within contemporary events.

Still 4   *Kampfgeschwader Lützow. Illustrierter Film-Kurier, Kampfgeschwader Lützow*, private collection.

As this suggests, there were many connections between Bertram's 'documentary' work, *Feuertaufe*, and the fictional representation of the Poland campaign in *Kampfgeschwader Lützow*. However, unlike Bertram's 1940 production, operations in the 1941 film are performed by individuals, individuals crafted as heroic, comradely and brave servants of the Reich. The individualization of the *Frontflieger* within the feature film, as opposed to the documentary, was most pronounced in the characterization of German fighter pilots and enemy bombers. Frequently, the cinematic discourse assumed the form of polarized and clear-cut contrasts: the audience is acquainted with the personal stories of the *Luftwaffe* pilots and their crews, whilst enemy airmen are denied individual identities, their faces often obscured or darkened. As Katje Kirste observed, 'on a visual level, the anonymity of the enemy is reinforced by enemy faces being made unrecognizable: the faces of enemy pilots in Nazi films are shown through the reflections of light and shadow'.[48]

However, it is notable that, although film-makers sought to capitalize on audience identification with individuals' stories and lives, at their core the characters in the air films only functioned in relation to the whole, in keeping with Nazi ideology pertaining to the relationship between the individual and the state. It is within the context of combat that selflessness and devotion to one's comrades is paramount. Bertram intended *Kampfgeschwader Lützow* to be a living document of the 'German struggle and German comradeship'.[49] This was embodied within the friendship between Paulsen and Eckhardt, heralded as the quintessence of soldierly spirit. *Filmwelt* asserted that 'the fate of the two friends is symbolic of the spirit of the whole squadron: ... comradeship proves its worth, giving strength to the individual and securing victory for the people'.[50] This sentiment was to be the cornerstone of militaristic propaganda in the films of the Third Reich and wider ideological discourses within it. It was a theme which was embraced across different cinematic genres, contributing to the attempt to create the Nazi *Weltanschauung*. This can be observed in another *Fliegerfilm* of the war years starring Heinz Rühmann, *Quax, der Bruchpilot* (Quax, the Crash-Happy Pilot, Kurt Hoffmann, 1941). In this comedy, Rühmann, assuming his typical persona of the 'little man' with 'familiar elements of petit bourgeois mentality',[51] plays a travel agent who wins a series of flying lessons in a competition. However, as Stephen Lowry noted, 'in flight school it is not just flying he has to learn ... but rather discipline, courage and above all comradeship'.[52] Rühmann, master of the slapstick, the grotesque and the childlike,[53] was able to capitalize on his experience as a pilot to perform some of the aerial stunts. In his Udet-Flamingo, a plane he recalled 'made out of wood and no longer the youngest [of aircraft] ... and without any brakes', Rühmann took a camera into the skies and shot much of the aerial footage himself.[54] Yet despite elements of the burlesque that this produced, it is a film conditioned by its wartime context. Within the publicity materials for the film, Terra reminded audiences that the star had flown for a short time as a courier for the *Wehrmacht*.[55] In a similar briefing, the studio also described Rühmann's characters as those with 'a visible modesty and atypical daring',[56] offering 'comic relief from the crisis of masculinity by focussing on the camaraderie in all male-groups'.[57] Within

Quax, der Bruchpilot these two characteristics collide, presenting an opportunity for an exploration of the daring of pilots and their innate comradeship. Although Quax's '"civilian" attitudes ... can be seen as a humorous protest against the military-style discipline of flight school or even as a satire of Nazi reality', Lowry argues that 'the potentially "subversive" force of comedy is quickly redirected into an affirmation of the status quo'. It is only by relinquishing his 'false individualism' that Quax progresses to become a flight instructor and wins the girl of his dreams. 'The infantalisation of the figure ... and submission to power are shown' by Hoffmann 'as the way to gain identity'. Within this environment, argued Lowry, 'voluntary submission proves to be the first step towards identification with and assumption of authority'.[58] In this way, the image of even the non-military aviator is militarized and politicized within varying film contexts, combining a focus on comradeship and the submerging of the individual into the mass and demonstrating that advancement in society is only gained by submission to authority. Here, the comedic overtones intended to soften the public message were, in reality, much more stark.

The most powerful expression of devotion to the virtues of comradeship and collective identity was death, and this finds ample treatment in the filmic representation of military aviation, particularly in films dating from 1941. *Kampfgeschwader Lützow* was no exception. Paulsen's death whilst attempting to save both machine and man tied in with wider Nazi wartime propaganda objectives. As Jay Baird has pointed out in his masterly analysis of the rituals of death in the Third Reich, 'with the coming of World War II, National Socialism had come full circle..., the will to battle had ever been the essence of the party and its Führer'. With the onset of *Blitzkrieg*, 'myth once more became the handmaiden to Mars'.[59] Initial hesitancy over the outbreak of war was gradually converted into euphoria with the victories of 1940, a period in which 'astounding German successes totally overshadowed considerations of death'. However, as Baird has noted, 'such overconfidence proved a brief phenomenon indeed and, in time, death loomed even larger in the German experience'.[60] It became clear that the subject of death had to be confronted in specific films and in wider propaganda. However, the transition from rapid victories to protracted war, from light casualties to heavy losses was complex, and did not bode well for propagandistic success. Bertram was almost certainly aware of this development, his works spanning both the period of ascendancy and the increasing need to tackle the issue of human losses on all fronts. In its final sequences, *Kampfgeschwader Lützow* becomes the embodiment of Hitler's pronouncement that 'the giving of one's own life for the existence of the community is the ultimate meaning of sacrifice'.[61] Paulsen, in making 'the last and highest sacrifice' for the nation, becomes forever entwined with the community. In dying, as the press book for the film proclaimed, 'his spirit lives on in hundreds, in thousands. And his sacrifice will never be forgotten'.[62] Paulsen's death is heralded as the ultimate expression of 'the fulfilment of one's duty and of comradeship'.[63] Here, as in other productions, death was 'something to be imitated'.[64] It was, in the words of director and later *Reichsfilmintendant*, Fritz Hippler, a 'condition' which was best articulated in 'poetry and the visual arts' in that it could be 'put into a larger philosophical context', the cumulative effect of this process serving to 'elevate [death] from the senseless and depressing sphere of nature into the world of values and ideals' in which 'dying itself becomes irrelevant..., merely a matter of medical record'.[65]

The possibility of death is articulated from a relatively early stage in the film and is an implicit thematic strand throughout, coming to the fore in the finale with the death of Paulsen. In a scene designed to steel comrades ahead of the task before them, Hellwig and Guggi (Gugsermos) engage in a discussion about death. In the process of writing to his mother to voice his anxieties, Hellwig lifts his head to ask his fellow solider:

Hellwig: Is it cowardly to think that one might die?

Guggi: Well, do you want to die?

Hellwig: I mean, things might kick off soon, mightn't they...

Guggi: Our teacher once told us of these three comrades he had. One of them never wanted to think about death and thought he could get away with it. But in the end it got him anyway and then he found it terribly hard. The other guy was into praying. He was a good guy, but what with all the praying he wasn't vigilant and got killed too. And then he had this other comrade... This guy, whenever things got difficult he would mentally detach himself. What will be will be. And then he would really go for it, like a bull, but always with his eyes wide open, just like a soldier should.

Hellwig: And did he get killed too?

Guggi: No. Not him. He was my father.[66]

As Kirste observed, the expected response to death was to be 'self-control and strength'.[67] The possibility of death is not denied, rather refined, becoming a positive virtue within the National Socialist propagandistic discourse, each individual encouraged to suppress anxiety and fear and face death as a liberation and contribution to the whole. The natural process of death cut across time in the propagation of the militaristic ideology of the Reich, and in *Kampgeschwader Lützow*, as in its prequel, bonds between the first and second world wars are established and nurtured. In both films, the elders are cast as educators and guides in death as well as in life. The two conflicts of the twentieth century are also linked in the portrayal of death in the Third Reich 'within the context of the flow of nature, which [demanded] sacrifice to bring about new life, as well as pain to heal a nation's wounds'.[68] Hitler frequently alluded to the eternal sacrifice of death, claiming that the 'glorious past ... was won and washed in the blood of countless German heroes'. Enveloping the solider in the rhetoric of the *Heldentod*, he implored contemporary men to 'be just as brave as those who went before [them]. We are now fighting for the same thing for which they once struggled. What was noble enough for them – if necessary – to die for, should find us ready to emulate at all times'.[69] Paulsen, like all those who were to give their lives in the conflict, was accorded eternal life by the regime. Victory, Hitler believed, would take vengeance for the deaths of his comrades of the Great War, 'their spirits ... [rising] from their graves [to] thank all those who by their courage and loyalty have at last avenged the horrible crime once committed against them by our people in an hour of weakness'.[70] As in *D III 88*, the example of World War I was used to forge continuity in the German experience, to justify militarism in the Third Reich and to idealize the Führer as first soldier of the nation. Accordingly, this process was a form of national palingenesis, seeking to extend the history of the Reich. Sacrifice was the *leitmotif* of this propagandistic strand and is visible throughout the *Fliegerfilme* of the period.

Given that *Kampfgeschwader Lützow* seemed to demonstrate the virtues of the *Luftwaffe* and of soldierly conduct, it was accorded particular praise on its release. The premiere, on 28 February 1941, was attended by leading Nazi officials and dignitaries, including Goebbels, Walther Darré and Heinrich Himmler together with diplomats and members of foreign military attachés.[71] The Reich Minister for Popular Enlightenment and Propaganda was particularly pleased with the film, noting in his diary on 14 February that it was 'a grandiose picture of the war-time *Luftwaffe*. With monumental images. A unique depiction of the milieu. I'm enchanted'.[72] Goebbels was confident that the film would enjoy popular success, as it was 'well made, clear, realistic, with wonderful takes and shots'.[73] Such was its status as 'a true war film for the people'[74] that in the final months of the Reich it was resurrected and re-released to inspire the population, the RMVP believing it could reinvigorate the German population, now under threat of invasion and defeat.[75]

Although the film was on general release and capitalized on the success of *D III 88* to bring cinema-goers to the theatres to see *Kampfgeschwader Lützow*,[76] the RMVP and the studio wished to target particular groups in their publicity for the film, indicating that it was intended for specific as well as popular consumption. This was a favoured technique of the film propagandists. Hake notes that both the Ministry and the studios had become adept at 'politicizing certain forms of movie going' by targeted screenings and advertising.[77] Special promotional campaigns were organized to attract the armed forces and the young. In a tie-in with Bertram's previous film, *Feuertaufe*, special premieres were organized locally in which a *Luftwaffe* orchestra played the song '*Wir fliegen gegen Engelland*' [sic] prior to the screening, attesting to the all-encompassing environment in which Nazi propaganda was constructed. Theatre-owners were encouraged to hand out leaflets promoting the film in barracks, in particular those used by the air force, and in schools.[78] Indeed, screenings of *Kampfgeschwader Lützow* were encouraged for the Hitler Youth.[79] After all, it would be the young who would ultimately be called upon to fight and die for the Fatherland, the educational curriculum informing young men that 'a man's greatest honour lies in death before the enemy of his country'.[80]

The connection between the young and death was explored in a later aviation film of that year, Karl Ritter's *Stukas*. The film followed what was becoming a rather rigid scenario for the *Fliegerfilme*: a series of individual events and sub-plots modelled around a basic structure – awaiting orders, camaraderie in the camp, the call to arms, extended aerial battle sequences, the flight home, landing and the consequences of battle.[81] Reinforcing the central tenets of previous films, *Stukas* sought to promote the virtues of camaraderie, discipline, preparedness and sacrifice, and differed little in this respect from its predecessors. Influenced heavily by the film's director, *Stukas* was intended as 'a hymn of devotion to the intrepid warriors of the air, joining elements of power, intellect and idealism'.[82] Known as a director with considerable sympathy for Nazi military values, Ritter, himself a pilot in World War I, held a fascination with air power and militarism, reflected in his previous productions such as *Patrioten* (Patriots, 1937) and *Pour le Merité* (For Honour, 1938). For him, *Stukas* represented the culmination of his cinematic achievements and his personal interest in aviation. He told *Filmwelt* in December 1940 that the film was partly inspired by his own enthralment with air war and his experiences: 'being a former aviator myself, I was extremely keen to get to know this miracle weapon and to experience its workings'. In preparing for the film, he continued, 'I let myself be posted to the Stuka unit where I studied the men and their machines for some weeks'.[83] Like Bertram, Ritter was insistent that the film reflect 'reality', generating an authentic feel to the fictional sub-plots. Ritter confirmed that 'we wanted to present a true, undistorted picture of the life of the German aviator, one which in its simple truth will also invalidate the enemy's hateful lies and propaganda'.[84] In the preparation of the script, alongside co-author Felix Lützkendorf, Ritter confirmed that 'reality always served as a gauge for me... We constantly checked our cinematic fiction against reality'.[85] By 1941, connecting realistic footage and scenarios with fictionalized plots and characters had become a favoured propagandistic technique. It had the advantage of heightening the authenticity and contemporary value of feature-length films and attempted to create identification with the audience, encouraging film-goers to internalize the film's central message. As with previous productions, Ritter used actual contemporary events to underscore the more ethereal and vague concepts forwarded in the film, such as comradeship and sacrifice.

Like the other films of this genre, comradeship is placed at the heart of the soldierly experience. Ritter's belief that his films 'deal with the insignificance of the individual' and that 'the personal has to be sacrificed to the cause' is given visual expression in *Stukas*.[86] Within the film, as Baird observed, comradeship is expressed through the 'boys' themselves, Ritter drawing on different sections of the community for characters, suggesting the correlation between comradeship and the concept of the *Volksgemeinschaft*. Unlike the representation in *Kampfgeschwader Lützow*, *Kameradschaft* operates outside of the construct of the Führer as the first soldier of the nation.[87] Instead, it stands as an independent and mutually reinforcing emotion between men, who through the love of battle and the nation sacrifice their individuality to the will of the mass. This sacrifice is typified in the film not only by giving the individual over to selfless duty but in submitting one's life to the nation, each soldier expecting and celebrating death, for, as Baird points out, 'heroic action' in the film 'is but a gateway to immortality, blessed by the gods'.[88] For the military, the eternal nature of death is a cause for celebration and allows the fallen soldier to enter the domain of divinity, Lieutenant 'Kücken' Prack (Johannes Schütz) commenting in the film that '*death*

Still 5   *Stukas. Images of comradeship in 'Stukas'.* Image from Bfi Stills, Posters and Designs.

was a dancer for Dionysus. For the fearful citizen, it is a skeleton with a scythe. Me, for my part, I believe in the dancer'. Many analyses have rightly focused on the exchange between Captain Heinz Bork (Carl Raddatz) and *Oberarzt* Dr Gregorius (O. E. Hasse) on the death of *Oberleutant* Jordan (Eugen Müller-Franken), whose mother contacts them to thank them for the return of his medal. Jordan's mother informs them of her pride, pushing aside her feelings of loss and bereavement to express her satisfaction at having given her son for the greater good of the nation. Gregorius reflects '*when a mother takes it like that, death no longer holds any weight'.* Bock agrees: '*One thinks more about the cause they died for. One remembers them forever as young gods'.* To give poetic expression to these sentiments, Gregorius recites Hölderlin's 'Death for the Fatherland':

> O take me, let me join that circle,
> so that I will not die a common death!
> I do not want to die in vain; but
> I would love to perish on a hill of sacrifice
>
> for the Fatherland, to bleed the blood of my heart,
> for the Fatherland – and soon it is done! To you
> dear ones! I come to join
> those who taught me to live and die!

And heralds of victory come down: We have
won the battle! Live on high, O Fatherland,
and do not count the dead! For you,
sweet one! Not one too many has died.[89]

It is in the characterization of death as godly and unearthly that filmic representations of casualties tended to expose a tension between the professed desire to represent the reality of war and the need to offer comfort to audiences by presenting it in surreal and idealistic terms, particularly as the number of dead began to rise exponentially. Newsreels were explicitly forbidden to carry pictures of dead German soldiers, and feature films complemented this 'pictorial abolition of death'.[90] Filmic conflict operated in a space in which individual death was presented 'only as an emblem of a theatrical scenario culminating in "ultimate victory"'.[91] It was in this cinematic environment that 'the stage magic of a battlefield in enemy territory gives the heroic struggle of destiny's community a mystical flair of irreality that conveys to the spectator at home in his theatre seat the feeling that stage and audience belong together',[92] distancing the film-goer from the harsh truths of war, despite the explicit intention of the film-maker to create a realistic picture of conflict. This exposes a fundamental tension between intent and image, and it is most pronounced in Ritter's 1941 production, a 'memorial to the fighting spirit and death defiance of our Stuka-men'.[93]

It was significant that death and sacrifice came to play an increasingly important role in filmic discourses by mid-1941, with *Stukas* premiered in June of that year. It was the last major film produced in the Third Reich on the subject of the air war. Ritter's next attempt to recreate the heroism and glory of the *Luftwaffe*, *Besatzung Dora* (Occupying Crew Dora, 1942-3), though completed, could not be issued on general release, the battle of Stalingrad proving that the German army was not invincible and that the bomber was no longer capable of single-handedly winning the war. The gap between the image and reality was such that not even harsh editing of Ritter's film could hide it. In February 1945, as the Reich was disintegrating, *Besatzung Dora* was shown in a private screening to members of the *Luftwaffe*.[94] Other later films, such as *Himmelhunde* (Daredevils, Roger Graf Normann, 1942) and *Junge Adler* (Young Eagles, Alfred Weidenmann, 1944), were merely propaganda to prepare the young for the forthcoming struggle in which they would have to play a significant role,[95] the latter meant to reflect the 'the spirit and joyfulness of modern youth'[96] but in fact little more than a call to arms.

The decline in aviation films in the Third Reich coincided with public disquiet over the prosecution of the air war and decreasing confidence in the *Luftwaffe*. After the propaganda surrounding the 'eighteen-day war', the public explicitly equated *Blitzkrieg* with a swift end to battles. With the attacks on Coventry and London in particular, certain sections of the German public began to speculate that the war would 'come to an end quicker than one would have expected'.[97] In the midst of the most ferocious attacks on the British mainland in July 1940, the German population fully anticipated that the assault would bring a 'sudden end for England'.[98] However, when immediate victory did not transpire, hopes of an early conclusion to the war faded. Fears of a protracted conflict intensified with British raids on German soil. Although the SD reported in August 1940 that 'confidence in the Führer was unlimited' and that 'everybody was full of anticipation of the *big event which would go down as one of the most devastating battles of all time*',[99] many feared that the attacks upon German cities, such as those in that month which left ten dead and twenty-eight injured in the capital, would lead to a much longer war.[100] Reports confirming that 'countless kilogram bombs' had been unleashed upon the population of London in 'their longest night in the air raid shelter', a night in which 'there were tremors all across the British Isles', could not dispel the increasing feeling of nervousness among the wider German population.[101] As long as the '*Britische Luftpiraten*' were still active in German skies,[102] the population were reminded that they were not completely safe from 'Tommy'.[103] This sat uneasily with the filmic portrayal of the *Luftwaffe* as the invincible, destructive force which knew no match and the ability of German defences to repel any attacker. Gradually, the spectre of death began to haunt the *Fliegerfilme*, indicating that the time for propagating the myth of impregnability had passed and that the time for sacrifice and 'total war' was upon them.

BRITAIN CAN TAKE IT! IMAGES OF THE BLITZ

In comparing the air films of Maisch, Bertram and Ritter with those produced on the subject of aerial bombardment in Britain in the same period, one is struck by the different approaches adopted by the democratic and authoritarian powers, a difference very much in keeping with each nation's ideological stance, cultural nuance and distinction and their position in the war. Notably, 'there was an element of defensiveness in British film propaganda' that simply could not be adapted to fit the German 'idealization of the Nazi fighter stereotype'. Significantly, British propaganda emphasized 'individual expression at the expense of sublimation and the community',[104] and this was fundamentally at odds with the forms of sacrifice and duty crafted by the RMVP. British film propaganda on the subject of *Blitzkrieg* fitted the nature of the conflict facing the nation throughout 1940 and 1941 and suited the democratic apparatus in which it operated. Although it has been claimed that the Blitz produced 'much less need for propaganda than had been expected',[105] propaganda on the subject of aerial bombardment functioned on multiple levels, from sustaining morale to mythologizing the dark days from September 1940 to May 1941, enabling the public retrospectively to make sense of 'the extraordinariness and the incongruity of everyday life'.[106] 'The blitz', Mark Connelly confirms, 'is very definitely a visual memory',[107] and it was for this reason that the myth of the Blitz was forged and developed, from an early stage, within the filmic medium, both in contemporary short films such as Harry Watt and Humphrey Jennings' *London Can Take It* (1940) to nostalgic fictional feature films such as *Unpublished Story* (Harold French, 1942) and *The Bells Go Down* (Basil Dearden, 1943).

Unlike its German counterpart, it was the impact of the Blitz that dominated the early cinematic outputs of the war years rather than the glorification of British air power. Although there were some initial attempts to create a positive image of the RAF, such as Korda's *The Lion Has Wings* and Maurice Baring's *The Warning* (1939), British film-producers outside the MoI, on the whole, turned to this theme a little later than their enemy, unsurprising given their relative positions within the war and the desirability for the propagandist to reflect their own audiences' experiences, thus matching popular opinion on contemporary events. The British public, however, were just as fascinated with aviation as their adversaries. Mass-Observation noted that the RAF was 'admired as a brilliant set of individuals'[108] and was the subject of much of the most popular literature of the period.[109] The level of veneration of the air force in the media and in the popular discourse is indicated by a report by the British Board of Film Censors (BBFC) on the film *The World Owes Me a Living*, in which they instructed the script writers to remove the line 'they're like little pansies' in reference to pilots.[110] The Home Intelligence Division demonstrated that 'public opinion studies have shown that there is great confidence in the RAF and that the continuous flow of air news (however monotonous it may be) has succeeded in keeping before the public the constant activity of the RAF', the population being 'reminded that the war in the air is unceasing'.[111] Newsreels featuring the RAF were consistently 'very well received'.[112] With such public interest in even the most mundane activities of the air force, the air war still did not become the central theme for British feature films in the early stages of the conflict. The film industry itself recognized the possible propagandistic and financial capital to be gained from a cinematic treatment of air power and began to push film-makers to give visual expression to the most appealing and popularized form of the wartime experience. Air films, as we have seen, could appeal to the wider home audience by successfully combining the contemporary with the escapist, Maurice Ostrer confirming in *Today's Cinema* that 'filmgoers have always enjoyed topical films… [A]ny film subject dealing with aerial warfare … cannot fail to thrill'.[113] However, it appears that, although there was a desire on the part of the film industry to produce a film focusing on the air war, the RAF was less than enthusiastic. In October 1940, film-producer Michael Balcon complained that he was 'dissatisfied with service film facilities'. Deeply disappointed by the fact that the air force had granted facilities to the US series *The March of Time*, he demanded why British film companies had not been allowed access to the same benefits.[114] Although cooperation between the film industry and the RAF improved considerably as the war progressed, the early years were beset with difficulties for the studios, leading to the last resort for a film industry desperate to show images of aerial warfare: the proposal to re-release *The Lion Has Wings*. In June 1940, *Kinematograph Weekly* suggested to the MoI that, in the face of 'total war, heralded by widespread air raids', the film industry should undertake

> an immediate re-editing of *The Lion Has Wings* in which the irrelevant professional acting is eliminated to admit new scenes depicting the cool behaviour of a disciplined public when a raid warning is given – the orderly trek to shelters, wardens going on duty, fire posts manned and ready, trains running and the good humour of the English crowd.[115]

Only this measure, they argued, could combat the 'pure destructiveness' of the raids and the fear they created.[116] Even here, film-makers proposed the repositioning of a film primarily designed to promote air power. The re-edited version of Korda's production refocused attention on the Blitz and the ordinary citizen's reaction to it. Aerial attack and defensive strategies were to form the master narrative of British filmic propaganda on the air war, and it was only later that attention was given to a more offensive outlook.

Officially British propagandists recognized from a relatively early stage that aerial bombardment had the potential to undermine public confidence in the war effort and lead to a collapse in morale. Planning for this possibility, therefore, was underway almost immediately, the MoI Home Publicity Division issuing a regional circular on 'hints for preventing or allaying panic in air-raids' in September 1939. Drawing on the advice of experts who had studied the Spanish Civil War, the British authorities produced guidelines to prevent the spread of rumours, educate the population about air power and incite anger towards the enemy. Above all, the MoI wished to stem the tide of fear which seemed to be welling-up in the aftermath of the outbreak of war. Concerned that 'fear . . . will come like a flood which . . . will spread dangerously', the Ministry intended to instruct the public to keep 'their mental poise and courage'. Regional Information Officers were drilled to inform their nervous populations that 'fear is only natural'. Resorting to the traditional British cure-all, they were informed that 'a cup of tea or coffee' would comfort the population in the wake of a raid.[117] For some, as Mass-Observation reported, the anticipation of aerial bombardment was far worse than the reality. Many displayed signs of anxiety, expecting the bombers to 'come in swarms'. However, 'the majority . . . gave the impression that they had made up their minds to the fact that [raids] were coming; that they believed they could see them through, and that they would be bad, but not unbearable'.[118] Nevertheless, as Tom Harrisson observed, 'deep down inside many of us were suppressing anxieties and consequently building up rather exaggerated pictures of what air-raids might mean'.[119] When at last the raiders attacked the British Isles, public opinion was by no means uniform 'either in emotion or in behaviour', the air-raid sirens provoking a range of reactions from 'annoyance, fear and calmness' to 'interest, curiosity or excitement'.[120] Although some reports confirmed that the Blitz was met with a determined resolve, a Home Intelligence report in late 1940 confirmed that 'heavy provincial raids' had led to anxiety and the fear that national defence was 'inadequate' which in turn prompted a 'rather lower state of morale'.[121] Propaganda had to respond to these diverse reactions to aerial attack and devise a sustained strategy which would simultaneously allay fears and strengthen resolve. In addition, concern over the impact of German air-raids on morale was not limited to a specific period in the war. It remained a constant and pressing theme of propaganda emanating from the MoI, a report in September 1941 reminding all Government Departments that publicity had to 'take into account the possibility of demoralisation, particularly under heavy and continuous bombing through a public feeling that the war has already gone on two years without it being clear how we are to win, and may go on for many more years'.[122]

Like the public reactions they sought to address, the aims of the MoI's propaganda relating to aerial attack were manifold, ranging from the practical and composed to incitement to anger and action. Firstly, government propaganda sought to create a sense of calm amongst the population by normalizing the air-raid experience. Churchill himself had asked the MoI to instruct broadcasters to 'handle air raids in a cool way and on a diminishing tone of public interest'. He hoped that people would become 'accustomed to treat air raids as a matter of ordinary routine', in time learning to take them 'as if they were no more than thunderstorms'.[123] Two months later, in August 1940, Tom Harrisson commented that raids had become 'a part of the routine of life, an unpleasant part like walking home from work in the snow or having mild indigestion'. The apocalyptic vision imagined prior to the first raids had not manifested itself, he added, and he was 'relieved to find how little bombs can do compared with the mental picture one had'.[124] The normalization of aerial attack was to be effectively combined with propaganda seeking to inspire confidence in the defence of the nation and its agencies. The MoI recognized from an early stage that

> the response of the country's nerves to severe air raids will depend on the general effi-
> ciency of ARP measures; on the supremacy of the RAF in defence and counter-attack;
> on popular faith in the Government; on hopes of ultimate victory in the war at large and
> not least on an absolute confidence in the justice of our cause.[125]

Propaganda, then, sought to encapsulate these general sentiments, forging them into a complete vision of the British response to German attack. It was within this context of defence that the Ministry attempted to 'improve home morale through the creation of an active front-line attitude among the whole population', carefully illustrating the role of the individual in the war effort. This was not to be achieved through 'exhortation but by systematically conveying to the public a picture of civilian war action of all kinds, at its best'.[126] The prevention of panic, the normalization of aerial bombardment, inspiring confidence in defence mechanisms and the creation of a homogeneous, unified and dedicated home front in the service of the war effort: ultimately, these were the aims of the wider propaganda campaign and formed the backdrop to filmic representations of Britain, and specifically London, under the veil of the Blitz.

Initially, there was some disquiet about making films about the Blitz. In late 1940, the director Sergei Nolbandov proposed a film which focused on the Battle of Britain. The film does not appear to have been released, as the air-raid sequences were considered to be 'too unpleasant … to appeal to most audiences'.[127] Even the soundtrack could easily prove to be alarming, the BBFC ordering the removal of sirens from various films throughout the war.[128] Harrisson had noticed that by August 1940 it was the 'sirens which [dominated] people's minds', with many recording that they 'upset them more than the actual raid'.[129] In addition, Mass-Observation reported that air raid sequences were 'probably the most unpopular sequences in films [this trend lay before the Blitz started…]. Only in one case', they continued, 'has a film of an air raid been entirely successful'. That film was Harry Watt and Humphrey Jennings' short *London Can Take It*. Mass-Observation attributed its success to the fact that it was 'intensely realistic, had no horror scenes, no characters who died or shots of dead bodies'. This seemed to be a winning formula for the Blitz films, as later productions demonstrated. The Blitz film had to relate to the audiences' own experience, and the directors were masters of realism, albeit in Jennings' case set within a rather surreal environment. Jennings' work naturally fitted the wartime milieu in which he worked. At once, he could capture the 'other-worldliness' of the Blitz, drawing on his own involvement in the surrealist movement, at the same time understanding and connecting with the real people of the cities who lived their lives from one night to the next with no rest, in deep, damp and dark shelters. He captured their existence on film. He understood them. He represented them. As Mass-Observation noted of Nolbandov's film, the Blitz sequence was something the audiences 'all know much about and they know too that the air raid depicted has no connection with what really happens'.[130] They concluded that 'films that attempt to show real people and real incidents are unquestionably successful if they are true to life'.[131] The public expressed a desire 'to see on the screen happenings at which they have themselves been spectators',[132] and Jennings' films, in particular, fulfilled that particular need. The feel of *London Can Take It* so aptly fitted the mood of the time and related intimately to the audiences' perception of the age in every way. Although historians have recognized that the Blitz was defined by its visual expression, its soundtrack was also distinctive, and it was the combination of the visual and the aural in Jennings' 1940 film which struck a chord with the audience. Mass-Observation confirmed that 'the most successful moment in *London Can Take It* was simply the sound of planes in the distance, then guns, then bombs, the soundtrack of a night raid. The audience recognised this [and] enjoyed it as part of their own experience'.[133] Although Jennings himself did not always fit with the Griersonian vision of documentary, some of his productions such as *Fires Were Started* (*I Was a Fireman*, 1943) including staged sequences, *London Can Take It* was the ultimate expression of his idea that 'if we are to persuade, we have to reveal; and we have to reveal in terms of reality'. This, according to Grierson, was the defining feature of British propaganda in the war years. For only by 'recognising this responsibility to the local and the particular' could the 'once-haunted concept of propaganda have a democratic interpretation'.[134]

London Can Take It was conceived as a film to underscore Britain's 'determination to show that indiscriminate bombing will not break [the] Britisher's morale'. The film scenario boasted: 'if this is Hitler's worst, then we have got him beat … it hasn't affected the war capacity of the country in the slightest. But better still, it hasn't affected the morale of the people. It's a bloody nuisance but everyone knows that we'll get our own back a hundredfold – and soon'.[135] This broadly reflected Jennings' own view that 'psychologically … this indiscriminate bombing is the greatest mistake Hitler could make'.[136] The film-maker's letters to his wife, Cicily, evacuated to the United States, demonstrate his deep compassion for the Blitzed and a love of British heritage and culture alongside a determined resolve to maintain public morale and defeat Nazism. This is amply demonstrated in his letter of

20 October 1940: 'Maybe by the time you get this one or two more 18th cent. churches will be smashed up in London: some civilians killed; some personal loves and treasures wrecked – but it means nothing: a curious kind of unselfishness is developing which can stand all that and any amount more'. Jennings celebrated the effect of 'the heart-breaking' damage inflicted on London by the German bomber, commenting of his film subjects, 'what warmth – what courage!... Everybody absolutely determined: secretly delighted with the *privilege* of holding up Hitler. Certain of beating him: a certainty which no amount of bombing can weaken: only strengthen'.[137] This was the essence of *London Can Take It*, illustrated by the commentary provided by the American journalist for *Collier's Weekly*, Quentin Reynolds.

The narration, delivered by '*the neutral reporter*' with a supposed air of detachment, together with the score by Vaughn Williams, provided for an uplifting short film in keeping with Jennings' own vision of the London spirit. On the front lines in the 'war for democracy', Jennings' '*people's army of volunteers ... brokers, clerks, peddlers, merchants by day* [and] *... heroes by night*' steel themselves for the bombers, civilians seeking refuge in the public shelters. Like the German air films which sought to obscure the individual visual identities of the enemy, Jennings turns the German bomber into '*a creature of the night...,* [melting] *away before the dawn ... [scurrying] back to the safety of their airdrome*'. It is in the aftermath of the raid, however, that the film becomes a hymn to determination, courage and resilience. When the new day breaks, '*London raises her head, shakes the debris from her hair and takes stock of the damage done ... London does this every morning*'. Like a '*great fighter*', she always gets up '*from the floor after being knocked down*' and '*faces the day with calmness and confidence*', the people resuming their natural routine as far as possible and greeting the destruction with good humour. The maintenance of morale is at the heart of *London Can Take It*, the people '*fused together not by fear but by surging courage of spirit the likes of which the world has never known*' and determined rather to '*face death than kneel down to face the kind of existence the conqueror would impose upon them*'. He concludes that '*there is no panic, no fear, no despair in London town*'. Rather, '*there is nothing but determination, confidence and high courage among the people of Churchill's Island*'. Further, contrasting Nazi and British values, and employing a similar technique to the Nazi 'documentaries of intimidation' in this one respect, Reynolds describes British defensive and offensive actions in the air thus: '*every night the RAF bombers fly deep into the heart of Germany, bombing munitions works, aeroplane factories, canals, cutting the arteries which keep the heart of Germany alive*'. Initially, neither protagonist in the conflict was prepared to promote the targeting of civilians, and here the theme of bombing industrial or military targets was used by propagandists as a means of setting one military power aside from the other whilst pointing to the indiscriminate bombing of their enemy. In any case, bombing, according to *London Can Take It*, was restricted in its impacts. Reynolds informs his audience that '*a bomb has its limitations. It can only destroy buildings and kill people. It cannot kill the unconquerable spirit and courage of London*'.

Although the film's commentary is infused with vague and higher concepts of the war for democracy, it was perceived as a reflection of reality. Public opinion of *London Can Take It* pointed to the favourable reception of the 'shots of London by night and the soundtrack of what every Londoner can hear'.[138] Moreover, film-goers 'seemed to like seeing people like themselves doing the things that they do'.[139] However, it was a reality which found expression in the sounds and feelings of war and its related emotions, if not in the visual reality of death which ensued. The treatment of death in *London Can Take It* operates within strictly defined boundaries. As Malcolm Smith points out, 'over 40,000 civilians were killed between September 1940 and May 1941, and it was not until late 1942 that total British uniformed casualties exceeded civilian'.[140] Mass-Observation commented that blitz films, such as Jennings and Watt's 1940 production, tended to be popular when they did not include horrific scenes of the dead or the physically mutilated. Ultimately, this was the real side of the Blitz that audiences did not see nor wish to see, despite claiming to want more gritty reportage of the aerial bombardment of British cities. Home Intelligence reported in 1940 that 'people wish to be told the worst and feel as if they are being treated as children if this is not done'.[141] Reynolds' commentary attempted to address this issue. Textually, *London Can Take It* was hard-hitting in its narrative of destruction and death. However, Jennings and Watt concede to a visual abolition of death and human injury. This appeared to be a wise decision, with the audiences recoiling from any film which was too overt or horrific in this respect. For some, *London Can Take It* had already overstepped the mark, Mass-Observation reporting that individual cinema-goers thought the film was the epitome of 'extreme bad taste' and commenting that it was 'difficult enough these days without being presented with scenes which are unfortunately before us every day of our life'.[142] Other productions, such as *Danny Boy* (1941), had suffered from being 'almost too realistic' in their depictions of the Blitz.[143] Yet, it is testament to the directors' skills as documentarists that they were able to represent London's suffering without dealing visually with its most profound impact. They crafted a reality which their audience could accept and one which fitted the cultural and social norms of the early 1940s. As Tom Harrisson commented, the dead 'as with those who die in the rhythm of ordinary times ... tended indeed to be looked past, to be put aside from continuing concern by those not directly connected'. He continued that, despite the Blitz, 'the extent or frequency of references to death seem remarkably small'. If anything, he observed, 'the normal human capacity to sweep death smartly under the carpet was if anything accentuated by blitzing'.[144] In its attitude to death and in its connection to the public mood, *London Can Take It* at the same time could capitalize on the popular obsession with the Blitz in the winter of 1940, the 'principal topic of conversation',[145] and could give it a visual identity, if a manufactured one.

In *London Can Take It*, public interest, meaningful representation of everyday experience and poetic expression collided, making the film an overwhelming popular success. Jennings was confident that the film would be well-received abroad as well as in the United Kingdom.[146] Careful not to alienate other sections of the British population, the concept of *London Can*

Take It was broadened for general and foreign release to *Britain Can Take It*, tying the effort of the regions to the wider conflict, the MoI pointing out that the film was 'representative of what is happening in every other British city and town, where resistance to intense aerial attack and powers of endurance are every bit as heroic'.[147] The film was considered to be particularly suitable for distribution in the 'neutral' United States of America, attested to by the choice of American war correspondents for the commentary. Initially, Watt had favoured Helen Kirkpatrick for the role, finally settling for Quentin Reynolds,[148] despite being deeply 'unimpressed' by the fact that he 'refused to leave the basement of the Savoy to report on the night raids' and the problems caused by his 'booming voice' and his lack of experience with the microphone.[149] Distributed by Warner Brothers, it was 'anticipated that the film [would] be shown in at least 15,000 American cinemas'.[150] Indeed, *Documentary News Letter* confirmed that *London Can Take It* had been a 'sensational ... success' in the United States,[151] a claim backed up by the box-office receipts which amounted to £11,180 by 13 March 1943.[152] Cull has claimed that the film 'opened the way for further British films'[153] in the United States, including *Christmas Under Fire*, '[revolutionising] British film propaganda in the U.S.'.[154] However, although the film was proclaimed an export success, just how valuable the film was as propaganda abroad was open to debate. John Grierson, writing from his base in Canada, had some doubts. Although he offered praise of the film as home front propaganda,[155] he contested its efficacy as foreign propaganda. Writing to his friend Sir Stephen Tallents in January 1941, Grierson 'thought its secondary effect wrong', arguing that 'once people had enjoyed the luxury of so much sympathy', American audiences 'felt they had discharged their duty'. He noted that 'sympathy is easy to get: support is more hardly won and can only be got by a tougher approach altogether', adding that 'in *London Can Take It*, there was the background suggestion of the old gentleman dying with dignity in the Horatian style, "Through the skies fall"'. Grierson contrasted this approach to 'the German war records', such as the films of Bertram, Maisch and Ritter, which were 'full of youth and going places ... certain of the future'. Highlighting the gulf between images of the period in relation to the bombers and the bombed, he added that this was not

> just a question of putting the light of the future in to their young men's eyes. The attitude is basic. The victory of France doesn't finish with the victory, but with rebuilding broken bridges and restoring things. [The Germans] seem to know the right answers in propaganda because they ask the right questions – in fact the questions so many people all over are asking. It may be a deception, but they work it with some effect on this side. Against the tide, of course one might say that the proportion of confidence in England is not so great as the proportion of sympathy with it. And this is the danger.[156]

For Grierson, from his perspective as 'a poor Scot', 'the "take it" business ... seemed psycho-logically curious for a nation that had known for so long how to hand it out'.[157] The effect of the film, he noted, was 'like a Landseer painting of a noble steer bleeding to death on a Scottish moor, but mutely asking no-one be sorry for it, therefore it is still "Monarch of the Glen"'.[158] Grierson favoured a more aggressive style of blitz propaganda, one which conveyed the status of the 'Monarch of the Glen' without the negative propaganda impacts requiring sympathy and little else. This explains why he thought Harry Watt's *Target for Tonight* (1941) a masterpiece, a film to which we will return.

Despite Grierson's concerns, home propaganda continued throughout 1940 to focus on the subject of the Blitz on British cities, particularly in short films issued by the MoI. Other films produced by the Crown Film Unit complemented *London Can Take It* and highlighted its central themes. *Ordinary People*, directed by J. B. Holmes and Jack Lee and released in 1942 primarily for overseas distribution, was intended to 'show a cross section of London life carrying on normally throughout a working day'.[159] It is clear from the film that the work of the Londoners continues despite the heartless bombing which takes place every night: the milkman delivers his produce as normal, the families who have lost their home clear up the debris calmly and quietly, factory production is maintained, the warden protecting the workers by spotting planes from the roof, and shoppers busily make their way around the stores in the West End. Amongst all of this, every ill and heartache is soothed by a cup of tea, echoing the Home Publicity Division's sentiment that after an air raid 'the most comforting thing ... was to have a cup of tea and get together to talk things over'.[160] Once again, the resilience of the British people was at the forefront of the Blitz propaganda, the film promoting 'the display of neighbourliness, of kindness, of cheerfulness, of uncomplaining suffering that is being given by ordinary people who secure no fame and who have no place in the headlines'.[161]

The subject of neighbourly behaviour during an air raid was the central theme of another short film produced by Strand films under instruction from the MoI, *Neighbours under Fire*, directed by Ralph Bond and released in late 1940. Here, in the world where '*the night brings the bombers*', comfort is found in the fact that '*everyone ... knows everyone else*'. Children forget '*in the warmth of their welcome, the horrors of their experience*'. Buoyed by the support of the church and connected in their Christian beliefs, the community pulls together to overcome the terror of aerial attack. This theme fitted well with the MoI's pronouncement that 'it is vital to show the inter-dependence of the individual and the community', urging 'co-operation between neighbours'.[162] In *Neighbours under Fire*, as in many British blitz films of 1940–2, the hero was the civilian. British film propaganda celebrated the everyman as opposed to the dynamic bravery of the airmen of the Nazi *Fliegerfilme*. The nation looked to the ordinary in search of victory, and it was to be the dedication of the 'people's army' on the home front which was to prove decisive, fighting alongside their comrades in the armed forces. As the scenario for *Ordinary People* stated, 'in this picture you will catch a glimpse of that spirit which is the surest bulwark of Britain against senseless and indiscriminate bombing by the half-civilized Hun. In brief', the film's producers continued, 'in this picture you will see why Hitler cannot win'.[163]

Although there were some problems with persuading cinema-owners to carry the films and the varying popularity of Ministry shorts, it remained one of the most effective mediums for delivering informational or inspirational messages to the British public, as well as one of the most prolific, with 1,400 films produced during the course of the war.[164] In many ways, the short film was perfectly suited to the subject of the Blitz. It allowed the film-maker to convey something of the everyday experience without running the risk of excess, as Mass-Observation recognized in their analysis of *London Can Take It*. In considering short film production relating to the aerial bombardment of British cities, it would be difficult to disagree with Chapman's conclusion that the five-minute films 'were no less important than commercial feature films; they just served a different purpose'. Feature films could convey 'images of national unity' and the long-term justification for war, wrapped up in a fictional story with individualized characterization, whereas the short film had a more practical and immediate purpose 'in putting over the more direct ... and urgent messages ... deemed necessary by the government'.[165] Short films could respond quickly to identifiable issues and tap into popular prevailing opinion. Indeed, the treatment of the Blitz seemed to be far more popular in the short film or documentary production of the war years than the feature length fictional film, as an analysis of two films dealing with this subject, Basil Dearden's *The Bells Go Down* (1943) and Harold French's *Unpublished Story* (1942), demonstrates.

Although, on the whole, MoI short films fulfilled their specific function in bringing key issues to the public's attention, they did not always meet the need for escapism. As one letter to *Picture-goer Weekly* commented, the shorts were 'tolerated with boredom and imitation', complaining that 'they deal with facts everyone is painfully familiar with, as all experience them'. The viewer went to the cinema to escape 'the encircling miseries of war', only to be presented 'with visions of raids, destructions and well-known facts'.[166] Entertainment could be a 'blitz beater'.[167] It was hoped that the MoI could successfully combine escapist entertainment with the higher propagandistic concepts of endurance, freedom and victory in their feature films relating to the Blitz experience, meeting the need to engage audiences in contemporary events whilst at the same time fulfilling their desires for fantasy and diversion. The Films Division recognized that the 'fictional touch is badly needed in our film propaganda'.[168] It was this element of the Blitz films that fictional feature-length studio productions could provide and, ultimately, that audiences sought.

In the midst of the dark days of the 1940s, humour was recognized as a means of lifting the general morale of the population, as well as an appeal to the spirit of the nation. The MoI acknowledged that 'the British capacity for humour in the midst of change and crisis is one of our strongest weapons',[169] and it is unsurprising that film-makers infused the Blitz spirit with comedy and good-natured banter. The public yearned for 'homely everyday humour', Mass-Observation commenting that films containing jokes 'have been almost invariably successful'.[170] As historian Paul Addison pointed out, this form of 'innocent propaganda' was far more likely to have 'the whole nation behind it. Leaving out the pain and the suffering, presenting the people with a cheerful image of themselves was probably the best thing'.[171] This sentiment was particularly fitting for representations of the Blitz. The shelter experience, the constant disruption of everyday life and the deprivation of sleep through incessant air raid warnings was certainly in need of an upbeat treatment. A number of music hall and comedy favourites found themselves in filmic depictions of the Blitz. In *Gert and Daisy's Weekend* (Maclean Rogers, 1941), comic duo and music hall sisters Elsie and Doris Waters were 'mistaken for volunteer escorts for a children's evacuation scheme' and forced into accompanying the children for a weekend in the country home of Lady Plumtree in the village of Little Pipham, an excursion which leaves the protagonists with the thought that 'after their weekend with the evacuees, even the Blitz will be quieter'.[172] Returning to their city home in Bow, which 'blitzed and undaunted carries on',[173] is some relief for Gert and Daisy. Although the storyline is primarily focused on the capture of a notorious jewel thief and the slapstick comedy which ensues, the contemporary *milieu* confirmed the fact that 'Gert and Daisy's pictures [were] topical as well as funny'. Their manager, Francis Baker, commented that through *Gert and Daisy's Weekend*, the public was 'now exercising its laughing facilities for the good of wartime morale over the comediennes' adventures with mischievous evacuee children'.[174]

Another music hall favourite, Tommy Trinder starred in a film which was primarily concerned with the Blitz experience, *The Bells Go Down* directed by Basil Dearden and released in 1943, which follows the fortunes of 'an East End AFS unit made good'.[175] Rather unwittingly Tommy Turk (Trinder) and his more serious sidekick Robert 'Bob' Matthews (Philip Friend), rejected from the army, which as Turk observed had '*come over all exclusive like a West End club*', join the Auxiliary Fire Service. In keeping with his identity as the East End wide-boy, Turk has a rather idealized vision of what life will be like in the AFS, informing Bob that '*I can see us now, climbing through the bombs and the flames, rescuing pretty girls in their nighties. Luverly grub!*' They soon discover that life in the AFS will not be as romantic as they had imagined, with young Ted Robbins (James Mason) in charge, who informs them on their arrival at the AFS station at the local school that '*playtime's over boys!*'

Soon the gravity of the situation hits home for Tommy and the crew, and they realize that training must begin in earnest. Mirroring the militarization of civilian life portrayed in *Quax, der Bruchpilot*, Chief District Officer MacFarlane informs his men that '*it's discipline that makes a good army or a good ship's crew and it's discipline that makes a good fire fighter. You've got to know your equipment inside out. You've got to learn every trick of it. In the light and in the dark. So that when the time comes, you'll know it like a soldier knows his rifle*'. Here, the AFS is transformed into a 'people's army'. Dearden confronts the perceived distinction between civilian and army life in the argument that breaks out in Pa Robbins' pub between some soldiers and Tommy's brigade. Accusing the AFS men of being behind the front lines and pointing to a medal won at Dunkirk, the soldiers laugh at the fire service. For Brookes (William Hartnell), a Spanish Civil War veteran, their mocking behaviour is tolerable as '*our cities are still behind the lines. When someone starts to pin medals on us, it'll mean they've moved right up to the front. It'll mean another Rotterdam, another Warsaw right here in England. They'll call us heroes if it comes to that. I'd rather they went on laughing*'. It is Brookes who delivers the stark reality of aerial warfare, Turk continuing to keep spirits high with his 'unbeatable Cockney spirit'. As the press book for *The Bells Go Down* confirmed, Trinder embodied 'the pluck of the Cockney', his character 'typical of the men whose heroism saved the Capital. With death at their elbow every second of those long nights, a joke was never far from their lips'.[176]

The film bore the hallmarks of popular comedy, its characters a stereotypical cross-section of '*the series of villages*' that make up London where the film is set: Tommy Turk the wise-cracking lovable rogue with his racing dog, Shorthead; Bob Matthews, the devoted husband and father; the authority figure, Chief District Officer MacFarlane (Finlay Currie); the serious and commited servant of the people, Ted Robbins; his glamorous and flirtatious girlfriend, Susie (Meriel Forbes); Bob's wife, Nan (Phillipa Hiatt); Sam (Mervyn Johns), the part-time crook on the run from the police for smuggling Guinness; and the staple tittle-tattling mother-figure in the form of Ma Robbins (Muriel George) and her long-suffering husband (Norman Pierce). However, the film's light tone is rather undermined by the more serious message it delivers in the concluding sequences, set in September 1940:

> with its terrific blitz, when all acquit themselves like heroes and comrades. Bob has to watch his dearly won little home go up in flames while he plays water in the opposite direction on a warehouse: meanwhile Nan has a baby in the middle of a raid. Tommy … dies in a fruitless attempt to save his chief MacFarlane, and even Sam fishes *his* special policeman out of a dock basin on the end of a boat hook. The film ends with the christening of Bob's baby. It is named 'Tommy' after the heroic little kennelman.[177]

It was the death of Tommy that caused the greatest shock and consternation among audiences. Having climbed into the burning hospital to save MacFarlane, the two are stranded on a ledge. Tommy lights up a cigarette, turns to his chief and says: '*Well I reckon that puts us off duty*'. As he does so, a wall collapses, killing them both. Tommy's effort to save MacFarlane was in vain. This was the most problematic aspect of Dearden's film. Although, as Robert Murphy observed, this sequence 'expresses the spirit of community, of pulling together with people one doesn't necessarily like…, it is a shocking moment in a film which until then has been essentially light-hearted and it drains the film of any sentimentality'.[178] Death was not a popular subject in films during the war. If the subject had to be addressed, the public preferred an optimistic representation of the afterlife, Mass-Observation reporting that films 'that showed the dead in heaven and still looking very much the same way they had always been and taking an interest in their loved ones below' were 'pretty certain to be a popular success'. With the Blitz, 'the next world [became] very much more real to everybody' and film, as a means of escape for many, did not need to remind the cinema-goer of the dreary reality that awaited them after the show was over.[179]

In part, it was also the act of killing off an audience favourite in Tommy Trinder that created a problem. The comedian was himself unsure of setting his 'cheery brand of humour … against a dramatic background', first showcased in *The Foreman Went to France* (Charles Frend, 1942). The press book for *The Bells Go Down* confirmed that 'it took a lot of persuasion to get [Trinder] to act in a film of this kind... Tommy preferred laughs without tears'. His role in *The Foreman Went to France* caused him concern: after all, 'he was a music hall star ... with a line in patter which didn't seem to fit into drama. The public expected comedy from him: he didn't want to break faith by doing a "Henry Irving" on them!'[180] Audiences *did* expect comedy from Trinder and consequently the closing sequences of *The Bells Go Down* did not match film-goers' expectations and brought the realities of war back into sharp focus.

The film also suffered from unfavourable comparison with another work released at the same time, Humphrey Jennings' *Fires Were Started*. In the publicity for *The Bells Go Down*, Ealing, the producing studio, emphasized the connection between the fictional story line and the reality of the Blitz, commenting that Dearden 'watched keenly as the panorama was being filmed with St. Paul's in the background. Having been among these East Enders for nearly three months to get real life atmosphere for this story of the Blitz and the AFS, he restrained the vendors when the performance became too enthusiastic for reality'.[181] The studio suggested numerous tie-ins to underscore the realism of the film and blur the distinction between fact and fiction. Cinema-owners were encouraged to 'secure the co-operation of your local fire service chiefs', organizing events to emphasize the contemporary

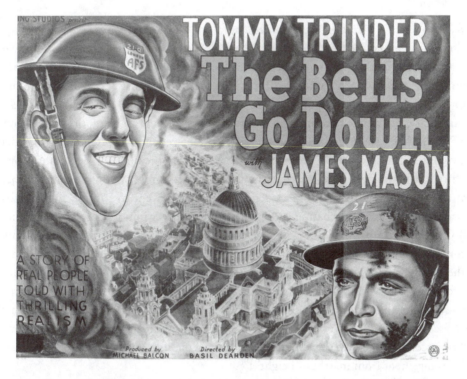

Still 6   *The Bells Go Down*. Promotional poster for 'The Bells Go Down'.
Reproduced by Bfi Stills, Posters and Designs.

connections such as exhibitions in film theatres and local fire stations of actual blitz photo-
graphs alongside stills from the film. Linking in with the story of Bob and Nan, local
newspapers and cinemas were to run firemen's wedding photo contests.[182] Despite this, however, it was the (albeit partially scripted) realism of Jennings' AFS film which triumphed.
The Times commented in April 1943 that:

> *The Bells go Down* is unfortunate in that it so quickly follows the documentary film *Fires
> Were Started*. It is by no means true that a documentary film must, by the very virtue of
> its office, be better than an imaginative reconstruction of events, but here the film which
> was acted by men who were actually in the NFS is superior at nearly every point.[183]

Although the critic found Trinder 'a most amiable and talented comedian', Dearden had
'allowed [Trinder's] personality to get out of hand, and his performance is that of a comedian out on his own – before the footlights and against the back-cloth of a burning city'.
Moreover, *The Times* continued

> his Cockney humour and good spirits are admirable so long as they spring naturally from
> character and circumstance, but there are moments when they are forced and deliberate,
> and the artificiality inherent in them and in a story which depends too much upon
> unconvincing personal relationships cuts a jagged tear across an otherwise commendable
> design.[184]

Here, the contrast with *Fires were Started* could not be more obvious. Jennings' film, according to the film critic for the *Evening News*, 'for three dimensional convictions, integrity
and dramatic intensity, has rarely been equalled'.[185] In its realism, it was proclaimed 'a
stirring piece of British social wartime history that speaks for itself'.[186] Although the film was
scripted, Jennings, by enlisting the NFS to 'star' in the production, had created the feel of a
documentary, the viewer becoming an observer to actual events. Taking the same theme as
The Bells Go Down, Jennings' 1943 production more successfully represented the experience
of a volunteer fire crew. Although the audience found that the film was 'deplorably slow for
the first half-hour', even here the pace embodied the tedium of waiting for the bomber in
contrast to the action of the Blitz sequences.[187] Jennings went to considerable lengths to
recreate realistic scenes, purchasing 100 smoke bombs with a 3-minute duration fuse ignition,
100 C-type smoke bombs, 80 18-inch election spray igniters, 12 practice bombs and 60
2-minute magnesium flares.[188] He requested 6–10 AFS uniforms. Such was the intensity
of the filming that Jennings did not think that they would be 'in a suitable condition for
returning'.[189] He even applied for special permission to film during the evening, informing
the authorities that 'in order to obtain a realistic atmosphere, it is proposed to film this
[blitz] section as late in the evening as possible, that is, as near as may be to blackout time. It
will be necessary to use overhead flares, probably magnesium flares suspended by a "fishing
rod" arrangement from masthead height'.[190]

Naturally, *The Bells Go Down* did not match *Fires Were Started* in terms of its realistic
depiction of the Blitz. However, Murphy has argued that *Fires Were Started* resulted in

an ethereal production despite its emphasis on the real, concluding that 'if Jennings' concentration on the mythological aspect of the war effort gives his film a magic lacking in more mundane efforts, a film like *The Bells Go Down* with its very human, fallible heroes, is a useful reminder that for most people the war was lived on a less exalted level'.[191] In all, the average cinema-goer preferred to see a comedy or a fictional representation which corresponded to their own experiences. Nevertheless, for Trinder, *The Bells Go Down* represented his last foray into the world of the Blitz. After 1943, he re-acquainted himself with his music hall persona starring in Cavalcanti's *Champagne Charlie* in 1944 and *Fiddler's Three* (Harry Watt, 1944), a reworking of his Palladium set, set in ancient Rome. With this, Trinder returned to the roguish identity he crafted in the 1930s, an essentially 'problematic type in wartime because of its emphasis on individualism rather than community values',[192] although this did not pose so much of a dilemma for the studios as the war drew to a close.

If *The Bells Go Down* was the comic representation of the Blitz, then *Unpublished Story* was the sinister one. The film follows the story of two newspaper reporters, Bob Randall (Richard Greene) and Carol Bennett (Valerie Hobson), in their attempt to track down fifth-columnists intent on undermining public morale in the Blitz. Under the cover of a pacifist organization, 'The People for Peace', German agents try to erode the Blitz spirit which manifests itself throughout the film. Again, London forms the backdrop for the action. In a similar sequence to that featured in Dearden's production, *Unpublished Story* uses the images of a blitzed St Paul's to underscore the iconic status of the city and the barbarism of a nation which launches attacks on churches, left standing as a reminder that Christian values will prevail. Here, as in other productions, the city of London offered recognizable symbols around which people could rally and the myth of the Blitz was formed. This acted as a means of positive reinforcement in propagandistic terms, the films reproducing images which had already entered into the public visual memory of the Blitz. The timing was also of significance. Like *The Bells Go Down*, Harold French's production was released after the most intense period of aerial attack on London. These films then performed a different function from 1942. They added to the development of the myth of the Blitz and the London spirit and acted as a form of memorial to the dark days of 1940. Involvement in the Blitz had been 'converted from a thing of terror to a symbol of pride and toughness', and both Dearden and French's film reflect the new found status of blitzed towns, each proclaiming according to Home Intelligence, '"our blitz was worse than yours – and look at us!"'[193] Churchill was keen in the later stages of the war to 'teach people about what happened in 1940, which very few realised completely at the time and which is already beginning to fade in memory'.[194] Through the appeal to the memory of the Blitz, propaganda was to 'stimulate [the] feeling that it is our privilege and honour to make the present age as glorious as our past'.[195] *The Bells Go Down* and *Unpublished Story* functioned as part of a campaign to reinvigorate the population, now under the strain of war-weariness, to convince them of their resilience and sacrifice in 1940-1 and to memorialize the Blitz experience, reminding the public what they

Still 7 *Unpublished Story. French's London Panorama.*
Reproduced with permission of Granada International Media.

were fighting for. The myth of the Blitz, therefore, was a propagandistic construct enacted at an early stage to both cope with the immediate problem of aerial bombardment and to enthuse the population at a later stage in their push for final victory. The Blitz films played an essential role in this process.

In crafting the identification with the audience, as previous film-makers had observed, French was careful to set his story against a realistic backdrop. The number 5 studio at Denham was transformed into a London scene, 'with burning buildings and firemen battling with the flames' in the reconstruction of the Blitzed docklands. *Kinematograph Weekly* commented that 'real flames roared in the wind, while through the billowing smoke begrimed firemen on the tops of escapes directed their hoses into the inferno. Roads and pavements were blocked with debris from the bombed buildings'. AFS men were on hand to give the director advice, 'several of them [involved in] ... fire-fighting in London, Bristol and other blitzed cities during the "black winter"'.[196] The blackout sequences were kept as realistic as possible, *Kinematograph Weekly* noting that 'for the first time on the screen the actual things that one glimpses in a complete blackout will be conveyed, and the sound of voices and footsteps, the flicker of car headlights'.[197] The producers even visited the tube stations to find extras for the shelter sequence, and 'genuine nightly visitors to the underground were selected to re-enact their real life experiences'.[198]

Nevertheless, *Unpublished Story* was intended as much more than a realistic reflection of past events. As *Today's Cinema* noted, 'the terrible and poignant spectacle of London's winter agony of 1940–41 is more than a mere reminder of those nightmare days – it is here made a symbol of the nation united by those famous Churchillian words "we will fight on the beaches ... we shall never surrender"'.[199] The film's producer, Anthony Havelock-Allen, 'was inspired by the Battle of Britain and the events of Dunkirk and the grim months that followed'[200] and was intent on creating a filmic record of 'British courage, told with a certain national pride'.[201] Pointing to the false rhetoric and the futility of pacifism and its use as an agent of enemy propaganda, Havelock-Allen and the film's co-creator Alan MacKinnon forged British courage in the crucible of the Blitz experience with stories of individual heroism and bravery. This functioned on an individual and communal level within the film. Ultimately, this provided a definition of the concept of blitz heroism: the ordinary member of society performing acts of individual heroism combined with a determined community response to aerial attack, characterized by steadfastness and blitz spirit. Ordinary men and women become the heroes of French's film, a fact noticed by *The Times* reviewer who commented that 'the director has imagination enough to be off-handedly matter-of-fact in his treatment' of the 'coolness and courage' of the everyman in the Blitz.[202] By focusing on the heroism of the individual and particularly of the 'everyman', French personalized the Blitz experience, making it accessible to the audience.

Individual heroism was an essential component of the myth of the Blitz, and it was prevalent in the storyline of *Unpublished Story* in the actions of Bob, Carol and, in particular, former pacifist Trapes (Frederick Cooper), who is shot trying to expose fifth-columnists. This is underscored by the publicity for the film, circulated by the film's producers, Two Cities. Cinema-owners were reminded that 'civil defence personnel and civilians have done heroic work; many have been rewarded, but there are a number of "unsung heroes of the Blitz" – people who have performed some heroic action, but for one reason or another have not been recognised'. Cinemas were encouraged to collect the names of heroes in the area and their stories of individual heroism. The press book instructed cinema-owners:

> Tell your patrons that you will give to the twelve heroes selected as having performed the most outstanding deed, season tickets for two persons, available for one month at your theatre. This competition should be run two weeks before you play the picture, and the stories of the deeds should be read out each day during the week previous to the picture being shown... Arrange, if possible, for two 'heroes' to appear on the stage each night during the playing of the picture.[203]

In this way, the positive message of the film was reinforced within the wider publicity for the production, offering the possibility for the film's central meaning to be conveyed in a more personal and direct manner and creating the atmosphere of acceptance prior to the screening of *Unpublished Story*, which in turn added an extra dimension of realism to French's fictional representation.

But heroism in the film did not solely focus on the individual hero. It also suggested that heroism could be found in communities, expressed through unity and spirit. Intended as 'a heroic drama of a nation's finest hour',[204] the film buttressed conceptions of togetherness and resilience in relation to the Blitz experience. This can be seen in one sequence in a public house which has just been bombed, but is open for business, in which the central characters in the film confront an enemy agent:

Agitator: How long do you think we're gonna stick this sort of thing out?

Landlord: We'll stick it alright!

Agitator: You heard what they did to Warsaw. Bombed it flat! Thousands killed. Rotterdam the same. Bombed it flat. Thousands killed.

Bob: It'd take them a heck of a long time to bomb London like that.

Warden: That's what I think.

Agitator: I'm being realistic. It's more than flesh and blood can stand, day after day.

Warden: Shut yer trap! I joined the fire service to dodge the army. But I just found out I gotta do my bit of fightin' too. And funnily enough I don't mind it.

These sentiments are cemented in the concluding sequences of the film, in which the editor of the newspaper, standing in the rubble of the offices blitzed in a night raid which claimed the life of his horoscope writer, a fate he clearly failed to predict, recites his editorial for the following day:

> The people of Britain know that night after night, through autumn and through winter, they must meet the German attack in their own streets. Marshal Göring announces that he strikes at us because we are the heart. Very well, the heart will go on beating. There are loved ones to avenge. There are all our hopes for the future to fight for. There is the most damnable tyranny which has ever threatened mankind to destroy. Knowing this, knowing what we're about, we say bombs will never break us. Panic will never stampede us. Britain will stick it out.

Although there is a strong sense of 'taking it' in the depiction of the Blitz spirit, the narrative of *Unpublished Story* indicates that this attitude was in the process of changing. The editor speaks of 'avenging' loved ones, whilst Bob, who signs up for duty in the RAF, decides that although he has '*applied for the fighters, I think I'll be asked to be transferred to the bombers*'. The style of propaganda had changed from 'tear dropped, job over'.[205] The period of 'taking it' was at an end. It was now the time to give it back.

It became apparent that as early as December 1940 people were 'getting a little tired of the slogan "Britain can Take it"'.[206] The public were 'now more concerned about "giving it"'.[207] Propagandists were aware this theme had been 'overplayed and we must strike a more offensive attitude'. The MoI recognized that 'the time has now come ... when we must change our tune'. This was particularly important in persuasive material sent to the United States. After all, the MoI conceded, 'everybody likes to back a winning horse and the more we can convince America that we are bound to win the more enthusiastic and whole-hearted support we shall receive'.[208] Echoing Grierson's views of *London Can Take It*, the Ministry understood that their blitz propaganda was having a disillusioning effect on the British public, commenting that 'a very large number of people do not expect from themselves much beyond an ability to "take it". They are not alive to the urgent need of fighting back'.[209] This was essential if British forces were to push for victory. There was a growing feeling 'in favour of retaliation and many people talk about retaliation [towards] civilians'.[210] 'Sympathy' was no longer 'enough', and British propaganda had to break out of its cathartic state to produce something that 'made the heart stir, the eyes see, and the muscles move' rather than a 'mere symphony of sadness'.[211] British propaganda had to become more aggressive. The MoI gradually recognized that 'in all our propaganda, we are tending to make one fundamental mistake, that is, we are all the time following the Germans... At the present moment, the only people with a propaganda plan seem to be the Germans ... we are always behind the Germans, who as far as propaganda goes, continually take the initiative'.[212] It became clear that the MoI had to 'learn from Germany that in total warfare the propaganda service is itself a fighting service'.[213] It was in this spirit that Harry Watt produced *Target for Tonight*, which reconstructed a bombing raid on Freihausen.[214]

The film was proclaimed to be 'a milestone in British film making ... the real thing ... actuality – grim, fascinating and engrossing with drama and chuckling humour both as spontaneous and real as the scenes inside Bomber Headquarters'. Released in mid-1941, the only criticism that *Today's Cinema* could offer was that 'this picture [was] not made twelve months ago'.[215] The film finally showed the British 'major striking weapon actually on the job, and [illustrated] the combination of planned efficiency on the ground and team work in the air that makes the Bomber Command of the RAF the most effective striking force in the world'.[216] Unlike the scenes in *The Lion Has Wings*, audiences not only got an indication of the awesome destructive power of the British air force in retaliatory and strategic operations inside Germany, but also an intimate portrait of Bomber Command at work and the personalities of the crew which made the film more personal for the cinema-goer. As the film's producer recognized, 'in the pleasing projection of these fellows' personalities lies 50% of our propaganda value'.[217] Herein lay the essential difference between British and German military propaganda. As Welch observed, the impact of the 'stilted dialogue' of the Nazi 'documentaries of intimidation' was limited when compared to the human touch of films such as *Target For Tonight*, 'where aviators, soldiers and civilians speak frankly about their feelings towards the war and the enemy'.[218] Watt did not discard the traditional apparatus of the aviation film, including some superb aerial sequences of the bomber above the clouds; rather he merged the action of the air war with the careful planning on the ground and highlighted the individual personalities of the pilots, drawing on their diversity (he included pilots and ground staff from England, Scotland and Canada) as an indication of strength rather than disunity. The various personalities and their 'exploits and experiences' are at the same time located 'within the narrative of a general process', with its focus on 'an operation requiring the interdependence of many people – metaphorically at least, situating the individual within the national, exploring the place of the individual within the nation'.[219]

The contrast with German propaganda relating to aerial attack could not have been more apparent. As Graham Greene observed, 'everything is natural; there is none of the bombastic language, the bragging and the threats that characterise the German film *Baptism of Fire*. What we see is no more than a technical exercise'. The response to Bertram's film had finally been delivered, argued William Whitebait in *The New Statesman*: 'Harry Watt's film is an answer. It has come pat on time'.[220] In producing *Target for Tonight*, British film propagandists could at last show themselves 'aware of the demands of the people in this country and of our friends in America and other parts of the world for a film which gives the war from our side'.[221] It appeared that the realism of Watt's film had triumphed over the over-inflated dialogue and propagandistic images of Nazi aviation. *Target for Tonight* was testament to the British 'flair' for 'understatement'.[222] But it was also a film which broke the one-sided discourse of 'taking it' and responded to the public need to 'give it back'. British propagandists began to understand the call for a response to Nazi propaganda. The services constructed their own film units to capture the war and reply to Goebbels, the War Office seeing the need to 'ensure that British film records should match those issued by the Germans ... and [try] to provide an answer [to] them'.[223] The British had recognized that a far more aggressive approach, albeit one which reflected democratic sensibilities, was needed to defeat the propaganda machine of the RMVP.

CONCLUSIONS

By mid-1940, it was clear that Britain and Germany were on quite different military trajectories. In the ascendancy across Europe and with the fall of France in June 1940, the *Luftwaffe* turned its might on the British Isles. Filmic representations of the battle that ensued responded to two very difference experiences of the 'black winter' of 1940–1, creating two very different conceptions of heroism. On the one hand, the *Fliegerfilme* of Maisch, Bertram and Ritter conceived of the German aviator as an idealized type, one set apart from the everyman and one who sublimated his identity for the greater good, working towards authority and losing his individualism to the ethereal concept of *Kameradschaft*. The individual was essentially meaningless, the ultimate expression of which could be found in the discourses of death presented within *D III 88*, *Kampfgeschwader Lützow* and *Stukas*. The British hero of the Blitz on the other hand was characterized by his identity and demonstrated that ordinary people were the heroes of the war, their individualism at the centre of their bravery and courage. Everyone could be a hero, even if they were essentially flawed characters, Tommy Turk and Sam the Guinness smuggler in *The Bells Go Down* being the ultimate examples. Moreover, heroism in British films was able to function on multiple levels, from individual acts of bravery to the communal courage of spirit expressed in the resistance to Nazi terror tactics. Here, attitude mattered as much as action. Victory, argued the Blitz films, could be founded in defiance and resilience. However, British propagandists recognized that this was not enough. The attitude that 'Britain Can Take It' was not only creating a general attitude that this was sufficient to win the war, but was gradually giving rise to a growing feeling of resentment and the desire for retribution. Harry Watt's *Target for Tonight* was publicly praised for demonstrating that Britain was on the offensive, not just militarily but in terms of propaganda. For just as the Germans had begun to recognize that blitzkrieg would not bring about the speedy victory they had hoped for and raids on their cities became more frequent, the British began to feel the 'turning of the tide' and changed their propaganda accordingly. Grierson recognized that 'if propaganda shows a way by which we can strengthen our conviction and affirm it more aggressively against the threat of an inferior concept of life, we must use it to the full or we shall be robbing the forces of democracy of a vital weapon for its own security and survival'.[224] British and German film propaganda did and had to adapt to changing circumstances and it was in this response to the needs of their audience that they found their greatest successes.

NOTES

1. Von Platen cited in W. J. Fanning Jr, 'The Origin of the Term "Blitzkrieg": Another View', *The Journal of Military History*, vol. 61, no. 2 (April 1997), pp. 283–302, here p. 288.
2. See W. J. Fanning Jr, 'The Origin of the Term "Blitzkrieg": Another View'.
3. Leslie Halliwell quoted in M. Paris, *From the Wright Brothers to Top Gun. Aviation, Nationalism and Popular Cinema* (Manchester University Press, 1995), p. 106.
4. Ibid.
5. M-O A: FR 253, 'A Report from Mass-Observation on Air Raids', July 1940, p. 2.
6. 'Front und Heimat', *Filmwelt*, 31 May 1940.
7. A popular term for the air-raid sirens. Cited in H. L. Mencken, 'War Words in England', *American Speech*, vol. 19, no. 1 (February 1944), pp. 3–15, here p. 12.
8. GP: G2:17, J. Grierson, 'Propaganda and Education', 15 November 1943.
9. Dilys Powell, Tribute to Anthony Asquith, Microjacket (Anthony Asquith), Bfi library, London.
10. Quoted in R. J. Overy, 'Hitler and Air Strategy', *Journal of Contemporary History*, vol. 15, no. 3 (July 1980), pp. 405–21, here p. 407.
11. At a regional level, see for example IWM FDC Unidentified and uncatalogued box of materials. SD report of the *Unterabschnitt-Leipzig* (Oschatz), II 225 Tgb. 3/40 Wa. 1 February 1940.
12. BArch NS 29/775, Albert Speer Collection, SD-Abschnitte und Unterabschnitte, Leipzig, 15 May 1940.
13. SD report, no. 89, 20 May 1940, in H. Boberach (ed.), *Meldungen*, vol. 4, p. 1151.
14. IWM FDC Unidentified and uncatalogued box of materials. SD report of the *Unterabschnitt-Leipzig* (Oschatz), II+225 Tgb. Nr. 3/40 Wa., 10 September 1940.
15. 'Kameradschaft Frontflieger', *Filmwelt*, 22 November 1940.
16. See for example, H. Hoffmann, *The Triumph of Propaganda. Film and National Socialism, 1933–45*, trans. J. A. Broadwin and V. R. Berghahn (Berghahn, Providence, RI, 1997), p. 108.
17. SDK 323 *D III 88*, Press book, p. 7.
18. S. Hake, *Popular Cinema in the Third Reich*, p. 75.
19. Cited in S. Hake, *Popular Cinema in the Third Reich*, p. 75.
20. J. Petley, *Capital and Culture*, p. 95.
21. Ibid., p. 98.
22. Commenting on *Legion Condor* which he viewed after the film had been cancelled, Goebbels praised Ritter for his 'direct' and 'primitive' approach to war films. E. Fröhlich (ed.), *Die Tagebücher von Joseph Goebbels. Sämtliche Fragmente*, vol. 4, diary entry for 11 March 1940, p. 69.
23. K. Kreimeier, *The Ufa Story. A History of Germany's Greatest Film Company* (University of California Press, Berkeley, 1996), p. 304.
24. D. Welch, *Propaganda and the German Cinema*, pp. 173–4.
25. J. Sywottek, *Mobilmachung für den totalen Krieg. Die Propagandistische Vorbereitung der deutschen Bevölkerung auf den Zweiten Weltkrieg* (Westdeutscher Verlag, Opladen, 1976), p. 170.

26. SDK Berlin, 323 *D III 88*, press book, p. 3.
27. SDK Berlin, 323 *D III 88*, Dr. Möhrke 'Weltkriegssoldat und Künstler Herbert Maisch der Regisseur von *D III 88*', in the press book, p. 3.
28. SDK Berlin, 323 *D III 88*, Lutz Heine 'Luftwaffe – im Spielfilm erlebt', in the press book, p. 13.
29. J. Sywottek, *Mobilmachung für den totalen Krieg*, p. 170.
30. SDK Berlin, 323 *D III 88*, Dr. Siska 'In der Hauptrolle: die Luftwaffe! Zum Film von der Deutschen Luftwaffe "D III 88"', p. 7.
31. SDK Berlin, 323 clippings 'Filme, die wir sahen: *D III 88*'.
32. Ibid.
33. Ibid.
34. Ibid.
35. Quoted in J. Sywottek, *Mobilmachung für den totalen Krieg*, p. 170.
36. SDK Berlin, 323 clippings 'Filme, die wir sahen: *D III 88*'.
37. Ibid.
38. SD report, no. 24, 4 December 1939, in H. Boberach (ed.), *Meldungen*, vol. 4, p. 527.
39. SDK Berlin, 3709 *Kampfgeschwader Lützow*, clippings: '*Kampfgeschwader Lützow*: Zur Berliner Uraufführung des großen Fliegerfilms', February 1941.
40. SDK Berlin, 3709 *Kampfgeschwader Lützow*, press book, p. 2.
41. Ibid., p. 1.
42. SDK Berlin, 3709 *Kampfgeschwader Lützow*, clippings, 'Start des *Kampfgeschwader Lützow*: Uraufführung in München und Berlin', 28 February 1941.
43. SDK Berlin, 2673 *Diesel*, original synopsis, *Filmabteilung*, 18 March 1942.
44. SDK Berlin, 3709 *Kampfgeschwader Lützow*, clippings, 'Start des *Kampfgeschwader Lützow*: Uraufführung in München und Berlin', 28 February 1941.
45. Ibid.
46. SDK Berlin, 3709 *Kampfgeschwader Lützow*, press book, p.1.
47. SDK Berlin, 3709 *Kampfgeschwader Lützow*, clippings, 'Start des *Kampfgeschwader Lützow*: Uraufführung in München und Berlin', 28 February 1941.
48. K. Kirste, 'Fliegen furs Vaterland – Tod und Patriotismus – eine interkulturelle Perspektive', in H. Kräh (ed.), *Geschichte(n) NS-Film – NS Spuren heute* (Ludwig, Kiel, 2000), pp. 75–96, here p. 95.
49. SDK Berlin, 3709 *Kampfgeschwader Lützow*, clippings: '*Kampfgeschwader Lützow*: Zur Berliner Uraufführung des großen Fliegerfilms', February 1941.
50. 'Kampfgeschwader Lützow', *Filmwelt*, 4 October 1940.
51. S. Hake, *Popular Cinema of the Third Reich*, p. 89.
52. S. Lowry, 'Heinz Rühmann – the Archetypal German' in T. Bergfelder, E. Carter, and D. Göktürk, (eds), *The German Cinema Book* (Bfi, London, 2002), pp. 81–90, here p. 84.
53. S. Hake, *Popular Cinema of the Third Reich*, pp. 93–4.
54. G. Ball and E. Spiess, *Heinz Rühmann und seine Filme* (Goldman, Munich, 1982), p. 107.
55. SDK Berlin, 2041 *Quax, der Bruchpilot*, Clipping from *Der Adler*, n.d. 'Ein neuer Film der Terra: "Rühmann macht Bruch"'.
56. Terra film advertisement, *Film-Kurier*, 6 February 1941, quoted in S. Hake, *Popular Cinema in the Third Reich*, p. 105.
57. S. Hake, *Popular Cinema in the Third Reich*, p. 93.
58. S. Lowry, 'Heinz Rühmann', p. 84.
59. J. Baird, *To Die for Germany. Heroes in the Nazi Pantheon* (Indiana University Press, Bloomington, 1990), p. 202.
60. Ibid.

61. Hitler in Reichspropagandaleitung/Hauptamt Kultur, *Die Heldenehrungsfeier der NSDAP* (Berlin, 1942), quoted in J. Baird, *To Die For Germany*, p. 202.

62. SDK Berlin, 3709 *Kampfgeschwader Lützow*, press book, p. 1.

63. SDK Berlin, 3709 *Kampfgeschwader Lützow*, press book, *Textvorschläge*.

64. H. Hoffmann, *The Triumph of Propaganda*, p. 155.

65. F. Hippler, 'Der Tod in Kunst und Film', *Der deutsche Film*, vol. 6, no. 6/7 (1941). Quoted in H. Hoffmann, *The Triumph of Propaganda*, pp. 155–6.

66. Also quoted in K. Kirste, 'Fliegen fürs Vaterland', p. 89. See also textual analysis of this speech in this essay.

67. Ibid.

68. J. Baird, *To Die For Germany*, p. 208.

69. 'Der Führer am Heldengedenktag 1940', Berlin, in Reichspropagandaleitung/Hauptamt Kultur, *Die Heldenehrungsfeier der NSDAP* (Berlin, 1942), quoted in J. Baird, *To Die For Germany*, p. 208.

70. Ibid.

71. SDK Berlin, 3709 *Kampfgeschwader Lützow*, clippings, 'Start des *Kampfgeschwader Lützow*: Uraufführung in München und Berlin', 28 February 1941.

72. E. Fröhlich (ed.), *Die Tagebücher von Joseph Goebbels. Sämtliche Fragmente*, Vol. 4, diary entry for 14 February 1941, p. 504.

73. Ibid., diary entry for 1 March 1941, p. 521.

74. Ibid.

75. BArch R 55/663, Reichsfilmintendant to Goebbels, 15 November 1944.

76. SDK Berlin, 3709 *Kampfgeschwader Lützow*, press book, p. 2.

77. S. Hake, *Popular Cinema of the Third Reich*, p. 71.

78. SDK Berlin, 3709 *Kampfgeschwader Lützow*, press book, advice to theatre-owners.

79. H. Hoffmann, *The Triumph of Propaganda*, p. 105; p. 109.

80. Speech by *Obergebietsführer* Stellrecht quoted in D. Welch, *Propaganda and the German Cinema*, p. 198.

81. W. Donner, *Propaganda und Film im 'Dritten Reich'* (TIP Verlag, Berlin, 1995), p. 104.

82. J. Baird, *To Die for Germany*, p. 196.

83. 'Professor Karl Ritter: "Stukas" Heldenepos der deutschen Luftwaffe', *Filmwelt*, 13 December 1940.

84. Ibid.

85. Ibid.

86. Ritter quoted in W. Donner, *Propaganda und Film*, p. 103.

87. J. Baird, *To Die for Germany*, p. 196.

88. Ibid.

89. I have used Baird's translation of this poem, translated from the original. J. Baird, *To Die for Germany*, p. 197.

90. K. Kreimeier, *The Ufa Story*, p. 307.

91. Ibid.

92. Hilmar Hoffmann quoted in K. Kreimeier, *The Ufa Story*, p. 308.

93. 'Professor Karl Ritter: "Stukas" Heldenepos der deutschen Luftwaffe', *Filmwelt*, 13 December 1940.

94. See K. Kreimeier, *The Ufa Story*, p. 347; M. Paris, *From the Wright Brothers to Top Gun*, p. 152.

95. K. Kirste, 'Fliegen fürs Vaterland', p. 77.

96. SDK Berlin, 6129 *Junge Adler*. Ingeborg Lohse, 'Ein Regisseur der Jugend. Gespräch mit Alfred Weidenmann, dem Regisseur des Ufa-Flms *Junge Adler*', in *Film-Kurier*, 10 March 1944.

97. IWM FDC Unidentified and uncatalogued box of materials. SD report of the *Unterabschnitt-Leipzig*, II 225 Tgb. Nr. 3/40. Wa. Leipzig, 19 November 1940.

98. IWM FDC Unidentified and uncatalogued box of materials. SD report of the *Unterabschnitt-Leipzig* (Oschatz), II 225 Tgb. Nr. 3/40 Wa., 10 July 1940.

99. IWM FDC Unidentified and uncatalogued box of materials. SD report of the *Unterabschnitt-Leipzig* (Oschatz), II 225 Tgb. Nr. 3/40 Wa., 29 August 1940. Emphasis in the original.

100. Ibid.

101. Ibid., 10 October 1940.

102. Ibid., 29 August 1940.

103. Ibid., 10 September 1940.

104. D. Welch, *Propaganda and the German Cinema*, p. 182.

105. M. Smith, *Britain and 1940. History, Myth and Popular Memory* (Routledge, London, 2000), p. 71.

106. Ibid., p. 70.

107. M. Connelly, *We Can Take It! Britain and the Memory of the Second World War* (Pearson, Harlow, 2004), p. 131.

108. M-O A: FR 886, 'Civilian Attitudes to the Navy compared with the R.A.F. and the Army', 30 September 1941.

109. M-O A: FR 1253–4, 'Air Superiority', 11 May 1942. Mass-Observation reported that 'most of the few outstanding war books so far are by or about the RAF'.

110. Bfi Special Collections, British Board of Film Censors (Hereafter BBFC) film scenarios, 1944, 91a, *The World Owes Me a Living* (British National Films), 4 August 1944.

111. TNA PRO HO 199/435, Home Intelligence to the MoI, public reaction to air force news, 23 July 1940.

112. M-O A: FR 394, 'Mass-Observation Film Work', L.E. 10 September 1940.

113. *Today's Cinema*, 1 January 1941, p. 14.

114. *Today's Cinema*, 5 October 1940, p. 1.

115. *Kinematograph Weekly*, 27 June 1940.

116. Ibid.

117. TNA PRO HO 199/434, MoI Home Publicity Division Regional Circular No. 12 'Hints for Preventing or allaying panic in air-raids', John Hilton, Director of Home Publicity, 20 September 1939.

118. M-O A: FR 253, 'Report from Mass-Observation on Air Raids', 5 July 1940.

119. M-O A: FR 313, 'Civilians in Air Raids', Tom Harrisson writing for *Picture Post* 1 August 1940.

120. M-O A: FR 253, 'Report from Mass-Observation on Air Raids', 5 July 1940.

121. TNA PRO INF 1/292, Home Intelligence Weekly Report, no. 9 25 November – 4 December 1940.

122. TNA PRO INF 1/251, Ministry of Information theme for propaganda, HP 852/33, 13 September 1941.

123. Winston S. Churchill Papers, Chartwell Collection, Churchill College Cambridge (hereafter Churchill Papers). CHAR 20/13 Churchill to the MoI, 26 June 1940.

124. M-O A: FR 313, 'Civilians in Air Raids', Tom Harrisson writing for *Picture Post*, 1 August 1940. For an extended discussion of civilian morale in the Blitz, see R. Mackay, *Half the Battle. Civilian Morale in Britain during the Second World War* (Manchester University Press, Manchester and New York, 2002), pp. 68–87.

125. TNA PRO HO 199/434, Crutchley to Lady Grigg, 13 December 1939.

126. TNA PRO INF 1/849, 'Memorandum for the Ministry of Information', Committee of Directors of Public Relations of the Civil Defence Executive Sub-Committee, 13 January 1941.

127. M-O A: FR 491, 'Battle for Britain' (not made), L.E., 13 November 1940.

128. For example, see Bfi Special Collections, BBFC scenarios, 1945, 64, *Here Comes the Sun* (John Baxter Productions Ltd,), 27 March 1945.

129. M-O A: FR 313, 'Civilians in Air Raids', Tom Harrisson writing for *Picture Post*, 1 August, 1940.

130. M-O A: FR 491, 'Battle for Britain', (not made), L.E., 13 November 1940.

131. Ibid.

132. *Today's Cinema*, 1 January 1941, p. 14.

133. M-O A: FR 491, from report on 'Battle for Britain', (not made), L.E., 13 November 1940.

134. GP G2:17, 'Propaganda and Education', 15 November 1943

135. TNA PRO INF 5/73, *London Front/London Can Take It*, film scenario, 1940.

136. Bfi Special Collections Humphrey Jennings Collection, Jennings to his wife, Cicely, 21 September 1940. Also reproduced in K. Jackson (ed.), *The Humphrey Jennings Film Reader* (Carcanet, Manchester, 1993), p. 7.

137. Ibid., 20 October 1940. K. Jackson (ed.), *The Humphrey Jennings Film Reader*, p. 8.

138. M-O A: TC 17/8/1, Len England, observing at the Gaumont, Streatham, 23 October 1940.

139. M-O A: TC 17/8/1, Len England, 25 October 1940.

140. M. Smith, *Britain and 1940*, p. 71.

141. TNA PRO HO 199/436, Special Report by Home Intelligence, 'Air raids: reactions and suggestions', July–August 1940.

142. M-O A: TC 17/5/A, Letters to *Picture-goer Weekly*, Len England, 13 January 1941.

143. *Monthly Film Bulletin*, vol. 8, no. 89, 31 May 1941, p. 55.

144. T. Harrisson, *Living through the Blitz*, pp. 98–9.

145. M-O A: FR 313, 'Civilians in Air Raids', Tom Harrisson writing for *Picture Post*, 1 August 1940.

146. Bfi Special Collections Humphrey Jennings Collection, Jennings to his wife, Cicely, 3 November 1940. Also reproduced in K. Jackson (ed.), *The Humphrey Jennings Film Reader*, p. 8.

147. TNA PRO INF 6/328, '*London Can Take It*', 1940.

148. IWMS 5367/5, interview with Harry Watt, October 1981.

149. N. Cull, *Selling War*, p. 107.

150. TNA PRO INF 6/328 '*London Can Take It*', 1940.

151. *Documentary News Letter*, August 1941, p. 144. The film was also screened to raise funds for the 'Refugees of England'. See *The New York Times*, 14 November 1940, p. 27. For reviews, see *The New York Times*, 24 October 1940, p. 30 and *The New York Times*, 27 November 1940, p. 133.

152. TNA PRO INF 1/58, Crown Film Unit film receipts from distribution up to 13 March 1943.

153. N. Cull, *Selling War*, p. 108.

154. Ibid., p. 139.

155. GP 4:20:6, John Grierson, 'Relations of the Government to the Film Industry in Time of War', an address to the National Board of Review, New York, 13 November 1942. Also available in the Library of the Academy of Motion Picture Arts and Sciences.

156. GP 4:25:2, Grierson to Tallents, 9 January 1941.

157. GP G4: N13, Grierson, 'A letter from England', c. 1941.

158. GP 4:26:20, Grierson to Elton, 1941.

159. TNA PRO INF 5/76, '*Ordinary People/London Carries on*: production of film', c.1940–1.

160. TNA PRO INF 1/316, Home Publicity Division minutes, 1 September 1939, as quoted in I. McLaine, *Ministry of Morale*, p. 27.

161. TNA PRO INF 6/330, '*Ordinary People* (wartime Londoners)', 1941.

162. TNA PRO INF 1/533, 'Propaganda on the Home Front', 27 May 1940.

163. TNA PRO INF 6/330, '*Ordinary People* (wartime Londoners)', 1941.

164. For an extended and superb analysis of MoI short film production, see J. Chapman, *The British at War*, esp. pp. 86–113.

165. Ibid., p. 113.

166. M-O A: TC 17/5/B, Letters to *Picturegoer Weekly*, 'British Films', n.d.

167. *Kinematograph Weekly,* 24 October 1940, p. 3.

168. TNA PRO INF 1/462, Mr Gates to Beddington, 19 February 1942.

169. TNA PRO INF 1/251, Ministry of Information theme for propaganda, HP 852/33, 13 September 1941.

170. M-O A: TC 17/8/B, 'Report on Audience Responses to MoI Short Films', Len England, 10 October 1940.

171. Paul Addison, quoted in 'George Formby Wins the War', *Times Higher Education Supplement*, 20 July 1973. In Bfi subject file, 'World War II and Film'.

172. Bfi, *Gert and Daisy's Weekend,* press book.

173. Ibid.

174. *Kinematograph Weekly*, 8 January 1942. Also quoted in R. Murphy, *Realism and Tinsel. Cinema and Society in Britain, 1939–1948* (Routledge, London, 1989), pp. 17–18.

175. *Monthly Film Bulletin*, vol. 10, no. 112, April 1943, p. 37.

176. Bfi, *The Bells Go Down*, press book.

177. Ibid.

178. R. Murphy, *Realism and Tinsel*, p. 41; see also A. Higson, *Waving the Flag*, p. 269.

179. M-O A: FR 2190, 'The Spiritual Trend in Films', 4 December 1942.

180. Bfi, *The Bells Go Down,* press book.

181. Ibid.

182. Ibid.

183. *The Times*, 15 April 1943, p. 6. Also quoted in J. Chapman, *The British at War*, pp. 177–8 and A. Aldgate and J. Richards, *Britain Can Take It*, pp. 240–1.

184. Ibid.

185. TNA PRO INF 6/985, A. Jympson-Hermon to Jennings, 4 December 1942.

186. TNA PRO INF 6/985, Introduction to the press book, quotation from the *London Daily Herald*.

187. TNA PRO INF 1/212, J.A. Bardsley Publicity Manager to Mr. Jarratt on screening in Preston, 5–7 December 1942.

188. TNA PRO INF 5/88, order of 7 January 1942.

189. Ibid.

190. TNA PRO INF 5/88, Hudson (Crown Film Unit) to the Chief of Fire Staff, Home Office, 11 February 1942.

191. R. Murphy, *Realism and Tinsel*, p. 40.

192. A. Spicer, *Typical Men: The Representation of Masculinity in Popular British Cinema* (I. B. Tauris, London, 2002), p. 17.

193. TNA PRO INF 1/292, Stephen Taylor, Home Intelligence, 'Home Morale and Public Opinion', a review of HI weekly reports, 1 October 1941.

194. Churchill Papers, CHAR 20/104, Churchill to Bracken, 19 July 1943.

195. TNA PRO INF 1/533, 'Propaganda on the Home Front', 27 May 1940.

196. *Kinematograph Weekly*, 21 August 1941, p. 26.

197. Ibid., 4 September 1941, p. 15.

198. Bfi, *Unpublished Story*, press book. For American coverage on how British studios coped with the Blitz, see *The New York Times*, 11 May 1941, p. SM15.

199. *Today's Cinema*, 27 March 1942, p. 23.

200. *Kinematograph Weekly*, 23 October 1941, p. 37.

201. *Today's Cinema*, 27 March 1942, p. 23.

202. *The Times*, 5 June 1942, p. 6.
203. Bfi, *Unpublished Story*, press book.
204. Ibid.
205. GP 4:26:20, Grierson to Arthur Elton, 1941.
206. TNA PRO INF 1/292, Home Intelligence Weekly Report, no. 11, 11–18 December 1940.
207. TNA PRO INF 1/292, Home Intelligence Weekly Report, no. 12, 18–24 December 1940.
208. TNA PRO INF 1/849, 'Publicity on America', 19 March 1941.
209. TNA PRO INF 1/849, 'Memorandum for the Ministry of Information', Committee of Directors of Public Relations of the Civil Defence Executive Sub-Committee, 13 January 1941.
210. TNA PRO HO 199/436, Special Report by Home Intelligence, 'Air raids: reactions and suggestions', July–August 1940.
211. GP 4:21:1, Grierson, 'Talking of Propaganda', n.d.
212. TNA PRO INF 1/533, J. Rodgers to Monckton, 24 May 1940.
213. TNA PRO INF 1/849, Draft Cabinet papers for discussion at the Policy Committee, 7 October 1940.
214. For a full and comprehensive analysis of this film, see K.R.M. Short, 'RAF Bomber Command's *Target for Tonight* – 1941 – UK Royal Air Force; documentary film', *Historical Journal of Film, Radio and Television*, vol. 17, no. 2 (June 1997), pp. 181–218.
215. *Today's Cinema*, 25 July 1941, p. 5.
216. TNA PRO INF 1/210, film scenario, 1941.
217. TNA PRO INF 1/210, Ian Dalrymple to Mr Mercier, 1 May 1941.
218. D. Welch, *Propaganda and the German Cinema*, pp. 181–2.
219. A. Higson, *Waving the Flag*, p. 208.
220. Greene and Whitebait quoted in K. R. M. Short, 'RAF Bomber Command', p. 192.
221. *The Times*, 2 July 1941. Quoted in K. R. M. Short, 'RAF Bomber Command', p. 192.
222. Roger Manvell, *Film*, 1st edn (Penguin, Harmondsworth, 1944), p. 97. Quoted in A. Higson, *Waving the Flag*, p. 210.
223. *Today's Cinema*, 2 December 1941, p. 1.
224. GP 4:2, 'Propaganda on the Offensive', n.d.

Hitler is no accident. He is the natural and continuous product of a breed which from the dawn of history has been predatory and bellicose… [The Germans are a] race of hooligans which is a curse to the whole world.

Sir Robert Vansittart, *Black Record*, 1941[1]

The English are firmly convinced that God is an Englishman. In their character mélange of brutality, mendacity, sham piety and sanctimonious Godliness, they are the Jews among the Aryan race.

Joseph Goebbels, *Das Reich*, 1940[2]

In any conflict, a primary task of the propagandist is to identify the enemy publicly thus creating a target for anger and blame and, potentially, crystallizing the nation in its focus and support for a just war. The often personalized nature of the representation of the 'enemy' in such associated propaganda continues to be potentially more effective than the dissemination of vaguer public concepts of nation or ideology and is able to give a real and meaningful focus to the war effort in tune with the primordial instincts of man. The image of the enemy intersects and complements many other aspects of war propaganda such that, as well as seeking to justify conflict, it must also provide explanation for suffering and loss and convince the population of ultimate victory. But it is also a form of propaganda *sui generis* which functions on four levels within the model of the defensive war, as most modern conflicts have been *perceived* to be: 'the mirror image, the coexistence of contradicting qualities, the dynamic nature of the image of the enemy and the need to dehumanise it'.[3] The propagandist seeks to provide a contrast between the 'heroic' victim and the enemy, portrayed as a mirror-image of the victim, in that positive values, such as innocence, humanity, pacifism, civility, fairness and morality, provide direct comparison with the negative image of the enemy's personification as barbarous, fanatical, cruel, ruthless, Godless and evil. This image can be simultaneously and interchangeably powerful and pitiful, depicting the enemy as a grand conquest or even a pathetic opponent. At the same time, 'enemy' propaganda is also infused with dehumanizing language, providing a philosophical distance and secular piety for the fighting forces, enabling them to carry out their task, and creating the atmosphere in which home populations can find a scapegoat for the ills that war inevitably brings. Fundamentally, then, 'the split of good and bad, holy and evil, and ultimately us and them, lies at the root of modern war', in which 'the enemy becomes the projected object' which in turn 'represents a direct (not symbolic) danger to oneself and one's group'.[4] These generic principles were at the heart of film images of the enemy during World War II in both democratic Britain and Nazi Germany, the unavoidable product of propaganda seeking to vilify the opponent. Although ideological differences remained, the driving forces behind both British and German enemy propaganda were relatively consistent. Both nations sought to place ultimate blame for the conflict upon the other, denigrate the adversary's system of government and avoid targeting the enemy populations directly, opting instead to concentrate on their leaders. For this was a war conducted in an era of interconnected media environments, where, the propagandists hoped, the right appeal to enemy nations could drive a wedge between the state and its fighting and producing people and force a premature end to conflict.

FORMULATING A CONSENSUS OF HATE? BRITISH FILM PROPAGANDA AND THE IMAGE OF THE NAZIS

Germany had been at the centre of the British wartime propaganda campaign from the outset. In determining what was 'at stake' if the British should suffer defeat, the Ministry of Information (MoI) was to inform the public that they stood to lose 'the ideal of a good life which men have created through two thousand years. A life based on equal justice, respect for the individual, family affections and the love of truth'. Their adversary would subject them to 'the justice of the Gestapo, the break up of the family and [a] truth distorted to serve ruthless party ends'. Britain would be unrecognizable, 'permanently disabled' and 'under the thumb of the strongest Continental power', the people of Europe 'enslaved' without 'hope of liberation'. The British people would lose their 'right to live, think, vote, talk and worship God' as they saw fit, and the new 'Satanic' religion would be victorious. It was time for the people to fight for 'justice and decency between man and man, nation and nation'.[5]

However, despite repeated appeals to the nation based around truth, freedom and the higher virtues of democracy, a June 1940 report by the Home Publicity Sub-Committee of the Ministry of Information regretted that the British people, who were 'patient, long-suffering, slow to anger and slower still to hate', were unfortunately 'harbouring little sense of real personal animus against the average German man or woman'.[6] The Committee recommended that the Ministry should conduct what they defined as an 'Anger Campaign' intended to '[heighten] the intensity of personal anger felt by the individual British citizen against the German people and Germany' for the purpose of 'increasing [the] war effort and preparing the British public for every emergency'.[7] They suggested that there were six main pre-existing sources of potential anger in Britain regarding the Germans which the campaign could exploit: anger at the Nazi attitude towards aggressive war, the denunciation of Christian values, the threat to democracy, unethical German military tactics, fear about the fate of Britain if left in Nazi hands, and anger at 'the inherent insanity of a race that seems never to learn better, never to be happy except when it is plunging the world into turmoil'.[8] The report acknowledged that it would be virtually impossible to extend the *types* of anger felt, recommending that the campaign should try to increase the 'intensity' of feeling already harboured by the British public. It had been suggested just two weeks earlier, on 4 June, that the Ministry should attempt to stir up a 'more primitive instinct' in the public.[9] The MoI was intent on reversing the fact that 'a good deal of the war-anger felt by the British people is not at present directed consciously at the Germans', and the campaign was to attempt to create intense reactions among the home population 'in such a way that [the anger would] appear to come quite spontaneously from the people themselves…, growing of its own accord'.[10]

This development signalled that British home propaganda had arguably changed direction due to a perceived crisis in public morale as a result of the retreat from Norway and the evacuation of Dunkirk. In January 1940, the War Cabinet adopted quite a different approach to the portrait of the Germans in home and foreign propaganda. It outlined the general principles guiding the Ministry of Information's wartime propaganda, arguing that a distinction should be drawn between the 'good' and the 'bad' German. 'With the German who accepts the essential principles of [the sanctity of absolute values, of the individual and the family, and of … nations],' Ministers concluded, 'we have no quarrel, but the German nation under its existing rulers does not accept [these values] and until it does so there can be no peace or security for the world'.[11] But by June that year, the situation had changed. The 'Anger Campaign' initiated in that month was designed to appeal to the more primeval instincts of man, targeting the population by class and gender in order to intensify the emotional reaction to Ministry propaganda. It sought to associate a 'healthy anger against a bully with the instinctive urge to hit him hard'. This was to be 'anger in action', a 'total attack',[12] which not only targeted the Nazi government but which also suggested continuities in German behaviour throughout the nation's history. After all, as the MoI stated, 'Germans will be Germans'.[13]

This was a far more aggressive style of propaganda than had been apparent previously and one which echoed contemporary debates. British propagandists gradually came to realize that their output 'should not permanently be on the defensive and often use silence as its principal arm' in response to German accusations at home or abroad.[14] This was a primary criticism of one of the most outspoken advocates of the baseness of the 'German character', Lord Robert Vansittart, Chief Diplomatic Adviser to the Government after 1938. Speaking in the House of Lords, he accused the MoI and the BBC of '[blaming the Germans'] crimes on one clique or even on one man'.[15] By avoiding placing responsibility for Nazi actions on the shoulders of the German population, British propaganda, he argued, had shown its inherent weakness, the product of the 'uncured spirit' of the more liberal elements of the MoI, such as Kenneth Clark.[16]

Clark advocated a more lenient approach to anti-German propaganda, one that did not emphasize the incurable 'German character', on the grounds that 'this attitude … is disastrous from the point of view of propaganda'. Looking to the future, he questioned 'if the Germans are really [incorrigible], what can be the outcome of the war? Are we hoping to exterminate 80 million people or to keep them in continual subjection?' Clark recognized that these were the questions most 'often in the mind of the average thoughtful man' and that they were creating a 'feeling of hopelessness'. In addition, memories of the Great War conditioned the mentality of many, who, if they followed Vansittart's line of argument, were left to believe that this war would merely be the precursor to the next, ultimately 'a depressing and disillusioning' prospect. Clark favoured a contrast between 1914 and 1939, arguing that it was the spectre of Nazism that the British people and their allies were attempting to chase from Europe and not 'the same old hun'.[17]

Clark's views seemed to reflect wider popular opinion, which was much more dynamic than some accounts suggest. Closer analysis points to the fact that public opinion on this issue fluctuated throughout World War II. Public opinion polls and Mass-Observation both emphasized that the public did not *consistently* take an overtly negative view of the Germans, much like the MoI itself, drawing a clear distinction between the German people and their Nazi leadership. In a British Institute of Public Opinion (BIPO) poll of June 1941, 46 per cent of those questioned felt that they were fighting for 'freedom, liberty and democracy', with only 14 per cent stating that it was to 'stop fascism, Hitlerism, Nazism [and] aggression', and fewer still, only 8 per cent, arguing that it was 'Britain V. Germany … it's them or us'.[18] In attempting to track the development of anti-German and anti-Nazi feeling, BIPO asked the public, over a period of four years from 1939 to 1943, whether the chief enemy of Britain was the German people or the Nazi government. In 1939, only 6 per cent held the German people responsible. In the immediate aftermath of the Blitz and the 'Anger Campaign' in 1940, this increased dramatically to 50 per cent. However, by April 1943, this figure fell to 41 per cent, with the majority of popular opinion shifting back to blame the Nazi government.[19]

Nevertheless, qualitative, as opposed to quantitative, sources reveal some significant tensions between popular opinions on the enemy. Home Intelligence reported in May 1942 that there was 'some criticism of the official attitude of hatred to Germany on the score that "England ought to be a civilising influence". [Hatred] might … eventually hamper a … reasonable settlement when the war is over'. The report stated '[a] *minority* view is that "there is not enough hate in this country" and that this is an "all out fight with all out methods"'.[20] Further, in the same year, Mass-Observation asked its observers to analyse British *private*, as opposed to public, opinion of the German people.[21] The report found that 54 per cent of opinion offered was 'pro-German', expressing notions of 'sympathy, not their fault, same as everyone else, not hatred [or] vindictiveness, [expressing no need for] punishment/retribution in any form'.[22] This view was reflected across 1941 and 1942 and looked to be increasingly tolerant towards the German people as the war progressed, despite the extension of war on all fronts and the mounting demands on the home front.[23] The fluctuation in popular opinion correlated with the peaks and troughs of military action and, in particular, the waves of aerial attacks on civilians. As such, opinion did not remain consistent. The effects of the anti-German Anger Campaign, if any, were short lived and limited to a distinct period, notably from August 1940 to May 1942, or appeared in the public consciousness after 1945.[24] The majority of the British public, then, as perceived by the Home Publicity Sub-Committee, were not displaying any significant signs of hatred towards the enemy. If signs of hatred did exist, they tended, on the whole, to be directed at the Nazi leadership, rather than at the German people, Mass-Observation confirming in 1943 that up to 60 per cent of people kept the distinction between Nazis and Germans more or less intact. They reported that the British considered 'in varying degrees that the [German] people have been foolish or misled, but feel that there are extenuating circumstances – that it is not mainly their fault'. Only a fifth to an eighth of those questioned felt any hatred, vindictiveness or need for retribution.[25] Even towns under heavy blitzing maintained a sense of perspective; 'the distinction between the German people and Nazis' was reported to be 'still widely felt [and] often explicit'.[26] British film propaganda focusing on the enemy during World War II was a product of this context, reflecting British public opinion in, for the most part, maintaining the division between the Nazi supporter and the German people. Once again, it is possible to observe a correlation between the popularity of themes in the cinema and public opinion on a given issue.

Immediately prior to the outbreak of war, films with an anti-Nazi theme were strongly discouraged and even banned, in order to avoid causing offence to the Third Reich.[27] A series of high-profile films fell victim to the BBFC's support of Chamberlain's policy of appeasement and consequent prevention of the antagonistic representation of German statesmen or policies.[28] This was aptly demonstrated by their objections to the *March of Time* film, *Inside Nazi Germany* (Jack Glenn, 1938), which was censored in February 1938. Colonel J. C. Hanna, Vice-President of the BBFC, noted of the script that 'the public exhibition of this picture in England would give grave offence to a nation with whom we are on terms of friendship'.[29] Equally, the BBFC declared that the film *Swastika* (1939), with its theme 'mainly concerned with relating the horrors of the Jewish persecution in Germany today', should be 'classed … as unsuitable for exhibition'.[30] *Professor Mamlock* (Adolf Minkin/Gerbert Rappaport, 1938), a powerful story of a Jewish professor persecuted by the Nazis produced in the Soviet Union, was not initially passed by the censor.[31] Despite Mass-Observation's comment that 'before the war not a single film about Germany was made'[32] and the BBFC's stringent policy of censorship, film producers continued to exhibit a topical interest in Nazism. There were indeed films produced with this focus, the most famous being the Boulting Brothers' *Pastor Hall* (1940), a dramatization of Ernst Toller's play focusing on the life of Martin Niemoeller.[33] *Pastor Hall* was submitted to the censor in July 1939 and met with the characteristic response: that the film had to be 'treated the same way as various other subjects which have been submitted to us recently … its exhibition at the present time would be very inexpedient'.[34] Roy Boulting recalled that 'the stench of appeasement was very much in the air' and the censor, 'endorsing Mr. Chamberlain's vain idea that the fascists, Mussolini and Adolf Hitler, could be bought off, said under no circumstances' would the BBFC 'give this film a certificate' if it were made. After Munich, when it became clear that 'Hitler had to be fought and we were going to have to fight him', *Pastor Hall* resumed production. The script was ready, and, now, 'the censor could not have said no'.[35]

In the initial years of the war, the Ministry's plan for film propaganda encouraged the portrayal of 'German ideals and institutions in recent history', urging film-makers to look to the German past, tales of Gestapo atrocities, German blunders and refugee stories for inspiration.[36] Film-makers were informed that the MoI was particularly interested in films which offered a historical reading of the German character, one which dealt with 'the growth of Pan-German ideas from Bismarck onwards'.[37] Despite the promotion of films of this nature through specialized series such as Glasgow's anti-Nazi film week in October 1939,[38] the representation of the enemy in film proved to be increasingly out of favour with the public, leaving film-makers with a crucial dilemma: should they sacrifice profits for propaganda? This was exacerbated by a 1940 Mass-Observation report which stated that, 'films about Nazi Germany are not popular … horror scenes cause disgust among the audience and the usual scenes of marching Germans … only boredom'.[39] They added, one month later, that 'women [in particular] dislike the sight of German troops in any circumstances',[40] a particular problem, as women made up the majority of home-front wartime audiences. Mass-Observation reported that a large number of people 'object to horror shots (e.g. dead bodies, explosions etc)',[41] an attitude confirmed by a letter to *Picture-goer Weekly* from a reader in Glasgow who commented, 'perhaps the Germans are brutal; perhaps they do atrocious things. But films which perpetuate these atrocities, which constantly remind us of them, will only undermine the peace offensive and keep the flame of hatred burning among nations. Let us adopt the good old Christian motto – forgive and forget – especially forget'.[42] The Home Publicity Sub-Committee maintained a policy in line with public opinion in this respect, commenting, in April 1941, that 'sheer horror stuff should be avoided' and that 'images should not be too extreme'. They were concerned that films with a theme of brutality and atrocity could 'arouse as much fear as anger unless very well done',[43] thus underlining the ultimate objective of their 'enemy' propaganda.

This presented a challenge for producers and screenwriters who were instructed by the MoI, at the beginning of the war, to deal with stories involving the Gestapo. The Ministry advised, however, that 'the activities of the Gestapo [should stress], as more easily credible, the sinister rather than the sadistic aspect'.[44] The BBFC, too, were conscious of the impact of horrific scenes on the cinema-going public. In finally agreeing the release of Anthony Asquith's 1940 film about a resistance movement in the Reich, *Freedom Radio*, they warned the film's producers that 'whilst during the war time our rule against the representation of living persons does not extend to enemy nationals, our ordinary standards of not allowing scenes of extreme horror or gross brutality will stand'.[45] Naturally, with their knowledge of the Gestapo and the persecution of Jews and political opponents, propagandists were keen to exploit the horrors of the Third Reich. However, the question of atrocity propaganda was a sensitive one, having been largely discredited in the aftermath of the Great War by the frequent exposés of fallacious stories in the contemporary press. Moreover, the British public did not enjoy scenes of barbarism and horror. In this context, the use of atrocity propaganda had to be handled particularly carefully.

The Boulting brothers, as fervent opponents of Nazism, were keen to highlight the barbarity of the Nazi regime in their 1940 film, *Pastor Hall*, and went to considerable lengths to stress that the production reflected the actual experiences of the German people. *Kinematograph Weekly* emphasized that 'great care has been taken to ensure the authenticity of the material used: for this purpose the Government White Paper on the subject of Nazi concentration camps was used as authority'.[46] The film was said to be 'as authentic as it is possible to achieve', owing to the extensive research conducted by the Boulting brothers.[47] In fact, such was this attention to detail that Mass-Observation reports suggested that *Pastor Hall* may have been a little too realistic in its treatment of Nazi atrocities for the average cinema-goer. In a special screening of the film for the MoI, observers concluded that there should be 'selected cuts to the tortures of the concentration camp. It should be horrifying but not to the point of the members of the audience shutting their eyes as I saw several of them doing', one viewer going as far as to suggest that 'these scenes would be bad for unbalanced individuals and in some the effect might be to compel them to some expression of violence which might take other forms than those desired by the Ministry'.[48] Pre-empting Mass-Observation's later findings, one female viewer expected that the film would 'have the most harmful effect on women's nerves, particularly on the nerves of women with men in the forces who may be taken prisoner by the Germans'.[49] Consequently, many scenes of Nazi brutality were toned down, leading Mass-Observation to comment that representations of German atrocities were highly deceptive and overly optimistic in their outlook. They reported in October 1940 that films depicting the Nazi terror system all 'have some message of hope at the end … escapes are made from concentration camps, which again creates the impression of hope. None of the films [analysed] contain characters who suffer and die unknown'.[50] Moreover, most representations of death were individual and there was no impression that the Nazis were pursuing a policy of genocide or widespread persecution.[51] The mass was consumed by the individual character, thus diluting the real meaning of terror in the Third Reich. This had little to do with the authentic representations of the persecution of the innocent the Boulting brothers wished to convey.

Commentators also expressed concern that horrific scenes set in concentration camps might not export well to neutral nations, such as the United States, as they had the potential to 'create a sense of distance in the native mind and a feeling of "Thank God we emigrated from Europe to a decent country"'.[52] The fear of exposing old wounds was also dominant in the minds of British propagandists, as demonstrated by the MoI's reaction to Korda's visit to the United States whilst promoting *The Lion Has Wings*. It was feared that tales of barbarism in exported films would prompt the 'feeling that it is the old armless-baby-act of the last war being worked all over again'.[53] Although *Pastor Hall* was potentially more popular in the United States than at home, distributed by James Roosevelt through United Artists with Eleanor Roosevelt providing a short introduction for American audiences,[54] British propagandists could not afford to generate the feeling that the experience of the Great War in relation to false atrocity stories was being repeated.

The most obvious and poignant reflection of this policy was the virtual exclusion of the suffering of the Jews from British cinema during World War II. Although in the initial months of the conflict film propagandists were advised to show details of the anti-Jewish pogroms,[55] by 1941 the Home Publicity Sub-Committee were advising propagandists to avoid the Jewish issue altogether. A memorandum of 21 April stated:

> sheer 'horror' stuff such as concentration camp torture stories repel the normal mind. In self-defence, people prefer to think that the victims were specially marked men – and probably a pretty bad lot anyway. A certain amount is needed but it must be used very sparingly and must always deal with the treatment of *indisputably innocent people. Not with violent political opponents. And not with Jews* [but the] ... *ordinary harmless individual.*[56]

That the Jews were mentioned alongside 'violent political opponents' not only reflected Whitehall perceptions in relation to the Jewish question but also anti-Semitism among sections of the British public, commented upon almost weekly in the Home Intelligence Reports commissioned by the Ministry and used to inform propaganda policy, and particularly reflected the fear of encouraging the development of such feeling in the wider public.[57] In addition, there was evidence to suggest that this theme did not play well with either home or foreign audiences. Analysing the impact of *Pastor Hall*, Grierson observed that

> [t]he comment that the Jewish motif is a bit of a bore is ... a great deal more typical than people will officially confess. Jewish maltreatment, concentration camps, sadistic lashings, are, one is afraid, old stuff, alien, slightly discredited and do not somehow command people's attention. This may represent escapism on the part of the American mind. On the other hand, it concerns distant people of whom they know or want to know little. The bond between democratic America and democratic Europe is not intimate enough, nor is this seemingly the way to make it so.[58]

Although the BBFC did not object to representations of the Jewish fate at the hands of the Nazis,[59] few British feature films of the period dealt with the issue of Jewish persecution in any real detail and those that did tended to emerge rather later. *Mr Emmanuel* (Harold French, 1944), produced by Two Cities and adapted from the novel by Louis Golding, focused on the story of an ageing Mr Emmanuel (Felix Aylmer) who vows to a young German refugee in Britain, Bruno, that he will travel to Berlin to find his mother. His treatment at the hands of the Nazis is spotlighted by French, who attempted to give the cinema-goer 'a rare insight into a people and country held in the grip of a regime which led to the present world-shattering events', contrasting 'light and shadow, the peaceful, lovely English countryside standing out against the more subdued atmosphere of Donnington's Magnolia Street [where the film is set], the brittle luxury of Berlin's night resorts and the drama of its sinister prisons'.[60] The film was intended to create a sense of anger among audiences, the US press book offering 'your money back if this picture doesn't make you mad'.[61] United Artists, the distributor, claimed that 'if you're a liberal minded, big-hearted, tolerant American with a true love for your fellow men, then you're going to get mad at the villains in this picture, ... the world villains of hate and prejudice and intolerance'.[62] The theme of vengeance, however, in keeping with popular opinion, was played down in the film. When Bruno, on discovering the fate of this mother, decides to take revenge, Mr Emmanuel gently tells him: '*No Bruno, it must not be* that *way ... it must be another sort of world ... no more hate, or it will be to do all over again...*'.

Although there was some recognition that atrocity stories could potentially 'increase the desire for a retributive peace', convincing the MoI that, by early 1942, it might be time to 'drop the kid-glove methods and stop playing cricket',[63] and that the public were on occasion 'roused from apathy' by reports of Nazi barbarity,[64] it was generally felt that film-goers did not 'want to go [to the cinema] to be more depressed. They go ... to forget the war for an hour or two. They hate horrors because they disturb their night's rest'.[65] This was obviously a complex issue. The film industry was facing pressures from the Ministry to produce films with an anti-German theme for a public who did not want to go to the cinema to see them. Moreover, the representation of Nazis in feature films often produced the opposite effect than that desired by the propagandist, Len England noting that 'the chief Nazi character is [often] portrayed not as a villain but as a good man gone wrong'. Referring to the first state-sponsored feature film of the war, *The Lion Has Wings*, the report continued 'that the Germans look, and were, the same as Englishmen'. This tended to prompt a strong feeling of 'sympathy' in the audience, where the Nazis are 'only misguided' and 'disappointed heroes'.[66] It was a comment which was to be made on a number of occasions, most notably of Michael Powell and Emeric Pressburger's 1941 film, *49th Parallel*.

Aside from the depiction of Nazi barbarism, the main features analysed so far had one thing in common: each featured a 'good German' alongside the evil Nazi. Mr Emmanuel is eventually rescued by Berlin cabaret singer Elsie (Greta Gynt) and Pastor Hall is the epitome of the good German, seeking to undermine the Nazi regime from within. Roy Boulting confirmed that *Pastor Hall* 'for the first time dealt with the Nazis and revealed them in all their infamy but also dealt with the Germans as human beings. They weren't all Nazis'.[67] Audiences noticed that 'the distinction between the German people and the Nazis' in the film 'was well brought out'.[68] However, perhaps the most powerful expression of the contrast between the Germany of the past and present was in the films of Powell and Pressburger both in their distinction between the 'good' and the 'bad' German and in their depiction of the destruction of classical German culture.

Their 1941 film *49th Parallel* tells the story of a group of six Nazis who escape an attack on their U-boat in the Hudson Bay.[69] The film tracks their journey through Canada, across the 49th parallel, to the 'neutral' United States and their encounters with the international community blocking their path. In their epic journey, they have to overcome the Canadians, the British, the Hutterites and the Inuit. As the *Documentary News Letter* commented in November 1941, 'in each encounter, the Nazis get an intellectual and/or physical poke in the snoot'.[70] They are portrayed in the film as being brutal and murderous, destroying all the vestiges of tradition, split by internal divisions and petty rivalries, and devoid of cultural appreciation. Each Nazi character in the film fulfilled a specific image of the enemy. Captain Bernsdorff (Richard George) was to be a man of blood and iron with an inherent belief in the redemptive power of war and the brutality of conflict, his life-philosophy grounded in Bismarck's battle cry that the German warrior should *leave them only their eyes to weep with*. His comrade, Lieutenant Ernst Hirth, was to be played by Eric Portman. Portman was to become familiar with the role of the over-zealous Nazi, his portrayal as Hirth a forerunner to his performance in *Squadron Leader X* (Lance Comfort, 1942).[71] Hirth is blinded by his fanaticism for the National Socialist cause. Powell found Portman's performance as Hirth compelling, the 'deep religious sincerity' of his character 'frightening'. Indeed, Portman's characterization of the obsessive Hirth was thought to be so powerful that 'Raymond Massey [who played soldier Andy Brock] … started a campaign with the other stars of the film to give him co-star billing'.[72] The atomizing nature of Nazism and the selfishness it produced was embodied in the character of Lieutenant Kuhnecke (Raymond Lovell), a failure in civilian life who takes pleasure in the demise of others. His fellow traveller is Vogel (Niall MacGuinness), indoctrinated by the Nazi political creed but who is desperate to reconnect with his inner-self. These characters are complimented by Lohrmann, a brazen opportunist who uses Nazism to forward his own ambitions and selfish aims. Collectively, these six characters represent the criticisms of the ardent Nazi: he is devoted to war, elevating it to a virtue, unquestioning and fanatical to the point where he will no longer listen to the voice of reason, petty, 'no superman, no sinister Nazi but a non-descript, rather pathetic little person',[73] a brainwashed fool, ill-educated in worldly values but well-versed in the evil ideology of Nazism, a 'simple peasant' who knows no better, and an opportunistic fraudster, capitalizing on the pain of others to benefit his own well-being. Although, as Kevin Macdonald observed, the structure of *49th Parallel* was highly schematic, 'the characters … are not stereotyped' and rather diverse.[74] In their depiction of the Nazis, Powell and Pressburger wanted to move away from 'the nostalgia and cosiness of *Goodbye Mr Chips*' and produce a film 'which realistically portrayed the brutality, sadism and proto-religious zeal' that the Third Reich encouraged. Frustrated by the pre-war BBFC rulings, they wanted to give visual expression to Britain's war aims and, 'as someone who had experienced Nazism first hand, Emeric [a Hungarian Jew who fled Germany after the *Machtergreifung*] thought it was his duty to tell it how it was'.[75]

Ultimately, the story functioned by contrasting western democratic views with Nazi authoritarian ideals in each episode, *Documentary News Letter* commenting in May 1942 that 'here was a film with an idea – the personal clash between individual Nazis of different types and a number of representative democrats'.[76] With each encounter, the renegade group is confronted with the antithesis of Nazi ideals: Johnnie Barras (Laurence Olivier), the loyal French Canadian and staunch advocate of royalty and liberty; Peter (Anton Walbrook) the Hutterite leader, the refugee who believes that he can never return to his native Germany for fear of persecution; Philip Armstrong-Scott (Leslie Howard), the intellectual with a love of art and culture, and Andy Brock (Raymond Massey), the 'everyman', the upholder of the right to democracy, who defends it with brute force, if need be. Together they represent a diverse international community united by the will to defeat Nazism. In many ways, *49th Parallel* emerges as the natural product of Clark's memorandum urging propagandists to 'stress the great difference between the Germany of 1914–18 and today by pointing out how in the last war all the best elements of German culture and science were still in Germany and were supporting the German cause, whereas now they are outside Germany and are supporting us'.[77] Two central scenes of *49th Parallel* adhere to the principles outlined by Clark in terms of propaganda content: the encounter with Philip Armstrong-Scott, a scene in which Nazi culture is seen to be base and meaningless and classical culture destroyed by the mindless fanaticism of Nazism, and the meeting of the Hutterite community in which their leader, Peter, denounces the Germany of today in relation to the Germany of the past.

The destructive nature of Nazism and its disregard for culture is emphasized in the scene in which the Nazis encounter the British intellectual Phillip Armstrong-Scott, who welcomes them into his encampment in the Rockies where he is studying the Black Foot tribe. The academic gradually becomes aware that he is entertaining the escaped Nazis after his guests reveal their true colours through their '*arrogance ..., stupidity,* [*and*] *... bad manners*'. Symbolically, in the ensuing conflict, Armstrong-Scott, the lover of the arts and culture, is tied to his bookcase to prevent any resistance. He shows no signs of fear or anger, until Lohrmann and Hirth set about destroying his manuscript, burning his books, and desecrating paintings by Matisse and Picasso. Denouncing his intellectualism and his love of the arts, they burn his paintings and books in a gesture reminiscent of the scenes in Berlin in 1933 and redolent of the MoI's 1941 short film *Battle of the Books* (Jack Chambers). Hirth throws Armstrong-Scott's copy of *The Magic Mountain* by Thomas Mann onto the fire, declaring '*We kicked this swine out of the Reich years ago*'. Menacingly, Lohrmann warns his captive, '*Think yourself lucky we don't burn you too!*' Here, a clear distinction is made between the uncultured Nazi, who finds pleasure in burning great works of art and literature and values weapons and war above all else, and the cultured Europeans and creators of the 'old Germany', echoing the sentiments of Clark. In order to demonstrate the need to protect European civilization physically, the next scene sees Armstrong-Scott resorting to force to defend his principles, turning a writer into a fighter. As the advert for the film stated, 'the kindly, cultured writer' is forced to retaliate against the 'Nazis who have ruined his books and pictures in an insane orgy of destruction'.[78] Capturing Lohrmann, Armstrong-Scott administers a beating. With each blow that he delivers, he declares '*That's for Thomas Mann! That's for Matisse! That's for Picasso! And that's for me!*', concluding: '*one armed superman against one unarmed democrat! I wonder how Dr. Goebbels will explain that!*'

This sequence, although powerful, was felt by some contemporaries to convey a somewhat disheartening message. *Documentary News Letter* was concerned that 'the Englishman is presented as a dilettante', an image which was bound to 'cause a certain amount of heart-burn' and 'play right into the Germans' hands'. Disturbingly, the depiction of the English academic was felt to be reinforcing the US belief that the British were 'soft and decadent'.[79] This reaction was intensified by some of Howard's lines in the film: on describing the hardships of war, he states '*they used to do you a very good lobster thermidor with a red Bordeaux. They still do the lobster but no more red Bordeaux. Nuisance isn't it, the war?*' The image of the effete and pretentious academic is underpinned and juxtaposed by Hirth, who questions '*what could these weaklings ever do to us? ... They're rotten to the core. There's no fight in them. They're soft and degenerate all through*'. In some ways, the development of Leslie Howard's character and his portrayal of the man of letters who is forced to resort to violence to reply to the Nazi thugs was 'a good propaganda stroke in the US'. As *Documentary News Letter* recognized: 'here the trick is to give your audience a picture of someone whom they wrongly think is representative, and turn the tables on them by revealing him as unexpectedly tough'.[80] However, Pressburger was less than impressed with Howard's performance. He was not pleased to arrive on set to find Howard shooting his scenes containing 'an entirely unknown text ... from a bit of paper'. Pressburger's fears for Howard's scenes were realized when he watched the rushes, commenting that there were 'new lines, twisted the wrong way. Lurid and bad'.[81]

The same could not be said of the scenes starring Anton Walbrook as Peter the Hutterite leader. Walbrook was well known as an actor who could successfully convey a sympathetic view of 'foreignness'. Walbrook, another refugee from Europe, had a persona that could easily be adapted to the wartime situation, Andrew Moor arguing that his characters were often used 'to illustrate how generous the Allied rhetoric of tolerant rapprochement is (differentiating it from its opposite, the rabid racism of Hitlerism)' and adding that within the 'hegemonic project of the People's War ... his alien status ... [is] downplayed'.[82] In *49th Parallel*, this is ultimately the function of Walbrook's character, the actor and his role merging to form a meaningful discourse on exile from Germany and the nature of 'Germanness'. On discovering the existence of the Hutterite community in Canada, Pressburger commented that he 'would very much like to see them in the picture',[83] representitative of Clark's view of the distinction between German 'nationals' past and present. Naturally, Pressburger, a native Hungarian, a Jew and an exile, found the storyline involving the Hutterite community particularly personal, his scripts throughout the 1930s and 1940s littered 'with crossed boundaries'.[84] This lies at the heart of Peter the Hutterite's soliloquy in the film in which he draws the distinction between past, present and newly formed German identities, clearly demarcating the 'good' and the 'bad' German:

> You call us Germans. You call us brothers. Yes, most of us are Germans. Our names are German, our tongue is German, our old hand-written books are in German script. But we are not your brothers. Our Germany is dead. However hard this may be for some of us older people, it's a blessing for our children. Our children grow up against new backgrounds, new horizons. And they are free ... You think we hate you. But we don't.

It is against our faith to hate. We only hate the power of evil which is spreading over the world. You and your Hitlerism are like the microbes of some filthy disease, filled with a longing to multiply yourselves until you destroy everything healthy in the world. No, we are not your brothers.

In Peter's speech, the distinction between Germans is distilled into evocative language with a clear propagandistic purpose matching the experiences of both screenwriter and actor. The acceptance of the Canadians is contrasted to the false exclusivity of the Nazis. Hitlerism is seen to have caused an irreparable split in German identities, dividing the decent, Godly and peaceful German and the fanatical warrior of the Reich. This is emphasized by Powell and Pressburger when Vogel, one of the escaped Nazis, vows to stay with the Hutterite community, rejecting Nazism. It was this portrait of Nazis and Germans, this distinction between people and leaders, which found the greatest acceptance from the British public.

Walbrook later extended his role as 'friendly alien', representing his status as a product of his national identity and his rejection of those elements of national identity subverted by the Nazis, in another Powell and Pressburger film, *The Life and Death of Colonel Blimp* (1943). Although the characterization of Peter in *49th Parallel* was showered with critical acclaim, not least from the screenwriter himself who was particularly impressed with Walbrook's blistering critique of Nazism, his later portrayal of Theodore Kretschmar-Schuldorff, the Prussian friend of the eponymous hero, was more controversial. Once again it was the alien's role to bring home the urgency of the fight with Nazism in an awe-inspiring speech, stressing that the methods of the past could not be used to defeat the Third Reich. The press book for the 1943 film illustrates some of the similarities in the depiction of Peter and Theo and the two scenes scripted by Powell and Pressburger, stressing the continuities in their work:

Still 8   *49th Parallel. Peter confronts the Nazis,
surrounded by the Hutterite Community.* Reproduced
with permission of Granada International Media.

People who have seen the film have compared this eloquent speech with the immortal Gettysburg Address … Commencing quietly, Walbrook paces his words slowly, but gradually the consuming depth of his hate for all things Nazi gathers impetus… They gather strength and force, and the listener is carried away on the tide of this man's great personal longing to leave the world of Nazi brutality behind him and take up a new free life in the land that his English wife, now dead, loved so devotedly.[85]

However, film could no longer inspire the hope that the Third Reich would collapse from within, a popular theme in early anti-Nazi cinematic polemics such as *Freedom Radio*.[86] It was clear by 1943 that Nazism would have to be overthrown from without. This tested British sensibilities over the distinction between Germans and Nazis, and it was within this atmosphere that the portrait of the German in feature film was challenged by the establishment. Although Lord Vansittart approved of the script for *The Life and Death of Colonel Blimp*,[87] the War Office, the Ministry of Information and the Prime Minister all raised objections. Powell and Pressburger were accused of showcasing German superiority in numerous scenes, specifically in the depiction of the duel between Clive Candy ('Blimp', Roger Livesey) and Walbrook's Theo and in the prisoner-of-war camp where German soldiers demonstrated their 'superior psychological position – their love of music and their refusal to fraternise with the British'.[88] Theo, they argued, was 'the most fully realised character in the film', appearing 'to have a wisdom and a sensitivity denied to any other of the characters except Edith (Deborah Kerr) – and it is significant that Edith marries him and that throughout the film the German has this superiority over the Englishman – he won the woman while the Englishman continually foozled his approach'. Even in his scene at the tribunal in which he requests asylum in Britain, the MoI complained that Theo 'appears only very weakly anti-Nazi'.[89] In all, for the authorities *The Life and Death of Colonel Blimp* 'asks for sympathy for the German (if not the Nazi) ideal. There is no serious distinction between Germanity and Nazidom and, although the total tone of the picture is not anti-British or pro-German, it is to a certain extent wantonly provocative'.[90]

Although Powell and Pressburger protested that they 'resented any suggestion that [they were] sympathetic to the German way of life',[91] Ministry views were echoed elsewhere, notably in the rather extreme and elaborate criticism offered by E. W. and M. M. Robson in the rather bizarre contemporary publication, *The Shame and Disgrace of Colonel Blimp: The True Story of the Film*. Although *Kinematograph Weekly* contended that the film 'exudes patriotism',[92] the Robsons argued that the 'wicked production' presented the English as 'softies and the Germans as hard-done-by victims of a superior caste', from a propagandistic view '[suiting] the Germans right down to the ground'.[93] To the Robsons, Powell and Pressburger had produced a film in which two characters contrasted at the extremes: 'the one will be a big, fat lollipop of a walrus-whiskered Englishman and the other, the noble, handsome, awe-inspiring, able and wise German'.[94] Although somewhat more restrained, *Documentary News Letter* offered criticism along similar lines, its critics left wondering 'who is the real hero of this film – the German who doesn't like Hitler or the Old Soldier who refuses to die?' They underlined the fact that it was 'the Prussian [in the film] who reneges on the Nazis' and it was Walbrook's character who teaches his friend 'a few elementary facts about international affairs'. Blimp, they argued, was an outmoded relic of the British past who has to be 'taught to adapt himself to modern life (and death) by a Prussian',[95] a view seconded by film critic C. A. Lejeune who questioned whether 'an ex-Prussian officer advocating the bombing of hospitals, the ruthless destruction of women and children, is the right man to teach us how to wage modern war'.[96]

This was not the first time that Powell and Pressburger had faced harsh criticism over their portrayal of the German character. There was a similar reaction to the portrait of the German escapees in *49th Parallel*. The *Documentary News Letter* of November 1941 commented that audiences always preferred the hunted to the hunter, thus generating a certain amount of sympathy for the Nazis on the run in the film.[97] The *New Statesman* agreed and argued that 'the natural heroes of [the film's] adventures are the campaigning Nazis. The further they get and the more hardships they have to undergo, the more inclined we shall be to sympathise'.[98] In addition, *Documentary News Letter* observed that although 'the actions of the Nazis throughout the film include brutalities of various descriptions, including cold-blooded murder ... the Nazi Commander gains a certain warmth at times, if only in terms of that blind and fanatical loyalty, which so far has been one of Hitler's major secrets of success'. Furthermore, it was 'a pretty poor show if six Germans can be at large for so long in hostile country'.[99] But it was precisely this depiction of the sympathetic German, such as Peter, Vogel and Theo, although not necessarily in the Nazi characters as indicated in the *New Statesman* or the *Documentary News Letter*, that played a role in making both *49th Parallel* and *The Life and Death of Colonel Blimp* popular successes. As Aldgate and Richards observed: 'the MoI found it exceedingly difficult to sell the idea to the British public that all Germans should be tarred with the same Nazi brush. Perhaps, in the final analysis, *49th Parallel* was a success precisely because, for all its evident intentions, it did not resort to the simple propagandist expedient of painting the enemy universally black',[100] a view which was in line with British popular opinion. The same could also be said of Powell and Pressburger's 1943 production. As with the films discussed thus far, successful film propaganda during World War II almost invariably managed to tap in to popular opinions on a given subject, reflecting and shaping them as opposed to creating them afresh.

Both Powell and Pressburger's 1941 and 1943 productions enjoyed considerable popular success. *49th Parallel* made a profit of £132,331 in box office receipts, justifying the Ministry of Information's investment in its production.[101] The film was also exported to the United States under the title *The Invaders*, its popularity there partially determined by the appearance of Raymond Massey and star of the 1939 blockbuster *Gone with the Wind*, Leslie Howard. Such success led Mass-Observation to comment: 'I should say that this film is going to have the greatest influence of any full length propaganda film yet made'. Interestingly, Mass-Observation found that the speeches on freedom and the mild violence against Nazis were particularly popular.[102] *The Life and Death of Colonel Blimp* found similar success. Audiences, unlike some critics, were refreshed by the fact that the film 'provided a diversionary glimpse of an English character that has its faults better known than its virtues'.[103] Others appreciated the representation of 'the true picture of the official English attitude towards the various problems of war, e.g. the old-young generation of soldiers; the attitude of non-hatred ... the non-sentimental ending'. This was 'propaganda that [did not] clash with reality too much'.[104] This combination of entertainment and political persuasion was the magical ingredient in Powell and Pressburger's wartime film propaganda. Pressburger recognised that his scripts had to be entertaining to be persuasive, noting that 'Goebbels considered himself an expert on propaganda, but I thought I'd show him a thing or two'. Naturally, he understood that his task was complicated by censorship. 'In a free country', he commented, 'if people had had enough of propaganda they just switch their radios off and go to the music hall. In Germany, there was nothing else to listen to'.[105] Powell and Pressburger knew that democratic propaganda had to be both attractive and meaningful. As *Documentary News Letter* observed in May 1942, the idea for their 1941 production 'was good as entertainment and was good as a propaganda opportunity. Within the simple theme of the film, propaganda and entertainment were fused – it was the propaganda itself that was entertaining'.[106] Although this was an essential component for wartime democratic propaganda, it was also an idea adopted by the RMVP in their pursuit of increasing the box office and persuading the public of ultimate victory.

Set in Canada, *49th Parallel*, although popular, did little to reinforce the fact that Britain was directly under threat from a similar Nazi invasion. The land was distant, foreign, and so was the potential danger. The Ministry recognized that it was important to show the consequences of invasion to the British public, especially given their fears that the British people were becoming apathetic and complacent about the prospect. In June 1940, when invasion looked increasingly likely, the Home Publicity Sub-Committee directed that, as a matter of urgency, propaganda should seek to illustrate 'what invasion would mean for the British way of life. When the Germans invade', the Ministry warned, 'if they come here, their terrible secret police and their brutal soldiers would come into our homes. Any knock at the door might mean prison and torture in prison'.[107] As the war progressed and the prospect of invasion became more distant, it is not surprising that the Ministry found that the British public became even more complacent about German occupation. In April 1941, the Home Publicity Sub-Committee were worried that an

> apathetic outlook of 'what have I got to lose even if Germany wins' [was arising] from ignorance of ways in which a Nazi victory would deprive a person who talks and thinks in these terms of liberties he or she now enjoys ... the middle class people ... do not understand that they would lose not some but all of their privileges. Women are particularly prone to it through simple war-weariness and ignorance of the issues.[108]

Clearly, the Ministry was anxious about levels of complacency concerning the possibility of invasion and its effects, even if the public wasn't.

The feature film was relatively late to pick up on this propaganda theme. In an analysis of anti-Nazi films, Mass-Observation concluded that contemporary productions created the impression that 'the Nazis harm those that disagree with them and who have authority but may well ignore the man in the street'. More worryingly from the point of view of the propagandist, the observers noted that 'there is never any attempt to link what is being shown on the screen with a feeling of "it might happen here". An audience seeing any of these films[109] would be unlikely to come away with the impression that what they had seen could happen outside Germany'.[110] This was clearly a problem for the propagandists. With little sense of what invasion would mean, the British public was unlikely to rally to the defence of the nation. The Ministry needed to ensure that everyone could at least conceive of the possible impact.

One of the few full-length feature films to deal with invasion was Alberto Cavalcanti's *Went the Day Well?*, unfortunately released in 1942, after the real threat of invasion had passed. It was based on Graham Greene's short story *The Lieutenant Died Last*, published in the US magazine *Collier's Weekly* on 29 June 1940.[111] Keeping some of the flavour of the original story, Greene worked on the script alongside Cavalcanti.[112] The title was derived from a quote located by the film's producer, Michael Balcon, which summed up the film's central message: 'Went the day well? We died and never knew. But, well or ill, freedom we died for you'.[113] Originally, the poem, published by J. M. Edwards during the Great War alongside three other epitaphs, had been intended as a memorial to those who 'died early in the day of battle,'[114] and it soon became a popular aspect of the military obituary in the last years of World War I and throughout the 1920s.[115] The alternative titles of the film give some indication that it was attempting to reflect the concerns of the Ministry relating to British complacence over invasion in their quintessentially English setting and its associated imagery. Titles such as 'They Came in Khaki', 'The Heart of the Country', 'Germans on the Green', 'Village in Arms', 'Somewhere in England', 'The Battle of Bramley Green' and 'Not Since Domesday' related specifically to the fact that the action was to take place on British soil, evoking the threat to English tradition and the historical background which were to become central to the plot of *Went the Day Well?*[116] The choice of title, on the film's release, was thought by some to be meaningless, *Documentary News Letter* asking: 'Why do people have to call films by these literary and impossible-to-remember titles? … What do these conglomerations of words mean to anybody who hasn't got a Boots' library subscription or a Golden Treasury handy?'[117]

The film, whose appearance was described as having 'been made with one eye on the clock and the other on a copy of the *Boy's Own Paper*',[118] tells the story of the village of Bramley End in the West of England, a small community-based village which is invaded by Germans disguised as British soldiers. The community welcomes the soldiers, who are supposedly on 'manoeuvres'. The Germans increasingly give themselves away through a number of careless mistakes and failed attempts to hide their inner character, and the community become suspicious. The Nazis finally reveal themselves to be brutal oppressors and imprison the villagers in the church and the local stately home. Helped by the local fifth-columnist, Oliver Wilsford (Leslie Banks), the village is cut off from the outside world. Through a series of brave and selfless acts, the community raises the alarm and is finally helped by the Home Guard of a neighbouring village, Upton, who join them in the fight to save Bramley End from the invaders.

The press book for *Went the Day Well?* stressed that the film was to be regarded as the epitome of 'British resolution, ingenuity and heroism ... it is, at the same time, an invasion warning, a disclosure of the value of our Home Guard and an illustration of Nazi ruthlessness and cunning'.[119] In keeping with the basic structures of 'enemy' propagaganda, the film contrasted the higher values of the heroic victim (in this case, the persecuted villagers) with their mirror-image (the barbarous invaders or, worse still, the fifth columnist). Cavalcanti depicted the Nazi as a brutal, cunning and ruthless murderer, who is willing to kill innocents, such as the vicar and the children; the Nazis have bad table manners and no respect for their hosts; they also make sloppy mistakes which betray their identity, a characteristic which tied in with the Ministry's instructions regarding the depiction of the Nazi, which noted that 'the Germans should be shown as making absurd errors of judgement',[120] avoiding the perpetuation of 'the legend of German efficiency'.[121] Their sloppiness in the film is sufficient to arouse the suspicions of the community. After all, 'English soldiers don't twist little boys ears (at least not both at once), we don't make sevens with a bar across the upright, our chocolate does not come from *Wien* and is not spelt "chokolade" [sic]'.[122] If the differences were not apparent to the audiences after all this, the film draws yet another distinction: the Germans drink coffee and the British drink tea.

In contrast, the British are presented as heroic, resilient and determined to liberate their village. They are brave and ingenious, despite being 'ordinary' citizens and not trained soldiers. Cavalcanti transfers the mantle of heroic resistance to the civilian population in line with recommendations from the Home Publicity Sub-Committee, which detailed in 1940 that 'we should play up, to their utmost, stories of individual heroism causing the tables to be turned on the Germans – especially by brave civilians.[123] This is precisely the central theme of *Went the Day Well?* However, the representation of 'Englishness' in relation to resistance and invasion is problematic in Cavalcanti's film. As Pierre Sorlin observes, 'resistance is a difficult, worrying problem, inasmuch as it raises unpleasant questions about people's collective and individual behaviour'.[124] *Went the Day Well?* simultaneously represents both the collective spirit and the alien 'Other'. The film challenges the newly established structures of order imposed upon the village, whilst maintaining strong cultural and social divisions, as well as overturning the classical discourse on class and loyalty. On the one hand, all sections of the community are represented in the struggle to liberate Bramley End. As the press book comments: 'You'll know them all',[125] encouraging audience identification and association. Like the wider propagandistic strand of the 'People's War', social divisions are recognized but at the same time submerged into the collective action. In Cavalcanti's film, this is particularly true of the female characters. The studio press book, suggesting a deliberate targeting of female film-goers in the preparation for invasion, details how each woman, representative of her social background, plays a part in the defence of the village: Mrs Collins (Muriel George), as the postmistress, martyred by the bayonet of the invader; Daisy the shop assistant (Patricia Hayes), 'beaten by a Nazi soldier, . . . manages to give useful service to the last'; the Land Army girls, Peggy (Elizabeth Allen) and Ivy (Thora Hird), play a crucial role alongside their men in defending the Manor House in the final battle sequence; Nora (Valerie Taylor), the mild-mannered vicar's daughter who guns down the village 'Quisling'; and finally Mrs Fraser (Marie Lohr), the Lady of the manor, who 'behind her social graces is revealed [as] a level-headed woman capable of playing her part in the tense and critical events that have suddenly come to her village'.[126] As with the images of the Blitz, individual identities remain but are channelled into the community, in which gender and social boundaries are transcended in the name of 'total war'. Societal division exists but the *action* of resistance is collective. This was essential for the audience in terms of credible propaganda outputs, the most successful films representing the *public's understanding* of class relationships and themselves.[127]

In one significant way, however, according to Sorlin, traditional discourses of class representation are overturned in *Went the Day Well?*, notably in the character of Oliver Wilsford. In classical narratives of invasion, 'it is an English gentleman, deeply rooted in the land, who foils the invaders' plans and helps defeat them'.[128] But in Cavalcanti's production, this is subverted. Wilsford is the 'Quisling' who contrives the collapse of the village from within. His role as Nazi agent defined, he is excluded from the community and eventually destroyed by them. The 'country squire' was the representation of the 'professional' fifth columnist, as opposed to the 'amateur' spreading 'doom and gloom'. Wilsford's mission 'is to assist [the German] armies in the event of invasion'.[129] His dual identity betrays his Englishness and defines him as the 'Other' in the film, alongside the invaders. After all, 'it just isn't cricket. [He's] playing for the other team'.[130] Here too Wilsford is the victim of inefficiency, having been identified and shot by Nora, the vigilant vicar's daughter, who is able to see past her heart and use her head in identifying the true identity of her former sweetheart.

Nevertheless, it is the propaganda of contrast which is particularly striking in *Went the Day Well?* The distinction between the British and Nazi way of life is illustrated in a scene in which Mrs Collins entertains her billet, a young Nazi soldier. Here Nazi and democratic moral values clash and old wounds from the Great War are exposed:

Collins: [Lulling the soldier into a false sense of security] Well, it's been a very pleasant surprise really after the way the papers have been carrying on about you Germans being fiends in human form and sticking babies on the ends of bayonets . . . You don't look at all that sort of man to me. A regular family man I should take you for.
Soldier: I'm not married. But I have two fine sons who will soon be old enough to fight.
Collins: [Giggling] Ooh, you don't say! Well, I'm broad-minded m'self and [turning sinister] accidents will happen. [Soldier starts banging the pepper pot to make pepper come out]

Still 9 *Went the Day Well? Daisy and Mrs Collins are confronted by the invaders.*
From Bfi Stills, Posters and Designs. Reproduced with permission from Canal+.

Here that silly pepper pot. I'll do it. I never had any children m'self. Mr Collins blamed me for it and I blamed him and then he was taken so we never found out. [Mrs Collins throws the pepper into the soldier's eyes. Mrs Collins grabs an axe and murders him].

In this sequence, Cavalcanti wished to demonstrate that 'people of the kindest character, such as people in that small English village, as soon as war touches them, become absolute monsters'.[131] Given the concerns of the MoI about representations of violence in film, *Went the Day Well?* was particularly horrific by contemporary standards: Mrs Collins butchers a Nazi soldier with an axe and is subsequently bayoneted to death as she tries to contact nearby Upton; the villagers set about overwhelming the invading force by beatings and shootings; the Land Army girls seize weapons from dead German soldiers; the Home Guard from Upton are violently assaulted on their way to rescue Bramley End, and in the final sequence, in her attempt to save the children, Mrs Fraser is killed by a grenade. Although these events work well in terms of underlining the potential consequences of invasion, there were two distinct problems with this form of propaganda, as the MoI recognized: 'one of the biggest difficulties that any general morale campaign has to face is the difficulty between fostering undue fear of the Germans on the one hand and of underestimating them and of engendering over-confidence on the other'.[132] In this respect, *Went the Day Well?* fell rather short: it both presented a terrifying image of the barbarity and brutalizing impact of war *and* suggested that the Nazi invaders could be defeated by a village defended primarily by women, pensioners and children.

The film received widespread publicity, including its adaptation into a radio play.[133] Cinema-owners were encouraged to 'show the flag, to decorate your house front and lobby in the best gala fashion, to interest the Services and Civic Heads'.[134] However, the test screening of the film in Croydon still revealed some tensions between the intended and actual messages conveyed by the production. Despite the explicit references, audiences were confused as to the identity of the invaders. The report on the screening detailed that, as the Germans were disguised as British soldiers, there was a 'worry over the similarity of the uniforms' and that the Germans and the English would be 'confused in the early stages of the film'. Moreover, Cavalcanti failed to convey 'the mood of urgency', essential for a film attempting to stress the impact of invasion. The film was considered 'too long' and the small sequences 'disjointed'.[135] The image of the Germans in the film also came in for some severe criticism from Caroline Lejeune of *The Observer*, who stated that 'it is a dangerous thing to show your opponents as clowns or bullies, who only get results by treachery, brute force or the long arm of coincidence. A director who does this merely cheapens his own countrymen, since victory over such people is empty and meagre'.[136] For *The Cinema*, the propaganda of contrast failed on all counts, objecting to the representation of the 'behaviour of Germans and villagers alike, [the] former merely marking time mostly beyond demonstrations of brutal aggression, while the latter seem strangely apathetic in the face of national emergency',[137] an observation reiterated by the audience for the test screening.[138] Ultimately, the film was judged 'unconvincing as a whole, its appeal relying mainly on star pull'. *Went the Day Well?*, *Kinematograph Weekly* concluded, was 'fair, average thick-ear fiction for the unsophisticated masses'.[139] Yet, even in the propaganda picture, it is wise not to underestimate the power of 'star pull' and a 'rattlin' good yarn',[140] as demonstrated by Marcel Varnel's 1940 production, *Let George Do It*.

Films with the ability to lift the public mood and fulfil audience desires to retreat from their everyday existences were popular in both Britain and Germany, where comedy, romance and historical dramas dominated the film programme throughout the war years. The escapist function of the cinema was among the most vital roles that film could play in the wider propaganda campaigns intending to support morale on the home front and the front lines. Fascination with the stars, their glamour and their familiarity, and the desire to alleviate wartime worries and stresses, converged, creating a powerful means of capturing the public imagination and distracting audiences from the context in which they lived, as this poem from an avid reader of *Picture-goer Weekly* from December 1940 demonstrated:

> In the shelter every night, I read by flickering candlelight
> My week's joy, it's *Picture-goer* and as my eyelids gently lower,
> I dream of Gable and MacMurray and therefore I'm in no hurry
> To wake to cold reality and find a bomb's dropped on me.
> As raiders drop their bombs once more, I dream again of stars galore.[141]

Although, as this suggests, the particular combination of star power and the desire for escapism was particularly potent in the dark days of 1940, this did not proclude films combining topical propaganda and diversion. As Ealing producer, Balcon, claimed, 'films with a war background [can] have escapist qualities'.[142] A number of comedies of the war years demonstrated that even the subject of the Nazis could be successfully adapted to fit the need to provide light relief from the exigencies of war. Tommy Trinder's *Sailors Three* (Walter Forde, 1940) and George Formby's *Let George Do It* were among the most successful productions of this genre, in that they 'had the effect of temporarily moving audiences away from the grim realities – yet both had war backgrounds'.[143] Here, propaganda functioned within the film on multiple levels, providing political and specific persuasive messages, whilst convincing the public that they were being entertained in keeping with film-goers' desires and patterns of film consumption. *Let George Do It* was an excellent example of this, although a closer analysis also reveals tensions between the propagandistic and escapist discourses within the film.

Described as a 'tonic for jaded nerves' and 'a sure cure for the blues',[144] *Let George Do It* sees Formby, the popular former music hall comedian, in a farcical comedy in which he finds himself at the centre of an espionage drama. A travelling entertainer, he is mistaken for a British spy and unwittingly helps to sink five U-boats. At the end of the film, George saves a British agent, Mary (Phyllis Calvert), from the Germans by posing as a German officer on a submarine. The film also contains two fantasy sequences in which George finds himself baked into a giant loaf of bread, and, in a topical dream sequence, saves the day by punching Hitler on the nose. The scene in which Formby attacks Hitler and the SA celebrate their liberation fitted well with existing trends in popular opinion, the leadership identified as the perpetrators of the war whilst the average Germans appeared relieved of all responsibility for Nazism, hoping for their liberation by the allied forces. Hitler was identified as a figure for particular vilification, so much so that Ealing found it difficult to cast the part in Formby's 1940 production and had to keep the name of the actor under wraps.[145] Film propaganda tended to adopt the approach that the leadership of Germany was responsible for the outbreak of war in 1939, a theme explored in both *Let George Do It* and short films such as Donald Taylor's *These are the Men* (1943), and indeed in wider propaganda campaigns, offering a point of comparison with the National Socialist propaganda of plutocratic leadership in Britain and war guilt. Both regimes sought to remove any stigma from enemy populations in their propaganda, a reasonable approach given both nations' investment in psychological incitement to enemy nations encouraging revolution, defeatism and the overthrow of their particular governments. Targeting enemy nationals served no practical or tactical advantage for either British or German propagandists, who wished to convert enemy nations, fundamentally weakening the position of those in power, and in direct consequence, the war effort.

Despite the good intentions of *Let George Do It*, the popular and critical reception was mixed. Mass-Observation commented that the film was regarded by the press as 'bad propaganda' by once again underestimating the enemy, with the British spies looking like careless fools. The dream sequence was felt by critics to be 'simply encouraging wishful thinking'.[146] The hope that Germany would be overthrown from within and that German spies could be easily defeated by the British 'everyman' was unrealistic. Yet, in many ways, it did not have to be 'true to life'. For the public, the most popular sequence in the film appeared to be the dream sequence, Mass-Observation reporting that audiences particularly enjoyed seeing George 'smacking Hitler on the jaw',[147] adding that, although *Let George Do It* enjoyed good box office returns and public praise, its 'topical references, with one exception, have not added much to its success, the one exception is the end of a dream sequence in which after George has knocked out Hitler, the Storm Troops [sic] go wild'.[148] It was clear that the sequence in Varnel's film was rather unique, successful in its confrontation with the iconic embodiment of the enemy. Generally, topical comedy was problematic, reflecting public desires for escapist cinema. In October 1940, Mass-Observation confirmed that 'topical jokes' in film 'were not popular and received little more than half the volume of response given to non-topical jokes in the same sequences'. Film faced a difficult task in respect of contemporary comedy based on current events. Compared to the live performer who could easily produce jokes 'sensitive' to public opinion and topical events, 'the film comedian, or the documentary film producer who wants to make the point with a touch of humour, is at a disadvantage here in having less contact with public opinion and therefore more need for a well-based understanding of probable trends', a challenge in the midst of fast-moving contemporary events. Film comedians, in many ways, were better advised to stick to perennial subjects which chimed in with the British sense of humour: 'ill-health, deformity, sexual abnormality or potential death (including war) situations', conforming to extant cultural traditions.[149]

Despite its shortcomings, *Let George Do It* was a popular success, as were the other films of the period starring Formby,[150] the film drawing sufficient public interest to warrant a re-release in March 1944.[151] Within this context, the historian should not underestimate the potential of escapism and star power in the propagandistically significant era of World War II. It became abundantly clear that the British public loved humour and comedies, and this found a practical application for the propagandist at war.[152] Mass-Observation noted, in September 1940, that 'comedies about war are much more popular than drama'.[153] Of the top ten British film stars, judged by box office receipts in 1940, comedians took four of the top spots with Formby at number one.[154] He remained in that position until 1944, when he was replaced by James Mason,[155] an indication of the increasing popularity of Gainsborough's escapist 'bodice rippers', such as *The Man in Grey* (Leslie Arliss, 1943) and *The Wicked Lady* (Leslie Arliss, 1945).[156] Of those questioned by Mass-Observation about Formby in *Let George Do It*, 86 per cent enjoyed his performance.[157] Formby, like other contemporaries such as Gracie Fields, Will Hay, Tommy Trinder and Max Miller, had 'created a new audience for British films', and it was claimed that he had 'almost wholly been responsible for certain large new circuits e.g. Odeon and County'. Attesting to the popularity of these familiar stars, Grierson commented that the 'native vitality of this music hall contribution has been strong enough to survive bad production, bad scripts and bad direction alike'.[158] Formby's strength as a popular performer lay in his regional and working-class identity, forming a bond with many cinema-goers who wanted films 'about *ordinary* people; we do get so tired of ... Oxford accents'.[159] Although Formby did not lose his Lancashire identity, he became 'a national star ... [a symbol] of the people. [He indicated] the truth of Patrick Joyce's contention that it was possible for people to be loyal simultaneously to family, street, town, county, nation and Empire: Formby ... embodied such multiple loyalties'[160] and in doing so connected with his film audience and represented the ultimate unity of the nation. Like Heinz Rühmann, in many ways his German counterpart, Formby represented the 'everyman' with a child-like, asexual simplicity which contributed to the Formby–Rühmann genre of comedy of the 1930s and 1940s. Although it would be reasonable to assume that his 'carp-like face, a mouth outrageously full of teeth, a walk that seems normally to be that of a flustered hen, ... a smile of perpetual wonder at the joyous incomprehensibility of the universe and the people in it'[161] and his simplicity of character 'would not survive the harsh reality of war', Formby became all the more popular, testament to the need to provide escapist comedy and to lift the spirits of the audience with the particular brand of humour that only Formby could provide: gentle, simple jokes accompanied by lively songs on the ukulele such as 'Oh! Don't the Wind Blow Cold', 'Grandad's Nightshirt', 'Mr Wu's a Window Cleaner' and the fitting blitz-beater 'Count your Blessings and Smile', all featured in Varnel's 1940 production.

For the propagandist, comedy and star power had a particular advantage over the conventional political drama or documentary. When questioned by Mass-Observation about the content of *Let George Do It*, 80 per cent did not think that the film was propaganda at all.[162] Mass-Observation frequently reported that the public did not want to see more propaganda when visiting the cinema. However, the MoI had correctly identified that the feature film was one of the most effective ways of conveying *subconscious* propaganda. As the initial plans for the use of film propaganda stated, it 'will be most effective when it is least recognisable as such'. It was imperative that 'the influence brought to bear by the Ministry on the producers of feature films, and encouragement given to foreign distributors must be kept secret'.[163] In addition, they added that 'the film, being a popular medium, must be good entertainment if it is to be good propaganda'.[164] It is no surprise, therefore, to find that George's knock-out blow to Hitler was favoured as a way of representing an anti-Nazi theme: a comic book hero, dealing with the world's most dangerous dictator by a good old-fashioned punch-up. Here comedy and topicality coincided and underlined the fact that 'we all want to laugh – so let George do it!'[165]

THE GERMAN RESPONSE: THEMES IN NAZI ANTI-BRITISH FILM PROPAGANDA

With the fall of France in June 1940, the Nazi armed forces turned on the population of the United Kingdom, this development in the war necessitating an intensification of propaganda relating to the enemy. On 23 June of that year, Goebbels instructed the German media to foreground 'the England theme', focusing on 'anti-British polemics' centred on Churchill and *The Times*' repeated claims that the island was now 'the last guardian of European liberty'.[166] In his desire to respond to British anti-Nazi propaganda, Goebbels kept a close eye on the persuasive techniques of his adversary at this critical period in the war.[167]

There were certain similarities in approach between Britain and Germany in respect of their 'enemy' propaganda, the most striking being the distinction between the leadership and the people, a division which added to the possibilities of converting potential sympathizers and establishing an environment in which instability could be nurtured. As early as 3 September 1939, the RMVP decreed that its media should not 'attack the English people, but the leading individuals who have guided England into this encirclement policy'.[168] Goebbels, like his British counterparts, recognized the potential for driving a wedge between leaders and their public. This was useful in both home and foreign propaganda alike, demonstrating that he not only appreciated the possibility for generating foreign unrest but the innate connection between populations under the strain of war, implied within the minutes of the ministerial conferences of July 1940. Mirroring the objectives of the British 'Anger Campaign' in the same period, Goebbels suggested that Nazi propaganda ought to '[buttress and strengthen] the very powerful mood of militancy inherent in the people', contending that the popular 'restraint of the past few weeks must be abandoned' in favour of 'entirely primitive arguments'.[169] Despite this need to increase anger amongst the general population, the distinction between leaders and led was to be strictly maintained, suggesting an important comparison with Britain in respect of the formation and execution of propaganda concerning the image of the enemy.

With the aim of generating a focus for anger, the RMVP directed its campaigns towards the vilification of the ruling classes. In July 1940, Goebbels instructed that 'even for the German public, the British plutocracy alone is to be attacked and not the British people as a whole'.[170] Vehement critiques were to be reserved for the leaders of the plutocratic caste governing the British Isles but 'never [directed at] the British nation as such'.[171] The concept of plutocracy, defined by Goebbels as 'that form of political and economic leadership in which a couple of hundred families rule the world without any right to do so',[172] was injected into much anti-British propaganda throughout the war years. Providing a connection to the principles of propaganda outlined by Britain in the early years of World War II, it was hoped that by avoiding stigmatizing the British population and appealing to them directly the Nazis could orchestrate an overthrow of the Churchillian War Cabinet, creating conditions conducive to invasion. Sensing this practical aspect of psychological warfare, Goebbels reminded his propagandists that 'it must always be the overall objective to incite the people against whatever government is in power', applying a similar policy in France and Britain alike.[173] In attempting to create a gulf between the people and their government, the RMVP were to 'make it clear to the British people that the plutocratic clique ruling them has nothing in common with them nor does it feel any ties to them … Mistrust must be sown of the plutocratic ruling caste, and fear must be instilled of what is about to befall [them]. All this must be laid on as thick as possible'.[174]

Ultimately challenging the propagandistic construct of the 'People's War', Nazi propaganda sought to accentuate class and social division, mocking the 'liberty' of democracies and their failure to provide adequate living conditions for the majority whilst the minority lived in palatial homes and dined on the finest produce. It was for this reason that Goebbels chose to target British leaders, such as Churchill, Chamberlain and Foreign Secretary Anthony Eden, drawing attention to their public school backgrounds, their privileged upbringing and their place in the plutocratic order. This distinction between the leaders and the people was maintained until a relatively late stage, Hitler proclaiming in late 1942 that 'we must persist in our assertion that we are waging war, not on the British people, but on the small clique who rules them'. He was confident that it was 'a slogan which promises good results'.[175] Equally, Goebbels was insistent that 'British differentiation between the German people and the National Socialist leadership must be kept out of our reports under all circumstances'. He was determined that the media should 'avoid at all costs publishing an enemy comment which attributes responsibility for the war to the National Socialists alone and proposes a differentiated treatment for Nazis and the rest of the people'.[176]

The image of the British leadership was a carefully crafted amalgam of pre-existing propagandistic strands which drew on extant popular conceptions,[177] merged to present the plutocrats as Jews, capitalists, imperialists, corrupt businessmen and cunning manipulators of world events, united in protecting the sanctity of the nation under the slogan 'right or wrong, my country',[178] Byron's perfidious Albion.[179] The RMVP focused on the London plutocrats' 'desire' to profit from conflict and to establish their hegemony in Europe in their attempt to justify the outbreak of war in 1939, brushing aside their commitment to the salvation of other nations unless such actions were in their own interest.[180] In this vein, propagandists of the Reich were encouraged to 'attack particularly the Jews, international capitalism and the financial interests',[181] 10 Downing Street characterized as

> the site of Britishness in its highest racial purity, the navel of British plutocracy and tyranny. It is here that they planned their attacks all over the world and hatched their sinister plots to rescue civilizations and freedom with bombs and grenades. Amongst the residents here have been the Jew Disraeli and Lord Rosebery, the Rothschild's son-in-law. It was here, as early as 25 years ago, that Winston Churchill planned the war.[182]

Using similar rhetoric to British propagandists attempting to warn their home populations of the fate awaiting them should the Nazis invade, Goebbels alerted the German public to 'the unmitigated misfortune for the whole world if [the English] were successful in this war. Humanity', he advised, 'would then have to travel a road of suffering which would never end'. In contrast to depictions of democratic culture in films such as *49th Parallel*, Goebbels argued that the 'greedy and cowardly' adversary had 'no understanding for ideas such as people, culture, humanity and civilization', concepts which were 'completely alien' to the British way of life. In short, he declared, 'we have nothing but hatred and contempt for the British plutocrats'.[183] It was this view that the RMVP sought to inculcate with its short and feature film productions of the early war years.

As in Britain, the short film was utilized in the Third Reich as a timely reinforcement of wider topical propaganda campaigns, the speed of production ensuring relevance to contemporary events and prevailing attitudes. Short films relating to the image of the enemy focused upon themes which capitalized on the short-term campaigns of the RMVP but also emerged as an extension of pre-Nazi strains of Anglophobia, as expressed in the works of Werner Sombert, Houston Stewart Chamberlain and Oswald Spengler among others. Such works presented the British as a mercenary 'nation of traders', disabled by their love of money, capitalist exploiters of minorities, frustrated and bound by tradition which prevented modernization and the establishment of equality between the classes, a nation with deep-seated megalomaniacal and avaricious tendencies, all hidden beneath a superficial veneer of gentlemanly behaviour and a deceitful pretence of 'fair-play', a pious and fundamentally uncreative people, unable to find their inner spirit, essential to the life-blood of a powerful state.[184] These elements of Anglophobic rhetoric, formed before the *Machtergreifung*, were to form the basis of two specific productions of the period 1940–2, *Gentlemen* (*Deutsche Wochenschau GmbH*, 1941) and *Soldaten von morgen* (Alfred Weidenmann, 1941).[185]

Soldaten von morgen, scripted, directed and conceptualized by Alfred Weidenmann, was primarily intended as a short film for educational use. It was passed by the censor on 3 July 1941, presumably for non-theatrical distribution in schools prior to its public release on 27 January 1942.[186] Weidenmann specialized in films depicting the experience of youth, such as his productions *Junges Europa Nr. 3* (Young Europe, 1942), *Hände Hoch!* (Hands Up!,1942) and *Junge Adler* (1944), his aspiration being 'to work with young people and, drawing on their experience, to create with them films that present a valid image of the aspiring German youth'.[187] In this respect, *Soldaten von morgen* was no exception. For this film, Weidenmann chose to expose the excesses and corruption of British plutocracy through a direct comparison between German and British youth, in which he employed the principles of 'enemy' propaganda by contrasting positive and negative values within the filmic narrative.

The film begins with a depiction of the *Hitlerjugend* (Hitler Youth, HJ) at play, mocking the decadence and mannerisms of the English plutocratic caste, their excesses and their hierarchy. The HJ boys dress accordingly, donning wigs and stockings and padding their svelte physiques with cushions to mimic the plump English schoolboy, fattened by years of overindulgence and intemperance. Indeed, clothing became a symbol of the British class system in both Weidenmann's film and in wider propagandistic rhetoric, Goebbels himself conjuring the image of British plutocrats as 'ravening wolves in dinner-jackets'.[188] The representation of Etonians and Harrovians in their top hat and tails or little caps and rugby shirts became a means of underscoring the division in society signified by, as the Reich

Minister for Popular Enlightenment and Propaganda suggested, 'the decadent "Haves" encircling the healthy "Have-Nots"'.[189] For the RMVP, the 'Eton School' was the 'breeding-ground of "gentlemanliness"'.[190] Nazi propaganda stressed the peculiarities of Etonian tradition, the inherent barbarities of their 'childhood' games and the connection between the leadership of the nation and the world of privilege and patronage that the public school system embodied. As *Filmwelt* observed in January 1940, 'in power in England today are the descendants of those men whose education at Eton ... included an annual celebration during which young men "were allowed" to chase an old sheep with sticks all across the playing field until it perished'.[191] Such stereotypical images promoted within the wider media, in newspapers and films such as *Soldaten von morgen*, were reinforced in the classroom. Some fifty years later schoolboy Willy Schumann recalled of his classes during the Third Reich:

> At school, we learned about the tradition of the English public schools and their role in training the political, social and military ruling class ... the exclusivity of these schools was denounced in our text books because they were there only for the privileged ruling classes, not for the people ... photographs of the school uniforms were shown and ridiculed ... We looked condescendingly upon such 'anti-diluvian' school uniforms, and we even felt a little sorry for our Etonian and Harrovian contemporaries in their 'straight-jackets'.[192]

Such visions were mirrored in *Soldaten von morgen*, in which boys from Eton and Harrow made the transition to the leadership of the nation, bringing with them the skewed values of the public school system. It was in the light of this perception that Weidenmann's film saw boys turned prematurely into men, ripped from their childhoods and propelled into the glutinous, corrupt and falsely superior world of the plutocrat. School primed them for their role as future leaders. In a scene which suggests the boys' future direction, the students grasp the globe, wrapping their arms around it as if to hold on to their imperialistic gains, those they will inherit, and to imagine the conquest of others. The young boys are depicted as mere reflections of their elders: they wear cologne, read *The Times* whilst languishing in an arm chair, smoke cigars and drink whisky and soda, served by a butler, all stressing a society divided by privilege and class.

Through this sequence, Weidenmann underlined the connection between the boys, the system and the contemporary British War Cabinet. As the narrator informs the audience *'everybody knows that the apple does not fall far from the tree'*. Eden is depicted as an effete and vain man,[193] his image edited to emphasize his decadent features and set against modern jazz music, *entartete musik*. However, the central target of *Soldaten von morgen*, in keeping with wider Nazi propaganda campaigns, was Churchill, his features and mannerisms a gift to the RMVP who portrayed him as 'the slave of the Jews and of alcohol',[194] 'a crazy fool ... [a] whisky-blissful-boozer ... [and a] big mouthed guzzler'.[195] He was depicted as a gangster, a brute and a barbarian, as well as the primary instigator of conflict and master of the plutocratic clique. For Goebbels, he embodied the ultimate plutocrat and all the ills of

British society; its arrogance, its false sense of superiority, its excesses, its decadence and its brutality. He was the archetypal 'John Bull'.[196] This formed the backdrop to *Soldaten von morgen*, the boys of Eton indicative of the men they will become, brought up in a society and education system which creates the circumstances in which the plutocratic caste are able to maintain their hold over the nation and their colonies.

In order to underscore these images, Weidenmann's production utilized the propaganda of difference. The presentation of the Eton boys is subsequently compared with the youth of the Third Reich. Set against scenes of natural beauty, as opposed to the smoky common-room of the public school, an idealistic portrait of Nazi childhood is offered. Underpinning the connection between British youth and their plutocratic destinies and highlighting the contrast to their German counterparts, the narrator informs the audience that '*Youth is the source of the future of the nation … Youth is the Volk of tomorrow*'. The German boys are active, not languid, their activities centred on the gymnasium and the countryside. They are fit and healthy. They box, hike, run cross-country, dive and ride horses. They are orienteers and mountaineers. Moreover, they are prepared for conflict and well educated in the art of survival. They row, shoot, arm-wrestle and fence. They learn the value of true comradeship. In a gymnastic scene reminiscent of Leni Riefenstahl's depiction of German youth at the 1934 Nuremberg rally in *Triumph des Willens*, the boys rely on their colleagues in a game of leap-frog, which teaches them the importance of trust and both mental and physical support, a key attribute in the armed forces. The boys also demonstrate their bravery by plunging from a building into a net, practising battle charges and indulging in war-simulation games. Here, Weidenmann glorifies preparedness, brute force, activity, comradeship, discipline, order, the natural world and the healthy body. This is in direct contrast to the decadence, avarice and excesses of a society ridden with internal division, in which the poor are sent out to fight for the power-lust of the rich and in which privilege dominates equality.[197] As *Filmwelt* suggested, 'the British people has been pushed into battle by the clique that is its government, while on the other side of the divide this battle is being fought by a united *Volk*. We Germans have not been betrayed in the belief and trust we placed in our leaders'.[198] Within films such as *Soldaten von morgen* as well as in the wider anti-British campaigns, the propagandistic function was twofold: firstly, as a means of direct contrast, positively reinforcing the values of German youth and the regime by comparison with the degeneracy of British society and secondly, as a means of reinforcing the policy of division between the British leaders and people, underpinning the wider campaign relating to plutocratic rule.

The concepts highlighted in *Soldaten von morgen* were extended to wider political and military commentaries in the *Deutsche Wochenschau* production *Gentlemen*, a film depicting the abandonment of British soldiers by their leaders, the fragility of the Anglo-French alliance, the deliberate targeting of civilians by British soldiers and the betrayal of the ordinary man by the War Cabinet. The title suggested the RMVP's reinterpretation and redefinition of the term to imply the superficiality of the British sense of 'fair-play' and ridicule their codes of social behaviour. Films such as *Gentlemen* attempted to reshape the stereotype of British 'sportsmanship', *Filmwelt* commenting in July 1940 that:

> The terms 'gentlemen' and 'fairness' originate from the English language. In reality, these English terms and others like it are expressions of the arrogance with which the English regard themselves as superior over other nations in every way … They represent one of the refined ways in which England has sought to disguise its megalomaniacal desire for world domination and to create motifs suitable to further its plans and serve its egotistical cause.[199]

Based upon this premise, *Gentlemen* suggested that British 'war plans … reveal their true character'[200] and that their enemy's claim to be fighting a just war was little more than empty rhetoric. *Filmwelt* argued that British military conduct was characterized by its 'barbarity' and 'cynical brutality', adding that 'the betrayal of its allies, the abuse of international law, assassination attempts, subversive work behind the enemy's front lines, inaccurate reporting, the misuse of flags and the arming of trading vessels are but the smallest perfidies in English warfare'.[201]

It was in order to reinforce these general themes that the RMVP re-released the 1933 film *Morgenrot* (Dawn, Gustav Ucicky) on two occasions after the outbreak of war, the production passing through the censor on 25 November 1939 and 12 February 1940.[202] Although the British government and the press objected to the depiction of the Navy in Ucicky's production,[203] the original film offered the view that the English were 'decent opponents and worthy enemies, to be treated with respect and even admiration'. Within Ucicky's work, as Petley observed, 'there is no real bitterness against the English sailors who sink the German submarine, even though they employ a ruse to do so. Instead the film seems to largely adopt the point of view … that the English sailors were only doing their duty'.[204] However, this interpretation was reconfigured in 1940 to emphasize the underhand methods of the British fleet and their dishonourable conduct in World War I. Commenting on the central plot, *Filmwelt* argued that 'in their methods of warfare, nations reveal their character. England regards it as permissible to arm its merchant navy and let it sail under an assumed flag. We Germans deplore this; no German trading vessel sails as an armed "trap"'.[205] The film demonstrated that 'the English have always been bad losers: they turned nasty whenever battle turned against them … The English character is both pious and base at the same time, both complex and mean, and for that very reason it is hard to see through it. The Englishman believes in his ideals, but only as long as they serve him well'. Moreover, continued the film magazine, 'we know what to think of England. The British island these days is populated by "gentlemen" who count on German chivalry, so as to make our annihilation more secure'.[206] By 1940 then, *Morgenrot* had been transformed into an example of British perfidy, one which served to buttress contemporary anti-British propaganda campaigns.

The general themes of anti-British short film propaganda were well connected to the wider objectives of the RMVP. Films such as *Soldaten von morgen* and *Gentlemen* maintained the distinction between the leaders and the people, stressing the underhand nature of British conduct in war and their attempt to establish hegemonic control over European and global affairs. The anti-Nazi alliance was depicted as unstable, and British society hopelessly divided by class and social inequalities. The British character was defined by its hypocrisy and its false 'gentlemanly' behaviour. Britain was presented as a nation dominated by capitalism, Jewry and a small clique of plutocrats, who kept the country under the yoke of oppression, serving their own needs rather than those of the country. Such themes were reinforced and fictionalized within the feature films of the Third Reich, forming a constructed and relatively consistent anti-British master narrative within the propaganda campaigns of 1940–2.

Feature films tended to focus on colonial rule, imperialism and the suppression of minorities. Indeed, a number of the most successful and powerful anti-British fictional feature films, such as *Der Fuchs von Glenarvon* (The Fox of Glenarvon, Max Kimmich, 1940), *Mein Leben für Irland* (My Life for Ireland, Max Kimmich, 1941) and *Ohm Krüger* (Uncle Krüger, Hans Steinhoff, 1941), were based on this general theme. This had not always been fertile ground for anti-British films of the Third Reich. Earlier representations such as *Die Reiter von Deutsch-Ostafrika* (The Riders of German East Africa, Herbert Selpin, 1934) were broadly sympathetic to the Anglo-German relationship and their collective pursuit of a 'place in the sun'. The general *amitié* was reflected in the friendship between the central protagonists Peter Hellhoff (Sepp Rist) and Robert Cresswell (Peter Voss). In many ways, *Die Reiter von Deutsch-Ostafrika* was the forerunner of Powell and Pressburger's *The Life and Death of Colonel Blimp*, its characters set on a similar plot trajectory to Clive Candy and Theo Kretschmar-Schuldorff. The Anglophile tendencies reflected in Selpin's production, if somewhat stereotypical in its characterization of the English, was such to warrant a ban in 1939 for 'pacifistic tendencies'.[207] Preventing positive images of Britain was not always possible in the Reich, however, as the case of Paul Wegener's 1934 film *Ein Mann will nach Deutschland* (A Man Must Return to Germany) demonstrates. The film offered a sympathetic treatment of a British camp commander, who refused to condone the internment of prisoners of war. Significantly, the production was banned in February 1940, only to be re-released in March after complaints from Ufa that the studio was losing box office receipts as a result, another example of where questions of finance and profit were more important than the need for propagandistic output.[208]

With Anglo-German co-operation at its zenith in 1935, with the signing of the Naval Agreement in June of that year, films such as *Das höhere Befehl* (The Higher Order, Gerhard Lamprecht, 1935), starring Lil Dagover and Karl Ludwig Diehl, uniting Britain and Prussia in the common aim of defeating Napoleon in 1806, found popular acceptance. Upon entering the age of appeasement, however, few films appeared which took Britain as a central theme. As Welch argued, this was 'surely no coincidence', adding that the omission was 'more likely a calculated move in order that Hitler's gesture of reconciliation [at Munich] should not be undermined'.[209] Moreover, it was this pattern of broadly sympathetic portrayals as well as the 'ambivalent' pronouncements in the early stages of the regime which provoked the Nazis to 'vent their frustrations and anger when the break finally came' in September 1939.[210]

Anti-British feature film propaganda after 1939 added a traditional dimension to modern commentaries like those contained within the short films such as *Soldaten von morgen* and *Gentlemen*, the newsreels and the print media. Historical narratives served to generate a sense of continuity in the British character and behaviour, further justifying the decisive showdown in which the *Volksgemeinschaft* was now embroiled, the culmination of centuries of conflict in which the British had consistently sought to curtail the development of opposing modern European nations. In this respect, both Britain and Germany employed similar tactics to exploit the misdemeanours of the past to rationalize the political developments of the present. The popularity of films of an historical nature combined with an unequivocal message to adversaries was demonstrated at a relatively early stage with Gustav Ucicky's 1935 production *Das Mädchen Johanna*, the story of a solitary heroine, Joan of Arc, who led the attempted rebellion against the English invaders with clear parallels to the *Führer-mythos*. Reviving the historic tradition in wartime, therefore, was a natural step for Nazi propagandists, who recognized the value of the genre as a means of combining persuasion and entertainment, films such as *Jud Süß* (Veit Harlan, 1940), *Der große König* (The Great King, Veit Harlan, 1943) and *Kolberg* (Veit Harlan, 1945) being examples of productions of this nature. Film propagandists found that they were presented with a wealth of scenarios ranging from the middle-ages to World War I to underpin Nazi conceptions of the modern British character. Naturally, the oppression of minorities played an important role in sketching the ubiquitous pursuit of Empire and the aggrandizement of British power throughout the ages. History was rich with examples.

Although there were some illustrations of the idealization of British colonial heroes, such as in the 1938 film *Kautschuk* (Eduard von Borsody), the story of smuggler Henry Wickham set in 1876, starring René Deltgen in the lead role, the majority of anti-British representations in historical dramas operated around the construct of the oppressed minority. Some films, such as Carl Froelich's *Das Herz der Königin* (The Heart of the Queen, 1940), demonized British leaders, whilst showing the persecution of minority counterparts, in this case, Mary Queen of Scots (Zarah Leander) by Elizabeth I (Maria Koppenhöfer) and exploiting the English–Scottish relationship.[211] Froelich's production intended to demonstrate that 'the figure of Elizabeth in this film will be the embodiment of English imperialism', *Filmwelt* opining that, 'in the Stuart tragedy lies the seeds of all English Empire-building and the British lust for world hegemony', the 'historical parallel [incorporating] in one symbol, all which remains topical ... and which has consequences for all continents and in all centuries right up to the present day'.[212] Historical representations of the persecution of the individual were supplemented by narratives of mass movements intent on reclaiming their homelands and ejecting the British occupiers. Such themes proved to be particularly popular with audiences. The SD reported in May 1940 that 'over the past few weeks a number of films depicting the liberation struggle of oppressed nations have generally been very well received, according to unanimous reports from all over the Reich'.[213] Of particular interest to Reich audiences were 'films expressing anti-English sentiments, such as *Leinen aus Irland* and *Der Fuchs von Glenarvon*'. The SD attributed the success of the propagandistic aspects of the films to their historical *milieu*, which prevented creating the impression that a definitive point of view was being advanced, reporting that there was 'particular approval of films whose anti-English sentiment originates directly in the historic plot without the issues being overstated by the director'.[214] Although the fictionalized plots relating to freedom movements against occupying forces were well-received by German audiences, the SD, recognizing the problematic question of national identities, felt it undesirable that films of this nature should be screened in occupied Poland or the Protectorate of Bohemia and Moravia, commenting that they were 'unsuitable and even dangerous' given 'that the Poles and Czechs can easily apply the plot of such films to their struggle of liberation from Germany'.[215]

Of the two films identified by the SD as significant in the presentation of the 'Irish problem', *Der Fuchs von Glenarvon* and *Leinen aus Irland*, only the former was focused for the most part on the minority struggle against British rule, a theme explored in Kimmich's subsequent cinematic endeavour, *Mein Leben für Irland*. With these films, Kimmich tapped into the pre-existing fascination with Ireland, both during and in the aftermath of World War I, and its resistance movement, which held a considerable amount of contemporary appeal for the German population.[216] In many respects, Irish republicanism offered Nazi propagandists a fertile ground on which to breed anti-English propaganda, naturally lending itself to a visualization of the oppression of a minority grouping by British imperialists. The German press were keen to emphasize that 'the dreadful, murderous work done against the Irish remains unforgotten today',[217] pre-war propaganda sowing the seeds for later manifestations of pro-republicanism in the period from September 1939. With Ireland declaring neutrality in World War II[218] and the developing relationship between the Irish resistance and the Third Reich, German propagandists were able to exploit the existing tensions between Britain and Ireland to extend their critique of the British imperial mission, as well as adding a further component to the complex matrix of justifications for war. Nazi rhetoric relating to the Irish question suggested that World War II was a war of liberation for those under the yoke of British domination, a 1940 publication entitled *Irland in der englischen Hölle* (Ireland in the English Hell) stating that 'for centuries the Irish people has fought a desperate battle for its vital rights in its own land against the robbery and murder of British greed. England's day will come'.[219] The depiction of the Irish problem also offered Nazi propagandists a means of removing themselves from isolation in their opposition to and hatred of the English. By demonstrating that in both the anti-colonial and Irish republican movements a growing resistance to British rule existed, Nazi Germany could argue that she had established a broad coalition in the fight against British world hegemony.

Such was the central contention of Kimmich's 1940 production *Der Fuchs von Glenarvon*. The story of the ruthless suppression of the Irish 'freedom' movement by the British Justice of the Peace Grandison (Ferdinand Marian) and the 'Hangman of India', Sir John Tetbury

Still 10 *Illustrierter Film-Kurier, Der Fuchs von Glenarvon*, private collection.

(Werner Hinz), provided the bridge between the Irish and colonial themes. Scripted by Hans Bertram and Wolf Neumeister, *Der Fuchs von Glenarvon* is a fusion of political propaganda styles, deploying symbols familiar to the German wartime audience: 'the woman [is depicted] as saviour-heroine', embodied in the character of Gloria, Grandison's wife, played by Olga Tschechowa, whose sympathy with the resistance is such that she falls in love with the revolutionary John Ennis (Karl Ludwig Diehl), fighting the brutality of Tetbury and her former husband; 'the splendour of British "plutocratic" ritual [is] contrasted with the misery caused by the English … [and] the gruesome hanging of the evil party',[220] Ferdinand Marian's character once again at the mercy of the hangman, as in his portrayal of the eponymous anti-hero in Veit Harlan's film of the same year, *Jud Süß*. Although the film deals with only one incident of the ruthless suppression of Irish nationalism, Kimmich 'fades in with a scene showing the conspirators and ends with the song of freedom and the image of Irish patriots endlessly and timelessly going into battle'.[221]

Set in 1921, Kimmich's production gave contemporary objections to British rule the validity afforded by history. As *Filmwelt* stressed,

The sea is eternally breaking against Ireland's rocky cliffs. Eternal too is the hatred felt by the Irish for their English oppressors who, with fire and sword, with violence and murder, have been causing havoc on this green isle for the past eight hundred years. Yet for any dozen who die in the battle for Ireland, hundreds more are ready to take their place until such a time when the thunderous noise of the breaking waves will be accompanied by the rejoicing, booming song of victory of a liberated country and nation.[222]

Once again, blame for the persecution of the Irish lies with the leadership. The publicity materials for Kimmich's film dated British oppression from the moment 'the Anglo Saxons and Normans first set foot on the green island, continuing with Cromwell brutally seeking to break popular resistance, the King greedily declaring the land to be [a] Crown Estate, noblemen expelling peasants, leading up to the terrible reign of Queen Victoria, celebrated in England, and the execution of Sir Roger Casement during the Great War'.[223] Historical parallel gave credence to contemporary representations of the British character in the short films produced in the same period and sought to reinforce extant stereotypes, the emphasis on the past a vehicle to convey the crimes of the present. As audiences were reminded, the story of *Der Fuchs von Glenarvon* was not purely a matter for scholars; rather it was 'of our time'.[224]

Der Fuchs von Glenarvon corresponded to the portrait of the English offered in *Gentlemen*. As *Filmwelt* observed of Kimmich's film,

These are the English as we know them; the greedy and unscrupulous civil servant who uses the methods of slander, betrayal and murder that he was taught by the secret service; the thoughtless and superficial society lady for whom hunting down people is but an exciting drama; the mercenary with no judgement or conscience who is prepared to do anything; the police trained to hunt down innocent people.[225]

The two central characters, Tetbury and Grandison, described as 'justices of the peace eaten up by greed for money and ambition for status',[226] were the embodiment of the callous and exploitative British occupier. In this respect, *Der Fuchs von Glenarvon* added to the creation of an image in which the Irish experience of the English merged with that of the National Socialist anti-British master narrative. Using the propaganda of contrast, a technique which dominated Nazi depictions of the enemy, Kimmich's film distinguished the heroism, honesty and bravery of the 'freedom' fighter from the underhand and brutal methods of the occupier.[227] It was a theme which formed the basis of Kimmich's subsequent production *Mein Leben für Irland*, a film which helped to reinforce the message of *Der Fuchs von Glenarvon*.

Mein Leben für Irland premiered at the Capitol cinema in Berlin on 17 February 1941. Set in the period 1903–21, the film focused on the story of the attempted 're-education' of the British of the son of an Irish insurgent, Michael O'Brien (Will Quadflieg playing the younger O'Brien, Werner Hinz, the elder) in a English-controlled 'boarding school'. In the course of the film, the school authorities and their English pupils reveal themselves to be spies and the barbaric oppressors of the innocent in their drive to rid the 'Green Isle' of the nationalist movement. With the imprisonment of Michael's mother, Maeve Fleming (Anna Dammann), the boys orchestrate an uprising to coincide with the rebellion masterminded by republican leader Robert Devoy (René Deltgen) in which both Devoy and Michael's friend, Patrick, sacrifice their lives. Once again, British tyranny is embodied within a specific, stereotypical character, Sir George Beverley (Paul Wegener). Challenging the concept of British 'fair-play', publicity materials for the film stressed the underhand methods employed to suppress national minorities in their fight for freedom, Tobis declaring that 'once again, the secret service employs "experts" for any requirements: polished experts in compromise as well as brutal henchmen, clever specialists in American propaganda as well as cold-blooded murderers'. However, Kimmich's film contended that 'neither the most sophisticated nor the most brutal methods could prevent the flame of freedom burning brighter and stronger in the country than ever before'.[228] As in *Der Fuchs von Glenarvon*, *Mein Leben für Irland* romanticized Irish uprisings against British despotism, the independence fighters elevated to heroic status. The glory of martyrdom and battle against the oppressor are embodied within the characters of Patrick and Devoy, their deaths opening the way for further challenges to British rule by inspiring a new generation. In a similar fashion to the filmic depiction of National Socialist heroes, Irish nationalists are honoured by sacrificial death, their spirit living on in the memory as martyrs, further emphasizing the contemporary connection between the struggles of minority groupings against British ambitions and the proclaimed purpose of World War II in Nazi propaganda.

The film was accepted by the Reich Minister in February 1941, who commented in his diary that, after some alterations 'it is now rather good. I'm happy with it'.[229] Like its predecessor, *Mein Leben für Irland* enjoyed a positive response from the public, an SD report from the Leipzig region commenting that the film 'was a big success'. Although 'the cinema attracted excellent audience figures for every showing', the SD observed some alternative insights into Kimmich's production, pointing to the tensions within the film and audience sensibilities, a film-goer commenting that '"In my view, the film which deals with the existential fight of the Irish people would have been better served if it hadn't been given this rather unusual love adventure as its plot". (A pupil falls in love with his best friend's mother)'.[230] Although there were occasions on which such minor criticisms were made, feature films focusing on the Irish question as a means of representing anti-British sentiment were positively received by German cinema audiences, the theme well suited to the desire for dramatic reconstructions of the past as well as presenting contemporary events in their 'historical context'. This proved to be a popular and successful method for conveying 'enemy' propaganda, one which formed the basis for other films representing similar themes, such as the masterwork of anti-British propaganda, Hans Steinhoff's 1941 film, *Ohm Krüger*.

Colonial rule, much like the oppression of Irish nationalism, offered Nazi propagandists yet another opportunity to exploit historical precedent in their claims to have 'exposed' the British character and to warn against the impact of British rule on defeated and occupied nations. Although the RMVP drew upon numerous historical incidents to illustrate the nature of 'perfidious Albion' and its brutality in suppressing resistance to the formation of Empire, such as the massacres in the Sudan in 1892 and the conduct of British troops in India, Egypt and Palestine, by far the most emotive episode exploited by Nazi propagandists was the struggle between the Boers and the British, reaching its climax in the period 1880–1902, in which, as *Filmwelt* recalled, 'thousands of women and children were … murdered'.[231] *Ohm Krüger*, which depicts the story of Paul Krüger, the controversial leader of the Boers in their struggle against British domination, fitted well with the propagandistic anti-imperial discourse within the German media[232] and capitalized on public interest in the question of the colonies, the SD reporting that, both nationally and regionally, audiences were fascinated with films focusing on the colonial question.[233] Naturally, with the German desire to expand their own colonies in Africa and create new ones in the push to the east and the extension of *Lebensraum*, any critique of British colonialism had to be set within the wider propagandistic framework of the anti-British campaign, highlighting the ruthlessness of British rule and pointing to the less than worldly objectives of their imperial mission. Much propaganda of this nature questioned the supposed 'moral purpose' behind the British colonial vision. In a speech to workers and soldiers in Berlin in November 1939, Goebbels questioned whether British leaders 'really care a straw for moral values. The whole story of Britain's colonial activities', he opined, 'bears the stamp of [an] utter lack of idealism, the same lack of moral consideration as made the British government stand up in 1939 against the definite liberation of the German people and the complete restoration of German sovereignty'.[234]

The memory of the Boer War was a contested historical space within propagandistic discourses of World War II. In Britain, representations of the conflict as a symbol of antiquated military practice became a bone of contention between film-makers Powell and Pressburger and the MoI over the controversial 1943 production, *The Life and Death of Colonel Blimp*.[235] In Germany, the symbolism of the conflict was much more clear-cut, delineated and served an obvious purpose as an iconic denouncement of British perfidy. Countering the impression that Britain was valued as the 'world's policeman' who sought out and 'fought against evil wherever she found it', National Socialist propaganda contended that there were 'enough examples showing that the British have only ever pursued their own selfish goals, even if they managed to disguise their pursuit of power'.[236] For the RMVP, the most important example of British colonial intentions was the 'rape of the Boers'. *Filmwelt* stated in November 1940, a few months before the release of *Ohm Krüger*, that 'the British, in the name of humanity and with their troops' tenfold superiority, managed to break the heroic resistance of this small and freedom-loving people … [T]his was when the world caught its first glimpse of Britain's notorious colonial policies'.[237] In highlighting the case of the Boers, Nazi propagandists could not only emphasize atrocities perpetrated against women and children of 'pure farming stock' by over-zealous and malicious British commanders in their concentration camps and illustrate the brutal oppression of the Boers struggling for their freedom and fighting injustice, they could also maintain their critical focus on leadership, past and present.

Ohm Krüger offered an opportunity to expose the insidiousness of royalty through Queen Victoria, and of capitalists and tyrants such as Cecil Rhodes, but also to draw clear parallels to contemporary leaders: Joseph Chamberlain, *Filmwelt* was eager to point out, was the 'father of Austen and Neville',[238] and, of course, Winston Churchill was a journalist at the time of the Boer War. The publicity materials for Hans Steinhoff's film ensured that audiences did not forget the Prime Minister's role in the atrocities of the late 1880s. The studio press book urged the local and national media to stress 'what Churchill learnt in the Boer War', 'Blood for Gold!' Tobis affirmed that this was 'the same Churchill who in South Africa saw his ideas about exterminating the Boers followed through, as the English rulers, voicing polished humanitarian slogans, while driven by mere greed, unleashed the most contemptible actions on a people under attack. [T]he same Churchill is now Albion's prime minister. We know', they concluded, 'his methods and his plutocratic clique which we shall fight to their end'.[239] Such pronouncements gave previous propaganda relating to the connection between British leadership past and present and the perpetual renewal of plutocratic power some continuity, further reinforcing the credibility of the image of the British created at the outbreak of war in 1939.

By drawing on a historical conflict, as with *Der Fuchs von Glenarvon* and *Mein Leben für Irland*, the RMVP and the producing studio, Tobis, could claim that *Ohm Krüger* could be relied upon as an accurate account of British conduct in the colonies and as a world power. Steinhoff's film was presented to the German public as 'true to history'[240] and as a human story of 'utmost topicality'.[241] The studio claimed that the authors, Harald Bratt (who also scripted *Leinen aus Irland*) and Karl Heuser, had gone to great lengths to research the film and ensure its 'authenticity'.[242] Tobis recognized that, in representing such atrocious crimes against the Boers, they risked alienating the film audience. Nazi propaganda was keen to expose British atrocity propaganda of World War I and a cynical audience might conclude that Steinhoff's production was merely another strain of the same form of persuasion. In preparation for the release of the film, therefore, Tobis primed film-goers through the production of a leaflet entitled '*Der Ohm-Krüger Film – erfunden? Die historischen Tatsachen* (*Ohm-Krüger* Film: Fictitious? The Historic Facts), authored by Dr Wilhelm Ziegler. The tract recognized that audiences were bound to ask themselves 'Is this film based on historic fact? … It is understandable that such doubts should arise. This film depicts so much horror and beastly [behaviour] that any normal human being would have to wonder whether there are, indeed, people who can come up with and execute such terrible deeds'. Tobis 'regretfully' informed films-goers that '*This is what happened. The film is based on history and it depicts events which actually took place in the Boer War*'.[243] To enhance the credibility of this statement, the leaflet contained excerpts of historical documents from a collection entitled *Works and Documents on English Humanitarianism*, printed in Berlin in 1940, covering 'The Torching of Boer Farms', 'The Shooting of Cattle Herds', 'Boer Women and Children as

Shooting Targets', 'Starvation and Death in the Concentration Camps' and 'Audiences at Hangings'.[244]

Tobis had every reason to be concerned about public reception of the historical interpretation presented in *Ohm Krüger*. Recording the critical comments of film-goers in May 1941, the SD reported that

> There is a danger that such propagandistic exaggerations could throw doubt on the credibility of the film's historic plot. According to reports, historically well-informed members of the audience in particular and the wider viewing public in general have repeatedly questioned whether the propagandistic tenor of the film is really necessary, considering that the downfall of the Boers, historically speaking, represented one of the most horrific chapters in English brutality. The question is whether by sticking more strongly to historic truth an equally persuasive or perhaps an even more persuasive film could have been made. It is common for audience members to think about particularly tendentious scenes afterwards, to see them as historically untrue and then to doubt the historic truth of other, larger sections of the film's plot.[245]

As this report demonstrates, although historical film offered a means of combining the escapist and propagandistic genre, it was not wholly successful. Tensions between the scenario, the propagandistic narrative and historical interpretation emerge from the SD report, suggesting that, at times, the cinema-goer was fully aware of the specific context in which film propaganda was screened and sought out and desired 'truth' in filmic representations.

That the audience reaction as presented in the SD report of 12 May 1941 focused on the partisan interpretative framework of this depiction of the Boer War was perhaps unsurprising given the desire of propagandists to compare the experience of English domination in the late nineteenth century with the contemporary experience of total war. As Tobis commented in the press book for Steinhoff's production, 'it is important, particularly now, to shed proper light on these historic events, because they provide the basis on which to judge the British and because they show up clearly the similarities with present-day English warfare'.[246] For *Filmwelt*, Krüger represented 'a human being whose fate requires interpretation and could be highly significant for our people in its current life battle', adding that 'basically, it is still the same battle which we are now taking to its victorious end. Paul Krüger was – and this is why he is so important to us – the first committed fighter against England'.[247] Such sentiments were reinforced in the wider press, the *Allgemeine Zeitung* reporting that 'during, what are for us, eventful times in which a new order is [to be] established for Europe, any expression of the German nation is geared towards the big aim of settling the score with England'.[248] In this sense, the story of the Boers was transformed into a 'film of the German people', a production which 'speaks to the heart of the *Volk*'.[249] Nazi propagandists sought to demonstrate that the past could never be considered as such, its contemporary significance always at the forefront of National Socialist polemics. At the same time, the RMVP attempted to create a perceivable distance between a film's subject matter and the cinema-goer, the latter a target for the propagandistic message hidden beneath the contours of the production. Unless this was particularly well done, audiences would recognize the propagandistic technique, undermining the overall impact of a particular piece, if not necessarily resulting in a complete rejection of the propaganda message itself, as the SD report of 12 May 1941 confirmed.

As *Filmwelt* recognized, the figure of Paul Krüger held the greatest meaning for German audiences in his Führer-like determination to guide his people through their epic struggle with the British oppressor. As with other productions dealing with the depiction of the enemy, propagandists sought to contrast the negative portrait of the British with an idealized counterbalance, in this case Paul Krüger and the Boers. This strategy appeared to have been largely successful, the SD reporting that 'the film did not exhaust itself in negative propaganda. Rather, its portrayal of the Boers' struggle for liberation gave expression, albeit in a highly glorifying manner, to ethical and national values'.[250] Praised by *Filmwelt* as 'having been the first to have managed to show the world the true nature of British imperialism',[251] Paul Krüger simultaneously embodied the solid, pure-blooded farmer, idealized in Nazi *Blut und Boden* imagery and rhetoric, and the leadership figure, endowed with the vision to guide his people in their greatest hour of need, a man who faces adversaries who do not recognize his genius. The actor chosen to portray 'the father of the Boers', Emil Jannings, was no stranger to screen personae with parallel lives to the Führer, having starred in Veit Harlan's 1937 film, *Der Herrscher*.[252] Jannings, producing as well as starring in Steinhoff's film, revelled in the role, as indicated by the various interviews he gave at the time of the film's release and in its production stages. He became fully engaged with the film's central propagandistic message, declaring in September 1940 that 'I made this film because its material was designed to start a battle that is only now [being] completed ... With Paul Krüger, the simple farmer from lonely South Africa, the world became conscious of the fact that national freedom, affluence and happiness are under threat from one of our culture's pernicious afflictions: the way in which the English exercise power'.[253] It becomes clear from Goebbels' diary entries relating to the production of *Ohm Krüger* that Jannings was deeply involved in its conception and execution. Moreover, the Reich Minister himself took a keen interest in the film, visiting Jannings on the set in the Grunewald studios in early March 1941[254] and viewing excerpts from the Steinhoff production as they became available.[255] He debated the proposed endings to the film, naturally concluding that 'the one written by me is the best and the one that will get used'.[256] Goebbels was so impressed with his experience on the set that he raised the question of whether the film ought to be screened in two instalments.[257] Such was the value of the message contained within the 1941 production that Goebbels resolved to create 'a new *Prädikat* for big films such as *Ohm Krüger*. Perhaps Film of the Nation. Link it with a ring of honour awarded to the main creator. That will encourage even more enthusiasm'.[258] Jannings's film was the first to be awarded the prestigious *Prädikat* of 'Film of the Nation'.[259] In addition, on 2 April 1941, the *Filmprüfung* bestowed the additional *Prädikate* of *staatspolitisch und künstlerisch besonders wertvoll, kuturell wertvoll, volkstümlich wertvoll* and *Jugendwert* on the film.[260] *Ohm Krüger* premiered two days later.

Steinhoff's film, as Welch observes, is constructed around 'a series of principles that Goebbels could apply to the contemporary war in Europe..., achieved by the contrasting use of archetype, in which simple black-and-white images of the enemy are manipulated in order to elicit the desired response from cinema audiences'.[261] Its main narrative a reflection of the Boer leader upon the fate of his people, *Ohm Krüger* opens in Switzerland, where Paul Krüger is nursed in his final years, dying there in 1904. Unscrupulous journalists, eager to gain his reaction to the news that Britain is to be the sovereign power in South Africa after the conclusion of the Boer War in 1902, force and bribe their way into his room, taking a flash photograph of the ailing Krüger despite being told by his nurse that he has an eye complaint. Here, the print media, specifically the *Berliner Tageblatt*, is demonized for its failure to understand the plight of the Boers, Linda Schulte-Sasse recognizing the connection between National Socialist anti-Semitic discourses in relation to the press and the character in *Ohm Krüger*. Seizing the newspaper from Krüger and warning him that *'newspapers are poison for you'*, the nurse, prompted by the former Boer President, reads the fallacious reports aloud to him, a scene in which 'oral history becomes a vehicle of Truth juxtaposed with the distorted truth propagated by the press as a "machine" of capitalism'.[262] Highlighting the individuality of the leader and the negative light in which the world's media portray him thus strengthening the parallel to the Führer, Krüger begins to reflect upon his life, inviting the cinema audience into his world, seeing the English oppressor through his eyes, warning that *'one can never reach an understanding with the English'*. Idealizing the Boer way of life, Krüger describes how his peaceful, farming peoples were driven from region to region by the English, content just to find a calm existence tending to their crops and animals, their one aim *'freedom and peace'*, a God-fearing people working hard to create a new life in their new territory. Finally settling in the Transvaal and the Orange Free State, the Boers thought that they *'could live in peace there ... But then the English came yet again'*.

The first visual encounter with the English tyrant comes with the revelation that Cecil Rhodes (Ferdinand Marian), financier, statesman and later Prime Minister of Cape Colony, intends to provoke war between Britain and the Boers in order to secure the gold he has discovered in the Transvaal. In a return to the theme of the capitalist exploiter, Rhodes embodies 'typically British character traits, such as inexhaustible energy, an almost foolhardy adventurousness and unscrupulous greed, all dangerously exaggerated'[263] and is possessed with a 'pathological craving for power'.[264] Marian, associated with his portrayals of the 'Other' in films of the Third Reich (as Süß Oppenheimer in the notorious 1940 Harlan film *Jud Süß* and as Grandison in *Der Fuchs von Glenarvon*), was praised for his 'realistic' characterization of Rhodes, *Völkischer Beobachter* remarking that 'there is a terrifying coldness in his eyes when he decides, in passing, to rob the Boers of their possessions; his words express morality, yet his actions are full of the British oppressors' cunning; he succeeds in creating a model of the classic plutocrat'.[265] The result of Rhodes' underhand machinations, ultimately revealing his English character, is demonstrated in the subsequent sequence in which pious missionaries hand out bibles and weapons to natives, against a backdrop of the British flag and to a soundtrack of *God Save the Queen*, a forceful and explicit critique of the moralizing rhetoric accompanying the British imperial vision.[266] In many ways, Marian was ideally suited to this role. His former on-screen personae, both reviled and revered, added to the mysterious charm and yet fundamentally evil character of Cecil Rhodes, the eroticization of his possession of Africa (caressing the globe, he declares '*I love this Africa like a woman*') bearing out Schulte-Sasse's interpretation of Marian as 'the attractive, gallant lover intensified by his southern looks, which in the Third Reich were considered foreign and forbidden'.[267]

The image of the devious Rhodes is supplemented by the depiction of Jameson (Karl Haubenreißer), Joseph Chamberlain (Gustaf Gründgens) and the supplier of arms, 'The White Mother', Queen Victoria (Hedwig Wangel). Victoria is complicit in the persecution of the Boers. 'The embodiment of the Empire',[268] 'in her regalia [representing] the power and toughness of a regime'[269] and driven by the acquisition of power and territories, she was described in the studio publicity material as lacking in 'magisterial stature': 'a small, fat woman with slightly protruding blue eyes, washed out facial features, in a black dress and an impressive widow's hat'.[270] Appearances can be deceptive, however, Tobis pointing out that 'the small, wilful mouth expressed a stubborn will, and the arrogant eyes remained distant at all times'.[271] The imperial mission, the characters of Chamberlain ('Sly Joe'[272]) and Victoria and the motif of the perfidious Albion come together in the following scene in which the British monarch and her Prime Minister discuss the situation in Africa:

Chamberlain: It is England's destiny to educate the minor, uneducated peoples. This is an established policy ... It is truly remarkable how unsophisticated this people's culture is.
Victoria: How can you tell?
Chamberlain: They refuse a great future: that of being subjects of your Majesty! They say they would rather die than become English.
Victoria: [Coughing, indicative of her declining health] These Boers have far too many friends: the French, the Dutch, the Germans. We English have no friends in the world. They take us for thieves. Are we thieves, Chamberlain?
Chamberlain: If I may, your Majesty, no other nation is as pious as the English.
Victoria: I've heard that the Boers are pious too.
Chamberlain: Yes, but not in the right way. They have remained poor. They have focussed on cattle and farming and have few needs.
Victoria: My medicine! [Medicine brought to her by Brown in a whisky bottle] And so do you really think we can just seize their state?
Chamberlain: It is our duty.
Victoria: Ach, Chamberlain, we have had enough trouble with India. But at least India is rich. Why must we bother with these poor peasants in Africa?
Chamberlain: Gold has been found in the Boers' land.

Victoria: Gold! Why didn't you tell me before? Naturally, that's significant … A lot of gold did you say?

Chamberlain: A great deal of gold, your Majesty. A great deal. So much that we will be eternally rich…

Victoria: Do the missionaries have enough munitions and arms?

Chamberlain: Her Majesty's Government knows nothing about it!

That gold is seen as sufficient grounds to prosecute war was a theme frequently expressed in feature films of the Third Reich. As Schulte-Sasse contends, gold was conceived as 'an object in itself possessing beauty and material value', filmic narratives of the 1930s and 1940s 'investing [it with an] enigmatic Otherness'. Within films such as *Ohm Krüger*, gold stands at 'the crossroads between a feudal and a capitalist society',[273] the two merging in attempts to retain or acquire it. As such, it becomes a contested and mystical object within film, the opening sequence to Karl Hartl's 1934 production *Gold* announcing that '*for gold, kinsmen, tribes, nations go to war; for gold, men cheat, persecute, slaughter each other*'.[274] In this respect, *Ohm Krüger* built upon established cinematic traditions, using them to add to the representation of the British avarice.

Still 11   *Images of Britishness in Ohm Krüger. Illustrierter Film-Kurier*, private collection.

In another parallel to films dealing with the Irish question, specifically *Mein Leben für Irland*, Steinhoff supplements his critique of the British leadership with the inference that they seek to corrupt youth, inculcating English plutocratic 'values' through their elitist education systems. In *Ohm Krüger*, it is Jan (Werner Hinz), Krüger's son, who is the victim of British perfidy. Educated in law at Oxford, Jan is the archetypal 'lost son', a reoccurring theme in films of the Third Reich. Although he eventually returns to the fold having seen the error of his ways, in many ways, he parallels the character of Claus (Kurt Meisel) in *Kolberg*, both having rejected their farming backgrounds for the cosmopolitan lifestyle, both pouring scorn upon the supposedly 'backward' ways of their families who chose to remain at home, never venturing out into the wider world, both seemingly representing 'worldly values' but in truth portrayed as having been fooled by the pretence of the city and foreign cultures. Both characters lose their lives, although in very different circumstances, Jan in the struggle for the freedom of his people, Claus so wedded to the world of the city *conservatoire* where he studies music that he loses his life attempting to save the symbol of his chosen lifestyle, his violin. In *Ohm Krüger*, Jan's father attempts to persuade his son to return, only to find that he has been corrupted by English 'education', become a committed pacifist and is only concerned with the superficial values of a corrupt society. This prompts a rift between them, which is only healed when Jan joins his father in their fateful struggle against the English oppressor, deciding to heed his father's advice that '*you don't study history, you make it!*'

The scenes involving Krüger and his son, by contrasting alternative values, highlight the accepted image of the people's leader, drawing parallels to the contemporary vision of the Führer. Krüger is a man of action, not a man of words. He is willing to fight to protect his people and their territory and does not respect international treaties if it undermines the sovereignty of his state. He remains unafraid of opposition, declaring that he does not care for parliamentary talk and that he does '*not need to strut around in a top hat and frock coat*' to earn respect. In his prevention of the sale of farmlands to the British, he is determined and resolute, recognizing the importance of the protection of *Blut und Boden*, his only descendants of pure 'Brandenburg farming blood'.[275] He is a leader who knows both the loneliness of power and the joys of being a father to his people. Although Krüger is portrayed as a kindly family man, taking obvious pleasure from his forty-five grandchildren, he is also 'like a father-figure to the Boers'.[276] He is inspirational, declaring that, in spite of all obstacles, he will '*lead [his] people in this struggle, [where] every single man ... will be a hero*'. His call to defend Boer land results in a flood of supporters flocking to oppose British rule, Krüger pronouncing that he had '*no idea we were so strong. The whole world is behind us and there's no going back now. We will march on and God will be with us!*' Krüger travels Europe, attempting to build a consensus against the British. Although some refuse to grant an audience to the Boer leader, naturally the Germans are keen to hear his case. Such is the growing feeling against British imperial methods and the fear of Krüger's diplomatic campaigning that on her deathbed Queen Victoria bemoans '*how much they hate us*', forewarning, '*I can see something terrible coming*'. Turning to her son, who has been recalled from a Paris nightspot to be by her side, indicating the decadence of the English plutocracy juxtaposed with the simplicity of the Boers, she warns: *'you must be very clever and prudent, my son. You must always remember that nations hate each other and the day they cease quarrelling, we are lost.'* The weak, feeble and destructive image of Victoria is contrasted to the idealized image of Krüger, the 'healthy, strong man of the house, proud of his large family; we see him amongst his fellow men who are both soldiers and farmers like he is; we see him talking to his enemies: relaxed, waiting, "a man like a rock"'.[277]

It is in the aftermath of the death of Victoria and in the subsequent bloody crusade against the Boers that the true English character is revealed. On being called into the fray, the barbaric Lord Kitchener declares that *'this is a colonial war and it must be fought with colonial methods. And that means no more humanity. The Boers must be hit where they are most vunerable. Their farms must be burned to the ground, their women and children incarcerated in concentration camps. We no longer recognize the distinction between soldiers and civilians'.* This pronouncement heralds the beginning of the scorched earth policy. The film's narrative climaxes in the desecration of Boer land and the attempted rape of their women. With dismay, although not with surprise, Krüger receives news that the English invaders used Boer women and children as *'a protective wall, as cannon fodder'*, the brave victims urging the Boer commander to shoot through them to defeat the enemy. The Boers also prove themselves to be a people of endurance. They are rounded up and marched to concentration camps, where they are starved and exposed to disease, a policy designed to limit the resistance movement and to bring their menfolk out of hiding.[278] Tobis reminded the audience of the enormity of the British atrocities against the Boers, claiming in their publicity materials that 'in December 1901 alone as many as 1767 children died in the camps! And the women! They were abused, offended, violated!'[279] In an explicit depiction of the cruelties of the camps, Steinhoff shows women and children starving whilst the camp commandant feeds prime cuts of meat to his dog. These barbarities exposed the English character within the film, hidden behind the suave and slick exterior of Chamberlain and Rhodes, fitting well with wider National Socialist rhetoric relating to the British imperial mission. As Goebbels stated in January 1942, Britain is a

> regime which could by war force a defenceless people in the interests of its capitalists to import opium, as the English did in China, [and] let captured women starve as in the Boer War, and even drive them in front of their troops to force the men to capitulate. Such a regime needs no judgement passed on it, it has already passed judgement on itself. We are not impressed by the supercilious manner of representing the worst cynicism as the mark of the real gentleman.[280]

The culmination of the acts of cruelty in the film is the execution of Krüger's son, Jan, who finds his wife Petra in the camp and is captured trying to liberate her. He is to be executed, the camp commandant ensuring that Petra has a front row seat. With his dying words, Jan assures this wife that *'I die for you, for our people, for our fatherland. Justice and*

Still 12 *British atrocity in Ohm Krüger. Illustrierter Film-Kurier*, private collection.

freedom have been taken away from us but belief in our cause is stronger than death … Curse England!' Jan is hanged and Petra, as a result of her protestations, shot. The film returns to the elderly Krüger recalling his story. In the concluding sequence of the film, the Boer leader warns that

> eventually the day of reckoning will come. I don't know when but so much blood cannot have been split in vain, so many tears were not shed for nothing. We were but a small and weak people. Great and powerful people will rise up against British tyranny. They will strike England to the ground. God will be with them. Then the way will be clear for a better world.

Filmwelt summarized the closing scenes thus:

> Yes, the English are a very clever lot! They are expert vampires, to perfection. No gang of thieves and murderers could know their business any better. The whole nation carries the mark of Cain, people either being thieves and murderers themselves or appropriating stolen goods and raising their standard of living from the fruits of murder and mass

murder. Like wolves in sheep's clothing, they represent themselves as benefactors to the world, only to be better able to lay into the nations they have targeted for exploitation and annihilation.[281]

Goebbels was more than satisfied with Steinhoff's final product, commenting, after a screening for select individuals at his home, that 'the film is outstanding. A huge achievement. Everybody is enchanted by it. Jannings has surpassed himself. The best anti-British film one can imagine'.[282] Such was the impact on Goebbels that four days later on 6 April he discussed the film with Hitler, recalling that 'he tells me what a deep impression the Boer War made on him when he was young. He really likes the character types in the film. He is full of praise for our theatre and film work. The film in particular has impressed him. He wants any profits from film or radio to be put into other areas of art, which is what I've said before'.[283] Even three months later, Goebbels was still praising the production, noting in July that 'the *Ohm-Krüger* film is definitely a cut above the rest. After all, it is a film that promises to be of utmost significance in our propagandistic efforts to reach the minds of our people'.[284]

Goebbels' instincts for the popularity of the film proved to be correct, Tobis declaring that *Ohm Krüger* attracted a quarter of a million patrons in four days, breaking all records in film theatres and adding that 'over the four days covered, cinemas showing *Ohm Krüger* reported audience figures of around 250,000 for some 210,000 seats'. Berlin's premiere cinema, the Ufa-Palast am Zoo, welcomed 50,788 film-goers from 5 to 14 April, whilst the Capitol in Cologne accommodated 25,242 in just four days.[285] The popularity of the film, as with other productions such as *Feuertaufe*, owed much to the pre-release studio publicity, the SD reporting in May 1941 that

> Reports from different regions of the Reich confirm that the extraordinarily high expectations created by intense press propaganda have been exceeded by the film's general impression on all sections of the public. The film is considered to be *the best in the current year* and there is particular acknowledgement of the fact that it achieves an outstanding unity of political conviction, artistic expression and acting performances. Its outstanding *popular success* is demonstrated not only by the fact that all showings have been sold out but also by the extensive word-of-mouth recommendations and many conversations about the film.[286]

The public were particularly impressed that such an elaborate film could be produced in wartime, indicating that 'this was regarded as special proof of the strength and ability of the German film industry'. The film was reported to have been well received in all sectors of the German population, the SD commenting that 'undoubtedly, the film fulfils its propagandistic function *vis-à-vis* the wider public'. In connection with the successful aspects of Steinhoff's production, they noted 'the film, despite having been adapted to suit a broad audience, does document English colonial history and as such substantially increases and reinforces the anti-English war sentiment. It is has created, particularly for younger viewers, a clear understanding of the decline of the Boer people'.[287] That *Ohm Krüger* was particularly popular with young audiences was confirmed by film surveys conducted for the Reich which placed the 1941 production in sixth place overall, behind *Der große König*, *Bismarck* (Wolfgang Liebeneiner, 1940), *Die Entlassung* (The Dismissal, Wolfgang Liebeneiner, 1942), *Friedrich Schiller* (Herbert Maisch, 1940) and *Heimkehr*, [288] five of the six films, including *Ohm Krüger*, historically based.[289] Moreover, such was the impact on youth that thirty years later some still recalled specific scenes such as the supply of arms and bibles to African natives.[290] Overall, the film prompted an increased interest in the colonial question and specifically the Boer War, the SD commenting that 'its effect is confirmed by the increased demand for literature on the Boers and their struggle for liberation'. Worthy of particular comment was 'the depiction of brutality on the part of the English' which proved to be effective, the SD adding that 'the construction of the plot has cleverly been made to chime with the German people's current mood *vis-à-vis* the English'.[291] Rejecting criticism that the scenes of English barbarity were too 'cruel', Goebbels commented that 'it has to be like this if it is to have an effect on the people. And that is its purpose'.[292] This debate was reflected in the SD report, which noted that 'the big scenes showing the executions of Boer women are widely seen as a particularly impressive climax. They are depicted with a degree of realism that comes close to being unbearable'.[293] As noted previously, critical voices, although few according to the SD, centred on the historical authenticity of these images and questioned to what extent they were propagandistically motivated.[294] Significantly, despite Tobis' publicity highlighting the issue of the Boers' 'pure blood', the public called attention to the question of race, character and colonialism within the film.[295] The report of 12 May detailed that,

> Knowledgeable viewers and experts on Africa … question whether it is useful to portray in such heroic terms the Boers whose racially positive characteristics are accompanied also by strong negative elements and who in terms of their character, their economic and political actions did not always play a positive role. There were conflicting elements in the character of this mixed nation, and with a view to the colonial tasks of post-victory Germany it could not be portrayed as a Germanic ideal.[296]

The sensitivity of this question did not escape the notice of the RMVP, historian Robert Herzstein asserting that 'Hitler did not feel comfortable in the role of liberator, especially of dark-skinned "natives". The result was a massive propaganda assault, not so much *for* national liberation, as *against* decadent British imperialism'.[297]

This was a theme to unite the Axis powers. Consequently, *Ohm Krüger* won the *Mussolini-Pokal* at the 1941 Venice Biennale as best foreign film. In awarding the honour to Steinhoff's film and drawing attention to the role of Jannings in promoting the film's central message, the Italian Minister for Popular Culture, Alessandro Pavolini, opined:

> This prize goes to a film that has made an overwhelming impression because it shows once again the immensely powerful political arguments which are uniting Europe against

> England ... At the same time, it is honouring Emil Jannings whose name stands for an achievement that in itself is like warfare and connects with the history of the German film in this war.[298]

Such was the national and international reputation of *Ohm Krüger* that in 1944, as the vision of the Reich collapsed before him, Goebbels re-released the film to coincide with the increased use of the *Volkssturm*.[299]

To return to the original premise of this chapter, both British and German film propaganda conformed to generic principles, reflecting 'the mirror image, the coexistence of contradicting qualities, the dynamic nature of the image of the enemy and the need to dehumanise it'.[300] Significantly, the filmic representation of the enemy in both British and German propaganda drew the distinction between leaders and the people. Neither state deviated substantially from that course despite the occasional blurring of the lines of demarcation. Representations of the enemy were not merely intended for internal consumption. Propagandists were keenly aware that critiques of the enemy civilian and fighting populations could be exploited by the enemy, thus undermining the strategic advantage that 'enemy' propaganda could create. In the early years of the war, both the British and the German leadership remained optimistic, if not realistic, about the possibility of inciting resistance leading to the overthrow of the enemy regime. Such filmic representations avoiding the vilification of the general population of combatant nations worked alongside overt propaganda to foreign populations on the radio, in leaflets and in the press, as well as psychological warfare initiatives.

Unsurprisingly, both British and German propagandists made considerable use of stereotypical images. Filmic narratives sought to undermine and subvert positive existing national stereotypes (British resilience, manners, social codes of behaviour, etiquette and gentlemanliness and German efficiency, determination and might) as well as pointing to negative perceived national characteristics (the British false sense of superiority, pretension, superficiality, the suppression of minorities and the seizure of territory in the name of Empire, the Nazi brutality, dictatorship, ruthlessness and persecution). This functioned particularly well in filmic terms by sharpening pre-existing values and preconceived popular sterotypes. Obviously, there were points of distinction in the national thematic strands, Nazi propagandists dealing with race and class in keeping with their professed ideology. Nevertheless, the points of similarity in approach suggest a key set of principles in 'enemy' propaganda campaigns, adhering to Zur's conceptualization of generic forms in war relating to the persuasive techniques of contrast and the need 'to dehumanise' the opponent.[301]

Both nations fused the historic and contemporary in their campaigns, demonstrating the continuity of the enemy's character, his unchangeable nature ultimately justifying a final showdown and underpinning more timely propagandistic pieces. The historical backdrop also partially fulfilled the desire of audiences to escape the trials of everyday life, offering the propaganda message inside the 'gilded pill'. This technique became increasingly popular as film-goers began to demand more escapist fare at the cinema as war-weariness took its toll on the peoples of both Britain and Germany. As a result, film propagandists turned to disguising their message beneath a veil of fantasy and escapism, a method revealed in propaganda relating to the depiction of leadership from 1940 to 1942 in Britain and Germany.

NOTES

1. R. Vansittart, *Black Record. Germans Past and Present* (Hamish Hamilton, London, 1941), pp. 12–16.
2. Joseph Goebbels, *Das Reich*, editorial, 16 June 1940. Quoted in D. Welch, *Propaganda and the German Cinema*, p. 222.
3. O. Zur, 'The Psychohistory of Warfare: the Co-evolution of Culture, Psyche and Enemy', *Journal of Peace Research*, vol. 24, no. 2 (June 1987), pp. 125–34, here p. 131.
4. Ibid., pp. 131–2.
5. TNA PRO INF 1/848, 'The Principles Underlying British Wartime Propaganda'. Paper approved by Cabinet on 30 January 1940. PC paper No. 3.
6. TNA PRO INF 1/849, HPC 'Anger Campaign', 17 June 1940.
7. Ibid.
8. Ibid.
9. TNA PRO INF 1/848, Policy Committee Minutes, 4 June 1940.
10. TNA PRO INF 1/849, HPC 'Anger Campaign', 17 June 1940.
11. TNA PRO INF 1/848, 'The Principles Underlying British Wartime Propaganda'. Paper approved by Cabinet on 30 January 1940. PC paper No. 3.
12. TNA PRO INF 1/849, HPC 'Anger Campaign', 17 June 1940.
13. TNA PRO INF 1/251, MoI Speaker's Notes, 'Germans will be Germans', 9 December 1940.
14. TNA PRO INF 1/867, 'German versus British propaganda', n.d.
15. Official Record of the House of Lords, 11 February 1943. Quoted in A. Goldman, 'Germans and Nazis: The Controversy over "Vansittartism" in Britain during the Second World War', *Journal of Contemporary History*, vol. 14, no. 1 (January 1979), pp. 155–91, here pp. 162–3.
16. Tate Gallery, Kenneth Clark papers, 8812.5.1.14, 'What should be our policy towards Germany? Discussion between G.D.H. Cole, C.E.M. Joad, Bertram Russell and Lord Vansittart, n.d.
17. TNA PRO INF/849, 'It's the Same Old Hun', memorandum to the Policy Committee, Kenneth Clark, 22 January 1941.
18. TNA PRO INF 1/292, Home Intelligence Report no. 41. 9–16 July 1941.
19. TNA PRO INF 1/292, 'British Institute of Public Opinion', April 1943.
20. TNA PRO INF 1/292, HI Report no. 86. 18–26 May 1942. Item 10. 'Hate Training School'.
21. For a further discussion of this distinction in the period, see T. Harrisson, 'What is Public Opinion?', *Political Quarterly*, vol. 4 (1940), pp. 368–83.
22. M-O A: FR 1104, 'Private Opinion on the German People', 27 February 1942.
23. M-O A: FR 1624, 'Private Opinion about the German People', 1 January 1943.
24. TNA PRO INF 1/292, 'British Institute of Public Opinion', April 1943.
25. M-O A: FR 1624, 'Private Opinion about the German People', 1 January 1943.
26. M-O A: FR 2000, 'Vengeance', 14 January 1944. This is also reflected in FR 1831 'Germany after the War', June 1943.
27. See J. Richards, *The Age of the Dream Palace. Cinema and Society in Britain 1930–1939* (Routledge & Kegan Paul, London, 1984), p. 125; J. Richards, 'The British Board of Film Censors and Content Control in the 1930s: Foreign Affairs', *Historical Journal of Film, Radio and Television*, vol. 2, no. 1 (1982), pp. 38–48.

28. Throughout the war years, the BBFC remained in operation, policing the moral and social aspects of censorship, whilst the MoI and service departments oversaw military security. For more details, see J. Croft and N. Pronay, 'British Film Censorship and Propaganda Policy during the Second World War', in J. Curran and V. Porter (eds), *British Cinema History* (Weidenfeld & Nicoloson, London, 1983), pp. 144–64; J. C. Robertson, *The British Board of Film Censors. Film Censorship in Britain, 1896–1950* (Croom Helm, London, 1985); *The Hidden Cinema: British Film Censorship in Action 1913–75* (Routledge, London, 1993); 'British Film Censorship Goes To War', *Historical Journal of Film, Radio and Television*, vol. 2, no. 1 (1982), pp. 49–64.

29. Bfi Special Collections. BBFC scenarios, (1938/19). J. C. Hanna quoted in J. Richards, 'The BBFC and Content Control in the 1930s', p. 40.

30. Bfi Special Collections, BBFC Scenarios, 1939, 58, *Swastika* (20th Century Productions), 15 August 1939.

31. M-O A: FR 57, 'Preferences for Themes in Films', March 1940. Also reproduced in J. Richards and D. Sheridan (eds), *Mass-Observation at the Movies*, p. 176.

32. Ibid.

33. For a full discussion of *Pastor Hall*, see J. Chapman, 'Why We Fight: *Pastor Hall* and *Thunder Rock*', in A. Burton, T. O'Sullivan, and P. Wells (eds), *The Family Way. The Boulting Brothers and Postwar British Film Culture* (Flicks Books, Trowbridge, 2000), pp. 81–97.

34. Bfi Special Collections, BBFC Scenarios, 1939, 48, *Pastor Hall*, 17 July 1939.

35. IWMS 4627/6, here 4627/1, Roy Boulting, interviewed in March 1980.

36. TNA PRO INF 1/867, 'Programme for Film Propaganda'. CC Paper no. 6. Foreign Publicity Business Advisory Committee, 1939.

37. Ibid.

38. *Kinematograph Weekly*, 19 October 1939, p. 19.

39. M-O A: FR 472, 'Impressions of Nazi Germany on Film', 30 October 1940. Len England.

40. M-O A: FR 491, 'Battle for Britain', 13 November 1940. Len England.

41. M-O A: TC 17/8B, 'Ministry of Information General Film Reports'. L.E. 'Uses of Intelligence for the Film', 9 October 1940.

42. M-O A: TC 17/5/C, 'Letters to *Picture-goer Weekly*', letter from F.M., Glasgow, n.d.

43. TNA PRO INF 1/251, Minutes. HPC Executive Committee, 21 April 1941.

44. TNA PRO INF 1/867, 'Programme for Film Propaganda'. CC Paper no. 6. Foreign Publicity Business Advisory Committee. 1939.

45. Bfi Special Collections, BBFC Scenarios, 1939, 64, *Liberty Radio* (later *Freedom Radio*) (C. Mann Ltd.), 6 October 1939.

46. *Kinematograph Weekly*, 16 May 1940, p. 24 A.

47. *Today's Cinema*, 12 April 1940, p. 14.

48. M-O A: TC 17/12/C, *Pastor Hall*, May 1940. Reaction from a male, 25–40, A.

49. M-O A: TC 17/12/C, *Pastor Hall*, May 1940. Reaction from a female, 40+, A.

50. M-O A: FR 472, 'Memo on the Impressions of Nazi Germany given by Various Films', 29 October 1940. Films analysed in the report were *Professor Mamlock*, *The Mortal Storm*, *Pastor Hall*, *Hitler – the Beast of Berlin*, *I was a Captive of Nazi Germany*, and *Night Train to Munich*.

51. See J. C. Robertson, *The British Board of Film Censors. Film Censorship in Britain*, p. 132.

52. GP G4:20: 3, John Grierson, 10 August 1940. Also quoted in J. Chapman, 'Why We Fight', p. 92. Ref: *Documentary News Letter*, September 1940, pp. 3–4.

53. Ibid.

54. N. Cull, *Selling War*, p. 50. The release of the film actually provoked an anti-Nazi riot in Times Square, New York, leading the Chicago authorities to issue an immediate ban through a 'by-law prohibiting the display

of "depravity, criminality or lack of virtue" in "a class of citizens of any race," although municipal authorities raised no comparable objection to the showing of the German propaganda film *Feldzug in Polen*' (Cull, p. 50).

55. TNA PRO INF 1/867, 'Programme for Film Propaganda'. CC Paper no. 6. Foreign Publicity Business Advisory Committee. 1939.

56. TNA PRO INF 1/251, HPC Executive Sub-Committee, 21 April 1941. My italics.

57. See L. London, *Whitehall and the Jews* (Cambridge University Press, 2000).

58. GP G4:20: 3, John Grierson, 10 August 1940. Also quoted in J. Chapman, 'Why We Fight', p. 92. Ref: *Documentary News Letter*, September 1940, p. 3–4.

59. See for example, Bfi Special Collections, BBFC Scenarios, 1940–1, 14, *The Sign of Colonel Britton* (Widgely Newman), 20 July 1941.

60. Bfi, press book, *Mr Emmanuel* (1944). This was Felix Aylmer's only starring role. The part of Mr Emmanuel had also been discussed with Paul Muni, Conrad Veidt and George Arliss. It is reported that Leslie Howard was on his way to talk about the role when he lost his life in an aircraft incident on 1 June 1943 over the Bay of Biscay. On the set itself, see *Kinematograph Weekly*, 17 February 1944, p. 13.

61. Bfi, US press book, *Mr Emmanuel* (1944).

62. Ibid.

63. TNA PRO INF 1/292, Home Intelligence, 'Home Morale and Public Opinion: a review of three months' findings, November 1941 – January 1942', 11 February 1942.

64. TNA PRO INF 1/292, Home Intelligence Report, no. 55, 13–20 October 1941.

65. M-O A: TC 17/12/C *Pastor Hall*, May 1940. Reaction from a female, 40+, A.

66. M-O A: FR 472, 'Impression of Nazi Germany on Film', 30 October 1940. Len England.

67. IWMS 4627/6, here 4627/1, Roy Boulting, interviewed in March 1980.

68. M-O A: TC 17/12/C, *Pastor Hall*, May 1940. Reaction from a male, 25–40, A.

69. The production history of *49th Parallel* has already been covered extensively elsewhere, notably in K. MacDonald, *Emeric Pressburger. The Life and Death of a Screenwriter* (Faber and Faber, London, 1994), pp. 165–82; A. Aldgate and J. Richards, *Britain Can Take it*, pp. 21–41.

70. *Documentary News Letter*, November 1941.

71. J. Robertson, *The British Board of Film Censors*, p. 119.

72. M. Powell, *A Life in Movies*, p. 359.

73. Bfi Special Collections, Thorold Dickinson Collection, Box 7, item 7. On Dickinson's Nazi character in *The Next of Kin* (1942): C. A. Lejeune in *The Observer*, 17 May 1942.

74. K. MacDonald, *Emeric Pressburger*, p. 171.

75. Ibid., p. 166.

76. *Documentary News Letter*, May 1942, p. 67.

77. TNA PRO INF/849, 'It's the Same Old Hun', memorandum to the Policy Committee, Kenneth Clark, 22 January 1941.

78. Advert for *49th Parallel* in *Today's Cinema*, 7 October 1941, p. 4.

79. *Documentary News Letter*, November 1941.

80. *Documentary News Letter*, November 1941.

81. Pressburger in K. MacDonald, *Emeric Pressburger*, p. 179.

82. A. Moor, 'Dangerous Limelight: Anton Walbrook and the Seduction of the English' in B. Babington (ed.), *British Stars and Stardom from Alma Taylor to Sean Connery* (Manchester University Press, Manchester, 2001), pp. 80–93, here p. 82.

83. Pressburger in K. MacDonald, *Emeric Pressburger*, p. 170.

84. A. Moor, 'Dangerous Limelight', p. 82.

85. Bfi, press book, *The Life and Death of Colonel Blimp* (1943).

86. For more on *Freedom Radio,* see J. Fox, '"The Mediator": Images of Radio in Wartime Feature Film in Britain and Germany', in M. Connelly and D. Welch (eds), *War and the Media. Reportage and Propaganda, 1900–2003* (I. B. Tauris, London/New York, 2005), pp. 92–112. In particular, pp. 97–101.

87. Letter from Vansittart to Powell, 25 May 1942. Reproduced in I. Christie (ed.), *Powell and Pressburger. The Life and Death of Colonel Blimp* (Faber and Faber, London, 1994), p. 26.

88. MoI Report on 'The Life and Death of Sugar Candy', signed R.B. 8 June 1942 and agreed by Jack Beddington, 9 June 1942. Reproduced in I. Christie (ed.), *Powell and Pressburger,* p. 35.

89. Ibid., p. 34.

90. Ibid., p. 36.

91. Memorandum from Powell and Pressburger to the Film's Division, MoI, 16 June 1942. Reproduced in I. Christie (ed.), *Powell and Pressburger,* p. 38.

92. *Kinematograph Weekly,* 10 June 1943, p. 13.

93. E. W. Robson and M. M. Robson, *The Shame and Disgrace of Colonel Blimp. The True Story of the Film* (The Sidneyan Society, London, n.d.), p. 4.

94. Ibid., p. 1.

95. *Documentary News Letter,* no. 5, 1943, p. 219.

96. C. A. Lejeune, *The Observer,* 13 June 1943. Reproduced in I. Christie (ed.), *Powell and Pressburger,* p. 57.

97. *Documentary News Letter,* November 1941, p. 215.

98. *New Statesman,* 18 October 1941 as quoted in K. MacDonald, *Emeric Pressburger,* p. 180; J. Richards and A. Aldgate, *Britain Can Take It,* p. 39.

99. *Documentary News Letter,* November 1941, p. 215.

100. J. Richards and A. Aldgate, *Britain Can Take It,* p. 41.

101. Ibid., p. 40.

102. M-O A: TC 17/8/A, 'Film Reports and Memos, 1940–1943, MoI'. '*49th Parallel*', 2 November 1941.

103. 'Writer, 20, Danbury', M-O directive (including a question on the most popular films of the war years), November 1943. Reproduced in D. Sheridan and J. Richards (eds), *Mass-Observation at the Movies,* pp. 220–91.

104. Ibid., 'Nursery assistant, 37, Oxford'.

105. Pressburger in K. MacDonald, *Emeric Pressburger,* p. 166.

106. *Documentary News Letter,* May 1942, p. 67.

107. TNA PRO INF 1/251, 'We Stand Fast', 28 June 1940

108. TNA PRO INF 1/251, HPC Executive Sub-Committee, 21 April 1941.

109. Films analysed in the report were *Professor Mamlock, The Mortal Storm, Pastor Hall, Hitler – the Beast of Berlin, I was a Captive of Nazi Germany,* and *Night Train to Munich.*

110. M-O A: FR 472, 'Memo on the Impression of Nazi Germany given by Various Films', 29 October 1940.

111. J. Richards and A. Aldgate, *Britain Can Take It,* p. 115.

112. M. Balcon, *Michael Balcon presents… A Lifetime of Films* (Hutchinson, London, 1969), p. 140.

113. Bfi Special Collections. Balcon Collection. F/7. Michael Balcon to Hugh Findlay, 14 July 1942.

114. J. M. Edwards, 'Four Epitaphs', *The Times,* 6 February 1918, p. 7. In Balcon's quotation, the word 'freedom' has replaced Edwards' original choice 'England'.

115. See references in the obituaries in *The Times* for 5 March 1918 and 1 July 1918. The references continue throughout the inter-war period and into World War II. See, for example, obituaries in *The Times* on 30 October 1919; 31 July 1920; 11 October 1924; 22 July 1929 and 22 July 1937.

116. Bfi Special Collections. Balcon Collection. F/7. Debate over Title of the Film. 10 August 1942.

117. *Documentary News Letter,* November–December 1942, p. 149.

118. Ibid.

119. Bfi, British press book, *Went the Day Well?*

120. TNA PRO INF 1/867, 'Programme for Film Propaganda'. CC Paper no. 6. Foreign Publicity Business Advisory Committee, 1939.

121. TNA PRO INF 1/849, HPC 'Anger Campaign', 17 June 1940.

122. *Documentary News Letter,* November-December 1942, p. 149.

123. TNA PRO INF 1/849, HPC 'Anger Campaign', 17 June 1940

124. P. Sorlin, *European Cinemas, European Societies, 1939–1990* (Routledge, London/New York, 1991), p. 56.

125. Bfi, British press book, *Went the Day Well?*

126. Ibid.

127. This was particularly true of films such as Noel Coward's *In Which We Serve*. For further discussion of this point, see A. Aldgate and J. Richards, *Britain Can Take It*, p. 208 and J. Fox, 'Millions Like Us? Accented Language and the "Ordinary" in British Films of the Second World War', *Journal of British Studies*, vol. 45, no. 4 (October 2006), pp. 819–45.

128. P. Sorlin, *European Cinemas*, p. 56.

129. TNA PRO INF 1/251, 'Hitler's Fifth Column: What it is. How it works. What we can do about it', planning committee, 25 June 1940.

130. Bfi, British press book, *Went the Day Well?*

131. E. Sussex, *The Rise and Fall of British Documentary* (University of California Press, Berkeley, 1975). Excerpt reproduced in I. Aitken (ed.), *The Documentary Film Movement. An Anthology* (Edinburgh University Press, Edinburgh, 1998), p. 195.

132. TNA PRO INF 1/849, HPC 'Anger Campaign', 17 June 1940.

133. Bfi, Special Collections. Balcon Collection. F8a.

134. Bfi, British press book, *Went the Day Well?*

135. Bfi Special Collections. Balcon Collection. F/7. Report on the Test Screening in Croydon, 10 August 1942.

136. Caroline Lejeune in *The Observer*, 1 November 1942. Quoted in A. Aldgate and J. Richards, *Britain Can Take It*, pp. 134–5.

137. *The Cinema*, 4 November 1942, p. 11.

138. Bfi Special Collections. Balcon Collection. F/7. Report on the Test Screening in Croydon, 10 August 1942.

139. *Kinematograph Weekly,* 29 October 1942, p. 20.

140. *Documentary News Letter*, November–December 1942, p. 149.

141. M-O A: TC 17/5/B, 'Letters to *Picture-Goer Weekly*, British Films', R.H., Battersea, 27 December 1940.

142. *Kinematograph Weekly*, 8 January 1942, p. 87.

143. Ibid.

144. Bfi, British press book, *Let George Do It*, 1940.

145. *Kinematograph Weekly*, 23 November 1939, p. 25.

146. M-O A: FR 435, '*Let George Do It*', 21 October 1940.

147. M-O A: FR 435, '*Let George Do It*', 21 October 1940.

148. M-O A: FR 394, 'Mass-Observation Film Work', Len England, 10 September 1940.

149. M-O A: FR 446, 'Social Research and the Film', October 1940. Reproduced in D. Sheridan and J. Richards (eds), *Mass-Observation at the Movies*, p. 214.

150. See for example, J. Poole, 'British Cinema Attendance in Wartime', p. 20.

151. *Today's Cinema*, 7 March 1944.

152. A study of British humour in film was conducted by Mass-Observation in June 1940. See M-O A: FR 198, 'Humour in Film', 13 June 1940. Also reproduced in D. Sheridan and J. Richards (eds), *Mass Observation at the Movies*.

153. M-O A: FR 394, 'Mass-Observation Film Work', 10 September 1940.

154. Poll from the *Motion Picture Herald* 1940: '1940 Opinion Poll for British Stars'. Reported in *The Cinema*, 1 January 1941. The stars were George Formby (1), Gracie Fields (3), Arthur Askey (4) and Will Hay (7). There has been much literature addressing the question of Formby's popularity. See in particular, J. Richards, *Stars in Our Eyes. Lancashire Stars of Stage, Screen and Radio* (Lancashire County Books, Preston, 1994); R. Murphy, *Realism and Tinsel*, pp. 191–219 (on music hall stars); R. McKibbin, *Classes and Cultures. England 1918–1951* (Oxford, Oxford University Press, 1998), pp. 436–7; S. Street, *British National Cinema* (Routledge, London, 1997), pp. 118–19.

155. R. Murphy, *Realism and Tinsel*, p. 193.

156. For an excellent discussion of the Gainborough melodramas, see S. Harper, *Picturing the Past: the Rise and Fall of the British Costume Film* (Bfi, London, 1994).

157. M-O A: FR 435, '*Let George Do It*', 21 October 1940.

158. GP G3:14:3, John Grierson, 'The Fate of British Films', reprinted from the *Fortnightly*, July 1937, p. 9.

159. M-O A TC 17/5/B, Letters to *Picture-Goer*: British Films. Letter from R.V., Harrow, 1 January 1941.

160. J. Richards, *Stars in Our Eyes*, p. 10.

161. A. Randall and R. Seaton, *George Formby* (W. H. Allen, London, 1974), pp. 16–17. Quoted in R. Murphy, *Realism and Tinsel*, p. 194.

162. M-O A: FR 435, '*Let George Do It*', 21 October 1940.

163. TNA PRO INF 1/867, 'Programme for Film Propaganda'. CC Paper no. 6. Foreign Publicity Business Advisory Committee, 1939.

164. Ibid.

165. *Kinematograph Weekly*, 25 July 1940, p. 18.

166. RMVP Ministerial Conference minutes, 23 June 1940 in W. Boelcke (ed.), *The Secret Conferences of Dr. Goebbels*, p. 59.

167. Ibid., 21 March 1941, p. 127.

168. Ministerial Conference Minutes, 3 September 1939. Cited in J. Petley, 'Perfidious, Albion: The Depiction of Great Britain in Films of the Third Reich', in C. Cullingford and H. Husemann (eds), *Anglo-German Attitudes* (Avebury, Aldershot, 1995), pp. 182–93, p. 187.

169. RMVP Ministerial Conference minutes, 24 July 1940, in W. Boelcke (ed.), *The Secret Conferences of Dr. Goebbels*, p. 70.

170. Ibid., 24 July 1940, p.70.

171. Ibid., 7 July 1940, p. 65.

172. Quoted in R. Herzstein, *The War that Hitler Won: The Most Infamous Propaganda Campaign in History* (Abacus, London, 1980), p. 330.

173. RMVP Ministerial Conference minutes, 2 June 1940, in W. Boelcke (ed.), *The Secret Conferences of Dr. Goebbels*, p. 49.

174. Ibid., 24 July 1940, p.70.

175. Quoted in R. Herzstein, *The War that Hitler Won*, p. 330.

176. RMVP Ministerial Conference minutes, 22 May 1942, in W. Boelcke (ed.), *The Secret Conferences of Dr. Goebbels*, p. 238.

177. On pre-existing Anglophobia, see J. Petley, 'Perfidious Albion', p. 185 and R. Herzstein, *The War that Hitler Won*, pp. 325–7. It should also be noted that there was also a sense of such Anglophile tendencies which ran parallel to this, as Petley observes and Welch details (D. Welch, *Propaganda and the German Cinema*, p. 219).

178. 'Englands Geißel über der Welt', *Filmwelt*, 12 July 1940.

179. Nazi propaganda made full use of Byron's 'Curse of Minerva', arguing that even Britons could see how the Empire devoured smaller nations in their quest for world hegemony. See for example 'Ihr "reizender Krieg"', Friedrich Hussong, *Filmwelt*, 27 September 1940, in which sections of the poem are reproduced alongside a blistering critique of contemporary and historical British war leadership.

180. See for example, R. Herzstein, *The War that Hitler Won*, p. 331. Herzstein gives a more detailed account of the history and pre-history of general anti-British propaganda than that presented here (which is focused on film). See for example, pp. 325–43.

181. Ministerial Conference Minutes, 3 September 1939. Quoted in J. Petley, 'Perfidious Albion, p. 187.

182. *Der Angriff*, 15 November 1939. Wiener Library cuttings collection, PC5/119D. For further examples of the vilification of Disraeli, see W. G. Knop (ed.), *Beware of the English! German Propaganda Exposes England* (Hamish Hamilton, London, 1939), pp. 31–2.

183. *Das Reich*, 3 January 1942. Wiener Library cuttings collection, PC5/101c.

184. For more details on these works and their relationship to Nazi anti-British propaganda, see R. Herzstein, *The War that Hitler Won*, pp. 325–7.

185. Dates and production details here from D. Welch, *Propaganda and the German Cinema*, pp. 220–1 (*Gentlemen*) and www.filmportal.de (*Soldaten von Morgen*).

186. It is unclear what was the direct distribution pattern of this film, as indicated by the discrepancy between the censorship and premiere dates (3 July 1941 and 27 January 1942 respectively). As records suggest that it was intended as an educational film, it would not be unreasonable to assume that the film enjoyed non-theatrical distribution in schools and youth groups prior to general release. For these dates and further information, see www.filmportal.de.

187. 'Ein Regisseur der Jugend. Gespräch mit Alfred Weidenmann, dem Regisseur des Ufa-Flms *Junge Adler*', Ingeborg Lohse, *Film-Kurier*, 10 March 1944.

188. *Das Reich*, 3 January 1942. Wiener Library cuttings collection, PC5/101c.

189. Quoted in D. Welch, *Propaganda and the German Cinema*, p. 221.

190. *Der Angriff*, 20 November 1939. Wiener Library cuttings collection, PC 5/101c.

191. 'Gentlemen auf der U-Bootfalle', *Filmwelt*, 26 January 1940.

192. W. Schumann, *Being Present: Growing up in Hitler's Germany* (Kent State University Press, Kent State, OH, 1991), p. 74.

193. 'Ihr "reizender Krieg"', Friedrich Hussong, *Filmwelt*, 27 September 1940. See also W. G. Knop (ed.), *Beware of the English!*, pp. 51–3.

194. Quoted in R. Herzstein, *The War that Hitler Won*, p. 336.

195. Ibid., p. 336.

196. 'Englands Geißel über der Welt', Hilde R. Lest, *Filmwelt*, 12 July 1940

197. See, for example, W. G. Knop (ed.), *Beware of the English!*, p. 74 and pp. 131–2.

198. *Filmwelt*, 17 May 1940.

199. 'Englands Geißel über der Welt', Hilde R. Lest, *Filmwelt*, 12 July 1940.

200. *Filmwelt*, 17 May 1940.

201. 'Englands Geißel über der Welt', Hilde R. Lest, *Filmwelt*, 12 July 1940.

202. Information from www.filmportal.de and www.deutsches-filminstitut.de.

203. For a further discussion of this, see J. Fox, '"A Thin Stream Issuing through Closed Lock Gates": German Cinema and the United Kingdom, 1933–45', in R. Van der Winkel and D. Welch (eds), *Cinema and the Swastika*.

204. J. Petley, 'Perfidious Albion', p. 182.

205. 'Gentlemen auf der U-Bootfalle', *Filmwelt*, 26 January 1940.

206. Ibid.

207. J. Petley, 'Perfidious Albion', p. 182.

208. D. Welch, *Propaganda and the German Cinema*, p. 219.

209. Ibid., p. 220.

210. Ibid., p. 219.

211. For an extended discussion of *Das Herz der Königin*, see J. Fox, *Filming Women in the Third Reich* (Berg, Oxford, 2000), pp. 26–31.

212. 'Ballade von Leben, Liebe und Tod. Bericht von der Formung des Ufa-Films *Das Herz einer Königin*', *Filmwelt*, 8 December 1939.

213. BArch R58/184, SD Report, 'Zur Aufführung von Filmen über völkische Freiheitsbewegung', 20 May 1940, also in H. Boberach (ed.), *Meldungen*, vol. 4, p. 1155.

214. Ibid.

215. Ibid.

216. See R. Herzstein, *The War that Hitler Won*, p. 342. An interesting contrast between German propaganda and British collaboration with Ireland can be seen in two specific SD reports in this respect: 15 July 1940 in H. Boberach (ed.), *Meldungen*, vol. 5, p. 1376 and 14 November 1940 in H. Boberach (ed.), *Meldungen*, vol. 5, p. 1764.

217. Reproduced in W. G. Knop (ed.), *Beware of the English!*, p. 168. This is an interesting book which demonstrates the circulation of wider German anti-British propaganda in the United Kingdom. It has a foreword by Stephen King-Hall, who himself was singled out by Nazi propagandists on occasion.

218. For new interpretations of this problem, see M. O'Driscoll and D. Keogh (eds), *Ireland in World War II: Neutrality and the Art of Survival* (Mercier Press, Cork, 2004). For the pre-war relationship between Ireland and Germany, see M. O'Driscoll, *Ireland, Germany and the Nazis: Politics and Diplomacy, 1919–39* (Four Courts Press, Dublin, 2004).

219. Quoted in R. Herzstein, *The War that Hitler Won*, pp. 342–3. Also quoted in J. Petley, 'Perfidious Albion', p. 189.

220. Ibid., p. 304.

221. 'Irische Passion. *Der Fuchs von Glenarvon* im Berliner Ufa-Palast am Zoo', 26 April 1940. Wiener Library cuttings collection, PC 15B/20A/8.

222. SDK Berlin, *Der Fuchs von Glenarvon*, clipping 'Filme, die wir sahen', *Filmwelt*, April 1940.

223. 'Irische Passion. *Der Fuchs von Glenarvon* im Berliner Ufa-Palast am Zoo', 26 April 1940. Wiener Library cuttings collection, PC 15B/20A/8.

224. SDK Berlin, *Der Fuchs von Glenarvon*, clipping 'Filme, die wir sahen', *Filmwelt*, April 1940.

225. Ibid.

226. Ibid.

227. The SD reported that the German public appreciated the fact the Diehl was released from the front to star in *Der Fuchs von Glenarvon*. See BA R58/184, SD Report, 'Zur Aufführung von Filmen über völkische Freiheitsbewegung', 20 May 1940, also in H. Boberach (ed.), *Meldungen*, vol. 4, p. 1155.

228. SDK Berlin, 4889 *Mein Leben für Irland*, press book.

229. E. Fröhlich (ed.), *Die Tagebücher von Joseph Goebbels. Sämtliche Fragmente*, vol. 4, diary entry for 2 February 1941, p. 488.

230. BArch NS 29/776, Albert Speer Collection, SD- Abschnitte und Unterabschnitte, Leipzig, 'Filmbericht für die Zeit vom 18.4–18.5.1941'.

231. 'Englands Geißel über der Welt', Hilde R. Lest, *Filmwelt*, 12 July 1940.

232. Critiques of British conduct in the Boer War were widely publicized in the Reich. Some examples can be found in W. G. Knop (ed.), *Beware of the English!*, p. 61 and p. 137.

233. See for example, SD report, 9 February 1940 in H. Boberach (ed.), *Meldungen*, vol. 3, p. 740 and SD report, 4 March 1940 in H. Boberach (ed.), *Meldungen*, vol. 3, p. 840.

234. Goebbels' Speech to workers and soldiers, Berlin, 12 November 1939. Wiener Library cuttings collection, PC5/101c, reel 98.

235. See I. Christie, *The Life and Death of Colonel Blimp*, p. 34.

236. '*Ohm Krüger*', *Filmwelt*, 29 November 1940.

237. Ibid.

238. Ibid.

239. SDK Berlin, *Ohm Krüger*, press book.

240. '*Ohm Krüger*', *Filmwelt*, 29 November 1940.

241. 'Emil Jannings: *Ohm Krüger* – Vorkämpfer gegen Englands Willkür', *Filmwelt*, 13 December 1940.

242. 'Burenschicksal- Englands ewige Schuld', *Völkischer Beobachter*, 5 April 1941.

243. Leaflet produced by Tobis, entitled '*Der Ohm-Krüger Film – erfunden? Die historischen Tatsachen*', Dr. Wilhelm Ziegler. In SDK Berlin, *Ohm Krüger* file.

244. Ibid.

245. BArch R58/160, SD report, No. 185, 12 May 1941. Also reproduced in H. Boberach (ed.), *Meldungen*, vol. 5, p. 2293.

246. SDK Berlin, *Ohm Krüger*, press book.

247. 'Emil Jannings: *Ohm Krüger* – Vorkämpfer gegen Englands Willkür', *Filmwelt*, 13 December 1940.

248. '*Ohm Krüger* – Zeitgemässe Gedanken zu meinen neuen Film', *Allgemeine Zeitung*, 13 September 1940. Clipping in SDK Berlin, *Ohm Krüger* file.

249. SDK Berlin, *Ohm Krüger*. Publicity materials for *Ohm Krüger*.

250. BArch R58/160, SD report, no. 185, 12 May 1941.

251. 'Emil Jannings: *Ohm Krüger* – Vorkämpfer gegen Englands Willkür', *Filmwelt*, 13 December 1940.

252. K. Kreimeier, *The Ufa Story*, p. 295.

253. '*Ohm Krüger* – Zeitgemässe Gedanken zu meinen neuen Film', *Allgemeine Zeitung*, 13 September 1940. Clipping in SDK Berlin, *Ohm Krüger* file.

254. E. Fröhlich (ed.), *Die Tagebücher von Joseph Goebbels. Sämtliche Fragmente*, vol. 4, diary entry for 5 March 1941, p. 526.

255. Ibid., diary entry for 10 February 1941, p. 498.

256. Ibid., diary entry for 26 March 1941, p. 553.

257. Ibid., diary entry for 5 March 1941, p. 526.

258. Ibid., diary entry for 21 March 1941, p. 547.

259. See *Straßburger Neueste Nachrichten* 8 April 1941 for further details of the press release. Wiener Library cuttings collection, PC5/106E.

260. SDK Berlin, *Zensurkarte* 55316, *Ohm Krüger*, 2 April 1941.

261. D. Welch, *Propaganda and the German Cinema*, p. 231.

262. L. Schulte-Sasse, *Entertaining the Third Reich*, p. 288.

263. 'Ohm Krüger, Held und Vater seines Volkes', Hilde R. Lest, *Filmwelt*, 4 October 1940.

264. '*Ohm Krüger*', *Filmwelt*, 29 November 1940.

265. 'Burenschicksal- Englands ewige Schuld', *Völkischer Beobachter*, 5 April 1941.

266. See W. G. Knop (ed.), *Beware of the English!*, p. 57 and p. 159.

267. S. Ziehnski and T. Maurer, 'Bausteine des Films *Jud Süß*', in *Jud Süss': Filmprotokoll, Programmheft und Einzelanalysen* (Spiess, Berlin, 1983), p.32. Quoted in L. Schulte-Sasse, *Entertaining the Third Reich*, p. 81. This is also the central contention of Schulte-Sasse in relation to Marian's role in *Jud Süß*.

268. *Englischer Krieg vor 40 Jahren und heute: zu dem Emil-Jannings Film der Tobis 'Ohm Krüger*', Book produced by Tobis to coincide with the release of the film. Copy held in SDK Berlin, *Ohm Krüger* file.

269. SDK Berlin, *Ohm Krüger*, press book.

270. *Englischer Krieg vor 40 Jahren und heute: zu dem Emil-Jannings Film der Tobis 'Ohm Krüger'.* Book produced by Tobis to coincide with the release of the film. Copy held in SDK Berlin, *Ohm Krüger* file.

271. Ibid.

272. *'Ohm Krüger'*, *Filmwelt*, 29 November 1940.

273. L. Schulte-Sasse, *Entertaining the Third Reich*, p. 247

274. Quoted in J. Petley, 'Perfidious Albion', p. 187.

275. 'Ohm Krüger, Held und Vater seines Volkes', Hilde R. Lest, *Filmwelt*, 4 October 1940.

276. *Illustrierter Film-Kurier*, No. 3196.

277. *Zur festlichen Aufführung des Emil-Jannings Film der Tobis 'Ohm Krüger'* (Tobis Film AG, no place of publication, n.d.), from the collections of the British Library, London. The British library catalogue suggests that the book may have been published c.1940. It is likely that the book would have been released to celebrate the premiere of the film, which would make the possible date of publication 1941.

278. *Illustrierter Film-Kurier*, no. 3196.

279. British Library collections, *Zur festlichen Aufführung des Emil-Jannings Film der Tobis 'Ohm Krüger'.*

280. *Das Reich*, 3 January 1942. Wiener Library cuttings collection, PC5/101c.

281. 'Ohm Krüger, Held und Vater seines Volkes', Hilde R. Lest, *Filmwelt*, 4 October 1940.

282. E. Fröhlich (ed.), *Die Tagebücher von Joseph Goebbels. Sämtliche Fragmente*, vol. 4, diary entry for 2 April 1941, p. 565.

283. Ibid., diary entry for 6 April 1941, p. 573.

284. E. Fröhlich (ed.), *Die Tagebücher von Joseph Goebbels. Teil II: Dikate 1941–45*, vol. 1, July–September 1941 (K. G. Saur, Munich, 1996), diary entry for 25 July 1941, pp. 124–5.

285. Figures from SDK Berlin, *Ohm Krüger* file.

286. BArch R58/160, SD report, No. 185, 12 May 1941. Italics in original report.

287. Ibid.

288. H. Hoffmann, *The Triumph of Propaganda*, p. 109.

289. For a further discussion of the function of historical films, see below pp. 197–200.

290. W. Schumann, *Being Present: Growing up in Hitler's Germany*, p. 74.

291. BArch R58/160, SD report, no. 185, 12 May 1941.

292. E. Fröhlich (ed.), *Die Tagebücher von Joseph Goebbels. Sämtliche Fragmente*, diary entry for 5 April 1941, p. 570.

293. BArch R58/160, SD report, no. 185, 12 May 1941.

294. See above p. 174.

295. For a reading of this aspect of *Ohm Krüger* as well as other films of the Third Reich, see L. Schulte-Sasse, *Entertaining the Third Reich*, p. 256.

296. BArch R58/160, SD report, No. 185, 12 May 1941.

297. R. Herzstein, *The War that Hitler Won*, p. 340.

298. Clipping relating to the Biennale, 16 September 1941 in SDK Berlin, *Ohm Krüger* file.

299. BArch R/55 663, Leiter Film/Reichsfilmintendant, den Reichsminister, 'Wiederanlauf nationaler Filme', 15 November 1944.

300. O. Zur, 'The Psychohistory of Warfare', p. 131.

301. Ibid.

A people that possesses a sovereign of the stature of Frederick the Great can think itself happy.

Adolf Hitler, 1941[1]

My birthday treat was to visit the ruins of the Carlton Club with the PM, who stumped in and wandered about amongst the wreckage... At the entrance steps the Prime Minister pointed to a piece of marble statuary half buried in rubble. Lifted up it was seen to be the head of Pitt.

John Martin, letter of 16 October 1940[2]

Leadership in the era of mass politics has often been the subject for historical scrutiny, lending itself to an exploration of the role of the individual in shaping the destiny and nature of the nation, historians seeking to understand the 'mass machines' of power and state by probing 'the frequently elusive ghosts within them'.[3] Few eras have elicited such debate over the question of leadership as that of World War II, its demagogues subjected to seemingly endless analyses of their styles, thus placing leadership at the forefront of national wartime destinies. It has increasingly been the historical trend to locate wartime leadership in a comparative context, historians such as Andrew Roberts in his work *Hitler and Churchill: Secrets of Leadership* drawing lessons for modern leaders from his analyses of the crises, victories and defeats of 1939–45.[4] Whether leadership in World War II is most appropriately dealt with through comparison has been the subject of recent historiographical debate, Richard Gott challenging Roberts by arguing that 'these two leaders and their relationships with their followers and their nations were so far apart, in terms of history, culture and programme, that they can hardly be fitted into the same conceptual framework'.[5] But can the same be said for *representations* of heroic leadership? An analysis of the projected image of leadership in this period adds a new dimension to this debate, shedding light on how the leader was perceived from within and offered to the public, and underlining shared characteristics as well as the uniqueness of the national example. In Max Weber's seminal works on charismatic leadership, there is some suggestion that the 'ambiguous qualities' of charisma could be applied to both 'totalitarian' and democratic leaders, an approach which may, in 'concentrating on the reciprocity of the charismatic leadership', help the historian to 'avoid the pitfalls of either a great-man theory or the neglect of the personal element in political history', providing an insight into the complex relationship between high politics, individuals, the mass and the myths associated with leadership.[6]

This chapter seeks to explore the functions of filmic depictions of leadership in Britain and Germany during World War II and offers an analysis of areas of similarity between the various depictions of Hitler and Churchill, as well as pointing to the essential uniqueness of Hitler's position in the Third Reich, which was at the mythic heart of the National Socialist movement. Naturally, the function of the leader in both Britain and Germany during World War II can be viewed as comparable in the sense that the central role was to provide a form of cohesion to a society being transformed by the catalytic effects of war. In both cases, the leader is presented as the inheritor and upholder of national values and unity, the embodiment of the national character, and, as such, the representative of the body politic and the mass; he is the 'projection of the national aspiration to greatness', the bearer of hope and the individual responsible for the fulfilment of the nation's destiny, created and dictated by history. The image of contemporary leadership was the product of inherent, but desirable, tensions: the leader is a man possessed of extraordinary genius and vision and yet simultaneously he feels an innate connection with the everyman. He is both beyond and of the people. He is of his time and yet ahead of his time, often the pioneer of new ways of thinking which brings him into conflict with his contemporaries, but eventually emerging as the visionary of future glory. For all these similarities in depiction, however, the mythic core of the *Führerprinzip* cannot help but differentiate the German case from its British counterpart. Within National Socialist ideology, Hitler assumed the position of the man of providence, of destiny, his genius at the head of a reconstructed *Volksgemeinschaft*, a development which heralded the long-awaited palingenesis of the German nation and spirit. Kershaw has argued that the significance of the concept of the Führer to the movement and to the nation is best explored through Weber's theory of charismatic authority, in which 'irrational hopes and expectations of salvation are projected onto an individual, who is thereby invested with heroic qualities'.[7] Although this may be used to explain other forms of charismatic leadership in the period, Kershaw contends that the specific construct of the *Führer-Mythos* in the Third Reich 'was both different in character and more far-reaching in impact than the charismatic forms seen anywhere else'.[8] This uniqueness resided in 'the specific form of rule [that Hitler] embodied and its corrupting influence on the instruments and mechanisms of the most advanced state in Europe', the Führer 'personifying … the "project" of "national salvation"', which found 'broad acceptance' and contributed to the 'internalization of the ideological goals by a new modern power élite'.[9] The way in which this phenomenon functioned also draws a clear distinction between the nature of British and German charismatic forms of leadership. As Michael Geyer shrewdly observed, the 'Hitler-mystique was not just "made". Goebbels was unquestionably a talented image maker. But only when his images were accepted by large segments of the population and when, in turn, popular sentiments influenced and transformed propaganda, the explosive fusion could occur that made the *Hitler-Mythos*'. Geyer identifies the innate connection between the propagandist and the mass, and the mutual reinforcement of the message and the collective desires that successful propaganda thrives upon. For Geyer, the 'triad' of 'propagandistic manipulations, Hitler's own actions, and the public creation of collective fantasies' explain the depths of the Hitler-myth and its impact on German society, a specific union which in itself was unique.[10]

However, despite these essential differences in the conception and conduct of leadership during World War II, it is striking that both British and German propagandists chose to represent contemporary leadership through historical analogy, avoiding direct representations of Hitler and Churchill. Although modern leaders were well acquainted with the filmic medium, few chose to be directly represented within the fictional and biographic feature film.[11] There were obvious exceptions. Most notably, in the Soviet Union, Stalin personally suggested his potential role in Mikhail Romm's *Lenin v oktjabre* (Lenin in October, 1937), in which he becomes the natural ally of and successor to the Bolshevik leader. Later, Stalin approved of his depiction in Mikhail Chiaureli's *Padenie Berlina* (The Fall of Berlin, 1949) by the Georgian Mikhail Gelovani, who secured the job of representing Stalin until the dictator's death in 1956.[12] Within Soviet films of this nature, a tradition of representing living political personalities was established and nurtured, creating the cinematic codes for audience acceptance and understanding of the genre. Such a transition did not occur in Nazi Germany, with depictions of the Führer as a fictionalized character 'considered blasphemy'.[13] Equally, in Britain, Churchill was not represented directly, his presence inferred, despite being proclaimed by cinema audiences in 1942 as 'one of the best screen stars of the present day'.[14] Lawrence Huntingdon's 1943 film, *Warn that Man*, about the attempted kidnap of an 'important person', was passed by the BBFC on the condition that the kidnapper's target 'is never mentioned by name', in line with their decision not to permit the depiction of living statesmen.[15] However, audiences were left in no doubt as to the leader's identity, the press book detailing that, in his impersonation of the personality in question, the main character 'swaggers out, smoking a huge cigar and talking airily of "blood, toil and sweat"'.[16] Both leaders and propagandists were aware that 'it is always difficult to depict contemporary political leaders on the screen. Only historical distance grants them credibility as people … In their own age, these monumental figures refuse to become life-like',[17] Churchill confirming that 'tributes if deserved come better after a man's death than in his lifetime'.[18] It was with this in mind that leaders were represented via historical analogy.

The historical film offered many benefits to the propagandist of World War II, partly conditioned by the way the public uses the past. The rationale for historical reflections centred on seeking explanation and searching for a golden age and through it 'the creation of an imagined landscape',[19] perhaps one in tune with the audiences' own cinematic fantasies. For propagandists, the historical genre developed a sense of familiarity, offering a form of 'validation', with 'the past [confirming] present attitudes and actions by affirming their resemblance to former ones'.[20] In this sense, as Virginia Woolf observed, 'the present when backed by the past is a thousand times deeper when it presses so close that you can feel nothing else'.[21] In a persuasive manner, the past could be reshaped to suggest that history offered guidance and solutions to contemporary challenges, drawing on 'valued attributes' to legitimize and glorify the present. Naturally, as Marcia Landy suggests, 'there is by no means unanimous agreement about the nature, role, or forms of historicizing' in filmic representations, although it has 'played a key role in consolidating notions of national, gendered, ethnic and racial identities, presenting deterministic and essentialist conceptions of time and human action', in this case leadership.[22]

For representations of leadership centring on the key figures of Churchill and Hitler, these functions were certainly mobilized by their nations' propagandists. In crafting analogous historical depictions of leadership, they sought to confer validity upon contemporary regimes and governments, suggesting innate connections to the past, the continuities of the national experience and crowning their leaders as the natural successors to great statesmen. During World War II, a direct line was drawn by film producers from Frederick the Great to Otto von Bismarck to Adolf Hitler, from William Pitt the Younger to Benjamin Disraeli to Winston Churchill, such representations not only validating specific forms of political rule, but also, through the individual, providing a distillation of leadership qualities and national identities, in itself not unusual within the biographical film. Through historical analogy, leaders could embody the sum of the nation and were released from their own age, whilst remaining innately connected to their contemporaries. As Fritz Hippler recognized, there was an instinctive bond between the people and their past, suggestive of the eternal nature of a nation's history: 'The only possible subjects for successful historical films are personalities and events from the past with which people of the present are familiar or with which they can identify. In other words, it must [give] meaning to life by means of the timeless authenticity of particular historical events, situations' and, above all, 'personalities'.[23]

The 'biopic' was not a new phenomenon. Silent cinema had often drawn on the leaders of the past for subject material. But, in the 1930s and 1940s, with the advent of sound, the 'biopic, the costume spectacle and the historical film' formed a means of popular representation of influential 'individuals and events associated mainly with traditional and watershed moments of a country's past … [which] celebrated significant events in the forging of national identity'. Such films functioned as a type of 'collective morality as well as a source of morale'. In this way, produced as they were 'on a grand scale and in the mode of "monumental history"', historical epics were 'instrumental in establishing conventions about the commercial cinema's uses of spectacle in the treatment of the past'.[24] The material selected by British and German propagandists, that of the period from the 1740s to the 1890s, had a cinematic pre-history, with its own particular and specific modes of address and resonances. In Germany, the filmic depiction of Frederick the Great had been in the public arena from the late nineteenth century, with the first film of the *Fridericus* genre appearing in 1896,[25] which was set alongside a wider 'literary and historiographical tradition' effectively 'glamorizing Prussian history' in the public consciousness.[26] In Britain, and indeed Hollywood, representations of Georgian and Victorian England, and in particular its leading personalities, proved to be popular with audiences. Films such as *Victoria the Great* (Herbert Wilcox, 1937), *Sixty Glorious Years* (Herbert Wilcox, 1938), as well as the earlier depictions of Disraeli in the 1916, 1921 and 1929 film versions of aspects of his life,[27] created cultural codes with which audiences could identify.[28] The historical film had the added advantage of appearing to satisfy cinema-goers, acting as an 'island of the past'. It became a 'desirable refuge from the pressures of modernising change',[29] typifying the feeling that one might '[find] in the past … much of the peace [the individual] could not get in contemplating the shifting scene of the present'.[30] Nowhere was change potentially as 'modern' or as fast as in the period 1939–45.

From the earliest days of the war, *Kinematograph Weekly* demanded that studios provide 'something that will offer as good a relief as possible from the anxiety which is never far below the surface of the British citizen in these days'. Studios, they argued, had a responsibility to offer 'vigorous, lively entertainment', and should not shun escapism. After all, they concluded, 'we sell it and the public buys it', a statement which underlined the ultimate consumerism that drove the industry even in times of crisis.[31] Indeed, the call for escapism was a prevalent theme throughout the war years in the trade newspapers, which were firmly of the opinion that film was to be the primary means of 'temporary escape from the trials and toils of civilization's fight for existence which affect every one of us in different degrees'. The fantasy or entertainment film '[refreshed] the human spirit', the cinema becoming a 'temporary *refuge* from the monstrous realities of these momentous times'. People turned to film, concluded P. L. Mannock, writing for *Kinematograph Weekly* in June 1942, 'in order to forget about the war for a time'.[32] Similar views were expressed in Germany, particularly during and after 1941, a report from the *Reichspropagandaleiter* in 1942 suggesting that entertainment films had enjoyed 'a rapid increase' in their box-office figures compared to those 'for war-based films'.[33] This goes some way to explaining the popularity of historical epics in both Britain and Germany during World War II. Although the historical genre had traditionally been successful, the fusion of escapism and opulence seemed to be particularly appealing in wartime, the Gainsborough melodramas of the late war period demonstrating the attraction for young female audiences in Britain,[34] whilst in Germany, cinema-goers flocked to see the latest historical drama, the SD confirming, in relation to the 1940 film *Bismarck*, that 'the comments made by the press long before the start of the Bismarck film and the general remarks about historical films had aroused people's interest, manifesting itself in a rare rush to the first performances. In some cases the cinemas had been sold out for days'.[35]

Propagandists recognized that they could capitalize on the popularity of the historical genre. The image of a past glory could potentially reinvigorate a flagging population, creating hope and propelling the nation towards a final victory, a victory, its history confirmed, it had every right to expect. The masses were encouraged to live up to their historical legacy. Both Britain and Germany sought ways of exploiting the historical film as a means of promoting a cohesive national unit and the genius of their wartime leadership, effectively reshaping and refining pre-existing cultural codes to support the notion of a nation engaged in 'total war' and distilling the central tenets of a national culture down to form a base construct for the prosecution of a 'people's war' with which the mass would identify. The historical film, then, offered the studio the possibility of popular success, which offset the extraordinary costs of 'epic films' and their demands on material resources, *and* provided propagandists with a means of appealing to popular desires whilst simultaneously injecting a central message into the filmic medium.

That both Britain and Germany chose to concentrate their analogous representations of leadership on one historical period, notably from the 1740s to the 1890s, and seemingly confined them to the period 1940–2, is also potentially significant. The eighteenth and nineteenth centuries provided sufficient distance from the audience, ensuring that the events depicted had been transferred from the realm of precise memory to historical matter, with its associated popular myths and fictions, although the tensions between fiction and historical reality were a source of contemporary unease, as Louis Gottschalk of the University of Chicago noted in his letter of 1935 to the President of Metro-Goldwyn-Mayer: 'If the cinema art is going to draw its subjects so generously from history, it owes it to its patrons and its own higher ideals to achieve greater accuracy. No picture of a historical nature ought to be offered to the public until a reputable historian has had a chance to criticise and revise it'.[36] The immediate concern of the propagandist, however, was to ensure that historical films at least played upon popular myth and recognized audience limits of acceptance. The dangers of not doing so were evident: audience responses to *Ohm Krüger*, whose level of atrocity was such that it led film-goers to question the veracity of the message. However, propagandists were not necessarily committed to historical accuracy, even though they claimed to be, often inviting the audience to suspend their critical faculties in the opening credits by asserting the crews' adherence to the 'historical facts'. In any case, it was far more comforting to portray the past two centuries than the recent past, with its direct associations of the horror and aftermath of the Great War. Few wanted a reminder of World War I, as Clark had warned the MoI in 1941.[37] Moreover, the period held a particular appeal with audiences enjoying the reminiscences of a perceived 'golden age', British audiences in particular reporting to Mass-Observers that they welcomed a 'form of escape' into the 'Victorian days'.[38] This period contained a series of events which were thought to represent significant moments in the formation and development of the nation and which offered contemporary audiences some comfort that the trials and ordeals of the past had always resulted in victory and a stronger state: from the military campaigns of the Seven Years War under Frederick the Great to the formation of the German nation under Bismarck; from the defeat of Napoleon under Pitt the Younger to the triumph of European diplomacy under Disraeli, each episode lent itself to historical analogy, proving valuable as a vital weapon in the propagandists' arsenal.

HISTORY, FILM AND THE HITLER-MYTH

As Aldgate and Richards have argued, Nazi propagandists set particular store by the creation of the Hitler-myth through historical analogy; more so, perhaps, than their British counterparts.[39] In contrast to British films of the same genre, German films offered a plethora of leadership figures drawn from a variety of artistic, cultural, military, scientific, as well as political backgrounds, resulting from the multi-faceted image of charismatic leadership promoted by the regime. This observation is unsurprising given that the Hitler-myth 'can be seen as providing the central motor for integration, mobilization and legitimation within the Nazi system of rule'.[40] The RMVP carefully crafted the image of Hitler as a master of many spheres of national life, as a patron of the arts, as a promoter of scientific endeavour, an entrepreneur and economist, as well as the political and military leader of the German nation.[41] Such a diversity of talents contributed to Hitler's representation as the 'bearer of specific gifts of ... mind that were considered "supernatural" (in the sense that not everybody could have access to them)'.[42]

To find an individual from the past who could embody all that Hitler had come to represent was a tall order, Nazi propagandists choosing to evoke the myths of a number of individuals, each possessed of a strand of the Führer's genius. Pre-dated by a series of films which captured aspects of charismatic authority in the Third Reich such as the 1935 production *Das Mädchen Johanna*, a film in which 'an overwhelming leader – personality saves the people from deepest distress as though through a miracle, forces the State to rise anew and brings peace to the people' with Joan of Arc becoming 'the Hitler of her day'[43], the films of the war years increasingly drew upon the past as a means of representing the contemporary construct of the Hitler-myth. As Felix Moeller points out, 'by spring 1942, numerous biographical films were already showing in the cinemas or were at the planning stage',[44] leading Goebbels to question whether he was 'making too many biographical films. Ultimately', Goebbels concluded, 'we must produce a likeness of life, and not just of a few great men'.[45] Nevertheless, in the period 1940–2, a series of high-profile films focusing on the lives and achievements of 'great men' in history appeared in the cinemas of the Reich: *Friedrich Schiller* (Herbert Maisch, 1940); *Bismarck, Ohm Krüger, Friedemann Bach* (Traugott Müller, 1941); *Carl Peters* (Herbert Selpin, 1941); *Der große König, Wen die Götter lieben* (Karl Hartl, 1942); *Andreas Schlüter* (Herbert Maisch, 1942); *Rembrandt* (Hans Steinhoff, 1942); *Die Entlassung, Diesel* and *Geheimakte WB 1* (Secret File WB 1, Herbert Selpin, 1942). After 1942, the flow of 'personality' films ebbed, with the only major films of this genre released in 1943 being *Paracelsus* (G.W. Pabst, 1943) and *Wien 1910* (Vienna 1910, E.W. Emo, 1943). Goebbels' diaries offer some explanation for the move away from the genre by this date, the entry of 16 August 1942 stating that propagandists were to 'generally get rid of these personality films and come back to themes about the matter in hand. The personality films', the Reich Minister argued, 'were a makeshift device at the beginning of the war to [get] German film production back on to the right route. And now we are back on the right route [and] can focus on films about [the] right issues again'.[46]

Although numerous film scenarios featuring key historical personalities, such as Edvard Grieg, Richard Wagner, Clara Schumann, Theodor Körner and Otto Lillienthal were rejected after 1942,[47] this did not mean that 'personality' films were dimissed out of hand, especially when the Führer himself had expressed a personal interest in their production. In

May 1942, Goebbels had proposed making a film of the life of Lola Montez, the famous mistress of King Ludwig I. Hitler was adamant that 'neither the fate of this woman nor the personality of King Ludwig I of Bavaria is in any way distorted'. He informed his Minister that, 'as regards the personality of Ludwig I, you must be careful too, not to portray him as first and foremost a 'skirt-chaser' [*Schürzenjäger*]. He was in every sense a great man, and was the finest architect of his time in Europe, ... a monarch whose visions ... embraced the whole Pan-German panorama'.[48] Hitler even went as far as concerning himself with possible actors for the part, commenting that Goebbels should not 'represent Ludwig I as a King of the Viennese charm school, something after the style of Paul Hörbiger, but rather as a worthy monarch, and I think Kayßler is the best man for the role'.[49] The following day in his diary, Goebbels confirmed that 'the Führer has read the film script and found it totally inadequate. It is true that [he] wants a film to be shot about Ludwig I, but then Ludwig I is not to be portrayed as an idiot or just as a womanizer. Ludwig I was a Pan-German prince of class who may be highly esteemed'. He added that Hitler had specified that Wolfgang Liebeneiner should be commissioned to direct the film, following his successes with *Bismarck* and in anticipation of his sequel, *Die Entlassung*, in production at the time.[50] It becomes clear from his interpretation of Ludwig I, as a patron of the arts, contributor to the life of Munich and perceived pioneer of Pan-Germanism, and his concern regarding his depiction that the Führer had 'become entangled in the popular image of himself', connecting with public fantasies and the Hitler-myth operating within the Third Reich.[51]

It becomes increasingly clear from contemporary observations that the 'personality films', in their heyday, fulfilled a specific function in the wider propagandistic campaigns of the RMVP maintaining the Hitler-myth and faith in leadership. As Gerhard Schoenberner observed, Germany's historic heroes, as refashioned by the films of the Third Reich, had much in common: 'All of them ... titans not understood by their contemporaries, but full of ... firm resolution to carry out their orders as determined by fate ... They do not fear falling into the abyss'.[52] In this way, film gave visual expression to the perception of National Socialist leadership principle. It was a natural partnership, the mythic qualities of film and the appeal of the cinema as a 'dream palace' reinforcing the ethereal image of the Führer and his historical predecessors. Moreover, the cult of personality and genius forged a bond between the doctrine of the Hitler-myth and the film industry itself. The construct of *Persönlichkeit* was essential to Nazism's 'reorganisation of cultural discourses and practices at every level and ... most significantly in film'.[53] As Erica Carter noted, the concept of personality had a well-established tradition in film-aesthetic writings of the 1930s, formed partly to challenge and distinguish German cinema from Hollywood productions of the same period.[54] After the *Machtergreifung*, personality had been mobilized as part of the National Socialist focus on spirit, the *Volk* and genius, created in reaction to the '"functional" leadership of the bureaucrat and the Party politician as the representatives of the impersonal "rational-legal" form of political dominion' under the Weimar Republic. Now, 'salvation could only be sought with a leader who possessed *personal* power and was prepared to take *personal* responsibility … [imposing] his own personal power upon the force of history itself'.[55] Moving beyond the translation of this idea onto the screen, the film industry of the Third Reich pivoted upon the reorganization of cinema around a cadre of 'creative personalities at the heart of the production process' through the artistic committees of the major film companies,[56] suggestive of the pervasiveness of film and its personalities in the maintainance of power.

The Führer cult complemented the emergence of a star system under the Third Reich based around charismatic 'Otherness'. Within the National Socialist film industry, star status was partly defined by 'situating stars as personalities of creative genius' and realigning the actors themselves as 'leadership figures embedded in a hierarchically organized Nazi State'.[57] It was within this environment that film personalities began to accept 'prominent roles in the *Volksgemeinschaft* by assuming public responsibilities that served the interest of the *Volk* and state', duties which went beyond the mere production of ideologically significant films, but into the promotion of State campaigns and organizations. Stars forged public bonds with the regime to the extent that, at times, the two merged in the mutual promotion of the cinematic arts and the state, through premieres which were frequently attended by party dignitaries, the press balls at which major stars performed and the assumption of managerial roles within the state structure.[58] These roles were merely intensified by war, with leading personalities involved in *Winterhilfswerk*, such as the actress Paula Wessely,[59] and *Truppenbetreuung* [care for the troops], which involved numerous personalities of stage and screen, such as Jenny Jugo, Luise Ullrich, Brigitte Horney and Olga Tschechowa.[60] Director Wolfgang Liebeneiner was proud that 'many … film actors and actresses have given up their free time to give joy and relaxation to each man and woman, strengthening [the resolve of] those in the service of protecting our homeland and places of work'.[61] Indeed, in the age of total war, as *Reichsfilmintendant* Hans Hinkel recognized, there were 'no apolitical artists'.[62]

Nowhere was this fusion between the film industry and the ideological core of National Socialist values more apparent than in the depiction of the leadership principle and specifically in the person of Emil Jannings, *Staatsschauspieler*. Speaking on the home broadcasting service in October 1942, Jannings, who depicted numerous leadership figures in the period 1937–42, such as Matthias Clausen in *Der Herrscher*, Paul Krüger in *Ohm Krüger* and finally Bismarck in *Die Entlassung*, stated that he felt that he 'had to represent not only a great man but the idea to which he gave his life and which gave him world-historical significance'. Emphasizing a publically observable correlation between the great Germans of the past and the Führer and embellishing the Hitler-myth, Jannings added that,

> such figures are … gifts sparingly given to a nation. They cannot be compared with ordinary individuals. They obey different laws and follow their own genius. Nevertheless, they and they alone are the essential embodiment of the spirit of the nation. It is the mission of the artist to bring home this unique significance of theirs, and in this tiny way become examples, or if you like, educators.[63]

Within this context, Jannings perceived his job as giving a personalized, historical and cinematic life to the *Führer-mythos* via historical analogy. History, according to Jannings, could convey 'our age, in which the ideal of the faithful and reliable man transcends all others'. Within the National Socialist state, he argued, 'film plays its part in the great national-political task of guiding the people towards their innate and characteristic ideals. Not only does history become film, but film must become history. It must enter into and become part of people's thoughts, and play its part in the central construction of the *Weltanschauung*'.[64]

As Jannings recognized, the historical film had a specific political and contemporary function to fulfil, and in this respect, the Reich's filmic histories and the destiny of the Führer dovetailed. As Kershaw has identified, in the initial years of World War II, it was Hitler's military image which came to dominate the discourses and images associated with the Führer-myth, the victories of 1940–1 representing the 'high peak [of his] popularity' culminating in the expected invasion of Britain.[65] Within this context, the Hitler-myth acted as a central psychological focus, 'deflecting [popular attention] from everyday grumbles and bolstering the basis of support for the regime'.[66] By 1941, public confidence in the Führer was 'unbounded'.[67] However, with stalemate in the East and West, increased reports of defeats in the field, aerial bombardment at home and the continuation of the war, the gulf between image and reality that the propagandists had tried so skilfully to hide was revealed. It was at this point that images of the Führer and associated analogies began to retreat deeper into myth and fantasy. Using Weber's construction of 'charismatic authority' in which power and influence is only maintained by the 'master as long as he "proves" himself',[68] Kershaw contended that 'failure [and] certainly a chain of failures, [meant] a fatal undermining of charisma', a notion which was at the heart of the Hitler-myth.[69] Although there is some evidence to suggest that, as late as September 1943, trust in the power and destiny of the Führer to rescue the nation from defeat and deliver the long-awaited *Vergeltung* was maintained by the populace, it appeared that, in the latter stages of the war,[70] belief in the Hitler myth began to fade in the public mind, and it was this deterioration in public confidence that Goebbels sought to limit with the historical films on leadership.

Despite his admission that the Führer-myth was his 'greatest propaganda achievement',[71] by 1941 Goebbels had begun to develop alternative methods to embrace the *Führerprinzip* without explicit reference to Hitler. At the same time that the charismatic leadership of Hitler was beginning to be questioned as a result of the stagnation of military conflict and the increasingly frequent reports of defeats,[72] Goebbels resolved to draw upon a corpus of pre-existing myths. These were to form the central focus of his propaganda in the latter years of the war. Long-term acceptance of the historical greatness of the leaders of the past, such as Bismarck and Frederick the Great, would add a new dimension to the perception of the leadership style of the Führer, attempting to bridge the emerging gulf between Hitler and the people. This propaganda strategy sought to forge a bond between the greatness of the German military past and the present war, legitimizing Nazi rule and its prosecution of World War II, as well as providing an escapist outlet for audiences now tiring of the constant beat of the propagandistic drum, reshaping the Hitler-myth in line with emerging trends in popular opinion. The significance of the historical film in this task could not be underestimated, Goebbels already understanding that 'film must remain contemporary, in order to have contemporary appeal. Although it may take and obtain its subjects for treatment from other countries and distant historical epochs, its problems must be adapted to the spirit of the period'.[73] For Goebbels, the past had to be reinterpreted in line with the needs of the present, and this was particularly true of the concept of leadership. As *Filmwelt* commented in February 1940, 'German film has … tried hard to show the character and merits of the German greats, emphasizing them in relation to the past and present of the German people, and to look beyond the role of an "historical personality", divesting him of being a mere character in the so-called "historical film" in favour of a more responsible historical interpretation'.[74] Within this interpretation, history was no longer a 'process but … a repetition of ever the same', Hitler as 'the personification of historic continuity'. Moreover, 'national history … found its climax in him as he seemed to complete the work begun by Frederick II and Bismarck'.[75] It was, therefore, to these figures in particular that Goebbels turned in 1940–2. In doing so, he was able to build upon the deep 'tracks' in the popular imagination that Prussian history had left behind, in particular the imagery and myths surrounding the forging of modern German power and nobility.

Used as they were within the cultural structures of the RMVP's broader mission, the historical films straddled what Sabine Hake has termed the dual but interrelated aims of Nazi film propaganda, notably *Wirklichkeitsnähe* (closeness to reality) and *Volkstümlichkeit* (popularity or popular appeal and 'folksiness'), drawing on the perception of authenticity that the historical genre naturally evokes, as well as the popular appeal of the epic costume drama and its connection to the folk myths of the past. It was, argued Hake, the 'concepts of *Wirklichkeitsnähe* and *Volkstümlichkeit*' which 'provided the shifting signifiers through which the strategic alliance between the official political culture and modern mass culture was to be accomplished'.[76] This sense of the connection between reality, popular art and culture was developed in relation to the historical portraits of leadership in National Socialist cinema, in which film became the official medium for reinterpreting national history for the masses, reaching the people in a way that scholars simply could not. As the press book for Liebeneiner's 1942 production, *Die Entlassung*, stated, the filmmaker could be of the

> conviction that he is capable of making the past come alive and to reproduce it 'as it really was'. And yet there will hardly be any doubt that neither he nor legitimate historiography itself can achieve this aim … The historical truth does not manifest itself by the simple means of reproduction. It will always be divided and graduated into foregrounds and backgrounds, condensed or stretched, depending on whether it is interpreted as insignificant and unimportant or as significant and important.[77]

What emerged from this process was a strange amalgam of reality, myth and the embodiment of the Führer, in which the image was constantly renegotiating its cinematic space with the propagandists' attempts to come to terms with what forms the historical film should take.

The image of the Führer and his style of leadership were developed within this construct. Hitler was very much the absent (in a literal sense) and yet omnipresent star of the feature films of the Third Reich from 1940 to 1942. This was a deliberate measure. As Schulte-Sasse observed, 'a fictionalized portrayal of, say, Hitler's rise to power might unwittingly have proven a deconstruction calling attention to the fictional nature of both "real" and represented Leader. In order to *be* Hitler, he had to remain beyond narrative representation'.[78] In many ways, 'no-one had to play Hitler because he was constantly there to play himself, whereas Frederick and the imaginary history he embodies depended on the series of representational forms that culminated in the movies'.[79] Edwin Ware Hullinger's attempt to make 'Mussolini into a movie star' who would become 'an attraction among the flickering marquee lights above the box office ... alongside Clark Gable' was not to be repeated in the Third Reich.[80] However, as with other aspects of the relationship between cinema and the Nazi state, the personalities of the screen converged with the concept of the Hitler mystique. It is significant that in the three major representations of historical leadership in the years from 1940 to 1942, *Bismarck*, *Der große König* and *Die Entlassung*, the central protagonists were played by *Staatsschauspieler*. Only Paul Hartmann, Otto Gebühr and, of course, Emil Jannings could lend their absent muse the gravitas his persona commanded. Historical analogy, then, functioned on many levels, evoking the sense of the past to legitimize and explain the present, as well as drawing upon the cult of personality extant in all areas of the Reich, but most importantly in the marriage between cinema and the state.

THE PRUSSIAN IDEAL

> My aim was to achieve feats of eternal glory. I never gave a damn about those idiots in the field.
>
> Frederick II, 22 October 1776[81]

The choice of Frederick the Great to represent the Führer in Veit Harlan's 1942 film *Der große König* was a natural one. The film's protagonist was a German cultural icon, both in the cinema and in the popular imagination, and Nazi propagandists sought to capitalize on the cinematic cult of Frederick the Great, using Otto Gebühr to play the King in films produced after 1933, 'in an attempt to maintain continuity with Weimar cinema'.[82] Nazi propagandists were able to build upon a 'ready-made terrain of pre-existing beliefs, prejudices and phobias ... onto which the "Hitler-myth" could be imprinted'.[83] As Schulte-Sasse observed, 'the cinematic *Frederick* cult dates back to the beginnings of German cinema, which had a predilection for glamorized Prussian history, and to an even older literary and historiographical tradition',[84] with 'German commercial cinema quickly [appropriating] both its narratives and ideology'.[85] Although Harlan's *Der große König* drew upon the cultural legacy of Prussian history, it was, at the same time, very much a product of the era in which it was made. The film depicted Frederick's triumph over adversity in the

Seven Years War and the bravery of his troops and his people in overcoming their own fears to serve the King in his struggle against the invading enemy. The propagandistic strength of a historical setting married with contemporary resonance meant that the propagandist could utilize both public familiarity with and the symbolic value of the cultural icons presented and reconfigure them within a context which was conducive to the conveyance of the intended message. As Pierre Sorlin noted, 'historical film is an indicator of a country's basic historical culture, its historical capital'.[86] It unites the audience in its provision of a cultural identifier – in this case, embodied within the person of Frederick the Great. Moreover, it enables interplay between fact and fiction: the audience is lulled into believing that they are witnessing an accurate representation of the past, particularly when they are informed that the film is based on historical documentation, as was the case with *Der große König*, the opening credits reassuring the film-goer, in a similar way to those in *Ohm Krüger*, that *'in its key scenes, it remains faithful to the historical facts and above all shows the tests of the Seven Years War to be stood by the king's outstanding personality ... The king's most significant words come from himself'*. Harlan went to considerable lengths to stress that he 'stuck strictly to historical facts when writing the script. But the real events of the Seven Years War often result in such a bewildering parallel to the events of our days that I deem it necessary to emphasize [them]'.[87] In this context, the propagandist is afforded the opportunity of creating a mythical representation, one which connected to the contemporary experience whilst maintaining the pretence of presenting an historically and factually accurate piece.

That the film concentrated on the individual, although many historical films have a tendency to do so to encourage audience identification,[88] is not without political significance in the Third Reich. The image of Frederick assumed a central importance in the production of Harlan's film, his identity contested within the filmic narrative, offering an interpretation of contemporary wartime events and reinforcing Hitler's position within the popular consciousness.[89] Frederick's identity is defined by his determination, his ability to rally his troops and people, his faith in his own military decisions above the advice of his generals and the solitude of leadership. Here, 'it is great leaders who make history, not history that makes great leaders'; the historical film was 'only relevant if it added meaning to the present'.[90] However, tensions emerge when consideration is given to the iconic status of Frederick the Great within a wider cultural context. As Schulte-Sasse contends, 'although Frederick was undoubtedly exploited for political purposes, ... we must again conceive the enduring fascination with this legend as an expression primarily of desire ... [relating] to the individual and social stability that Nazism and earlier anti-modern movements perceive as "lost"', Frederick's filmic presence functioning as 'an object to which [the masses] can cling'[91] and a bridge to a less contested past. Within the Third Reich, the location of the image of leadership within the wider classical cinema both draws upon the tradition of 'Prussiana' and suggests that propagandists almost certainly recognized the value of pre-existing cultural codes and harnessed them for the purposes of promoting the Hitler mystique, the two functioning in a synchronous and mutually reinforcing way within *Der große König*.

That *Der große König* was conceived of as a contemporary parallel is suggested by the publicity materials from Tobis, who used Hitler's speeches as a basis for promoting Harlan's production, the press book emphasizing: '"Today you have a Frederickian Germany in front of you!"', the Führer's pronouncements in his speech of 19 September 1939 at Artushof cited as 'the reason for commissioning Veit Harlan to write the film-script'.[92] Goebbels was determined to manage Harlan's portrait of the Prussian King, ensuring that the representation served to reinforce the central tenets of the Hitler-myth. It was a task made all the more pressing by the fact that the Führer had cast himself in the mould of Frederick, emulating and idolizing him in public and private. As Schulte-Sasse noted, the Great King 'functioned as … a fantasy object for the Führer himself. Hitler repeatedly invoked Frederick as a historical model, likened the early struggle of National Socialism with Frederick's assertion of Prussia against great powers, and kept a picture of Frederick above his desk, which gave him "new strength, when bad news threatens to oppress me"'.[93] Goebbels clearly intended to detail the parallel lives of past and present leaders, confirming in his diary on 25 January 1942 that Harlan's film 'shows the King in his greatness and loneliness and offers surprising parallels to the present … The times that Frederick the Great had to go through during the Seven Years War have an awful lot in common with the times we are dealing with today. From this example the German people may thus realize where we stand and the direction in which we have to go'.[94] Here, *Der große König* was intended to mobilize the Hitler-myth in order to reinvigorate the population in their struggle against the Allies, Goebbels stressing that 'undoubtedly, Frederick the Great is a noble example especially for our time. The film … is a good mechanism in the struggle for the soul of our people and in the process of the permanent growth of the German power of resistance necessary to win this war'.[95] It is unsurprising, therefore, that both Goebbels' diaries and Harlan's memoirs chronicle the Minister's constant interference in the project and his particular concern over the image of the King, contrived as it was to the reflect the image of the Führer himself.

Goebbels invested much political and ideological capital in *Der große König*, priding himself that he 'was intensely engaged in this film project'.[96] His interventions, however, became a problem for the production team, and most notably for the film's director Veit Harlan. Whilst preparing for his next project, *Agnes Bernauer*, Harlan had received a commission from the RMVP to produce a film focusing on the life and career of Frederick the Great. Harlan claimed that he intended to 'stick exclusively to the historical facts' in his treatment of the Great King, consulting, in particular, the works of Thomas Carlyle and Thomas Mann's 1915 book, *Friedrich und die große Koalition* [*Frederick and the Great Coalition*], alleging that Goebbels had personally recommended the latter 'despite his loathing of the author'.[97] Harlan asserted that he had 'decided to demystify the King and to [create] a human being and, above all, to break with "tradition"' by casting Werner Krauss as the eponymous hero instead of Otto Gebühr.[98] It was in this aim that Harlan first found himself in conflict with Goebbels and, significantly, the Führer, who had opposed the replacement of Gebühr, commenting that it was a 'betrayal' of the public's adoration of the actor in the role he had executed with considerable skill in the past. Moreover, it undermined the connection between the films of the past and Harlan's new production, Tobis ensuring that audiences associated Gebühr's previous characterizations with his portrait in 1942 by stating in their publicity materials that 'after the Fridericus films, still well-known from the silent film era…, the new Tobis film *Der große König* reintroduces us to Otto Gebühr as Frederick the Great'.[99] The actor and the role had been drawn into a symbiotic relationship in which Gebühr had almost assumed the persona of Frederick. In an interview with the *Hamburger Fremdenblatt*, Gebühr contended that 'it is said that a married couple will resemble each other within time. This is similar to how I felt with Frederick … [I] felt I was coming closer to the portrait from day to day, how the masking, the uniform, the typical movements and the words helped me to grow into the familiar character once more'.[100] This merging of character and actor was essential to the activation of the cultural codes associated with the Prussian myth and contributed to the positive reception of Gebühr's portrayal, as stressed in the SD report of 28 May 1942.[101] This was a view shared by the character's inspiration, Adolf Hitler, who on viewing the film instructed Goebbels to confer the title *Staatsschauspieler* upon the ageing Gebühr,[102] reaffirming the connection between star status and the Hitler-myth operating within the Third Reich.

Still 13   *Otto Gebühr as 'Der große König'*. From Bfi Stills, Posters and Designs.

The tensions between Harlan and Goebbels were exacerbated by the director's intention to depict the King more authentically than in previous productions, reflecting the 'face of reality'.[103] In an article for the studio entitled *History and Film*, Harlan elucidated his vision of the King:

> I dispensed with any heroic pose. I wanted to look into the careworn face of a man collapsing, after the lost battle, under the responsibility that he has taken upon himself ... Often his face is distorted by reluctance, sometimes overwhelmed by weakness, but again and again strengthened and rejuvenated by his faith in gaining victory. In my film, you will not find any of the many famous anecdotes or affable tales formerly told in an attempt to bring their greatest king closer to the German people. Instead you will see the King the way I believe he was – he must have been.[104]

However, it was this harsh new depiction which broke from some of the pre-existing representations of the Great King and exposed the differing interpretations of *Wirklichkeitsnähe*, history and the representation of leadership in operation. Goebbels actively sought to tone down the negative representation of Frederick's character. After an evening pre-release screening of the film in August 1941, at which Harlan was present, Goebbels concluded that alterations had to be made, as the final product still did not conform to his expectations. 'It is true' he stated 'that [the King] ought to come off his pedestal, but he must not be vulgarized. Harlan has gone too far with this, especially when he lets the Great King talk with a Berlin accent, which makes the film seem obtrusive and tasteless after a while'.[105] Harlan was required to dub 'all the scenes in which the King spoke German with a Berlin accent or French', the director recalling that his insistence that the film was grounded in historical 'fact' met with the characteristic response: that Harlan had 'impudence beyond measure'.[106] Not only did the depiction of the 'new Frederick' cause debate between the production team and the RMVP, it also sparked a popular discourse upon the film's release, the SD reporting that the audience had both appreciated and questioned Harlan's more nuanced interpretation of the historical icon. The report of 28 May 1942 remarked:

> The new image of the king depicted in the film is the focus of interest and mostly the centre of the conversations about the film. Only in a few isolated cases, ordinary cinemagoers regretted that they had not recognized 'their Old Fritz'... The new image of Frederick, on the other hand, makes an immensely attractive and fascinating impression on wide sections of the population. The film therefore ... frees Frederick's genius from his popular [myths] and shows the king undisguised in his severity and human greatness. There is hardly anything left of the radiant 'Fridericus' of the silent film and nothing at all of the popular father of the soldiers and the people as depicted in legend. So in spite of numerous critical arguments, the film is suitable to rid Prussia's history of the romantic veils, the patriotic pathos and the bourgeois morality and to give our people a notion of how lonely and icy the atmosphere around a leader is who has to bear the responsibility for the destiny of a nation.[107]

Such reactions to *Der große König* not only encapsulate the fusion of and tensions between public desires for myth and reality and their reception of the propaganda of war and leadership in relation to contemporary events, but also demonstrate that the central tenets of the *Führer-Mythos* as expressed within Harlan's film had been fully recognized, if not internalized, by audiences within the Reich.

That film-goers also recognized that Hitler was to be perceived as the modern incarnation of Frederick the Great was also confirmed by the SD report, which detailed that 'the audience had considered the film mainly as "a reflection of our own time". Many had compared the Führer with the King and, when the film was released, remembered a ... newsreel presenting the Führer alone in his headquarters'.[108] In this respect, the report corroborates other evidence which suggests the total and pervasive impact of the media environment within the Third Reich and also establishes the connection in the public mind between the images of leadership past and present, a sentiment evoked throughout *Der große König*.

Although Harlan sought to reconceptualize Frederick II, there are many elements within his film which demonstrate both the reconfiguration of the image of the Great King in line with the *Führerprinzip* and the endurance of the legends surrounding him. The mythic presence of the King is felt throughout the filmic narrative. At various points in the film, as well as in the publicity material, the spirit of the Hitler-myth is invoked by Harlan, suggesting contemporary parallel and reinforcing the popular conception of leadership. Gebühr 'has to portray the suffering and fighting Frederick, nearly crushed by destiny, nevertheless enduring with immense and superhuman stamina and defying the weakness of faith in his circle'.[109] He was to embody the 'notion of the highest [form] of self-discipline as the most striking expression of "Prussianness"', a 'symbolic representation of the German essence'.[110] The parallels between the charismatic leadership of Frederick and Hitler were brought to the fore with Tobis' declaration that 'Frederick and the Führer stand [together] in the fight for victory or downfall; then as now [it is a fight] not for wealth, expansion or success, but only for life, existence and durability'.[111] Harlan presents a series of episodes which highlight this comparison further, reiterating the essential characteristics of charismatic authority. Both Hitler and Frederick are depicted as being invested with the ability to rise from defeat, Frederick reversing the humiliating trouncing at Kunersdorf, thus suggesting that the Führer will deliver a similar miracle. Both have the ability to inspire a flagging population, restoring their faith in the personalized leadership. Both are men of destiny, propelled by fate into assuming positions of authority under difficult circumstances. Although they stand alone as the head of State, their destinies are somehow intertwined with the destiny of the nation, bonded with their people in an historic struggle for national glory.[112] Both men demonstrate that they are willing to stand up to world opinion for the best interests of the nation, and both are depicted as having the skills with which to manage contemporary opposition, particularly the short-sighted generals who should know not to question the genius of the leader. *Der große König* is striking in its representation of the solitude of the authority figure and the rejection of the private sphere in favour of the public, emphasizing that the principle of *Gemeinnutz vor Eigennutz* has particular resonance for the leader, such depictions resurrecting the uniqueness of both Frederick and Hitler's personal genius and recreating a mythic portrait of a man of destiny who, in the final hour, stands alone at the head of his nation.

The contemporary parallels offered by the selection of the defeat of Kunersdorf as the starting point for Harlan's narrative are obvious. The depiction of the fading Bernburg regiment under the command of '*der alte Fritz*' creates the possibility for the regeneration of the spirit of charismatic leadership and the reinstallation of Frederick as the 'Great King' of historical legend, as well as presenting the opportunity for the re-emergence of hope for the future and encouraging trust in the ability of the Führer to lead the Reich to a similar revival of military fortunes. Leaders, the film suggests, have to undergo a rite of passage, entailing the loss of public confidence and contemporary political and social opposition. Nowhere is this more apparent than in the exchange between the miller's daughter, Luise, played by Kristina Söderbaum, and Frederick. Goebbels originally opposed the inclusion of the female character on the grounds that the director was merely creating the role for his wife, a view confirmed by audiences who noted that her performance was 'colourless and soulless' and questioned whether all Söderbaum's dramatic roles were generated as a result of her marriage rather than her talent.[113] However, the relationship between Frederick and Luise becomes a central mechanism in the film by which the audience can judge the rehabilitation of the 'Great King' in the public consciousness and demonstrate the connection between the leader and his followers, Luise gradually coming to recognize Frederick's compassion for his people and her 'duty to recognize his charisma'.[114] In defining the proximity between charismatic authority and the people, the destinies of Luise and the King are intertwined, giving visual expression to the mythically constructed connection between centre and periphery propagated in the Third Reich. Initially blaming the King for the loss of family members and the destruction of her home and her mill, Luise comes to realize that their destinies are one and freely succumbs to her duty to be led, Harlan informing cinema-goers that the miller's daughter and her sweetheart, Paul Treskow (Gustav Fröhlich), 'sense their king's greatness, finding their way back to their faith in the justice of his cause for which they are prepared to die. These traditional characters', claimed the director, 'are not idealized as heroes, but they fight for their heroism, they acquire it in order to possess it. After all, they are Prussians – they are Germans, with their weaknesses and with their extraordinary strength of sacrifice and love'.[115] Such distinctions between leader and led are revealed in the sequence in which Frederick returns to his people after his victory at Schweidnitz in 1762:

Frederick: Are you alone? I am also alone.
Luise: Your Majesty is not alone though!
Frederick: Oh yes.
Luise: But the Prussian people…

Frederick: Hate me! They have even pronounced it – here in this house.

Luise: Does my child hate me if he doesn't understand me?

Frederick: Do my people know how I love them? [Luise nods]. And do they understand that I was only waging this war to secure their future?

Luise: What we can't grasp with understanding, our hearts tell us.[116]

Surrounded by public jubilation, the leader is destined to follow a solitary, yet noble, path. As *Filmwelt* emphasized: 'The loneliness of the Great is not voluntary. Destiny and circumstance require it'.[117] This distinctive 'Otherness' is highlighted in this scene, in which only the leader has the genius to understand and the people must be content to follow unquestioningly. That the leader is dedicated to his people as opposed to his private life can also be observed in his reaction to the impending death of his son, when he chooses duty over the opportunity to see his child for the last time: 'Frederick lost what he loved, what gave meaning and value to his private life', stressing that he only exists in his national, and not private, persona.[118] Moreover, each subject is rendered child-like by both sequences, the average Prussian infantalized by lack of understanding, as emphasized by the symbolism of Luise's analogy between the leader and his people and her own baby, and the rejection of one child by the King in favour of all his children – the nation.

In other ways too, Harlan underscores the master narrative of solitude throughout the film, most notably in Frederick's exchanges with his generals and world opinion. Drawing upon the wider propaganda campaign surrounding Hitler's position in relation to the declaration and conduct of the war, Frederick is seen to possess the courage to stand in the face of misguided world opinion and to challenge the short-sighted generals who surround him. Regardless of the views of his contemporaries, he relies on his own genius and vision to lead the nation to victory. Tobis ensured that the parallels with the Seven Years War were not lost on audiences, their press book proclaiming that 'the German people are nowadays caught in a struggle against a part of the world's opinion with which clever "opinion managers" have been indoctrinating the world public for decades ... using all the means of a well-established virulent propaganda with the result that distrust, fear and hatred against Germany have, without any reason, taken over'. *Der große König*, claimed the studio, offered historical precedent, asserting that

> it is the path followed by the Great Frederick, misunderstood and taunted, then feared and hated by a world that would not be thrown off the supposed balance of their old political ideas and aims until the superhuman efforts of German soldiers and the never-ending resistance of a single man led, by force, to a new world and another time against their will, until they began to recognize and respect that power.[119]

Not only is Frederick forced to confront world opinion, but he faces an insolent barrage of criticism from his generals, exposing their inexperience in military matters and accentuating the King's genius. Such depictions naturally caused some heartburn for the OKW. Goebbels recorded in his diary that they complained about the depiction of 'the defeatism of the past generals',[120] commenting later that their critiques of Harlan's film were

> short-sighted as well as foolish, and can only derive from a bad conscience as to the attitude of the circles concerned in the present. I will not admit such a tendency under any circumstances. If this becomes a habit, you cannot even take dramatic material out of history, not to mention the present. For today everybody feels offended if his profession or class is depicted in a film at all, unless in near-angelical surroundings and performances.[121]

Such was the vehemence of the debates created by *Der große König* that, symbolically given the subject matter, the Führer had to intervene to resolve the dispute.[122]

However, by 1942, the sensibilities of Hitler's Generals were not of particular concern to Goebbels. His attention had shifted to the prosecution of total war. To the Reich Minister, the most important function of Harlan's film was to 'give the people the right attitude towards the war. The opinion of the Generals is not so important at home. More important is that the front fights the war and that the home front understands [it]'.[123] For Goebbels, *Der große König* not only offered the opportunity to reinforce the central elements of the Führer-myth, but allowed for the possibility of propagating an image of stoic popular resilience in times of national crisis, local cinemas offering special screenings for war wounded and armaments workers.[124] It was the destiny of the *Volk* to rise from the ashes of defeat to enjoy an era of renewed prosperity, a new golden age forged in loss, pain and endurance. Harlan's film functioned as a rallying cry to a flagging population, proffering the possibility of a favourable outcome in its analogy with the battle of Schweidnitz. As the Tobis press book noted, 'for today as in those days it is about the liberty, justice and recognition of a nation whose destiny has, from its historic beginning, been nothing but struggle'. It added that 'in those days like today, however, victory is not only gained with the genius of the military commander and the courage of the soldiers, but also with the people's strong heart', a sentiment which is suggestive of the relationship between the charismatic authority of the leader, his followers and their combined fate. It was this propagandistic function which was best characterized by the role of Luise, Söderbaum herself interpreting the part in these terms:

> She is particularly interesting for me because I play a genuine woman and her emotions during the war, her genuinely feminine attitude of feelings towards the issues and hardships of war *and* towards the demands in times of need, of the state and towards the king, rising from hostility derived from rather subjective reasons to an enthusiastic willingness to make sacrifices for her king.[125]

Numerous women of the Reich must have been asking themselves the same questions of the war by 1942. Here was no 'historical personality' to act as a role model but a 'person of flesh and blood'.[126] Luise suggested the path they should take in the face of seemingly insurmountable odds.

For all the 'realism' Söderbaum suggested, *Der große König* was still infused with the same mysticism that had characterized earlier filmic portraits of Frederick's achievements, most notably expressed in the body and personality of the King himself. In numerous sequences, the film exposes a complex interplay between the desire to emphasize Frederick's mythic presence and the stated intent of the film's director to 'demystify' the traditional image of the 'Great King'.[127] Pointing to the fusion of myth and the attempt at *Wirklichkeitsnähe*, Schulte-Sasse emphasizes that in the image of Frederick 'an all too human fragility collides with a titanic iconography'.[128] Representations of the King form a ubiquitous backdrop to the central plot. His portrait is present in his first encounter with Luise and is the focus of their discussion; it is Treskow who rebels against the caricature of Frederick on a chalk board in a local inn, his removal of the image suggestive of his rejection of the 'demystification' of the 'Great King'; on his return to Sanssouci, Frederick's shadow is cast across the palace, his reminiscences of the halcyon days of the flute concert redolent of the early films of the *Fridericus* genre, infused with legend and myth. However, it is the final sequence, described by Schulte-Sasse as a 'scene that shows the "fascist" potential of the Frederick legend, [epitomizing] the disavowal of war as Beauty and simultaneously [synthesizing] the genre's attempted sublation of modernity and premodernity',[129] which calls into question Harlan's intent to 'demystify' the King in the popular imagination. The scene

> attempts to *show* Frederick's omnipotent gaze in cinematic terms. Multiple exposures superimpose Frederick's giant eyes over the windmill that throughout the film stands metaphorically for *Heimat*, over a plough cutting the earth and over peasants ploughing and sowing fields... By superimposing Frederick's eyes over privileged icons of romantic anti-capitalism, nation and *Volk*, the sequence amalgamates Mother and Father, nurturance and discipline, the bodily and the abstract, icon and verbal text.[130]

Here, the God-like Führer has brought prosperity to his once war-torn nation and offers his continued protection and devotion, gazing upon his subjects from the heavens. It is at this point that the mythic image of the charismatic leader is re-imposed upon Harlan's filmic text. Its meanings were not lost on the audience. Commenting on the visual challenge to religious iconography, the SD noted that 'The "Eye of Frederick" had aroused the embarrassing notion of the "Eye of God" ... whereas other sources emphasize that especially the closing scene with the "Eye of the King" had had a wonderful effect in the film'.[131]

Originally intended to premiere on 30 January 1942, coinciding with the ninth anniversary of the *Machtergreifung*,[132] *Der große König* was first screened at the Ufa-Palast am Zoo on 3 March 1942 to a specifically invited audience of dignitaries, *Ritterkreuz* holders, war wounded and armaments workers, mirroring the relationship between centre and periphery depicted in the film.[133] Goebbels was more than satisfied with Harlan's finished product, awarding it the highest *Prädikat, Film der Nation*.[134] The Reich Minister contended that the film was 'propaganda in the best sense of the word',[135] 'a major victory in the 'battle for souls'.[136] He noted in his diary that 'here the film becomes a first-class political means of education. It is just what we need nowadays. We are living in a time that needs the Frederickian spirit',[137] an age which required 'the internal front of resistance'.[138] By 22 April, Goebbels was able to report profits topping RM 5.5 million, a figure only exceeded by Josef von Baky's film *Annelie* (1941).[139] So proud was the Reich Minister of what he considered to be partly his achievement that he arranged a special screening for the film's central inspiration, Adolf Hitler, who was so enchanted with the production that it led him to consider building a grand cinema in his hometown of Linz which would include a gallery dedicated to the pioneers of German film.[140] Goebbels commented that 'you can imagine what a soothing effect the depiction of the great king's personality had on him. [The Führer] has asked me to provide him with a copy of this film. He intends to send it to the Duce together with an accompanying letter'.[141] This cultural exhange of films was not limited to Hitler, however. Churchill too sent Roy Boulting and David Macdonald's 1943 film *Desert Victory* to Franklin D. Roosevelt and Joseph Stalin[142]. In an even more striking parallel, Churchill brought Stalin's attention to another film which had touched him, Alexander Korda's *That Hamilton Woman* (1941).[143] The film detailed the plight of Horatio Nelson in his battle against the dictators of Europe, a leader engaged in the struggle of his career, offering parallels to Churchill's own contemporary situation.

Overall, the SD reported that *Der große König* had been received favourably by the German population, concluding that 'this cinematographic work produces an extraordinary and lasting effect and is received with enthusiasm by the population, particularly by wide circles of cinema-goers'.[144] This enabled Goebbels to brush aside any criticisms. He reported that the widespread celebration of Harlan's production had been marred by the disapproval of just one city: Vienna. This was hardly surprising given the depiction of decadent Viennese politicians in Harlan's film. Even Goebbels admitted in the early stages of the film's production that 'the Austrian complex has turned out to be somewhat too critical and aggressive. We cannot afford this at the moment because the film is supposed to be a guiding model not only for the Prussians, but for the whole of Germany'.[145] Although Goebbels had previously vowed to break the 'cultural hegemony of Vienna' and reprimanded the city's inhabitants for having the temerity to express disapproval of the Führer,[146] a factor perhaps reflected in their rejection of *Der große König*, Harlan's depiction went a step too far. Indeed, Harlan contended in his memoirs that Goebbels had used the excuse of the anti-Austrian angle to ban *Der große König*, especially as Austrians were now to be considered *Reichsdeutsche* and that the Führer was of Austrian descent.[147] This, it later transpired, was a smokescreen for a far deeper set of problems facing the Reich in 1942.

It was the representation of General Czernitscheff (Paul Wegener) that had caused the RMVP to rethink the film's scenario, leading to a temporary ban of *Der große König*. When Harlan began to film in 1940, the Nazi–Soviet Pact of August 1939 was still valid, and the political situation allowed for a sympathetic portrait of the Russian ally. Now, however, the image of the Russian general, who had in reality been a close associate of Frederick's, was subject to historical manipulation in line with the teaching of the battle of Schweidnitz in schools, which omitted the decisive role of Czernitscheff. Students were to learn that 'it was the Prussians who achieved the victory simply by virtue of the brilliant strategy of their king'.[148] In response to this, Harlan claimed that he was ordered to reshoot the sequences involving Czernitscheff, much to the delight of Paul Wegener, who demanded that he was paid according to his going rate: RM2,000 per day.[149] However, the alterations created tensions between the on-screen portrait and the public understanding of the Russian's role in the battle, the SD commenting that 'some reports include comments that the Russian General Tschernitscheff [sic.] has been misrepresented in the film, [that] in reality the general is "a passionate admirer of Frederick"'.[150] It became clear that this issue had inadvertently resulted in the questioning of the historical veracity of Harlan's film, leading to more probing questions on the part of German film-goers. Audiences began to criticize the propaganda function of the film, suggesting that 'the parallels between the situation of Prussia at that time and the situation of today's Germany are drawn "far too roughly"' and '"grossly exaggerated"'.[151] Not only did the parallels point to the magnificence of the King but they also demonstrated the yawning gap which began to open between the image presented by the Third Reich and its reality as experienced by the people. Reports from across the Reich were suggesting the pervasiveness of war-weariness, audiences even rejecting depictions of past wars in their attempt to escape from the everyday reality of conflict. The SD in Leipzig noted that the comment '"war again and again; even war in films" could frequently be heard' in relation to Harlan's production,[152] whilst the national report confirmed that 'women had rejected the film arguing that there was "too much war" in it and watching the film proved to be too much of a nervous strain… In some places, they had started a downright whispering campaign"'.[153] Moreover, filmgoers began to question whether Hitler's military leadership *was* in fact akin to Frederick's, leading to unfavourable comparison, especially in the light of the protracted war in the East and increased Allied bombing of German cities. Indeed, such was the concern over these unwanted assessments that it was reported that Goebbels had requested the press to tone down analogous comments after the film's release.[154] It was a problem that Goebbels was to encounter again in his representations of the genius of Bismarck.

In the propagandistic campaigns of the Third Reich, Bismarck was portrayed as the natural successor to Frederick the Great and the forerunner of Hitler, making him the perfect subject for film treatment. By using Bismarck as the embodiment of the modern German age and nation, the image of *Preußentums* could be brought into the later nineteenth century, offering even closer parallels to National Socialist Germany, with the leader confronting modern problems which had arguably led to the formation of attitudes still held in German society. Bismarck's status as the father of the German nation, as well as his legendary significance in the popular imagination, himself the subject of a personality cult in his own age and beyond,[155] led to the production of two films about his life during World War II, *Bismarck* (1940) and *Die Entlassung* (1942), both directed by Wolfgang Liebeneiner. Like *Der große König*, the main purpose of these films was to give visual expression to the *Führerprinzip*, drawing parallels between past and present and offering analogous commentaries on the special genius of Hitler, whilst once again invoking the memory of past leaders whom Hitler himself respected and admired.[156]

The central aim of Liebeneiner's 1940 film was to legitimize the rule of law by an authoritarian leader. *Bismarck* offered audiences a critique of the democratic process, reflecting upon the perceived weaknesses of the Weimar Republic and the western democracies that Germany was now fighting, thus adding an extra dimension to the criticism, in particular, of Britain and France. The Bismarckian period allowed Liebeneiner, like Harlan, to capitalize on the past to reinforce and justify authoritarian approaches to modern problems and point to the efficacy of rule by 'blood and iron', paralleling contemporary events and political processes and resurrecting the victories of Bismarck's rule, notably in the field of world affairs and in the creation of the German nation.

Like *Der große König*, the 1940 production laid emphasis on the genius of the charismatic leader, Bismarck bringing order and strength to a political system fatally flawed by debate, a system which had lost the ability to make executive decisions. Within the main narrative of *Bismarck*, liberal democracy is shown to produce few results, and democrats are demonstrably disassociated from the will of the nation and the national momentum. Liberal politicians are concerned with petty power politics, placing pacifity above the national spirit. In Bismarck's (Paul Hartmann) exchanges with Rudolf von Virchow (Karl Haubenreißer), it becomes clear that the exponents of democracy are dangerously out of touch with the population, Bismarck informing his adversary that '*it is an honour for me to be called an enemy of the people by Virchow. Herr Virchow does not know the people at all! He really meant "enemy of the Landtag". In fact, I desire the hatred of the* Landtag'.[157] Frustrated by the hesitancy of his opponents and the futility of debate, Bismarck negotiates with the King to bring about the mobilization of the armed forces, sensing the threat posed by other European powers, asserting that '*by the time the grumblers in parliament get around to doing anything about it, we will be ready and mobilized!*' The film suggests that parliamentary democracy obstructs the path to greatness, *Der Angriff* commenting that 'one is deeply shocked by the speeches and oppositional counter-speeches held by Bismarck's political enemies, and one realizes again and again that hollow parlamentarianism has always been an obstacle to the real leader and genius'.[158] It was a subject which found particular resonance with audiences in 1940, the SD commenting that 'as reported, particular notice is taken of the parliamentary scenes ("luckily we do not have such debating clubs in Germany any more!") and of those film parts that depict Bismarck's struggle'.[159] The rejection of the parliamentary system reflected in this comment bolsters Kershaw's view that 1940 was very much the 'high peak' of Hitler's popularity and belief in the *Führerprinzip*, the results of the *Blitzkrieg* in eastern and western Europe seemingly offering a positive endorsement of the power of the executive authoritarian leader, in contrast to the western parliamentary democracies.[160]

This theme is reinforced in the depiction of the charismatic leader in Liebeneiner's film. Overcoming the *Landtag* is Bismarck's rite of passage. *Bismarck* highlights that it is only by 'blood and iron' rule that a nation is able to aspire to greatness, and once again this is spearheaded by a man of exceptional ability, an 'other-wordly' man, whose 'genius' is able to rise above the 'the seething chaos of the *Landesfraktionen*'.[161] In a similar vein to the representation of Frederick the Great in *Der große König*, the exceptional status of the leadership figure is revealed through the sacrifice of his private existence for the nation and his duty to the *Volk*. As the Tobis press book detailed, 'Everything for Germany – that was the motto of his life. He was prepared to sacrifice anything for the idea of Germany: honour, personal happiness, enjoyment of a family and the cheap applause of the short-sighted masses'. In Liebeneiner's film, therefore, Bismarck was intended to embody the key characteristics of the charismatic leader, reflected in both the Hitler-myth and in analogous historical films. He is a man of vision, the quintessence of the nation he founded. Through his solitude and self dedication to his mission as dictated by destiny, he is elevated to the pantheon of great German leaders, a 'titan who envisioned the German Reich'. As with *Der große König*, *Bismarck* stresses the difficulties of leadership and the trials associated with the accomplishment of great national tasks. As the publicity materials for the 1940 film suggested, 'everyone knows the Iron Chancellor... But who still thinks about what battles and agonies this genius had to go through before he fulfilled his great work'?[162] Tobis was able to claim that 'the greatest merit of the film is the credible depiction of the great man in his tenderness as well as in his toughness. Both sides were inherent to Bismarck, in rare unity and purity, and together they made him a genius'.[163] Personality is at the heart of the film, and Tobis certainly conceived of Liebeneiner's production in relation to other films of this genre, promoting it alongside Maisch's *Friedrich Schiller*, which was released in the same month.[164] Moreover, Hartmann's status as *Staatsschauspieler* ensured that the bond between the star system and the Hitler-myth remained intact. In a similar way to Gebühr, character and star became conflated, reviewers commenting that 'one might boldly claim that the genuine and authentic Bismarck of the year 1862, conjured up on the screen, would not seem more convincing to the masses of spectators than Paul Hartmann in his mask'.[165] In this way, the cult of the star and his embodiment of the character worked in conjuction with the myth surrounding the protagonist and the pervasive presence of Hitler in the film's narrative.

As with *Der große König*, Tobis went to considerable lengths to promote *Bismarck's* historical 'authenticity'. Described as a 'document of history and a document of German contemporary cinematics',[166] the studio informed audiences that 'it is a historical film in which the reality of an overwhelming story and an exceptional man knows how to hold both the spectators and a whole nation spellbound'.[167] Moreover, the location of 'factual' history within the fictional feature appeared to be having the desired propagandistic impact, the SD reporting that 'according to the majority of spectators *this film had an extraordinary power of persuasion and documentary intensity* ... which, from the start, one would not consider to be [associated with the] "feature film" ... The performance, lasting barely two hours, proved time and time again to be a highly topical "history lesson"'.[168]

Once again, audiences perceived that *Bismarck* drew parallels to the present day. Sensing the modern-day analogy to the Nazi–Soviet Pact of August 1939, the SD noted that the public appreciated that policy had to be

> continously adapted to reality. When Bismarck explained to the King that a change in attitude towards Austria was inevitable, and spoke of the fact that this was 'politics and diplomacy', parts of the audience made a connection to the relationship between Germany and the USSR. Also, the allusion that in the realm of foreign policy a certain amount of double-dealing could not be avoided at all times, was seen as a reference to the present.[169]

Moreover, the SD recognized that 'it could be judged from the conversations about the film, that, and to what extent, particularly those who were not well-versed in history drew *parallels* between Bismarck's struggle for a unified German Reich and the *Führer's efforts at achieving unity*'.[170] Tobis ensured that such associations were made through the promotion of the film as a reflection of nation-building past and present, the press materials asserting that Bismarck laid 'the cornerstone of German Unity, which, a few generations later, by the work of Adolf Hitler, was to be crowned by the creation of Greater Germany'.[171] It was to be billed as a film that 'every German simply has to see',[172] viewing becoming the duty of every German, the studio using a similar promotional technique to that deployed in respect of Bertram's 1940 production *Feuertaufe*. Not only were the parallels made clear within the filmic narrative and the publicity materials issued by the studios, but audiences had already been pre-conditioned to equate the Third Reich and its charismatic leader with the Second Reich under Bismarck. Kershaw observed that, as early as April 1933, in celebration of Hitler's forty-fourth birthday, Goebbels had already begun the process of linking the new Chancellor with his predecessor.[173] Such connections had also been established at a local level. The citizens of Bochum in the Ruhr, for example, made Hitler an honorary citizen, the town's petition stating that 'as prince Bismarck forged together the Reich, Adolf Hitler is forging together the nation into a united people',[174] a statement reflective of the SD report on Liebeneiner's film. Moreover, it is conceivable that Hitler began to think of himself in a similar fashion. His comment that 'I shall not cease to think that the most precious possession a country can have is its great men. If I think of Bismarck I realize that only those who have lived through 1918 could fully appreciate his worth' was just one of many references to the 'Iron Chancellor' in the endless hours of his 'table-talk'.[175] That Hitler saw the 'great men' films as being representative of his own character is revealed in his reactions to another production detailing the life of Bismarck, Liebeneiner's *Die Entlassung*.

Audiences of Liebeneiner's first production were disappointed that the 1940 film did not go beyond the Kaiser's proclamation at Versailles to explore the 'difficulties of the founding of the Reich from 1871', the 'tragic final years of Bismarck's chancellorship' and his dismissal from office.[176] Such complaints were addressed in the sequel to *Bismarck*, released in October 1942, just seven months after Harlan's *Der große König*. *Die Entlassung*, set in 1888, begins with the accession of Wilhelm II to the throne at a time of great international instability, in which Bismarck is recalled to bring calm to a volatile Europe. However, it is admidst the political plotting and machinations of Wilhelm's short-sighted bureaucrats that Bismarck is left with no choice but to tender his resignation. It was an historical episode which Hitler felt was a great 'injustice committed by the Kaiser at Bismarck's expense'. The Führer declared that the foolhardy monarch had 'treated the founder of the Reich with ... ingratitude' and berated the German people for 'allowing such an injustice to be committed'.[177] As Welch observed, it was 'a strange choice to include in the historical film cycle',[178] with its depiction of the defeat of a political and national icon. Moreover, the central sub-plot, Bismarck's negotiations to avoid a war on two fronts through the Treaty of 1887, did not augur well for favourable comparison between the statesmanly achievements of Bismarck and the contemporary military situation. Goebbels was well aware of the problems posed by the film's central contention, commenting in his diary in December 1941:

> As far as the Russia problem is concerned, it is presented in the film as if Bismarck wanted a treaty of reassurance with Russia at any cost and for all time. Even if historically this cannot be entirely discounted from a certain point of view, it does not fit into the present political landscape. Here, too, we have to take the view that Bismarck regarded the reassurance treaty with Russia to be only temporary and did not consider it as made for eternity. After all, the film must not provide evidence against the current war against the Soviet Union.[179]

Naturally, this necessitated some changes.[180]

As Welch suggests, it may well have been that Goebbels prematurely predicted the end of the war in the east, envisaging that the film would be released after the conquest of the Soviet Union.[181] As such, the film's intention was to be very much in line with previous historical analogies to the *Führerprinzip*, Goebbels confirming in his diary that the film was meant to be an artistic expression of the 'life, acts and dismissal of this genius'.[182] The centrality of the man of genius was once again reinforced by the casting of a *Staatsschauspieler*, Emil Jannings, as the protagonist, an actor publically associated with portraits of charismatic leadership, an identification which facilitated the merging of image and star cult.[183] Once again, Jannings took it upon himself to promote the connections between the past and present, drawing parallels between Hitler and Bismarck's attitude towards Britain and his treatment of the 'menace' of socialism.[184] For Jannings, there was a clear historical line to be drawn, mirroring that depicted in the films of the Third Reich: 'Frederick the Great – Bismarck – Hitler... The perspective is right because ... those three names highlight the same historical situation: One man against the world!' He added that, 'in the repeated reading of his speeches, his writings, his letters I learnt to see Bismarck through the eyes of the present; as one of those great historical personalities who, left to their own devices and trusting no-one but themselves, release the people's powers that others no longer dare to believe in'.[185] Painting Bismarck as the 'first soldier of the nation' and, at the same time, a man of peace, he remarked that the pronouncements of the Iron Chancellor were reminiscent of those of the Führer.[186] In a striking comment on the relationship between star, image and the *Führerprinzip*, Jannings concluded:

> I wanted to and I had to play Bismarck. Not only the great figure in history, but the ... bearer of a vision of global history, the visionary who, while others waver and torment themselves, always takes the right step with uncanny sureness... He called this the Prussian way of life, and he knew well that such an existence of sacrifice and labour for the common good was not for everyone ... [Bismarck] created the Reich. But it was a partial solution. Undoubtedly he unified the German peoples, but he could not give them the room necessary for their new, strong life. This heritage he left to the future – and today we know that this task will find its fulfilment.[187]

However, that Bismarck's legacy would be perceived as being fulfilled by the Führer was a matter for some concern in the RMVP, and was an issue brought to the fore by *Die Entlassung*. The film raised considerable problems in relation to the image of the Führer, problems which Hitler himself had recognized. Speaking privately in August 1942, he questioned whether the Ministry 'should ... now release the film.[188] The dismissal of Bismarck undoubtedly shattered the nation, and not only the fact itself but the manner in which it was accomplished; for Bismarck, after all, was the symbol of national unity'.[189] It was not timely to recall the humiliating dismissal of the founder of the Reich when Hitler's own authority was beginning to be called into question, and when some were beginning to doubt the Führer's own command over public confidence. Moreover, the film raised uncomfortable questions about such historical analogies. Whereas Bismarck prevented a war on two fronts, Hitler could not, a realization which threatened the image of the Führer as the man of destiny sent to fulfil the 'Iron Chancellor's' legacy.

It was for this reason that the RMVP arranged a test-screening of Liebeneiner's production in Stettin on 15 September 1942, the local press invited to comment upon the audience's reaction.[190] Reporting on the event, Goebbels recorded the following day that 'never had a film been launched in Stettin with such phenomenal success, as has now been the case with the Bismarck film. Not one critical voice has been heard. Even the generals are deeply impressed by the masterwork of Liebeneiner and Jannings'. The film required one more vote of approval: that of the Führer, to whom Goebbels was to present his findings in the coming days.[191] Goebbels' enthusiasm, however, was not shared by Party ideologue Alfred Rosenberg who personally wrote to Martin Bormann urging him to ban Liebeneiner's production on the grounds that it supported Allied propaganda claims regarding war guilt and World War I, adding that the production was 'a ghastly mistake, and will do nothing to enhance domestic policy'.[192] Although Goebbels proclaimed the film to be a success and conferred the *Pradikät* of *Film der Nation* upon it,[193] *Die Entlassung* was not released amidst the usual pomp and circumstance that accompanied such high-profile productions. In fact, Goebbels instructed the press to 'emphasise the differences between Wilhelm II's system of government and that of the Third Reich'[194] and banned the film's export.[195]

Die Entlassung confirmed that the era of the historic film, pronounced as 'the child of our time' by Tobis in 1942,[196] was drawing to a close, only to make one last major reappearance with Veit Harlan's 1945 epic *Kolberg*. It became apparent that positive analogies with the past were becoming increasingly problematic as the contemporary situation became ever more desperate. Moreover, as Kershaw has observed, the comparison between past and present, far from drawing leader and people closer together in their fight for the collective destiny of the nation, merely accentuated the apparent distance between Führer and *Volk*. By the end of 1942, 'Hitler became an increasingly distant figure. Without new triumphs to proclaim, he appeared less and less in public, and seldom made speeches'. The analogy with the Great King could not have been more poignant: a leader whose war had drawn him further and further away from his people, the 'war lord' who was seen 'more and more in terms of an unyielding, scarcely human harshness which was out of touch with the interests and problems of ordinary people'.[197] The diversionary escapism of the historical analogy had, rather inadvertently, touched upon the ultimate reality of the war and the increasing isolation of its creator.

BRITISH CHARISMATIC LEADERSHIP, HISTORY AND FILM [198]

It becomes clear from a cursory glance at the historical films produced during World War II that the 'cinematic mobilization of history ... was much less all-embracing and much more selective' in Britain than in Germany.[199] Of the films of this genre that were released in this period, two in particular offered an historical analogy to contemporary leadership and style: *The Prime Minister* (Thorold Dickinson, 1941) and *The Young Mr Pitt* (Carol Reed, 1942). As in the Third Reich, history could reconstruct a 'social relationship which, using the pretext of the past, reorganizes the present'.[200] British propagandists also capitalized on their ability to refashion history, sensing its ability to show simultaneously the continuities between the past and present, to reaffirm and validate the existing course of action, to establish hope for the future and, of course, to give visual expression to a shared heritage and identity, serving to unite rather than underline divisions in society.[201] Propagandists recognized that 'a collectivity has its roots in the past', and that they could reinterpret 'the treasures of the past' to give meaning to the present, a particularly powerful construct when the very essence of the nation was under threat.[202] Writing in *The Citizen* in July 1939, S. C. Leslie realized 'what a powerful leaven in the world's thought would be the spectacle, successfully conveyed, of Britain refreshing her own awareness of the historic roots of her social and political life, and remaking that life accordingly'.[203] Historical analogy had to take a specific form if it was to be successful, Grierson commenting more broadly that propaganda films should avoid 'pictures of pennants flying and guns popping and rhetoric', concentrating on the depiction of 'how men live, should live and where creative forces that fulfil men's honest needs reside'.[204] It was for this reason that historical representations were to centre on leadership, and as such upon the individual, recognizing that 'spectators quickly became accustomed to a simple, often touching and involving vision of the past',[205] rather than on vague and ethereal expressions of national identity. Grierson recognized that propagandists could capitalize on the fact that 'England's international reputation and England's leadership in the deeper matters of human progress are complementary'.[206]

Films such as *The Prime Minister* and *The Young Mr Pitt* tied perceptions of England's international reputation to leadership, drawing on times of national crisis in relation to foreign affairs as their inspiration. These films shared some common features. Harper recognized that they 'endorsed one favoured view, [presenting] the past as a cycle of misery and oppression from which the audience should learn to value the present and its liberties … [and an] all [endorsing] charismatic leadership [with] a broadly conservative interpretation of history'.[207] Significantly these films attempted to correspond to popular opinion regarding the wartime leader, Churchill, and his principles of leadership. Naturally, as in the films of National Socialist Germany, if the historic leaders depicted could be related to contemporary visions of leadership, reflecting pre-existing belief systems and patterns of popular opinion as well as the more specific characteristics of the individual leader and their actions, the propagandists would have a greater chance of success. Where this was not the case, as with the depiction of leadership in *Die Entlassung*, tensions between leadership styles could be exposed and act as a conduit for negative comparisons with past leaders and their leadership methods. In Britain, as in Germany, the connection between past and present was to be primarily generated by the publicity surrounding the release of the films and by the creation of an intricate web of psychological connections, established through the use of press books, publicity placement, reporting in the trade press and promotions within individual cinemas exhibiting the films. However, unlike Nazi Germany, the patterns of governmental manipulation were far more reserved and complex. As Harper noted, 'historical features … enjoyed the discreet approval of the Ministry', whose influence was 'indirect', so indirect in fact that, due to 'the cumbersome nature of the MoI's methods of encouragement and permission, there were examples of "slippage": films were made exemplifying an MoI perspective on history well after the MoI had shifted its views'.[208]

At times, however, the depictions rendered in films of the historical genre were at the very least redolent of the wider campaigns outlined by the MoI. One prominent strand in the MoI's early propaganda operations centred on forging a bond between leadership and people and the creation of a sense of collective responsibility if the war was lost. It indicated that this was to be 'the nation's war', informing its people that 'you will be responsible, as well as your leaders, if it ended in defeat'.[209] The MoI recognized that historical films could prove a valuable tool in promoting such ideas, suggesting that those relating to the British life and character, ideas and institutions would make for excellent treatments. Cinematic productions should attempt to show, they argued, 'our independence, toughness of fibre, sympathy with the under-dog', considering 'films of heroic actions [and] histories of national heroes' to be of particular value.[210] It was envisaged that 'ideas such as freedom, and institutions such as parliamentary government [be] made the main subject of a drama or treated historically', with the MoI suggesting that 'it might be possible to do a great film on the history of British Liberty and its repercussions in the world'. This was to be contrasted with 'German ideals and institutions in recent history', in which Bismarck would be one of the central targets. Films were to emphasize that 'British character [is] ... capable of great sacrifices' and that 'British institutions ... [have been] won and retained' through them.[211] Such ideas could be profitably articulated in the depiction of the past, the MoI contending that 'human history has been marked by certain definite advancements, each one of which produced its own special contribution to the improvement of Man'; these were values which were now under attack by the Nazi system.[212] Moreover, propaganda to boost morale, they argued, 'should use the powerful aid of history and the Anglo-Saxon "tradition of victory" and should show that this record of victory is not due to accident or to military power alone, but to qualities in the Anglo-Saxon character engendered by the Anglo-Saxon way of life'. History was to be a powerful weapon to mobilize 'active-minded' men and women, who 'work and fight better if they feel they are marching in step with history, and are not simply defending the past, but helping the birth of the future'.[213] All of these themes found visual expression in *The Prime Minister* and *The Young Mr Pitt*, capitalizing on the fact that film and other forms of propaganda could build upon the popular appeal of leadership in war and the specific popularity of Winston Churchill, tapping into pre-existing sentiments to give visual and personal identities to the vague notions forwarded by the Ministry.

It was only with the reinvention of British wartime leadership in May 1940 that such historical analogies began successfully to relate to the people, who in July 1940 were expressing a deep-seated mistrust of political leaders, born out of the crisis of appeasement and the perceived failures of Chamberlain.[214] They felt distanced from politics, Mass-Observation commenting that 'people do not, for the most part, feel themselves personally involved in political problems'.[215] Further reports claimed that the public had very little specific understanding of or interest in political values and issues. Awareness was 'certainly not focused on Parliament [nor] on the House of Commons', which seemed 'too remote',[216] a trend which was identified by the propagandists of the MoI, who recognized that democracy could not be explained only as a 'set of abstract political principles' but rather 'as a way of life'.[217] Where public interest and politics coincided, however, was in the popular fascination with personality.[218] The British found a distinctive, iconic personality in Churchill who, in comparison to his predecessor, had attained a high level of popularity. The Mass-Observers recorded that Chamberlain had never reached the 80 per cent popularity ratings accorded to his successor,[219] noting that

> much of what people think about the Government and the whole democratic machinery is tied up with what they think about the Prime Minister... The very fact of a strong and exciting personality tends, as things are at present, to heighten the prestige of this particular system to the minds of ordinary people who are not very interested in the details.[220]

It is no surprise to find, therefore, that the filmic medium sought to fuse the ideals of parliamentary democracy with the concept of leadership, the two being already tied together in the public imagination. The location of this construct within the historical genre only made the propagandistic effect all the more powerful.

In filmic terms, fictional features were also able to capitalize upon the popularity of images of leadership in the newsreels. Although Chamberlain's representation elicited 'a steady and accelerating decline in favourable audience response', despite public pressure to be 'loyal to your Prime Minister, especially in wartime', other leaders such as Charles de Gaulle were consistently more popular with film-goers. The image of royal leadership was also particularly well-liked by audiences, a concept equally relevant to the question of national identity in this period.[221] Naturally, the desire to elicit a public reaction to the war effort and to the vague concepts of 'what we are fighting for' meant that personality became the embodiment of national values and characteristics. Audiences could more easily identify with an individual, with the ideas and values they represented having a popular resonance in the wake of discussions centring on character. Historical epics could exploit public interest in personality and leadership, producers carefully constructing film propaganda disguised by the dislocation of time and by the escapism of costume drama. Wartime Prime Ministers and monarchs, therefore, provided an excellent opportunity for filmmakers in 1940 and beyond to explore national values, and, by May 1940, Britain had an appropriate icon, a leader who could not only represent the modern condition but could also be aligned with the past. As Grierson noted in 1941, 'for the propagandist, Churchill … is simply the dramatic form in which the drums of Drake have been brought out from the English subconscious and beaten again'.[222] For both the MoI and the studio, this mystical connection between past and present offered a golden opportunity to attain that elusive combination of propaganda and entertainment film. This was increasingly precious to propagandists because it provided the veil with which to disguise the propaganda content, exacerbating its effect, and to the studios because they were not keen to jeopardize profits. Film was, after all, a business, as well as a tool in the battle for hearts and minds.

An analysis of the two major feature films of this genre, *The Prime Minister* and *The Young Mr Pitt*, demonstrates how closely the past was connected to the present. In a similar fashion to Germany, the central motor in this process was the studio promotional activity which sought to refashion the image of past leadership to fit the contemporary mould. Although textual references within the film obviously reflected the specific construction of the image, promotional materials attempted to reinforce the cinematic portrayal either by planting the idea before audiences entered the cinema or retrospectively reinforcing the filmic image through reflection. In this way, studios, and indeed propagandists, could ensure that the central connection to the present was not lost. Moreover, such sources indicate that the studios were actively promoting parallels between past and present in a variety of ways. This form of persuasion had a potentially dualistic impact on audiences, either by playing upon the popular desire to apply personal meaning to events in the past, making them more relevant, or by drawing on the escapist appeal of historical costume drama. It was a similar tactic to that used by the German studios in the same period.

It is significant that films such as *The Prime Minister* and *The Young Mr Pitt* tapped into public perceptions of the Churchillian premiership. They were both set within a wartime context, with Britain fighting against an autocratic continental aggressor determined to ensure territorial expansion. Disraeli and Pitt the Younger were depicted as men of their time, but timeless, their values the embodiment of 'Britishness'. They were both in conflict with their contemporaries, seeking to challenge the 'Establishment' and yet innately a part of it. Both men submitted to a rite of passage in confronting the European dictators, upholding their beliefs in spite of political and popular harassment. Both protagonists emerge from a period of desperation to regain the trust and adoration of their public, their unique vision triumphing over the short-sightedness of their opponents. Most importantly, however, the image of the 'men of destiny' depicted in the films also corresponded to public perceptions of Churchill's qualities. In April 1941, Mass-Observation asked the public to describe the Prime Minister in one word. The responses could be easily mapped onto past wartime leaders as they were depicted in British feature films from 1940 to 1942. In the popular mind, Churchill represented 'hope', 'genius', greatness, versatility, Britishness; he possessed tactical brilliance and nobility. He was the nation's 'bulldoggish' wartime leader, who was 'alright for a war', but 'not in peacetime'. Churchill was also described as 'historic',[223] an image borne of the times in which he lived, but also deliberately cultivated by propagandists. The promotional film poster for *This England* (David Macdonald, 1941), in which the Prime Minister was portrayed as the most recent chapter in Britain's victorious history, provides a clear example that Churchill had inherited the mantle of British wartime leadership, displayed as he was alongside other wartime leaders: Elizabeth I, Francis Drake and Nelson. In short, Churchill was *already* recognized as being bound up with the nation's history, the films depicting the 'men of destiny' only serving to accentuate and shape pre-existing attitudes.

The first major feature film to represent leadership in this way was Thorold Dickinson's 1941 production, *The Prime Minister*, originally titled *An Empire Was Built*,[224] starring John Gielgud as Disraeli. Dickinson's film centred on the distinctive 'Otherness' of the protagonist and his essentially unique character.[225] The object of broad adulation, 'admired by women, idolised by artists, received in all circles with great distinction and appreciation',[226] Disraeli was characterized in the film as possessing unsurpassed *'courage, spirit and a command of language'*. A man of exceptional genius, he is convinced by his soon-to-be wife, Mrs Wyndam-Lewis, that his 'destiny' was to 'serve England'. Marriage, like the German examples of the same genre, did not indicate that he was to be denied his period of solitude, the death of his wife at a critical moment in the affairs of the nation reinforcing the fact that ultimately the leader is alone, offering a similar parallel to Nazi portraits of charismatic leadership.

In a further comparison to National Socialist images of the leader, the figure of Disraeli was to be 'England's man of destiny' in press releases, general advertising and exhibitor displays, which emphasized that, like Churchill, 'Disraeli ... found ... a fertile ground for his genius in foreign affairs', where Britain had always considered itself great.[227] Drawing a parallel to recent events in Britain, Warner Bros. announced that 'in Disraeli's time too ... England's Empire was threatened by appeasers within and strong men without'.[228] Such analogies were envisaged by the film's director who, in shooting the sequence in which Disraeli announces to the House that war has been forestalled at the 'eleventh hour', informed the '250 assembled extras that it was a parallel [to] the Munich affair, a threat of war and a method of dealing with it. The House should, therefore, show the appreciation of these issues by the intensity of its feeling, just as the House had risen to the Premier when war was averted in September 1938'.[229] One scene in particular underlined pre-war debates, reliving them through the cinematic depiction of Cabinet discussion, with Disraeli fitting the model of Churchillian leadership. On hearing that the Russians have mobilized against Turkey, protected by a guarantee offered by Britain, a debate erupts in Cabinet as to the appropriate course of action. When it is suggested that '*some attempt at appeasement*' should be made, Disraeli replies:

> Appeasment? Of an autocrat? ... In an autocracy, the leader is the people. And Europe, at the moment, is at the mercy of the most ruthless band of autocrats that the world has yet seen. I know these dictators, these men of 'blood and iron'. They have one weakness; they're always in a hurry... They hold themselves a race apart, divinely ordained to rule the world to the exclusion of all others. That is a form of madness that must eventually destroy the world or be destroyed. It cannot be appeased by soft words or good neighbourliness. All the civilized methods of approach to international agreements are signs of weakness to these men. They recognise one argument and one argument alone: force. That is the argument I beg you to use now. With all your heart and with all your soul, for the sake of peace and for the sake of England.

This '*mobilization to prevent war*' against the triumvirate of Germany, Russia and Austria at a time when the Nazi–Soviet pact was still in force could not have failed to resonate with audiences in early 1941, the US press book ensuring that the contemporary parallel was not missed: 'Disraeli, more than any other statesman, is well aware of the subterranean moves in German diplomacy and is determined to make his country recognize the dangers of the German Chancellor Bismarck's purposes. Then, as so recently, there were many who could not believe that there was anything but good intentions behind the assurances of the European dictator'.[230]

More specific reference was made to the link between Churchill and Disraeli, *The Cinema* observing that the film was 'a very mirror of events today...: Then, as now, we had a Prime Minister entirely motivated by his devotion to his country and his high regard for her honour'.[231] It was the cult of the personality and the importance of the Prime Minister to British identity and democracy, rather than its institutions or processes, which was foregrounded by Dickinson's production. In their advice to exhibitors, Warner Bros.

encouraged theatres to run essay-writing contests in schools, and run Disraeli quizzes in local newspapers. Extravagantly, the studio suggested that exhibitors mount lobby displays of a full-size blow up portrait of Disraeli, with a theatre attendant reading the 'Wit and Wisdom of Disraeli' via a PA system behind the display.[232]

The production of *The Prime Minister* quickly became entangled with the history of the period in which it was made, serving as a reflection of contemporary experiences in Britain. The studio connected the film and 'a crucial period in Britain's history', proclaiming that 'English actors were anxious to appear in the production in any part to show that nothing could halt them'.[233] As the press book commented, Gielgud's speeches were seen as 'mighty portentous words to utter while the RAF kept watch over the Teddington England studios, where the enthralling drama was shot'.[234] This was made all the more poignant with the news that, as filming ended, Nazi bombers had inflicted a direct hit on the studio, killing its manager. The studios stressed not just the thematic proximity of the film to wartime events, but also its literal proximity, a tactic mobilized two years later by Gaumont British when advertising Carol Reed's 1942 production *The Young Mr Pitt*.

Still 14　*The Prime Minister. John Gielgud as Benjamin Disraeli.*
Still from Bfi Stills, Posters and Designs.

Although *The Prime Minister* was intended to 'show the best of Britain', an expression of 'the major things Britain has done, can do and will do again',[235] the reviews were mixed. Although *Kinematograph Weekly* was generous in its praise for the film,[236] the production did not enjoy a universally favourable response. *The Times*, in particular, was critical of Dickinson's interpretation of history and its use as a contemporary parallel, commenting that the film 'oversimplifies complex issues, and writes nineteenth-century history with an eye on the present year of 1941'. In doing so, argued the reviewer, the production 'did not take the advantage of the Disraeli legend as it might legitimately have done'.[237] Despite the newspaper's praise for Gielgud's performance, film-goers did not always agree, one letter to *Picture-goer Weekly* arguing that the actor was 'a little too old to play his heroes'.[238] Gielgud himself went to considerable lengths to offer an authentic portrait of the statesman, consulting the son of Disraeli's valet to perfect the 'mannerisms which eccentric "Dizzy" affected, such as pretending to have coughing fits whenever he was stuck for words or quick explanations'.[239] However, as Harper has noted, this resulted in a rather effeminate portrait, devoid of the virility expected of a wartime leader, with Gielgud 'constantly [fussing] with his hair, face and gloves'.[240] Even those involved in production were not satisfied with the final piece. Dickinson recalled that the film was 'just a hack-job … thoroughly commercial',[241] while Gielgud noted that it 'could have been exploited a good deal more than it has been from a wartime propaganda standpoint'. Here was 'a golden opportunity missed'.[242] It was clear that the cult of personality, either that of the star or of the leader he attempted to play, did not positively dominate the film. Audiences looked to a more dynamic and young leader for inspiration, portrayed by a glittering star of the screen. This combination was delivered by Carol Reed's production, *The Young Mr Pitt*, which found greater success than its forerunner.

Robert Donat's portrayal of William Pitt the Younger in Reed's 1942 production owed some of its success to the popularity of the film's star.[243] Donat had real star power, being voted second most popular British screen actor in 1940, behind George Formby.[244] *The Young Mr Pitt* details the story of the Georgian Prime Minister, his great rivalry with Charles James Fox, the successes and failures of his career and the two military campaigns of his premiership against France in 1793 and during the Napoleonic wars of 1803–5.[245] Like Dickinson in his portrait of Disraeli, Reed was said to have been 'struck by the parallel with the wartime situation – England under the threat of invasion from the Continent by the victorious Napoleon had an obvious relevance to Hitler's war'.[246] That the film was intended to be a direct parallel between the past and present was confirmed in an interview with Reed some years later.[247] Viscount Castlerosse agreed to write the story and additional dialogue, for later adaptation by the script writing duo Frank Launder and Sidney Gilliat.[248] *The Young Mr Pitt* began filming in July 1941.[249]

Press coverage promoted the attempts by the studio to create an historically accurate picture of the Georgian period and its politics to lend the production an air of authenticity. *Kinematograph Weekly* confirmed that 'history is in the remaking at Denham'.[250] Elaborate sets were constructed, 'studio draughtsmen Carter and Bowden, under art director Vetchinsky, [spending] a fortnight drawing the plans'. Reconstructions ensured that the smallest detail was given attention, 'fifteen scale drawings ... needed for ... moulding, panelling, benches, [and the] Speaker's chair'.[251] *Kinematograph Weekly*, who followed the film closely in its production stages, reported that 'make-up and wardrobe ... received birthdate charts of all historical characters, so that their appearances may be suitably altered as the period of the film proceeds'. Similar charts were provided to the props team 'for each scene from 1768 to 1805, so that floral decorations, scenic backings, costumes, will correspond'.[252] The art department were required to recreate the Luxembourg Gardens in Paris, in which Napoleon was to preside over an 'elaborate fireworks display'. Louis Levy, the film's musical director, was dispatched to the British Museum to 'unearth some [manuscripts] of unknown Georgian composers'.[253] This attention to detail was extended to the cast. In order to deal with a scene in which 'Pitt is attacked at night by a mob hired by his political enemies' in a '[reconstructed] Old Bond Street',[254] both Donat and John Mills (William Wilberforce) were coached by 'Bombardier' Billy Wells, heavyweight champion of Britain and Europe.[255]

Particular attention was given to sets which sought to reinforce the parallel to 1940s Britain within the public consciousness. When filming scenes at Walmer Castle of the proposed invasion of Britain by Napoleon,[256] Gaumont British informed the press, in October 1941, that Churchill had just become Warden of the Cinque Ports, of which Walmer Castle was a residence. This served as an 'historical reminder' for audiences of *The Young Mr Pitt*.[257] Evoking a sense of the distant as well as the more recent past, *Kinematograph Weekly* remarked that 'Donat as William Pitt will be seen living in the famous castle, which was built in the reign of Henry VIII', adding that 'it was from this retreat that Pitt was recalled to save the British from Napoleon – a strange coincidence with recent events in the life of our own Prime Minister'.[258] Reporters, witnessing the filming of scenes at 'historic Walmer', were also reminded how closely the past as reflected in the film mirrored the present situation, commenting that 'in the reproduction of the Walmer Castle scene after Pitt had been recalled to aid his country in its direst need, it sounded all too familiar with the ever-present threat of Nazi invasion hanging over us', a threat which must have seemed all the more immediate as cast and crew looked over the channel whilst filming. *Kinematograph Weekly* commented on a further scene with contemporary parallels, informing their readers that 'Donat has a visitor who brings news almost as odd as the rumours that followed the arrival of Hess. Hugh McDermott, playing an American who, in the midst of war, came as a negotiator of peace terms between England and France. That he failed dismally is also reminiscent of Hess's arrival'. The reporter naturally concluded that *The Young Mr Pitt* bore a 'very close resemblance to current history'.[259]

As with *The Prime Minister*, the studio seized the opportunity to reinforce the contemporary parallel by promoting the literal proximity of the actors and film-makers to the war. Articles for placement in the press stressed the problems of wartime filming. The production of *The Young Mr Pitt* was, stated Gaumont British, 'a race against the bombs', the press book detailing that filming in London's Guildhall, the setting of the great banquet chamber finale, was hampered by 'fallen masonry and fire-wrecked timbers'. Attempts to shoot the scenes in the House of Commons were continually thwarted by aerial bombardment, the producers eventually moving the set from the 'blitzed Parliament ... to the still-standing House of Lords'.[260] The destruction of sites of national heritage and tradition tied in with the propaganda image of the uncultured aggressor highlighted in films such as *49th Parallel*. Artistry and creativity were pitted against the barbarous destruction perpetrated by the enemy, a theme stressed, not only in cinematic terms, but also in the promotional material. In detailing the work of the set designers, the studio proclaimed: 'The weeks of designing and draughtsmanship on *The Young Mr Pitt* was a race against the Nazis, the three draughtsmen making their drawings of houses, streets and doors, Adam fireplaces, Georgian sidewalks, praying that they would get their old London replanned before further bombs obliterated the landmarks and the relics from which they were gaining their inspiration'.[261] The refusal of the artistic directors and producers to leave the city, despite the fact that 'bomb destruction in London ... removed many of the original buildings required for the film',[262] not only underlined the timely comparison forwarded by *The Young Mr Pitt* but strangely paralleled the premier's decision not to leave the capital. Operating from the secure rooms of the No. 10 Annexe at Storey's Gate, Churchill finally relented to Air Ministry pressure that he should 'sleep in reasonable safety' if he were to stay in London,[263] although he still insisted on 'using No. 10 itself whenever it was reasonably safe to do so', despite the residence remaining '"totally insecure" from bombs and later from flying bombs and rockets'.[264] Churchill could be near to the Londoners, touring blitzed sites and offering them his support, his car often being mobbed accompanied by cries of 'It was good of you to come Winnie. We thought you'd come. We can take it. Give it 'em back'.[265] In this way, the setting, scenario and even the contemporary experience of filming in wartime London, all reinforced the contemporary parallel with Churchill, a parallel only extended when one turns to the film itself.

The central aim of *The Young Mr Pitt* was to carve a portrait of idealized wartime leadership, stressing 'the duty of giving all for the country to which we owe all that we have and are', bound up within a celebration of the British past and its key personalities.[266] *The Young Mr Pitt* was to be 'an epic of what a brave man can do when supported by soldiers and sailors of British blood. England called for a man whom the spoils of office could not buy, a man who, possessed of a strong will and opinions ... loved honour and his country above all'.[267] Like his filmic counterparts, Pitt must endure a rite of passage through the House and through war, and gives up the love of his life in the name of honour and duty. As the press book noted, Eleanor Eden (Phyllis Calvert) was 'the girl who shared his hopes and dreams but waited while he *challenged dictatorship!*'[268] The sacrifice that Pitt makes in the name of his country is not limited to the rejection of a personal existence. Ultimately, the strain on his health, caused by the long hours and dedication to the cause, results in his untimely death.

Throughout the filmic narrative, Pitt is revealed to be a man of passion and fervour, representing the future, challenging the establishment and yet ultimately shaping what it will become. This was embodied in Pitt's statement to Fox on being offered the job of Prime Minister: '*the ideas of yesterday are dead and those of today are dying. It's being in step with the ideas of tomorrow that counts. We are men of the future*'. As a young leader, who 'as Prime Minister at 24 ... smashes tradition',[269] Pitt was to be an inspiration for future leaders. The studio encouraged cinema-owners to launch competitions in local newspapers in which readers submitted 'a list of the ten most important personages in the world today who are under forty' together with 100 words as to which 'they [considered] ... the most important', the winners and runners-up receiving 'war stamps or guest tickets' to a screening of the film. Entrants were naturally reminded that 'many young men are playing major roles in today's historic struggle to beat the Axis, much as Pitt did when Napoleon threatened the continent of Europe'.[270] Although not offering a direct comparison to Churchill, who was sixty-six years of age at the time of the film's release, campaigns of this nature further bolstered the cult of personality. As with films in the Third Reich, the publicity surrounding key productions merged the on-screen persona with the cult surrounding the leading man,

Still 15   *Robert Donat as 'The Young Mr Pitt'.* From Bfi Stills, Posters and Designs.

Donat described by the studio as the 'handsome, romantic gentleman of stage and screen' who was 'the supreme example of a man whose faith in himself and whose natural courage carried him to world stardom after enduring bitter adversity';[271] a mirror of the depiction of Pitt in Reed's film.

In keeping with the propaganda objectives of the film, the 1942 production was to be a sanitized version of Pitt's life. Such was the importance of the virtue of the leader that the script writers found themselves in conflict with Reed and Donat over the image of Pitt. Launder and Gilliat wanted to show Pitt's 'human imperfections',[272] including a scene where Pitt makes a drunken speech in the House of Commons. Gilliat noted that he wanted to show that 'under the stress of trying to run a war, people do not behave impeccably, and that if somebody is pissed making a speech, this is a moving thing'. This, according to Gilliat, would have injected a little life into the historic portrait of the Prime Minister, adding that 'Pitt was known as a bit of a cold fish in his day'. Reed and Donat would 'not have [this] at any price',[273] the two writers completing the script according to the limitations placed upon them,[274] still convinced that, as Launder put it, 'untainted heroes, unless biblical, are bores'.[275] Pitt was to be a 'paragon of virtue' and the film was to be a 'simple yet spectacular tale of one man's unremitting labours in the cause of England ... a present day parallel in the threat of invasion, [underlining] the almost magical resilience of an unflagging courage ... a film of yesterday for today'.[276] In Britain as in Germany, then, the depiction of leadership and specifically the human side of leaders, their imperfections and failings, were a subject of intense debate, and revealed conflicting visions of the proper treatment of the wartime leader.

In another parallel to the German representation of leadership, both the film and the studio publicity explicitly made clear references to analogies between past and present. Billed as 'a story of a generation like ours' and 'a thrilling drama of a great nation, challenged by a power-mad dictator', the press book encouraged exhibitors to 'sell its amazing time-lessness'.[277] The press book specifically quoted Pitt's speeches in an attempt to stress the historical parallels, which were often used with tie-ins serving to promote the film and its message. One example was the use of the following speech in the publicity campaign for the 1942 film:

> We are called to struggle for the destiny not only of this country alone, but of the civilized world ... our highest exultation ought to be that we hold out a prospect to nations, now bending under the iron yoke of tyranny, of what exertions of a free people can effect. I trust that we shall at last see that wicked fabric destroyed which brought with it more miseries, more horrors than are to be paralleled in any part of the annals of mankind.[278]

The speech was used to prompt a flurry of promotional activities in theatres and local communities, appealing to a wide variety of cinema-goers from adults to children. The studio advised exhibitors and the press to use this stirring and timely speech as an incentive for editorial comment in your paper. Blow it up for inclusion in your lobby displays, and use it on handouts, book-marks, and school and library bulletin board posters. It might serve as the basis of a school essay contest, with history teachers cooperating in asking their students to compare the situation in Pitt's time with that of today.[279]

The film was certainly intended to establish a link not just to the problems of the past and present, and the difficulties of leadership, but more specifically to Winston Churchill personally. In the promotion of the film, as with Warner Bros. publicity for *The Prime Minister*, Gaumont British did not disguise its intention to depict Churchill as the Pitt of his day. Under the heading 'amazing parallel with to-day's events', the press book for the film stated:

> Where Mr Churchill stands this day, four square against the hatred of the Hun, there stood in George III's time a similar man in No. 10 Downing Street, a bold, earnest figure braced with the steadfast faith of the whole people of Britain. His name was William Pitt. And now, at a time when the spirit of Pitt is embodied in Winston Churchill, the great saga of a valiant statesman who in his time defied as brutal an aggressor, has been brought to the screen.[280]

That the press book provided a template for wider distribution of reports on specific films is confirmed by the fact that this excerpt found its way, word for word, into the trade newspaper, *Kinematograph Weekly*.[281]

Such parallels were brought out in the film itself, Pitt's speeches forming the central propagandistic discourse throughout. Choosing similar themes to *The Prime Minister* and mirroring contemporary debates, Pitt is shown to be the staunch advocate of a policy of action, opposing appeasement and all it represents. Rejecting '*platitudes*', Pitt recognizes that the only answer to dictators is to '*fight or surrender ... and we shall fight*'. As the only man to understand the expansionist intentions of Napoleon, underscoring his characterization as a man of vision who is possessed of exceptional genius setting him apart from his contemporaries, allies as well as adversaries, Pitt tells the House that it is only through action and bravery that one is promised a secure future in the face of '*a danger which threatens all the nations of the earth... [W]e shall meet it undaunted. Determined to stand ... by the laws, liberties and religion of our country*'. Rejecting the call for peace, in terms of the popular and political voice of the nation, Pitt determines a strong course of action, seeing through the rhetoric to the heart of dictatorship: '*We must realise that we are fighting a nation of armed fanatics led by an arch-fanatic. We must work together with a single mind and a single purpose. We must put aside all personal affairs, renounce leisure, family, even sleep, to this one imperative duty*'. It is his unswerving commitment to the security of the nation and his determination to defeat the menace of Napoleon that both define his premiership and offer parallels to the contemporary situation. Mirroring the master narrative offered in *The Prime Minister*, depicting Britain as the defender of liberty and protector of minor states, Pitt informs the House:

> It is not enough for us to say that Bonaparte is a mad man and will pay the price of his madness and folly. We must take care that we do not pay it first. We are called to struggle for the destiny not of this country alone but of the civilized world... [O]ur highest exultation ought to be that we hold out to countries now bending under the iron yolk of tyranny... [F]or the benefit of the world at large and for the honour of mankind, I say that the spirit of Bonaparte and the principles he cherishes must be extinguished, and that other principles shall prevail.

In both the film text and the promotional materials, then, the parallel between Britain of the late eighteenth and early nineteenth and mid-twentieth centuries is carefully drawn, the two methods of propaganda reinforcing the central message to be internalized by the audience.

However, the link to the past was not merely defined through identification with the leader. Audiences themselves were encouraged to feel a form of personal association with the story and the times. Not only did the studios sell the historical similarities between Britain in 1793 and 1940 through the image of leadership, but they also sought to publicize the experience of the 'everyman'. The strapline for the film hinted at this inclusivity: 'The Story of a Generation like Ours – With a Job to Do'. Similarly, the press book drew on the contemporary experience of many men and women in wartime Britain, observing that:

> In this day, the famous William Pitt faced a situation parallel to that which confronts us today! Across the Channel was a ruthless dictator and an army waiting to invade England. Pitt's problem was much like that of millions of men today. He hears his country's call. Shall he give up the woman he loves and devote his life to fight for freedom? Pitt made his decision, and it is stirringly told in *The Young Mr Pitt*.[282]

This reinforced the link to the people, adding a new strand to the image of leadership. With this identification, the audience was led to believe that leaders were not unlike themselves – they are men of the people as well as men of destiny. Exhibitors were advised to 'get this timely, interest-catching situation across to your movie-goers'.[283] In contrast to the National Socialist films of leadership, Pitt was connected to the people in every way. Although the special genius of Pitt is recognized, the average cinema-goer could be expected to empathize with his plight, his form of sacrifice comparable to theirs, and not separated from it in his isolation as the closing sequence of *Der große König* suggested to German audiences.

As a key vehicle for encouraging this personal identification, a powerful tool to the propagandist and entertainer alike, the love story between Pitt and Eleanor Eden refocused the theme of sacrifice, love and war.[284] Exhibitors were persuaded to mount giant stills from the film in the foyer, one of which was to bear the caption: 'Like a million lovers today, they waited their country's call, sacrificing love for duty!' In addition, local press tie-ins were encouraged, stressing the impact of war on relationships, and encouraging strength and patience in the face of adversity. Exhibitors could use this angle to gain additional publicity for their screenings. The press book offered the following suggestion:

In *The Young Mr Pitt*, Robert Donat, playing the title role, heeds the call of duty to his country and gives up the woman he loves. Similar problems face many a young man today going off to war. For an excellent 'Inquiring Reporter' question or newspaper contest, you might offer this problem to moviegoers, asking for the best letters giving arguments for and against marrying before entering the army.[285]

This combination of personal identification with the leadership figure, a factor not particularly prominent in the representation of Disraeli in Dickinson's 1941 production, allied with a depiction of charismatic leadership, proved to be popular with audience and critics alike, *Kinematograph Weekly* heralding Reed's film as having a 'surging and compelling power' and lavishing praise on its 'strong human as well as historical and moral angle'. The trade newspaper was also full of admiration for the use of historical parallel, stating that *The Young Mr Pitt* 'proves how uncannily history can repeat itself. Every inch of the turbulent real-life story has its lesson' making it an 'invaluable example' in its 'almost complete reconstruction' of history past and present. Commenting on the interpretation of wartime leadership, the review concluded that the film was 'Churchillian in power, purpose and poise', offering 'a shining tribute to a great man, an imperishable personal experience and a lofty example to our own leaders and ourselves'.[286] Nevertheless, some disquiet about using the past and escapism as veils for contemporary propaganda began to emerge with the production of *The Young Mr Pitt*, not least from the Prime Minister himself. Reed's production 'was reportedly seen by Churchill, who was said to have approved' of it,[287] giving the artistic directors of the film special permission to use his study in Downing Street.[288] The film was shown to MPs, including members of the War Cabinet,[289] and the King and Queen.[290] However, the Prime Minister did not back comparisons between his leadership and times and those of Pitt the Younger. Although he recognized occasions when the House turned to historical analogy to explain the present,[291] Churchill was always careful to draw the distinction between the two. In an introduction to Pitt's speeches in 1940, he commented that

> No historical analogies can be exact, and in one respect our situation is very different from what it was in Pitt's day... There can be no comparison... in the scale of civilization between the Nazi system and that of the Napoleonic Empire; nor could the humane, free-spirited French people ever have become the docile instruments of such barbarism as now issues from Berlin.[292]

It was a sentiment the Prime Minister was to reiterate in the House of Commons, telling his fellow parliamentarians in May 1941 that 'some have compared Hitler's conquests with those of Napoleon... It must be remembered, however, that Napoleon's armies carried with them the fierce, liberating and equalitarian winds of the French Revolution, whereas Hitler's empire has nothing behind it but racial self-assertion, espionage, pillage, corruption and the Prussian boot'. As such, the comparison offered by *The Young Mr Pitt* was neither approved nor endorsed by the film's inspiration.

Others too questioned the validity of the historical analogy presented in Reed's film. The *New Statesman and Nation* contended that Pitt was no match for the Prime Minister and that the film had unfairly rewritten history. In casting the striking Donat, argued the periodical, Reed had reinvented the 'ungainly figure with an interminable turned-up nose and what George III called a "damned long obstinate upper lip" ..., every future schoolboy' now thinking of Pitt as 'a graceful and handsome young man with a flawlessly aquiline nose'. Moreover, they observed 'the film world, presumably because of the money bags behind it, is always resolutely anti-liberal; Dizzy is always a hero, Gladstone a skunk. So now Fox is the villain – and, what is more, an effeminate villain'. The film's parallels were declared to be 'misleading', Pitt having 'neither Churchill's virtues nor his deficiencies. He was by nature a man of peace – indeed, he began as an appeaser, and he fought Napoleon chiefly by subsidizing foreign armies'.[293] The problems of the historical analogy were evident. In reconstructing an historical memory and suggesting the continuities between the past and present for propagandistic purposes, tensions were bound to occur.

Despite the critics, *The Young Mr Pitt* was considerably more popular and well-received than *The Prime Minister*. At face value, the two seemed to propose similar portraits of wartime leadership. Both *The Prime Minister* and *The Young Mr Pitt* were reflections on dogged determination in the face of a continental aggressor and the nature of leadership in wartime, and both made a clear and unambiguous comparison with Churchill. Both films were promoted by Warner Bros. and Gaumont British in a similar way, stressing the timely nature of the story, the iconic status of the individual leader, enshrined in the Prime Minister and the historical parallel. However, an analysis of the publicity reveals that there is one glaring difference between the promotional activity for each film – that of the importance of personal identification. Whereas the publicity for *The Prime Minister*, and to some extent the film too, stressed the historical importance of Disraeli and his work – in short, telling the story 'from above'– the advertising and promotional activity for *The Young Mr Pitt* went further, building a bridge between the leader and the people. The filmic Pitt was promoted as a man with problems like the everyman. Audiences could identify with his dilemmas, simply because many were facing the same challenges themselves.

While *The Young Mr Pitt* and *The Prime Minister* were both released in a similar period, 1940-2, this did not mean that depictions of wartime leadership were confined to those years. Britain's propagandists could delve deep into the past to create legitimacy, hope, morale and promises of victory. Although Nigel Mace 'discounts' Laurence Olivier's 1945 production, *Henry V*, from the genre of the historical parallel films on the grounds that despite 'its obvious jingoism, [it] still had Shakespeare's play as its basic text',[294] it was an important expression of British heritage and leadership. Even the use of Shakespeare's text becomes a statement on the former, demonstrating that British propagandists were not merely honouring political and military leaders, but, by association, promoting British cultural icons, looking to Shakespeare to give expression to leadership as the war drew to a close. Moreover, the film added a dimension to previous films in that it dealt with royal leadership, a popular point of reference for British audiences during World War II, making it worthy of inclusion in a discussion of the historical genre. Although centred on monarchy, *Henry V* bore significant similarities to both *The Young Mr Pitt* and *The Prime Minister*, not least in the representation of a resolute, determined leader of a nation facing a European expansionist force.

In many ways, the sheer scale of the production and the commitment of the players were perceived as patriotic gestures and a celebration of the closing stages of the conflict in Europe. Although Carol Reed, the director of *The Young Mr Pitt*, was originally intended to be the director of *Henry V*,[295] Laurence Olivier was permitted to return from the Fleet Air Arm in August 1943 to star in and direct *Henry V*, suggesting the importance of the film to national morale and the approval of the MoI.[296] Olivier's potential discharge had been the subject of much controversy in 1942 when the Ministry had refused to release him for Powell and Pressburger's *The Life and Death of Colonel Blimp*.[297] That they chose to release him one year later for *Henry V* indicates at least a tacit approval. The film had always been intended as a contribution to the nation's propaganda campaigns in its 'desire to produce a picture which could bring to life to the war-suffering people the beauty and wisdom of the greatest universal poet', functioning as a means of national expression and escape.[298] Olivier stated that in his mind the film was to be a 'national gesture'.[299] If this was to be its purpose, then the choice of *Henry V* was apt. As C. Clayton Hutton, the author of the contemporary publication *The Making of Henry V*, noted, the play 'speaks for England ... not only in Henry's famous orations but in the words and deeds of his several soldiers, the humblest of them being the most expressive of all. Furthermore', he continued, 'it is propaganda for our country with a long view so that if the present war finished next month, it would still create a most healthful and salutary effect'.[300] The propaganda impact was obvious. Timed to coincide with the end of the war, Alan Dent, the screenwriter for the production, commented that *Henry V* 'was the most patriotic, the most pro-England play that Shakespeare ever penned', depicting the 'overwhelming defeat ... [of] an enemy which was to all appearances incomparably stronger'.[301] In order to exacerbate the parallels between Shakespeare's play and contemporary events, Dent resolved to make changes to the text, Harper commenting that 'the final script [was] extremely selective; [omitting] ... the negative aspects of Henry's character and the positive aspects of the French. Also missing are the suggestions of internal dissent, and the paeans to Divine Right', the edited film left to 'concentrate on leadership, without the inconvenience of metaphysics'.[302] In this way, the screen writer '[removed] any doubts about national unity and references to the unchivalrous aspects of medieval warfare'.[303] The original play was thus transformed into a film script which 'bore the hand of Brendan Bracken', as the *Boston Post* observed,[304] and deliberately intended to 'evoke the maximum emotional response by narrowing and intensifying definitions of national culture'.[305]

Henry V, like its predecessors, took the opportunity to venerate modern-day wartime leadership, thinly veiled by the historic setting, a fact not overlooked by contemporary observers. Scholar Stafford A. Brook, in correspondence with Dent, commented that the 'King is great minded [embodying] ... that which makes the heart of England great ... [his] words might almost have been written of the Battle of Britain in the autumn and winter of 1940'.[306] Dent himself expressed Henry V's style of leadership as 'appropriate to the times' in which the film was made.[307] War was depicted as 'a miracle of quiet, temperate, austere judgement',[308] and the subject matter 'a poem [of the] ... glorification of the dauntless spirit and invincible endurance of Englishmen'.[309] As Dent noted, it was the perfect example of the 'little man' being inspired by 'famous orations' to great words and deeds,[310] a film which would demonstrate that unity under a strong leader could 'defeat ... an enemy which was to all appearances ... stronger'.[311] Olivier was to be the very embodiment of the monarch. With the 'looks, defiance and glamour of a King', he delivered the ultimate image of a wartime leader, the expression of 'British dignity' in war, a 'quality', remarked E. T. Carr of the Eagle Lion Studios in a letter to the star of the film, possessed by 'no other race of people'.[312] This sentiment was in keeping with the obvious propaganda content which was promised to Jack Beddington, head of the films division of the MoI, by Two Cities, the film's producers.[313] Dent suggested that the publicity materials for *Henry V* should stress that it is 'the most eloquent reminder of the "glories of our blood and state ever penned by mortal man, and as such its ringing message should be repeated now more urgently than at any other period in the whole of English history"'.[314] In short, *Henry V* was to be yet another endorsement of British wartime leadership through the mobilization of the past.

However, as with the history of virtually all other productions of this nature, the studio experienced problems. The challenges for the production team of *Henry V* lay in the use of language, particularly when it came to exporting to the United States. Although Clayton Hutton was sceptical about the American public's appreciation of 'dignity and tremendous action, two things', he argued, 'which they in pictures have never been able to achieve but which they always strive to do',[315] Olivier was still keen to export the production. However, from the very outset, he found himself in conflict with the Hays Office. On hearing that the American distributors were requesting drastic cuts, fearing that *Henry V* was too long for the US market, and the censors insisting on alterations to the language, Olivier retorted that 'the point of making classical pictures is to attempt to win the admiration of people who know what we are talking about. If we are not going to worry about those people', he concluded, 'then we should not have made a classical picture, and if the American distributors are only worried about the great unwashed, then we had best only make the sort of pictures that the great unwashed are going to like and leave it at that'.[316] Moreover, Olivier objected to the editing of the Shakespearean language to suit the sensibilities of American audiences, the Hays Office requesting changing the word 'bastard' to 'darstard' and the removal of all 'references to the Almighty'.[317] Smarting from these *diktats*, an incandescent Olivier replied:

> It might be helpful to remind the Board of Censors that the picture has been [seen] and approved by over a million members of the English-speaking public including the King, the Queen, the two princesses, the Archbishop of Canterbury, the Prime Minister

and President Roosevelt, and we cannot believe that there is 'owt in it to disturb the morals of the naughtiest little boy on the East side or the wickedest little girl in the dust bowl.[318]

Adding to the battles over the export of *Henry V* to the United States, battles which made Olivier comment that the whole affair had caused his 'blood [to boil and freeze] at odd intervals' and had to 'stifle [his] impulses to burst into the arena and crack a few whips',[319] the production team were also under pressure from the US distributors to make the historical analogy more relevant to American film-goers, a move which Two Cities resisted on the grounds that 'any parallel would be obviously crude and irritating to the cinema audience'.[320] Del Guidice of Two Cities informed the US distributors that Olivier could not be persuaded on this issue: 'no such tie-up ... between the men of Agincourt and the British shock troops in this last war can logically be extended to include our Allies from America, and any attempt to do so would, I think, appear obviously straining; ... the result on screen would appear pompous and over-important'.[321] It was no surprise to find that Olivier's production was not even nominated for an Academy Award in 1947, the Rank Organisation declaring that 'we are simply livid with rage at the whole thing. It was certainly a "stop Britain at any price" year in Hollywood'.[322]

Distribution in Britain presented fewer problems and reception of the film was, on the whole, positive. As with some similar German productions, as noted by the SD reports, the pre-publicity surrounding the film certainly added to the positive reception of the film after release, Olivier recognizing that there was 'immense curiosity ... already provoked in the minds of sections of the public that have heard about [*Henry V*]' and strongly recommending that 'this curiosity should be given time and opportunity to spread itself to the millions'.[323] The positive reaction to the film was not only generated in the public mind and through positive reviews,[324] but was apparent to the film community. For the director Anthony Asquith, Olivier had succeeded in giving the impression of 'intense reality' as if he had been 'watching the most natural and living people in the most natural settings'.[325] Eagle Lion studios commended Olivier on making a film that left the viewer 'quietly feeling ... proud to be British – at the same time thoroughly entertained'.[326] Of course, supplementing the patriotic and entertaining overtones of *Henry V* was the titanic image of Olivier himself, the embodiment of star power, heightened by his marriage to actress Vivian Leigh, star of the 1939 blockbuster *Gone with the Wind*, which ensured that he was never out of the public eye both in Britain and abroad. Olivier also had a sense of national duty, and had been one of the first stars to return to work in British studios and volunteer for service on the outbreak of war. This was greatly appreciated by British cinema-goers, the reluctance of some stars to return from Hollywood causing a storm of controversy in the early years of the conflict.[327]

The contribution to the war effort was a theme emphasized not only in Olivier's persona but in the publicity for the film. The director suggested that, before general release, *Henry V* should be screened to British and Allied troops, Olivier commenting that 'Allied soldiers on the fighting fronts should have a chance to see it and all of H.M. ships. [It] should be a sincere gesture, please the public and heighten speculation and interest'.[328] The promotion of the film in local cinemas also capitalized on the past, with Two Cities advising cinema-owners that 'there is an extraordinary comparison between Henry V's landing at Harfleur and the D-Day landing of the Allies'. They suggested that 'these might form the basis of an interesting display [in foyers] comparing the actual landing carried out by the Allies on D-Day'.[329] Such connections were not lost on the cinema-audience, one fan living in the United States writing to Olivier to tell him that 'Dunkirk and the year after when England stood alone made [Americans] wonder where we got the tenacious strength to hold on… Seeing *Henry V* has given us the knowledge of where you have gotten the strength to carry on against the odds, as in past war'.[330]

However, the time for drum beating had passed. Many objected to the fact that the 1945 production had, in the words of Olivier, 'exaggerated [Shakespeare's] historical discrepancies a wee bit'.[331] It became clear that, by now, as Harper has observed, 'the lessons of history were less relevant as peace approached',[332] as was the premiership of Churchill, the British public perceiving, as early as November 1942, that the premier was predominantly a wartime, and not a peacetime, leader.[333] Thoughts were turning to peace and the post-war world, and in this atmosphere, the 'picture of our ancient customs, our picturesque villages our cathedrals and the like' had given way to discussions of how the nation's 'social progress in health, housing and education is being affected by the war', Basil Wright contending that 'the best [slogan] we could use in our wartime film propaganda would be the phrase "preparing for peace"'.[334]

By 1943, the veil of escapism of the Prime Ministerial roles of Gielgud and Donat had been reborn in the style of the Gainsborough melodrama. Although textual readings are invariably more complex, the films pointed to the fact that cinema was as much about relaxation as persuasion, *The Cinema* arguing in July 1942 that 'the masses today more than ever need entertainment with amusement'.[335] The popularity of the luxurious Gainsborough films and their increased production in the latter stages of the war, despite a 'Board of Trade watch on studio clothes',[336] demonstrated that the time for dramatic stories of heroic leadership past and present was over and that the public had begun to explore new 'historical pleasures'.[337]

Historical films offered much to the propagandist of World War II, as the cases of Britain and Germany suggest. In drawing on the recent and distant past, both British and German propagandists recreated the glories of a golden age, offering the hope of future victories and a stronger sense of a shared heritage to their peoples in the hope of encouraging greater unity and commitment to 'total war'. The very production of epic films, at a time of rationing of resources, such as film stock, set materials and costumes, let alone the everyday items such as fuel and food, hinted at victory and power, the sumptuous film sets indicating to cinema-goers that the nation was not on the brink of collapse and was withstanding the ravages of conflict, as the SD reports and commentaries in trade newspapers in both Britain and Germany indicated.[338]

In their leaders, film-makers found examples for the conduct of the average citizen in terms of self-sacrifice, honour, hard work and endurance, as well as expressions of genius, of the 'Otherness' that set them apart from the everyman. The qualities of the wartime leader were similar: dedication to nation above personal life, the denial of the pleasures of a private existence, determination, the ability to overcome adversity and the survival of rites of passage, emerging all the more powerful, rising out of their early defeats like the phoenix from the flames. They had vision and were connected to the people but not necessarily of the people; the 'men of destiny' were men of their own time but timeless. Although these leaders had much in common, the uniqueness of the Hitler-myth necessarily meant that the German heroes were invested with an 'other-worldliness', a god-like persona, in keeping with the Führer's image of omniscience and omnipotence propagated by the Third Reich. Historical analogy also served leaders in another way, notably as a means to legitimize and justify contemporary military and political decisions, implying historical precedent, subsequent victory and the recurrent past. That, for the most part, both regimes confined these analogies to the years 1940–2 is significant, suggesting that such films somehow met a contemporary need to be led through a turbulent period in the nation's history, a period in which strong leadership gave comfort and optimism to populations faced with the uncertainty of the future. That both British and German propagandists turned again to the past to give a visual identity to victory, such as that of Agincourt in *Henry V*, and to defeat, as detailed in Veit Harlan's 1945 production *Kolberg*, is also noteworthy, indicating that World War II by implication had itself become history and that their great sacrifices, whether in triumph or depair, would enter into the annals.

Hitler once remarked that he drew confidence from the example of Frederick the Great, 'who had luck in defeating by superior skill, adversaries who were numerically . . . superior'.[339] When it became clear that the Reich was collapsing and that Hitler was not possessed of the same genius as the 'Great King', it was to Frederick that the Führer turned once more, placing his portrait on the wall of the bunker. Hitler was facing his own Kunersdorf and could only hope for the same revival of fortunes as his role-model, a hope which was never to be realized. Here, the script could not be amended as in the dream palaces. For Winston Churchill, however, the script had already been rewritten, his mythic status as wartime leader set within both historical and contemporary memory.

NOTES

1. *Hitler's Table Talk 1941–45* (Weidenfeld and Nicolson, Bungay, 1953), p. 14. Entry for 26 July 1941.
2. John Martin, letter of 16 October 1940. Quoted in M. Gilbert, *Finest Hour. Winston S. Churchill 1939–1941* (Minerva, Aylesbury, 1989), p. 844.
3. J. Gottlieb and R. Toye, 'Introduction' to J. Gottlieb and R. Toye (eds), *Making Reputations: Power, Persuasion and the Individual in Modern British Politics* (I. B. Tauris, London, New York, 2005), p. 1.
4. A. Roberts, *Hitler and Churchill: Secrets of Leadership* (Weidenfeld and Nicolson, London, 2003).

5. Richard Gott in the *New Statesman*, 24 February 2003.

6. H. te Velde, 'Charismatic Leadership, c. 1870–1914. A Comparative European Perspective', in J. Gottlieb and R. Toye (eds), *Making Reputations*, pp. 42–55, here pp. 53–5.

7. I. Kershaw, 'Hitler and the Uniqueness of Nazism', *Journal of Contemporary History*, vol. 39, no. 2 (April 2004), pp. 239–54, here, p. 245.

8. Ibid.

9. Ibid., p. 253.

10. M. Geyer, review of '*Der Hitler-Mythos: Volksmeinung und Propaganda im Dritten Reich*' by I. Kershaw, *Journal of Modern History*, vol. 4, no. 54 (December 1982), pp. 811–12.

11. For a detailed discussion of Churchill's relationship with film, see J. Fox, 'Winston Churchill and the "Men of Destiny": Leadership and the role of the Prime Minister in wartime feature films' in J. Gottlieb and R. Toye (eds), *Making Reputations*, pp. 92–109, esp. pp. 93–7; D. J. Wenden and K. R. M. Short, 'Winston S. Churchill: Film Fan', *Historical Journal of Film, Radio and Television*, vol. 11, no. 3 (1991), pp. 197–214; D. J. Wenden, 'Churchill, Radio and Cinema' in R. Blake and W. Roger Louis (eds), *Churchill* (Clarendon, Oxford, 1993), pp. 215–41.

12. I am indebted to Dr Sarah Davies for her guidance and information on sources on filmic representations of Stalin in this period. See, N. Hülbusch, 'D[zhacek]uga[shacek]vili der Zweite. Das Stalin-Bild im sowjetischen Spielfilm (1934–1953)', in K. Heller and J. Plamper (eds), *Personality Cults in Stalinism – Personenkulte im Stalinismus* (V&R Press, Göttingen, 2004), pp. 207-39.

13. D. Welch, *Propaganda and the German Cinema*, p. 124.

14. TNA PRO INF1/293, MoI Home Intelligence Special Report No. 13, 'First Summary of Films Correspondents' Reports on News Reels', 23 March 1942.

15. Bfi Special Collections, BBFC Scenarios, 1941–43, f. 57, *Warn that Man* (Associated British Picture Corp.), 7 January 1943. John H. C. Hanna.

16. Bfi, press book, *Warn that Man* (1943).

17. Thomas Wiseman, *The Guardian*, 14 July 1972.

18. Churchill Papers, CHAR 20/143, f. 46. Churchill to Harold Laski, 21 September 1944.

19. D. Lowenthal, *The Past is a Foreign Country* (Cambridge University Press, 1985), p. 25.

20. Ibid., pp. 39–46.

21. Virginia Woolf, *Moments of Being*. Quoted in D. Lowenthal, *The Past is a Foreign Country*, pp. 47–8.

22. M. Landy, 'Introduction' in M. Landy (ed.), *The Historical Film. History and Memory in Media* (Athlone Press, London, 1980), pp. 1–25, here p. 2.

23. Fritz Hippler, *Betrachtungen zum Filmschaffen* (Berlin, 1942), p. 94. Quoted in D. Welch, *Propaganda and the German Cinema*, pp. 138–9.

24. M. Landy, 'Introduction' in M. Landy (ed.), *The Historical Film*, p. 8.

25. L. Schulte-Sasse, *Entertaining the Third Reich*, p. 93. The other main films, as identified by Schulte-Sasse were *Fridericus Rex* (Arsen von Cserépy, 1922), *Der alte Fritz* (Gerhard Lamprecht, 1927), *Das Flötenkonzert von Sanssouci* (Gustav Ucicky, 1930), *Die Tänzerin von Sanssouci* (Friedrich Zelnik, 1932), *Der Choral von Leuthen* (Carl Froelich, 1933), *Der alte und der junge König* (Hans Steinhoff, 1935) and *Fridericus* (Johannes Meyer, 1936). Also cited, and discussed, in D. Welch, *Propaganda and the German Cinema*, p. 147. For a full and annotated filmography, see W. Jacobsen and K. Nothnagel, 'Vorbemerkung zur kommentierten Filmografie "Preußen im Film"', in A. Marquardt and H. Rathsack (eds), *Preußen im Film* (Rowohlt, Reinbeck bei Hamburg, 1981), pp. 234–83.

26. Ibid., pp. 93–4.

27. Warner Brothers' 1929 production *Disraeli*, directed by Alfred E. Green proved to be extremely popular with audiences, earning $1,498,000 and earned George Arliss the Academy Award for Best Actor in a

Leading Role in 1929–30. See M. Glancy, 'Warner Bros' Film Grosses, 1921–51: The William Schafer ledger – Warner Bros. Inc.; Jack Warner's Executive Secretary', *Historical Journal of Film, Radio and Television*, vol. 15, no. 1 (March 1995), pp. 55–74.

28. For an excellent account of British costume films prior to World War II, see S. Harper, *Picturing the Past*, pp. 8–64.

29. D. Lowenthal, *The Past is a Foreign Country*, p. 50.

30. T. P. Peardon, *The Transition in English Historical Writing 1760–1830* (Columbia University Press, 1933), p. 244 (on Robert Southey). Quoted in D. Lowenthal, *The Past is a Foreign Country*, p. 49.

31. *Kinematograph Weekly*, 19 October 1939.

32. *Kinematograph Weekly*, 25 June 1942.

33. BArch NS18/357, *Reichspropagandaleiter* to Tießler, 13 November 1942. GP/Ir/St.

34. S. Harper, 'Historical Pleasures: Gainsborough Costume Melodrama', in M. Landy (ed.), *The Historical Film*, pp. 98–122. See also S. Harper, *Picturing the Past*.

35. BArch R 58/157, SD report *Zur Aufnahme der Filme 'Bismarck', 'Friedrich Schiller', 'Feinde'*, 27 January 1941.

36. Cited in R. A. Rosenstone, 'The Historical Film: Looking at the Past in a Postliterate Age', in M. Landy (ed.), *The Historical Film*, pp. 50–66, here, p. 50.

37. TNA PRO INF/849, 'It's the Same Old Hun', memorandum to the Policy Committee, Kenneth Clark, 22 January 1941.

38. M-O A: FR 446, 'Social Research and the Film: MoI Films', November 1940. Also reproduced in D. Sheridan and J. Richards (eds), *Mass-Observation at the Movies*, pp. 213–15.

39. A. Aldgate and J. Richards, *Britain Can Take It*, pp. 156–7.

40. I. Kershaw, *The 'Hitler Myth'. Image and Reality in the Third Reich* (Oxford University Press, 1987), p. 257.

41. Ibid., pp. 253–4.

42. G. Roth and C. Wittich (eds), M. Weber, *Economy and Society*, vol. II (University of California Press, Berkeley, 1978), p. 1112.

43. *Observer*, 12 May 1935. Wiener Library cuttings collection, reel 46.

44. F. Moeller, *The Film Minister: Goebbels and the Cinema in the Third Reich*, trans. M. Robinson (Edition Axel Menges, Stuttgart, 2000), p. 108.

45. Goebbels' diary entry, 22 July 1941. Quoted in F. Moeller, *The Film Minister*, pp. 108–9.

46. Goebbels' diary entry, 16 August 1942. Quoted in F. Moeller, *The Film Minister*, p. 109.

47. F. Moeller, *The Film Minister*, p. 109.

48. *Hitler's Table Talk*, p. 505. Entry for 29 May 1942.

49. Ibid., p. 506.

50. Imperial War Museum, Department of Documents, (IWMD) Goebbels' Diaries, unpublished fragments. EDS 250 EAP. 21-g-16/5c. AL 1904/2. 30 May 1942, pp. 57–8.

51. M. Geyer, review of '*Der Hitler-Mythos*', p. 812.

52. G. Schoenberner, 'Das Preußenbild im deutschen Film. Geschichte und Ideologie', in A. Marquardt and H. Rathsack (eds), *Preußen im Film*, pp. 9–38, here, p. 29.

53. E. Carter, *Dietrich's Ghosts. The Sublime and the Beautiful in Third Reich Film* (Bfi Publishing, London, 2004), p. 26.

54. Ibid., pp. 26–7.

55. I. Kershaw, *The 'Hitler Myth'*, p. 255.

56. E. Carter, *Dietrich's Ghosts*, p. 35.

57. Ibid., p. 62.

58. Ibid., p. 63.

59. BArch materials of the former Berlin Document Center (hereafter BDC) Paula Wessely, RKK2600, Box 0229, File 14, WHW to Wessely, 15 November 1938.

60. See for example BArch R56 VI/000005, from Dr Müller-Goerne to the RKK, Berlin, 8 March 1945. Dr. MG/Pe; BDC Olga Tschechowa file, RKK 2600, Box 0214, File 06, Hinkel to Goebbels, 28 August 1943; Hinkel to Goebbels, 1 September 1943.

61. BArch R56I/110, Wolfgang Liebeneiner, *Alle müssen zur Stelle sein!* In a collection of documents intended for publication, 1944.

62. BArch R56 I/110, Hans Hinkel, Paper entitled *Kampf bis zum Endsieg!*, 1944.

63. Talk by Emil Jannings, 'History becomes Film, Film becomes History: The Function of the Historical Film'. German Radio Home Service, 1293m, 8 October 1942. Broadcast at 18.45 (14 Mins). Wiener Library cuttings collection. Reel 105 and 106E.

64. Ibid.

65. I. Kershaw, *The 'Hitler Myth'*, p. 151.

66. Ibid., p. 157.

67. Ibid., p. 159.

68. M. Weber, *Economy and Society*, p. 1113.

69. I. Kershaw, *The 'Hitler Myth'*, p. 9.

70. Se, for example, G. Kirwin, 'Waiting for Retaliation – A Study in Nazi Propaganda Behaviour and German Civilian Morale', *Journal of Contemporary History*, vol. 16, no. 3 (July 1981), pp. 565-83. Quoting an SD report from the *Hauptaußenstelle Schwerin* (14 September 1943), which stated that 'people believe these words of the Führer unconditionally because they consider it quite impossible that in this darkest hour of the war the Führer would feed them with cheap hopes', Kirwin contends that some semblance of the Hitler myth remained in tact (p. 571). Geyer concurs, stating 'it is hard to believe … that the Hitler mystique was consumed by the war'. M. Geyer, review of '*Der Hitler-Mythos*', p. 812.

71. Goebbels quoted in I. Kershaw, *The 'Hitler Myth'*, p. 4.

72. I. Kershaw, 'Hitler and the Germans', in R. Bessel (ed.), *Life in the Third Reich* (Oxford University Press, 1987), pp.41–55, here, p. 53.

73. *Cinema Quarterly*, Autumn 1935.

74. H.-W. Betz, 'Große Deutsche, wie der Film sie sah', *Filmwelt*, 23 February 1940.

75. G. Schoenberner, 'Das Preußenbild im deutschen Film', p. 29.

76. S. Hake, *Popular Cinema of the Third Reich*, p. 174.

77. SDK Berlin 333, *Die Entlassung*, 'Die Kamera schreibt Geschichte', publicity booklet, *Kamera läuft … Sonderheft zu dem Emil Jannings-film der Tobis: Die Entlassung*, pp. 3–5.

78. L. Schulte-Sasse, *Entertaining the Third Reich*, p. 105.

79. Ibid., p. 106.

80. S. Falasca-Zamponi, 'The "Culture of Personality": Mussolini and the Cinematic Imagination', in K. Heller and J. Plamper (eds), *Personality Cults in Stalinism*, pp. 83–109, here, p. 83, quoting Hullinger.

81. Frederick II quoted in H. Hoffmann, *The Triumph of Propaganda*, p. 44.

82. D. Welch, *Propaganda and the German Cinema*, p. 147. For a further discussion of the *Fridericus* films of the Weimar Republic, see H. Regel, 'Die Fridericus-Filme der Weimarer Republik' in A. Marquardt and H. Rathsack (eds), *Preußen im Film*, pp. 124-35. This volume also contains some other excellent essays. Of particular relevance are; H.-W. Betz, 'Das Preußenbild im deutschen Film. Geschichte und Ideologie', pp. 9–39; H. Feld, 'Potsdam gegen Weimar oder Wie Otto Gebühr den Siebenjährigen Krieg gewann', pp. 68–74; and F. P. Kahlenberg, 'Preußen als Filmsujet in der Propagandasprache der NS-Zeit', pp. 135–64.

83. I. Kershaw, *The 'Hitler Myth'*, p. 4.

84. L. Schulte-Sasse, *Entertaining the Third Reich*, pp. 92–3.

85. J. C. Horak, 'Eros, Thanatos, and the Will to Myth: Prussian Films in German Cinema', in B. A. Murray and C. J. Wickham (eds), *Framing the Past: The Historiography of German Cinema and Television* (Southern Illinois University Press, Carbondale, IL, 1992), pp. 121–40, here, p. 122.

86. P. Sorlin, *The Film in History. Restaging the Past* (Blackwell, Oxford, 1980), p. 21.

87. SDK Berlin 329, *Der große König*, V. Harlan, *Geschichte und Film*, press book.

88. P. Sorlin, *The Film in History*, pp. 21–2.

89. D. Welch, *Propaganda and the German Cinema*, pp. 147–55.

90. Ibid., p. 154.

91. L. Schulte-Sasse, *Entertaining the Third Reich*, pp. 95–6.

92. SDK Berlin 329, *Der große König*, press book, p. 5.

93. L. Schulte-Sasse, *Entertaining the Third Reich*, p. 99.

94. IWMD, Goebbels' Diaries, unpublished fragments. EDS 250 EAP. 21-g-16/5c. AL 1904/2. 25 January 1942, p. 34.

95. Goebbels diary entry, 19 February 1942. E. Fröhlich (ed.), *Die Tagebücher von Joseph Goebbels: Teil II Diktate 1941–1945*, vol. 3, p. 340.

96. IWMD, Goebbels' Diaries, unpublished fragments. EDS 250 EAP. 21-g-16/5c. AL 1904/2. 25 January 1942, p. 34.

97. V. Harlan, *Souvenirs ou le cinema allemand selon Goebbels* (éditions france-empire, Paris, 1974), pp. 180–1. Harlan's memoirs prove useful to the historian in a variety of ways, despite being an obvious defence of his actions under National Socialism. There are occasions when the account given by Harlan matched the account offered by Goebbels in his diaries, a source which is also problematic. The memoirs have been used here to add an extra dimension to the extant diaries of the Reich Minister for Popular Enlightenment and Propaganda. Other comments from the Harlan memoirs are treated as allegations within the main text.

98. Ibid., p. 181.

99. SDK Berlin 329, *Der große König*, press book, p. 44.

100. 'Die Rolle wird zum Schicksal. Ein Schauspieler-Leben für Fridericus – Typisierung auf der Film-Leinwand', *Hamburger Fremdenblatt*, 23 March 1942. Wiener Library cuttings collection, reel 106E.

101. SD Report No. 287, 28 May 1942. In H. Boberach (ed.), *Meldungen*, vol. 10, p. 3759.

102. Goebbels diary entry, 28 January 1942. E. Fröhlich (ed.), *Die Tagebücher von Joseph Goebbels: Teil II Diktate 1941–1945*, vol. 3, p. 207.

103. SDK Berlin 329, *Der große König*, V. Harlan, *Geschichte und Film*, press book.

104. Ibid.

105. Goebbels diary entry, 6 August 1941. E. Fröhlich (ed.), *Die Tagebücher von Joseph Goebbels: Teil II Diktate 1941–1945*, vol. 1, pp. 180–2. Further changes were requested on 28 January 1941 (vol.3, p. 207), and final checks by Goebbels took place on 19 February 1942 (p. 340) and 3 March 1942 (p. 401).

106. V. Harlan, *Souvenirs*, p. 187.

107. SD Report No. 287, 28 May 1942. In H. Boberach (ed.), *Meldungen*, vol. 10, pp. 3759–60.

108. Ibid., p. 3759.

109. SDK Berlin 329, *Der große König*, press book, p. 15.

110. Ibid., p. 44.

111. SDK Berlin 329, *Der große König*, press clipping, Munich, 1942. Unidentified.

112. SDK Berlin 329, *Der große König*, press book, p. 59.

113. IWM FDC Unidentified and uncatalogued box of materials. SD report of the *Unterabschnitt-Leipzig*, III G3 Film-Spielfilme Gd/J, 'Spitzenfilm, *Der große König*', 12 May 1942.

114. M. Weber, *Economy and Society*, p. 1113.

115. SDK Berlin 329, *Der große König*, V. Harlan, *Geschichte und Film*, press book.

116. Text from D. Welch, *Propaganda and the German Cinema*, pp. 150–1. Original sequence.

117. Günther Sawatzki, 'Sein Herz schlug für Preußen', *Filmwelt*, 29 November 1940.

118. Ibid.

119. SDK Berlin 329, *Der große König*, press book, p. 52.

120. Goebbels diary entry, 28 January 1942. E. Fröhlich (ed.), *Die Tagebücher von Joseph Goebbels: Teil II Diktate 1941–1945*, vol. 3, p. 207.

121. Ibid., Goebbels diary entry, 2 March 1942, p. 400.

122. Ibid., Goebbels diary entry, 20 March 1942, p. 506.

123. Ibid., Goebbels diary entry, 28 January 1942, p. 208.

124. IWM FDC Unidentified and uncatalogued box of materials. SD report of the *Unterabschnitt-Leipzig*, III G3 Film-Spielfilme Gd/J, 'Spitzenfilm, *Der große* König', 12 May 1942.

125. SDK Berlin 329, *Der große König*, E. von Csisaky, 'Besuch bei Kristina Söderbaum und Veit Harlan. Auch zu Hause ist ein Schneidetisch und Vorführraum', *Information Tobis. Sonderdienst.*

126. Ibid.

127. V. Harlan, *Souvenirs*, p. 181.

128. L. Schulte-Sasse, *Entertaining the Third Reich*, p. 108.

129. Ibid., p. 121.

130. L. Schulte-Sasse, *Entertaining the Third Reich*, pp. 121–2.

131. SD Report No. 287, 28 May 1942. In H. Boberach (ed.), *Meldungen*, vol. 10, p. 3760.

132. Goebbels diary entry, 25 January 1942. E. Fröhlich (ed.), *Die Tagebücher von Joseph Goebbels: Teil II Diktate 1941–1945*, vol. 3, p. 187.

133. Ibid., 4 March 1942, p. 412.

134. IWMD, Goebbels' Diaries, unpublished fragments. EDS 250 EAP. 21-g-16/5c. AL 1904/2. 4 March 1942, p. 20. This was also widely reported in the press alongside short reviews. See for example, *Hamburger Fremdenblatt*, 4 March 1942. Wiener Library cuttings collection, reel 106E.

135. IWMD, Goebbels' Diaries, unpublished fragments. EDS 250 EAP. 21-g-16/5c. AL 1904/2. 2 March 1942, p. 20.

136. Ibid., 1 June 1942, p. 26.

137. Ibid., 4 March 1942, p. 20.

138. Goebbels diary entry, 14 April 1942. E. Fröhlich (ed.), *Die Tagebücher von Joseph Goebbels: Teil II Diktate 1941–1945*, vol. 4, p. 95.

139. Ibid., 22 April 1942, p. 147.

140. IWMD, Goebbels' Diaries, unpublished fragments. EDS 250 EAP. 21-g-16/5c. AL 1904/2. 30 May 1942, p. 56–7.

141. Goebbels diary entry, 20 March 1942. E. Fröhlich (ed.), *Die Tagebücher von Joseph Goebbels: Teil II Diktate 1941–1945*, vol. 3, p. 506.

142. Churchill Papers, CHAR 20/92, Telegram from Churchill to Roosevelt, accompanying a copy of *Desert Victory*, 5 March 1943; CHAR 20/109 f. 35 T428/3, Telegram from Stalin to Churchill, thanking him for his copy of the film, 29 March 1943.

143. W. S. Churchill, *History of the Second World War. Vol. 6: Triumph and Tragedy* (The Reprint Society, London, 1952, 1956), p. 218.

144. SD Report No. 287, 28 May 1942. In H. Boberach (ed.), *Meldungen*, vol. 10, p. 3758.

145. Goebbels diary entry, 28 January 1942. E. Fröhlich (ed.), *Die Tagebücher von Joseph Goebbels: Teil II Diktate 1941–1945*, vol. 3, p. 207.

146. See for example, IWMD, Goebbels' Diaries, unpublished fragments. EDS 250 EAP. 21-g-16/5c. AL 1904/2.

147. V. Harlan, *Souvenirs*, p. 185.

148. Ibid., p. 186.

149. Ibid., p. 187.

150. SD Report No. 287, 28 May 1942. In H. Boberach (ed.), *Meldungen*, vol. 10, p. 3759.

151. Ibid.

152. IWM FDC Unidentified and uncatalogued box of materials. SD report of the *Unterabschnitt-Leipzig*, III G3 Film-Spielfilme Gd/J, 'Spitzenfilm, *Der große* König', 12 May 1942.

153. SD Report No. 287, 28 May 1942. In H. Boberach (ed.), *Meldungen*, vol. 10, p. 3759.

154. See DKD report, 5 March 1943. 'Seven Years War Parallel to be Toned Down'. Wiener Library cuttings collection, PC5/106E, reel 105.

155. I. Kershaw, *The 'Hitler Myth'*, p. 15.

156. See for example, *Hitler's Table Talk*, p. 325.

157. The full exchange between Bismarck and Virchow is reproduced in D. Welch, *Propaganda and the German Cinema*, pp. 142–3.

158. SDK Berlin, *Bismarck*, clipping from review in *Der Angriff*, December 1940.

159. BArch R 58/157, SD report *Zur Aufnahme der Filme 'Bismarck', 'Friedrich Schiller', 'Feinde'*, 27 January 1941.

160. See I. Kershaw, *The 'Hitler Myth'*, pp. 151–68.

161. SDK Berlin, *Bismarck*, clipping from review in *Völkischer Beobachter*, December 1940.

162. SDK Berlin, *Bismarck*, publicity materials from the press book.

163. SDK Berlin, *Bismarck*, clipping from unidentified review, December 1940.

164. SDK Berlin, *Bismarck*, publicity materials from the press book.

165. 'Das Antlitz Bismarcks im Film', *Münchener Neueste Nachrichten*, 21 December 1940. Wiener Library cuttings collection, reel 106E.

166. SDK Berlin, *Bismarck*, clipping from *Der Angriff*, December 1940.

167. SDK Berlin, *Bismarck*, clipping from *Deutsche Allgemeine Zeitung*, December 1940. Positive reception was confirmed by the SD report of 27 January 1941. BArch R 58/157, SD report '*Zur Aufnahme der Filme 'Bismarck', 'Friedrich Schiller', 'Feinde'*, 27 January 1941.

168. Ibid.

169. Ibid.

170. Ibid.

171. SDK Berlin, *Bismarck*, press materials and reports (1940).

172. SDK Berlin, *Bismarck*, instructions to theatre owners.

173. I. Kershaw, *The 'Hitler-Myth'*, p. 57.

174. Cited in J. V. Wagner, *Hakenkreuz über Bochum* (Bochum, 1983), pp. 219–20. Quoted in I. Kershaw, *The 'Hitler Myth'*, p. 55.

175. *Hitler's Table Talk*, p. 325. Entry for 21 February 1942.

176. BArch R 58/157, SD report *Zur Aufnahme der Filme 'Bismarck', 'Friedrich Schiller', 'Feinde'*, 27 January 1941.

177. *Hitler's Table Talk*, p. 36. Entry for 21 September 1941.

178. D. Welch, *Propaganda and the German Cinema*, p. 144.

179. Goebbels diary entry, 1 December 1941. E. Fröhlich (ed.), *Die Tagebücher von Joseph Goebbels: Teil II Diktate 1941–1945*, vol. 2, p. 410.

180. Ibid. This is confirmed in a previous diary entry for 30 November 1941, p. 404.

181. D. Welch, *Propaganda and the German Cinema*, p. 145.

182. Goebbels diary entry, 25 October 1941. E. Fröhlich (ed.), *Die Tagebücher von Joseph Goebbels: Teil II Diktate 1941–1945*, vol. 2, p. 176.

183. See for example, SDK Berlin 333, *Die Entlassung*, 'Der Weg zur Leistung: Wolfgang Liebeneiner über seine Zusammenarbeit mit Emil Jannings in dem Emil-Jannings-Film der Tobis, *Die Entlassung*', publicity booklet, *Kamera läuft … Sonderheft zu dem Emil Jannings-film der Tobis: Die Entlassung*, p. 2.

184. Ibid., p. 15.

185. See for example, SDK Berlin 333, *Die Entlassung*, E. Jannings, 'Emil Jannings: Bismarck in dieser Zeit', in the press book for *Die Entlassung*, p. 3

186. Ibid.

187. Ibid., p. 4.

188. This actually refers to *Die Entlassung* rather than Liebeneiner's previous production of 1940.

189. *Hitler's Table Talk*, pp. 646–7. Entry for 20 August 1942.

190. D. Welch, *Propaganda and the German Cinema*, p. 146.

191. Goebbels diary entry, 16 September 1942. E. Fröhlich (ed.), *Die Tagebücher von Joseph Goebbels: Teil II Diktate 1941–1945*, vol. 5, p. 511.

192. BArch NS 18/283, letter from Rosenberg to Bormann, 27 July 1942. Quoted in D. Welch, *Propaganda and the German Cinema*, p. 146.

193. Goebbels diary entry, 7 October 1942. E. Fröhlich (ed.), *Die Tagebücher von Joseph Goebbels: Teil II Diktate 1941–1945*, vol. 6, p. 88.

194. D. Welch, *Propaganda and the German Cinema*, p. 146.

195. R. Herzstein, *The War that Hitler Won*, p. 306.

196. SDK Berlin 333, *Die Entlassung*, 'Kurz Notizen'.

197. I. Kershaw, *The 'Hitler Myth'*, pp. 180–1.

198. A much shorter and specific version of some of the ideas presented here has been published in J. Fox, 'Winston Churchill and the "Men of Destiny". Some sections of this chapter have been reproduced with the kind permission of Julie Gottlieb, Richard Toye and I. B. Tauris.

199. N. Mace 'British Historical Epics in the Second World War', in P. Taylor (ed.), *Britain and the Cinema in the Second World War*, pp. 101-20, here, p. 102.

200. P. Sorlin, *The Film in History*, p. 79.

201. D. Lowenthal, *The Past is a Foreign Country*, pp. 21–49.

202. Simone Weil quoted in D. Lowenthal, *The Past is a Foreign Country*, p. 44.

203. GP G3: P5, S.C. Leslie, 'The Formation of Public Opinion', *The Citizen*, July 1939, pp. 3–7, here p. 3.

204. GP G4:19.20, John Grierson, draft of introduction to Rotha's writings, n.d.

205. P. Sorlin, *European Cinemas*, p. 179.

206. GP 4.12.20, Grierson notes (c.1940).

207. S. Harper, *Picturing the Past*, p. 91.

208. Ibid.

209. TNA PRO INF 1/848, 'The Principles and objectives of British Wartime Propaganda'. Paper approved by Cabinet, n.d.

210. TNA PRO INF 1/867, 'Programme for Film Propaganda'. CC Paper no. 6. Foreign Publicity Business Advisory Committee, 1939.

211. Ibid.

212. TNA PRO INF1/251, Home Planning Sub-Committee 'Theme for Propaganda', n.d., c.1941.

213. Ibid.

214. M-O A: FR 257, 'Should Leaders Lead?' Critique of broadcast by Professor Gilbert Murray who accuses the public of ignorance and apathy, 6 July 1940

215. M-O A: FR 496, 'Popular Attitudes to Wartime Politics', 20 November 1940, p. 2.

216. Ibid., p. 16.

217. TNA PRO INF1/251, Home Planning Sub-Committee 'Theme for Propaganda', n.d., c.1941.
218. M-O A: FR 496, 'Popular Attitudes to Wartime Politics', 20 November 1940, p. 4.
219. Ibid., p. 3.
220. Ibid., pp. 5–6.
221. M-O A: FR 446, 'Social Research and the Film', October 1940. Reproduced in D. Sheridan and J. Richards (eds), *Mass-Observation at the Movies*, p. 213.
222. GP G4. N13, John Grierson, 'A letter from England', 1941, p. 1.
223. M-O A: FR 654, 'Churchill: Public Opinion', April 1941.
224. *Kinematograph Weekly*, 31 October 1940.
225. See for example, the press materials in Bfi British press book *The Prime Minister* (1941).
226. Ibid.
227. Ibid.
228. Ibid., 'Film has parallel between Disraeli's time and our own'.
229. *Kinematograph Weekly*, 31 October 1940.
230. Bfi, *The Prime Minister*, US press book.
231. *The Cinema*, 12 March 1941. Quoted in A. Aldgate and J. Richards, *Britain Can Take It*, p. 143.
232. Bfi, *The Prime Minister*, British press book.
233. Ibid.
234. Ibid.
235. *Kinematograph Weekly*, 31 October 1940.
236. Ibid., 13 March 1941.
237. *The Times*, 5 March 1941.
238. M-O A: TC 17/5/B, 'Letters to *Picture-goer Weekly*', DJ, Kenton, MX, 10 November 1940.
239. Bfi, *The Prime Minister*, US press book.
240. S. Harper, *Picturing the Past*, p. 89.
241. Bfi Special Collections. Dickinson Collection. Box 48. Item 1. Full unedited transcript of 'Interview with Thorold Dickinson', later published in *Film Dope*, no. 11, Jan 1977.
242. Gielgud quoted in *Kinematograph Weekly*, 24 July 1941.
243. That star power was important to the average film-goer is confirmed in a Mass-Observation survey of letters to *Picture-goer Weekly* conducted in December 1940, which found that 47 per cent of all letters concerned stars, with films, the next highest percentage, attracting only 15 per cent of comments. See M-O A: TC 17/5/A, analysis of 1536 letters, 23 December 1940.
244. *The Cinema*, 1 January 1941, p. 5. It is claimed by Nicholas Wapshott that MGM Studios refused to release Donat from his studio contract. Mayer gave in after Donat reportedly told him that he was 'depriving hundreds of people … in the most difficult period in Britain's history'. Reported in N. Wapshott, *The Man Between: A Biography of Carol Reed* (Chatto & Windus, London, 1990), p. 153.
245. Full story synopsis released by the studio (Gaumont British) can be found in the British press book, *The Young Mr Pitt*, 1942. In Bfi library.
246. B. Davies (ed.), *Carol Reed* (Bfi Publishing, London, 1978), pp. 5–6. Also confirmed in *Kinematograph Weekly*, 23, October 1941, p. 37.
247. Ibid., p. 20. This was confirmed in an interview with Charles Thomas Samuels.
248. Ibid., p. 6.
249. *Kinematograph Weekly*, 31 July 1941, p. 17.
250. Ibid., 28 August 1941.
251. *The Cinema*, 1 October 1941, p. 5.
252. *Kinematograph Weekly*, 7 August 1941.

253. Ibid., 4 September 1941.

254. Ibid., 11 September 1941.

255. *Today's Cinema*, 17 September 1941, p. 5.

256. *Kinematograph Weekly*, 23 October 1941.

257. Ibid., 2 October 1941.

258. Ibid., 2 October 1941, p. 39.

259. Ibid., 23 October 1941.

260. Bfi, British press book *The Young Mr Pitt* (1942).

261. Ibid.

262. Ibid.

263. Churchill Papers, 20/8, 'Personal', 15 September 1940. Cited in M. Gilbert, *Finest Hour*, p. 782.

264. M. Gilbert, *Finest Hour*, p. 783, citing Sir John Peck's notes to Gilbert, 10 November 1982.

265. Churchill Papers, 4/198, notes enclosed with a letter from Major General Hastings Ismay to Churchill of 26 November 1946. Cited in M. Gilbert, *Finest Hour*, p. 775. A further account of a similar nature is recounted in A. Calder, *The People's War* (Literary Guild, London, 1969), p. 158.

266. Rachel Reid reviewing *The Young Mr Pitt*, *Sight and Sound*, Autumn 1942, p. 51.

267. *Today's Cinema*, 22 May 1942, p. 3.

268. Bfi, British press book *The Young Mr Pitt* (1942).

269. *Kinematograph Weekly*, 14 August 1941.

270. Bfi, British press book *The Young Mr Pitt* (1942).

271. Ibid.

272. Interview with Frank Launder and Sidney Gilliat in G. Brown (ed.), *Launder and Gilliat* (Bfi Publishing, London, 1977), p. 104.

273. Ibid.

274. Ibid., p. 105.

275. Ibid., p. 104.

276. *The Cinema*, 17 June 1942, p. 4.

277. Bfi, British press book *The Young Mr Pitt* (1942).

278. Bfi, British press book, *The Young Mr Pitt* (1942).

279. Ibid.

280. Ibid.

281. *Kinematograph Weekly*, 28 May 1942. Quoted in A. Aldgate and J. Richards, *Britain Can Take It*, p. 152.

282. Bfi, *The Young Mr Pitt*, British press book.

283. Ibid.

284. Donat also recognized the 'great singlemindedness and loneliness' of the eponymous hero, and even went as far as criticizing his decision, stating 'I think [giving her up] was a mistake myself'. See *The New York Times*, 20 July 1941, p. X3.

285. All information here from Bfi, British press book *The Young Mr Pitt* (1942).

286. *Kinematograph Weekly*, 18 June 1942. A similarly positive review was given by *The Cinema*, 17 June 1942, pp. 3 and 14.

287. N. Wapshott, *The Man Between*, p. 154.

288. S. Harper, *Picturing the Past*, p. 89.

289. *The Cinema*, 7 July 1942.

290. *The Cinema*, 15 July 1942.

291. See, for example, a comment on the Pitt administration in W. S. Churchill, *History of the Second World War Vol. 4. The Hinge of Fate* (The Reprint Society, London, 1953), p. 335.

292. Introduction to the third edition of Pitt's speeches (Oxford University Press, 1940). Quoted in M. Gilbert, *Finest Hour*, p. 844.

293. *New Statesman and Nation*, 11 July 1942. Reproduced in S. Aspinall and R. Murphy (eds), *Bfi Dossier 18: Gainsborough Melodrama* (Bfi, London, 1983), p. 67.

294. N. Mace, 'British Historical Epics', p. 103.

295. Laurence Olivier Archive, British Library Manuscripts Collection (hereafter L-O), Box 93, Filippo del Giudice (Managing Director of Two Cities Films, the producer of *Henry V*) to Jack Beddington, 1 January 1943.

296. Ibid. Olivier's contract was agreed on 18 August 1943. Olivier was also released for his work of Anthony Asquith's 1943 film *The Demi-Paradise*.

297. Letter from S. G. Gates (MoI) to Michael Powell, 25 June 1942. Reproduced in I. Christie (ed.), *The Life and Death of Colonel Blimp*, pp. 40–1.

298. L-O, Box 93, Observations of C. Clayton Hutton.

299. L-O, Box 93, Olivier to Del Giudice, 6 December 1944.

300. L-O, Box 93, C. Clayton Hutton to Olivier, 23 March 1945.

301. L-O, Box 93, synopsis of *Henry V*, Alan Dent.

302. S. Harper, *Picturing the Past*, p. 87.

303. G. Crowdes, '*Henry V*', *Cineaste*, vol. 22, no. 1 (April 1996).

304. *Boston Post*, 7 April 1946. Quoted in S. Harper, *Picturing the Past*, p. 88. The distortion of history was a criticism also levelled at *The Young Mr Pitt* by American reviewers. For example, see *The New York Times*, 14 March 1943, p. X3.

305. S. Harper, *Picturing the Past*, p. 88.

306. L-O, Box 93, Stafford A. Brooke, notes by Alan Dent during the production of *Henry V*, 1943.

307. L-O, Box 93. Alan Dent, notes for publicity matter, July 1944.

308. L-O, Box 93, Stafford A. Brooke, notes by Alan Dent during the production of *Henry V*, 1943.

309. L-O, Box 93, Sir Edmund Chambers, writing in 1925. Notes by Alan Dent during the production of *Henry V*, 1943.

310. L-O, Box 93, Synopsis of *Henry V*, Alan Dent, 1943.

311. Ibid.

312. L-O, Box 93, E. T. Carr, Eagle Lion to Olivier, 24 July 1944.

313. L-O, Box 93, Filippo Del Giudice to Jack Beddington, 11 January 1943.

314. L-O, Box 93, Alan Dent, notes for publicity matter, July 1944.

315. L-O, Box 93, C. Clayton Hutton to Olivier, 23 March 1945.

316. L-O, Box 94, Olivier's notes on the American release of *Henry V*, March 1945.

317. L-O, Box 94, Olivier to Denham Studios, 23 July 1945; Olivier to Phil C. Samuel of Two Cities, 8 April 1945. The tussle was reported in *The New York Times* on 15 July 1945.

318. L-O, Box 94, Olivier to Denham Studios, 23 July 1945.

319. L-O, Box 94, Olivier to Del Guidice, 29 August 1945.

320. L-O, Box 94, Samuel to Del Guidice, 13 November 1945.

321. L-O, Box 94, Del Guidice to US distributors, 7 January 1945.

322. L-O, Box 94, J. Eiry, Rank organization memorandum, 17 March 1947.

323. L-O, Box 93, Olivier to Del Guidice, 6 December 1944.

324. See, for example, a wide selection of reviews duplicated in the studio press book. Bfi, British press book, *Henry V* (1945).

325. Bfi Special Collections, Anthony Asquith collection, personal notebook 4.

326. L-O, Box 93, *Eagle Lion* to Olivier, 24 July 1944.

327. See, for example, *Kinematograph Weekly*, 27 June 1940 and M-O A: TC 17/5/A, 'Letters to *Picture-Goer Weekly*', 23 December 1940.

328. L-O, Box 93, Letter from Olivier to Del Giudice, 6 December 1944.

329. Bfi, British press book, *Henry V* (1945).

330. L-O, Box 94, Letter from Annie R. Winter to Olivier, 9 October 1946.

331. L-O Box 94, Olivier to Del Guidice, 4 April 1945. Box 94 contains many letters relating to historical discrepancies in the film from film-goers and scholars.

332. S. Harper, *Picturing the Past*, p. 91.

333. M-O A: FR 2024, 'Churchill: Replies to Question about whether Churchill should continue to be Prime Minister after the war', 8 February 1944, p. 1.

334. GP G3:17:5, Basil Wright in *The Spectator*, 13 October 1939.

335. *The Cinema*, 1 July 1942.

336. *The Cinema*, 17 February 1942.

337. S. Harper, 'Historic Pleasures', p. 98. Sue Harper has conducted much excellent research on the subject of Gainsborough melodramas, which can be found in this essay and also *Picuring the Past*, pp. 119–46.

338. In Britain, see for example, *Today's Cinema* on *Henry V*, 24 November 1944.

339. *Hitler's Table Talk*, p. 646. Entry for 20 August 1942.

The year 1943 was to be one of celebration for the German film industry. A grand ceremony to mark the 25th anniversary of Ufa was to be held in early March, the Führer honouring the 'pioneers of film' and the studio premiering its latest offering, a spectacular version of the life and times of Baron Münchhausen, the nobleman who recounted fantastic tales of his adventures. Formal proceedings were to last over two days, featuring music, speeches by leading members of the film industry, a gala reception in the Hotel Kaiserhof hosted by the Reich Minister for Popular Enlightenment and Propaganda, and culminating in the conferring of the title 'Professor' on two of the Third Reich's most prominent directors, Wolfgang Liebeneiner and Veit Harlan.[1] Swastika flags adorned the Ufa-Palast am Zoo, as the many guests, among them Reich Finance Minister Walther Funk, head of the German Labour Front, Robert Ley, and the old supporter of the early movement and media mogul Alfred Hugenberg, as well as stars from the silver screen, packed into the auditorium.[2] Ludwig Klitzsch, named chairman of Ufa's board of directors during the celebrations, set the tone for the festivities in his speech to the assembly, proclaiming that 1933 heralded a 'great era for the German film industry', with cinema defining the 'struggle for the soul of the German people' and strengthening their 'will to live'.[3] Klitzsch served as the warm-up act for the star speaker, Joseph Goebbels, who seized upon the opportunity to underline the importance of film to the cultural development of Germany as well as its vital functions in wartime, declaring that 'one can no longer imagine the history of the last or this world war without films'.[4] Placing the National Socialist influence at the heart of the industry's revival, the Reich Minister opined, 'this people's art (*Volkskunst*) … exudes its strength, encompassing individuals as well as the whole nation, from the Reich's most representative film theatre, the Ufa-Palast am Zoo in Berlin, to the village cinema in the smallest hamlet of our Fatherland'.[5] Sensing the mood of the occasion and noting its proximity to the city of Berlin, which was under heavy bombardment, Goebbels added that 'the 25th anniversary of Ufa is taking place in the midst of the German people's struggle for existence. Ufa was founded during the World War; it can now look back, during a greater world war, on a quarter-century of service to people and the Reich. During this quarter-century', he concluded, 'it has, [as] a pioneer of the art of the screen, paved the way for the cinema from mere "flicks" to its present importance'.[6]

It was clear that, by 1943, Goebbels had come to view film as an essential weapon in Germany's arsenal. Conflating war and the arts, the Reich Minister intended to use the

Ufa celebrations to award war service crosses to industry personnel for their exceptional contribution to the cinema under the Third Reich. The original list of intended recipients gives some indication of the works Goebbels considered the most important to the war effort. Director Eduard von Borsody was to receive the award for his work on the 1940 film *Wunschkonzert*; Willi Forst for *Operette* and *Wiener Blut*; Helmut Käutner for *Auf Wiedersehen Franzsiska, Anuschka, Wir machen Musik* and *Romanze in Moll*; Herbert Maisch for *D III 88, Friedrich Schiller, Ohm Krüger*; and *Andreas Schlüter* and Hans Steinhoff for *Robert Koch, Die Geierwally, Ohm Krüger* and *Rembrandt*. Actors and actresses were also to be honoured, notably Willy Fritsch, Ferdinand Marian, Käthe Dorsch, Heidemarie Hatheyer, Hilde Krahl, Kristina Söderbaum and Paula Wessely. The most prestigious award, the first-class *Kriegsverdienstkreuz*, was reserved for Klitzsch, Dr Max Winkler, Reich Commissioner for the Film Industry, and directors Veit Harlan for his work on *Der große König* and Wolfgang Liebeneiner for his work on the Bismarck films.[7] That Hitler and Goebbels perceived the importance of film to the war effort quite differently, however, was revealed by the Führer's refusal to accede to his Minister's requests, denying the award of war crosses to stars of the screen. In 'total war' priorities had to change. In February, Goebbels was informed that 'the Führer now exercizes the utmost restraint in presenting war service crosses. This is particularly true for *Kriegsverdienstkreuze 1. Klasse*'.[8] Under direct instruction from the Führer, Goebbels was forced to rethink his plans, reflecting some days later that 'this anniversary would have been, in times of peace, a good reason for awarding a great number of honours which would have been conferred upon deserving men of the German film industry. With consideration for the situation, these honours are to be postponed with the exception of a few cases which I put in the hands of the Führer'.[9]

In the light of this, the Minister recommended that because, 'the German film has achieved such paramount importance as an instrument of propaganda, … I consider it appropriate to honour the achievements of some leading men amongst German film-makers during the war'.[10] It was with this in mind that the Minister resolved to confer the title 'Professor' upon both Harlan and Liebeneiner for their work on the Führer-myth films of 1940–3. The importance of these works to the war effort and to the Nazi movement was expressed in Goebbels' recommendation for the two directors. Liebeneiner was considered to be, alongside Harlan, the 'first director' of the nation, his work on *Bismarck* and *Die Entlassung* of 'outstanding artistic [quality]', serving as a 'fine example as to the importance of films as a medium of propaganda'. For the Reich Minister, Liebeneiner's films provided the German people with a 'propagandistically significant fragment of their political history' central to the current war. Harlan too had contributed to the sense of 'war mobilization', his films *Jud Süß* and *Der große König* perceived by Goebbels to have 'fortified national powers of resistance' in all sectors of society.[11] Harlan had, according to the Reich Minister, been in no small part responsible for the depiction of national 'glory' during wartime, strengthening the 'moral resilience' of the *Volk*.[12]

The tensions, however, between the films singled out for particular praize and the Ufa celebration were clear. Firstly, that both Liebeneiner and Harlan were honoured for films depicting the relationship between the leader and his people merely spotlighted the absence of Hitler himself from the celebrations, Goebbels charged with conferring the titles on the Führer's behalf, further drawing attention to the increasing distance between Hitler and the German people. Secondly, the film chosen to mark Ufa's 25 year anniversary highlighted the studio's and the RMVP's retreat from the political propaganda film, a response to war-weariness which had prompted German audiences to boycott the newsreels.[13] Moreover, the film seemed to contradict the less extravagant celebrations ordered by the Führer. *Münchhausen* was a film evoking sumptuous opulence in its excessive costumes and sets, its set designers, Emil Haßler and Otto Guelstorff producing over 2,000 designs and individual sketches and fashioning thirty different set samplers.[14] The film was to be 'an absolute triumph of fantasy, a delicious jump over all barriers of reality into the magical gardens of dreams... For two hours one believes the incredible and succumbs with pleasure to the charm of magic'.[15] Josef von Baky, the film's director, had created a 'fairy-tale world'[16] in which audiences were invited to take 'a journey through wonderland'.[17] Film-goers were presented with a colourful variety of characters: 'sultans and ladies of the harem, a Tsarina and wild Russians, courtiers, hunters and even moon-dwellers... in their milieux of palace and fun-fair, carnival and encampment, as well as the bizarre landscape of the moon and the gondolas of the "city of lagoons"'. The characters 'dance and fight, they play and booze, they kiss and betray each other, they fly through the air'. In all, there were over two hundred film roles in von Baky's colour production, but none surpassed that of the eponymous hero, Baron Münchhausen, played by Hans Albers.[18] It was clear from the scenario that, as the *Deutsche Allgemeine Zeitung* recognized, 'Ufa's anniversary film courageously punctures the façade of reality, a breakthrough for fantasy. And the film-goers follow Ufa curiously and happily on a journey into the colourful, magical world of the unreal'.[19]

Still 16   *Münchhausen. Münchhausen meets a moon-dweller.*

Goebbels fully understood the potential of such images. Divorced from overt propaganda content, *Münchhausen* offered the opportunity to distract German audiences from the everyday realities of war, film-goers escaping into the mythic world of the heroic Baron. As early as March 1942, the Reich Minister recognized that German films needed more 'light and entertaining characters', ones which could lift the burden of the people in this 'difficult time'.[20] He knew that to maintain the 'good mood' of the people was 'important to the [conduct of the] war'.[21] Cinema audiences were actively rejecting Nazi propaganda, the *Tätigkeitsberichte* reporting that 'the interest in the German weekly newsreel has in recent times diminished... Run a weekly newsreel after the main feature and one can see that 50% of the cinemagoers leave the theatre after the main feature'.[22] Goebbels knew that the public required more escapist fare in the film programme, his intention to use film as a means of raising popular morale reflected in his decision to extend and enhance the provision of free tickets to the war wounded and those involved in armaments production and the *Winterhilfswerk*.[23] Naturally, films for this purpose were to be made available at no charge by the film companies' marketing departments.[24] *Münchhausen* too was screened to the war-wounded as part of Ufa's 25th anniversary celebrations, *Film-Kurier* reporting that soldiers from Berlin's military hospital were treated to a special viewing, during which Albers himself appeared 'in the name of Ufa, [to] greet the soldiers from the Front who were recovering in [the capital]'.[25]

Despite the RMVPs attempts to bring the festivities into line with the contemporary military situation, tensions remained. The opulence of the 25th anniversary celebrations and the extravagant luxury in *Münchhausen* stood in stark contrast to the everyday reality of living in the Third Reich. Just two nights before the festival, Allied bombers had, once again, penetrated Berlin's airspace, high explosives raining down on the city. As the dignitaries flocked to the Ufa-Palast am Zoo to bask in the glory of Nazism, 'many Berliners were picking their way through the bombed parts of the city, assessing the damage, inquiring after their friends and relatives'.[26] The stark contrast between the two worlds was recognized by the star of *Münchhausen*, Albers, remarking that as 'bombs are falling, the battle of Stalingrad is already lost..., Ufa celebrates its anniversary'.[27] British operatives working in Berlin noted that, by 1944, morale was 'probably lower ... than in any other town at any other time during the war. Life', they noted, had 'become primitive', concluding that 'the twilight of the gods is casting lengthening shadows over ... the German Reich. Soon – and Berlin knows it – night must fall'.[28]

The decline of the Reich was becoming increasingly apparent not only to the population but also to the film industry. The Ufa celebrations displayed an inner confidence in the film business which belied the impact of the war on production. Goebbels' view that the industry was a 'real money-spinner' for the state finally gave way to the pressures of the war economy.[29] Rationing of materials, fuel and luxuries greatly affected the industry's ability to produce extravagant films. More seriously, by 29 July 1944, the RMVP were actively looking to economize. It became necessary to lower the cost of individual films; productions in general were not to exceed RM600,000. Colour film, such as that used for *Münchhausen*, was to be used only with special permission from Goebbels.[30] The length of films had been reduced just seven days earlier, as a memorandum from *Reichsfilmintendant* Hans Hinkel noted: 'feature films can only be 2,200 m in length and culture films only 300 m in length. Exceptions need my personal permission.'[31] In consultation with Winkler, Goebbels had identified the problem of spiralling costs by January 1942, noting in his diary that the budgets for 'a normal film ... are really enormous'. He concluded that 'politically important state films are being produced in great numbers these days, and they cost so much in manpower as well as material that they are barely affordable. What is missing is the fine, good value light entertainment film'.[32] However, even after this, costly historical epics and fantasy films continued to form the backbone of state political productions. By 1944, the RMVP were paying the price and had to fall back on a series of re-releases. Such a policy had been in practice since April 1942, film companies deciding that the circumstances of the war necessitated further use of re-runs, no matter how undesirable.[33] By November 1944, under the pretext of reinvigorating the German population, the *Reichsfilmintendant* ordered the reissue of ideologically significant films, among them the epics of the *Führerprinzip*, such as *Bismarck*, *Die Entlassung*, *Der größe König* and *Der Herrscher*, alongside films designed to demonize the enemy, such as *Der Fuchs von Glenarvon*, *Ohm Krüger* and *G.P.U*, as well as more popular depictions of sacrifice and war such as *Annelie*.[34]

War also affected film personnel. Sensing the impact of the aerial raids on the health of studio employees, Dr Müller-Goerne, of the *Reichsfilmintendanz*, was concerned about the 'difficulties in finding personnel for films to be produced in Berlin... Film-makers give many reasons, supply sick notes signed by prominent doctors etc. so that it usually proves impossible to attribute [their illness to] fear of bombs'.[35] Moreover, such was the national crisis that the industry began to lose manpower. Liebeneiner, in his role as the *Leiter der Fachschaft Film* [Head of the Professional Film Association], called for all personnel to be 'on the spot', encouraging stars to adopt additional duties such as 'guest performances and tours of the front', which, he predicted, would have the effect of 'giving pleasure and relaxation to those men and women whose hard and demanding service protects our homeland, ... our living spaces and work places'.[36] Hinkel went further, telling the industry in 1944 that, during breaks in filming, personnel should report to local armaments factories for duty.[37] The national emergency not only affected the studios and the stars, however; it extended to the cinemas themselves, some theatres closing as their projectionists were drafted into the Services or armaments production.[38]

Increased Allied bombing also wreaked havoc on the film industry. Whilst the RMVP stepped up operations to provide entertainment for those affected by aerial raids in December 1943,[39] the studios themselves were increasingly subject to attack, the Tempelhof studios receiving a direct hit in March 1944,[40] with the main Babelsberg studios bombed just weeks before.[41] The Ufa Headquarters in central Berlin was hit by two high-explosive bombs in May 1944, causing 'light property damage'.[42] Whereas the Ufa offices escaped relatively unharmed, Tobis was not so fortunate. In an attack on their administrative centre in February 1945, the detonation of two powerful high explosives killed forty people, injuring a further ten. With the building no longer habitable, the head of production and his team were moved out to Grunewald.[43] Naturally, such activities disrupted production, the filming of one of the final cinematic productions of the Reich, appropriately entitled *Das Leben geht weiter* (Life goes on), constantly halted due to air-raid warnings and attacks.[44] Such was the pressure on studios such as Ufa, Tobis, and other companies under the newly formed Ufi conglomerate, that some filming was moved to Prague in the final years of the war. Reflecting the continuing importance of film to the Reich, the Barrandov and Hostivar studios maintained production facilities well into March and April 1945, Goebbels, in a visit to the former in November 1944, declaring Prague to be a future extension of the German 'film enterprise'. The actress, Olga Tschechowa, recognized that 'Prague is now the Mecca of film-makers'.[45] The 'Prague bunker', as it became known, offered directors a relatively tranquil environment in which to continue film production, the cameras of Willi Forst and Hans Steinhoff still rolling as Soviet troops surrounded the Reich capital. It was only the invasion of Czechoslovakia from the east that threatened to halt production. Characteristically, on 19 April 1945, Steinhoff warned his cameramen that they would be arrested if they thought about fleeing, which he himself promptly did the following day. Attempting to fly to Berlin, however, proved to be a misadventure. His plane was shot down by the Soviets and his body recovered from Luckenwalde in Brandenburg shortly afterwards.[46]

Individual cinemas and holding stations for film stock were also affected. Air raids had begun to impact upon box-office figures, Goebbels being informed that 'with the beginning of the intensification of the air-terror, a tremendous drop [in attendance is apparent] from about the middle of 1943. Since October 1943, the box office figures are, for the first time, below that of the previous year'.[47] Back in Britain, by January 1945, newspapers were reporting that 'allied bombers and the general pressure of war have put out of business all but 31 of Berlin's 400 cinemas'.[48] Daily reports of damage caused by bombing began to pour into the offices of the Propaganda Ministry. Raw film materials and film copies were destroyed, and cinemas were levelled.[49] All this represented a crisis for the industry, one which had the potential to affect civilian and military morale, Hinkel stressing that 'the movie experience is often the only opportunity left for lifting the hearts or relaxing the nerves of our fighting comrades'.[50]

The extent of the damage to the film industry caused by the end of the war is revealed in a report carried by the British newspaper the *Daily Telegraph* in January 1945. The function of cinema as a means of diversion, even in the darkest days for the Reich, was still as important as ever. William Mundy, the correspondent, confirmed Hinkel's observations, reporting that his contact in Berlin had informed him that the city's inhabitants 'trudge miles across their city to see films they have already seen half a dozen times. For the lucky ones, able to secure tickets, it represents two hours of escapism'. Moreover, he noted, 'the cinemas are the only warm places above ground in Berlin today. There is no heating of course, but everybody sits well wrapped-up in coats and scarves; everybody is smoking and we all sit huddled in a thick fug of pleasant warmth'.[51] Such was the importance of this facility to Berliners that many theatres, such as the *Deutsches Opernhaus*, were converted into makeshift cinemas. The *Alt Bayern Theater* in Friedrichstraße became a cinema exclusively for soldiers. There was little point having theatres anyway, the correspondent's informant continued, as many actors were either 'at factory benches or touring *Wehrmacht* camps'. In this atmosphere, the cinemas ran shows throughout the day, from 9:30a.m. to 6:30p.m., tickets costing from 90Pf. to RM4. Queues were long for every screening. The normal practice of allowing those in uniform, whether party or military, to go straight to the head of the line was increasingly abandoned, as this caused 'serious dissatisfaction among civilians who rate Berlin today as one of the toughest war fronts', suggesting not only the continued conflation of front lines and home front but also the breakdown of party authority. Nevertheless, war workers were issued with 'special permits' to allow them to book in advance for fear of 'losing valuable man-hours' as individuals waited in queues. Screenings were frequently disturbed by air-raid warnings, but the fact that cinemas were fundamentally unsafe did not deter the population from seeking entertainment to lighten their burden.[52] The contrast between the decline of the film industry, culminating in these Berlin scenes of January 1945, and the scenes of celebration in the Ufa-Palast am Zoo in March 1943 and its gala presentation of *Münchhausen* could not have been more obvious. The regime was in a spectacular state of 'self-denial'.[53] For whilst they revelled in the excesses of Ufa's 'magic kitchen', spending summers 'on location in Venice, floating about on gondolas on the closed-off Grand Canal in front of palaces with Goblins hanging in the windows', the Berlin front had begun its fight for survival.[54] It was in this context that Goebbels produced his final masterwork, Veit Harlan's 1945 film *Kolberg*, a fusion of the mythic world of Nazi cinema, which sought solace in the past, and the reality of the home front.[55]

In 1942, the Reich Minister for Popular Enlightenment and Propaganda was confident that 'by the end of the war, film will, without doubt, be, and will remain, one of the most important instruments of leading and influencing a nation'.[56] The perceived importance of film to the final days of the Reich was illustrated by the relative effort directed towards the production of the feature film *Kolberg*, the fictionalized representation of the defence of the town from the Napoleonic invasion of 1806–7. From a reading of the Goebbels diaries and the memoirs of Veit Harlan, it is possible to overstate the impact that the film was expected to have on the population. Comparatively greater resources were made available to Harlan's team, the film costing over RM8 million to produce due to its extravagant battle scenes. However, although Goebbels may well have intended the film to be his cinematic legacy as suggested by his aide Rudolf Semmler,[57] neither Hitler nor his Propaganda Minister thought that the film could change the course of the war. As historian Peter Paret has argued, 'the two men were not that foolish, and even Harlan never claimed *that* much power for his films'.[58] Nor was it intended as a means of expressing political tensions between the SA and the SS.[59] Rather it was a product of the time of its inception.

Harlan was officially instructed by Goebbels to produce *Kolberg* in June 1943, the Reich Minister said to have conceived of the idea as early as 1941.[60] Certainly, his intentions for the film are revealed in his diary entries from May 1943. Goebbels hoped that *Kolberg* would serve as 'an example of manly courage and a civilian populace's strength to resist when facing a desperate situation. This film', he continued, 'will above all offer a powerful lesson in regions subject to air raids'. It was hoped that it would be ready for screening by Christmas of that year.[61] At that stage, Goebbels was confident that 'the nation [was] prepared to sacrifice everything for the war'.[62] The developing course of the war indicated that, by 1943, hopes of victory were increasingly turning to mere survival, which necessitated widespread mobilization. It was in the wake of Goebbels' 'total war' speech of 18 February of that year that *Kolberg* was born, accompanying the veritable flood of propaganda that followed encouraging the German population to give themselves wholly to the war effort. The conflict was increasingly characterized as a 'people's war' in which, 'without sacrifice', the population could not expect 'victory'.[63] Although the RMVP dictated that 'on no account must publicity be given to slogans such as "Life or death"',[64] newspaper reports increasingly printed articles which suggested the turning of the tide, *Der Angriff* noting just days after this edict that the current conflict centred on Germany's right to 'be or not to be'; it was either 'victory or downfall'.[65] Goebbels' own commitment to the mobilization of the nation can be seen in his acceptance of the role of Reich Plenipotentiary for Total War in July 1944, the ultimate fusion of propaganda and war. It was the culmination of two years of intensive propaganda activity in which he had attempted to convince the German people that 'the harder the climate, the more dogged becomes the determination to get the better of all difficulties. For experience has shown', he informed the *Volk*, 'that those peoples on which life has been hardest do not lose but gain in strength. We Germans would be of a different mettle had everything been made easy for us'.[66] The original function, therefore, of Harlan's production was to encourage the population to adapt to their new role in defending the nation and the transformation of the home front into an active battlefield.

Naturally, the formative intentions of the Minister and the production team were transformed by developments in the war, the film gradually becoming a hymn to the resilience of the *Volkssturm* and the swan-song of the Reich. Goebbels himself postulated the eventual fate of *Kolberg*, writing in his diaries in May 1943 that *Kolberg* would fit 'the political and military landscape that we shall probably have to record by the time this film is shown',[67] adding some days later: 'who knows in what position we will find ourselves'.[68] Delays on the film, created by modifications to the script and the scenarios, meant that Harlan did not begin filming until 27 October, with some scenes being re-shot as late as 17 July 1944. The rough cut was produced on 30 November of that year.[69] As a result of these constant postponements, *Kolberg* began to assume new meanings and forward new messages, consistent with the changing trajectory of the war and the perceptions of both film-makers and cinema-goers. It was in this environment that the film was proclaimed by Goebbels to have a similar 'meaning for the mood of the German people ... as a battlefield victory'.[70]

Goebbels intended the film to be less epic than Harlan's other productions, its central purpose being to connect with the people. At the same time, *Kolberg* was to play down the realities of war, striking a balance between the human interest angle and the 'nationalist concept', avoiding 'too simple a patriotic tone'.[71] Goebbels requested that Harlan 'cut down a bit on his monumental plans and shape a film a bit more in the style of *Mrs. Miniver*', a reference to the 1942 American production which offered a reflection on the human, everyday experience of war. William Wyler's film remained one of Goebbels' personal favourites into the final months of the war.[72] The importance of the depiction of the 'ordinary' in war films to the propaganda campaigns of the Ministry was exemplified by the production *Das Leben geht weiter*, directed by Liebeneiner, who on 13 October 1944 was invited to a screening of *Mrs Miniver* with Goebbels to stimulate ideas for his production.[73] *Das Leben geht weiter* was intended to be a testament to civilian morale as a means of countering the devastation of aerial bombardment. It was not, however, completed, the arrival of British troops halting the shoot on 15 April 1945.[74]

Kolberg, alongside its 'companion' film, *Das Leben geht weiter*, was intended to appeal to the individual and personal, as well as the collective, experience of war.[75] Goebbels was

Still 17 *Kolberg. Nettelbeck and Maria in the final scenes of the film.*
Still from the Bundesarchiv Filmarchiv, Berlin.

concerned that Harlan 'pays too much attention to the disaster scenes and misses the more intimate moments'.[76] Although the Reich Minister had initially resisted the inclusion of a dominant love story, claiming that the director had, 'as is often the case with him, made a Söderbaum film out of a Nettelbeck film [a central character in the film, played by Heinrich George]',[77] it was the final sequence between Maria [Söderbaum] and Nettelbeck which gave visual expression to his initial conception of a testament to the spirit of 'total war', in the same way that Harlan's insertion of the relationship between Luise and Frederick the Great had defined the essence of the *Führerprinzip* in *Der große König*.[78] In the final scene, Maria, reflecting on the loss of her sweetheart, Lieutenant von Schill [Gustav Diesel], is comforted by Nettelbeck. The dialogue brings together each strand of the RMVP's 'total war' propaganda, Nettelbeck reminding Maria that, '*You have sacrificed everything, Maria. But it wasn't in vain. Death is part of victory. The greatest achievement always stems from pain. If one bears the pain, one will be great again. You're great, Maria! You did your duty and were not afraid of death. You're victorious too, Maria! You too!*' In a final justification of the losses at the front and a continuation of the mythic discourse on destiny offered in the early *Fliegerfilme*, Nazi cinema bolstered the image of heroic death, Gneisenau [Horst Caspar] in *Kolberg* celebrating that '*now we can die together!*' Nonetheless, *Kolberg* did not merely emerge as a film of the lost and the fallen. It also became a film of new beginnings. From defeat, the subtext of the film suggests, nations can be resurrected, a sentiment which corresponded to Nazi propaganda surrounding the *Machtergreifung*. As Goebbels stated in the final months of the Reich, 'one day the shining hour of victory will rise up from the graves of our dead, our noble fallen'; *Kolberg* offered a visual embodiment of this concept.[79] For Goebbels, Harlan's film had come to represent his legacy. On 17 April 1945, he informed his RMVP associates, who were hoping to be granted a release from the Ministry so that they could flee Berlin, that they should internalize the central message of *Kolberg*, promising them everlasting life on the silver screen of the future: 'Gentlemen, in a hundred years' time they will be showing another fine colour film describing the terrible days we are living through. Don't you want to play a part in this film', he asked them, 'to be brought back to life in a hundred years' time?' Urging them to 'stand fast', Goebbels affirmed that this was every individual's 'chance to choose the part that he will play in the film a hundred years hence'. The film was going to be 'a fine and elevating picture'.[80] It was clear to all in the room that the Reich was facing its *Götterdämmerung*, and it was in this moment of total collapse that its Reich Minister chose to take his inspiration from *Kolberg*.

The town of Kolberg proved to be an unfortunate choice, however. Goebbels closely followed its demise during the closing stages of World War II in his diaries,[81] often conflating its fictional representation in Harlan's film with contemporary events, an indication of how removed he had become from the stark reality of war that he had attempted to present in his famous speech at the *Sportspalast* in February 1943. The Reich Minister regretfully commented on 18 March 1945 that the town of Kolberg had been evacuated, remarking that it had been 'defended with such extraordinary heroism, [but] could no longer be held.

I will ensure that the evacuation of Kolberg is not mentioned in the OKW report. In view of the severe psychological repercussions on the Kolberg film, we could do without that for the moment'.[82] Just over one month later, the crown jewel of the German film industry, the Babelsberg studios, fell into Soviet hands. Watching the 'Soviet tanks ... making their way over torn-up pavements and along streets dotted with dead horses', one observer commented that 'this street had been constructed for the film *Flüchtlinge*. Back then, this was all props; now it is a horrible reality'.[83] As the remnants of the German army seized civilian clothes from Ufa's costume department to disguise their identity, it was clear that the era of Nazi cinema had come to an end.[84]

Portents of this fateful moment surrounded the release of Harlan's film in January 1945. Attempting to lift the spirits of the troops, Goebbels sent a copy of *Kolberg* to the *Festungskommando* in La Rochelle, informing them that:

> The film is an artistic eulogy to the courage and the desire to prove themselves of those prepared to make the greatest sacrifices for nation and homeland... May you and your brave soldiers experience this film as a record of the unshakeable steadfastness of a nation which, as one with the fighting front in these days of world-embracing struggle, is willing to match the greatest examples of its glorious history. *Heil unserem Führer!*[85]

Back in Berlin, tensions between the film's central message and the gala premiere were exposed. The film could only be shown at two of the city's Ufa-cinemas – Alexanderplatz and Tauentzienstraße. All other venues normally booked for premieres had been destroyed.[86] Actors were instructed to return from evacuation to attend the premiere in order to maintain the façade of normality. Söderbaum recalled that she had returned to the city to find her house in ruins, and was forced to stay with a neighbour. It was hardly the luxury accommodation normally afforded to film stars and other dignitaries, the neighbour's home having no windows, the empty frames covered only with a thin layer of paper. Preparing for the premiere, the actress had to cajole another neighbour into sharing her bath, exchanging her pullovers for an evening gown. Aware that aerial bombardment was always a possibility and making her way to the cinema through streets strewn with debris and rubble, Söderbaum thought that, under these circumstances, 'it was ridiculous to go to a film premiere'.[87] The premiere reflected the 'self-denial' that the RMVP had been practising since the Ufa celebrations of March 1943, the surreal smokescreen a dismal attempt to hide the collapse of the 'thousand year Reich'.

The attempt to maintain an idealistic vision of National Socialism, one which seemed increasingly at odds with reality, was challenged by some film-makers, the German film industry essentially fragmenting, with various strands of filmic activity emerging from 1943: the 'official' Nazi narrative of survival and rebirth, the escapist state of denial offered by the fantasy features and the emergent new realism represented by the works of, amongst others, Helmut Käutner, which whilst not appropriately classified as 'resistant' cinema, certainly offered a counterpoint to accepted National Socialist film during this period. Undercurrents of resistance activity emerged during the closing years of the war, however. From their respected positions in society, some stars were able to remain critical of the regime, Kreimeier arguing that even 'from among the significant number of well-trained actors who were popular with the public, [the state] was never able to produce the homunculus of the "new era"'.[88] Although 'many stars did not find social trafficking with high Nazi officials any imposition' and were willing to at least coexist with the regime that paid their salaries,[89] some were prepared to use their status to defend less fortunate colleagues, among them Henny Porten (herself the subject of some persecution as a result of her marriage to a Jew),[90] Käthe Dorsch, Brigitte Horney, and the star of *Münchhausen*, Hans Albers.[91] Albers infuriated the Reich Minister, refusing to take part in the *Winterhilfswerk*, telling Goebbels that he simply had 'no time'.[92] Albers was also reported to be enraged at Porten's persecution simply because she refused to leave her husband, the events resonating with the actor's own experience of having to send his own partner, Hansi Burg, to Switzerland in 1934. Burg's father later died in Auschwitz.[93] He had to be reminded by Jobst von Reiht-Zanthier, head of casting at Ufa since 1931, that making oppositional remarks was a dangerous enterprise: he warned him to 'just wait. One only has to be able to survive all this'.[94] In 1943, as Kreimeier recognized, 'survival is all: ... that was the secret (or openly embraced watchword) in Ufa-City, for the stars and for the rank and file, for the outspoken and for the silent, for the opponents and, increasingly, even for the adherents of the regime'.[95]

Von Reiht-Zanthier's advice to Hans Albers appeared to be good counsel from a friend. Although the regime was perceived to be grinding to a halt, persecutions and arbitrary arrests were not. Fritz Kaelber, Fritzsch's replacement as chief executive of Ufa, opened the senior management meeting of 14 April 1944 with the news that 'the press chief of Terra-Filmkunst had been sentenced to death by the "People's Court" for subversive statements particularly hostile to the army'. From this it is possible to gain an insight into the pervasive sense of terror in the film industry, and more generally in Nazi society.[96] Shortly afterwards, in May, Richard Düvell, Ufa's press chief, was arrested after having been denounced for making 'defeatist' comments. Despite protestations by film director Wolfgang Liebeneiner, Düvell was found guilty by the 'People's court' and beheaded. At least, joked Kaelber darkly, 'he would only need a short coffin'.[97] The fate of the press chief was reminiscent of the case of Herbert Selpin, which came to the attention of the film community one year earlier. In February 1942, the director began shooting the epic *Titanic*, the story of the fated 1912 transatlantic voyage which resulted in the loss of over 1,500 lives. Naturally, the film was to be infused with Nazi ideology, suggesting that the disaster was the result of the 'unscrupulousness and the greed of British magnates of the stock exchange', a tale of 'self-sacrifice, silent heroism, blatant egoism and faithful love' which tied in with previous propaganda campaigns focused on British plutocracy.[98] In order to capture the scenes on board the Titanic and recreate the chaos which ensued as the ship hit the iceberg and plunged to the depths of the ocean, the production team were loaned a barracks ship for filming, the *Cap Arcona*, together with 3,000 extras. Tensions soon emerged between the extras and Selpin, mirrored in the increasing antagonism between the director and his script-writer Walter Zerlett-Olfenius. Pressures on the set soon became apparent to the *Reichspropagandaleiteramt* in Danzig-Westpreußen. The film, being on location, was under their jurisdiction, and they promptly initiated a frantic 'paper war' with the *Reichsfilmintendanz*, complaining of the behaviour and disorder on board the *Cap Arcona*.[99] Events culminated in an extraordinary argument over dinner in Zoppot which resulted in the resignation of Olfenius, who informed Tobis that he could no longer work with such an 'inept' director, particularly one who revelled in the 'abuse' of soldiers and the Navy, 'dragging [the name] of the *Wehrmacht* through the mud'.[100] On 11 July, Selpin was summoned to answer directly to Hans Hinkel, on the grounds that he had been overheard making 'demoralizing utterances' during an angry outburst whilst on location in Gotenhafen. The *Reichssicherheitshauptamt* was informed. In fact, the Gestapo 'had declared the situation a harmless one; Selpin was not an enemy of the state. He could be cautioned and make a donation to the *Winterhilfswerk*'.[101] However, the case came to the attention of the Reich Minister for Popular Enlightenment and Propaganda, who insisted on confronting the errant director, requiring him to answer before an *Ehrengericht*. Selpin's refusal to retract his comments resulted in his imprisonment. Faced with few alternatives, Selpin took his own life, hanging himself with his braces, whilst in custody at the Gestapo headquarters in the Prinz-Albrecht Palais on the evening of 1 August 1942.[102] The arrest and subsequent suicide of Selpin reportedly prompted widespread protest across the film community of Berlin in opposition to the violent methods employed by the Ministry to ensure conformity.[103] Justifying the RMVP's actions against Selpin, *Der Film* reminded the industry of the inevitable consequences of 'defaming and insulting German soldiers' and undermining 'war morale'.[104] In a further example of the bizarre world in which the film industry was operating by 1942, Selpin's fate was recorded directly below an article reporting 'dance and music in abundance'.[105]

Despite the severe recriminations associated with dissent, by 1944, the collapse of the regime offered film-makers an alternative means of expressing a counter-cultural viewpoint. The work of Helmut Käutner in the final years of the war offered a new realism. Filmed from within the ruins of the Reich, Käutner's films, specifically *Große Freiheit Nr. 7* (Great Freedom no. 7) and *Unter den Brücken* (Under the Bridges), began to create a new identity for the German cinema, one which was to provide the basis for the development of German film in the post-war period. In many ways, Käutner was the perfect director for this task. His roots were firmly located in the bohemian culture of the Weimar era, finding work as a 'cabaret artist, satirical singer/song-writer [and] feature writer', his particular 'area of expertise' being 'literary parody'.[106] Associated with the cabaret *Die Vier Nachrichter*, Käutner enjoyed a career as a satirist, abandoning his doctoral study on the Swabian Passion Plays in 1932 to pursue his theatrical ambitions. These aspirations ended in 1935 with the newly established *Reichsministerium für Volksaufklärung und Propaganda* closing the cabaret and accusing the players of being 'destructive' and 'demoralizing',[107] even though their form of satire was social and not political, reflecting the all-encompassing nature of the Nazi cultural *Gleichschaltung*.[108] Käutner continued working in the arts, turning his attention to the cinema. During the Third Reich, he produced a series of popular films such as *Kleider machen Leute* (Clothes Make the Man, 1940), *Auf Wiedersehen, Franziska!* (Goodbye, Franziska, 1941), *Anuschka* (1942) and *Wir machen Musik* (We're Making Music, 1942). Two films in particular brought Käutner into conflict with Goebbels and the RMVP. The 1939 film, *Kitty und die Weltkonferenz* (Kitty and the World Conference), with its sympathetic depiction of the English Secretary of State for Commerce, disappeared from Reich cinemas soon after its release and was banned in the aftermath of Britain's guarantee to Poland in 1939.[109] Käutner's *Romanze in Moll* (Romance in a Minor Key, 1943), a sympathetic portrait of a woman trapped in a loveless marriage who attempts to bring meaning to her life through an adulterous affair, was not a particular favourite of the Reich Minister either.[110] Although Käutner was not overtly resistant to the regime, Witte has argued contentiously that through these films, and his works of 1944-5, Käutner displayed an '"aesthetic opposition" to National Socialism', a 'poetic style' that can be read as a 'vehicle for a veiled critique of the bombast of much Third Reich entertainment'.[111] The director's final productions of the war years not only display this tendency but reveal much about the conditions on set and the disintegration of the Ministry in the period from 1944 to the collapse of Nazi Germany.

Käutner's penultimate film of the war years, *Große Freiheit Nr. 7*, portrayed the touching story of a former seaman Hannes (Albers) and his quest for companionship. The film, set on the street in Hamburg which lends its name to the title, depicts the relationship between Hannes and the ex-lover of his dying brother Gisa (Ilse Werner), the seaman wanting to settle down and build a life for them both. Gisa, however, falls in love with a young deckhand (Hans Söhnker), Hannes returning to sea to forget. The concept of the film began to take shape in early 1943, passing to the *Reichsfilmdramaturg* on 18 March.[112] Filming began at the Ufa studios in Babelsberg on 5 May.[113] Allied bombing meant that production had to move first to the Tempelhof studios in mid-July and then, later, on to the 'Prague bunker'. Käutner and his team returned to Hamburg, struggling to shoot the sequences depicting the lively streets, by this stage totally destroyed by aerial bombardment,[114] the cameramen attempting to 'present the viewer with the impression of an intact port'.[115]

That the film was intended as an important contribution to the cinema of the closing years of the war is confirmed by the facilities and materials afforded to Käutner and his production team. Albers' fee for his appearance was an astronomical RM406,000,[116] his co-star Ilse Werner receiving RM40,000.[117] Despite economy measures ordered by the Ministry, *Film-Kurier* reported on 17 March 1944 that, in keeping with the bright signs of Hamburg's Reeperbahn, the film was to be shot using Agfa-colour film stock, enthusing that 'by night-time the *Grosse Freiheit* is anything but grey. What colours even in the smoky pub where a blue-grey haze lies on all faces and objects!... The red-yellow lights of the street lamps glimmer in the dark harbour alleys under a veil of mist'.[118] As this suggests, Käutner's film offered an alternative vision of the life of a seaman, no longer the glorified heroism of the Navy but a rather sad and dingy existence in the bars and back streets of Hamburg, the gaudy colours of *Film-Kurier*'s report suggestive of a cultural underworld – immoral, hard and real. This vision was obviously far-removed from the idealized image of the *Kriegsmarine*, provoking Admiral Dönitz to object to Käutner's production on the grounds that it damaged the prestige of the German Navy in the public mind.[119]

More controversial still was the film's title. Originally named *Die Große Freiheit*, the word 'freedom' created some cause for concern. Under the pretext of suggesting that the title did not accurately represent the fact that the film was about a location rather than a concept, the RMVP changed the title twice, firstly to *Auf der Großen Freiheit* in early July 1943 and finally, by the end of the month, to *Große Freiheit Nr. 7*.[120] The idea of 'great freedom' obviously caused more than a little heartburn within a dictatorship, the censors having previously gone as far as to remove the final line of Maisch's *Friedrich Schiller* in which the eponymous hero whispers '*freedom!*' As Schulte-Sasse points out, this was a particularly odd gesture in a film with a consistent subtext of rebellion, such a script alteration only being explicable 'if we read the Duke and his school as a stand-in for Nazism, which … runs up against many features of the text'.[121] It is possible that the RMVP, especially in the context of 1943–4, did not want to leave any room for popular misinterpretation, confusing National Socialist conceptions of 'freedom' with alternatives less desirable to the functioning of the Nazi state.

In line with Goebbels' original conception that Käutner's film was intended to lift the spirits of a nation at war and given the setting, it was envisaged that *Große Freiheit Nr. 7* would premiere in Hamburg. The *Reichsfilmintendanz* rejected Gauleiter Forster's suggestion that Danzig, given its contested past, offered a prime location for a gala performance, stating 'in our opinion the premiere has to take place in Hamburg! In case there is no luxurious film palace left following the terror attacks, it has to be released in five or ten emergency film theatres so that the citizens of Hamburg, who were hit so fiercely by enemy terror, are the first to be shown their film'.[122] Plans for the premiere were halted with the characteristic intervention of the Reich Minister. Demanding further alterations to the final cut of *Große Freiheit Nr. 7*, Käutner was instructed to adjust a number of sequences amounting to an additional two or three months' work. These changes delayed the release of the film in Germany indefinitely. Käutner's film was released for foreign distribution, premiering in Prague on 15 December 1944, but was only screened to the German population after the collapse of the Reich, the debut of an edited version taking place in the Western sector of Berlin on 9 September 1945.[123]

Although passing through the *Filmprüfstelle* on 1 March 1945, Käutner's final production of the war years, *Unter den Brücken*, was also not screened until after the fall of Nazi Germany. The film, thought to be lost, was found in Zurich and premiered in Locarno on 1 September 1946, exactly seven years after the first shots were fired across the Polish border initiating the conflict which would eventually consume the empire of its instigators. *Unter den Brücken* bore the characteristic hallmarks of Käutner's new realism: the story of two men, Hendrik (Carl Raddatz) and Willy (Gustav Knuth), living on a barge and looking for a way of settling down, their lives changed forever by a chance meeting with a young woman, Anna (Hannelore Schroth). Described as the 'most beautiful and most liberal film of the war years', the film presented 'an aesthetic [antithetical to] its time'.[124] Even a dissenting aesthetic, which may have drawn the attention of Goebbels and his censors previously, was consumed by the total destruction and confusion which characterized the final months of the war. Walter Ulbrich, who co-wrote the screenplay with Käutner, recalled, 'when we started our film, chaos was already waiting. One order addressed to the film industry [followed] another. What was valid today was forbidden tomorrow; what had been forbidden today was ordered tomorrow and forgotten the day after'.[125] In any case, the RMVP 'was occupied with defending its last line of propaganda, with the film *Kolberg*. The imbalance between atrocious reality and film can be seen as absolutely shameless'.[126] How much Goebbels would have personally concerned himself with their production anyway is a matter for speculation. As demonstrated in reference to *Der große König*, *Die Entlassung* and *Kolberg*, for example, the Reich Minister had the capacity to be highly disruptive to the creative process of making a film, interfering with some productions almost incessantly. However, these films were regarded by Goebbels as being central to the propaganda campaigns of the Reich and, as such, required his 'expert' attention. As Michael Kater has argued, an analysis of Goebbels' diaries reveals that 'as a politician with many duties, he could not be on top of everything at all times'. Rather, his attention was focused on a few 'prestige' films. Beyond this, his role as the ultimate film censor was 'on a par with reading a good book or listening to a Furtwängler recording; these activities were challenges worthy of his intellect and artistic sensibilities'.[127] Indeed, Goebbels 'scrutinized very few war films', using 'pure' entertainment films as a means of escape, redolent of the way he expected such productions to serve the German people.[128] Given his own film viewing and censorship habits, it is possible that, with the multiple tasks facing him in 1944–5, Käutner's film may not have been his first priority. Nonetheless, *Unter den Brücken* does receive some comment from the Reich Minister in a diary entry of 28 December 1944. Goebbels recognized that the film had the trademark 'maverick' characteristics of its director, noting that the film was 'a remarkable work of art which impresses in particular because of its clever, psychological direction as well as its modern psychology. Käutner is the "avantgardist" among the German directors'. He concluded, 'despite the quality of this cinematic work of art, I can't muster the right measure of interest'.[129]

The very production of *Unter den Brücken* defined its distance from the reality of the Reich, the crew's cameras rolling on the banks of the Havel whilst in the background Berlin was fighting for its survival. The production team recalled that filming *Unter den Brücken* was, in itself, a form of escapism.[130] Some years later, Ulbrich commented that it was important to recall the circumstances under which the film was made, so that one might appreciate how much *Unter den Brücken* meant to its producers, offering another commentary upon the parallel disintegration of National Socialism and its film industry.[131] The film was intended as a '*Großstadtmelodie*',[132] and the production team were well aware that, as well as creating a hymn to the city of Berlin, they were filming its requiem. The contrast between the filmic idyll constructed on the Havel and the fate of the capital just a few miles away was obvious to the star of the film, Carl Raddatz:

> Our back-drops: Glienicke Bridge, the river Havel, Ketzin, Havelwerder – it was an idyllic, almost romantic, time of filming during which streams of bombs drifted to Berlin above our heads. A few minutes later, mushroom clouds rose up on the horizon; the sky darkened, it thundered and the ground shook softly while frogs croaked around us, the wind blew through the reeds and the Havel carried on flowing leisurely as if nothing had happened.[133]

The film-makers were careful to ensure that 'work carried on' regardless. After the 'sounding of the alarm', the 'spot lights went out' and the crew hurried 'speedily to the bunker of the brewery'. But after 'the all-clear, [they] continued shooting until the morning'.[134] As reflected in Raddatz's comments, war became the defining and uniting experience on set. Käutner's team, although working without extensive interference from the RMVP, was also without essential materials. Ulbrich recalled:

> In the end, the simplest aids were missing. Bomb attacks disrupted the telephone connections, [there were] power cuts, petrol for our transport often had to be siphoned off from the *Wehrmacht*'s vehicles – we called this 'direct acquisition'. Important skilled workers were forced into the *Volkssturm* and had to be brought back by employing a variety of tricks… On other occasions we saw the fire clouds towering high above Berlin while we were filming outside on the Havel. A good many had to ask themselves whether their houses were still standing, or whether their families were still alive or who might have been hit today. Some were in danger of losing their cool.[135]

Whilst Käutner's team hid in the bunkers on the banks of the Havel to avoid Allied bombers, their colleagues at Ufa were also underground. On 25 April, a middle manager at the studio wrote in his diary that over two hundred people were secreted in the cellars, amongst whom were thirty employees of the film company. Reporting that 'some SS men have fought their way through to us' under instruction from the RMVP intent on defending 'the Ufa building at all costs', the manager quickly realized that the situation was hopeless. In a frantic exchange, the SS officer informed his captives that the advancing Soviet armies would not 'take him alive'. The diarist astutely understood that that would 'be the end of us civilians'. Tensions reached a climax as the building came under fire on 1 May. Their hideout was alight, flames surrounding the cellar on three sides. The next day, Soviet tanks 'rolled into Dönhoffplatz … and fired into the cellars and bunkers'. As negotiations began with the invading force, the SS officer 'blew himself and a comrade up with a hand grenade'.[136] Meanwhile, the day before, the Reich Minister had achieved the highest position in the Reich, succeeding his beloved Führer as Reich Chancellor. He lasted in this post for one day. Magda Goebbels, sensing that the post-war world would hold little for the children of one of the most notorious criminals of the Nazi era, poisoned their six offspring. Shortly after, her husband shot her in the courtyard of the bunker before turning the gun on himself. The era of the Reich Ministry of Popular Enlightenment and Propaganda had come to an end, the charred remains of its champion waiting to be discovered by the advancing troops.

A new world had begun for the film-makers of the Third Reich, one which revolved around rapidly changing identities and coming to terms with the past. *Unter den Brücken* and *Große Freiheit Nr. 7* became films which defined a new aesthetic, a mode of expression which was somehow resistant to the cultural principles of National Socialism. Yet, as Robert C. Reimer has argued, Käutner's films 'never entirely escape the ideological constraints' of the RMVP.[137] Contending that *Unter den Brücken* 'neither directly nor indirectly makes reference to a battle-scarred Berlin', Reimer forwards that the 1945 production fitted well with Goebbels' concept of escapism as propaganda, allowing the viewers to experience a different city, a pre-war city 'outside of temporal space'.[138] By providing pre-war visions of familiar landmarks and places, Käutner reminded his audiences to 'forget what was outside the theatre, in spite of the reminders of the city that the locations provide', albeit for a short period of time.[139] It was the war, argues Reimer, that prevented the general release of *Unter den Brücken*, and it was the post-war context, when the film was finally screened, that allowed for a reinterpretation of the production: 'avoiding all reference to the Third Reich' not only fitted with Goebbels' vision of escapist propaganda but also meant that the 'images could [simultaneously] appeal to post-war sensitivities'.[140] Focusing on Detlev Peukert's definition of 'passive consent' in the Third Reich, in which 'accepting the regime as a given and being prepared to do one's day-to-day duty', thus permitting the continuance of the Nazi state, Reimer reverses the testimony of Ulbrich.[141] Suddenly an act of dissent, in the production of a 'realist' film in the midst of war, the survival of which is testament to the film-makers' commitment to their task, is transformed into an act of conformity, an act which ultimately allowed the film to 'offer dreams and help its intended audience turn inward and forget reality for a while'.[142] How seditious the storyline of Käutner's films may have appeared is also tempered when placed alongside other productions. In their post-war context, films such as *Große Freiheit Nr. 7*, *Auf der Reeperbahn nachts um halb eins* (On the Reeperbahn at Half Past Midnight, Liebeneiner, 1957) and *Das Herz von St. Pauli* (The Heart of St Pauli, Eugen York, 1957) took on new meanings. As Sabine Hake observes, 'in all three films, Albers' infatuation with a much younger woman forces him to accept the impossibility of returning home, of belonging. Unwilling to mourn his loss, he seeks refuge in melancholy'. Such actions are reinterpreted in the light of the collapse of the Reich, with 'what might have had subversive effects … now reduced to sentimental recollections, nostalgic re-enactments, selective memories and, above all, acts of wilful forgetting'.[143] In the cold light of day, the film stars of the Third Reich were forced to accept a post-war existence in which they would have to come to terms with their past, and if they could not, self-delusion and denial were always other options. From the remnants of the film industry, many different existences emerged, the two most extreme examples being represented by the directors who have been at the centre of this chapter, Helmut Käutner and Veit Harlan.

Although Käutner's films occupy a contested space in the history of Nazi cinema and indeed in patterns of dissent and conformity, his post-war persona was very much grounded in the former. The director disputed his association with National Socialism in the aftermath of World War II, informing the occupying forces that his films were 'pure light entertainment films without an ideological way of looking at a problem and had, therefore, been permitted without difficulties'; they mostly received the *Prädikate "'künstlerisch besonders wertvoll'*", never *"staatspolitisch wertvoll"* or *"Film der Nation"*'.[144] Distancing himself and some of his compatriots from the Third Reich, Käutner argued: 'my professional success is based on the acceptance of my work abroad. If some of it was also effective in Germany, it is, in the first instance, due to the fact that the best part of the German audience turned away from Nazi propaganda films to look for relaxation in pure art where that was offered'.[145] For Käutner and others, the post-war era meant facing the concept of passive consent, not only in filmic terms but in a wider social sense as well. Reflecting on *Kristallnacht*, he lamented that 'we were implicated in this ... Germans had done this or had not prevented it. We had. I also felt guilt personally without realizing exactly why'.[146] As this suggests, Käutner had begun to confront the controversial idea of 'collective guilt' at an early stage. Accepting its problematic nature, he added that:

> Even a whole nation can become guilty, but only a free nation which responsibly chooses its own representatives to carry out its wishes. The German nation was such a nation when it voted for Hitler. Therefore, it is collectively guilty for the reign of National Socialism and its consequences: the downfall of human rights, the war, Europe's destruction, for deprivation and misery in the whole world resulting from the former. The fact that the German people did not know what it did in 1933 does not acquit it from such guilt, but it makes that guilt understandable and tragic.[147]

Extending the notion, he concluded that 'All of Europe's free nations, well, all of the world's [nations], are not free from collective responsibility ... it was late in the day when they decided to fight for freedom and human rights'.[148] Käutner keenly felt the need for answers and for the prosecution of those who had brought the German nation to its knees, morally and literally. It was in the post-war era that, in the search for an acceptable future and responses to an unacceptable past, individuals sought a catharsis. Käutner turned his attentions to one of the most notorious directors of the Third Reich: Veit Harlan.

Harlan's experience of the post-war world was turbulent. The director was the only major film-maker to stand trial, accused of 'crimes against humanity, complicity in persecuting others on racial grounds, and to have collaborated with the planning of such crimes'.[149] The trial focused on Harlan's 1940 production *Jud Süß*, and raised issues germane to the related questions of compulsion and complicity, probing the essential relationship between propaganda, film and popular opinion.[150] The prosecution had to demonstrate that the message of Harlan's film had compelled others to commit crimes against humanity, and that Harlan had willingly and knowingly contributed to propaganda for this explicit purpose. The trial exposed how fragmented the filmic community had become after 1945, one of Harlan's accusers being the actor Gustav Fröhlich, star of the director's 1943 film *Der große König*. The post-war pain of involvement with the Nazi regime also came to the fore.[151] The widow of Ferdinand Marian, who played the eponymous anti-hero in *Jud Süß*, appeared in court to give evidence in favour of Harlan. On 7 August 1946, Marian, who had been prohibited from working as a result of his involvement in the 1940 production, was involved in a fatal car accident near Munich. It was thought that he had attempted to end his life.[152] Maria Byk-Marian, deeply affected by the death of her husband and having exonerated Harlan before the tribunal, committed suicide just days later. In a letter to friends, she expressed her frustration at the post-war situation in which artists found themselves.[153]

Although Harlan was found not guilty, since the direct link between the propaganda and resultant actions could not be legally demonstrated, further accusations followed. As *The New York Times* observed, 'through the vagaries of de-Nazification, Harlan [had been] cleared in three separate trials. This left him legally unblemished, but morally far from clean in the eyes of Germans of goodwill. No matter what the courts said', the reporter continued, 'the reek of gas ovens is inseparably associated with his name'.[154] Harlan's attempt to resume his filmic career with the production *Unsterbliche Geliebte* (1950) prompted two further court appearances questioning his Nazi past.[155] Erich Lüth, Hamburg's press chief and *Senatsdirektor*, used the 1951 German Film Week to call for a boycott of Harlan's films. Lüth asserted that 'anyone who has been as outstanding a director of Nazi movies as the co-creator of *Jud Süß* ... should be blackballed in disgust by all decent Germans mindful of the tears that still flow at millions of Jewish graves. ... Harlan's re-emergence will open wounds which have hardly closed. ... It is the duty even more than the right of all decent Germans to be ready, not only to protest against – but to boycott – Veit Harlan'.[156] Harlan took Lüth to court for defamation of character. Lüth was subsequently prevented from initiating further similar campaigns against the director.[157] The court's decision proved to be unpopular, prompting widespread protests and boycotts in Berlin, Munich and Heidelberg.[158] Hans Habe, who had worked for the Propaganda and Psychological Warfare Detachment of the 12th Army and had stayed on in Germany as a editor and writer, observed similar scenes in Freiburg, where 'the showing of the new Harlan picture was only prevented by students who protested even when they were cruelly beaten and severely punished by the police'.[159] Protests were further fuelled by a newspaper article which appeared in the *Hamburger Abendblatt* on 7 January 1951. The author of the open letter to Lüth was Helmut Käutner. Käutner informed the *Senatsdirektor* that in the last months of the war he had seen a script for Harlan's next production – an adaptation of Shakespeare's *The Merchant of Venice*. Käutner openly and publicly contended that:

This script in its unscrupulous, anti-Semitic maliciousness coupled with its falsification of history and misuse of Shakespeare's genius put the film *Jud Süß* in the shade ... I know for certain that this film was in pre-production and that Werner Krauss was to play Shylock, Christina [sic] Söderbaum Portia and Bettina Moissi the part of Jessica. I find it incomprehensible why this renewed attempt of the *Jud Süß*-director to work in the same vein as with the first rabble-rousing propaganda film has remained unknown to the public.[160]

In this way, Harlan's Nazi associations continued to haunt him. His involvement with *Jud Süß* and the Nazi regime was to define his past, present and future. Harlan had hoped that the resumption of his career would be possible, writing to a theatre owner in April 1948 that 'The world is round. One day my wife will be back on the silver screen and I will once again be next to a camera'.[161] However, although the Allied authorities began to re-release some of his pre-1945 films, from 1951 onwards,[162] it was a *passé qui ne passe pas*. Film-makers, like others in German society, had to undergo a form of *Vergangenheitsbewältigung*, choosing either to confront their Nazi past, to deny it or to reconfigure it within the 'collective amnesia of the post-war world' in which 'powerless employees of the studios ... could not be held responsible for cases of political infiltration and manipulation'.[163] The Harlan trial proved that, in a legal sense, film could not be subject to prosecution in the same way as other weapons of war. The interpretative framework within which film operates, functioning as part of a persuasive construct but without clearly defined, identifiable and isolated impacts, obviated any successful legal case against film-makers of the Reich. It is clear from the post-war histories of those involved in the Nazi 'dream factory' that, although the trial against Harlan gave legal closure, it did not bring a satisfactory conclusion to the underlying emotional tensions within German society. If anything, the pressures were exacerbated by the post-war process of 'de-nazification', as the protests in Hamburg, Berlin, Munich and Heidelberg suggest. Moreover, the history of Nazi film in the immediate post-war period reveals the tortured existences many film-makers were forced to lead, uncertain of the meaning of film in the wider discourses of active and passive resistance or conformity. Nazi film was, and still is, a contested space with multiple identities, which offer little opportunity for a meaningful resolution of these complex issues. The re-release of the films of the Nazi period, however, allowed 'a new generation of film-makers and movie-goers ... to use these filmic discourses to reflect on the possibilities of a German cinema able simultaneously to accept and move beyond the burdens of the past'.[164] In this sense, at least, the afterlife of Nazi cinema had a positive outcome.

If Nazi film offers the historian the opportunity to witness the collapse of a nation through the silver screen, then British film in the same period presents a story of reconstruction and renewal. In many ways, film in Britain during World War II not only reflected debates relating to the post-war world but shaped them, giving visual expression to calls for modernization and reform. From an early stage, the film industry began to ask questions not only about its own place in the post-war era but about the future of British society. War became the defining feature of the British film industry, both during the conflict and beyond, film-makers recognizing the opportunities circumstance had afforded which in essence had delineated the British war experience and set the course of future production. In short, as Basil Wright observed, 'world events [in 1939] were ... to force the industry to grow up, and fast'.[165]

As the war drew to a close, there was an obvious need in Europe, the British film industry perceiving that it would be a primary exporter of films as direct propaganda to liberated nations. Film followed the Allied forces as they hit the beaches of Normandy in June 1944. The MoI agreed a specific programme of films for each nation, reflecting the diverse needs of the liberated populations. Employing the full filmic arsenal from fictional features to MoI shorts to newsreels and British Council shorts, the programme was intended to address particular propaganda objectives, notably to promote Allied cooperation in the face of the Axis powers, to demonstrate the unity of the British Empire, to reassure populations that there had been some form of retribution (here Churchill's film *The Biter Bit* was resurrected), to provide an immediate and general history of the war, and to reflect the wider wartime experience. Films such as Jennings and Watt's *London Can Take It* could now be seen as a stoical representation of resilience and a memorial to the dark days of British suffering. Moreover, with the entry of British troops into European territories, the MoI saw the opportunity for a course of cultural conditioning, easing the way for the Allied occupation and liberation and, simultaneously, promoting the British way of life. Productions selected by the MoI for distribution in Northern France, liberated European territories and North Africa were specifically chosen for 'their portrayal of Britain and the British character under war conditions' and intended to show 'events and living conditions with which countries now liberated have for so long been out of touch'. Films such as *Fires Were Started*, *The Gentle Sex* (Maurice Elvey/Leslie Howard, 1943), *In Which We Serve* (Noel Coward, 1942), *Millions Like Us* (Sidney Gilliat and Frank Launder, 1943) and *Salute John Citizen* (Maurice Elvey, 1942) were particularly suited to this form of cultural propaganda. Foregrounding the 'quality of production and entertainment value', the Ministry was actively promoting the portrait of 'co-operation between the "free" and underground national movements and the Allies'.[166] It was, after all, in the Allied interest, temporarily at least, to win over populations and avoid the problematic questions surrounding the gradations of complicity and assent which existed in Nazi occupied nations.

In the immediate aftermath of victory, it was the MoI and the industry's contention that 'the peoples of the liberated territories, who for years have laboured under the heels of the oppressor, can best have their lives brightened through the motion picture'. It was essential, they argued, that Allied propaganda 'plugged home that all problems are soluble and that good inevitably triumphs over evil'.[167] Calls for Britain to prepare for the collapse of Nazi rule in Europe in filmic terms had been made as early as 18 February 1943. Whilst Goebbels was appealing to the German population to embrace the concept of 'total war' in Berlin's

Sportspalast, Kinematograph Weekly was lobbying for the British Government to formulate a 'plan to supply the European post-war market with film entertainment'. Concerned that US interests would inevitably overwhelm the new Europe, the film trade urged the MoI to 'evolve some scheme by which selected British films of high quality [could] be subtitled or dubbed' into, amongst others, French, Flemish, Dutch, Norwegian, Czech, Polish, Greek, Swedish and Italian, so that as soon as Allied troops landed, films could be circulated. *Kinematograph Weekly* pointed out that 'entertainment will figure high in the predominant requirements of the occupied peoples when their countries are freed', the 'harassed and oppressed inhabitants' not wishing to see another 'German [film] as long as they live'. Entertainment provided for their 'morale', giving them 'cheer', the liberated peoples 'avid for something other than the aggressive, swashbuckling pictures extolling Nazi deeds and expressing Nazi *kultur*'.[168]

As well as providing for the needs of European audiences, film producers were convinced that the medium could bridge the divide between peace and war, softening the heightened emotions brought on by conflict and acting as an agent of peace as Allied triumph moved closer. Sensing the approach of victory, *The Cinema* predicted the 'turning point in democracy's war against the murderous treachery of dictatorship', congratulating the British film industry on their determination to stand 'the supreme test of carrying on under fire with the unflinching steadfastness that characterises the British people'. However, 'having so well solved the trying problem of war', it would now have to 'turn confidently to the more pleasant problems of peace'.[169] It was the cinema's role, as Charles W. Korner, Vice-President and General Manager of RKO Pictures, observed, to assume the 'front rank in keeping the world peaceful and happy so that the sacrifices will not have been made in vain'.[170] Whereas in Germany the occupying forces experienced problems in prosecuting those who used film as a weapon of war, in Britain debates centred on the transformation of that weapon in peacetime, focusing on its ability to heal division and its potential to unite the peoples of Europe. Studios recognized that the 'screen has a deeper duty to mankind'. As Jack Cohn, Vice President of Columbia Pictures, commented:

> the peace to come will find scars that will take a long time to heal. Men trained to hate will find it difficult to readjust their mental processes so that they are able to think in terms of justice, amity and brotherly love. It is to the task of helping to bring about this psychological readjustment that the motion picture industry should devote at least part of its efforts in the post-war period to come.[171]

Film was to 'assist in the improvement in human relationships',[172] the director Anthony Asquith urging his colleagues to embrace a new, international humanity and produce 'films that extol those precious qualities of mercy and human kindness'.[173] Although the post-war film developed a focus on the nation in the longer term emerging out of war propaganda which sought to use the construct of a shared, collective national identity to unify the population, film-makers looking toward the post-war world evoked a novel sense of internationalism in their plans for post-1945 production. It would be the responsibility of film, suggested David E. Rose, Managing Director of Paramount, to '"introduce" nations, one to the other; to show how each other lives – their expression of national life, methods of education and outlook'. 'Film consciousness', he forwarded, was 'a universal characteristic. From the shack in Africa to the cathedrals of entertainment in London and New York, peoples throughout the world can receive simultaneously the same messages of good will through the medium of the screen'.[174] Moreover, the Chairman of the Board of Directors at Paramount Pictures felt that film could meet the 'crying need throughout the world today for understanding, both among peoples and between peoples'. Now, propaganda could be used to create 'bonds of sympathy'.[175]

In the longer term, there was a growing feeling within the industry that it needed to reinvent itself for the challenges of the post-war era. War was no longer expected to provide the focal point for productions. Many film producers recognized that Britain's 'social world will be completely different and this obviously means that kinema [sic] audiences will be of a new character'. Soon the end of the war would be upon the studios, and their pictures would be screened to a 'people reacting to the security of peace..., building homes and tasting once again the happiness of family life'.[176] It was in this changing environment that the studios began to reshape their role. Reflecting upon the experience of conflict, Twentieth Century Fox urged the industry to 'focus and channelise the world's thinking if we are to be worthy of our trust and if we are to contribute our share toward making this a better and more decent world'.[177] Film centred on the twin issues of progress and reconstruction in order to shape its post-war identity.[178] Naturally, the industry itself, suffering under the pressures of wartime shortages and the effects of bomb damage, required its own form of reconstruction.[179] However, film's role in terms of progress did not purely confine itself to the industry. It was to reflect the visions of the post-war world in a broader sense, relating to the hopes of the nation and of the wider world. The film studios saw cinema's new peacetime role in terms of a 'community asset', asserting its 'importance ... both as an entertainment and as a community centre', its task in this respect 'receiving full recognition in municipal schemes of post-war rehabilitation'.[180] Turning his attention to the future, Asquith, acting in his role as President of the Association of Cine-Technicians, asked why 'if films can teach us to be good soldiers ... should they not be equally capable of teaching us to be good citizens?' Extending the analogy further, he implored the Government to use this filmic army 'whose weapons need not be scrapped but ... turned in the twinkling of an eye from swords to plough shares'.[181] Even George Formby could be mobilized in peace as well as war, *Kinematograph Weekly* reporting in May 1944 that his next production was to have a 'post-war planning theme'.[182]

The central role of the filmic medium which seemed to be emerging from the discussions of the latter years of the war was educational, working in tandem with political developments that resulted in the Butler Act of 1944. War brought an increasing desire by some elements of the film industry to move away from the image of cinema as a 'glorified peep-show' and toward a higher purpose, to reflect the 'brave new world'. It was time to end the extant 'bitter prejudice against education, culture and taste', argued screenwriter and producer Anatole de Grunwald, and give the public something other than 'hokum..., sob-stuff and crude sex appeal'.[183] The screen now had to have a social conscience, a 'duty to provoke thought',[184] and become a 'social force',[185] a role it had started to assume during the war, resulting in increased credibility for film as an educational tool. With the effects of war on film production, educational films had been passed over for more propagandistic pieces, with the outcome that many productions of this nature had become scarce and out of date.[186] The industry began to realize that there was a 'need for more ... work in education',[187] not just as a 'teaching aid but also as an art'.[188] Such a focus on the educational value of film reflected the wider socio-political discussions on the nature of the state in the post-war era, becoming an instrument at the disposal of Government for the process of reconstruction.[189] Moreover, it became an acceptable means of approaching the post-war use of propaganda in a more realistic way than in 1918. Instead of defining the phenomenon as a weapon of war and dismantling the propaganda machinery, profitable use could be made of persuasive output in an educational environment. Grierson, who was to head the post-war reincarnation of the MoI, the Central Office of Information,[190] observed that in 'recognising the deeper levels of understanding and exposition into which information in a democracy must inevitably reach, it is possible to appreciate that even the once-haunted concept of propaganda may have a democratic interpretation, and that its democratic interpretation makes propaganda and education one'.[191] In a reconfigured format, media became conduits for 'new education and waiting instruments of an enlivened democracy',[192] transforming seamlessly from a weapon of war into a mechanism for the communication of peace. Nowhere was this idea more expressly conveyed than in the proposal to hand the 16mm projectors used by the forces over to schools in 1945.[193]

Although war strained the mechanics of production, the industry suffering from the call-up, the restriction of studio space and a shortage in materials,[194] film-makers realized that the post-war world would offer new possibilities for film's continued expansion, its reinvention partly conditioned by having to confront the threat posed by the new medium of television.[195] Pronouncing on the future direction of the film industry, the trade press began to carve out new identities for the cinema, effectively smoothing the passage between war and post-war worlds whilst maintaining the centrality of film to the needs and desires of the nation. That film was conceived of as a medium which could satisfy the requirements of both peace and war suggests its flexibility as a form of communication and the overt appeal of the cinema, as well as its rapid evolution: from 1941 film was being discussed as a means to heal the divisions created by conflict, herald the new age of reconstruction, educate, provide entertainment to the liberated peoples of Europe, *and* offer hope of international reconciliation.

At the forefront of these developments was the documentarist. Reflecting the nature of post-war social problems was a natural extension of the documentary form, emerging from the pre-war foundation of the movement. In its formative years, the documentary move-ment sought to 'throw a light into the dark corners of human endeavour, to bring alive the factual drama of communications and of public services, [...promoting] understanding on topical problems of [the] every day'.[196] Prior to the outbreak of war, the documentary sought to 'throw much of its weight into the struggle for social equality and a more equitable distribution of the benefits of civilized life. It was able to produce films which analysed the evils of bad housing, malnutrition, unemployment and bad education. It was concerned not only to expose these evils but to point the way to their redress'.[197] War temporarily refocused the work of the movement, but ultimately provided it with some of its most compelling material, the drama of conflict lending itself to more realistic treatments of extraordinary events. The trade began to recognize the significance of their film work, *Kinematograph Weekly* noting that 'almost every subject they touch upon represents something of our national existence which is now at stake'.[198] Although the early conflicts with the MoI were internally divisive,[199] the aims of both documentary and the overt propaganda objectives of the Ministry were ultimately complementary. In its self-professed *raison d'être*, the documentary movement claimed 'a special expertise in the use of films for propaganda and informational purposes ... working to a thesis of public enlightenment', which fitted exceptionally well with both the needs of Government and the MoI's concept of propaganda for democracy, one which was proclaimed to be innately tied to information, education and 'truth'. However, although the war gave the movement a higher profile in the industry and in the wider public, certain elements within the documentary school longed to return to its deeper objectives. Peace gave the movement an opportunity to reconnect to its roots and to each other.[200]

The documentarists thrived on the idea of 'forward-looking propaganda themes'[201] and, in this respect, sought to make 'peace exciting'.[202] The reconstruction of the post-war world and the social issues associated with it allowed the movement to revisit its original objectives of bringing societal problems to the fore and re-engage with the more activist aspects of their agenda. Although their images of war were ultimately to form the backbone of their legacy, it was the confrontation of the transition from war to peace and the rebuilding of national and world societies which were of contemporary interest to the film-makers themselves. Criticizing American productions such as *Mrs Miniver* and *This Above All* (Anatole Litvak, 1942), *Documentary News Letter* urged film-makers to take a more radical stance, not to present images 'intended to satisfy a public appetite for progress without raising the revolutionary manifestations of progress'. Such films, they argued, 'seek to persuade us that simply by beating the Axis we shall attain a comfortable, kindly world which will make no more demands upon us than can be satisfied by regular attendance at church, the occasional perusal of a book of patriotic questions and a belief in Father Christmas'. This was not a time for 'blind faith' but for 'thinking'. As the war drew to a close, the documentarists advocated that film-makers 'remember the miseries, frustrations and inept leadership of the pre-war years' and demanded that the Government clarify its position in relation to the 'new order..., [reminding] us that the horrors of peace can equal and even exceed in their apparent hopelessness the horrors of war'.[203] Film was now to become the central driver of change, holding the Government to account for social promises made during the course of the war and shedding light on the problems of reconstruction, this purpose ultimately resurrecting the original documentary idea. The movement wanted to see the 'brass tacks' and prevent the people from being led away into a 'cloud-cuckoo-land of pious social aspiration'.[204] In short, it wanted to see the realization of meaningful social and economic change. As Grierson noted, 'these changing times of ours do not represent ordinary changes. There are periods in history when the whole basis of truth is re-examined and when the operative philosophies are revolutionised and renewed. This is one of them'.[205]

It was from this position that documentary 'concerned itself not only with mobilization for war but also with mobilization for the world beyond war'.[206] And in some ways the two objectives combined; a promising vision of the future could potentially 'infuse [the population] with a fresh enthusiasm for their country, [stimulate and liven up] their pride', providing 'both an antidote to war-weariness and a stimulus to effort'.[207] However, the MoI's campaign to elucidate Britain's war aims and to buoy morale through a discussion of the post-war world met with some significant opposition, most notably from the Prime Minister. Despite a desire by the Ministry to engage at the very least with the developing popular interest in reconstruction, Churchill refused 'to make a clear statement on war aims'. Harold Nicolson, Parliamentary Secretary to the MoI, was frustrated by the Prime Minister's insistence that 'precise aims would be compromising, whereas vague principles would disappoint'.[208] Churchill remained consistent in this view. A memorandum of January 1943 instructed Ministers to avoid raising

> false hopes as was done last time by speeches about 'Homes for Heroes' etc. The broad masses of the people face the hardships of life undaunted but they are liable to get very angry if they feel they have been gulled or cheated... It is for this reason of not wishing to deceive the people by false hopes and airy visions of Utopia and Eldorado that I have refrained so far from making promises about the future.[209]

Although Churchill's opinions were clear, the Ministry, from time to time, felt compelled to respond to popular desires for a discussion of the peace, giving support, for example, to a series of BBC broadcasts on the issue in April 1941, although their eventual release was postponed indefinitely due to the opposition of the Prime Minister.[210] The slightest hint of publicity on the matter was enough to send Churchill into a rage. When Nicolson gave a private talk to the Fabian Society in February 1941 which was subsequently picked up by the New York magazine, *Nation*, and the *Manchester Guardian*, the Prime Minister 'blew up, and sent a stinking note to Duff [Cooper, Minister of Information] asking by what right I was writing about war aims when he himself had deprecated any mention of them'. Such was the anger in Churchill's letter that Nicolson feared that he might lose his job.[211]

The Ministry found itself in a difficult position. It could not issue any propaganda dealing with peacetime aspirations to a public which was desperate to hear it. The popular voice was increasingly formulating its hopes for the post-war era, in terms of the eradication of unemployment, the possibility of better health care and social provision, 'occupational and economic security', the 'levelling' of the classes and 'an equal chance for all children'.[212] Meanwhile, as long as the Prime Minister maintained his strict ban on the articulation of the Government's position, all the MoI could do was collect Home Intelligence reports on the matter. The public clamour for clear promises for the future met with a 'deafening silence'. Even with the publication of the Beveridge Report, the Government went to considerable lengths to suppress publicity.[213] The public became suspicious that the report was little more than hot air, the majority fearing that it would 'either be shelved, mutilated, or whittled away, or else an inferior substitute put forward instead'.[214] Subsequent reforms, such as the Education Act of 1944 and the White Paper on the National Health Service, were viewed by the public as attempts to renege on Beveridge's proposals. The propagandists were in a position where they could do little 'without appearing to be protesting too much about the Government's pure intentions'.[215]

It was in this environment that film-makers, and in particular members of the documentary movement, found themselves giving visual expression to the popular voice in the face of Government, and specifically the Prime Minister's, intransigence. Using their expertise in social issues and joining with other media forces such as the press, they began to put pressure on the Ministry and the Cabinet to engage with public desires and shape the possibilities for Britain's future. As early as June 1941, the documentarists wanted to create 'propaganda campaigns ... based on a forward-looking conception which is prepared here and now for the permanent jettisoning of all the brakes on progress, represented by "bitter greybeards", the mentally stunted reactionaries, and the bloodless bureaucrats who live, of their own free will, in a Hades of paper, tape and rustling typewriters'.[216] To some extent, the Films Division of the MoI managed to respond to this call and circumnavigate wider missives emanating from Number 10, reflecting the potential vagaries of Cabinet Government, particularly within a War Cabinet which did not consistently involve the Minister himself and within a Ministry with overlapping and confused structures. That the Films Division and the documentarists working within them were permitted to raise these otherwise taboo issues suggests that their work was considered by the Government to be of secondary importance to the propaganda campaigns of World War II, a view echoed in some subsequent historical examinations.[217] As a result, the output of the Films Division could more closely relate to public concerns in relation to the peace, drawing on their own training within documentary to offer a social commentary on the 'new order'.

One of the first filmic representations of the desires of the people in relation to the post-war world was the Boulting Brothers' 1941 production *Dawn Guard*, in which two members of the Home Guard, each from a different generation (Percy Walsh and Bernard Miles), discuss the war and their hopes for post-war Britain.[218] Roy Boulting recalled that the aims of the film were closely tied to the memories of pre-war deprivation and depression:

> If the war … was to have any meaning at all, it was going to be fought not to return to the England of the thirties, not to return to the England of mass unemployment, of appeasement, of class division and so on; it was going to be fought and hopefully won on the basis that the inequalities, the disparities and the poverty and the suffering was going to be ameliorated, if not eliminated entirely, at least, the lot of the ordinary man or woman was going to be improved. Very ingenious, very idealistic, deeply felt and that is the film we made.[219]

In the Boultings' film, it is the younger of the two guardsmen who articulates his vision of the future, drawing on extant discourses of unity and the 'people's war' to inform his commentary:

> We made a fine big war effort. Well, when it's all over we've got to see to it that we make a fine big peace effort. There's no two ways about it. Can't go back now we've made a start… Look at that Dunkirk. Wasn't no unemployed there. Everyman had a job to do and he done it. That's what we gotta see they 'ave in peacetime – a job. There'll be work enough when this lot's over. Building up something new and better 'an what's been destroyed. There mustn't be no more chaps 'anging around for work what don't come. No more slums neither. No more dirty filthy back streets and no more 'alf starved kids with no room to play in.

The film received mixed reviews. It was poorly received in Scotland due to its failure to include the 'British' in its vision of the 'people's war'.[220] Scottish audiences feared that 'someone is trying to put something over on them [through] … insincere propaganda', preferring more solid statements on intent rather than vague and idealistic sentiments.[221] However, as Petley has observed, 'the message of [*Dawn Guard*] could hardly be clearer: the values of "old" and "new", rural and urban England need to be forged together in social unity if the people's peace is to succeed'.[222] Indeed, the film responded to popular opinion of the same period, Home Intelligence reporting in January, the same month that *Dawn Guard* enjoyed its public premiere, that trends in relation to peace aims revealed 'an absence of thought along conventional party lines'. Instead, 'the main cleavage is not between class and class, but between the young and old… On the home front, it is hoped that the extremes of wealth and poverty will be swept away, and that there will be a greater degree of social security for all'.[223] Roy Boulting's sentiments regarding his 1941 film neatly underline Geoff Eley's observation that the vision of the 'people's war' and post-war reconstruction were inextricably linked to

> a complex of democratic traditions stressing decency, liberalism, and the importance of everyone pulling together, in a way that honoured the value and values of ordinary working people. More elaborately, it evoked images of the Depression and its social misery, which a broad consensus believed should never be repeated, and here the patriotic

comradeship of war was reworked into a social democratic narrative of suffering and social justice.[224]

It was this that the documentarists wanted to convey in their short film work, focusing on 'the desires, so often vague and unformulated, of ordinary people'.[225]

Dawn Guard laid the foundations of later Ministry productions, which fused conceptions of the collective spirit and ideas of post-war reconstruction, giving form to the trends in public opinion beginning to emerge from late 1941. *Post 23* (Ralph Bond), a film about an air-raid warden station released in early 1942, provides a further example of how discourses relating to the 'people's war' became conflated with ideas on the future of Britain, extending the concept of wartime mobilization into the post-war era. Communities, argued the film, had been forged as a result of the exigencies of conflict, which could not and should not disintegrate once hostilities ceased. As one warden comments, '*Funny how things change. You know, before the war I hardly knew a soul in this neighbourhood… Now, well, I feel I know every household, every family in the area. I feel I belong to this neighbourhood, these people*'. Home Intelligence began to receive reports which implied that the public had begun to think in similar terms, a summary of trends in public opinion in the Midlands in April–May 1942 reporting that the public had been engaging in 'a certain amount of "self-criticism" both as regards individuals and as a nation'. Publicity given to the plight of working mothers, and problems in the mining industry, as well as to achievements in the agricultural sector, stimulated the mass to consider the ignominy of the past and the potential of the future: people now had a sense of 'what can be done when [the population is] put to it'. The report added that 'ARP activities have brought together people living in the same area and awakened in them (very slightly) some idea of local co-operation … [and offered] greater opportunities for an exchange of views'.[226] Moreover, Home Intelligence noted that war-weariness was beginning to take its toll, the public 'suffering from feelings of depression, frustration and disinterestedness'. However, the report concluded, 'because of continued indifference, frustration and reverses, and together with the self-criticism, the public is ripe for new ideas that are put to them in an enthusiastic way and promise well for the future'.[227]

This was ultimately the function of the short film *Post 23*, which suggested that individuals, who had previously felt alone in an atomized state, learnt that they had a role to play in a post-war community, drawing on their wartime experiences to enable them to participate in the rebuilding of the nation and take on the burden of collective responsibility for the future of Britain. Here the physical destruction of war is turned into a positive opportunity:

- I've been thinking about the gaps between the houses. What comes down has to go up again, you know.
- Not like it used to be I 'ope. Not all those slums and tenements.
- That's just the point. We've got to see that the job's done decently this time… If we can work together now to look after the lives of the people here, I don't see why we

couldn't work together afterwards to clean up the mess and help build a better world in which these things can't happen.

– I'll second that. It's people like us that've been doing the work of the war and it's people like us that're gonna do the work of the peace.

The desire for a more active citizenship as expressed here, the promotion of which was one of the central foci of the documentary movement, was a theme reiterated in the 1943 short film *Words and Actions* (Max Anderson), which delineated Government and citizens' power to craft the prospects for post-war Britain. Voicing the questions coming to dominate popular discourses, the narrator informed audiences that '*every man and woman*' was now

> taking an active part in the smaller … things and in the wider issues. The war will be won by ordinary people tackling all the problems and overcoming them. Peace will bring even more problems. What will it be like to work in Britain? [shot focuses on copy of the Beveridge Report] What will living conditions be like? What sort of social services will we have? These questions will be decided by people who think things out for themselves, who think things out and go all out to get it. These are the people who will make victory and make it a stepping stone to a worthy peace.

Whilst some films such as Ronald Riley's 1943 short for the Army Bureau of Current Affairs appealed to returning soldiers to form the backbone of the 'new order', others looked increasingly to the next generation to fulfil the nation's hope and dreams. Jennings' 1945 production *A Diary for Timothy* embodied this sentiment. A record of the final years of the war, the film detailed the aspirations of the 'people's army', serving as an *aide-mémoire* to Timothy's generation, born as the conflict drew to a close. Jennings characterized the central aim of the film as representing 'the turn-over from war to peace – in the film we present Tim to the world and the world to Tim'. It was not to be 'a war picture but a background behind a baby's life', reflecting the existences of 'some of the people in this Island … who in war and peace are working for Timothy without either knowing it', creating a point of identification with the individual and their future.[228] The film, as the producer Basil Wright recalled, was 'literally a diary, not only of the life of the baby and of the arbitrarily selected real characters, such as the locomotive driver, the wounded air pilot and the equally damaged coalminer, but also of what, unpredictably day by day, was happening during the last months of the European war'.[229] As such, questions could not be directly answered, the director choosing instead merely to reflect the concerns of the average man, one individual in the film observing, '*I was sitting thinking about the past. The past war, the unemployment, broken homes, scattered families. And then I thought that has all this really got to happen again?*' Until the final sequence in the film, Timothy plays a passive role: he is a 'spectator', according to Jennings.[230] Turning to the citizens of the future, represented by Timothy, Michael Redgrave, reading the words of E. M. Forster, activates the baby as a future citizen, asking:

> Up to now, we've done the talking. But before long, you'll sit up and take notice. And what are you going to say about it and what are you going to do?... Are you going to have greed for money or power, ousting decency from the world as they have in the past? Or are you going to make the world a different place, you and the other babies?

The result was, according to Wright, 'a rather cosy, liberal, middle-class statement about some aspects of the war',[231] although some sequences shot in the Rhondda valley were directly intended to represent a 'truly socialist community'.[232] 'The approach to the staging and direction of individual episodes' not only directly countered Grierson's original documentary idea and pointed to the different approaches within the movement with regard to 'realism', but also resulted in a scenario which was 'not particularly warm'. Indeed, concluded Wright, 'compared with *Fires were Started* and *Listen to Britain*, it is cerebral' but nonetheless 'communicates an emotional immediacy'.[233]

Although some in the MoI felt that *A Diary for Timothy* was 'nonsense' and 'a waste of public money',[234] Beddington was quick to realize that Jennings' rather less overt approach suited Ministry sensibilities over the thorny issue of peace aims. Both the active and the passive socialist approach endorsed by the Ministry and the services' short films should not be misinterpreted. As McLaine noted, 'it would be wrong to conclude ... that ... [the] half-hearted aspirations [espoused within Ministry memoranda] issued from socialist conviction ... they had little affinity with socialism, as defined in the classical Marxist sense. What was wanted, in fact, was a half-way house to socialism in which most people would be content to reside'.[235] The seeds of this desire for the Ministry to remain 'balanced' can be seen in the early decisions of its personnel department, who in March 1940 warned against the over-employment of 'persons of left-wing tendencies'. The then Minister of Information, Sir John Reith, whilst accepting that 'the greater proportion of persons likely to be of use to the Ministry in a creative capacity would be of a left wing tendency, ... thought it necessary to pay some attention to public opinion', which had apparently indicated some discomfort with the 'left-wing bias' of the MoI. Reith instructed his officers to 'recruit accordingly'.[236]

Nevertheless, whereas the Ministry's vision of socialism and activism was more restrained, the same could not be said for some documentarists. The most revolutionary of the films produced in the final years of the war was *Land of Promise*, directed by Paul Rotha, which called for the re-mobilization of the 'people's army' in the nation's new war against the problems of peace. *Land of Promise* directly challenged society's elites and the Government to confront social problems and treat them in the same way as the battle to defeat Nazism:

> What about this war against ill health and unhappiness? This is another war for freedom. And don't let's have anyone getting up and saying that's different. It isn't. But its battlefields are our thickly crowded areas and the slums are its front line... Come on then, you leaders! Come on, where are you? Architects, doctors, planners, engineers, social workers – step out into the light!... Are you going to use your right or will you shut your eyes and let yourselves and us be led into one crisis after another, into worse depression, worse poverty, worse slums, worse sickness? Come on! Make up your minds!

If you lose this chance, it may never come again. There are millions of us, you and me. We are the British people! No power on earth can stop us once we've the will to win!

Rotha's film was not, unsurprisingly, commissioned by the MoI, but by the Gas Board. Even the new Labour government, elected in the landslide victory of 1945, did not wish to be associated with such radical approaches to social problems. *Land of Promise*, the director recalled, 'probably the most socially progressive film to be made [in] Britain about the problems of planning and housing', was 'offered free to the new Minister of Health in 1945... The film was rejected', Rotha complained, 'because it was "thought" that an actual rent-strike march in the East End shown in the film "had been Communist inspired"'.[237] *Land of Promise,* he stormed, 'was uncomfortable... Times had changed. No longer did the Labour people want films to expose bad housing conditions... They wanted films to instruct local authorities how to build pre-fabs. The emphasis had passed from attack to construction'.[238]

Moreover, Rotha realized that the new regime was not going to support the idea that the documentary should take its place in 'the world community of nations'.[239] Rotha's 1943 production *World of Plenty* sought to extend the principles of home post-war planning to the wider world. Sir John Orr, narrating the film, informed audiences:

Tell me, what are we fighting for if not something revolutionary? What do people like you and me hope to get out of this war if not a better world? The empty slogans 'A World Safe for Democracy', 'A Land fit for heroes' – these mean nothing! Plain people know what they want. They want security ... and that doesn't mean doles, relief or charity. The common man everywhere demands freedom from want. He demands it not only for himself but for all men. There must be no forgotten people.[240]

Still haunted by the ghost of *Feuertaufe* in 1945, the film-makers contrasted their film of hope and generosity with the Nazi 'documentaries of intimidation'. British documentarists, argued Rotha, were free to engage with the 'fundamental need of Mankind' – food. Rotha was 'proud to have made this film because it speaks the truth. It shows what *can* be done for the common peoples of all nations. It puts in front of all who see it the goal of a world of plenty – to be won by using science, labour and knowledge for the common good'.[241] The international approach to film, typified by Rotha's 1943 production, was heralded by *Documentary News Letter* as the wave of the future, enabling British film-makers to reject the parochialism of the past and embrace 'a world outside its own back-porch', to move away from 'photographing the moon – our own special British moon – through the bottom of Nat Gubbins' upturned beer mug'. Its editorial opined, 'other countries ... have cultures and traditions of their own of which they are proud. The [Films] Division often seems to assume, not only that everything British is best, but that every country recognises this as a law of creation'.[242] This came a little too close to threatening the basis of Empire. Rotha recalled that 'a great deal of pressure on both sides of the Atlantic was brought to bear to stop *World of Plenty* and [its sequel] *The World is Rich* ... from reaching the public screens'.[243]

Both *Land of Promise* and *World of Plenty* were, according to Rotha's fellow documentarist Basil Wright, 'very, very difficult and [a] dangerous way of making film because it didn't permit any form of escape for the audience. This is why', he continued, 'there was such an attempt to stop some of those films, particularly *World of Plenty*, on the part of various authorities. It was too near the knuckle, because if you ask the audience to answer that sort of question, the answer is going to be very embarrassing to authority'.[244] This explanation was little consolation for Rotha. Bemoaning the fact that the Labour movement 'had no ear for such an imaginative approach to public service and public education', he lambasted their 'rusty outlook'. Documentarists, he confessed, had celebrated the Labour victory, hoping that the new Attlee Government would 'implement an imaginative and purposeful national information service'.[245] It was not to be, and the documentary movement was left 'bitterly disappointed'.[246] Rotha saw this as the beginning of the end for Grierson's 'documentary idea'. From this point, he argued 'British documentary went into its decline from ... a social point of view'.[247]

However, it is not to the documentary shorts, by their very nature sidelined as a form of mainstream culture, to which the historian must look to view the real impact of the movement. As Pronay observed, 'as far as the war effort was concerned, the country could have dispensed with the whole lot without an iota of difference. The real propaganda *war* was carried out in the commercial cinemas..., not in any significant way by the documentary film'.[248] As the war progressed, producers of fictional commercial feature films came to recognize that 'everyday life does not lack drama'.[249] *Documentary News Letter* noted in May 1940: 'Only the documentary makers have so far looked habitually beyond the lay figures of screen romance for their characters. It now becomes the task of the fiction film producer to people his world, not with synthetic aristocrats, outrageous eccentrics and the music-hall's conception of the proletariat, but with the inhabitants of this country'.[250] In this respect, the studios increasingly looked to the documentary style for inspiration. Basil Wright recalled that 'it was not unnatural for the feature-film makers to turn in [the documentarists] direction ... nearly all producers, willingly or unwillingly kept a close eye on documentary and, in particular, the Crown Film Unit'.[251] It was this marriage between the fictional feature and the documentary style which ultimately gave popular expression to the concepts forwarded by short film productions during the period 1939–45, defining their legacy and most significant contribution to the war effort.

The feature film, in many ways, was the perfect vehicle for representing the people. It was, after all, *their* medium and had a far better chance of appealing to the masses than the short film: as Mass-Observation noted, producers of short films and documentary were perceived to be 'in a world of their own'.[252] Although some film-makers believed that feature and non-fiction films were entirely distinct in their aim and purpose,[253] studio productions in the latter half of the war demonstrated that the feature film could reflect the public perception of 'real life' as effectively as the documentary,[254] capitalizing on Grierson's idea that in order to 'persuade, we have to reveal; and we have to reveal in terms of reality'.[255] Grierson also recognized that 'the ordinary affairs of people's lives are more dramatic and more vital than all the false excitements you can muster'. Make 'war films', he instructed Allied film-makers, 'but more films too about the everyday life, the values and the ideals which make life worth living'.[256] As Dilys Powell observed, demand grew for more 'imaginative interpretations of everyday life'. The public had, he identified, multiple desires, demanding of their film programme a variety of genres. The war, argued Powell, created an environment in which serious commentaries could comfortably sit alongside 'the farce, the musical, the banal screen fairy-tale'. Where the documentary and fiction were merged, the result was even more powerful, fusing the escapist needs of the wartime audience with a social message, audiences internalizing the central idea through identification with a series of fictional characters.[257] In this way, propaganda messages could be introduced more subtly, using the 'gilded pill' of popular stars and by creating on-screen environments which the audience either recognized or perceived as escapist.[258] As *Kinematograph Weekly* observed, the strength of British films could be found in the 'authenticity of the actual dramatic happenings of today; the human problems are posed and answered and mirrored by people easy to believe in'. Such representations were 'more than realistic, they were just real'.[259]

Of the more 'down to earth' films produced in the latter years of the war, Launder and Gilliat's productions *Millions Like Us* (1943) and *Waterloo Road* (1945) stand out for their treatment of the problems of the peace.[260] Wright observed that these films, in particular, 'showed the reaction of the so-called "little men", the semi-educated, the tongue-tied with their memories of unemployment, the Means Test, malnutrition – to the crisis of war. It is in these films', he argued, 'that we can most clearly see the reasons why the British people, as soon as the war was over, rejected the Conservatives (including the man who had led them to victory) in favour of men who were less guilty of the neglect, cruelty and incompetence of the ruling administrations between the wars'.[261] Features, as Wright recognized, had begun to involve themselves in the social issues spearheaded by the documentary movement, Launder and Gilliat's 1943 production, *Millions Like Us*, a good example of how the studios sought to draw out the social angle presented in Ministry shorts and the work of documentarists. Indeed, Rotha claimed the initial idea for the film as his own. Recalling an occasion when Beddington called a meeting of the 'ideas committee' involving both documentary and commercial film-makers in 1942, a move which, according to Rotha, 'broke down the barrier which had existed between feature and documentary', the producer contended that his film *Night Shift* (Jack Chambers, 1942) had been the inspiration for *Millions Like Us*, which was screened one evening to the committee members.[262] Here was an example, argued Wright, of two feature producers 'who'd really dived headfirst into the documentary conception and come up with this very simple ... but ... very moving, very beautiful, very true film'.[263] As Coultass has contended, Launder and Gilliat's production demonstrated that 'it was possible to borrow from the documentary movement and to put onto the screen characters who were at least tolerable approximations to real people'.[264]

The aim of *Millions Like Us* was to inform the wider discourses of the 'people's war', paying particular attention to the redefined roles of women. The press book proudly announced that, in her experience as a factory girl, Celia, the central female protagonist, meets 'every type, rich and poor alike... She quickly makes friends with her roommates; Gwen, a Welsh girl whose wise-cracking remarks hide a kind heart; Annie, who comes from Lancashire; and Jennifer, a rich society girl who finds her changed life difficult'.[265] The film revealed a complex picture of the 'people's war' which was full of tensions and uncertainty, one which was perhaps in tune with audiences' contemporary understanding of national unity. On the one hand, coming from very different backgrounds, the factory girls find companionship in unlikely places, Launder and Gilliat presenting a unified community, working collectively towards the war effort. *Millions Like Us*, in this respect, represented the changing social panorama of Britain, as reflected in the reports of Mass-Observation from August 1945. Their surveys noted that war had transformed social attitudes, bringing 'people into contact with each other who in peacetime would never have met. The whole tendency during the war', they continued, 'has made for the mixing of social classes'. Mirroring the on-screen existence of Celia, one report contended that conflict had altered the 'sociability of some previously repressed types. There are some people who are quite capable of leading a normal social life but are too shy to make the attempt. When war conditions throw them into the companionship of others, these people unfold like a Japanese flower in water'.[266] One Mass-Observation panel member offered comment on a friend:

> When the war broke out, she was timid ... and old-fashioned in her dress... She lived in dreams of becoming a great Prima Donna, and had never earned a penny in her life. When the war began, she joined the NFS, became trim and efficient, earns her own living ... has in fact become a normal human being – and one can say that the war has definitely done her good.[267]

The same could be said for the character of Celia, whose identity was defined by service to her father and sisters, her timid persona increasingly transformed into a confident woman who marries and survives the trauma of losing her new husband and who can pull her weight in a factory. Moreover, her early romanticized dreams of service, alongside the armed forces, which she hoped would put her into contact with a series of dashing young suitors, are quickly transformed into a far better reality. Here, the film offers a comment on the cinema experience itself: do not lay all your hopes in fairy-tales. For although, as Jennifer states in *Millions Like Us*, '*You must escape sometime*', the reality can be just as fulfilling and more exciting.

Whereas Celia's wartime existence, whilst not wholly positive, is uplifting, Jennifer's is rather more disappointing. Jennifer's transformation comes through 'negative' social movement, attempting to come to terms with a new existence in a factory instead of the luxurious lifestyle to which she had become accustomed. As Mass-Observation noted, 'the war has thrown nearly everyone into a new environment, whether the novelty is to do without servants, to drop bombs, to calm frightened old ladies or to have an eggless breakfast. Sudden changes like these act as a challenge which is either overcome so as to lead to a fuller life, or proves too great an obstacle'.[268] Jennifer rises to some challenges, such as coping with factory life, but is unable to surmount the problems created by her class, falling in love with Charlie, the factory foreman. In a poignant comment on the uncertainty of the peace and the true meaning of the 'people's war', Charlie and Jennifer find their class differences, and the social stigma attached to their different identities, too overwhelming. Charlie's realistic vision of the post-war world prevails over Jennifer's rose-tinted aspirations for the future:

Charlie: Ah, we've precious little in common.
Jennifer: Practically nothing.
Charlie: That's nothing to do with it. If that was all, I might take a chance.
Jennifer: Are you thinking of my parents?
Charlie: Partly.
Jennifer: 'Cause I can handle them. Anyway, they'd approve of you.
Charlie: But would I approve of them? I doubt it.
Jennifer: You know, Charlie, when it comes to pride, you're worse than a blue-blooded grandee!
Charlie: P'rhaps I have more to be proud of. The world's made up of two kinds of people. You're one sort and I'm the other. Oh, we're together now there's a war on – we need to be. What's going to happen when it's over? Shall we go on like this or are we going to slide back? That's what I'd like to know! And I'm not marrying you until I'm sure. I'm turning you down without even asking you. D'you understand?

The relationship remains unresolved by the end of the film, the questions posed by Charlie turned back on the audience. Charlie's fears were also reflected in the reports by Mass-Observation in the final years of the war, who noted the 'renewal of hostility between class and class with the coming of peace'. The reality of the supposed 'levelling of classes', which the MoI had claimed had already occurred by October 1941,[269] was exposed by the peace. Citizens feared that the perceived constructed social unity would evaporate with the end of the war, Mass-Observation echoing this sentiment by reporting the views of individuals who thought that 'many people would suddenly realize with some bitterness that the apparent unity with which the war had been pursued by almost all sections of the people would prove the sham that it always was'.[270]

In this sense, *Millions Like Us*, in its tensions and contradictions, could be said to be the contemporary 'mirror of modern life as it may well be so known by many families throughout the land'. *The Cinema* contended that this was 'the secret of the picture's certain appeal'.[271] Audiences applauded Launder and Gilliat's presentation of 'Britain and life as it is', commending the film's 'truth and integrity'.[272] Film-goers felt that the production 'really was true to its title. These were real people, people one knew and liked, not film actors and actresses',[273] a feeling Launder and Gilliat were trying to achieve by drafting in women 'from a Midlands aircraft factory and … a Government training centre in London' as extras.[274] Such characters undoubtedly bolstered the audiences' identification with the plot and the protagonists, one viewer commenting that 'it was like spending an evening with a delightful variety of people and enjoying with them all the humour of everyday life now and in the delicious glimpse of the joys of holidays in the pre-war world', evoking memories of the past to cement the relationship between the filmic individuals and the spectator.[275] In a comment redolent of the Griersonian mission of documentary, one cinema-goer argued that 'films dealing with the everyday occurrences of life in wartime … make the significance of our everyday lives more vivid'. Praising the film-makers for avoiding 'unmitigated propaganda', viewers were appreciative of the fact that 'no attempt [was] made to give the film a happy-ending, which again seems more realistic'.[276]

However, as Poole notes, 'films which reconstructed … boredom and banality … did less than average business'.[277] Although the realism cinema of the final years of the war received critical acclaim and arguably tapped into the public's understanding of the class system and their fears for the post-war order, it did not necessarily fulfil the needs and desires of British cinema audiences. Rather than the expected euphoria on the declaration of peace, Mass-Observation reported in August 1945 that 57 per cent of those questioned were experiencing feelings of 'depression', whilst only 39 per cent felt 'cheerful'. Many did not appreciate the distinction between peace and war, fearing the problems that war had created: 'insecurity on an enormous scale, famine, disease and death'. On the declaration of the end of the war, many expected 'a sudden change for the better', a majority feeling 'jaded' when it did not arrive. People began to get the sense that 'the peace problems [would be] as great as the war ones'. Mass-Observation reported, '"The killing's stopped but everything else will be as bad or worse" is the average opinion. One gets the feeling that people are lost and perplexed, astray in a dark forest'.[278] In this environment, it is unlikely that audiences wanted to be reminded of their uncertain future, preferring instead to lose themselves in the magic of the cinema, Poole pointing to the success of comedies and glossy melodramas which became the vehicles for escapism in the final years of the war.[279] For whilst cinematic methods had adapted to public desires for realistic depictions of the contemporary on screen, public desires themselves were undergoing a process of change driven by war-weariness and the aspiration of audiences to escape the real using the cinema as a gateway to the fantastic. By the end of 1942, as the fortunes of war began to shift and its toll demanded that film move towards more escapist cinema, it was no longer enough for film-makers to assume that identification *only* took place where audiences were confronted with themselves, but that a more powerful identification was felt when the ordinary was placed within the extraordinary, affirming the cinema's place as a 'dream palace', which goes some way to explaining the enduring popularity of the Hollywood musical or the Gainsborough melodrama.

Both Britain and Germany, then, used film as a means to give a visual identity to the end of World War II and to the uncertainty of the post-war world their citizens would have to face. The cinema was a means through which both nations sought to define their legacies, their aspirations and their hopes for the future world, as well as a means of reviewing the past conflict, making sense of the drama and the losses. In Britain and Germany, film in 1945 was a vehicle for coming to terms with an uneasy past. In Britain, the cinema confronted the impact of the 1930s, the depression, the failure to address social problems and deprivation, and in Germany the screen's role in dealing with the Nazi era was only just beginning to be realized, starting its journey on the long road to its own *Vergangenheitsbewältigung*. Both nations used film to reverse their reactions to the Great War: in Britain, by dealing with the consequences of years of social neglect and heading towards a meaningful realization of a land fit for heroes, a 'new Jerusalem'; in Germany, by recognizing the environment in which extremism could grow and painfully reviewing its consequences. German and British cinema emerged from the war with two distinctive national cinemas, each born of their wartime experience. British cinema embraced a new realism, whilst simultaneously delving deeper into the myth of the 'people's war', the Blitz and the victory of 1945,[280] whilst German cinema in the post-war era frequently became a means of exploring the past and facing it head on, German film-makers engaging in a process of 'self-reflection' in the aftermath of defeat.[281]

EPILOGUE

As the war drew to a close and as Goebbels sat in his bunker under the *Reichskanzlei*, the RMVP finally fulfilled one last objective: Nazi film filled the screens of London cinemas. From comedies and musicals such as *Hallo Janine* (Carl Boese, 1939), *Frau Luna* and *Wir tanzen um die Welt* (Karl Anton, 1939), to popular dramas, *Auf Wiedersehen Fransiska!*, *Die Reise nach Tilsit* (Veit Harlan, 1939), to the banned production of *Titanic*, even the most propagandistic and overtly political productions of the Reich were shown, many of which had a distinctly anti-British flavour, such as the notorious *Feuertaufe*, *Ohm Krüger*, and *Der Fuchs von Glenarvon*. The context was somewhat different from that desired by the Reich Minister for Popular Enlightenment and Propaganda. His productions were now 'Films in Prize', the spoils of war. The victors sat in numerous locations in London including the MoI cinema in Malet Street, the Curzon and the War Office Cinema, poring over the filmic record of the National Socialist regime.[282] They were not admiring the work of the Nazi studios, rather deciding their fate. The Allies were now faced with the task of finding an acceptable use for the products of the Nazi 'dream factory' and defining their legacy for the German people.

NOTES

1. BArch R55/879, Memorandum to the Reichsminister (Goebbels), 'Ufa Jubilaum', January 1943.
2. K. Kreimeier, *The Ufa Story*, p. 322.
3. Wiener Library cuttings collection, 101c. German Home Service Broadcast, via Frankfurt, 4 March 1943 (18:30).
4. Ibid.

5. Goebbels' speech reported in *Hamburger Fremdenblatt*, 6 March 1943. Wiener Library cuttings collection, 101c.

6. Wiener Library cuttings collection, 101c. German Home Service Broadcast, via Frankfurt, 4 March 1943 (18:30).

7. BArch R55/879, Memorandum to the Reichsminister (Goebbels), 'Ufa Jubilaum', January 1943.

8. BArch R55/879, Memorandum to the Reichsminister, 'Ehrung zum Ufa Jubilaum', 4 February 1943.

9. BArch R55/879, 'Kopfbogen Minister', 16 February 1943.

10. Ibid. Goebbels also mentioned this in his speech: 'The seriousness of the present situation, however, precludes a celebration on a large scale. Nevertheless, the Führer has not refrained from bestowing distinctions on a few men whose national services to the German cinema will have an effect on periods to come': Wiener Library cuttings collection, 101c. German Home Service Broadcast, via Frankfurt, 4 March 1943 (18:30).

11. BArch R55/879, 'Vorschlag für die Verleihung des Titels Professor', Reichsminister für Volksaufklärung und Propaganda, 16 February 1943.

12. BArch R55/879, Goebbels' speech to mark the 25th anniversary of Ufa, 4 March 1943. Reproduced in *Hamburger Fremdenblatt*, 6 March 1943. Wiener Library cuttings collection, 101c, and *Film-Kurier*, 5 March 1943.

13. See for example, BArch R55/601, *Tätigkeitsbericht*, 19 December 1944.

14. SDK Berlin, *Münchhausen*, Rolf Marben, 'Märchenwelt im *Münchhausen*', clippings collection.

15. SDK Berlin, *Münchhausen*, *Leipziger Neueste Nachrichten*, 24 July 1943.

16. SDK Berlin, *Münchhausen*, Rolf Marben, 'Märchenwelt im *Münchhausen*', clippings collection.

17. SDK Berlin, *Münchhausen*, report on the gala opening of von Baky's film, clippings collection.

18. SDK Berlin, *Münchhausen*, Ilse Urbach, 'Zwei Jubiläumsfilme der Ufa. *Münchhausen* und *Damals*', *Das Reich*, 14 March 1943.

19. SDK Berlin, *Münchhausen*, Werner Fiedler in *Deutsche Allgemeine Zeitung*, 5 March 1943.

20. IWMD, Goebbels' Diaries, unpublished fragments. EDS 250 EAP. 21-g-16/5c. AL 1904/2. 13 February 1942, pp. 20–1.

21. Goebbels diary entry, 27 February 1942. E. Fröhlich (ed.), *Die Tagebücher von Joseph Goebbels: Teil II Diktate 1941–1945*, vol. 3, p. 377.

22. See for example, BArch R55/601, *Tätigkeitsbericht*, 19 December 1944. This was reported to have caused a problem in some instances. The SD in Leipzig reported that women, in particular those with sons at the Front, wanted the newsreel to be shown always at the beginning of the film programme. Their viewing of the newsreel was consistently disturbed by individuals leaving the theatre. See, IWM FDC Unidentified and uncatalogued box of materials. SD report of the *Unterabschnitt-Leipzig*, WS 572, III C3, 'Film', WS 572, 26 August 1941.

23. See for example, BArch R56 VI/30, Reichsfilmkammer *Rundschreiben*, no. 95/42, S. no. 98/42: to the Central and Affiliated Member Firms, 'Freivorstellung der deutschen Filmtheater für Verwundete', 3 August 1942; Reichsfilmintendant, *Rundschreiben* No. 1/4943, S No. 1/1943, 'Winterhilfswerk 1942–1943', 4 January 1943.

24. BArch R56VI/30, Reichsfilmintendant, *Rundschreiben*, no. 1/4943, S. no. 1/1943, 'Winterhilfswerk 1942–1943', 4 January 1943.

25. SDK Berlin, *Münchhausen*, '*Münchhausen* für Verwundeten', *Film-Kurier*, 6 March 1943.

26. K. Kreimeier, *The Ufa Story*, p. 323.

27. *Münchhausen*, Ufa-Magazin No. 19, Deutsches Historisches Museum (1992).

28. TNA PRO AIR 24/264. To HQ in Groups from HO BC. 'Battle of Berlin'. BC/S. 30329/Intl. Assessment No. 20 prepared by Air Staff Intelligence, HDc, 1944.

29. Goebbels diary entry, 22 August 1941. E. Fröhlich (ed.), *Die Tagebücher von Joseph Goebbels: Teil II Diktate 1941–1945*, vol. 1, p. 292.

30. BArch R55/656, Minutes of meeting between Hinkel and Goebbels, 29 July 1944.

31. BArch R56I/110, Memorandum from Hinkel, 21 July 1944. For more details on cost-cutting measures in the film industry as a result of the war, see J. Fox, *Filming Women*, pp. 73–6.

32. Goebbels diary entry, 9 January 1942. E. Fröhlich (ed.), *Die Tagebücher von Joseph Goebbels: Teil II Diktate 1941–1945*, vol. 3, p. 200.

33. BArch R 56VI/30, Fachgruppe Inländische Filmvertrieb, *Rundschreiben*, no. 65/42, S. no. 65/45, 30 April 1942.

34. BArch R55/663, Leiter Film/Reichsfilmintendant, to Reichsminister, 'Wiederanlauf nationaler Filme', 15 November 1944.

35. BArch R 109 II/29. Cited in H. Theuerkauf, *Goebbels' Filmerbe. Das Geschäft mit unveröffentlichten Ufa-Firmen* (Ullstein, Berlin, 1998), p. 29.

36. BArch Wolfgang Liebeneiner, *Alle müssen zur Stelle sein!*, 1944.

37. BArch R56 I/110, Hans Hinkel, *Kampf bis zum Endsieg!*, 1944.

38. BArch R56VI/30, Reichsfilmkammer, *Rundschreiben*, no. 71/42, S. No. 71/42, 22 May 1942.

39. BArch R56VI/110, 'Kunst unter Bombenterror', December 1943.

40. BArch R109II, Ufa Minutes, No 1562, 31 March 1944.

41. BArch R109II, Ufa Minutes, No. 1561, 15 March 1944.

42. BArch R55/663, Leiter F.i.V. Bearbeiter den ORR Dr Bacmeister to the Reichsminister, Berlin, 24 May 1944.

43. BArch R55/663, 'Bombenschäden auf der Filmsektor', *Reichsfilmintendant* to the *Reichsminister*, 7 February 1945.

44. See, for example, the *Aktennotiz*, 6 December 1944 reproduced in *Unter den Brücken*, Ufa-Magazin no. 21, Deutsches Historisches Museum (1992). See also the commentary of director Oscar Fritz Schuh on the filming of *Ein toller Tag* in H. Theuerkauf, *Goebbels' Filmerbe*, p. 37.

45. O. Tschechowa, *Mein Uhren gehen anders* (Munich, 1973), p. 195. Cited in M. Krützen, *Hans Albers. Eine deutsche Karriere* (Quadrige, Berlin, 1995), p. 274.

46. All information here from K. Kreimeier, *The Ufa Story*, pp. 339–40.

47. BArch R55/663, from Leiter K.i.V. OKR Schmitt-Halin to the Reich Minister. Berlin, 26 April 1944.

48. 'Berliners Queue for Escape in Cinemas' *Daily Telegraph*, 3 January 1945. Wiener Library cuttings collection, 106e.

49. See for example the report on the attack on Afifa in Tempelhof in December 1944. The attack destroyed over 75 per cent of the mass production capabilities of the business and obliterated much raw film stock and film copies. BArch R55/663, 'Schwere Schäden bei den Aififa-Tempelhof', *Reichsfilmintendant* to the *Reichsminister*, 7 December 1944.

50. BArch R56 I/110, Hans Hinkel, *Kampf bis zum Endsieg!*, 1944.

51. 'Berliners Queue for Escape in Cinemas' *Daily Telegraph*, 3 January 1945. Wiener Library cuttings collection, 106e.

52. Ibid.

53. J. Hembus and C. Bandmann, *Klassiker des deutschen Tonfilms 1930–1960* (Citadel – Filmbücher, Goldmann, Munich, 1980). Cited in K. Kreimeier, *The Ufa Story*, p. 330.

54. K. Kreimeier, *The Ufa Story*, p. 330.

55. *Kolberg* has been the subject of much scholarly attention and, as a result, I have decided to focus my attention on the salient aspects pertaining to the intentions behind the production in relation to the war effort. For a wider analysis of the film itself, see R. Aurich, 'Films als Durchhalteration: *Kolberg* von Veit Harlan', in H.-M. Bock and M. Töteberg (eds), *Das Ufa-Buch. Kunst und Krizen; Stars und Regisseure; Wirtschaft und Politik* (Zweitausendeins, Frankfurt am Main, 1992); D. Culbert, '*Kolberg* (Germany, 1945): The Goebbels Diaries and Poland's Kołobrzeg Today', in J. Whiteclay Chambers II and D. Culbert (eds), *World War II:*

Film and History (Oxford University Press, 1996), pp. 67–77; F. P. Kahlenberg, 'Preußen als Filmsujet'; P. Paret, '*Kolberg* (Germany, 1945): As Historical Film and Historical Document', in J. Whiteclay Chambers II and D. Culbert (eds), *World War II*, pp. 47–66; R. Taylor, *Film Propaganda*, pp. 196–207; D. Welch, *Propaganda and the German Cinema*, pp. 186-98; *Kolberg*, Ufa-Magazin No. 20, Deutsches Historisches Museum (1992) and D. Culbert, *Kolberg: Film, Film Script and Kołobrzeg Today's Historical Journal of Film, Radio and Television*, vol. 14, no. 4 (1994), pp. 449–66.

56. IWMD Goebbels' Diaries, unpublished fragments. EDS 250 EAP. 21-g-16/5c. AL 1904/2. 21 February 1942, p. 17.

57. R. Semmler, *Goebbels. The Man next to Hitler* (Westhouse, London, 1947), p. 194. Diary entry for 17 April 1945.

58. P. Paret, '*Kolberg*, p. 48.

59. Ibid., p. 49.

60. V. Harlan, *Souvenirs*, pp. 258–9.

61. Goebbels diary entry, 7 May 1943. Reproduced in D. Culbert, '*Kolberg*', p. 70.

62. Goebbels diary entry, 18 September 1941. E. Fröhlich (ed.), *Die Tagebücher von Joseph Goebbels: Teil II Diktate 1941–1945*, vol. 1, p. 449.

63. Helmut Sündermann, 'Hart Sein – härter werden', *Der Angriff*, 26 January 1943. Wiener Library cuttings collection, 113a. For more on the German concept of the 'people's war', see 'Mit Siegesmut in den weiteren Kampf' ('Dieser Krieg ist ein Volkskrieg'), *Danziger neueste Nachrichten*. Wiener Library cuttings collection, 101c.

64. RMVP Ministerial Conference minutes, 6 January 1943 in W. Boelcke (ed.), *The Secret Conferences of Dr. Goebbels*, p 314.

65. 'Sein oder Nichtsein', *Der Angriff*, 27 January 1943. Wiener Library cuttings collection, 113a.

66. Goebbels, 'The New Year', reproduced in *Das Reich* (January 1942) and broadcast on the German Home Service on 2 January 1942 at 18:45. Wiener Library cuttings collection, 101c.

67. Goebbels diary entry, 25 May 1943. Reproduced in D. Culbert, '*Kolberg*', p. 70.

68. Ibid., diary entry for 5 June 1943.

69. D. Culbert, '*Kolberg*', p. 71.

70. Goebbels diary entry, 1 December 1944. Reproduced in D. Culbert, '*Kolberg*', p. 71.

71. Ibid., diary entry for 14 June 1943.

72. D. Culbert, '*Kolberg*', p. 75.

73. H.-C. Blumenberg, *Das Leben geht weiter: Der letzte Film des Dritten Reiches* (Rowohlt, Berlin 1992), pp. 118–23; See also, H. Theuerkauf, *Goebbels' Filmerbe*, pp. 88–94.

74. Ibid. For more on *Das Leben geht weiter*, see H.-C. Blumenberg, *Das Leben geht weiter*.

75. D. Culbert, '*Kolberg*', p. 75.

76. Ibid., diary entry for 15 July 1943.

77. Goebbels diary entry, 6 June 1943. E. Fröhlich (ed.), Die Tagebücher von Joseph Goebbels: Teil II Diktate 1941–1945, vol. 8, p. 425.

78. See above, pp. 212–14.

79. Goebbels quoted in J. Baird, *To Die for Germany*, p. 240.

80. R. Semmler, *Goebbels. The Man next to Hitler*, p. 194. Diary entry for 17 April 1945.

81. See the diary entries for the following dates in 1945: 28 February; 4 March; 5 March; 10 March; 13 March; 16 March; 18 March; 20 March. Reproduced in D. Culbert, '*Kolberg*', p. 74.

82. Goebbels diary entry, 18 March 1945. Reproduced in D. Culbert, '*Kolberg*', p. 74.

83. Cited in K. Kreimeier, *The Ufa Story*, p. 362.

84. Ibid.

85. DNB Presseschreibfunk (Inland), 12.43, 10.41, 31 January 1945. Wiener Library cuttings collection, 106e.

86. V. Harlan, *Souvenirs*, p. 272.

87. IWMS 2933/2. Interview with Söderbaum, n.d.

88. K. Kreimeier, *The Ufa Story*, p. 295.

89. Ibid.

90. For more on this, see J. Fox, *Filming Women*, pp. 152–4.

91. K. Kreimeier, *The Ufa Story*, p. 295.

92. M. Krützen, *Hans Albers*, p. 249.

93. M. Kater, 'Film as an Object of Reflection in the Goebbels Diaries: Series II (1941–1945)', *Central European History*, vol. 33, no. 3 (2000), pp. 391–414, here, p. 413.

94. J. von Reiht-Zanthier, *Sie machten uns glücklich* (Ehrenwirth, Munich, 1967), p. 230.

95. K. Kreimeier, *The Ufa Story*, p. 330.

96. BArch R109I/1716, Minutes of Management Meeting, 1563, 14 April 1944. Cited in K. Kreimeier, *The Ufa Story*, p. 361.

97. H.-C. Blumenberg, *Das Leben geht weiter*, p. 52.

98. SDK Berlin, *Titanic* (1943), press book – suggested straplines. For a further discussion of the campaigns centred on British plutocracy, see in particular, pp. 160–6.

99. K. Wetzel and P. Hagemann, *Zensur*, p. 132.

100. SDK Berlin, *Titanic* (1943), press materials produced for the release of the film by *Filmverleih Südwest GmbH*, 18 July 1955. The outburst is reported in J. Wulf, *Theater und Film im Dritten Reich. Eine Dokumentation* (Sigbert Mohn Verlag, Gütersloh, 1964), p. 299. Arriving on set to discover that little preparatory work had been completed, Selpin was reported to have said, 'Ach, du mit Sch … soldaten, du Sch … leutnant überhaupt mit deiner Sch … Wehrmacht'.

101. J. Wulf, *Theater und Film*, p. 299.

102. K. Wetzel and P. Hagemann, *Zensur*, pp. 132–4. For more on the fate of the film, see pp. 134–5. For the post-war life of the film and British attempts to ban the film after occupation due to its anti-English tendencies, see SDK Berlin, *Titanic* file, specifically *Briefdienst Kultur*, 7 April 1950.

103. SDK Berlin, *Titanic* (1943), press materials produced for the release of the film by *Filmverleih Südwest GmbH*, 18 July 1955.

104. *Der Film*, 8 August 1942. Reproduced in K. Wetzel and P. Hagemann, *Zensur*, p. 134.

105. Ibid.

106. SDK Berlin, personal file *Helmut Käutner*, 2042, autobiographical statement, 5 June 1945.

107. Ibid.

108. R. C. Reimer, 'Turning Inward: An Analysis of Helmut Käutner's *Auf Wiedersehen, Franziska*; *Romanze in Moll* and *Unter den Brücken*' in R. C. Reimer (ed.), *Cultural History through a National Socialist Lens. Essays on the Cinema of the Third Reich* (Camden House, Rochester NY, 2000), pp. 214–40, here, p. 224.

109. K. Witte, 'Film im Nationalsozialismus', in W. Jacobsen, A. Kaes and H. H. Prinzler (eds), *Geschichte des Deutschen Films* (J. B. Metzler, Stuttgart/Weimar, 1993), p. 138; p. 532. See also SDK personal file *Helmut Käutner*, clipping from *Der Spiegel*, 19 August 1959.

110. H. Fraenkel, *Of Fine Films that were Banned* (1957). Original Transcript. Bfi library, p. 161.

111. E. Carter, 'The New Third Reich Film History', *German History*, vol. 17, no. 4 (1999), pp. 71–80. Carter is reviewing Karsten Witte's *Lachende Erben, toller Tag. Filmkomödie im Dritten Reich* (Vorwerk 8, Berlin, 1995). Further discussion of this aspect of Witte's argument can be found in 'Im Prinzip Hoffnung, Helmut Käutners filme', in W. Jacobsen and H. H. Prinzler (eds), *Käutner* (Edition Filme, Volker Spiess, Berlin, 1992), pp. 62–109.

112. K. Wetzel and P. Hagemann, *Zensur*, p. 71.

113. SDK Berlin, 1094 *Große Freiheit Nr. 7*, *Film-Kurier*, 6 May 1943.

114. K. Wetzel and P. Hagemann, *Zensur*, p. 72.

115. Cited in K. Kreimeier, *The Ufa Story*, p. 349.

116. K. Wetzel and P. Hagemann, *Zensur*, p. 72. Goebbels sought to reduce salaries in the final years of the war, as recounted by H. Theuerkauf, *Goebbels' Filmerbe*, p. 101.

117. BArch BDC RKK 2701. Box 0022. File 04.

118. SDK Berlin, 1094 *Große Freiheit Nr. 7*, Werner Krein, 'Effekte im Farbfilm', *Film-Kurier*, 17 March 1944.

119. SDK 1094 Berlin, *Große Freiheit Nr. 7*, 'Hafenromanze – in Farben. Start des Films *Große Freiheit*', *Film-Bühne*, Vienna, 8 September 1945.

120. K. Wetzel and P. Hagemann, *Zensur*, p. 72. See also article from *Film-Kurier*, 22 July 1943, reproduced on the same page.

121. L. Schulte-Sasse, *Entertaining the Third Reich*, p. 172. See also M. Kater, 'Film as an Object of Reflection', p. 408; p. 413. The difficulties with the word 'freedom' in the title are also recounted in P. Cornelsen, *Helmut Käutner. Seine Filme – sein Leben* (Heyne Filmbibliothek, Munich, 1980), p. 62.

122. BArch R55/665. Cited in K. Wetzel and P. Hagemann, *Zensur*, p. 73.

123. K. Wetzel and P. Hagemann, *Zensur*, p. 73.

124. *Unter den Brücken*, Ufa-Magazin no. 21, Deutsches Historisches Museum (1992).

125. SDK Berlin , *Unter den Brücken*, clipping from the *Helmut Käutner Archiv*, 'Walter Ulbrich: Die Entstehung des Films *Unter den Brücken*', *Neue Zürcher Zeitung*, 11 May 1947.

126. Ibid.

127. M. Kater, 'Film as an Object of Reflection', p. 406.

128. Ibid., p. 408.

129. Goebbels diary entry, 28 December 1944. E. Fröhlich (ed.), *Die Tagebücher von Joseph Goebbels: Teil II Diktate 1941–1945*, vol. 14, p. 476.

130. *Unter den Brücken*, Ufa-Magazin no. 21, Deutsches Historisches Museum (1992).

131. SDK Berlin, *Unter den Brücken*, clipping from the *Helmut Käutner Archiv*, 'Walter Ulbrich: Die Entstehung des Films *Unter den Brücken*', *Neue Zürcher Zeitung*, 11 May 1947.

132. SDK Berlin, *Unter den Brücken,* clipping from *Film-Kurier*, 11 July 1944.

133. SDK Berlin, *Unter den Brücken,* clipping from SDK publication *Berlin und das Kino*. Interview with Carl Raddatz, ZDF, 1973/1. Raddatz, in fact, married his co-star Hannelore Schroth. The witness to their marriage was Helmut Käutner. See P. Cornelsen, *Helmut Käutner*, p. 69.

134. Ibid.

135. SDK Berlin, *Unter den Brücken*, clipping from the *Helmut Käutner Archiv*, 'Walter Ulbrich: Die Entstehung des Films *Unter den Brücken*', *Neue Zürcher Zeitung*, 11 May 1947.

136. Cited in K. Kreimeier, *The Ufa Story*, p. 363. For a further discussion of the fall of the studio, see H. Theuerkauf, *Goebbels' Filmerbe*, pp. 31–9.

137. R. C. Reimer, 'Turning Inward', p. 214.

138. Ibid., pp. 230–2.

139. Ibid., p. 232.

140. Ibid., p. 233.

141. Ibid., p. 234.

142. Ibid., p. 233.

143. S. Hake, *Popular Cinema of the Third Reich*, p. 228.

144. SDK Berlin, personal file *Helmut Käutner*, 2042, autobiographical statement, 5 June 1945.

145. Ibid.

146. SDK Berlin, personal file *Helmut Käutner*, 2042, Käunter, 'Polit. Stellung'.

147. SDK Berlin, personal file *Helmut Käutner*, 2042, Helmut Käutner 'Kollektivschuld'.

148. Ibid.

149. TNA PRO FO 1060/1233, *Anklageschrift gegen Veit Harlan*, 15 July 1948.

150. Notes on the proceedings and associated papers can be found in TNA PRO FO 1060/1233. Harlan gives an account of the trial and his post-war experiences in his memoirs (V. Harlan, *Souvenirs*, pp. 304-41), as does K. Söderbaum, *Nichts bleibt immer so. Rückblenden auf ein Leben vor und hinter der Kamera* (Hestia, Bayreuth, 1983), pp. 223-7.

151. This was not just in terms of the film community. *The New York Times* reported that a Jewish witness for the prosecution was attacked and jeered (15 April 1950, p. 5). These actions resulted in a public statement from Konrad Adenauer, expressing his regret at the '"shameful way" in which his fellow-countrymen were behaving towards the Jews' (16 April 1950, p. 34). See also *The New York Times*, 30 April 1950, p. 5. For details of Fröhlich's accusations, see V. Herlon, Souvenirs, pp. 307–8 and K. Söderbaum, Nichts bleibt immer so, p. 224.

152. For a further discussion of this issue, see F. Knilli, *Ich war Jud Süß. Die Geschichte des Filmstars Ferdinand Marian* (Henschel, Berlin, 2000), pp. 181-9.

153. Reproduced in K. Söderbaum, *Nichts bleibt immer so*, p. 226.

154. *The New York Times*, 22 April 1951, p. 97.

155. H. Fehrenbach, *Cinema in Democratizing Germany: Reconstructing National Identity after Hitler* (University of North Carolina Press, Chapel Hill, NC, 1995), p. 195.

156. Lüth cited in H. Fehrenbach, *Cinema in Democratizing Germany*, p. 203.

157. Details of the judgement against Lüth can be found in BVerfGE 7, 198 Federal Constitutional Court (First Division), 15 January 1958. Viewed at http://www.ucl.ac.uk/laws/global_law/german-cases/cases_bverg.shtml?15jan1958, November 2005. See also T. Henne and A. Riedlinger (eds), *Das Lüth-Urteil aus (rechts-)historischer Sicht. Die Konflikte um Veit Harlan und die Grundrechtsjudikatur des Bundesverfassungs gerichts* (Berliner Wissenschaftsverlag, Berlin, 2005).

158. For an example of open protest against Harlan, see SDK Personal Film, *Veit Harlan*, 318, clipping 'Kein Platz für Harlan', 6 March 1952.

159. H. Habe, *Our Love Affair with Germany* (Putnam, New York, 1953), p. 136. See also reports in *The New Tork Times*, 2 February 1951, p. 31 and 22 April 1951, p. 97.

160. SDK Berlin, Personal Film, *Veit Harlan*, 318, 'Käutner und Bettina Moissi gegen Harlan', *Hamburger Abendblatt*, 7 January 1951. Documents relating to the production, including fragments of the script can be found in the Hamburg State Archive, Erich Lüth papers, 622/1, 27/1 vol. 3 1/1–15/2/51. I am grateful to Susan Tegel for drawing my attention to these documents.

161. SDK Berlin, Personal Film, *Veit Harlan*, 318, Harlan to H. B. Heisig, owner of the Waterloo Theatre, Hamburg, 19 April 1948.

162. Details on this process can be found in TNA PRO FO 1023/182.

163. S. Hake, *Popular Cinema of the Third Reich*, p. 212.

164. Ibid., p. 229.

165. B. Wright, *The Long View* (Secker & Warburg, London, 1974), p. 177.

166. Bfi Microjacket (Asquith), Ministry of Information circular, 'British Films for Liberated Europe', 1 August 1944.

167. *The Cinema*, 3 January 1945, p. 26E.

168. *Kinematograph Weekly*, 18 February 1943.

169. *The Cinema*, 6 January 1943, p. 9.

170. *The Cinema*, 3 January 1945, p. 21.

171. *The Cinema*, 5 January 1944, p. 16.

172. *The Cinema*, 12 April 1944, p. 3.

173. *Today's Cinema*, 8 January 1941, p. 11.

174. *The Cinema*, 3 January 1945, p. 25.

175. *The Cinema*, 3 January 1945, p. 12.

176. S. F. Ditcham, Managing Director, General Film Distributors in *Kinematograph Weekly*, 13 January 1944.

177. Darryl F. Zanuck, Vice President in charge of production at 20th Century Fox in *The Cinema*, 5 January 1944, p. 10.

178. See for example, on progress, *Kinematograph Weekly*, 13 April 1944.

179. For the problems of reconstructing the film industry's infrastructure in the post-war period, see *Kinematograph Weekly*, 14 January 1943, p. 13.

180. *Kinematograph Weekly*, 4 May 1944.

181. *Kinematograph Weekly*, 23 April 1942.

182. *Kinematograph Weekly*, 11 May 1944.

183. *The Cinema*, 5 January 1944, p. 26A.

184. *The Cinema*, 3 January 1945, p. 34.

185. *Today's Cinema*, 29 August 1944, p. 3.

186. TNA PRO INF1/947, 'History of Film during the Second World War', 1944, p. 9.

187. *Today's Cinema*, 29 August 1944, p. 3.

188. *Documentary News Letter*, February 1943, p. 176.

189. See, for example, *Documentary News Letter*, February 1943, p. 176.

190. For more on this transition, see M. Grant, 'Towards a Central Office of Information: Continuity and Change in British Government Information Policy, 1939–51' in *Journal of Contemporary History*, vol. 34, no. 1 (Jan. 1999), pp. 49–67.

191. GP G4:19, 'Propaganda and Education', 15 November 1943. Also reproduced in F. Hardy (ed.), *Grierson on Documentary* (Faber & Faber, London/Boston, 1979), pp. 141–55, here, p. 155.

192. Ibid., p. 153.

193. *The Cinema*, 5 January 1944, p. 3.

194. See, for example, *Kinematograph Weekly*, 30 July 1942 on shortage of manpower and restrictions on studio space; *Kinematograph Weekly*, 14 January 1943 on the impact of bombing on film 'showmanship' on the Kent Coast; *Kinematograph Weekly*, 13 January 1944 on re-issues; *Today's Cinema*, 10 February 1943 on the rationing of film stock; S. Aspinall and R. Murphy (eds), *Bfi Dossier 18: Gainsborough Melodrama* (Andre Deutsch, London, 1998), interview with Maurice Carter conducted by Sue Harper, p. 55 on the impact of the call-up and requirements of the Service Film Units.

195. *Kinematograph Weekly*, 29 June 1944.

196. Edgar Anstey 'Documentary Item', *New York Times*, 12 December 1937.

197. *Documentary News Letter*, June 1941, p. 104.

198. *Kinematograph Weekly*, 1 August 1940.

199. See J. Fox, 'John Grierson, his "Documentary Boys"'.

200. The movement experienced a major split during the war, which essentially focused on two schools of thought: one which suggested that the movement ought to co-operate with the MoI and partly abandon its agenda in favour of overt state propaganda (Arthur Elton) and one which wanted to maintain the integrity of Grierson's original documentary idea (Paul Rotha). For more details on this split, see J. Fox, 'John Grierson, his "Documentary Boys".

201. *Documentary News Letter,* June 1941, p. 105.

202. GP G4:N6, 'The Film at War'. Also reproduced in F. Hardy (ed.), *Grierson on Documentary*, pp. 86–9, here, p. 88.

203. *Documentary News Letter*, January 1943, p. 161.

204. Ibid.

205. GP G4:19:1, John Grierson 'Education and the New Order', Winnipeg, 1941.

206. GP G4:24:136, Letter from Grierson to 'Moe', 10 June 1940.

207. TNA PRO INF 1/234, Robert Fraser to Lord Davidson, 19 March 1941. Cited in I. McLaine, *Ministry of Morale*, p. 176.

208. Harold Nicolson, diary entry of 22 January 1941 in N. Nicolson (ed.), *Harold Nicolson. Diaries and Letters 1939–45* (Collins, Fontana Books, Bungay, Suffolk, 1967), p. 137.

209. TNA PRO CAB 66/33, Prime Minister's memorandum, 12 January 1943. Cited in I. McLaine, *Ministry of Morale*, p. 183.

210. I. McLaine, *Ministry of Morale*, p. 174.

211. Harold Nicolson, diary entry of 11 February 1941 in N. Nicolson (ed.), *Harold Nicolson. Diaries and Letters*, p. 141.

212. TNA PRO INF1/864, Memorandum by S.G. Gates, 21 April 1942. Also cited in I. McLaine, *Ministry of Morale*, p. 179.

213. A. Calder, *The People's War*, p. 531.

214. TNA PRO INF1/293, Home Intelligence Special Report, 31 May 1944. Also cited in I. McLaine, *Ministry of Morale*, p. 185.

215. I. McLaine, *Ministry of Morale*, p. 185.

216. *Documentary News Letter*, June 1941, p. 105.

217. For a summary of the historiography on MoI short film production, see J. Chapman, *The British at War*, p. 87.

218. Copies of many of the films discussed in the section can be found in the BBC2 series *Propaganda with Facts* ('The New Jerusalem'), a historical commentary by Nicholas Pronay. See also N. Pronay, '"The Land of Promise": the projection of peace aims in Britain' in K. R. M. Short (ed.), *Film and Radio Propaganda*.

219. IWMS 4627/6, Interview with Roy Boulting, March 1980.

220. M. Paris, 'Filming the People's War: *The Dawn Guard, Desert Victory, Tunisian Victory* and *Burma Victory*', in A. Burton, T. O'Sullivan and P. Wells (eds), *The Family Way*, pp. 97–109, 97.

221. *Documentary News Letter*, July 1941, p. 129. Cited in J. Chapman, *The British at War*, p. 102.

222. J. Petley, 'The Pilgrim's regress: the politics of the Boultings' films', in A. Burton, T. O'Sullivan and P. Wells (eds), *The Family Way*, pp.15–35, here, p. 17. For a further discussion of the Boulting Brothers' films in relation to the 'people's war', see M. Paris, 'Filming the People's War'. Paris argues that the language of the films constantly reinforced the unity of the nations fighting the Nazis in its use of the words 'we' and 'us' throughout (p. 101).

223. TNA PRO INF 1/292, Home Intelligence Weekly report to the MoI, no.22, 26 January 1941.

224. G. Eley, 'Finding the People's War: Film, British Collective Memory, and World War II', *American Historical Review*, vol. 106, no. 3 (June 2001), pp. 818–38, here, pp. 820–1.

225. *Documentary News Letter*, February 1941, p. 21. Cited in J. Chapman, *The British at War*, p. 102.

226. TNA PRO INF1/679, To Mr Parker (H.I.) from Senior Assistant Officer, Midland Region, no. 9. 'Summary of Trends in Public Opinion during the period April 20th–May 18th 1942'.

227. Ibid.

228. TNA PRO INF6/1917, notes on *A Diary for Timothy*.

229. B. Wright, *The Long View*, p. 202.

230. Bfi Special Collections, Humphrey Jennings Collection, Item 3, 'Diary for Timothy'. Broadcast on the French Service, 1945.

231. B. Wright, *The Long View*, p. 202.

232. TNA PRO INF6/1917, notes on *A Diary for Timothy*.

233. B. Wright, *The Long View*, p. 202.

234. IWMS Interview with Basil Wright, 6231/1.

235. I. McLaine, *Ministry of Morale*, p. 180.

236. TNA PRO INF1/848, Minutes of meeting of the Policy Committee, item 9 'Employment of Persons of Left-Wing Tendency', 15 March 1940.

237. P. Rotha, *Documentary Diary. An Informal History of the British Documentary Film, 1928–1939* (Secker & Warburg, London, 1973), p. 280.

238. Foreword to Rotha's 1951 edition of *Documentary Film*. Cited in E. Sussex, *The Rise and Fall of British Documentary. The Story of the Movement founded by John Grierson* (University of California Press, Berkeley, 1973), p. 163.

239. Ibid.

240. Text from *World of Plenty* (1943). Reproduced in P. Rotha and E. Knight, *World of Plenty. The Book of the Film* (Nicholson and Watson, London, 1945).

241. Ibid.

242. *Documentary News Letter*, 49th Issue, 1945, p. 87.

243. P. Rotha, *Documentary Diary*, p. 284.

244. Interview with Wright in E. Sussex, *The Rise and Fall of British Documentary*, p. 138.

245. P. Rotha, *Documentary Diary*, p. 281.

246. Interview with Rotha in E. Sussex, *The Rise and Fall of British Documentary*, p. 161.

247. Ibid.

248. N. Pronay, '"The Land of Promise"', p. 72.

249. 'The Man on the Screen', *Documentary News Letter*, May 1940, p. 4.

250. Ibid., p. 3.

251. B. Wright, *The Long View*, p. 177.

252. M-O A: 'Home propaganda: A report prepared by Mass-Observation for the Advertising Service Guild', *Bulletin of the Advertising Service Guild*, no. 2, 31.

253. B. Wright, *The Long View*, p. 109.

254. For more on the debate on the role of the documentary and the feature film in representing the real see S. Hood, 'John Grierson and The Documentary Movement', in J. Curran and V. Porter (eds), *British Cinema History*, pp. 99–113. In particular, see p. 110.

255. GP G4:19, 'Propaganda and Education', 15 November 1943. Also in F. Hardy (ed.), *Grierson on Documentary*, p. 155.

256. GP G4:20:4, 'Films and the War'. Speech by Grierson to the National Film Society of Canada, n.d.

257. D. Powell, *Films since 1939* (The British Council, Longman, London/New York, 1947), p. 39.

258. For more on the MoI's recognition of star power in films, see TNA PRO INF 1/251, 'Five minute shorts', Home Publicity Committee minutes. 13 November 1940. This is also reiterated in TNA PRO INF 1/679, Rowntree memorandum on 'Home Propaganda', 25 April 1942, 3 (b).

259. *Kinematograph Weekly*, 19 April 1944.

260. For a more detailed discussion of the problems of depicting the 'ordinary' in relation to the concept of the 'people's war' as opposed to the peace (as dealt with here), see J. Fox, 'Millions Like Us?'

261. B. Wright, *The Long View*, p. 195.

262. Interview with Rotha in E. Sussex, *The Rise and Fall of British Documentary*, pp. 140–1.

263. Interview with Wright in E. Sussex, *The Rise and Fall of British Documentary*, p. 140.

264. C. Coultass, *Images for Battle. British Film and the Second World War 1939–1945* (Associated University Presses, London, 1989), p. 126.

265. Bfi, *Millions Like Us* (1943), press book.

266. M-O A: FR 2275, 'Character in War and Peace', August 1945.

267. Ibid.

268. Ibid.

269. TNA PRO INF 1/292, Stephen Taylor, Home Intelligence. 'Home Morale and Public Opinion: A review of some conclusions arising out of a year of Home Intelligence weekly reports', 1 October 1941.

270. M-O A: FR 2270A, 'The General Election', July 1945.

271. *The Cinema*, 24 September 1943, p. 8.

272. Responses to M-O directive, November 1943. Reproduced in D. Sheridan and J. Richards (eds), *Mass-Observation at the Movies*, p. 238.

273. Ibid., p. 277.

274. *Today's Cinema*, 27 January 1943, p. 21.

275. Responses to M-O directive, November 1943. Reproduced in D. Sheridan and J. Richards (eds), *Mass-Observation at the Movies*, p. 277.

276. Ibid., p.278.

277. J. Poole, 'British Cinema Attendance in Wartime', p. 30.

278. M-O A: FR 2278B, 'Feelings about the Peace', August 1945.

279. J. Poole, 'British Cinema Attendance in Wartime', p. 30.

280. See, for example, P. Gillett, *The British Working Class in Postwar Film* (Manchester University Press, Manchester/New York, 2003), pp. 26–38; S. Harper and V. Porter, *British Cinema of the 1950s: The Decline of Deference* (Oxford University Press, 2003).

281. S. Hake, *Popular Cinema of the Third Reich*, p. 211.

282. TNA PRO INF 1/633, A full list of films screened can be found in this file, as well as details on the use of 'films in prize'. For a further discussion, see J. Fox, 'A Thin Stream'.

The rival banners of warring parties wave in the breeze and under them march propagandists, academes and citizens alike in one wild army of bedevilled unreality.

John Grierson[1]

We return to where we began: the writings of a film propagandist, John Grierson. Constant observer and critic of the art throughout World War II, specialist in the psychology of film, he offers the historian a contemporary perspective on the issues raised in this book, his writings detailing the dilemmas that film propagandists faced in total war and drawing our attention to the fact that during the conflict film propaganda was conceived of and operated within a comparative environment. Grierson knew that the conflict had altered contemporary understandings of propaganda, conceptions of authoritarian and democratic persuasion emerging from the experience of psychological manipulation in the period from 1939 to 1945. Undermining the pervasive view in the early years of the war that propaganda was 'an exotic' which could only be 'grafted onto the democratic machinery' with some difficulty,[2] the controversial documentarist confronted the key tensions facing propagandists. Theorizing on models of democratic and authoritarian propaganda, Grierson put forward his ideas on the application and functioning of the phenomena under the two distinct forms of government. 'A democracy,' he argued, 'by its very nature and by its very virtues lies wide open to division and uncertainty. It encourages discussion; it permits free criticism; it opens its arms wide to the preaching of any and every doctrine'. In this environment, contended Grierson, the task of the propagandist becomes all the more complex. The maintenance of morale, far from being a 'relatively easy and straightforward' undertaking,[3] is complicated by the existence of multiple and overtly expressed opinions, with little or no systematic means of controlling them. It was for this reason that Grierson asserted that

> instead of propaganda being less necessary in a democracy, it is more necessary. In the authoritarian state, you have powers of compulsion and powers of repression, physical and mental, which in part at least take the place of persuasion. Not so in a democracy. It is your democrat who most needs and demands guidance from his leaders. It is the democratic leader who most must give it. If only for the sake of quick decision and common action, it is democracy for which propaganda is the more urgent necessity.[4]

For British propagandists, then, on the one hand, moving towards victory had an obvious advantage. But they were also faced with targeting a population free to express dissent overtly and covertly, and were unable to create an intoxicating environment in which the population were subject to multiple compulsive pressures and in which propaganda and terror functioned hand-in-hand to create a theoretically inescapable atmosphere of horizontal and vertical manipulation and repression. According to Grierson, Nazi propagandists found themselves confronted with a different set of issues. The democrats, he noted, at least had the advantage of being able, with increasing victories and the nature of the state, to draw on their 'liberal tradition', capitalizing on the fact that 'the truth must command goodwill everywhere and, in the long run, defeat the distortions and boastings and the blatancies of the enemy'.[5] Essentially contending that the *élan vitale* was more important to man than the *élan morale*, the National Socialists were always arguing the more troubling case. After all, argued Grierson, 'you can't start blatantly talking of conscience as a chimera; morals as an old wives' tale; the Christian religion as a dream of weaklings; and the pursuit of truth as *bourgeois* fiddle-faddle, without raising a few doubts in the heart of mankind'.[6]

Grierson essentially cut to the heart of the problem, highlighting the tensions between the propagandistic strategies and problems facing democrats and authoritarians. Both Britain and Germany faced some different challenges, but ultimately, as Grierson recognized, both were faced with the task of putting 'propaganda on the offensive'. He knew too that by 1939 the nature of war had changed. The Germans perceived that in the modern war propaganda was no longer 'an auxiliary in political management and military strategy'. It was 'the first and most vital weapon' in modern combat. Trench warfare was 'blown to smithereens by the development of the internal combustion engine. Fast moving tanks and fast troop carriers could get behind the lines. Aeroplanes and flying artillery could get behind the lines. War', Grierson informed propagandists, 'in one of its essentials, has become a matter of getting behind the lines and confusing and dividing the enemy'.[7] Aeroplanes had also brought the possibility of mass bombardment of enemy cities. Guernica demonstrated to the world the awesome fire power of the bomber. Now, front and homeland became conflated; the towns and streets now bore the scars of the front lines. This necessitated total war both physically and psychologically. In this new atmosphere, propaganda had to learn to 'integrate the loyalties and forces of the community' in the name of given ideologies. Propaganda on the home and front lines served to 'crystallize' the aims of the war, a real force in society which provided 'the patterns of thought and feeling which [made] for an active [population]' at times of crisis, fitting 'the particular circumstances' of the era.[8] Being a film-maker, Grierson knew that the cinema was going to play a key role in this process. 'There,' he stated, 'in the vast machinery of film production, of theatres spread across the earth with an audience of a hundred million a week, was one of the great new instruments of war propaganda. It could make people love each other or hate each other. It could keep people to the sticking point of purpose'.[9] Both British and German propagandists recognized the power of the cinema and afforded film a central place in their persuasive campaigns of World War II.

Obviously, natural tensions have emerged in this study between the film industries of Britain and Germany in this period, the nature of the states determining particular structures and pressures in relation to film production. The mechanisms for production and delivery in the two nations were quite different. The cascading organization of the central RMVP to the RKK to the RFK and to local levels through the *Reichspropagandaleiter* meant that cinema was bound by more obvious strictures. The mechanisms for obtaining finance, nationalization, the eventual merging of film studios and companies, and overt state sponsorship for 'politically significant' productions meant that the Reich Ministry had a far more explicit means of bringing film production to heel and under the command of the Nazi state. In organizational terms, the structures of control were delineated and clear, although, at times, the practicalities meant that a limited independence was tolerated in respect of insignificant productions. The arts, including the cinematic arts, were *gleichgeschaltet*, in theory at least. Such a system of control was not, and could not be, replicated in a democracy. The British Ministry of Information had a rather less overt and more complicated relationship with the industry, their influence on production discreet, complex and indirect.[10] Where British feature films were overt in their approach to propaganda themes, in the majority of cases the central message was *redolent* or reflective of rather than explicitly directed by MoI policies. Although the Ministry did promote and occasionally finance feature films, such as Powell and Pressburger's *49th Parallel*, for the most part, the studios worked towards the needs of the Ministry's propaganda campaigns, predicting and reflecting the development of the war. There is certainly an observable correlation between the Ministry and the Home Publicity Sub-Committee's objectives and the filmic outputs of the era, one which reflects the vagaries of the relationship between the state and the industry and is more in keeping with a general flow of information and ideas between the two bodies facilitated by unofficial groups such as Beddington's 'Ideas Committee'. The pressure exerted by the Ministry on the studios is relatively difficult to reconstruct in an empirical sense. It was nebulous, flexible and blurred in character, making stark pronouncements on the exact processes at work in relation to a particular film difficult. In keeping with the rhetoric surrounding the democratic conception of propaganda, it was imperative that 'the influence brought to bear by the Ministry on the producers of feature films, and encouragement given to foreign distributors be kept secret',[11] thus complicating the historian's task, and making direct comparison with Nazi Germany more difficult in concrete terms.

Nonetheless obvious examples point to the innate differences in terms of processes involved in censorship and propaganda outputs, the 1943 production *The Life and Death of Colonel Blimp* demonstrating the essential 'Otherness' of the German system of control. That the Ministry could not, and did not want to, ban the film, despite protestations from the War Office and the Prime Minister, suggests that the democratic system guaranteed that the MoI at least attempted to remain constant in its promise to 'tell the truth, nothing but the truth, and (in so far as is safe) the whole truth'.[12] It could not do otherwise, for fear of compromising the basis of the guiding principles of its propaganda campaigns. There was much more flexibility in resisting Government demands. It was true that the Ministry and other offices of state could curtail and attempt to hinder the activities of a production team, the release of materials and personnel and restrictions on export just two weapons in their arsenal, but they could not prevent the release of the production itself. The RMVP was not bound by the same democratic strictures of accountability. Even in the midst of collapse, the RMVP still possessed the power to prevent the distribution of a film, *Titanic* and *Große Freiheit Nr. 7* being clear examples.

It is also impossible to draw distinctions between the operations of the two film industries in this period without reference to the importance of terror as a means of maintaining consensus in the Third Reich. Significantly, as the regime began to experience a collapse in popular morale and a resurgence of patterns of dissent, opposition and resistance, the explicit ruthlessness of the terror increased. Ultimately, as Kershaw has recognized, 'the escalation of terror in the latter years of the regime was no incidental development. It denoted the collapse of any form of consensus in Germany except the one most unacceptable to the regime – a consensus for ending the war. And with the collapse of any popular base of support for the regime, the ultimate powerlessness of Nazi propaganda was complete'.[13] The intricate relationship between the terror state and the propaganda apparatus defined the Nazi system, accounting for its successes and mitigating the failures of the latter in relation to the maintenance of the dictatorship. Although Goebbels idealistically proclaimed, on taking up the position which he would fill for the next thirteen years, that his Ministry would not be 'satisfied … with the knowledge that it has 52% behind it while terrorizing the other 48%',[14] circumstances pushed terror to the fore, forcibly maintaining compliance and, at the very least, passivity among the general populace. The final expression of the failure of propaganda alone to 'revolutionize' the national consciousness was that terror and persuasion worked hand in hand in the Nazi state, not only by disguising the iron fist within the velvet glove, but also allowing for the systematic repression of cultural freedom and the extinction of divergent ideological codes. Where propaganda failed terror could succeed, providing a safety net for Goebbels' campaigns, if necessary. Both aspects of the state functioned within a mutually reinforcing environment. This process, combined with attempts at *Gleichschaltung*, sets the RMVP apart from its British counterpart.

The central conceptions of the role of propaganda in society at the outset of the conflict in Britain and Germany were also at odds. For the Nazi state, propaganda was an active, revolutionary process, aimed at enacting a palingenesis within German society, one which rectified the past and set the course for the future. It was intended to be aggressive and total. For the far-right, the Great War had been a defining experience. No more would Germany be in a position of psychological weakness; now she would mobilize the full force of propaganda and popular enlightenment to bolster the state and promote the political, ideological, social and military objectives of the National Socialist movement. The modern nation demanded the use of modern methods of psychological manipulation and mobilization. World War I also set the course for the British. Gearing up for the possibility of conflict from 1935, their propagandists shied away from the aggressive and deceptive use of communications, the memory of the shame of the inter-war years and exposure of the techniques of the last war leaving an indelible print on the minds of the pre-war planners. British propagandists were more cautious and were more sceptical about the power of persuasion to alter the course of military events. However, although the MoI went to great lengths to stress the distinctiveness of the British approach to propaganda, Goebbels also distancing himself from the 'poor psychological' policies of the enemy,[15] the two nations had much in common when war broke out in September 1939. In many ways, war was a levelling process in relation to such discourses, both British and German propagandists confronted with a series of generic problems associated with modern warfare; the justification for entering a conflict against the popular will and the promotion of the concept of the 'defensive' war; the psychological and physical impacts of aerial bombardment; the definition and vilification of the enemy; the persuasion of neutrals and the support of allies; the conflation of home and front; the changing fortunes of war and the need to explain defeats and promote the importance of victories; and the need to boost morale in periods of stagnation, confronting war-weariness and devising methods for overcoming it. What emerges from a comparative analysis of the filmic outputs of Britain and Germany in this period is a perspective on how each nation responded to these challenges, which in turn reveals much about the reactions of democratic and authoritarian propagandists to their tasks, as well as the popular reactions to their outputs.

Naturally, Britain and Germany were on very different military trajectories in the period from 1939 to 1945. It is not possible to speak of parallel experiences throughout the war and in relation to certain topics, specifically in relation to the racial agenda of the Third Reich. However, the comparative framework allows for a re-evaluation of points of similarity, whilst, at the same time, highlighting the distinctive 'Otherness' of the Nazi state and its representation of its own identity. Outwardly, the film productions of the initial years of the conflict seemingly reflected the approaches of the RMVP and the MoI to propaganda. The Nazi 'documentaries of intimidation' screamed the mission of the German military, a 'blood and thunder' approach matching their deployment of weapons of mass persuasion. The British responded with *The Lion Has Wings*, a production which to the modern, and to some extent the contemporary, eye presented a Britain which had not quite understood the nature of the war to come, overly optimistic in their national defences and the awesome power of the RAF, with its potential to penetrate German soil. Initially, the British response to German propaganda was not much more than rhetoric, commentators repelled by the explicit nature of Nazi threats, contrasting the brash claims of the enemy with the power of the understatement. And yet, even at this early stage, despite seeming at opposite poles, the initial productions of the war years suggested that each nation had begun to lay the foundations for its future propagandistic success and failure. As Kershaw argues, 'from September 1939 the chief aim [of the RMVP] switched to the preservation of morale during the war. And in this aim propaganda encountered growing failure. Distrust of German propaganda, coupled with boredom at its dull monotony, paved the way even in the period of German military triumph for the later drastic collapse of confidence'.[16] As the Germans 'flooded the world with pictures of action, of their young troops on the march and going places, of deeds done', British propagandists looked on, privately wishing that they too could, 'without running over into harshness and blatancy, ... put [their] propaganda more on the offensive'.[17] However, this process had, in fact, already begun. Even *The Lion Has Wings*, in its own way, was direct and aggressive propaganda. As Grierson noted, the film contained 'no peace... [This] was Britain actually at war, zooming and roaring above the clouds. It was also the film at war'.[18] British propagandists worked at putting the film industry on a war footing, their messages becoming ever more aggressive in tone and nature, moving from the mentality of merely taking it to giving it back; *The Biter Bit* and *Target for Tonight* just two examples. The seeds of collapse were already apparent in the German propaganda of the same period. 'Where the Germans failed,' noticed Grierson, 'was in the fact that their cold-blooded cynicism spilled over and was spotted'.[19] What was suitable for short-term propaganda, as Goebbels himself knew, did not necessarily work for a longer, total war.[20] Frustrated by the constant pronouncements of success by the OKW, the Reich Minister understood that even the initial 'conscious efforts may not necessarily engage the deeper loyalties of the subconscious. In propaganda you may all too easily be here today and gone tomorrow'.[21]

Although these differences emerge, this study has also identified similarities in approach to specific challenges faced by the propagandist at war. Despite the variation in specific images of the enemy, both British and German propagandists revealed a desire to avoid demonizing the enemy population as a whole. Both nations chose instead to focus attention on the leadership. This was a natural instinct for the propagandist seeking both to drive and prevent a wedge being driven between leaders and their people, undermining popular trust in the enemy's management of the war effort and encouraging the populace to rise up against the governing body, fundamentally weakening the state and its ability to function. This mission was all the more important in a total media environment, with the technical capacity to reach enemy nationals in their own homes through the radio. Filmic propaganda, unsurprisingly, reflected this trend. Producing a negative image of the enemy population served no tactical purpose whatsoever. Indeed, Vansittartism and its encouragement to see the Germans as a collective unit, was described as a 'gift to Goebbels', reinforcing the Reich Minister's own propaganda which told the German people 'we sink or swim together'. Goebbels frequently commented that Vansittart's pronouncements were 'music to my ears', encouraging him to continue supplying 'grist for [my] propaganda mill'.[22] Both British and German film-makers concentrated their efforts on the ruling clique, whether Nazi or plutocrat.

Despite experiencing the extremes of defeat and victory at various points in the conflict, both Britain and Germany also faced a period of stagnation and stalemate in the middle years of the war, resulting in the feeling of entrenchment, uncertainty and war-weariness on the part of the population. Both were faced with the task of overcoming this, maintaining morale and propelling their people towards greater sacrifice and commitment. This trend in popular opinion affected patterns of consumption, and particularly the desires for fantasy and escapism as well as information. More than ever before, both populations needed the cinema to resume its place as a 'dream factory', a place where they could go for a couple of hours and forget about the long working days, disturbed sleep, the threat of aerial bombardment and the consequences of war. Film-makers in both Britain and Germany knew that they had to respond to public needs in this field and offer a mixed programme. Both the RMVP and the MoI, and their respective film industries, understood the interplay between entertainment and propaganda and specifically the need for strands of filmic propaganda to work alongside one another.

Recent studies have focused on what Goebbels termed the 'orchestra principle' to explain the apparent inconsistencies in the *modus operandi* of the RMVP and its outputs. 'We do not expect everyone to play the same instrument,' Goebbels argued, 'we only expect that people play according to a plan',[23] a comment reflective of film's uneasy relationship with the seemingly 'totalitarian' structures of the Nazi propaganda machine. Eric Rentschler reiterated that '[n]ot every instrument plays the same tune when we hear a concert; still the result is a symphony'.[24] Every film genre contributed to the whole, representing a significant and crucial element of Goebbels' orchestra. Rentschler's statement that 'cinema in the Third Reich involved a division of labour between heavy hands and light touches'[25] is not merely a comment on the nature of productions: it could equally be applied to the organizational processes of the propaganda machinery and the sometimes inconsistent messages of the final image. Equally, Goebbels, for the most part, appreciated the power of 'light touches' and the value of entertainment as a form of propaganda. For the Reich Minister, diversion was just as important to the maintenance of morale as the overt political feature. In Britain, too, film-makers recognized the need for 'more fluff' in the cinematic programme.[26] As the reports by Mass-Observation consistently demonstrated, if the propagandistic intent of a particular piece was 'obvious: presto! The film is a flop. Pictures should never be labelled propaganda. The public has a tremendous resistance to *obvious* propaganda done with the mechanical approach'.[27] Like Germany, Britain created a film programme which allowed for the coexistence of propaganda and entertainment; documentary and political propaganda could, in fact, comfortably sit alongside 'the farce, the musical, the banal screen fairy-tale'.[28] This combination, in both countries, had a propaganda purpose of its own, making every kind of filmic production a contribution to the campaigns of the propagandist. If audiences were distracted for a few hours by the latest musical or melodrama, thus boosting morale, relaxing the patron and diverting their attention from the drudgery or horror awaiting them beyond the foyer, this too had a function for the nation at war, as well as raising revenues for the industry.

The mixed programme of news, documentary, entertainment, political propaganda and escapism became particularly important as the nations entered the phase of 'total war' and the period of extensive war-weariness. How British and German propagandists conceived of and presented the specific challenges this period brought reveals, according to David Culbert, some interesting parallels. Reflecting upon Harlan's production *Kolberg* and the film's central message of 'never surrender', he has suggested that the rhetoric of 'total war' in Nazi Germany was akin to official pronouncements in Britain. He questioned whether Nettelbeck's determination was

> so different from Churchill's brilliant calculation when he delivered his speech to the House of Commons in June 1940? . . . What is the literal difference between Churchill's 'we shall never surrender' and Nettelbeck's 'Kolberg must not surrender'? The phrases are virtually identical, which is not to ignore for a moment the enormous differences in context. Still, it is important to ensure that the test for speeches urging last-ditch sacrifice on a civilian populace not be simply a moral judgement as to the worthiness of the speaker or the government in question.[29]

As Culbert recognizes, the essential difference here is context and timing. For whilst Churchill's call for total sacrifice came early on in the war, at a time when war-weariness had not really had the chance to set in, and before the effort was truly needed, Goebbels' call at the *Sportspalast* came rather later, if not too late. The success of the evocation of the concept of 'total war' was dependent upon the political and military time. It was easier by far to have to deal with great sacrifice at the outset, predictions relating to the new means of warfare never really materializing, than to have to face the twin evils of war-weariness and stagnation and fear of defeat. Despite having warned against overly optimistic predictions as to when the war would end, Goebbels was now facing an uphill struggle. As Kershaw noted, the Reich Minister's '"realism propaganda" restored credibility for a while, but the downward spiral was [evident]. By 1944 the failure was all but total. If temporary and partial successes could still be registered, the general effectiveness of propaganda in this phase was minimal'. It was in this environment that Goebbels was forced to fall back on propaganda's 'counter-foil, present since the beginning but now reaching its apogee: terroristic repression'.[30] As consensus collapsed in the Third Reich, the temporary nature of the euphoria surrounding the *Blitzkrieg* was exposed. Within the Nazi state, it became increasingly clear that Goebbels had not achieved his aim of cultural, social and political revolution. It became evident that 'if [the nation's] mental and emotional loyalties are not engaged in the cause [the propagandist presents], if they are not lifted up and carried forward, they will fall down on you sooner or later when it comes to total war . . . their morale will break'.[31] For the German people, calls to total war could not override the increasing popular scepticism of the ideological programme of the Nazi state and could not disguise the course of the war, bringing the real possibility of defeat into sharp focus. With little relief, the population was left to fear the worst, and even Goebbels' almighty propaganda machine could not reverse that trend. For Britain, having experienced the 'dark days' earlier on in the war, progression provided hope. There was nothing like the propagandistic value of victories to ease war-weariness and raise expectations for the eventual outcome.

For all the similarities in representing certain aspects of the war, this study has also re-vealed a number of clear differences between British and German propaganda, which point to the essential 'Otherness' of the Nazi state and its aims. The comparative study of the *Fliegerfilme* of the Third Reich and Britain indicate a visual representation of the nature of the relationship between centre and periphery in authoritarian and democratic regimes. Comparing the 'documentaries of intimidation' with Watt's *Target for Tonight* highlights the failure of the 'stilted dialogue' of the Nazi films when compared to the human touch of British productions of the same genre, 'where aviators, soldiers and civilians speak frankly about their feelings towards the war and the enemy'.[32] As Graham Greene observed, 'everything is natural; there is none of the bombastic language, the bragging and the threats that characterise the German film *Baptism of Fire*. What we see is no more than a technical exercise'.[33] Moreover, within films such as *D III 88*, *Kampfgeschwader Lützow* and *Stukas*, the individual was subordinated to the will of the state, individual existences and identities essentially meaningless. The individual only acquires any form of status when he sacrifices his life for the Fatherland, in keeping with the wider ideological tenets of Nazism. The British hero, on the other hand, was *characterized* by his individual identity. Each individual, despite contested, fractured and multiple identities, could play an essential role in the 'people's war'. Successful propaganda suggested that the war could not eliminate the sense of different existences; rather, it encouraged individuals to work together for a common aim, regardless of background. Here, the individual is central to the functioning of the war effort, his or her bravery and courage operating on multiple levels, from individual acts to the communal courage of spirit expressed in the resistance to Nazi terror tactics. These relationships between the centre and periphery expressed the essential differences in the two systems of rule. Equally revealing in this respect is the study of leadership. For although the two film industries chose to depict the leader through historical analogy and many generic qualities of the wartime leader emerge, such as dedication to nation above personal life, the denial of the pleasures of a private existence, determination, the ability to overcome adversity and the survival of rites of passage, the uniqueness of the Hitler-myth is central to an understanding of the function and processes of leadership propaganda in the Third Reich. In this context, the relationship between leader and people is not negotiated; it is dictated. The population is reduced to unquestioning obedience, sharing the leader's mystic destiny. German heroes were invested with an 'other-worldliness', a god-like persona, in keeping with the Führer's image of omniscience and omnipotence propagated by the Third Reich. In many ways, Hitler was depicted as being almost above terrestrial leadership, providing a direct contrast to the Churchillian image in the same period.

The visual identity of the relationship between centre and periphery in this study is supplemented by an analysis of vertical and horizontal processes in relation to the functioning of propaganda. As noted at the outset, Steinert identified that 'every state leadership, be it democratic, [or] authoritarian … requires a certain degree of acclamation to exercise power in the long run. Without the consensus, whether forced or passive, of a broad social stratum, no government can long survive in the age of the masses'.[34] Although it is frequently asserted that democratic propagandists have to be responsive to trends in popular opinion, as the power to grant office ultimately lies in the hands of the electorate, studies of authoritarian states are beginning to understand the importance of popular opinion in relation to the basic functioning of the regime. This process can be seen clearly in relation to propaganda. As Steinert observed, 'the ... propaganda policy of the Third Reich, which was to mould and direct the opinion of the *Volk*, was not only a reaction to public opinion but was also frequently inspired by it, as well as often decisively forming the public mind. It can thus be confirmed ... that "public opinion and propaganda mutually limit and influence each other"'.[35] In this environment, and in keeping with broader studies on the Third Reich, it is no longer possible for the historian to speak of an authoritarian state completely divorced from its public. Goebbels knew that he had to be

> the man with the greatest knowledge of souls. I cannot convince a single person of the necessity of something unless I understand how to pluck the string in the heart of his soul that must be made to sound... The propagandist must know not just the soul of the people in general but he must understand the secret swings of the popular soul from one side to another. The propagandist must understand not only how to speak to the people in their totality but also to the individual sections of the population... The propagandist must always be in a position to speak to people in the language they understand. These capacities are the essential preconditions for success.[36]

Goebbels understood that propaganda functioned by tapping into the pre-existing beliefs of his target, and, in attempting to create the new man of the Nazi era, he needed to recognize trends in popular opinion in order to 'sculpt and "garden" a better, purer society while simultaneously moulding society's human material into a more ... conscious and superior individual'.[37] It was for this reason that 'hardly a National Socialist organization existed that did not, at least occasionally or in specific areas, deliver public opinion reports', from the Gau to the national level, from the party organizations to the state.[38] A study of film propaganda, like other studies of the Third Reich, reveals a far more flexible and fluid connection between the centre and periphery than extant totalitarian models allow. The philosophies of Goebbels combined with a study of the processes of filmic propaganda in Nazi Germany suggest the possibility that popular views had the potential to shape propaganda outputs alongside wider ideological and centrally directed campaigns. An SD report from 1940, for example, attempted to put pressure on the RMVP to renege on lucrative American film contracts, the public feeling that the showing of American productions, 'solely in order to make money, is not in keeping with National Socialism'.[39] Here, the popular voice seemed to be more reflective of Nazi ideology than the RMVP itself, which was, at times, bound by the pragmatism required to respond to short-term issues. This process highlights the complex interplay between propaganda and public needs and desires which ran parallel to and occasionally engaged with the dominant ideological narratives within the Third Reich. Whilst the popular voice may not have been able to shape and alter the central aims of the ideological form, it could affect and shape the process in which specific outputs were received. Even within authoritarian societies such as the Third Reich, studies of film propaganda relate a far more complex picture of the processes, popular and political, at work in the Nazi state, connecting to a wider historiography seeking to challenge the vertical and monolithic conceptions of the dictatorial state and its society.[40]

Our understanding of democracies and propaganda are also challenged. The very existence of propaganda, theoretically speaking, runs somehow counter to the liberal traditions and democratic values espoused by the MoI. As Ellul observed, 'some of democracy's fundamental aspects paralyse the conduct of propaganda. There is, therefore, no "democratic" propaganda. Propaganda made by the democracies is ineffective, paralysed, mediocre'.[41] However, with the increasing recognition by British propagandists that their output would have to go on 'the offensive', there was, at the same time, a partial release from the sensibilities which frustrated propagandistic success at the beginning of the war. The historian must, therefore, be careful not to apply blindly the rhetoric of the Ministry to the actual practices. They were, after all, propagandists, with the aim of shaping perceptions and manipulating cognitions; they were deliberately and decisively '[attempting] to influence the opinions of an audience through the transmission of ideas and values for a specific persuasive purpose, consciously designed to serve [their interests], either directly or indirectly'.[42] While their overall aims remained broadly consistent, the methods of achieving them were more fluid, responding to trial and error, opportunism, resource constraints and circumstance, a process which, at times, exacerbated the tension between the use of propaganda and the nature of the democratic state. This conflict pervaded discussions in Britain over the appropriate place for psychological manipulation and persuasion in the war effort, the MoI and the public gradually coming to terms with the phenomenon as the war progressed. That democrats knew that their propaganda had to go on the offensive, *Target for Tonight* being the filmic recognition of this, suggests a diminishing sense that propaganda was only the tool of dictators.

Patterns of reception, both in dictatorships and in democracies, are notoriously difficult to ascertain. Naturally, the historian has to recognize national difference within this context. Grierson contended that propaganda did not have to be 'like the chameleon, [taking] its colour from the country or the community in which it is operating'.[43] However, this study has attempted to assess the reception of films in their national context, response patterns varying partly due to the nature of the state as well as to more generic factors. Nevertheless, some common trends emerge. In both nations, the success of a particular feature film was largely dependent upon predicting the popular patterns of consumption and the ability of the film to move over the waves of popular trends, as opposed to depending on direct and immediate topical references. This was the function of the short film, which could be assembled far more quickly than the feature and could respond to a rapidly changing environment. A study of the most successful propaganda feature films in both Britain and Germany reveals that there was a close correlation between contemporary public desires and viewpoints and the films' central messages. In other words, films with which audiences could identify, which reflected *pre-existing* audience opinions and desires, found success in wartime. This trend fits much of the existing literature relating to wider propaganda theory and practice, Aldous Huxley observing that propaganda can only 'give force and direction to the successive movements of popular feeling and desire; but it does not do much to create these movements. The propagandist is a man who analyses an already existing stream. In a land where there is no water, he digs in vain'.[44] In this environment, British and German propagandists (and indeed the studios, for it is important not to forget that the film industry was also a business in both nations) had to pay close attention to popular needs and desires and political timing, Duff Cooper correctly asserting that 'the power of propaganda, as of all other weapons, must depend very largely upon the time when it is used'.[45] This was particularly true for the politically or ideologically motivated feature. With the fast pace of military events and the length of time needed to produce a feature film, propagandists could so easily miss the opportune moment for the film's release, thus failing to connect the message and popular sentiment. It is perhaps for this reason that both Britain and Germany came to depend on the escapist angle in their propagandistic outputs. The fantasy feature was not bound by the same problems of political and military time, transcending the exact moment of its release to engage with popular needs and desires. It was the combination of fantasy and escapism that made the entertainment feature such a powerful means of propaganda, both in its function and, at times, in its underlying message. It is within this context that popular cinema fulfilled its role as 'a historically specific articulation of social fantasies and mentalities'.[46]

The filmic medium was particularly appropriate as a form of propaganda, well equipped as it was to exploit pre-existing beliefs. It was able to draw upon extant cultural codes, on many occasions having previously formed them in the public mind, connecting contemporary messages with past symbols and memories. As demonstrated by the analysis of the use of history and analogous representations of leadership, propagandists were attuned to the possibility of exploiting popular myths to press home a political point, thinly disguising their message under the veil of escapist historical drama. At the heart of these representations were pre-existing cultural codes and cinematic forms, with which the audience would have been familiar. Here, the propagandist was tapping into 'an already existing stream'. This is particularly, although not exclusively, significant to the study of the cinema of the Third Reich. As Hake observed, such approaches stress 'the continuities on the aesthetic, cultural, social and economic levels that haunt the history of German film beyond all ideological divisions and political ruptures', pointing to 'an acute awareness of the paradoxical, asymmetrical, and non-synchronous relationship between cinema and politics'.[47] Within this restructured conceptual terrain, as Lowry has demonstrated, the Third Reich emerges as having promoted 'a host of countless residual ideologies which in their fragmenting form derail, divert or block the articulation of social lacks, experiences and interests', the aim of Nazi propaganda serving more as a 'structuring presence in content than [forming] unconscious discursive strategies which set parameters for institutionally sanctioned discourse'.[48] To what extent, then, World War II and its cinemas, both British and German, represented a rupture from the past is open to question, the implications of which, particularly in relation to the Nazi state, raise problematic issues for cultural and political historians alike.

A comparative analysis of film propaganda in Britain and Germany naturally raises a series of questions relating to the nature of cinematic persuasion and the form it takes within democracies and dictatorial regimes. The period from 1939 to 1945 also highlights a significant shift in perceptions about propaganda as a modern phenomenon. In Britain, there was a gradual recognition that democracies, at the very least, had to attempt to put their propaganda on a war footing. This was necessary to respond to Nazi psychological aggression in kind, to 'match conviction with greater conviction and make the psychological strength of the fighting democracies shine before the world'. As Grierson understood, 'it behoves us to match faith with greater faith and, with every scientific knowledge and device, secure our own psychological lines'.[49] Propaganda was increasingly seen as a necessity, partly reversing the view that it was 'something dishonest, totalitarian, undemocratic'.[50] By 1945, propagandists had come to understand that the phenomenon could just as easily be used to win the peace, as well as the war. In contrast to 1918, propaganda was not to be judged negatively by its wartime use but emerged as a powerful means of communication which could profitably be employed within a peacetime and democratic context, a realization produced by an understanding of the way in which overt, white propaganda had been used and had increasingly come to serve the masses in giving expression to their multiple identities. By contrast, the German experience forced a reinterpretation of the nature of propaganda. Rather than being seen as the herald of the modern age and an important weapon in warfare, it became tied to the evils of 'totalitarianism'. The horror of propaganda, its potential impacts and its identification with falsehoods were revealed with the peace. It was now seen in its wider European context as a pejorative force, a pervasive view which still persists to some extent, Goebbels being widely recognized as the 'master of propaganda' and his use of communications often equated with 'brainwashing', despite numerous studies pointing to the occasional subtlety of his methods and the flexibility of his psychological manipulation. As Rentschler noted, 'propaganda does not show or suggest; it speaks. Sometimes it whispers; usually it shrieks'.[51]

Effectively, the myth of propaganda, established in the inter-war years, had been debunked. It could not win wars. It could not, alone, affect military outcomes. It was also not the sole preserve of the dictators. Propaganda was inescapable for the modern state, and democracies came to formulate an acceptable use for it in peacetime. The inter-war years had produced an unrealistic and idealistic response to propaganda, Grierson observing that 'we revolted from the bottom of our hearts against any attempt to batter our minds into an over-simplified mould. We resisted what we thought to be an assault on human freedom'. However, with the emergence of the dictatorships of Europe, democracies realized that greater human freedoms were in peril. The world recognized that 'in spite of all [its] protests, [there had been] an even greater development of propaganda' since 1918. The dictatorships began to deploy psychological forces on a massive scale: the Soviet Union forcing its way into power 'not without a great and deliberate use of propaganda'; Germany emerging from 'the sackcloth and ashes of a defeated nation and [becoming] an even more destructive force than before, again through the instruments of propaganda'. With the progress of the war, the democracies too 'reached the point where there is no longer anything gruesome in the thought that [they were] as deeply involved in the war for men's minds as other countries'.[52] The 'old point of view' gradually became submerged into the greater need and was reinterpreted to meet the challenges of the new world. In that new world, film was to find its role in the process of re-creating the once divided nations of Europe. It reflected their identities and desires during wartime and now it was to be redeployed to give visual expression to their hopes for the post-war world. For both nations, this process involved coming to terms with the past: in Britain, the progress towards the 'new Jerusalem' was not without a painful confrontation of the ills of the 1930s; for Germany, a more recent past had to be faced. It was in the light of the needs of reconstruction and peace that film found its new place in the post-war world, standing down from its post as a weapon of war and reconnecting with its role as communicator and mirror of peacetime needs and desires.

NOTES

1. GP G4:19:20, notes by Grierson, n.d.
2. Lord Reith, *The Reith Diaries*, 27 March 1940, p. 244
3. I. Kershaw, 'How Effective was Nazi Propaganda?', pp. 181–2.
4. GP G4:21, 'The Nature of Propaganda'. Also reproduced in F. Hardy (ed.), *Grierson on Documentary*, pp. 108–9.
5. Ibid., p. 104.
6. Ibid., p. 108.
7. Ibid., p. 101.
8. GP G4:19, 'Propaganda and Education'. Also reproduced in F. Hardy (ed.), *Grierson on Documentary*, p. 143.
9. GP G4:N6, 'The Film at War' (1940). Also reproduced in F. Hardy (ed.), *Grierson on Documentary*, p. 86.
10. S. Harper, *Picturing the Past*, p. 91.
11. TNA PRO INF 1/867, 'Programme for Film Propaganda'. CC Paper no. 6. Foreign Publicity Business Advisory Committee, 1939.
12. Monckton papers. MSS DEP Monckton Trustees Papers (Balliol). Box 4. f. 152. 'Matters of Moment', Walter Monckton, 31 March 1941. 1st draft.
13. I. Kershaw, 'How Successful was Nazi Propaganda?', p. 201.
14. Goebbels cited in R. Taylor, 'Goebbels and the Function of Propaganda', p. 36.
15. '"Engländer – schlechte Psychologen". Unterredung mit Dr. Goebbels über die Kapitalfehler der Plutokraten', in *Der Angriff*, 24 March 1940. Wiener Library cuttings collection PC 5/101c.
16. I. Kershaw, 'How Successful was Nazi Propaganda?', p. 201.
17. GP G4:21, 'The Nature of Propaganda'. Also reproduced in F. Hardy (ed.), *Grierson on Documentary*, p. 107.
18. GP G4:N6, 'The Film at War' (1940). Also reproduced in F. Hardy (ed.), *Grierson on Documentary*, p. 88.

19. GP G4:21, 'The Nature of Propaganda'. Also reproduced in F. Hardy (ed.), *Grierson on Documentary*, pp. 107–8.
20. RMVP Ministerial Conference minute, 19 June 1940. In W. Boelcke, *The Secret Conferences of Dr. Goebbels*, p. 57.
21. GP G4:21, 'The Nature of Propaganda'. Also reproduced in F. Hardy (ed.), *Grierson on Documentary*, p. 106.
22. A. Goldman, 'Germans and Nazis', p. 167.
23. Goebbels quoted in Rentschler, *Ministry of Illusion*, p. 20.
24. Rentschler, *Ministry of Illusion*, p. 20.
25. Ibid.
26. GP G4:N6, 'The Film at War' (1940). Also reproduced in F. Hardy (ed.), *Grierson on Documentary*, p. 87.
27. Frank Tuttle, 'People's Daily World', 8 July 1939. GP G3:8:2, Grierson's notes at symposium on 'channels of communication' at the Institute of Public Opinion and Propaganda, UCLA, 14 July 1939.
28. D. Powell, *Films since 1939*, p. 39.
29. D. Culbert, '*Kolberg*', p. 73.
30. I. Kershaw, 'How Successful was Nazi Propaganda?', p. 201.
31. GP G4:21, 'The Nature of Propaganda'. Also reproduced in F. Hardy (ed.), *Grierson on Documentary*, p. 102.
32. D. Welch, *Propaganda and the German Cinema*, pp. 181–2.
33. Greene quoted in K. R. M. Short, 'RAF's Bomber Command', p. 192.
34. M. G. Steinert, *Hitler's War and the Germans*, p. 1.
35. Ibid., p. 3. Here Steinert is quoting P. R. Höfstatter, *Psychologie*, p. 148.
36. Goebbels cited in R. Taylor, 'Goebbels and the Function of Propaganda', p. 38.
37. P. Holquist, '"Information is the Alpha and Omega of our Work": Bolshevik Surveillance in its Pan-European Context', *Journal of Modern History*, vol. 69 (September 1997), pp. 415–50, here, p. 417. I am grateful to Dr. Sarah Davies for drawing my attention to this article.
38. M. G. Steinert, *Hitler's War and the Germans*, p.1.
39. IWM FDC Unidentified and uncatalogued box of materials. SD report of the *Unterabschnitt-Leipzig*, II 225 Tgb. Nr. 3/40 Wa. 1 August 1940. II 214.
40. Two excellent examples of work challenging these conceptions are R. Gellately, *The Gestapo and German Society: Enforcing Racial Policy 1933–1945* (Clarendon, Oxford, 1990) and I. Kershaw, *Popular Opinion and Political Dissent in the Third Reich : Bavaria 1933–1945* (Clarendon, Oxford, 1983).
41. J. Ellul, *Propaganda: The Formation of Men's Attitudes*, p. 241.
42. D. Welch, 'Propaganda' in N. Cull, D. Culbert and D. Welch (eds), *Propaganda and Mass Persuasion*, p. 322.
43. GP G4:21, 'The Nature of Propaganda'. Also reproduced in F. Hardy (ed.), *Grierson on Documentary*, p. 105.
44. A. Huxley, 'Notes on Propaganda', *Harper's*, 174 (December 1936), p. 39. Quoted in N. Cull, D. Culbert and D. Welch (eds), *Propaganda and Mass Persuasion*, p. 320.
45. Duff Cooper, speech to the House of Commons, 3 July 1941. Quoted in N. Cull, D. Culbert and D. Welch (eds), *Propaganda and Mass Persuasion*, p. 321.
46. S. Hake, *Popular Cinema in the Third Reich*, p. viii.
47. Ibid.
48. J.-C. Horak, review of Lowry's *Pathos und Politik. Ideologie im Spielfilm des Nationalsozialismus* in *Historical Journal of Film, Radio and Television* (June 1996).
49. GP G4:21, 'The Nature of Propaganda'. Also reproduced in F. Hardy (ed.), *Grierson on Documentary*, p. 104.

50. M-O A: TC 43/2/C, 'Typed report on Morale/Propaganda', 1940. I am grateful to Mindy Jhittay for drawing my attention to this reference.
51. E. Rentschler, *Ministry of Illusion*, p. 11
52. GP G4:19, 'Propaganda and Education'. Also reproduced in F. Hardy (ed.), *Grierson on Documentary*, p. 141.

SELECT FILMOGRAPHY

ENTRY FORMAT

Title, year; production company; *prod*: producer; *asst dir*: assistant director; *dir*: director; *scr*: screenplay; *comm*: commentary; *narr*: narration; *st*: original story; *cast*: principal cast; *P*: *Prädikat* (Germany only).

Prädikate (Germany only): aw: *anerkennenswert*; bw: *besonders wertvoll*; FN: *Film der Nation*; Jf: *Jugendfrei*; jw: *Jugendwert*; kbw: *künstlerisch besonders wertvoll*; küw: *künstlerisch wertvoll*; küw: *kulturell wertvoll*; Lf: *Lehrfilm*; sbw: *staatspolitisch besonders wertvoll*; skbw: *staatspolitisch und künstlerisch besonders wertvoll*; ST: *Staatspreisfilm*; sw: *staatspolitisch wertvoll*; vb: *volksbildend*; vw: *volkstümlich wertvoll*.

BRITAIN

COMMERCIAL FEATURE FILMS

The Bells Go Down, 1943; Ealing Studios; *prod*: Michael Balcon; *dir*: Basil Dearden; *scr*: Roger Macdougall, Stephen Black; *cast*: Tommy Trinder, James Mason, Mervyn Johns, Philip Friend.

A Canterbury Tale, 1944; Rank/The Archers; *prod/dir/scr*: Michael Powell and Emeric Pressburger; *cast*: Eric Portman, Sheila Sim, Sgt John Sweet, Dennis Price, Hay Petrie, Edward Rigby, George Merritt.

The Day Will Dawn, 1942; GFD/Paul Soskin; *prod*: Paul Soskin; *dir*: Harold French; *scr*: Terence Rattigan, Anatole de Grunwald, Patrick Kirwan; *cast*: Hugh Williams, Griffith Jones, Deborah Kerr, Ralph Richardson, Finlay Currie, Francis L. Sullivan, Roland Pertwee.

The Demi-Paradise, 1943; Two Cities; *prod/scr*: Anatole de Grunwald; *dir*: Anthony Asquith; *cast*: Laurence Olivier, Penelope Dudley Ward, Marjorie Fielding, Margaret Rutherford, Felix Aylmer.

The First of the Few, 1942; British Aviation Pictures; *prod/dir*: Leslie Howard; *scr*: Miles Malleson, Anatole de Grunwald; *st*: Henry C. James, Kay Strueby; *cast*: Leslie Howard, David Niven, Rosamund John, Roland Culver, Derrick de Marney, Filippo Del Giudice.

For Freedom, 1940; Gainsborough Pictures; *prod*: Edward Black; *dir*: Maurice Elvey, Castleton Knight; *scr*: Leslie Arliss, Miles Malleson; *comm*: E. V. H. Emmett, Vice-Admiral J. E. T. Harper; *cast*: Will Fyffe, Anthony Hume, E. V. H. Emmett, Guy Middleton, Albert Lieven, Hugh McDermott.

The Foreman Went to France, 1942; Ealing Studios; *prod*: Michael Balcon; *dir*: Charles Frend; *scr*: John Dighton, Angus McPhail, Leslie Arliss; *st*: J. B. Priestley; cast: Clifford Evans, Tommy Trinder, Constance Cummings, Gordon Jackson, Robert Morley, John Williams.

49th Parallel, 1941; GFD/Ortus Films; *prod*: John Sutro, Michael Powell; *dir*: Michael Powell; *scr*: Emeric Pressburger, Rodney Ackland; *cast*: Leslie Howard, Lawrence Olivier, Anton Walbrook, Raymond Massey, Eric Portman, Glynis Johns, Finlay Currie, Niall MacGinnis.

Freedom Radio, 1941; Two Cities; *prod*: Mario Zampi; *dir*: Anthony Asquith; *scr*: Anatole de Grunwald, Jeffrey Dell, Basil Wood; *cast*: Clive Brook, Diana Wynard, Raymond Huntley, Derek Farr.

The Gentle Sex, 1943; Two Cities/Concanen; *prod*: Derrick de Marney; *dir*: Maurice Elvey, Leslie Howard; *scr*: Moie Charles, Aimee Stuart, Roland Pertwee; *cast*: Joan Gates, Jean Gillie, Joan Greenwood, Lili Palmer, Joyce Howard, Rosamund John, Barbara Waring, Mary Jerrold.

Henry V, 1944; Two Cities/Rank; *prod*: Laurence Olivier; *dir*: Laurence Olivier; *scr*: Alan Dent, Laurence Olivier; *cast*: Laurence Olivier, Leslie Banks, Felix Alymer, Griffith Jones, Ernest Thesiger, Robert Newton, George Robey, Renée Asherton.

In Which We Serve, 1942; Two Cities; *prod*: Noel Coward; *dir*: Noel Coward, David Lean; *scr*: Noel Coward; *cast*: Noel Coward, John Mills, Bernard Miles, Celia Johnson, Kay Walsh, Richard Attenborough.

Let George Do It, 1940; Ealing Studios; *prod*: Michael Balcon; *dir*: Marcel Varnel; *scr*: Angus MacPhail, Basil Dearden, Austin Melford, John Dighton; *cast*: George Formby, Romney Brent, Phyllis Calvert, Bernard Lee, Garry Marsh.

The Life and Death of Colonel Blimp, 1943; The Archers, Rank; *prod*: Michael Powell, Emeric Pressburger; *dir*: Michael Powell, Emeric Pressburger; *scr*: Michael Powell, Emeric Pressburger; *cast*: Roger Livesey, Anton Walbrook, Deborah Kerr, Roland Culver, James McKechnie.

The Lion Has Wings, 1939; London Film Productions; *prod*: Alexander Korda; *dir*: Michael Powell, Brian Desmond Hurst, Adrian Brunel; *scr*: Ian Dalrymple, Adrian Brunel, E. V. H. Emmett; comm: E. V. H. Emmett; *cast*: Ralph Richardson, Merle Oberon, Derrick de Marney, June Duprez.

Millions Like Us, 1943; Gainsborough Pictures; *prod*: Edward Black; *dir*: Frank Launder, Sidney Gilliat; *scr*: Frank Launder, Sidney Gilliat; *cast*: Patricia Roc, Anne Crawford, Eric Portman, Gordon Jackson, Basil Radford.

Mr Emmanuel, 1944; British Lion; *prod*: William Sistrom; *dir*: Harold French; *scr*: Gordon Wellesley; *cast*: Felix Aylmer, Greta Gynt, Ursula Jeans, Walter Rilia, Peter Mullins.

The Next of Kin, 1942; Ealing Studios; *prod*: Michael Balcon; *dir*: Thorold Dickinson; *scr*: Thorold Dickinson, Angus MacPhail, John Dighton, Basil Bartlett; *cast*: Mervyn Johns, John Chandos, Nova Pilbeam, David Hutcheson, Jack Hawkins.

One of Our Aircraft is Missing, 1942; British National; *prod*: John Cornfield; *dir*: Michael Powell; *scr*: Emeric Pressburger; *cast*: Eric Portman, Godfrey Tearle, Bernard Miles, Hugh Williams.

Pastor Hall, 1940; Charter Films; *prod*: John Boulting; *dir*: Roy Boulting; *scr*: Leslie Arliss; *cast*: Marius Goring, Seymour Hicks, Wilfred Lawson, Eliot Makeham, Nova Pilbeam, Brian Worth.

Pimpernel Smith, 1941; British National; *prod*: Leslie Howard; *dir*: Leslie Howard; *scr*: Anatole de Grunwald; *cast*: Peter Gawthorne, Mary Morris, Francis L. Sullivan, Leslie Howard.

The Prime Minister, 1941; Warner Bros. British Productions; *prod*: Max Milder; *dir*: Thorold Dickinson; *scr*: Michael Hogan, Brock Williams; *cast*: Fay Compton, John Gielgud, Will Fyffe, Stephen Murray, Owen Nares, Diana Wynyard.

San Demetrio, London, 1943; Ealing Studios; *prod*: Michael Balcon; *dir*: Charles Frend; *scr*: Charles Frend; *cast*: Robert Beatty, Walter Fitzgerald, Gordon Jackson, Mervyn Johns, Ralph Michael.

This England, 1941; British National; *prod*: John Corfield; *dir*: David Macdonald; *scr*: A. R. Rawlinson, Bridget Boland, Emlyn Williams; *cast*: Constance Cummings, Esmond Knight, Frank Pettingell, John Clements, Emlyn Williams.

This Happy Breed, 1944; Two Cities, Cineguild; *prod*: Anthony Havelock-Allen, Noel Coward; *dir*: David Lean; *scr*: Anthony Havelock-Allen, Ronald Neame, David Lean; *cast*: Stanley Holloway, Celia Johnson, Robert Newton, Kay Walsh, John Mills.

Unpublished Story, 1942; Columbia; *prod*: Anthony Havelock-Allen; *dir*: Harold French; *scr*: Sidney Gilliat, Lesley Storm, Allan MacKinnon, Patrick Kirwan; *cast*: Roland Culver, Richard Greene, Valerie Hobson, Basil Radford.

The Way Ahead, 1944; Two Cities; *prod*: John Sutro, Norman Walker; *dir*: Carol Reed; *scr*: Eric Ambler, Peter Ustinov; *cast*: James Donald, William Hartnell, Stanley Holloway, Raymond Huntley, David Niven.

The Way to the Stars, 1945; Two Cities; *prod*: Anatole de Grunwald; *dir*: Anthony Asquith; *scr*: Terence Ratigan; *cast*: Bonar Colleano, Trevor Howard, Rosamund John, Douglass Montgomery, Michael Redgrave, John Mills.

Went the Day Well?, 1942; Ealing Studios; *prod*: Michael Balcon; *dir*: Alberto Cavalcanti; *scr*: John Dighton, Diana Morgan, Angus MacPhail from story by Graham Greene; *cast*: Elizabeth Allan, Leslie Banks, Frank Lawton, Basil Sydney, Valerie Taylor, Muriel George, Thora Hird.

The Young Mr Pitt, 1942; Gainsborough Productions; *prod*: Edward Black; *dir*: Carol Reed; *scr*: Frank Launder, Sidney Gilliat; *cast*: Robert Donat, Robert Morely, Phyllis Calvert, John Mills, Herbert Lom.

DOCUMENTARY FEATURE AND SHORT FILMS

ABCA, 1943; Army Film and Photographic Unit; *prod*: Ronald Riley; *dir*: Ronald Riley; *scr*: Jack Saward.

All Hands, 1940; Ealing Studios; *prod*: Michael Balcon; *dir*: John Paddy Carstairs.

The Biter Bit, 1943; Coombe Productions; *prod*: Alexander Korda; *scr*: Michael Foot.

Christmas under Fire, 1941; Crown Film Unit; *dir*: Harry Watt; *scr*: Quentin Reynolds.

Coastal Command, 1943; Crown Film Unit; *prod*: Ian Dalrymple; *dir*: Jack Lee; *scr*: Jack Lee.

Dangerous Comment, 1940; Ealing Studios; *prod*: Michael Balcon; *dir*: John Paddy Carstairs.

The Dawn Guard, 1941; Charter Films; *prod*: John Boulting; *dir*: Roy Boulting; *scr*: Anna Reiner.

Desert Victory, 1943; Army Film and Photographic Unit and RAF Film Production Unit; *prod*: David MacDonald; *dir*: Roy Boulting; *scr*: James Lansdale Hodson.

A Diary for Timothy, 1946; Crown Film Unit; *prod*: Basil Wright; *dir*: Humphrey Jennings; *scr*: Humphrey Jennings.

Fires Were Started, 1943; Crown Film Unit; *prod*: Ian Dalrymple; *dir*: Humphrey Jennings; *scr*: Humphrey Jennings.

The First Days, 1939; GPO Film Unit; *prod*: Alberto Cavalcanti; *dir*: Humphrey Jennings, Harry Watt, Pat Jackson.

The Heart of Britain, 1941; Crown Film Unit; *prod*: Humphrey Jennings; *dir*: Humphrey Jennings.

Journey Together, 1945; RAF Film Production Unit; *prod*: John Boulting; *dir*: John Boulting; *scr*: Terence Rattigan; *cast*: Richard Attenborough, Jack Watling, Edward G. Robinson, Bessie Love.

Listen to Britain, 1942; Crown Film Unit; *prod*: Ian Dalrymple; *dir*: Humphrey Jennings, Stewart McAllister.

London Can Take It, 1940; GPO Film Unit; *dir*: Harry Watt, Humphrey Jennings; *scr*: Quentin Reynolds.

Men of the Lightship, 1940; GPO Film Unit; *prod*: Alberto Cavalcanti; *dir*: David Macdonald; *scr*: Rodney Ackland.

Now You're Talking, 1940; Ealing Studios; *prod*: Michael Balcon; *dir*: John Paddy Carstairs.

Post 23, 1941; Strand; *dir*: Ralph Bond; *scr*: Ralph Bond.

Rush Hour, 1942; 20th Century Fox; *prod*: Edward Black; *dir*: Anthony Asquith.

The Silent Village, 1943; Crown Film Unit; *prod*: Humphrey Jennings; *dir*: Humphrey Jennings; *scr*: Humphrey Jennings.

Squadron 992, 1940; GPO Film Unit; *prod*: Alberto Cavalcanti; *dir*: Harry Watt; *scr*: W. D. H. McCullough.

Target for Tonight, 1941; Crown Film Unit; *prod*: Ian Dalrymple; *dir*: Harry Watt; *scr*: Harry Watt.

The True Story of Lili Marlene, 1944; Crown Film Unit; *prod*: J. B. Holmes; *dir*: Humphrey Jennings; *scr*: Humphrey Jennings.

They Speak for Themselves, 1942; Seven League; *prod*: Paul Rotha; *dir*: H. M. Nieter.

The True Glory, 1945; British Army and Photographic Unit and American and Allied Film Services; *prod*: Carol Reed, Garson Kanin; *dir*: Carol Reed, Garson Kanin; *scr*: Eric Maschwitz, Arthur Macrae, Jenny Nicholson.

Tunisian Victory, 1944; Army Film and Photographic Unit and US Service Film Units; *prod*: Hugh Stewart, Frank Capra; *dir*: Hugh Stewart, Frank Capra; *scr*: James Lansdale Hodson, Anthony Veiller.

Western Approaches, 1944; Crown Film Unit; *prod*: Ian Dalrymple; *dir*: Pat Jackson; *scr*: Pat Jackson.

Words and Actions, 1943; Realist; *prod*: Edgar Anstey; *dir*: Max Andersen, G. A. Simmonds.

Words for Battle, 1941; Crown Film Unit; *prod*: Ian Dalrymple; *dir*: Humphrey Jennings; *scr*: Humphrey Jennings.

World of Plenty, 1943; Rotha Productions; *dir*: Paul Rotha; *scr*: Eric M. Knight.

GERMANY

COMMERCIAL FEATURE FILMS

Achtung Feind hört mit!, 1940; Terra; *asst dir*: Hans Müller; *dir*: Arthur Maria Rabenalt; *scr*: Kurt Heuser; *cast*: Michael Bohnen, Rolf Weih, Christian Kayßler, Lotte Koch, Josef Sieber, Karl Dannemann, Armin Münch, Rudolf Schündler, Adolf Fischer, Ernst Waldow, René Deltgen; *P*: sw.

Andreas Schlüter, 1942; Tobis; *asst dir*: Heinz-Günther Schulz; *dir*: Herbert Maisch; *scr*: Helmut Brandis, Herbert Maisch; *cast*: Heinrich George, Mila Kopp, Olga Tschechowa, Dorothea Wieck, Theodor Loos, Karl John, Herbert Hübner, Marianne Simson, Ernst Fritz Fürbringer, Eduard von Winterstein, Emil Heß, Robert Taube, Max Gülstorff, Christian Kayßler, Trude Haefelin, Paul Dahlke, Franz Schafheitlin, Otto Graf; P: skbw, vw.

Annelie, 1941; Ufa; *asst dir*: Walter Wischniewsky; *dir*: Josef von Baky; *scr*: Thea von Harbou; *cast*: Luise Ullrich, Karl Ludwig Diehl, Werner Krauß, Käthe Haack, Albert Hehn, Axel von Ambesser, Ilse Fürstenberg; *P*: skbw, vw.

Auf Wiedersehen, Franziska!, 1941; Terra; *asst dir*: Rudolf Jugert; *dir*: Helmut Käutner; *scr*: Helmut Käutner, Curt J. Braun; *cast*: Marianne Hoppe, Hans Söhnker, Fritz Odemar, Rudolf Fernau, Hermann Speelmans, Margot Hielscher, Herbert Hübner, Josefine Dora, Frida Richard; *P*: küw.

Bismarck, 1940; Tobis; *asst dir*: Peter Pewas, Siegfried Krügler; *dir*: Wolfgang Liebeneiner; *scr*: Rolf Lauckner, Wolfgang Liebeneiner; *cast*: Paul Hartmann, Friedrich Kayßler, Lil Dagover, Käthe Haack, Maria Koppenhöfer, Walter Franck, Ruth Hellberg, Werner Hinz, Margret Militzer, Karl Schönböck, Günther Hadank; *P*: skbw, jw.

Carl Peters, 1941; Bavaria; *dir*: Herbert Selpin; *scr*: Ernst von Salomon, Walter Zerlett-Olfenius, Herbert Selpin; *cast*: Hans Albers, Karl Dannemann, Fritz Odemar, Hans Leibelt, Erika von Thellmann, Toni von Bukovics, Rolf Prasch, Friedrich Otto Fischer, Herbert Hübner; *P*: skw, kuw, vb, jw.

D III 88, 1939; Tobis; *dir*: Hans Bertram, Herbert Maisch; *scr*: Hans Bertram, Wolf Neumeister; *cast*: Christian Kayßler, Otto Wernicke, Heinz Welzel, Hermann Braun, Horst Birr, Adolf Fischer, Fritz Eberth, Karl Martell, Paul Otto, Carsta Löck; *P*: sbw, jw.

Die Entlassung, 1942; Tobis; *asst dir*: Leo de Laforgue, Hilde Vissering; *prod*: Emil Jannings; *dir*: Wolfgang Liebeneiner; *scr*: Curt J. Braun, Felix von Eckhardt; *cast*: Emil Jannings, Margarethe Schön, Christian Kayßler, Theodor Loos, Karl Ludwig Diehl, Hildegard Grethe, Werner Hinz, Werner Krauß, Otto Graf, Paul Hoffmann, Paul Bildt, Walther Süßenguth, Franz Schafheitlin,

Herbert Hübner, Rudolf Blümner, Fritz Kampers, Werner Pledath, Heinrich Schroth, O. E. Hasse, Friedrich Maurer, Otto Stoeckel, Karl-Heinz Peters; *P*: FN, skbw, kuw, vw, aw, vb, jw.

Feinde, 1940; Bavaria; *asst dir*: Auguste Reuß-Barth; *dir*: Viktor Toujansky; *scr*: Emil Burn, Arthur Luethy, Viktor Tourjansky; *cast*: Brigitte Horney, Willy Birgel, Ivan Petrovich, Karl-Heinz Peters, Carl Wery, Nikolaj Kolin, Hedwig Wangel, Reinhold Lütjohann, Gerd Höst, Arthur Fritz, Arnulf Schröder, Hannes Keppler, Beppo Brem; *P*: sw, küw, jw.

Friedemann Bach, 1941; Terra; *asst dir*: Ulrich Erfurth; *dir*: Traugott Müller; *scr*: Helmut Brandis, Eckart von Naso; *cast*: Gustaf Gründgens, Leny Marenbach, Johannes Riemann, Camilla Horn, Eugen Klöpfer, Wolfgang Liebeneiner, Hermine Körner, Gustav Knuth; *P*: kuw, küw.

Friedrich Schiller, 1940; Tobis; *asst dir*: Walter Steffens; *dir*: Herbert Maisch; *scr*: Walter Wassermann, C. H. Diller; *cast*: Horst Caspar, Heinrich George, Lil Dagover, Eugen Klöpfer, Paul Henckels, Friedrich Kayßler, Herbert Hübner, Hannelore Schroth, Hildegard Grethe, Lore Hansen, Albert Florath; *P*: sw, küw, jw.

Der Fuchs von Glenarvon, 1940; Tobis; *asst dir*: Willy Zeyn; *dir*: Max Kimmich; *scr*: Wolf Neumeister, Hans Bertram; *cast*: Olga Tschechowa, Karl Ludwig Diehl, Ferdinand Marian, Joachim Pfaff, Traudl Stark, Albert Florath, Lucie Höflich, Else von Möllendorff, Richard Häußler, Ellen Bang, Elisabeth Flickenschildt, Curt Lucas, Paul Otto, Werner Hinz; *P*: küw.

GPU, 1942; Ufa; *dir*: Karl Ritter; *scr*: Karl Ritter, Felix Lützkendorf, Andrews Engelmann; *cast*: Laura Solari, Andrews Engelmann, Marina von Ditmar, Will Quadflieg, Karl Haubenreißer, Helene von Schmithberg, Vladimír Majer, Hans Stiebner, Maria Bard, Karl Klüsner.

Große Freiheit Nr. 7, 1944; Terra; *asst dir*: Rudolf Jugert; *dir*: Helmut Käutner; *scr*: Richard Nicolas, Helmut Käutner; *cast*: Hans Albers, Ilse Werner, Hans Söhnker, Gustav Knuth, Günther Lüders, Hilde Hildebrand, Ethel Reschke, Kurt Wieschala, Helmut Käutner, Richard Nicolas.

Der große König, 1942; Tobis; *asst dir*: Wolfgang Schleif, Herbert Kiehne; *dir*: Veit Harlan; *scr*: Veit Harlan; *cast*: Otto Gebühr, Kristina Söderbaum, Gustav Fröhlich, Paul Wegener, Paul Henckels, Elisabeth Flickenschildt, Kurt Meisel, Hilde Körber, Claus Clausen, Klaus Detlef Sierck, Herbert Hübner, Otto Wernicke, Otto Graf; *P*: FN, skbw, kuw, vw, vb, jw.

Die große Liebe, 1942; Ufa; *dir*: Rolf Hansen; *scr*: Rolf Hansen, Peter Groll; *cast*: Zarah Leander, Grethe Weiser, Viktor Staal, Paul Hörbiger, Wolfgang Preiss, Hans Schwarz Jr, Leopold von Ledebur, Julia Serda, Victor Janson; *P*: skw, vw.

Das Herz der Königin, 1940; Ufa; *asst dir*: Harald Braun, Rolf Hansen; *dir*: Carl Froelich; *scr*: Harald Braun, Jacob Geis, Rolf Beissmann; *cast*: Zarah Leander, Willy Birgel, Maria Koppenhöfer, Lotte Koch, Axel von Ambesser, Friedrich Benfer, Will Quadflieg, Walther Süßenguth, Bruno Decarli, Ruth Buchardt, Anneliese von Eschstruth, Margot Hielscher, Lisa Lesco, Ernst Stahl-Nachbaur; *P*: küw, kuw.

Heimkehr, 1941; Wien-Film; *asst dir*: Wolfgang Schubert; *dir*: Gustav Ucicky; *scr*: Gerhard Menzel; *cast*: Paula Wessely, Peter Petersen, Attila Hörbiger, Ruth Hellberg, Berta Drews, Elsa Wagner, Gerhild Weber, Carl Raddatz, Werner Fuetterer, Otto Wernicke; *P*: FN, skbw, jw.

Himmelhunde, 1942; Terra; *dir*: Roger von Norman; *scr*: Philipp Lothar Mayring; *cast*: Malte Jaeger, Lutz Gotz, Albert Florath.

Jud Süß, 1940; Terra; *asst dir*: Wolfgang Schleif, Alfred Braun; *dir*: Veit Harlan; *scr*: Veit Harlan, Eberhard Wolfgang Moller, Ludwig Metzger; *cast*: Ferdinand Marian, Heinrich George, Hilde von Stolz, Werner Krauß, Eugen Klöpfer, Kristina Söderbaum, Malte Jaeger, Albert Florath, Theodor Loos; *P*: skbw, jw.

Junge Adler, 1944; Ufa; *asst dir*: Carl Merznicht, Zlata Mehlers; *dir*: Alfred Weidenmann; *scr*: Herbert Reinecker, Alfred Weidenmann; *cast*: Willy Fritsch, Herbert Hübner, Dietmar Schönherr, Gerta Böttcher, Albert Florath, Karl Dannemann, Aribert Wäscher, Paul Henckels, Josef Sieber; *P*: sw, küw, jw.

Kadetten, 1941; Ufa; *asst dir*: Gottfried Ritter; *dir*: Karl Ritter; *scr*: Karl Ritter, Felix Lützkendorf; *cast*: Mathias Wieman, Carsta Löck, Andrews Engelmann, Theo Shall, Josef Keim, Erich Walter, Wilhelm Kaiser-Heyl, Willy Krüger, Bernd Rußbült, Klaus Detlef Sierck, Martin Brendel, Jürgen Mohbutter, Rolf Ullmann-Schienle, Hans-Otto Gauglitz, Gert Witt, Klaus Storch.

Kampfgeschwader Lützow, 1941; Tobis; *asst dir*: Rudolf Hilberg, Fritz Wendel; *dir*: Hans Bertram; *scr*: Wolf Neumeister, Heinz Orlovius, Hans Bertram; *cast*: Christian Kayßler, Hermann Braun, Heinz Welzel, Hannes Keppler, Marietheres Angerpointner, Carsta Löck, Adolf Fischer, Horst Birr, Helmut vom Hofe, Peter Voss, Ernst Stimmel; *P*: skbw, vw, jw.

Kitty und die Weltkonferenz, 1939; Terra; *asst dir*: Boleslaw Barlog, Rudolf Jugert; *dir*: Helmut Käutner; *scr*: Helmut Käutner; *cast*: Hannelore Schroth, Fritz Odemar, Christian Gollong, Maria Nicklisch, Max Gülstorff, Paul Hörbiger, Charlott Daudert.

Kolberg, 1945; Ufa; *asst dir*: Wolfgang Schleif, Kurt Meisel; *dir*: Veit Harlan; *scr*: Alfred Braun, Veit Harlan; *cast*: Heinrich George, Kristina Söderbaum, Paul Wegener, Horst Caspar, Gustav Diessl, Otto Wernicke, Irene von Meyendorff, Kurt Meisel, Hans Hermann Schaufuß, Franz Schafheitlin, Theo Shall; *P*: FN, skbw, kuw, vw, aw, vb, jw.

Leinen aus Irland, 1939; Styria Film for Wien Film; *dir*: Heinz Helbig; *scr*: Harald Bratt; *cast*: Otto Treßler, Irene von Meyendorff, Rolf Wanka, Friedl Haerlin, Georg Alexander, Hans Olden, Maria Olszewska, Oskar Sima, Siegfried Breuer, Tibor von Halmay; *P*: sw, küw.

Mein Leben für Irland, 1941; Tobis; *asst dir*: Willy Zeyn; *dir*: Max W. Kimmich; *scr*: Max W. Kimmich, Toni Huppertz; *cast*: Anna Dammann, Werner Hinz, René Deltgen, Will Quadflieg, Eugen Klöpfer, Heinz Ohlsen, Paul Wegener, Karl Dannemann, Friedrich Maurer, Claus Clausen, Karl John, Siegfried Drost; *P*: sw, küw, jw.

Münchhausen, 1943; Ufa; *dir*: Josef von Baky; *scr*: Erich Kästner; *cast*: Hans Albers, Hans Brausewetter, Käte Haack, Brigitte Horney, Ferdinand Marian, Hermann Speelmans, Ilse Werner; *P*: kbw, vw.

Ohm Krüger, 1941; Tobis; *prod*: Emil Jannings; *dir*: Hans Steinhoff; *scr*: Harald Bratt, Kurt Heuser; *cast*: Emil Jannings, Lucie Höflich, Werner Hinz, Ernst Schröder, Friedrich Ulmer Joubert, Eduard von Winterstein, Hans Adalbert Schlettow, Max Gülstorff Reitz, Walter Werner Kock, Elisabeth Flickenschildt, Hedwig Wangel, Alfred Bernau, Gustaf Gründgens, Ferdinand Marian, Flockina von Platen, Karl Haubenreißer, Franz Schafheitlin, Otto Wernicke; *P*: FN, skbw, kuw, vw, vb, jw.

Quax, der Bruchpilot, 1941; Terra; *asst dir*: Toni Thermal, Fritz Aeckerle; *dir*: Kurt Hoffmann; *scr*: Robert A. Stemmle; *cast*: Heinz Rühmann, Karin Himboldt, Werner Holten, Lothar Firmans, Harry Liedtke, Elga Brink, Hilde Sessak, Beppo Brem; *P*: küw, vw, jw.

Rembrandt, 1942; Terra; *asst dir*: C. A. H. van der Linden, Roland von Rossi; *dir*: Hans Steinhoff; *scr*: Kurt Heuser, Hans Steinhoff; *cast*: Ewald Balser, Gisela Uhlen, Hertha Feiler, Elisabeth Flickenschildt, Aribert Wäscher, Theodor Loos, Paul Henckels; *P*: küw.

Romanze in Moll, 1943; Tobis; *asst dir*: Siegfried Breuer, Rudolf Jugert; *dir*: Helmut Käutner; *scr*: Willy Clever, Helmut Käutner; *cast*: Marianne Hoppe, Paul Dahlke, Ferdinand Marian, Siegfried Breuer, Eric Helgar; *P*: kbw.

Stukas, 1941; Ufa; *asst dir*: Conrad von Molo; *dir*: Karl Ritter; *scr*: Karl Ritter, Felix Lützkendorf; *cast*: Carl Raddatz, Hannes Stelzer, Ernst von Klipstein, Albert Hehn, Herbert Wilk, O. E. Hasse, Karl John, Else Knott, Egon Müller-Franken, Günther Markert, Adolf Fischer; *P*: sw, küw, vw, jw.

Titanic, 1943; Tobis; *asst dir*: Erich Frisch; *dir*: Herbert Selpin, Werner Klinger; *scr*: Walter Zerlett-Olfenius, Hansi Köck, Herbert Selpin; *cast*: Sybille Schmitz, Kirsten Heiberg, Hans Nielsen, Ernst Fritz Fürbringer, Karl Schönböck, Charlotte Thiele, Otto Wernicke, Franz Schafheitlin, Theo Shall, Theodor Loos, Sepp Rist.; *P*: skw

U-Boote westwärts, 1941; Ufa; *asst dir*: Wolfgang Wehrum; *dir*: Günther Rittau; *scr*: Georg Zoch; *cast*: Herbert Wilk, Heinz Engelmann, Joachim Brennecke, Wilhelm Borchert, Karl John, Clemens Hasse, Carsta Löck, Herbert Klatt, Ingeborg Senkpiel, Agnes Windeck, Claire Reigbert; *P*: sw, küw, vb.

Unter den Brücken, 1946; Ufa; *asst dir*: Rudolf Jugert; *dir*: Helmut Käutner; *scr*: Walter Ulbrich, Helmut Käutner; *cast*: Hannelore Schroth, Carl Raddatz, Gustav Knuth, Ursula Grabley, Hildegard Knef.

Wunschkonzert, 1940; Cine-Allianz Tonfilm Produktion for Ufa; *dir*: Eduard von Borsody; *scr*: Eduard von Borsody, Lützkendorf; *cast*: Ilse Werner, Carl Raddatz, Heinz Goedecke, Joachim Brennecke, Ida Wüst, Hedwig Bleibtreu, Hans Hermann Schaufuß, Hans Adalbert Schlettow, Malte Jaeger, Walter Ladengast, Albert Florath, Elise Aulinger, Wilhelm Althaus, Marika Rökk, Heinz Rühmann, Paul Hörbiger, Hans Brausewetter, Josef Sieber, Willy Fritsch, Weiß-Ferdl; *P*: sw, küw, vw, jw.

DOCUMENTARY FEATURE AND SHORT FILMS

Feldzug in Polen, 1939; Deutsche Filmherstellungs-und-Verwertungs-GmbH; *dir*: Fritz Hippler.

Feuertaufe, 1940; Tobis; *dir*: Hans Bertram; *scr*: Hans Bertram, Wilhelm Stöppler; *narr*: Herbert Gernot.

Gentlemen, 1941; Deutsche Wochenschau-GmbH.

Sieg im Westen, 1941; Deutsche Filmherstellungs-und-Verwertungs-GmbH; *dir*: Svend Noldan; *scr*: Svend Noldan, Fritz Bruscha.

Soldaten von Morgen, 1941; Deutsche Filmherstellungs-und-Verwertungs-GmbH; *dir*: Alfred Weidenmann; *scr*: Alfred Weidenmann.

SELECT BIBLIOGRAPHY

ARCHIVAL RESOURCES

BUNDESARCHIV, BERLIN

R55 *Reichsministerium für Volksaufklärung und Propaganda*
R56/I *Reichskulturkammer*
R56/VI *Reichsfilmkammer*
R58 *Reichssicherheitshauptamt*
R109 I/II *Records of Ufa, Terra, Tobis, Wien and Berlin Film Companies*
BDC *Files of the former Berlin Document Center*

BUNDESARCHIV FILMARCHIV

HOOVER INSTITUTION FOR WAR, PEACE AND REVOLUTION, STANFORD UNIVERSITY, CALIFORNIA

Papers of Hans Hinkel, *Reichsfilmintendant*, speeches and writings 1924–44. IDCSU2YY222-A

STIFTUNG DEUTSCHE KINEMATEK, BERLIN SCHRIFTGUTS ARCHIV

Select film and personal files. In particular files relating to the following films:

Achtung! Feind hört mit!
Bismarck
D III 88
Damals
Diesel
Die Entlassung
Feinde
Feldzug in Polen
Feuertaufe
Friedrich Schiller
Fronttheater
Der Fuchs von Glenarvon
Germanin
G.P.U.
Große Freiheit No.7.
Der Große König
Hauptsache Glücklich
Ich brauche dich
Junge Adler

Kadetten
Kampfgeschwader Lützow
Leinen aus Irland
Mein Leben für Irland
Münchhausen
Ohm Krüger
Der Postmeister
Quax, der Bruchpilot
Reitet für Deutschland
Rembrandt
Robert Koch
Titanic
Über Alles in der Welt
Unter den Brücken

Personal files relating to:

Rolf Hansen
Veit Harlan
Helmut Käutner
Wolfgang Liebeneiner
Gustav Ucicky
Zensurkarte

WIENER LIBRARY, LONDON

Cuttings collection.

BRENDAN BRACKEN PAPERS, CHURCHILL COLLEGE, CAMBRIDGE

BRITISH FILM INSTITUTE LIBRARY, LONDON

Press books, publicity materials and cuttings collection.

BRITISH FILM INSTITUTE, SPECIAL COLLECTIONS, LONDON

Anthony Asquith Collection
Michael Balcon Collection
Thorold Dickinson Collection
Humphrey Jennings Collection
British Board of Film Censors records
Film Society Collection

KENNETH CLARK PAPERS, TATE GALLERY, LONDON

WINSTON CHURCHILL PAPERS, CHURCHILL COLLEGE, CAMBRIDGE

JOHN GRIERSON PAPERS, SPECIAL COLLECTIONS, UNIVERSITY OF STIRLING, SCOTLAND

IMPERIAL WAR MUSEUM, DUXFORD. FOREIGN DOCUMENTS COLLECTION

IMPERIAL WAR MUSEUM, LONDON. WRITTEN ARCHIVES

IMPERIAL WAR MUSEUM, LONDON. FILM ARCHIVE

IMPERIAL WAR MUSEUM, LONDON. SOUND ARCHIVE

LAURENCE OLIVIER COLLECTION, BRITISH LIBRARY, LONDON

MASS-OBSERVATION ARCHIVES, SPECIAL COLLECTIONS, UNIVERSITY OF SUSSEX
File Reports and Topic collections.

MONCKTON PAPERS, DEPARTMENT OF SPECIAL COLLECTIONS AND WESTERN MANUSCRIPTS, NEW BODLEIAN LIBRARY, UNIVERSITY OF OXFORD

NATIONAL ARCHIVES, KEW
AIR *Air Ministry*
INF1 *Ministry of Information: General memoranda and correspondence*
INF5 *Records of the GPO and Crown Film Units*
INF 6 *Records of the Films Division*
FO *Foreign Office*
PREM4 *Prime Ministerial correspondence*

SELECT NEWSPAPERS AND TRADE NEWSPAPERS
Der Angriff
Documentary News Letter
Film-Kurier
Filmwelt
Filmwoche
Illustrierter Film-Kurier
Kinematograph Weekly
Monthly Film Bulletin
New York Times
Picturegoer Weekly
Das Reich
Sight and Sound
The Times
Today's Cinema
Völkischer Beobachter

WORKS PUBLISHED PRIOR TO 1945
Harrisson, T., 'What is Public Opinion?', *Political Quarterly*, vol. 4 (1940), pp. 368–83.
Hippler, F., *Betrachtungen zum Filmschaffen* (Max Hesses Verlag, Berlin, 1942).
Hitler, A., *Mein Kampf*, trans. R. Manheim (Hutchinson, London, 1992).

IHERING, H., *Emil Jannings. Baumeister seines Lebens und seiner Filme* (Hüthig, Heidelberg, Berlin, Leipzig, 1941).

KNOP, W. G. (ed.), *Beware of the English! German Propaganda Exposes England* (Hamish Hamilton, London, 1939).

KRIEGK, O., *Der deutsche Film im Spiegel der Ufa. 25 Jahre Kampf und Vollendung* (Ufa, Berlin, 1943).

MADGE, C. and Harrisson, T., *Britain by Mass-Observation* (Penguin, Harmondsworth, 1939).

ROBSON, E. W. and M. M., *The Shame and Disgrace of Colonel Blimp: The True Story of the Film* (The Sidneyon Society, London, n.d.).

ROTHA, P. and Knight, E., *World of Plenty. The Book of the Film* (Nicholson and Watson, London, 1945).

SANDER, A. U., *Jugend und Film* (Franz Eher Verlag, Berlin, 1944).

SHIRER, W., *Berlin Diary. The Journal of a Foreign Correspondent, 1934–1941* (Hamish Hamilton, London, 1941).

SINGTON, D. and Weidenfeld, A., *The Goebbels Experiment. A Study of the Nazi Propaganda Machine* (John Murray, London, 1942).

UFA, *Zur festlichen Aufführung des Emil Jannings Films der Tobis: Ohm Krüger.*

UFA, *Freedom Calling! The Story of the Secret German Radio by the Representative in Great Britain of the Freedom Station* (Frederick Muller, London, 1939).

WARE, J., *The Lion Has Wings: The Epic of the Famous Korda Film*, from the film written by Ian Dalrymple (Collins, London, January 1940).

AUTOBIOGRAPHICAL WORKS

BALCON, M., *Michael Balcon Presents... A Lifetime of Films* (Hutchinson, London, 1969).

CLARK, K., *The Other Half: A Self Portrait* (John Murray, London, 1977).

CLARKE, T. E. B., *This is Where I Came In* (Joseph, London, 1974).

FRÖHLICH, G., *Waren das Zeiten. Mein Film-Heldenleben* (Herbig, Munich, 1984).

HARLAN, V., *Souvenirs ou le cinema allemand selon Goebbels* (éditions france-empire, Paris, 1974).

HIPPLER, F., *Verstrickung: Einstellungen und Ruckblenden* (Verlag Mehr Wissen, Düsseldorf, 1981).

JANNINGS, E., *Theater, Film – Das Leben und ich* (Zimmer & Herzog, Berchtesgarten, 1951).

KÄUTNER, H., *Abblenden* (Moewig, Munich, 1981).

KRAUSS, W., *Das Schauspiel meines Lebens. Einem Freund erzählt*, ed. H. Weigel (Goverts, Stuttgart, 1958).

MAISCH, H., *Helm ab – Vorhang auf. Siebzig Jahre eines ungewöhnlichen Lebens* (Lechte, Emsdetten, 1968).

MILLS, J., *Up in the Clouds Gentlemen Please* (Weidenfeld and Nicolson, London, 1980).

POWELL, M., *A Life in the Movies: An Autobiography* (Mandarin, London, 1986).

REIHT-ZANTHIER, J. von, *Sie machten uns glücklich. Erinnerungen an große Schauspieler in goldenen und nicht nur goldenen Jahren* (Ehrenwirth Verlag, Munich, 1967).

SEMMLER, R., *Goebbels. The Man Next to Hitler* (Westhouse, London, 1947).

SÖDERBAUM, K., *Nichts bleibt immer so. Rückblenden auf ein Leben vor und hinter der Kamera* (Hestia, Bayreuth, 1983).

WATT, H., *Don't Look at the Camera* (Paul Elek, London, 1974).

PUBLISHED DOCUMENT COLLECTIONS

AITKEN, I. (ed.), *The Documentary Film Movement. An Anthology* (Edinburgh University Press, Edinburgh, 1998).

BEHNKEN, K. (ed.), *Deutschland-Berichte der SOPADE*, 6 vols (Verlag Petra Nettelbeck, Zweitausendeins, Frankfurt am Main, 1980).

BOBERACH, H. (ed.), *Meldungen aus dem Reich. Die geheimen Lageberichte des Sicherheitsdienstes der SS, 1938–1945*, 17 vols (Pawlak Verlag, Herrsching, 1984).

BOELCKE, W., *The Secret Conferences of Dr. Goebbels. October 1939–March 1943*, trans. E. Osers (Weidenfeld and Nicolson, London, 1966 and 1967).

CHRISTIE, I. (ed.), *Powell and Pressburger. The Life and Death of Colonel Blimp* (Faber and Faber, London, 1994).

FRÖHLICH, E. (ed.), *Die Tagebücher von Joseph Goebbels. Sämtliche Fragmente. Teil I: Aufzeichnungen 1924–1941*, 4 vols (K. G. Saur, Munich/New York/London/Paris, 1987); *Die Tagebücher von Joseph Goebbels. Teil II: Diktate 1941–1945*, 15 vols (K. G. Saur, Munich/New York/London/Paris, from 1993) .

HARDY, F. (ed.), *Grierson on Documentary* (Faber and Faber, London, 1979).

JACKSON, K. (ed.), *The Humphrey Jennings Film Reader* (Carcanet, Manchester, 1993).

KUROWSKI, U. (ed.), *Deutsche Spielfilme, 1933–1945*, 3 vols (Münchner Filmzentrum, Munich, 1980).

NOAKES, J. (ed.), *Nazism: The German Home Front in World War II*, vol. 4 (University of Exeter Press, Exeter, 1998).

SHERIDAN, D. and Richards, J. (eds), *Mass-Observation at the Movies* (Routledge & Kegan Paul, London/New York, 1987).

SUSSEX, E., *The Rise and Fall of British Documentary* (University of California Press, Berkeley, 1975).

TREVOR-ROPER, H., (ed.), *Hitler's Table Talk 1941–45* (Weidenfeld and Nicolson, Bungay, 1953).

WULF, J. (ed.), *Theater und Film im Dritten Reich. Eine Dokumentation* (Ullstein, Frankfurt am Main/Berlin/Vienna, 1966).

GENERAL WORKS PUBLISHED AFTER 1945

BADSEY, S. and Taylor, P. M., 'The Experience of Manipulation: Propaganda in Press and Radio', in J. Bourne, P. Liddle and I. Whitehead (eds), *The Great World War 1914–1945*, vol. 2: *The People's Experience* (HarperCollins, London, 2000).

BALFOUR, M., *Propaganda in War 1939–1945. Organisations, Policies and Publics in Britain and Germany* (Routledge & Kegan Paul, London, Boston and Henley, 1979).

CARRUTHERS, S., *The Media at War: Communication and Conflict in the 20th Century* (Macmillan, London, 2000).

CULBERT, D. and Whiteclay-Chambers, J. (eds), *World War II, Film and History* (Oxford University Press, Oxford, 1996).

CULL, N. *et al.*, *Propaganda and Mass Persuasion: A Historical Encyclopaedia, 1500 to the Present* (ABC-CLIO, Santa Barbara, 2003).

ELLUL, J., *Propaganda: The Formation of Men's Attitudes* (Vintage, New York, 1973) (First published by Alfred A. Knopf, New York, 1965).

Fox, J., '"The Mediator": Images of Radio in Wartime Feature Film in Britain and Germany', in M. Connelly and D. Welch (eds), *War and the Media. Reportage and Propaganda, 1900–2003* (I. B. Tauris, London/New York, 2005).

Furhammer, L. and Isaksson, F., *Politics and Film*, trans. Kersti French (Praeger, New York, 1971).

Fussell, P., *Wartime: Understanding and Behaviour in the Second World War* (Oxford University Press, Oxford, 1989).

Goldfarb-Marquis, A., 'Words as Weapons: Propaganda in Britain and Germany during the First World War', *Journal of Contemporary History*, vol. 13, no. 3 (July 1978), pp. 467–98.

Jackall R., (ed.), *Propaganda* (University of New York Press, New York, 1995).

Jowett, G. and O'Donnell, V., *Propaganda and Persuasion* (Sage, Newbury, CA, 1992) .

Landy, M. (ed.), *The Historical Film. History and Memory in Media* (Athlone Press, London, 1980).

Paris, M., *From the Wright Brothers to Top Gun. Aviation, Nationalism and Popular Cinema* (Manchester University Press, 1995).

Reeves, N., *The Power of Film Propaganda: Myth or Reality?* (Cassell, London/New York, 1999).

Rhodes, A., *Propaganda: The Art of Persuasion. World War II* (Angus & Robertson, London, 1975) .

Richards, J., *Visions of Yesterday* (Routledge and Kegan Paul, London, 1973).

Short, K. R. M. (ed.), *Feature Films as History* (Croom Helm, London, 1981).

Short, K. R. M. (ed.), *Film and Radio Propaganda in World War II* (Croom Helm, London, 1983).

Short, K. R. M. and Dolezel, S. (eds), *Hitler's Fall: The Newsreel Witness* (Croom Helm, London, 1988) .

Sorlin, P., *European Cinemas, European Societies, 1939–1990* (Routledge, London/New York, 1991).

Sorlin, P., *The Film in History. Restaging the Past* (Blackwell, Oxford, 1980).

Qualter, T., *Propaganda and Psychological Warfare* (Random House, New York, 1962) .

Taithe, B. and Thornton, T. (eds), *Propaganda: Political Rhetoric and Identity, 1300–2000* (Sutton, Stroud, 1999).

Taylor, P. M., *Munitions of the Mind: A History of Propaganda from the Ancient World to the Present Era* (Manchester University Press, Manchester, 1995).

Taylor, P. M., 'Propaganda and the Origins of the Second World War', in R. Boyce and J. Maiolo (eds), *The Origins of World War Two: The Debate Continues* (Palgrave Macmillan, Basingstoke, 2003).

GENERAL WORKS PUBLISHED AFTER 1945 (BRITAIN)

Adamthwaite, A., 'The British Government and the Media, 1937–1938', *Journal of Contemporary History*, vol. 18, no. 2 (April, 1983), pp. 281–97.

Aitken, I., *Film and Reform: John Grierson and the Documentary Film Movement* (Routledge, London, 1990).

Aldgate, A., 'Creative Tensions: *Desert Victory*, the Army and Anglo-American Rivalry', in P. M. Taylor (ed.), *Britain and the Cinema in the Second World War* (Palgrave, Basingstoke, 1988).

Ashby, J. and Higson, A. (eds), *British Cinema, Past and Present* (Routledge, London/New York, 2000).

Babington, B. (ed.), *British Stars and Stardom from Alma Taylor to Sean Connery* (Manchester University Press, Manchester, 2001).

Barr, C., *Ealing Studios* (Studio Vista, Dumfriesshire, 1993).

BARR, C. (ed.), *All Our Yesterdays. 90 Years of British Cinema* (Bfi Publishing, Worcester, 1986).

BIRKENHEAD, F. W. S., *Walter Monckton. The Life of Viscount Monckton of Brenchley* (Weidenfeld & Nicolson, London, 1969).

BUCKMAN, K., 'The Royal Air Force Film Production Unit, 1941–5', *Historical Journal of Film, Radio and Television*, vol. 17, no. 2 (1997), pp. 219–45.

BURTON, A., 'Projecting the New Jerusalem: The Workers' Film Association, 1938–1946' 1942', in D. Thoms and P. Kirkham (eds), *War Culture: Social Change and Changing Experience in World War Two Britain* (Lawrence & Wishart, London, 1995).

CALDER, A., *The Myth of the Blitz* (Jonathan Cape, London, 1991).

CALDER, A., *The People's War. Britain 1939–45* (The Literary Guild, London, 1969).

CARRUTHERS, S., '"Manning the Factories": Propaganda and Policy on the Employment of Women, 1939–47', *History*, vol. 75, no. 244 (June 1990), pp. 232–56.

CHAPMAN, J., *The British at War. Cinema, State and Propaganda 1939–1945* (I. B. Tauris, London/New York, 2000).

CHAPMAN, J., 'British Cinema and the People's War', in N. Hayes and J. Hill (eds), *'Millions Like Us'? British Culture in the Second World War* (Liverpool University Press, Liverpool, 1999).

CHARMLEY, J., *Duff Cooper: The Authorized Biography* (Weidenfeld & Nicolson, London, 1986).

CONNELLY, M., 'The British People, the Press, and the Strategic Air Campaign against Germany', *Contemporary British History*, vol. 16, no. 2 (2002), pp. 39–58.

CONNELLY, M., *Reaching for the Stars: A New Interpretation of Bomber Command in the Second World War* (I. B. Tauris, London, 2001).

CONNELLY, M., *We Can Take It! Britain and the Memory of the Second World War* (Pearson, Harlow, 2004).

COOK, P., *Fashioning the Nation. Costume and Identity in British Cinema* (Bfi, London, 1996).

COULTASS, C., 'British Feature Films and the Second World War', *Journal of Contemporary History*, vol. 19, no. 1, Historians and Movies: The State of the Art: Part 2 (Jan. 1984), pp. 7–22.

COULTASS, C., *Images for Battle: British Film and the Second World War* (Associated University Presses, London/Toronto, 1989).

CULL, N. J., *Selling War: The British Propaganda Campaign against American 'Neutrality' in World War II* (Oxford University Press, New York, 1995).

CURRAN, J. and Porter, V. (eds), *British Cinema History* (Weidenfeld and Nicolson, London, 1983).

DICKINSON, M. and Street, S., *Cinema and State* (Bfi, London, 1985).

DOHERTY, M., 'The Attack on the Altmark: A Case Study in Wartime Propaganda', *Journal of Contemporary History*, vol. 38, no. 2 (2003), pp. 187–200.

ELEY, G., 'Finding the People's War: Film, British Collective Memory, and World War II', *American Historical Review*, vol. 106, no. 3 (June 2001), pp. 818–38.

FOX, J., 'John Grierson, his "Documentary Boys" and the British Ministry of Information, 1939–1942', *Historical Journal of Film, Radio and Television*, vol. 25, no. 3 (August 2005), pp. 345–69.

FOX, J., 'Winston Churchill and the "Men of Destiny": Leadership and the Role of the Prime Minister in Wartime Feature Films', in J. Gottlieb and R. Toye (eds), *Making Reputations: Power, Persuasion and the Individual in Modern British Politics* (I. B. Tauris, London, New York, 2005).

FOX, J., 'Millions Like Us? Accented Language and the "Ordinary" in British Films of the Second World War', *Journal of British Studies*, vol. 45, no. 4 (October 2006), pp. 819–45.

GILLETT, P., *The British Working Class in Postwar Film* (Manchester University Press, Manchester/ New York, 2003).

GLANCY, M., *When Hollywood Loved Britain: The Hollywood 'British' Film 1939–45* (Manchester University Press, Manchester, 1992).

GLEDHILL, C. and Swanson, G. (eds), *Nationalising Femininity: Culture, Sexuality and British Cinema in the Second World War* (Manchester University Press, Manchester, 1996).

GOLDMAN, A., 'Germans and Nazis: The Controversy over "Vansittartism" in Britain during the Second World War', *Journal of Contemporary History*, vol. 14, no. 1 (Jan. 1979), pp. 155–91.

GOTTLIEB, J. and Toye, R. (eds), *Making Reputations: Power, Persuasion and the Individual in Modern British Politics* (I. B. Tauris, London, New York, 2005).

GRANT, M., 'Towards a Central Office of Information: Continuity and Change in British Government Information Policy, 1939–51', *Journal of Contemporary History*, vol. 34, no. 1. (Jan. 1999), pp. 49–67.

HARPER, S., *Picturing the Past: Rise and Fall of the British Costume Film* (Bfi Publishing, London, 1994).

HARPER, S., *Women in British Cinema: Mad, Bad and Dangerous to Know* (Continuum, London, 2000).

HARPER, S. and Porter, V., *British Cinema of the 1950s: The Decline of Deference* (Oxford University Press, 2003).

HARRIS, J., 'War and Social History: Britain and the Home Front during the Second World War', *Contemporary European History*, vol. 1 (1992), pp. 17–35.

HARRISSON, T., 'Films and the Home Front – An Evaluation of their Effectiveness by M-O', in N. Pronay and D. W. Spring (eds), *Propaganda, Politics and Film 1918–1945* (Macmillan, London, 1982).

HARRISSON, T., *Living through the Blitz* (Collins, London, 1976).

HAYES, N. and Hill, J. (eds), *'Millions Like Us'? British Culture in the Second World War* (Liverpool University Press, Liverpool, 1999).

HIGSON, A., *Waving the Flag: Constructing a National Cinema in Britain* (Clarendon Press, Oxford, 1995).

HIGSON, A. (ed.), *Dissolving Views: Key Writings on British Cinema* (Cassell, London, 1996).

HIGSON, A. (ed.), *Young and Innocent? The Cinema in Britain, 1896–1930* (University of Exeter Press, Exeter, 2002).

HOOD, S., 'John Grierson and the Documentary Film Movement', in J. Curran and V. Porter (eds), *British Cinema History* (Weidenfeld and Nicolson, London, 1983).

HURD, G. (ed.), *National Fictions: World War II in British Films and Television* (BFI Publishing, London, 1984).

KROME, F., 'The True Glory and the Failure of Anglo-American Film Propaganda in the Second World War', *Journal of Contemporary History*, vol. 33, no. 1 (Jan. 1998), pp. 21–34.

KUHN, A., 'The Camera I: Observations on Documentary', *Screen*, vol. 19, no. 2 (1978), pp. 71–83.

KUHN, A., *An Everyday Magic: Cinema and Cultural Memory* (I. B. Tauris, London, 2002).

KUHN, A., *Women's Pictures: Feminism and Cinema* (Verso, London, 1994).

LANDY, M., *British Genres: Cinema and Society, 1930–1960* (Princeton University Press, Princeton, 1991).

LANT, A., *Blackout: Reinventing Women for Wartime British Cinema* (Princeton University Press, Princeton, 1991).

LONGMATE, N., *How We Lived Then* (Hutchinson, London, 1971).

MACKAY, R., *Half the Battle. Civilian Morale in Britain during the Second World War* (Manchester University Press, Manchester and New York, 2002).

MACKENZIE, S. P., *British War Films, 1939–45: The Cinema and the Services* (Hambledon and London, London, 2001).

MCKIBBIN, R., *Classes and Cultures. England 1918–1951* (Oxford University Press, 1998).

MCLAINE, I., *Ministry of Morale. Home Front Morale and the Ministry of Information in World War II* (George Allen & Unwin, London, 1979).

MACNAB, G., *J. Arthur Rank and the British Film Industry* (Routledge, London, 1993).

MANVELL, R., *The Film and the Public* (Penguin, Harmondsworth, 1955).

MANVELL, R., *Films and the Second World War* (Dent, London, 1952).

MANVELL, R., *What is a Film?* (Macdonald, London, 1965).

MARWICK, A., 'People's War and Top People's Peace? British Society and the Second World War', in A. Sked and C. Cook (eds), *Crisis and Controversy: Essays in Honour of A. J. P.Taylor* (Macmillan, London, 1976).

MURPHY, R., *British Cinema and the Second World War* (Continuum, London/New York, 2000).

MURPHY, R., *Realism and Tinsel. Cinema and Society in Britain 1939–1948* (Routledge, London/ New York, 1989).

MURPHY, R. (ed.), *The British Cinema Book* (Bfi Publishing, London, 1997).

NEALE, S., 'Propaganda', *Screen*, vol. 18, no. 3 (1977), pp. 9–40.

NICHOLAS, S., *The Mass Media in Twentieth Century Britain* (Palgrave Macmillan, Basingstoke, 2001).

OSLEY, A., *Persuading the People* (HMSO, London, 1995).

PARIS, M., *Warrior Nation: Images of War in British Popular Culture, 1850–2000* (Reaktion Books, London, 2000).

POOLE, J., 'British Cinema Attendance in Wartime: Audience Preference at the Majestic, Macclesfield, 1939–1946', *Historical Journal of Film, Radio and Television*, vol. 7, no. 1 (1987), pp. 15–34.

POWELL, D., *Films since 1939* (Longman, London/Toronto, 1947).

PRONAY, N., '"The Land of Promise": The Projection of Peace Aims in Britain', in Short, K. R. M. (ed.), *Film and Radio Propaganda in World War II* (Croom Helm, London, 1983).

PRONAY, N. and Croft, J., 'British Film Censorship and Propaganda Policy during the Second World War', in J. Curran and V. Porter (eds), *British Cinema History* (Weidenfeld and Nicoloson, London, 1983).

PRONAY, N. and Spring, D. W. (eds), *Propaganda, Politics, and Film, 1918–45* (Macmillan, London, 1982).

PRONAY, N. and Thorpe, F., *British Official Films in the Second World War: A Descriptive Catalogue* (Clio, Oxford, 1980).

RAMSDEN, J., 'Refocusing "The People's War": British War Films of the 1950s', *Journal of Contemporary History*, vol, 33, no. 1 (1998), pp. 35–63.

RICHARDS, J., 'The British Board of Film Censors and Content Control in the 1930s: Foreign Affairs', *Historical Journal of Film, Radio and Television*, vol. 2, no. 1 (1982), pp. 38–48.

RICHARDS, J., *The Age of the Dream Palace: Cinema and Society in Britain, 1930–1939* (Routledge & Kegan Paul, London, 1984).

RICHARDS, J., *Films and British National Identity: From Dickens to Dad's Army* (Manchester University Press, Manchester, 1997).

RICHARDS, J., *Stars in Our Eyes. Lancashire Stars of Stage, Screen and Radio* (Lancashire County Books, Preston, 1994).

RICHARDS, J., *Visions of Yesterday* (Routledge & Kegan Paul, London, 1973).

RICHARDS, J. (ed.), *The Unknown 1930s: An Alternative History of the British Cinema, 1929–39* (I. B. Tauris, London, 1998).

RICHARDS, J. and Aldgate, A., *Best of British: Cinema and Society, 1930–1970* (Blackwell, London, 1983).

RICHARDS, J. and Aldgate, A., *Britain Can Take It: The British Cinema in the Second World War* (Edinburgh University Press, Edinburgh, 1986/1994).

ROBERTSON, J. C., *The British Board of Film Censors. Film Censorship in Britain, 1896–1950* (Croom Helm, London, 1985).

ROBERTSON, J. C., 'British Film Censorship Goes to War', *Historical Journal of Film, Radio and Television*, vol. 2, no. 1 (1982), pp. 49–64.

ROBERTSON, J. C., *The Hidden Cinema: British Film Censorship in Action 1913–75* (Routledge, London, 1993).

ROSE, S., *Which People's War? National Identity and Citizenship in Britain 1939–1945* (Oxford University Press, Oxford, 2003).

ROTHA, P., *Documentary Diary: An Informal History of the British Documentary Film 1928–1939* (Secker and Warburg, London, 1973).

ROTHA, P., *The Film till Now: A Survey of World Cinema* (Vision, London, 1949/1963).

ROTHA, P., *Rotha on the Film: a Selection of Writings about the Cinema* (Faber and Faber, London/ Boston, 1968).

SHORT, K. R. M., 'RAF Bomber Command's *Target for Tonight* – 1941 – UK Royal Air Force; Documentary Film', *Historical Journal of Film, Radio and Television*, vol. 17, no. 1 (June 1997), pp. 181–218.

SHORT, K. R. M., *Screening the Propaganda of British Air Power. From RAF (1935) to The Lion Has Wings* (Flicks, Trowbridge, 1997).

SMITH, H. (ed.), *War and Social Change: British Society in the Second World War* (Manchester University Press, Manchester, 1986).

SPICER, A., *Typical Men: The Representation of Masculinity in Popular British Cinema* (I. B. Tauris, London, 2002).

STANSKY, P. and Abrahams, W., *London's Burning. Life, Death and Art in the Second World War* (Stanford University Press, Stanford CA, 1994).

STREET, S., *British National Cinema* (Routledge, London, 1997).

SUMMERFIELD, P., 'Mass-Observation: Social Research or Social Movement?', *Journal of Contemporary History*, vol. 20, no. 3 (1985), pp. 439–53.

SWANN, P., *The British Documentary Film Movement* (Cambridge University Press, 1989).

TAYLOR, P. M., 'British Official Attitudes towards Propaganda Abroad, 1918–39', in N. Pronay and D. W. Spring (eds), *Propaganda, Politics and Film, 1918–45* (Macmillan, London, 1982), pp. 23–49.

TAYLOR, P. M., *British Propaganda in the Twentieth Century: Selling Democracy* (Edinburgh University Press, Edinburgh, 1999).

TAYLOR, P. M., 'Film as a Weapon in the Second World War', in D. Dutton (ed.), *Statecraft and Diplomacy in the Twentieth Century: Essays presented to P. M. H. Bell* (Liverpool University Press, Liverpool, 1995).

TAYLOR, P. M., '"If War Should Come": Preparing the Fifth Arm for Total War 1935–1939', *Journal of Contemporary History*, vol. 16, no. 1; The Second World War: Part 1 (January 1981), pp. 27–51.

TAYLOR, P. M. (ed.), *Britain and the Cinema in the Second World War* (St. Martin's Press, New York, 1988).

THOMS, D., 'The Blitz, Civilian Morale and Regionalism, 1940–1942' in D. Thoms and P. Kirkham, *War Culture: Social Change and Changing Experience in World War Two Britain* (Lawrence & Wishart, London, 1995).

THOMS, D. and Kirkham, P., *War Culture: Social Change and Changing Experience in World War Two Britain* (Lawrence & Wishart, London, 1995).

TIRATSOO, N., *England Arise! The Labour Party and Popular Politics in 1940s Britain* (Manchester University Press, Manchester, 1995).

WENDEN, D. J. and Short, K. R. M., 'Winston S. Churchill: Film Fan', *Historical Journal of Film, Radio and Television*, vol. 11, no. 3 (1991), pp. 197–214.

WILLIAMS, T., *Structures of Desire: British Cinema, 1939–1955* (State University of New York Press, Albany, NY, 2000).

WILLCOX, T., 'Projection or Publicity? Rival Concepts in the Pre-war Planning of the British Ministry of Information', *Journal of Contemporary History*, vol. 18, no. 1 (Jan., 1983), pp. 97–116.

WINSTON, B., *Claiming the Real: The Griersonian Documentary and its Legitimations* (Bfi, London, 1995).

WRIGHT, B., *The Long View* (Secker & Warburg, London, 1974).

WRIGHT, B., *The Use of the Film* (Bodley Head, London, 1948).

YASS, M., *This is your War: Home Front Propaganda in the Second World War* (HMSO, London, 1983).

WORKS ON SPECIFIC FILMS AND ARTISTS PUBLISHED AFTER 1945 (BRITAIN)

AITKEN, I., *Cavalcanti: Strange Realisms* (Flicks Books, Trowbridge, 2000).

ASPINALL, S. and Murphy, R. (eds), *Bfi Dossier 18: Gainsborough Melodrama* (Bfi, London, 1983).

BABINGTON, B., *Launder and Gilliat* (Manchester University Press, Manchester, 2002).

BROWN, L., *Launder and Gilliat* (Bfi Publishing, London, 1977).

BURTON, A., O' Sullivan, T. and Wells, P. (eds), *The Family Way: The Boulting Brothers and British Film Culture* (Flicks Books, Trowbridge, 2000).

CARTMELL, D., 'Through a Painted Curtain: Laurence Olivier's *Henry V*, 1942', in D. Thoms and P. Kirkham (eds), *War Culture: Social Change and Changing Experience in World War Two Britain* (Lawrence & Wishart, London, 1995).

CHAPMAN, J., '*The Life and Death of Colonel Blimp* (1943) Reconsidered', *Historical Journal of Film, Radio and Television*, vol. 15, no. 1 (1995), pp. 19–36.

CHRISTIE, I., *Arrows of Desire* (Faber and Faber, London, 1994).

CHRISTIE, I. (ed.), *Powell, Pressburger and Others* (Bfi Publishing, London, 1978).

CHRISTIE, I. and Moor, A. (eds), *The Cinema Of Michael Powell: International Perspectives on an English Film-Maker* (Bfi, London, 2005).

DAVIES, B. (ed.), *Carol Reed* (Bfi Publishing, London, 1978).

HOUSTON, P., *Went the Day Well?* (Bfi, London, 1992).

JACKSON, K., *Humphrey Jennings* (Picador, London, 2004).

JENNINGS, M.-L. (ed.), *Humphrey Jennings: Film-maker, Painter, Poet* (Bfi, London, 1982).

KENNEDY, A. L., *The Life and Death of Colonel Blimp* (Bfi, London, 1997) .

KORDA, M., *Charmed Lives. A Family Romance* (Allen Lane, London, 1979).

KUHN, A., '"Desert Victory" and the People's War', *Screen*, vol. 22, no. 2 (1981), pp. 45–68.

KULIK, A. K., *Alexander Korda: The Man Who Could Work Miracles* (W. H. Allen, London, 1975).

LAZAR, D. (ed.), *Michael Powell: Interviews* (University of Mississippi, Jackson, MS, 2003).

MACDONALD, K., *Emeric Pressburger. The Life and Death of a Screenwriter* (Faber and Faber, London/ Boston, 1994).

MOOREHEAD, C., *Sidney Bernstein. A Biography* (Jonathan Cape, London, 1984).

O'SHAUGHNESSY, M., '"What Wouldn't I Give to Grow up in a Place Like That": *A Canterbury Tale*', in D. Thoms and P. Kirkham (eds), *War Culture: Social Change and Changing Experience in World War Two Britain* (Lawrence & Wishart, London, 1995).

RICHARDS, J., 'Humphrey Jennings: The Poet as Propagandist', in M. Connelly and D. Welch (eds), *War and the Media. Reportage and Propaganda, 1900–2003* (I. B. Tauris, London/New York, 2005).

RICHARDS, J., *Thorold Dickinson* (Croom Helm, London, 1986).

RICHARDS, J., 'Wartime British Cinema Audiences and the Class System: The Case of *Ships with Wings* (1941)', *Historical Journal of Film, Radio and Television*, vol. 7, no. 2 (1987), pp. 129–41.

WAPSHOTT, N., *The Man Between. A Biography of Carol Reed* (Chatto and Windus, London, 1990).

WINSTON, B., *Fires were Started* (Bfi, London, 1999).

GENERAL WORKS PUBLISHED AFTER 1945 (GERMANY)

ALBRECHT, G., *Nationalsozialistische Filmpolitik. Eine soziologische Untersuchung über die Spielfilme des Dritten Reiches* (Ferdinand Enke, Stuttgart, 1969).

ALBRECHT, G., *Der Film im Dritten Reich. Eine Dokumentation* (Schauburg, Karlsruhe, 1979).

ASCHEID, A., *Hitler's Heroines: Stardom and Womanhood in Nazi Cinema* (Temple University Press, Philadelphia, 2003).

BAIRD, J., *To Die for Germany. Heroes in the Nazi Pantheon* (Indiana University Press, Bloomington, 1990).

BAIRD, J., 'Goebbels, Horst Wessel, and the Myth of Resurrection and Return', *Journal of Contemporary History*, vol. 17, no. 4. (Oct. 1982), pp. 633–50.

BAIRD, J., 'The Myth of Stalingrad', *Journal of Contemporary History*, vol. 4, no. 3 (July 1969), pp. 187–204.

BARKHAUSEN, H., *Filmpropaganda für Deutschland im Ersten und Zweiten Weltkrieg* (Olms Presse, Hildesheim/Zürich/New York, 1982).

BATHRICK, D. and Rentschler, E. (eds), *German Film History* (Telos, New York, 1993).

BAUER, A., *Deutscher Spielfilm Almanach 1929–1950* (Filmladen Christoph Winterberg, Munich, 1976).

BECHDOLF, U., *Wunsch-Bilder? Frauen im Nationalsozialistischen Unterhaltungsfilm* (Tübinger Vereinigung für Volkskunde, 1992).

BECKER, W., *Film und Herrschaft. Organisationsprinzipien und Organisationsstrukturen der national-sozialistischen Filmpropaganda* (Volker Spiess, Berlin, 1973).

BELACH, H. (ed.), *Wir tanzen um die Welt. Deutsche Revuefilme 1933–1945* (Carl Hanser, Munich, 1979).

BENZ, W., *Herrschaft und Gesellschaft im nationalsozialistischen Staat* (Fischer, Frankfurt am Main, 1990).

BERGFELDER, T., Carter, E. and Göktürk, D. (eds), *The German Cinema Book* (Bfi, London, 2002).

BEYER, F., *Die Ufa-Stars im Dritten Reich. Frauen für Deutschland* (Heyne, Munich, 1991).

BOCK, H. M. and Töteberg, M., *Das Ufa-Buch. Kunst und Krisen; Stars und Regisseure; Wirtschaft und Politik* (Zweitausendeins, Frankfurt am Main, 1992).

BORGELT, H., *Die Ufa, ein Traum: hundert Jahre deutsche Film: Ereignisse und Erlebnisse* (Edition Q, Berlin 1993).

BRADY, R., 'The National Chamber of Culture' in B. Taylor and W. van der Will (eds), *The Nazification of Art: Art, Design, Music, Architecture and Film in the Third Reich* (Winchester Press, Winchester, 1990).

BRANDT, H.-J., *NS-Filmtheorie und dokumentarische Praxis: Hippler, Noldan, Junghans* (Max Niemeyer, Tübingen, 1987).

CADARS, P. and Courtade, F., *Histoire du Cinéma Nazi* (Eric Losfeld, Paris, 1972).

CARTER, E., *Dietrich's Ghosts. The Sublime and the Beautiful in Third Reich Film* (Bfi Publishing, London, 2004).

CARTER, E. 'The New Third Reich Film History', *German History*, vol. 17, no. 4 (1999), pp. 71–80.

CHALMERS, M. (ed.), *The Diaries of Victor Klemperer 1933–1945: I Shall Bear Witness – To the Bitter End* (Phoenix Press, London, 1998; 2000 edn).

CUOMO, G. R. (ed.), *National Socialist Cultural Policy* (St Martin's Press, New York, 1995).

CZIFFRA, G. von, *Es war eine rauschende Ballnacht. Eine Sittengeschichte des deutschen Films* (Ullstein, Frankfurt am Main/Berlin, 1987).

DELAGE, C., *La vision nazie de l'histoire: Le cinema documentaire du Troisième Reich* (L'Age d'Homme, Lausanne, 1989).

DONNER, W., *Propaganda und Film im 'Dritten Reich'* (TIP Verlag, Berlin, 1995).

DOOB, L., 'Goebbels' Principles of Propaganda', *Public Opinion Quarterly*, vol. 14, no. 3 (Autumn 1950), pp. 419–42 .

DREWNIAK, B., *Der deutsche Film, 1938–1945. Ein Gesamtüberblick* (Droste, Düsseldorf, 1987).

ETLIN, R. A. (ed.), *Art, Culture, and Media under the Third Reich* (University of Chicago Press, Chicago IL, 2002).

FEHRENBACH, H., *Cinema in Democratizing Germany: Reconstructing National Identity after Hitler* (University of North Carolina Press, Chapel Hill, NC, 1995).

FOX, J., *Filming Women in the Third Reich* (Berg, Oxford, 2000).

FOX, J., '"Heavy Hands and Light Touches": Approaches to the Study of Cinematic Culture in the Third Reich', *History Compass* (2003).

GELLATELY, R., *Backing Hitler: Consent and Coercion in Nazi Germany* (Oxford University Press, Oxford, 2001).

GELLATELY, R., *The Gestapo and German Society: Enforcing Racial Policy 1933–1945* (Clarendon, Oxford, 1990).

HAKE, S., *German National Cinema* (Routledge, London, 2002).

HAKE, S., *Popular Cinema of the Third Reich* (University of Texas, Austin, 2001).

HAGENLÜCKE, H., 'The Home Front in Germany', in J. Bourne, P. Liddle and I. Whitehead (eds), *The Great World War 1914–1945* vol. 2: *The People's Experience* (HarperCollins, London, 2000).

HAPPEL, H.-G., *Der historische Spielfilm im Nationalsozialismus* (R. G. Fischer, Frankfurt am Main, 1984).

HEMBUS, J. and Bandmann, C., *Klassiker des deutschen Tonfilms 1930–1960* (Citadel – Filmbücher, Goldmann, Munich, 1980).

HERZSTEIN, R., *The War that Hitler Won: The Most Infamous Propaganda Campaign in History* (Abacus, London, 1980).

HOFFMANN, H., *The Triumph of Propaganda. Film and National Socialism, 1933–45*, trans. J. A. Broadwin and V. R. Berghahn (Berghahn, Providence, RI, 1997).

HORAK, J.-C., 'Eros, Thanatos, and the Will to Myth: Prussian Films in German Cinema', in B. A. Murray and C. J. Wickham (eds), *Framing the Past: The Historiography of German Cinema and Television* (Southern Illinois University Press, Carbondale, IL, 1992).

JACOBSEN, W., Kaes, A. and Prinzler, H. H. (eds), *Geschichte des deutschen Films* (Metzler, Stuttgart, 1993).

JACOBSEN, W. (ed.), *Babelsberg. Ein Filmstudio, 1912–1992* (Stiftung Deutsche Kinematek, Berlin, 1992).

KANZOG, K., *'Staatspolitisch besonders wertvoll'. Ein Handbuch zu 30 deutschen Spielfilmen der Jahre 1934 bis 1945* (Schaudig und Ledig, Munich, 1994).

KATER, M., 'Film as an Object of Reflection in the Goebbels Diaries: Series II (1941–1945)', *Central European History*, vol. 33, no. 3 (2000), pp. 391–414.

KERSHAW, I., 'Hitler and the Germans', in R. Bessel (ed.), *Life in the Third Reich* (Oxford University Press, 1987), pp. 41–55.

KERSHAW, I., *The 'Hitler Myth'. Image and Reality in the Third Reich* (Oxford University Press, 1987).

KERSHAW, I., 'Hitler and the Uniqueness of Nazism', *Journal of Contemporary History*, vol. 39, no. 2 (April 2004), pp. 239–54.

KERSHAW, I., 'How Effective was Nazi Propaganda?', in D. Welch, *Nazi Propaganda* (Croom Helm, London, 1983).

KERSHAW, I., *Popular Opinion and Political Dissent. Bavaria 1933–45* (Clarendon, Oxford, 1983).

KERSHAW, I., 'Popular Opinion in the Third Reich' in J. Noakes (ed.), *Government, Party and People in Nazi Germany* (University of Exeter Press, Exeter, 1980).

KIRWIN, G., 'Waiting for Retaliation – A Study in Nazi Propaganda Behaviour and German Civilian Morale', *Journal of Contemporary History*, vol. 16, no. 3 (July 1981), pp. 565–83.

KLEINHANS, B., *Ein Volk, ein Reich, ein Kino. Lichtspiel in der braunen Provinz* (PapyRossa, Cologne, 2003).

KRACAUER, S., *From Caligari to Hitler: A Psychological History of German Film* (Princeton University Press, 1947).

KRÄH, H. (ed.), *Geschichte(n) NS-Film – NS Spuren heute* (Ludwig, Kiel, 2000).

KRAMER, T., *Terra: Ein Schweizer Filmkonzern im Dritten Reich* (Chronos, Zürich, 1991).

KREIMEIER, K., *The Ufa Story. A History of Germany's Greatest Film Company* (University of California Press, Berkeley, 1996).

LANGE, G., *Das Kino als moralische Anstalt. Soziale Leitbilder und die Darstellung gesellschaftlicher Realität im Spielfilm des Dritten Reiches* (Lang, Frankfurt am Main, 1994).

LEISER, E., *Nazi Cinema*, trans. Gertrud Mander and David Wilson (Secker and Warburg, London, 1975).

LOIPERDINGER, M. (ed.), *Märtyrerlegenden im N-S Film* (Leske & Budrich, Opladen, 1991).

LOWRY, S., *Pathos und Politik. Ideologie in Spielfilmen des Nationalsozialismus* (Niemeyer, Tübingen, 1991).

MAIWALD, K.-J., *Filmzensur im NS-Staat* (Nowotny, Dortmund, 1983).

MARQUARDT, A. and Rathsack, H. (eds), *Preußen im Film* (Rowohlt, Reinbeck bei Hamburg, 1981).

MOELLER, F., *The Film Minister: Goebbels and the Cinema in the Third Reich*, trans. M. Robinson (Edition Axel Menges, Stuttgart, 2000).

MOSSE, G., *The Crisis of German Ideology: Intellectual Origins of the Third Reich* (Schocken, New York, 1981).

MOSSE, G., 'Two World Wars and the Myth of the War Experience', *Journal of Contemporary History*, vol. 21, no. 4 (Oct. 1986), pp. 491–513.

MÜHL-BENNINGHAUS, W., 'The German Film Credit Bank, Inc.: Film Financing during the First Years of National Socialist Rule in Germany', *Film History*, vol. 3, no. 4 (1989), pp. 31–44.

NOAKES, J. (ed.), *The Civilian in War: The Home Front in Europe, Japan and the USA in World War II* (University of Exeter Press, Exeter, 1992).

NOAKES, J., 'Leaders of the People? The Nazi Party and German Society', *Journal of Contemporary History*, vol. 39, no. 2 (April 2004), pp. 189–213.

NOAKES, J. (ed.), *Government, Party and People in Nazi Germany* (University of Exeter Press, Exeter, 1980).

PETLEY, J., *Capital and Culture. German Cinema 1933–45* (Bfi, London, 1979).

PETLEY, J., 'Film Policy in the Third Reich' in T. Bergfelder, E. Carter and D. Göktürk (eds), *The German Cinema Book* (Bfi, London, 2002).

PETLEY, J., 'Perfidious Albion: The Depiction of Great Britain in Films of the Third Reich' in C. Cullingford and H. Husemann (eds), *Anglo-German Attitudes* (Avebury, Aldershot, 1995).

PEUKERT, D., *Inside Nazi Germany. Conformity, Opposition and Racism in Everyday Life*, trans. R. Deveson (Penguin, Harmondsworth, 1989).

PHILLIPS, M. S., 'The German Film Industry and the New Order', in P. Stachura (ed.), *The Shaping of the Nazi State* (Croom Helm, London, 1978).

PHILLIPS, M. S., 'The Nazi Control of the Film Industry', *Journal of European Studies*, vol. 1, no.1 (1971), pp. 37–68.

QUANZ, C., *Der Film als Propagandainstrument Joseph Goebbels'* (Teiresias, Cologne, 2000).

RAACK, R., 'Nazi Film Propaganda and the Horrors of War', *Historical Journal of Film, Radio and Television*, vol. 6, no. 2 (1986), pp. 189–95.

RABENALT, A. M., *Film im Zwielicht. Über den unpolitischen Film des Dritten Reiches und die Begrenzung des totalitären Anspruchs* (Olms, Hildesheim/New York, 1978).

REIMER, R. C., 'Turning Inward: An Analysis of Helmut Käutner's *Auf Wiedersehen, Franziska!; Romanze in Moll* and *Unter den Brücken*', in R. C. Reimer (ed.), *Cultural History through a National Socialist Lens. Essays on the Cinema of the Third Reich* (Camden House, Rochester, NY, 2000), pp. 214–40.

REIMER, R. C. (ed.), *Cultural History through a National Socialist Lens: Essays on the Cinema of the Third Reich* (Camden House, Colombia, SC, 2000).

RENTSCHLER, E., *The Ministry of Illusion. Nazi Cinema and its Afterlife* (Harvard University Press, Cambridge, MA/London, 1996).

REUTH, R. G., *Goebbels*, trans. K. Winston (Harcourt Brace, New York, 1993).

SAKMYSTER, T., 'Nazi Documentaries of Intimidation: *Feldzug in Polen* (1940), *Feuertaufe* (1940) and *Sieg im Westen*', *Historical Journal of Film, Radio and Television*, vol. 16, no. 4 (1996), pp. 485–514.

SAKKARA, M. (ed.), *Die große Zeit des Deutschen Films, 1933–1945* (Druffel, Leoni am Starnberger See, 1980).

SALTER, S., 'Structures of Consensus and Coercion: Worker's Morale and the Maintenance of Work Discipline, 1939–1945', in D. Welch (ed.), *Nazi Propaganda* (Croom Helm, London, 1983).

SCHOENBERNER, G., 'Ideologie und Propaganda im NS-Film. Von der Eroberung der Studios zur Manipulation ihrer Produkte', in U. Jung (ed.), *Der deutsche Film. Aspekte seiner Geschichte von den Anfängen bis zur Gegenwart* (Wissenschaftlicher Verlag, Trier, 1993).

SCHULTE-SASSE, L., *Entertaining the Third Reich. Illusions of Wholeness in Nazi Cinema* (Duke University Press, Durham, NC/London, 1996).

SHANDLEY, R., *Rubble Films: German Cinema in the Shadow of the Third Reich* (Temple University Press, Philadelphia, 2001).

SILBERMAN, M., *German Cinema: Texts in Context* (Wayne State University Press, Detroit, 1995).

SILBERMAN, M., 'Shooting Wars: German Cinema and the Two World Wars', in R. Grimm and J. Hermand (eds), *1914/1939: German Reflections of the Two World Wars* (University of Wisconsin Press, Madison, 1992).

SPECTOR, S., 'Was the Third Reich Movie-Made? Interdisciplinarity and the Reframing of "Ideology"', *American Historical Review*, vol. 106, no. 2 (April 2001), pp. 460–84.

SPIKER, J., *Film und Kapital. Der Weg der deutschen Filmwirtschaft zum nationalsozialistischen Einheitskonzern* (Volker Spiess, Berlin, 1975).

STEINERT, M. G., *Hitler's War and the Germans: Public Mood and Attitude during the Second World War*, trans. E. J. T. De Witt (Ohio University Press, Athens, OH, 1977).

STEINWEIS, A. E. (ed.), *Art, Ideology and Economics. The Reich Chambers of Music, Theatre and the Visual Arts* (University of North Carolina Press, Chapel Hill/London, 1993).

SUDOWL, G., *Geschichte der Filmkunst* (Fischer, Frankfurt am Main, 1982).

SYWOTTEK, J., *Mobilmachung für den totalen Krieg. Die propagandistische Vorbereitung der deutschen Bevölkerung auf den Zweiten Weltkrieg* (Westdeutscher Verlag, Opladen, 1976).

TAYLOR, B. and Van der Will, W. (eds), *The Nazification of Art. Art, Design, Music, Architecture and Film in the Third Reich* (Winchester Press, Winchester, 1990).

TAYLOR, R., *Film Propaganda in Soviet Russia and Nazi Germany*, 2nd edn (I. B. Tauris, London/New York, 1998) .

TAYLOR, R., 'Goebbels and the Function of Propaganda', in D. Welch (ed.), *Nazi Propaganda* (Croom Helm, London, 1983).

TEGEL, S., '"The Demonic Effect": Veit Harlan's Use of Jewish Extras in *Jud Süss* (1940)', *Holocaust and Genocide Studies*, vol. 14, no. 2 (2000), pp. 215–41.

TEGEL, S., *Jew Süß* (Flicks Books, Trowbridge, 1997).

TEGEL, S., 'Veit Harlan and the Origins of Jud Süss, 1938–1939: Opportunism in the Creation Of Nazi Anti-Semitic Film Propaganda', *Historical Journal of Film, Radio and Television*, vol. 16, no. 4 (1996), pp. 515–33.

THEUERKAUF, H., *Goebbels' Filmerbe. Das Geschäft mit unveröffentlichten Ufa-Firmen* (Ullstein, Berlin, 1998).

TOEPLITZ, J., *Geschichte des Films. Band 4. 1939–45* (Henschel, Berlin, 1983).

VAN DER WINKEL, R., 'Nazi Germany's Fritz Hippler, 1909–2002', *Historical Journal of Film, Radio and Television*, vol. 23, no. 2 (June 2003), pp. 91–9.

VAN DER WINKEL, R. and Welch, D. (eds), *Cinema and the Swastika: The International Expansion of the Third Reich Cinema* (Palgrave, Basingstoke, 2006).

WEINBERG, G., *Germany, Hitler and World War II: Essays in Modern German and World History* (Cambridge University Press, Cambridge, 1995).

WELCH, D., *Germany, Propaganda and Total War, 1914–1918: Sins of Omission* (Rutgers University Press, New Brunswick, NJ, 2000).

WELCH, D., 'Manufacturing a Consensus: Nazi Propaganda and the Building of a "National Community"', *Contemporary European History*, vol. 2 (1993), pp. 1–15.

WELCH, D., 'Nazi Film Policy: Control, Ideology and Propaganda', in G. R. Cuomo (ed.), *National Socialist Cultural Policy* (Macmillan, Basingstoke, 1995).

WELCH, D., 'Nazi Propaganda and the *Volksgemeinschaft*: Constructing a People's Community', *Journal of Contemporary History*, vol. 39, no. 2 (April 2004), pp. 189–213.

WELCH, D., *Propaganda and the German Cinema, 1933–1945*, 2nd edn (I. B. Tauris, London/New York, 2001).

WELCH, D., *The Third Reich: Propaganda and Politics*, 2nd edn (Routledge, London, 2002).

WELCH, D., '"Working Towards the Führer": Charismatic Leadership and the Image of Adolf Hitler in Nazi Propaganda"', in A. McElligott and T. Kirk (eds), *Working Towards the Führer. Essays in Honour of Sir Ian Kershaw* (Manchester University Press, Manchester, 2004).

WELCH, D. (ed.), *Nazi Propaganda: The Power and the Limitations* (Croom Helm, London and Canberra, 1983).

WENDTLAND, K., *Geliebter Kintopp. Sämtliche Deutsche Spielfilme von 1929–1945* (Medium Film, Berlin, n.d.).

WETZEL, K. and Hagemann, P. A., *Zensur – Verbotene deutsche Filme 1933–1945* (Volker Spiess, Berlin, 1978).

WINKLER-MAYERHÖFER, A., *Starkult als Propagandamittel. Studien zim Unterhaltungsfilm im Dritten Reich* (Ölschläger, Munich, 1992).

WITTE, K., 'Film im Nationalsozialismus', in W. Jacobsen, A. Kaes and H. H. Prinzler (eds), *Geschichte des Deutschen Films* (J. B. Metzler, Stuttgart/Weimar, 1993).

WITTE, K., 'The Indivisible Legacy of Nazi Cinema', *New German Critique*, vol. 74 (Spring–Summer 1998), pp. 23–31.

WITTE, K., *Lachende Erben, Toller Tag. Filmkomödie im Dritten Reich* (Vorwerk 8, Berlin, 1995).

ZEMAN, Z., *Nazi Propaganda* (Oxford University Press, Oxford, 1964).

WORKS ON SPECIFIC FILMS AND ARTISTS PUBLISHED AFTER 1945 (GERMANY)

AURICH, R., 'Films als Durchhalteration: *Kolberg* von Veit Harlan', in H.-M. Bock, and M. Töteberg (eds), *Das Ufa-Buch. Kunst und Krisen, Stars und Regisseure, Wirtschaft und Politik* (Zweitausendeins, Frankfurt am Main, 1992).

BALL, G. and Spiess, E., *Heinz Rühmann und seine Filme* (Goldman, Munich, 1982).

BLUMENBERG, H. C., *In meinem Herzen, Schatz... Die Lebensreise des Schauspielers und Sängers Hans Albers* (Fischer Taschenbuch, Frankfurt am Main, 1991).

BLUMENBERG, H. C., *Das Leben geht weiter: Der letzte Film des Dritten Reiches* (Rowohlt, Berlin, 1992).

CADENBACH, J., *Hans Albers* (Universitas, Berlin, n.d.).

CORNELSEN, P., *Helmut Käutner. Seine Filme – sein Leben* (Heyne Filmbibliothek, Munich, 1980).

CULBERT, D., '*Kolberg* (Germany, 1945): The Goebbels Diaries and Poland's Kołobrzeg Today', in J. Whiteclay Chambers II and D. Culbert (eds), *World War II: Film and History* (Oxford University Press, 1996).

FRICKE, H., *Spiel am Abgrund. Heinrich George. Eine politische Biographie* (Mitteldeutscher Verlag, Halle, 2000).

GNADENBACH, J., *Hans Albers. Lebensbilder* (Ullstein, Frankfurt am Main/Berlin/Vienna, 1983).

GRAHAM, C. C., '*Sieg im Westen* (1941): Interservice and Bureaucratic Propaganda Rivalries in Nazi Germany', *Historical Journal of Film, Radio and Television*, vol. 9, no.1 (1989), pp. 19–44.

HOLBA, H., *Emil Jannings* (Günther Knorr, Ulm, 1979).

JACOBSEN, W. and Prinzler, H. H. (eds), *Käutner* (Edition Filme, Volker Spiess, Berlin, 1992).

KLOTZ, M., 'Epistemological Ambiguity and the Fascist Text: *Jew Süss, Carl Peters* and *Ohm Krüger*', *New German Critique*, vol. 74 (Spring–Summer 1998), pp. 91–125.

KNILLI, F., *Ich war Jud Süß. Die Geschichte des Filmstars Ferdinand Marian* (Henschel, Berlin, 2000).

KRÜTZEN, M., *Hans Albers. Eine deutsche Karriere* (Quadriga, Berlin, 1995).

LAREGH, P., *Heinrich George. Komödiant seiner Zeit* (Langen Müller, Munich, 1992).

LUTZ, R. C., 'False History, Fake Africa, and the Transcription of Nazi Reality in Hans Steinoff's *Ohm Krüger*', *Literature/Film Quarterly*, vol. 25, no. 3 (1997), pp. 188–92.

MONK, D., *Erich Kästner im NS Deutschland* (Peter Lang, Frankfurt am Main/Bern, 1981).

PARET, P., '*Kolberg* (Germany, 1945): As Historical Film and Historical Document', in J. Whiteclay Chambers II and D. Culbert (eds), *World War II: Film and History* (Oxford University Press, 1996).

INDEX